Portugal

Julia Wilkinson
John King

D1495493

Portugal

1st edition

Published by
   Lonely Planet Publications
   Head Office: PO Box 617, Hawthorn, Vic 3122, Australia
   Branches: 155 Filbert St, Suite 251, Oakland, CA 94607, USA
                  10 Barley Mow Passage, Chiswick, London W4 4PH, UK
                  71 bis rue du Cardinal Lemoine, 75005 Paris, France

Printed by
   Colorcraft Ltd, Hong Kong
   Printed in China

Photographs by

Vicki Beale	Bethune Carmichael	John King
Damien Simonis	Rob van Driesum	Tony Wheeler
Julia Wilkinson		

Front cover: Tiles on façade of house in Viseu (John King)

First Published
   May 1997

Although the authors and publisher have tried to make the information as accurate as possible, they accept no responsibility for any loss, injury or inconvenience sustained by any person using this book.

National Library of Australia Cataloguing in Publication Data

   Wilkinson, Julia
   Portugal.

   1st ed.
   Includes index.
   ISBN 0 86442 467 1.

   1. Portugal - Guidebooks. I. King, John (John S.). II.
   Title. (Series : Lonely Planet travel survival kit).

914.690444

text & maps © Lonely Planet 1997
photos © photographers as indicated 1997

Julia Wilkinson & John King

Julia set out with her first backpack at the age of four in a moment of tempestuous independence and has been hooked on travel ever since. After finishing university in England in 1978 she headed for Australia but got sidetracked in Hong Kong, where she worked in publishing and radio until going freelance as a writer and photographer. Since then she has travelled throughout Asia, writing for various international magazines. She has contributed to guidebooks on Hong Kong, Tibet and Laos, and authored others on Portugal and Thailand. In 1994 Julia updated the Portugal chapters for LP's *Western Europe* and *Mediterranean Europe* guides. When she wants to get away from it all she takes to the skies, flying hot-air balloons.

John grew up in the USA, destined for the academic life (in past incarnations he was a university physics teacher and an environmental consultant), but in a rash moment in 1984 he headed off to China for a look around and ended up living there for half a year. During that time he and Julia crossed paths in Lhasa, the Tibetan capital. After a three-month journey across China and Pakistan they decided they could manage joint housekeeping, and have since split their time between south-west England and remoter parts of Hong Kong.

In 1988 John wrote Lonely Planet's *The Karakoram Highway*, and, with Julia, took up full-time travel writing. John is also co-author of LP's *Central Asia*; *Russia, Ukraine & Belarus* (formerly the *USSR* guide); *Pakistan*; *Czech & Slovak Republics*; and the *Prague city guide*.

Since 1995 they have been assisted and entertained by their son, Kit, with whom they travelled around Portugal to research this book and the Portugal chapters of *Western Europe* and *Mediterranean Europe*.

From the Authors

Three offices of ICEP (Investimentos, Comércio e Turismo de Portugal) provided excellent help. We're particularly indebted to Pilar Pereira of ICEP London for assistance and logistical support. Thanks also to her colleagues in the Lisbon and Porto ICEP offices, who provided answers to our seemingly endless questions.

Several municipal turismos (tourist offices) stood out from the rest: Aveiro, Bragança, Coimbra, Estremoz, Évora, Figueira da Foz, Lisbon, Sintra and Tavira. Thanks in particular to Paula Oliveira at the Lisbon turismo, Amélia Paulo Vieira at Sintra, Paulo Jorge Neves at Coimbra and Maria Manuela Ferreira da Silva at Évora. Turinfo at Sagres also deserves a special mention.

Another organisation which extended ready help was the Fundação Calouste Gulbenkian, via Carlos Baptista da Silva, secretary to the board of trustees. Thanks to Luisa Gomes for timely post-trip research.

Among those in the UK who came to the rescue were Melissa Hutchings at Eurolines' fittingly named publicity office, Beehive Communications; Paul Gowen, Touring

Information & Research Manager at the RAC; and Sue Hall of the Cyclists' Touring Club. Various staff at STA Travel and Campus Travel offices around the globe helped us with bus, train and plane fares and schedules.

Thanks to fellow author George Wesely for helping us find and enjoy *Iberian Villages*. We're grateful to Steve Lee (UK) and Markus Salchegger (Austria) for information on cycling in Portugal. Cheers to fellow travellers Dr Ollis R Miller and Susan B Gerber (Jordan), Coleman Higgins (Ireland) and Andrew Oddo (USA) for good letters.

LP Melbourne people endured our delays and alterations with patience, tact and incredibly good humour; nobody ever had a better support crew. Thanks especially to editors Brigitte Barta and Karin Riederer and designer Lyndell Taylor. And we also owe a lot to the LP authors who laid the groundwork with the Portugal chapter of the first edition of *Western Europe*, Deanna Swaney and Robert Strauss.

Our son, Kit, sends thanks and *beijinhos* (kisses) to the many people who looked after him while his mum and dad pounded the pavements. Warm thanks especially to Amélia Paulo Vieira and her daughter Andreia in Sintra; Maria Olivete Lobo da Costa and her family at Campeã near Vila Real (especially Rui for tractor rides and his father for donkey rides); Nuno Miguel Soares Vilacova and his family for soup and smiles at Restaurante O Padeiro in Porto; and the big-hearted staff at Porto's Infantário Pãe América, especially Maria Amélia and Julia.

Finally, *obrigada/o* from all of us to Barry Girling for his house and the soft landing it gave us on arrival.

From the Publisher

This 1st edition of *Portugal* was edited in Lonely Planet's Melbourne office by Brigitte Barta with assistance from Karin Riederer, Paul Harding, Adrienne Costanzo, Janet Austin, Suzi Petkovski, Miriam Cannell and Liz Filleul. Lyndell Taylor drew the maps and illustrations and laid out the book. Additional mapping assistance was provided by Trudi Canavan, Tony Fankhauser, Sally Jacka, Jacqui Saunders, Rachel Scott, Michelle Stamp and Geoff Stringer. David Kemp designed the cover. Brigitte did the index.

Warning & Request

Things change – prices go up, schedules change, good places go bad and bad places go bankrupt – nothing stays the same. So, if you find things better or worse, recently opened or long since closed, please tell us and help make the next edition even more accurate and useful.

We value all of the feedback we receive from travellers. Julie Young coordinates a small team who read and acknowledge every letter, postcard and e-mail, and ensure that every morsel of information finds its way to the appropriate authors, editors and publishers.

Everyone who writes to us will find their name in the next edition of the appropriate guide and will also receive a free subscription to our quarterly newsletter, *Planet Talk*. The very best contributions will be rewarded with a free Lonely Planet guide.

Excerpts from your correspondence may appear in updates (which we add to the end pages of reprints); new editions of this guide; in our newsletter, *Planet Talk*; or in the Postcards section of our web site – so please let us know if you don't want your letter published or your name acknowledged.

Contents

Boxed Asides

Map Legend

BOUNDARIES

............International Boundary
............Provincial Boundary

ROUTES

............Freeway
............Highway
............Major Road
............Unsealed Road or Track
............City Road
............City Street
............Railway
............Underground Railway
............Narrow Gauge Railway
............Walking Track
............Walking Tour
............Ferry Route
............Cable Car or Chairlift

AREA FEATURES

............Parks
............Built-Up Area
............Pedestrian Mall
............Market
............Cemetery
............Forest
............Beach or Desert
............Rocks

HYDROGRAPHIC FEATURES

............Coastline
............River, Creek
............Rapids, Waterfalls
............Lake, Intermittent Lake
............Aqueduct
............River Flow
............Swamp

SYMBOLS

☼ CAPITAL		............National Capital
◉ Capital		............Regional Capital
CITY		............Major City
● City		............City
● Town		............Town
● Village		............Village

............Place to Stay, Place to Eat
............Cafe, Pub or Bar
............Post Office, Telephone
............Tourist Information, Bank
............Transport, Parking
............Museum, Youth Hostel
............Caravan Park, Camping Ground
............Church, Cathedral
............Stately Home, Synagogue

............Embassy, Petrol Station
............Airport, Airfield
............Swimming Pool, Gardens
............Shopping Centre, Zoo
............Golf Course, Metro Station
............Hospital, Police Station
............One Way Street, Route Number
............Stately Home, Monument
............Castle, Mountain Range
............Mountain or Hill, Lookout
............Lighthouse, Pass
............Beach, Spring
............Archaeological Site or Ruins
............Ancient or City Wall
............Railway Station

Note: not all symbols displayed above appear in this book

Portugal Map Index

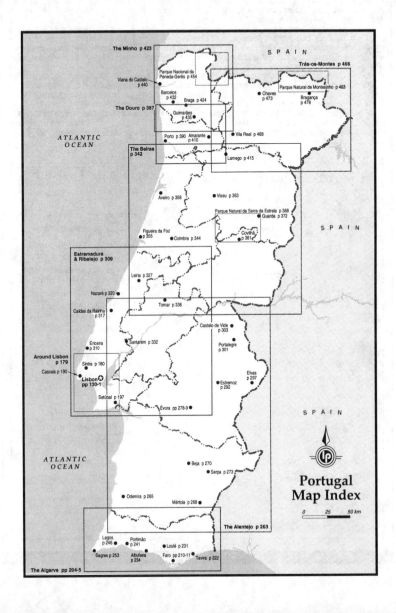

The Minho p 423

S P A I N

Trás-os-Montes p 466

Parque Nacional da Peneda-Gerês p 454

Viana do Castelo p 440

Parque Natural de Montesinho p 483

Barcelos p 432

Braga p 424

Chaves p 473

Bragança p 478

The Douro p 387

Guimarães p 435

Porto p 390

Amarante p 410

Vila Real p 468

ATLANTIC OCEAN

The Beiras p 342

Lamego p 415

Aveiro p 358

Viseu p 363

Parque Natural da Serra da Estrela p 368

Guarda p 372

S P A I N

Figueira da Foz p 355

Coimbra p 344

Covilhã p 381

Estremadura & Ribatejo p 309

Leiria p 327

Nazaré p 320

Tomar p 336

Caldas da Rainha p 317

Castelo de Vide p 303

Ericeira p 310

Santarém p 332

Portalegre p 301

Around Lisbon p 179

Sintra p 180

Elvas p 297

Cascais p 190

Lisbon pp 130-1

Estremoz p 292

Setúbal p 197

Évora pp 278-9

S P A I N

ATLANTIC OCEAN

Beja p 270

Serpa p 273

Odemira p 265

Mértola p 268

Portugal Map Index

0   25   50 km

The Alentejo p 263

Lagos p 246

Portimão p 241

Loulé p 231

Sagres p 253

Albufeira p 234

Faro pp 210-11

Tavira p 222

The Algarve pp 204-5

Carving Up Portugal

Traditionally Portugal was composed of seven loosely defined provinces *(províncias)* – the Minho (after the Rio Minho), the Douro (after the Rio Douro), Trás-os-Montes ('beyond the mountains'), the Beira ('border'), the Estremadura ('furthest from the Rio Douro'), the Alentejo ('beyond the Rio Tejo') and the Algarve (after the Moorish *al-gharb*, for 'west country').

In the 1830s the boundaries of these provinces were firmed up and they were subdivided into administrative districts *(distritos)*, each named after its main town. In the 1930s three provinces were broken into smaller pieces – the Beira into Beira Litoral (coastal), Beira Alta (upper) and Beira Baixa (lower); the Estremadura into Estremadura and Ribatejo; and the Alentejo into Alto Alentejo and Baixo Alentejo.

The chapters of this book correspond to the traditional provinces, defined by their 1830s borders – with the exceptions of a separate chapter for Lisbon and its surroundings, and the inclusion in the Douro chapter of the entire Douro valley all the way to the Spanish border (even though some towns in the valley are properly part of Beira Alta or Trás-os-Montes).

To complicate matters, ICEP, the Portuguese tourism authority, has invented its own geographically based 'tourism regions' *(regiões de turismo)*. Their brochures and maps, and the locations of regional tourist offices, are all based on these regions whose borders don't correspond exactly with any of the political ones. ■

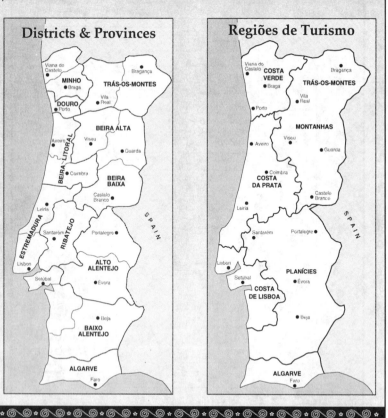

Introduction

Portugal has long been overlooked on the traveller's European itinerary. This is a land apart, at the westernmost corner of Europe, its development hindered for hundreds of years by poverty and political turmoil. Ruled by Romans and Moors for centuries, and perennially in the threatening shadow of Spain, it finally established its independence and its frontiers in the 13th century (making it one of Europe's oldest countries). Two hundred years later its mariners ventured into the unknown, ultimately discovering a sea route to India and turning Portugal into one of the richest and most powerful kingdoms in the Western hemisphere. But the gold and glory were short-lived. Portugal slipped into chaos and obscurity on the forgotten hem of Europe.

Wracked by political upheaval, including 48 years of dictatorship and a revolution in 1974, it has only recently begun to emerge from the shadows. In 1986 it joined the European Union and looked to a future within Europe. Thanks largely to massive EU funding, changes since then have been fast and furious: new highways to Spain, new urban development, new enterprises and new confidence. But the long isolation, especially the xenophobic period of dictatorship under Salazar, has left much of the country extraordinarily, often appealingly, old-fashioned. This includes the capital, Lisbon, which, despite ferocious redevelopment in the run-up to Expo '98, remains one of Europe's most attractive and relaxing cities. Although stretches of the country's 800 km of Atlantic coastline are terribly polluted and the southern Algarve coastline has long

hosted tourists (and paid the price with its ugly coastal development), there's plenty left that's wild, unspoilt and stunningly beautiful. That's true of the interior too. For such a small country there's a remarkable natural diversity, ranging from the south's undulating plains and Mediterranean landscapes to the north's dramatic mountain ranges and lush valleys. While the south, particularly the Alentejo, is chequered with vast farming estates (originally founded by the Romans) and yawning vistas of cork oaks and wheat, the north reflects an even older agricultural system of tiny smallholdings supporting maize, vegetables and vines. Socially, too, there are obvious north-south divisions: southern Portuguese tend to be outgoing and 'Mediterranean', whereas northerners are more conservative and religious, taking their festivals and folklore very seriously indeed. In parts of the rural north, where EU funds have yet to trickle down, life has changed little in hundreds of years. Poverty is so ingrained that many families depend on money sent by menfolk who have emigrated to France and Germany in search of work, following a tradition dating from the 17th and 18th centuries. Their home villages of granite and shale houses, bullock carts and donkeys seem hardly touched by Portugal's new winds of progress, though even here roads are slowly being upgraded and farm machinery is being introduced.

As a traveller in this little-explored corner of Europe, you've got some enviable choices to make: you can stick to the Algarve with its lively resorts, golf courses and water sports; loiter in Lisbon with its up-beat attitude and lively nightlife, including music ranging from *fado* – Portugal's own soul-searing blues – to immigrant African sounds; trek into remote mountains where the Portuguese themselves rarely go; follow a cultural trail through the art and architecture of half a dozen UNESCO World Heritage sites, including Évora, Batalha and Alcobaça; or meander up the beautiful Lima, Douro and Minho valleys in the north. Of course there are hiccups – phones are infuriating, reliable information is scarce and many officials are incurably inefficient. On the other hand, transport and accommodation are excellent and reasonably priced. Food, if not refined, is certainly plentiful, and Portuguese wine is perhaps the country's best and most addictive bargain. Add to this a generous supply of sunshine and you've got one of the most attractive destinations in Europe.

Facts about the Country

HISTORY
Pre-Roman & Roman
The Iberian Peninsula is known to have been inhabited for at least 500,000 years but the earliest evidence of human habitation in Portugal is some Neanderthal-type bones and the recently discovered Palaeolithic rock carvings beside the Rio Cóa in northern Portugal, which are believed to have been executed some 20,000 years ago. The first distinct cultures can be traced back to the Neolithic-era *castro* culture of fortified hilltop settlements and to settlements in the lower Tejo valley dating from 5500 BC.

During the first millennium BC, Celtic people started to trickle into the peninsula, settling in northern and western areas of Portugal around 700 BC. They merged their culture with that of the castro culture, creating dozens of *citânias* or fortified villages (especially in the northern Minho district), complete with huge defence walls and several moats. Many, including the formidable citânia of Briteiros near Braga, which still shows evidence of its complex fortifications, continued to be used right up to Roman times.

Meanwhile, further south, Phoenician traders, followed by Greeks and Carthaginians, set up coastal stations and mined metals inland. The Carthaginians held sway until their defeat by the Romans in the Second Punic War (218-202 BC). When the Romans swept into southern Portugal in 210 BC, they expected easy victory. But they hadn't reckoned on the Lusitani. This Celtic warrior tribe, based between the Tejo (Tagus) and Douro rivers, fought ferociously against the invaders for some 50 years. Only when their brilliant leader, Viriathus, was deceived and assassinated in 139 BC by three of his followers did the resistance collapse. The name Lusitania lived on as one of the later Roman provinces, but by 19 BC the Romans had subdued all other signs of Lusitanian independence. By then, under Decimus Junius Brutus, and later Julius Caesar, a capital had been established at Olisipo (Lisbon) in 60 BC and major colonies founded at Scallabis (Santarém), Pax Julia (Beja), Bracara Augusta (Braga) and Ebora (Évora).

Around 25 BC, Augustus divided this part of the Roman Empire – called Hispania Ulterior – into several different provinces, including Lusitania (covering the area south of the Douro), and Baetica (Andalusia). In the 3rd century AD, the Minho district became part of a new province called Gallaecia (Galicia). It was around this time, too, that Christianity was established, with important bishoprics at Évora and Braga.

By the 5th century AD, when the Roman Empire had all but collapsed, Portugal's inhabitants had had some 600 years of Roman rule. What did they get from it? Most usefully, roads and bridges (still in evidence throughout Portugal), but also the introduction of wheat, barley, olives and vines; a system of large farming estates (called *latifúndios* and still in existence in the Alentejo); a legal system; and, above all, a Latin-derived language. No other invader left Portugal such an influential legacy.

Moors & Christians
The gap left by the Romans was quickly filled by barbarian invaders from beyond the Pyrenees: Vandals, Alans, Visigoths and Suevi. The Germanic Suevi tribe had the greatest impact, settling between the Minho and Douro rivers in about 411 AD and ruling from Braga and Portucale (the Roman settlement near the mouth of the Douro, which later became known as Porto). For a time, the Suevi had tenuous control over most of the peninsula, but in about 469 AD the Arian Christian Visigoths got the upper hand, encouraged by the Romans. Internal disputes paved the way for the Visigoths' downfall and for Portugal's next great wave of invaders: in 711, Muslim forces from Africa were

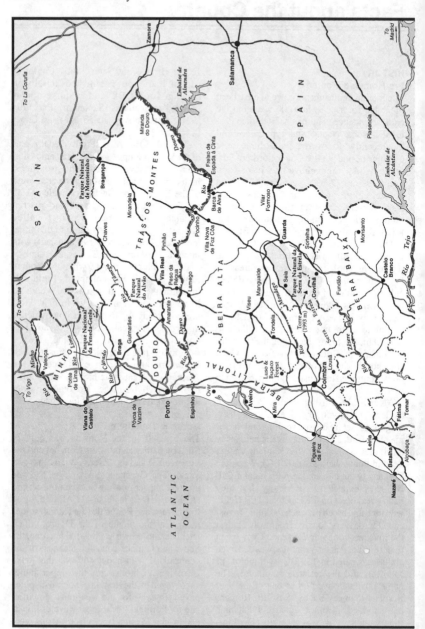

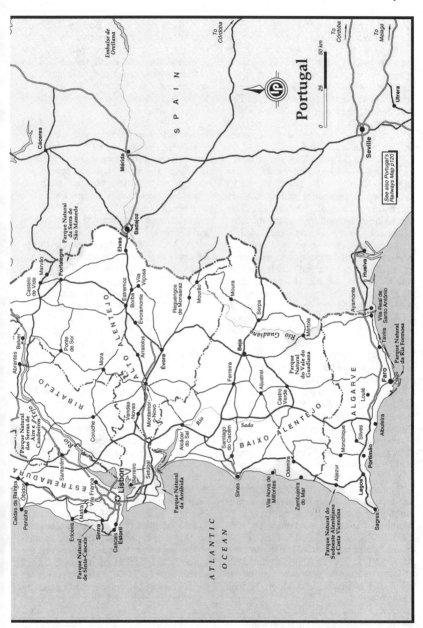

invited to come and help one of the squabbling Visigoth factions. The Moors were only too ready to move northwards. Commanded by Tariq ibn Ziyad, they rapidly occupied Portugal's southern coastal region. Egyptians settled in the Beja and Faro area, while Syrians mostly settled between Faro and Seville, an area they called al-Gharb al-Andalus. The north – known as the county of Portugal – remained unstable, unsettled and predominantly Christian.

Under the Moors (who established a capital at Silves, then called Shelb), the Portuguese living in the south enjoyed a civilising and productive period. The new rulers were tolerant of both Jews and Christians. Christian smallholding farmers, called Mozárabs, were allowed to keep working their land and were encouraged to try out new methods of irrigation and new crops, especially citrus fruits and rice. It was from this period, too, that Arabic words began to filter into the Portuguese language, and Arabic influences into the local cuisine. In particular there was an increasing obsession with cakes and desserts of unsurpassable sweetness.

Meanwhile, in the north, Christian powers were gaining strength. The symbolic kickstart to the Reconquista was the Christian victory over a small force of Moors in 718 at Covadonga in the Asturias, northern Spain. Around this kernel of Christianity the tiny kingdom of Asturias-León slowly expanded. It gradually took over Castile, Aragón, Galicia, and the land of Portucale, including Porto which was taken by the Christians in 868.

By the 11th century Portucale had become an important regional power, for a time autonomous under the dynastic rule of Mumadona Dias and her family. By 1064 Coimbra was also included in the Christian sphere, governed by a Mozárab. In 1085 Afonso VI, king of the Christian kingdoms of León and Castile, took the bull by the horns and conquered the Moors in their Spanish heartland of Toledo. A colourful character, Afonso is said to have gambled on securing Seville by playing a game of chess

with its cultured emir. But the following year, Afonso faced a tougher enemy: the ruthless Almoravids from Morocco who answered the emir's call for help. They defeated Afonso and established a harsh rule, driving out the Mozárabs. Worse was to follow with the arrival of the even more fanatical Almohads.

When Afonso, in his turn, called for foreign help, European crusaders were quick to rally against the 'infidels'. Among them were Henri of Burgundy and his cousin Raymond who won more than honour and glory on the battlefield: they won the hands of Afonso's daughters. Henri married Teresa (and became Count of Portucale), Raymond married Urraca (and became Lord of Galicia and Coimbra).

On Afonso's death, however, things became messy: while Urraca's son, Afonso Raimúndez (later Afonso VII), took control of León, Teresa, acting as regent for her son, Afonso Henriques, after the death of her husband in 1112, favoured a union with Galicia, thanks to her dalliance with a Galician. But she reckoned without the nationalist ideas of her young son. In 1128, Afonso took up arms against her, roundly defeating her forces near his capital, Guimarães. At first, he still had to bow to the superior power of his cousin, Afonso VII. But by 1143, after a dramatic victory against the Moors at Ourique in 1139, Afonso was formally acknowledged as Afonso I, King of Portugal, a title confirmed in 1179 by the pope (on condition extra tribute was paid, of course).

By then, Afonso had also retaken Santarém and Lisbon from the Moors (crusaders en route to the Holy Land helped with Lisbon's siege in 1147). By the time of Afonso's death in 1185, the Portuguese frontier was secure to the Rio Tejo. Yet in spite of the assistance frequently given by the crusaders (another hoodlum bunch helped capture Silves in 1189), it was to take almost another century before the rest of the country – the Alentejo and the Algarve – was wrested from the Moors. Finally, in 1297, after several disputes with the neighbouring

Spanish power, Castile, the boundaries of the Portuguese kingdom (much the same as today) were given official recognition in the Treaty of Alcañices. The kingdom of Portugal had arrived.

The Burgundian Era

During the time of the Reconquista, the 400,000 inhabitants of the country – most of whom lived in the north – were faced with more than war and turmoil: in the wake of the Christian victories they faced the arrival of new rulers and new Christian settlers (especially in Trás-os-Montes and the Beiras, and later in the Algarve). The powerful military orders, such as the Knights Templar and the Hospitallers, took control of much of the land south of the Tejo, while the Cisterian religious order developed the Alcobaça area.

The Church and its extremely wealthy clergy were the greediest landowners – so much so that Afonso II and his successors had to hold frequent royal commissions to recover illegally taken land. Next in the land-owning pecking order came a hundred or so nobles from the aristocratic warrior class, followed by a thousand or so minor nobles. During the rule of Afonso Henriques' son, Sancho I, many municipalities *(concelhos)* were enfranchised and given special privileges embodied in charters. Many Muslims, too, were enfranchised, though slavery among the Moors persisted in some places right up to the 13th century. And both Moors and Jews continued to live in segregated areas – called *mourarias* for the Moors and *judiarias* for the Jews.

So although in theory free, most common people were still subjects of the landowning classes, working on their lord's land, their rights controlled by the terms of the charters. In the south, especially, many were also recruited as foot soldiers for ongoing raids into Muslim territory. The first hint of democratic rule came with the establishment of the *cortes* (parliament): an assembly of nobles and clergy who first met in 1211 at Coimbra, which was then the capital. Municipal representation – allowing commoners (mostly wealthy merchants) to attend the cortes – followed in 1254. Six years later, Afonso III moved the capital to Lisbon.

However, although Afonso III can take credit for these important constitutional changes, and for standing up to the power of the Church, it was his son Dinis (1279-1325) who started to really shake Portugal into shape. A far-sighted and cultured man, Dinis brought the judicial systems under royal control, initiated progressive afforestation programmes, suppressed the dangerously powerful Knights Templar by refounding them as the Order of Christ, and encouraged internal trade. He also cultivated music, education and the arts, founding a university in Lisbon in 1290, which later transferred to Coimbra.

His foresight was spot on when it came to defending Portugal's frontiers: Dinis built or rebuilt some 50 fortresses along the eastern frontier with Castile, and signed a pact of friendship with England in 1308, which formed the basis of a future, long-lasting alliance.

It was none too soon. Within 60 years of Dinis' death, Portugal was at war with Castile over rival claims to the Portuguese throne. Fernando I, the last of the Burgundian kings, had done much to provoke the clash by playing a dangerous game of alliances both with Castile and with the English as represented by John of Gaunt, Duke of Lancaster. He had, for instance, promised his only legitimate child, Beatriz, to John of Gaunt's nephew when the English arrived in 1381 to help with an invasion of Castile. In the event, Ferdinand made peace with the Castilians halfway through the campaign and offered Beatriz to Juan I of Castile instead, thereby throwing Portugal's future into Castilian hands.

On Ferdinand's death in 1383, his wife, Leonor Teles, ruled as regent, but she, too, was entangled with the Spanish, having long had a Galician lover. While the nobility and bishops supported her, the merchant classes turned to a more Portuguese option: João, Grand Master of the Order of Avis, and a son (albeit illegitimate) of Ferdinand's father,

Pedro I. João assassinated Leonor's lover, Leonor fled to the King of Castile, and the Castilians duly invaded. But João had the support of the common people, who rose in revolt not only against the invaders but also against those Castilian nobles who had settled in Portugal.

The showdown came in 1385 when João faced an imposing force of Castilians at Aljubarrota. Even with Nun' Álvares Pereira (the 'Holy Constable') as his military right-hand man, and a force of English archers as support, the odds were stacked against him. João vowed to build a monastery to the Virgin if he won. The victory sealed Portugal's independence – and delivered the superb architectural legacy of Batalha Abbey. It also sealed Portugal's alliance with England: the 1386 Treaty of Windsor was followed by the marriage of João with John of Gaunt's daughter, Philippa of Lancaster. Peace with Castile was finally concluded in 1411. Portugal was ready to look further afield for its adventures.

The Age of Discoveries

Morocco was the obvious first outlet for the military energies of João and his supporters:

in 1415 Ceuta fell to his forces. Although João's successor, Duarte, unsuccessfully tried to capture Tangier in 1437, these overseas advances marked the start of something very big indeed. It was João's third son, Prince Henry 'the Navigator', who focused the spirit of the age – a combination of crusading zeal, love of martial glory and desire for gold and riches – into some extraordinary explorations across the seas, transforming the small kingdom into a great imperial power (see the boxed aside).

Using the resources of the wealthy Order of Christ, Prince Henry established a kind of 'think-tank' with experts on shipbuilding, map making, astronomy and navigation. Expeditions were organised and sent forth into the unknown. Madeira and the Azores were the first lands to be discovered, in 1419 and 1427 (colonisation followed in 1445). In 1434 Gil Eanes sailed beyond the much-feared Cape Bojador on the west coast of Africa and discovered that the world did not fall into hell. By the 1460s the Cape Verde Islands had been discovered and the Gulf of Guinea had been reached. And in 1487 Bartolomeu Dias rounded the Cape of Good Hope. The way was now open to India: in

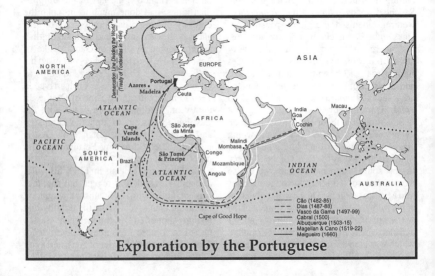

Exploration by the Portuguese

1497, during the reign of Manuel I (who titled himself 'lord of the conquest, navigation, and commerce of India, Ethiopia, Arabia and Persia'), Vasco da Gama reached Calicut. With gold (and slaves) from Africa and spices from the East, Portugal soon became enormously wealthy.

Spain, however, had also jumped on the

Prince Henry the Navigator

Henrique, Infante de Portugal (Prince of Portugal), was born in Porto in 1394, third of four half-English sons of João I and Philippa of Lancaster. By the time he died 66 years later, he had almost single-handedly set Portugal on course for its so-called Age of Discoveries, turning it from Spain's little brother into a wealthy maritime power, and in the process transforming seaborne exploration from a groping, semirandom process to a near science.

At the age of 18, Henry and his older brothers, Duarte and Pedro, keen to prove themselves in battle, convinced their father to invade Ceuta in Morocco. The city fell with ease in 1415 and Henry was appointed its governor. Though he spent little time there, this stirred his interest in North Africa, and with several ships now at his disposal, he began to sponsor exploratory voyages. Two of his protégés discovered the islands of Porto Santo and Madeira (actually rediscovered them, as Genoese sailors had already stumbled across them in the 14th century).

In 1419 Henry became governor of the Algarve, moved to the south coast and began collecting the best sailors, map makers, shipbuilders, instrument makers and astronomers he could find in order to get Portuguese explorers as far out into the world as possible. The usual story is that he did this at Sagres, and while he did found the new town of Vila do Infante there, much of the work may actually have gone on at Lagos, where many of his expeditions sailed from.

The next year, at the age of 26, Henry was made Grand Master of the Order of Christ, which superseded the crusading Knights Templar, and his efforts went into high gear thanks to money available through the order. His strategy was indeed as much religious as commercial, aimed at sapping the power of Islam by siphoning off its trade and ultimately, as it were, by finding a way around it by sea, all the while converting newly discovered peoples. All his ships bore the trademark red cross of the Order of Christ on their sails. Henry took no vows, though he lived simply and chastely, and remained single all his life.

One of the major accomplishments of Henry's sailors during the reign of his brother Duarte as king was psychological as much as physical: the rounding of Cape Bojador on the West African coast by Gil Eanes in 1434, breaking a maritime superstition that this was the end of the world. The newly designed, highly manoeuvrable Portuguese caravel made it possible.

In 1437 Henry and his younger brother, Prince Fernando, embarked on a disastrous attempt to take Tangier. The defeated Portuguese army was only allowed to leave on condition that Fernando remain behind as a hostage. Fernando died six years later, still in captivity, a source of lifelong guilt for Henry and probably an added incentive for his work.

He carried on under the regency of his brother Pedro and the rule of his nephew Afonso V. In 1441, as unease was mounting over his lavish spending on exploration, ships began returning with West African gold and slaves. Within a few years the slave trade was galloping, and Henry's interest gradually began to turn from exploration to commerce. He founded his own trading company in Lagos, having been granted by Afonso the sole right to trade on the coast of Guinea.

The last great discovery to which Henry was witness was of several of the Cape Verde islands by the Venetian Alvise Cá da Mosto and the Portuguese Diogo Gomes. The furthest his sailors got in his lifetime was present-day Sierra Leone, or possibly the Ivory Coast. His last military adventure, at the age of 64, was the capture, with Afonso, of Alcácer Ceguer in Morocco. Two years later, on 13 November 1460, he died at Sagres – heavily in debt in spite of revenues from the slave and gold trade. ■

The Portuguese Discover Australia

It's believed by many historians that Portuguese explorers reached the Australian coast in the 16th century, 2½ centuries before the arrival of Captain James Cook. At least one Australian historian, Kenneth McIntyre, is convinced that by 1536 they had secretly mapped three-quarters of the coast. In September 1996 a 500-year-old Portuguese coin was discovered by a treasure-hunter on the Mornington Peninsula, on the Victorian coast, adding further weight to this theory. ■

the exploration bandwagon and was soon disputing some of Portugal's claims to foreign land. Columbus' 'discovery' of America for Spain in 1492 led to a fresh outburst of jealous conflict. It was resolved by the pope with the extraordinary Treaty of Tordesillas of 1494, by which the world was divided between the two great powers along the line 370 leagues west of the Cape Verde Islands. Spain won the lands to the west of the line, Portugal those to the east – including Brazil, the existence of which they may have known about already (it was officially claimed for Portugal in 1500).

In the following years, as Portuguese explorers reached Timor, China and eventually Japan, Portugal consolidated its imperial power and world trading status by establishing garrison ports and strategic trading and missionary posts: Goa in 1510, Malacca in 1511, Hormuz in 1515 and Macau in 1557. Back home, the monarchy, taking its 'royal fifth' of trading profits, became the richest in Europe, and a lavish 'Manueline' style of architecture marked the exuberance of the age, notably in the Mosteiro dos Jerónimos and Torre de Belém.

It couldn't last, of course. By the 1570s, the huge cost of the expeditions and the maintenance of the overseas empire began to take its toll. The riches gained went little further than the monarchy and nobility, while domestic agriculture declined and prices in Europe fell. The expulsion of many commercially minded refugee Spanish Jews in 1496

and the subsequent persecution of converted Jews ('New Christians' or *marranos*) only worsened the financial situation.

The final straw came in 1557 when the young idealist Sebastião took the throne, determined to bring Christianity to Morocco. He rallied a huge force of 18,000 and set off in 1578, only to be disastrously defeated at the Battle of Alcácer-Quibir. Sebastião and 8000 others were killed, including most of Portugal's nobility. Over the next few years, Sebastião's aged successor, Cardinal Henrique, had to drain the royal coffers in paying ransoms for those captured. On his death in 1580, Sebastião's uncle, Philip II of Spain, seized the opportunity to claim the throne, defeating Portuguese forces at the battle of Alcântara. The following year he was crowned Felipe I of Portugal. It marked the end of the Avis dynasty and centuries of independence; the end of Portugal's Golden Age and its glorious moment on the world stage.

Spain's Rule & Portugal's Revival

The start of Hapsburg rule looked promising: Felipe I promised to preserve Portugal's autonomy and to frequently call on the long-ignored cortes. However, the common people strongly resented Spanish rule and held onto the dream that Sebastião was still alive: pretenders to the Sebastião role continued to pop up right until 1600. And though Felipe was honourable, his successors were considerably less so, using Portugal to raise money and men for Spain's wars overseas and appointing Spaniards to Portuguese offices of government. Meanwhile, Portugal's empire was slipping out of its grasp. In 1622, the English seized Hormuz, and by the 1650s the Dutch had taken Malacca, Ceylon and part of Brazil.

Portuguese resentment against the Spaniards finally exploded in 1640 when an attempt was made to recruit Portuguese forces to crush a revolt in Catalonia. Encouraged by the French (who were at war with Spain at the time), a group of nationalist-minded leaders forced the unpopular governor of Portugal from her office in

Lisbon and drove out the Spanish garrisons. The Duke of Bragança, grandson of a former claimant to the throne and head of a powerful landowning family, reluctantly stepped into the hot seat and was crowned João IV.

With a hostile Spain on the doorstep, Portugal searched for allies: in 1654 it signed a treaty with the English Commonwealth, followed by the Treaty of 1661 by which Charles II of England married João's daughter, Catherine of Bragança, promising arms and men for the war with Spain, in return for Portugal ceding Tangier and Bombay. Preoccupied with wars elsewhere, Spain made only half-hearted attempts to recapture Portugal and, after losing a series of battles on the frontier, it finally recognised Portuguese independence with the 1668 Treaty of Lisbon.

The moves towards democracy, which had been started with municipal representation at the cortes over 400 years previously, were stalled during the reigns of João's successors. During this time the Crown hardly bothered to call the cortes at all, thanks to its new power of financial independence following the discovery of gold and precious stones in Brazil at the end of the 17th century. Economically, too, the country was in trouble: after a short burst of economic sense, when Pedro II's Superintendent of Finance managed to boost exports and restrict the import of luxury goods, another era of profligate expenditure ensued. This was epitomised by the gigantic baroque monastery palace of Mafra, which required a workforce of some 50,000 men when it was built between 1717 and 1735. The most notable event on the economic front was the 1703 Methuen Treaty, which stimulated Anglo-Portuguese trade by providing preferential terms for the import of English textiles to Portugal and for Portuguese wines to England. But even this wasn't as beneficial as it first appeared, since it increased Portugal's dependency on Britain, reduced its own textile industry and distracted efforts at increasing the production of wheat.

Into this increasingly chaotic scenario stepped the man for the moment: the Marquês de Pombal, chief minister of the hedonistic José I (who was more interested in opera than affairs of state). Popularly described as an enlightened despot, Pombal dragged Portugal into the modern era, crushing any opposition with brutal efficiency. He reformed trade and industry by setting up state monopolies, curbing the power of the British merchants and boosting agriculture and home industries as the Brazilian gold production declined.

He abolished slavery in mainland Portugal and the distinctions between old and 'new' Christians, and emancipated the Jesuits' Indian protégés in Brazil (to the fury of the Jesuits). He founded royal schools and reformed the universities, eliminating the Jesuits' influence and establishing faculties of science. And when Lisbon suffered a devastating earthquake in November 1755, causing the deaths of up to 40,000 people, he acted swiftly and pragmatically to deal with the crisis and rebuild the city. Pombal was then at the height of his powers. In the following years he got rid of his main enemies – the powerful Jesuits and several noble families – by accusing them of a mysterious attempt on the king's life in 1758.

He may well have continued his autocratic rule had it not been for the accession of the extremely devout Maria I in 1777. The anti-clerical Pombal was promptly dismissed, put on trial and charged with various offences, though he was not imprisoned. Although his religious legislation was repealed, his economic, agricultural and educational policies were largely maintained, helping the country back towards prosperity. But turmoil once again was on the horizon, as Napoleon swept through Europe.

The Dawn of a Republic

In 1793 Portugal found itself back at war when it joined England in sending naval forces against revolutionary France. After a few years of uneasy peace, Napoleon threw Portugal an ultimatum: close your ports to British shipping or we'll invade. There was no way Portugal could turn its back on Britain – Portugal depended on its old ally for half its trade (especially in cloth and wine) and for protection of its sea routes. In 1807 Portugal's royal family fled to Brazil (where they stayed for 14 years), and General Junot led Napoleon's forces right into Lisbon, thereby sweeping Portugal into the so-called Peninsular War (France's invasion of Spain and Portugal which lasted until 1814). Invoking the British alliance, Portugal soon had the help of Sir Arthur Wellesley (later Duke of Wellington) and Viscount William Beresford, leading a force of seasoned British troops. After a series of setbacks, the joint Portuguese-British army finally drove the French back across the Spanish border in 1811.

Free but seriously weakened, Portugal was administered by Beresford while João IV and his court remained in Brazil. In 1810 Portugal had lost its profitable intermediary trading role between Brazil and Britain, when it gave Britain the right to trade directly with Brazil. The next humiliation was when Brazil was proclaimed a kingdom in 1815. With soaring debts and dismal trade, Portugal was at one of the lowest points in its history, its status reduced to that of a colony of Brazil and a protectorate of Britain.

Meanwhile, resentment was simmering in the army, not only about the continued presence of the unpopular Beresford but also about lack of pay and promotion. Influenced by liberal ideas circulating in Spain, a group of rebel officers took advantage of Beresford's absence from the country in 1820 to call a cortes and draw up a new, liberal constitution in 1822. Based on the ideals of the Enlightenment, it abolished clerical privileges and the rights of the nobility and instituted a single-chamber parliament, to be chosen every two years by an electorate of men (excluding clergy). Faced with this *fait accompli*, João returned and accepted its terms – though his wife and his son Miguel were bitterly opposed to it, a sentiment that won widespread support in rural areas. João's elder son, Pedro, also had other ideas: left behind to govern Brazil, he immediately snubbed the constitutionalists by declaring Brazil independent in 1822 and himself its

emperor. When João died in 1826, leaving no obvious successor, the stage was set for civil war.

Offered the crown, Pedro first drew up a new, less liberal charter and then abdicated in favour of his seven-year-old daughter Maria, provided she marry her uncle Miguel, and he vowed to accept the new constitution. In 1827, Miguel duly took the oath and was appointed regent, only to abolish Pedro's constitution – still considered unpalatably progressive to many Portuguese – proclaim himself king and revert to the old monarchist system. The liberals rallied under Pedro and, encouraged by the French, British and Spanish liberals, forced Miguel to surrender at Évora-Monte in May 1834.

Pedro died the same year but his daughter Maria, now Queen at the age of 15, kept his flame alive with her fanatical support of his 1826 charter. The supporters of the liberal 1822 constitution, especially the more radical members, were even more active and vociferous. By 1846, with urban discontent exacerbated by economic recession, the prospect of civil war loomed once again. The Duke of Saldanha (a 'Chartist' supporting the 1826 charter) sought the intervention of the British and Spanish, and peace was restored in 1847 with the Convention of Gramido.

For the next five years, Saldanha steered the country through more stable waters. A compromise was reached between the progressive and conservative liberals by using the charter of 1826 but restricting suffrage to 36,000 voters (increased to 500,000 by 1910), and by rotating power between the so-called 'Historicals' (radicals) and the 'Regenerators' (moderates such as Saldanha). Another notable Regenerator was Fontes Pereira de Melo, who created the Ministry of Public Works and set about modernising the country's infrastructure by organising the building of roads, bridges, railways and ports.

Although these improvements helped Portugal's economy, the country was still in dire straits by the turn of the century. Industrial growth lagged far behind that of its

European neighbours, its budgets were rarely balanced, and foreign involvement (notably British) left a quarter of Portugal's trade and industry out of its control. With the development of tobacco manufacture and sardine canning industries, rural areas were depopulated in favour of the cities, and emigration (especially to Brazil) became increasingly popular among the villagers of the poor northern Minho area, their remittances a vital prop to the country's balance of payments.

Much was changing, but for many the changes weren't fast enough. The industrial workers were poorly paid and protected, their organisations lacking political clout. Urban discontent grew, as did support for socialism and trade unions. The humiliation suffered when Britain forced Portugal to withdraw its claim to land between Angola and Mozambique was another blow to the monarchist government.

A radical and nationalist republican movement started to sweep the urban lower-middle classes in Lisbon, Porto and the rural south. When Dom Carlos allowed his premier, João Franco, to rule dictatorially, resentment reached its crisis point and the republicans responded with an attempted coup in 1908. It failed, but the following month, the king and crown prince were assassinated while driving through the streets of Lisbon. Carlos' younger son, Manuel II, and his ministers feebly tried to appease the republicans, but it was too late. On 5 October 1910, after an uprising by both military and naval forces, a republic was declared. Manuel 'the Unfortunate' sailed into exile in Britain where he died in 1932.

The Rise & Fall of Salazar

Hopes were high among the republicans after their landslide victory in the 1911 elections, but it was soon clear that the sentiment expressed in the 1910 national anthem ('Oh sea heroes, oh noble people…raise again the splendour of Portugal…!') wasn't going to be realised any time soon. Under the increasingly dominant leadership of Afonso, Costa's leftist Democrat Party, power was maintained by patronage and a divisive form of anticlericalism that was bitterly opposed in rural areas. Some of Costa's more controversial actions were the expulsion of the religious orders and the internationally criticised persecution of Catholics.

Meanwhile, the economy was in tatters, a situation exacerbated by the financial strain of military operations in WWI when Portugal made the economically disastrous decision to join the Allies. In the recessionary postwar years, political chaos deepened: the various republican factions continued to squabble, workers and their trade unions were repressed despite frequently exercising their new right to strike, and the military became increasingly powerful. The new republic soon had a reputation as Europe's most unstable regime. Between 1910 and 1926 there were 45 changes of government, often installed by military intervention. Yet another coup in May 1926 heralded the familiar round of new names and faces again, until one rose above all the others – António de Oliveira Salazar.

A renowned professor of economics at Coimbra University, Salazar was appointed minister of finance by the new president, General Óscar Carmona, and given sweeping powers to bring some order into Portugal's economy. This he did with such success that by 1932 he was prime minister, a post he was to hold for 36 years. The following year he announced a new constitution and a 'New State': a corporatist republic that was nationalistic, Catholic, authoritarian and repressive. Political parties were banned except for the National Union, a loyalist movement that provided the National Assembly with all its elected members. Strikes were banned and workers were organised into national syndicates or associations that were controlled by their employers. Censorship, propaganda and brute force kept society in order. The feared Polícia Internacional e de Defesa do Estado (PIDE) was the most sinister development, a secret police force that didn't hesitate to use imprisonment and torture to suppress opposition. Not surprisingly, various attempted coups during Salazar's rule quickly came to nothing.

The only good news about life under Salazar was that the economy markedly improved. The country's debt was reduced, as was its dependence on British investment; and although agriculture stagnated because it mechanised too slowly, industry and infrastructure development responded well to encouragement. During the 1950s and 1960s Portugal experienced an economic boom with a growth rate of some 7% to 9% a year in the industrial sector.

Internationally, Salazar played a two-faced game, unofficially supporting Franco's Nationalists during the Spanish Civil War, and supporting the British during WWII despite official neutrality (and despite continuing to sell wolfram to the Germans until 1944). But it was something else on the international scene that finally brought down the Salazar rule, economically and politically: the movement of decolonisation. Refusing to relinquish the colonies, Salazar was faced with increasingly costly military expeditions that were internationally deplored and domestically unpopular, even among the military. In 1961, Goa was occupied by India and local nationalists rose up in Angola. Similar guerrilla movements soon followed in Portuguese Guinea and Mozambique.

In the event, Salazar himself didn't have to face the consequences. In 1968 he fell off a chair and had a stroke, dying two years later. His successor, Marcelo Caetano, made some attempt at reform which only stirred up more unrest, and military officers who sympathised with the African freedom fighters became increasingly reluctant to continue serving in the colonial wars. Several hundred of them formed the Movimento das Forças Armadas (MFA) and, led by General Costa Gomes and General António de Spínola, they carried out a nearly bloodless coup on 25 April 1974, later nicknamed the Revolution of the Carnations (the victorious soldiers apparently stuck carnations in the barrels of their rifles). But although the coup was generally popular (a record 92% of voters turned out in April 1975 to vote for the Constituent Assembly), the year was to be marked by unprecedented chaos and confusion.

From Revolution to Democracy

The first major change took place where the revolution began: in the African colonies. Independence was granted almost immediately to the newly named Guinea-Bissau, and was followed the next year by the decolonisation of the Cape Verde Islands, São Tomé e Príncipe, Mozambique and Angola. Independence wasn't always peaceful for the colonies. A huge civil war broke out in Angola, and when East Timor was relinquished, it was immediately invaded by Indonesia, whose massacre of the Timorese and continuing aggressive occupation is still widely criticised and resented. For Portugal, too, the effects of decolonisation were turbulent. Suddenly it had to cope with nearly a million refugees from the African colonies – a social upheaval that it eventually managed remarkably well.

Politically and economically, however, the country was in a mess. There were widespread strikes and a tangle of political ideas and parties, although the two most powerful groups were the communists (who dominated the trade unions) and a radical wing of the MFA. It was at this time that private banking, insurance firms, transport and the media were nationalised and peasant farmers seized some of the huge latifúndio estates in Alentejo to establish their own communal farms (few of which succeeded and most of which were later returned to their owners).

As the political parties polarised and the MFA factions splintered, the divisions in the country became increasingly obvious, with more traditional conservatives in the north (led by Mário Soares and his Socialist Party, the Partido Socialista or PS) and revolutionaries in the south. In August 1975 a more moderate government was formed, bitterly opposed by the Communist Party (Partido Comunista Português or PCP) and the extreme left. Finally, on 25 November 1975, a radical leftist coup was crushed by moderate forces under General Ramalho Eanes. The revolution had ended.

The Rocky Road to Stability

The new constitution of April 1976 committed Portugal to a blend of socialism and democracy, with a powerful president, an Assembly elected by universal suffrage, and a Council of the Revolution to control the armed forces. After parliamentary elections, Mário Soares formed a minority government and General Eanes won the presidential election.

Only a year later, Soares' government faltered and there followed a series of failed attempts by coalition governments and non-party candidates, including Portugal's first female prime minister, Maria de Lurdes Pintassilgo. In the 1980 elections a new political force emerged: the conservative Democratic Alliance (Aliança Democrática or AD), a combination of right-leaning parties led by the Social Democrat, Francisco de Sá Carneiro. After Carneiro's death in a plane crash that same year, Francisco Pinto Balsemão took over as prime minister and persuaded the socialists in the Assembly to agree to a series of constitutional changes to establish full civilian rule. These included abolishing the Council of the Revolution and reducing the president's powers. Marxist phraseology was also removed from the constitution. Other about-turns favoured by both the public and the government were reprivatisation of the nationalised economy and the abolition of communal farming methods. The first steps were also made to join the European Community (EC), renamed the European Union (EU) in 1992.

It was partly to satisfy the requirements for admission to the EC and to keep the IMF happy that a new coalition government of socialists and social democrats under Mário Soares was forced to implement a strict economic policy and a programme of modernisation. Not surprisingly, the belt-tightening wasn't popular. The most vocal critics were Soares' right-wing partners in the Social Democrat Party (Partido Social Democrata or PSD), led by the dynamic Aníbal Cavaco Silva. And the most active critics were the communist trade unions in the industrial and transport sectors, which organised massive strikes. Adding to this unrest was an increase in urban terrorism, mainly by the radical left-wing group Forças Populares de 25 Abril (FP-25). In June 1984 more than 40 suspects were arrested, including the former revolutionary leader Lieutenant Colonel Otelo Saraiva de Carvalho. At the same time, controversial legislation was passed establishing a new security intelligence agency.

By June 1985 the coalition government had collapsed over disagreements about labour and agricultural reform. At the October elections the PSD emerged as the narrow winner, forming a minority government led by Cavaco Silva as prime minister. Not that it marked the end of Soares' political career: in presidential elections in February 1986, the veteran socialist leader became president, the country's first civilian head of state for 60 years. Another political record was reached in 1987 when parliamentary elections returned Cavaco Silva and the PSD with the first clear majority since 1974. With a repeat performance four years later, it looked as if Portugal had finally reached calm waters.

In January 1986 Portugal was at last admitted to the EU, after nine years of negotiations. Flush with EU funds it now raced ahead of many of its equally poor EU neighbours, recording an unprecedented 4.5% to 5% annual economic growth rate. The new prosperity gave Cavaco Silva the power to push ahead with his programme of radical economic reform and free enterprise. Privatisation continued and fundamental changes were made to the agriculture, education and media sectors.

But there was considerable resistance among industrial workers to the government's attempts at reforming the labour laws (to the employees' disadvantage). During the 1980s, industrial unrest simmered and boiled, leading to major strikes in March 1988 (an estimated 1.5 million workers participated in a 24-hour general strike) and in

January 1989 (10,000 protested in Lisbon). The controversial legislation was finally passed in February 1989, but labour unrest continued with demands by various sectors of the workforce that wage increases should match inflation.

Despite its troubles, the PSD managed to keep most of its seats in elections to the European Parliament in June 1989 (when the Portuguese Greens won their own first seat). However, at municipal elections in December, the scandal-ridden PSD suffered a serious reverse, and the Socialist Party, backed by the communists and the Greens, took control of Lisbon and other major cities. The canny Cavaco Silva fought back with a surprise reshuffle of his cabinet in January 1990, removing the scandal-tainted ministers. But further scandal erupted in February when the socialist governor appointed by Soares to rule Macau (the Chinese territory administered by Portugal until 1999) was involved in a bribery accusation.

Nevertheless, the hugely popular Soares won an outright victory in the presidential elections in January 1991. Even more surprisingly, perhaps, the PSD renewed its absolute majority in the legislative elections that followed in October. The electorate may have been disgusted by the scandals and worried about the increasing problems of unemployment and inflation, and the severe shortcomings in the health and education services, but they were still attracted by the PSD's promise of continued economic growth and political stability.

Portugal Today

It was soon obvious that the PSD promise of prosperity was going to be pretty hard to keep. In 1992, the year Portugal held the presidency of the European Community, all EC trade barriers fell and Portugal was faced with the threat of growing competition, especially for its small and middle-sized companies. Fortunes faltered as recession set in, and disillusion with the PSD grew as Europe's single market revealed the backwardness of Portugal's agricultural sector. Uncontrolled profiteering, pollution and corruption were also undermining the PSD's reputation and the improvements that had been made in infrastructure, transport, health and welfare. Politically, too, there was trouble brewing. Tensions between the socialist Soares and his centre-right prime minister became increasingly evident, with President Soares frequently exercising his right of veto to stall or modify controversial legislation.

Throughout 1993 and 1994 there were strikes (mainly in support of wage increases), charges of corruption (among other cases, the Minister of Finance was investigated over missing EU funds), and student demonstrations, protesting about increases in university fees. The government was further shaken when Amnesty International expressed public concern about allegations of torture by Portuguese police and prison officers.

At local elections in 1993 and elections to the European Parliament, voters showed how the tide was turning, giving the Socialist Party (PS) more seats than the PSD. By the end of 1994, although the government managed to survive a vote of no confidence, criticism was increasingly public, with the president warning darkly of a 'dictatorship of the majority.'

Cavaco Silva saw the writing on the wall. In an astute move, which many saw as a way to save his reputation for presidential elections in 1996, he announced his resignation as leader of the PSD in January 1995. He continued as prime minister until the legislative elections of October 1995, when the PS, under the dynamic leadership of 46-year-old António Guterres, gained the largest number of seats (although without an overall majority) and 10% more votes than the PSD. As expected, Cavaco Silva ran for the presidency in January 1996 on the expiry of Soares' second and last term of office. But his defeat by the socialist mayor of Lisbon, Jorge Sampaio, who won 54% of the vote compared to Cavaco Silva's 46%, confirmed how the populace had tired of Cavaco Silva. The outcome of both elections marks the end of a decade in power by the PSD, and it's the first time since 1974 that the president and prime minister have come from the same party (socialist).

António Guterres had led his party's campaign on a platform of social reform but in most ways he offers little change in his programme of government. Indeed, one of the first announcements made within a month of winning the election was that there would need to be two years of economic stringency before the government could hope to meet its pledges on social reform. But people are hopeful: the days of uneasy coalitions and economic instability that marked the 1970s and early 1980s are over. The business community has been reassured by Guterres' commitment to budgetary rigour and his determination to join the European Monetary System in 1999. The atmosphere is one of cautious optimism that Guterres can fulfil at least some of his promises, such as regional devolution in mainland Portugal and the establishment of a minimum guaranteed income. However, if improvements in health care, education and policing take too long and if unpopular budgetary cuts are needed to qualify for monetary union, the new-look, market-oriented Socialist Party could well be in trouble.

GEOGRAPHY

Together with Ireland, Portugal lies at the westernmost edge of Europe. Covering an area of 92,389 sq km and being only 560 km north to south and 220 km east to west, it's one of Europe's smallest countries (about the size of Austria). But it's also one of the most geographically diverse. Bordered on the west and south by the Atlantic Ocean and on the east and north by Spain (a country five times bigger), it offers everything from dramatic mountain ranges and lush, green valleys in the north to flat, dry plains and undulating landscapes in the south. You can take your pick of beaches from over 830 km of coastline and your choice of mountain hiking from a series of *serras* that reach their highest point with the Torre peak (1993m) in the Serra da Estrela range.

Dividing the country roughly in half is the Rio Tejo, which flows north-east to south-west, draining into the Atlantic at Lisbon, one of Portugal's few natural harbours. To the north of the Tejo are most of the country's mountains: 90% of the land here rises above 400m, although only a fraction is higher than 700m. This region, together with Spanish Galicia, comprises the mountainous border of the Meseta (a major plateau region of the Iberian Peninsula), which is also the source of three of Portugal's most important rivers, the Douro, Tejo and Guadiana.

While the fertile and heavily populated north-west Minho region is characterised by rolling plateaus and rivers flowing through deep gorges, the adjacent provinces of Beira Alta ('upper' Beira), Douro and Trás-os-Montes (literally 'behind the mountains'), are marked by high plateaus of granite, schist and slate. This region rises to 800m and is billed the *terra fria* (cold country). In the eastern and southern stretches of the Alto Douro is the *terra quente* (hot country), a region of sheltered valleys with dark schists that trap the heat, creating the perfect microclimate (described by locals as nine months of winter and three months of hell) for growing Portugal's port wine grapes.

Further south, the high Beira plains are *serra* country, featuring several major mountain ranges, notably the Serra da Estrela, which are a continuation of Spain's central sierras. The mountain chain extends southwest, where the Serra do Açor and Serra da Lousã feature as some of the loveliest and least visited ranges in the land.

The border between Beira Baixa ('lower') and Alto ('high') Alentejo at the Rio Tejo is marked by the sudden drop of the plateau from an altitude of 480m to 215m. South of here is the low-lying and often marshy coastline of Beira Litoral and Estremadura, stretching southwards along the Atlantic seaboard and characterised by lagoons and salt marshes at the river mouths. Inland, between the Tejo and the Guadiana, the Alto Alentejo features a series of plateaus, a continuation of the Spanish tablelands. Further south, in northern Baixo Alentejo, are ridges of quartz and marble, a vast undulating landscape of wheat, cork and olive trees, which rarely rises above 150m.

This southern half of the country is predominantly flat: some 63% of the country below 400m is found here. Only the eastern Serra do Caldeirão and western Serra de Monchique break the monotony, acting as a division between the Alentejo and the Algarve provinces and a buffer against the northern climate for the Algarve, which basks in a protected Mediterranean climate and semitropical landscapes.

The various provinces serve as administrative areas as well as distinct geographical regions for most guidebooks (including this one). But you'll also find that the national tourist board's literature divides the country into five main regions: the Montanhas refers to Trás-os-Montes, the inland Beiras and part of the Douro; Costa Verde refers to the Minho and the rest of the Douro; Costa de Prata to Beira Litoral, Estremadura and Ribatejo (except Lisbon and surroundings); Planícies to inland Alentejo; Costa de Lisboa to the coastal region from Lisbon to just below Sines; and the Algarve, which is the same as the provincial region. Within these regions are further divisions, eg Costa Azul refers to the Setúbal area; Rota do Sol to the Leiria area; Rota da Luz to the Aveiro area; and Região de Turismo dos Templários to the Tomar region. The headquarters for each of these regional tourism divisions has the most detailed information for the area.

The islands of Madeira and the Azores (originally colonised in the 15th century) are also part of metropolitan Portugal, although too far away to be considered in a peninsular visit: Madeira (a popular destination in its own right) lies 900 km to the south-west (off the west coast of Africa), while the nine-island archipelago of the Azores is spread in the Atlantic Ocean about 1440 km west of Lisbon. The last remaining overseas territory still under Portuguese administration is Macau, which returns to Chinese rule in 1999.

CLIMATE

Portugal is in a unique position in Europe,

falling both in the Atlantic and the Mediterranean climatic zones. It's the Atlantic, however, that influences the country the most, especially in the north-west Minho province, which has noticeably milder, damper weather than the rest of the country. As much as 2000 mm of rain a year can fall here (2500 mm on higher ground), compared to an annual average of 300 mm in the interior of the Algarve, 686 mm in Lisbon and a national average of 1100 mm. The Atlantic also helps to moderate the dry Mediterranean climate of the southern coastal regions, where summer temperatures average a comfortable maximum of 28°C (the highest recorded temperature for Faro in the last 30 years is 40°C). Average summer maximums in Lisbon and Porto are slightly less (27°C and 25°C), and rain is a rarity everywhere in July and August. Even winters are mild in these coastal regions, averaging 13°C in Lisbon, 12°C in Porto and 16°C in Faro.

Inland, however, there's greater temperature variation, thanks to continental winds blowing from the interior. Summers can be painfully hot in the upper Douro valley and Alentejo (expect temperatures as high as 40°C), with drought often lasting for a month or more. Further south, drought can last even longer, with the Azores high-pressure system ensuring a long, dry summer. Spanish influences (high pressure conditions from the Meseta plateau region), as well as Siberian anticyclones, are also responsible for the relatively severe winters in the mountainous Serra da Estrela and north-easterly Bragança areas – temperatures often drop to freezing levels in Bragança in January. In the Serra da Estrela you can usually ski from January to March, or you can join the queue of traffic to find the last remnants of snow on the Torre peak as late as May. The national winter average temperature, however, is a mild 11°C.

Sun-seekers receive a warm welcome in Portugal: there's an average 12 hours of sunshine a day during a typical Algarve summer (six hours in the winter). In the north, the average drops to about four hours daily during winter but a balmy 10 during summer.

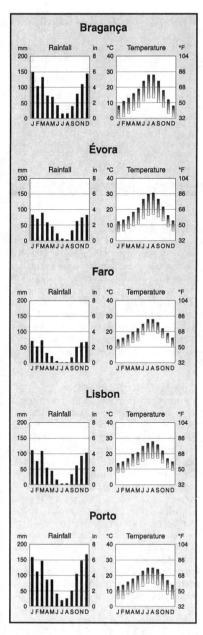

Bragança

Évora

Faro

Lisbon

Porto

ECOLOGY & ENVIRONMENT

Portugal has been relatively slow to wake up to the environmental problems it faces, notably soil erosion, pollution, rubbish disposal and the effects of mass tourism on its delicate coastal areas. Of growing concern, too, are the rapid spread of eucalyptus plantations and the consequences of several years of drought leading to the first stages of desertification in some areas.

Significantly, despite the country's outstanding natural attributes and some unique flora and fauna, none of the seven sites on the World Heritage List are in the category of natural importance (they're all listed for their cultural value). Right now, Portugal has more environmental problems to sort out than achievements to boast about.

For visitors, the effect of mass tourism is the most immediately obvious problem, especially in the overdeveloped southern Algarve region, with its ugly rash of hotel, holiday flat and condominium development. Building restrictions were widely ignored after the 1974 revolution and although they are now back in place, the damage has already been done in areas around Albufeira, Lagos and Portimão. However, despite the obvious coastal destruction, the Algarve's sunny climate, sandy beaches, excellent water sports and golf facilities continue to draw in the majority of Portugal's tourists. Of the nearly 10 million or so tourists the country hosts every year, at least 40% stay in the Algarve.

Almost everywhere in Portugal, whether at popular seaside resorts or inland cultural sites such as Évora, the sudden influx of summer visitors – as many as 40,000 on a village population of 2000 is not uncommon – causes enormous pressure on the environment as services and infrastructure are stretched to the limit. Environmentally conscious travellers could help alleviate the situation by limiting their stays in these popular places to a couple of days at most, avoiding them altogether, or visiting them off season (a far more pleasant experience almost everywhere, in fact). And any tourist would be wise to avoid the polluted seas

The Eucalpytus Onslaught

One of Portugal's biggest consumers of water is the eucalyptus. Quick to grow (it's tall enough for felling in 10 years), it's one of the most profitable trees on the market, much in demand by paper pulp companies. By the 1990s, paper-pulp was earning Portugal as much as US$2 billion a year. Eucalpytus plantations have continued to spread over the hillsides all over the country, much to the concern of many local farmers who are seeing their traditional smallholdings of olive and cork disappear. Environmental groups are even more vociferous: critics argue that the eucalyptus drains the soil both of water and nutrients, and that the huge plantations are destroying the region's wildlife habitat.

According to Marion Kaplan in her book *The Portuguese*, government officials have tried to reassure the protesters by saying that eucalyptus forests will be kept to a maximum of 20% of the forest area (in 1989 it was already at 14%). But as Carlos Pimenta, Portuguese member of the European Parliament, has said: '...short-term private profit almost always has won over the defence of our common values and heritage of those living or yet to be born. Public awareness and information are important in the fight to save our habitat'. ■

around heavily populated or industrial centres such as Porto, Estoril and Sines. Indeed, Porto's coastline is so notoriously filthy from industrial and sewage waste it's considered a major health risk to swim anywhere near the city: move south or north at least 20 km before dipping your toes into this water.

Water – or rather the lack of it – is at the heart of another increasingly controversial environmental issue in Portugal. After four years of drought – the worst dry cycle this century – there's increasing concern about Spain's National Hydrographic Plan, a mammoth scheme that includes diverting water from the rainy north to the south of the country. Unfortunately for Portugal, three of its most important rivers – the Douro, Tejo and Guadiana – come from Spain. And like Spain, Portugal desperately needs the water from these rivers for farming purposes (which account for 76% of water use in Portugal), hydroelectric production and for the environment generally (see the boxed aside). But if Spain's plan goes ahead (heated discussions between the two countries have been going on for years), Portugal's water supplies – especially from the Douro – could be seriously affected.

Of more immediate concern is the Guadiana, vital to Portugal for irrigating the arid Alentejo plains. Work has now resumed on a long-delayed giant dam at Alqueva, near Beja, for both irrigation and electricity purposes. But Spain has recently increased its intake of waters from the Guadiana and has plans to take even more for its own irrigation purposes, leaving scarcely enough for Portugal's own supplies, let alone for the environment. Spain's response to the alarm is that Portugal is worrying too much since the plan has yet to get the official go-ahead. If the cycle of drought continues, then the tug-of-war over the rivers is bound to escalate.

Environmental Organisations

The most active environmental group in Portugal to tackle these and other issues is Quercus: Associação Nacional de Conservação da Natureza (National Association for the Conservation of Nature, ☎ 01-353 05 40; fax 01-315 20 39), 139 Rua do Salitre 3-A, 1200 Lisbon. Established in 1986, it now has some 10,000 members and branch offices in Aveiro, Beja, Braga, Bragança, Coimbra, Covilhã, Faro, Guarda, Ourém, Porto, Portalegre, Viana do Castelo, and Vila Real, as well as environmental education centres (Centros de Educação Ambiental) in Setúbal, Monsanto and Porto. In addition to carrying out studies of Portugal's flora, fauna and ecosystems, its members also bring environmental issues to the attention of the public and government through regular campaigns. Some of its more active branch offices (eg Aveiro, Coimbra, Porto) also arrange field trips to nearby natural parks or reserves: call the head office for contact details. If you read Portuguese, you'll find its monthly magazine, *Teixo*, packed with the latest environmental horror stories.

Another group worth contacting if you're interested in joining like-minded locals in weekend trips to environmentally special areas is GEOTA: Grupo de Estudos de Ordenomento do Território e Ambiente (Study Group of the Environment, ☎ 01-395 61 20; fax 01-395 53 16), Travessa do Moinho de Vento 17, 1200 Lisbon. The cost of these trips ranges from 5000$00 to 10,000$00 per person, depending on the location.

Less obviously active environmental organisations include Liga para a Proteção da Natureza (League for the Protection of Nature, ☎ 01-778 00 97), Estrela do Calhariz de Benfica 187, Lisbon; and Associação Portuguesa de Ecologia e Amigos da Terra (Portuguese Association of Ecology and Friends of the Earth, ☎ 01-395 18 66),

Calçada Marquês de Abrantes 10, 3/f, Lisbon.

In 1998 the environmental spotlight will fall on Portugal when it hosts Expo '98, which is dedicated to preserving the oceans (it coincides with the United Nations' International Year of the Oceans and the 500th anniversary of Vasco da Gama's discovery of the sea route to India). In addition to building the biggest oceanarium in Europe, Portugal is planning to use the occasion to boost its world role in the management, study and preservation of the oceans. In particular, it's hoping to win the bid to provide a headquarters in Lisbon for a major international organisation concerned with marine resources.

For more on Expo '98, see the Lisbon chapter.

FLORA & FAUNA
Flora
Like its climate, Portugal's flora is a mixture of Mediterranean and Atlantic (or European)

Cork
Travel through the vast Alentejo plains and you'll see thousands of them: tall, round-topped evergreen trees with glossy, holly-like leaves, and wrinkled bark that's often stripped, leaving a strangely naked, ochre trunk. One of Portugal's most profitable indigenous products – *quercus suber* or cork oak – grows abundantly throughout the country, supplying some 700 factories with about 160,000 tons of cork a year, a third of which is manufactured by one family firm, Corticeira Amorim. Lucky Amorim: Portugal's prodigious cork output (accounting for 60% of world output, twice that of Spain) makes it the world's leading supplier – not bad for a tree that's as slow and traditional as a vintage port wine. Cultivators have to wait 20 years before they can cut the first bark (probably 30 years before the bark is of commercial quality), and then cut (always by hand) as skilfully as a barber to guarantee future harvests for the next 100 years or so of the tree's life.

So valuable is this tree that there's a law against stripping its bark until the tree's circumference has reached a certain size (usually when it's about 15 years old). And from then on it can only be stripped every ninth year. Such repeated strippings are possible because the tree continually grows new tissue, though care has to be taken not to damage the deeper layers.

Cork has long been prized for its lightness (it's only one-fifth as heavy as water) and its insulating and watertight qualities. More versatile than any synthetic product, it's used for everything from footwear to floor-covers, gaskets to girders, baseball bats to fishing-rod handles. And most obviously, of course, it's used as a bottle stopper. Spirits such as whisky and gin gave up cork in the 1960s, cheap wine resorted to plastic, and synthetic cork stoppers from Norway barged in on the market, but for superior wines there's no alternative. The world's victuallers obviously agree – 25 billion corks are used a year. Cork's all-natural assets (no smell, no taste, no toxicity) make it the unbeatable bottle stopper for posh wines such as champagne, which is particularly fussy about its corks. Portugal comes up with the goods: about 30 million corks a day, and 500 million a year just for champagne. ■

species, with European plants dominating. Only a third of the species are typical of the Mediterranean. The country's geography reflects the division: European species are found largely in the mountainous, rainy north, while Mediterranean species are found in the sunny south. As many as a third of the species are of foreign origin, mostly introduced during Portugal's colonisation era (though the exotic thuja firs, enormous sequoias and araucarias you'll see in Sintra were introduced much later, in the 18th and 19th centuries when such novelties were fashionable). Throughout the country, scrub and steppe are far more common than woodland, with most of the mixed deciduous wood limited to the north and the thickest forests to the Beira Alta region.

The most common types of European vegetation you'll come across are pine and oak (especially black and British oak), as well as chestnut, elm and poplar, heather, broom and juniper. Pine and eucalyptus forestation is widespread. Among the Mediterranean species, the most widespread is, of course, the olive. This tree prefers the sunny climate of the south but since Roman times it's also taken root in parts of the north. Other Mediterranean species that give the southern Algarve its Moorish flavour are almonds, carobs, vines and figs and the whole range of citrus fruits.

Perhaps the plant that most characterises Portugal is the cork oak, especially in the southern Alentejo province, where dry plains are extensively covered by both cork and holm oak as well as cistus scrub. The white-flowering cistus gum is also widespread in the Algarve, where it's often dried and used as fuel for village bread ovens. Orchid-lovers will find the Algarve their richest hunting ground, especially around Faro in springtime. A wide variety of orchid species thrive in the limestone soil here.

If you're interested in seeing how the cork oaks are stripped, then visit Alentejo's cork plantations between May and early September. Late September to early October is the time to watch the harvesting of the port-wine grapes in the upper Douro valley.

Fauna

Portugal's fauna is a mixture of European and North African species. Most commonly seen in the countryside are foxes, rabbits and Iberian hares, while less easily spotted are wild goats, wild boars and deer, which tend to roam the more mountainous interior (especially in the Parque Nacional da Peneda-Gerês). Wild ferrets, otters and badgers, genets (a kind of civet cat), and Egyptian mongooses are other species, which, although widespread, aren't eager to be noticed.

You'd be extremely lucky, too, to see two of Portugal's rarest mammals – the Iberian wolf (see Endangered Species in this chapter), whose last major hide-out is in the Parque Natural de Montesinho, and the lynx, whose habitat is preserved in the tiny Reserva Natural da Serra da Malcata of Beira Alta.

But if you're an ornithologist, you'll have a field day. Portugal is on the winter migratory route for many northern and central European species and on the spring migratory route for birds flying between Africa

---

The Portuguese Water-Dog

What do you get when you cross a dog and a duck? Answer: the Portuguese (or Algarve) water-dog. This curious breed (no descendant of the duck) looks very like a poodle at first glance, with its clipped black or brown hair. However, it has the unique characteristic of webbed feet (strictly speaking, a membrane between the toes). This makes it a great little swimmer, able to dive down to depths of six metres.

Traditionally these pedigree dogs have been a fisherman's best friend: they can dive for fish that have escaped from nets, paddle from boat to shore with ropes in their mouths and retrieve broken nets drifting in the sea. Now practically extinct (dog-fanciers in the USA have snapped up many in recent years), they're getting a new lease of life at the Quinta de Marim headquarters of the Parque Natural da Ria Formosa, where there's a special programme for breeding the species and restoring its unique place in the webbed-feet, wagging-tail world. ■

and northern Europe. Among those you may well spot are avocets, spoonbills, white storks, greater flamingoes, black-winged stilts, griffon vultures and hundreds of ducks. Portugal's parks and nature reserves are also home to hundreds of bird species including several unusual or rare ones such as the red-billed jackdaw, azure-winged magpie, great bustard, collared pratincole and sultan chicken (see Endangered Species below, and the Organised Tours section in the Getting Around chapter for information on bird-watching tours in Portugal).

Cruelty to Animals

Hunting It's not as bad as in France, perhaps, but the macho urge to pick up a gun and shoot any wild bird or animal that comes within range is surprisingly deep-rooted among Portuguese men. There are over a quarter of a million licensed hunters in the land and many more illegal, unlicensed ones taking their own private pot shot. Migratory birds have long been a favourite target, as well as rabbit, quail, partridge, duck and wild boar. In fact, pretty much anything from wolves to songbirds have frequently fallen prey to Portugal's hunting passion.

Since 1988, hunting has become more organised with newly defined hunting zones. It's also become a popular and profitable business with special *zona de caça turística/associativa* hunting reserves geared specifically for visitors or private associations. These are often created from the large estates of the Alentejo region and have facilities for both game and clay-pigeon shooting. Red deer, pheasant and red-legged partridge are the most popular species reared for hunters in these zones, but even the protected wild boar can be culled under licence when its numbers are considered to have become excessive.

There are laws, of course. During the open season, hunting is restricted to Thursdays, Sundays and public holidays. Landowners can forbid hunting on their land (red and white metal markers by the roadside indicate what areas are out of bounds), and trapping of small birds is illegal. But policing the laws is an almost impossible task. Even the vast, organised hunting reserves aren't as simple a solution as they may appear to the pro-hunting lobby: at the very least they hinder rural development and also affect long-established grazing rights. And birds of prey – although themselves protected – suddenly find they're unwelcome intruders as they swoop up the profits from the land that was once freely theirs.

Bullfighting This is even more controversial than hunting. Although not as popular in Portugal as in Spain, it's still considered by many Portuguese to be a spectacular form of 'entertainment' and a noble cultural tradition dating back 2000 years. At least 300 *touradas* or bullfights are held every March-to-October season (traditionally from Easter Sunday to All Saints' Day), many in tourist areas such as the Algarve (especially Albufeira). To alleviate foreigners' distaste, the posters for these events often carry the headline, 'The bull isn't killed!'. Don't be deceived – the bulls do suffer. And they are killed. You just don't get to see the final fatal blow.

Bullfighting supporters point out that the Portuguese *tourada* is far less brutal and bloody than the Spanish version. There's a good deal more skilled horsemanship, more artistry, more valour and bravado. The most obvious differences are that the bull is initially fought by a man on horseback, then by a team of young men who tackle the bull by hand; and the fight is not to the death (at least, not in public: the gory death of a nobleman, Count dos Arcos, in 1799, put a stop to that). Another difference is that the bulls' horns are covered in leather or capped with metal balls.

However, none of this can disguise the fact that bullfighting is basically a cruel sport. If you must see for yourself, read the Spectator Sports section in the Facts for the Visitor chapter so that you know what to expect.

The anti-bullfighting lobby in Portugal is vocal but small. Most Portuguese are either impartial or simply surprised at the protests. If you feel strongly enough, you could write to the *turismo* (tourist office) and *câmara municipal* (town hall) of places such as Albufeira that promote bullfighting for tourists' entertainment (popular protests finally led Tossa de Mar in Spain to actually ban bullfights and related advertising).

The following organisations are worth contacting for more information and advice about what action you can take.

People for the Ethical Treatment of Animals (PETA)
England: PO Box 3169, London NW1 2JF (☎ 0171-388 4922; fax 0171-388 4925)
USA: 501 Front St, Norfolk VA 23510 (☎ 757-622-PETA; fax 757-622-1078
Germany: Peta Deutschland e.V., Postfach 31 1503, 70475 Stuttgart (☎ 711-866 6165; fax 711-866 6166)
World Society for the Protection of Animals (WSPA)
England: 2 Langley Lane, London SW8 1TJ (☎ 0171-793 0540; fax 0171-793 0208; e-mail wspahq@gn.apc.org)
USA: PO Box 190, Boston MA 02130 (☎ 617-522-7000; fax 617-522-7077; e-mail wspa @world.std.com)
Canada: 44 Victoria Street, Suite 1310, Toronto, Ontario M5C 1Y2 (☎ 416-369-0044; fax 416-369-0147; e-mail 102232.3627@compuserve.com)

Liga Portuguese dos Direitos dos Animais (Portuguese League for Animal Rights), Rua João Ortigão Ramos 31-D, Lisbon (☎ 01-764 81 86)

Endangered Species

Portugal's protected areas (see National Parks) harbour several endangered species of bird, such as the royal eagle and woodland screech owl in the Parque Nacional da Peneda-Gerês, and the sultan chicken (also called the purple gallinule) in the Parque Natural da Ria Formosa, where the estimated population of the bird is less than 30. Ria Formosa is also home to the strictly protected chameleon (introduced to Portugal from Africa about 70 years ago). Outside the parks, your best chance of seeing an endangered or strictly protected species is in the southern Alentejo – in Mértola where white storks nest in spring, or in the Castro Verde region, which is a favourite haunt of the great bustard, Europe's heaviest bird (adult males can weigh up to 18 kg).

Among endangered mammal species in Portugal, the most controversial is the

Wolves

It's thought that there are fewer than 200 Iberian wolves left in Portugal (out of an estimated 1500 in the entire Iberian peninsula). Most of these are believed to live in the Parque Natural de Montesinho in north-east Trás-os-Montes. Fully protected by law, the wolf is still illegally shot, trapped or poisoned.

As elsewhere in the world, it is widely feared and hated for supposedly attacking cattle and domestic animals (though in fact many of these attacks are by wild dogs).

Now in danger of extinction in Portugal (an estimated 20 wolves are illegally killed every year), the wolf has at least some friends working on its behalf: Grupo Lobo, an independent, nonprofit association established in 1985, wins support for the wolf and the preservation of its habitat by publishing booklets and pamphlets and operating a travelling exhibition. It also helps run a Centro de Recuperação do Lobo Ibérico (recuperation centre) in Malveira, about 40 km north of Lisbon. Originally established by Robert Lyle in 1989, the centre's 17 hectares of secluded woodland provide a refuge for over 20 wolves that have been rescued from traps, snares or miserable captive conditions. You can visit the centre if you call in advance (see Mafra in the Around Lisbon chapter) or you can support the cause by joining Grupo Lobo for 1600$00 a year or by 'adopting' a wolf at the centre for 5000$00 a year. ■

Iberian wolf. There are also declining numbers of dolphins in the Sado Estuary and a few lynx hiding out in the Lynx Reserve of the Reserva Natural da Serra da Malcata in Beira Alta.

National Parks

Strictly speaking, Parque Nacional da Peneda-Gerês is the only national park in Portugal. The 10 other parks are called *parques naturais*. You're hardly likely to notice the difference: Peneda-Gerês meets certain international requirements (including the setting aside of a part of the park for research only) and features a vast area with ecosystems little changed by humans, while a parque natural features both natural or seminatural and landscaped areas where human activities have integrated with nature. There are also eight *reservas naturais*, three *áreas de paisagem protegida* and 10 *sítios classificados*. Altogether, these protected

---

Portugal's Parks & Nature Reserves

Following are contact details for Portugal's national/natural parks and reserves:

Park Name	Contact Details
Parque Nacional da Peneda-Gerês (north-east Minho district)	Quinta das Parretas, Rodovia, 4700 Braga (☎ 053-6131 66)
Parque Natural do Alvão (Trás-os-Montes, near Vila Real)	Rua Alves Torgo 22, 3rd floor, 5000 Vila Real (☎ 059-32 4138)
Parque Natural da Arrábida (south of Lisbon, near Setúbal)	Praça da República, 2900 Setúbal (☎ 065-52 40 32, ☎ 065-52 69 93)
Parque Natural de Montesinho (north-east Trás-os-Montes)	Bairro Salvador Nunes Teixeira, Lote 5, 5300 Bragança (☎ 073-38 14 44, ☎ 073-38 12 34)
Parque Natural da Ria Formosa (Algarve coastline, near Olhão)	Quinta de Marim, Quelfes, 8700 Olhão (☎ 089-70 4134)
Parque Natural da Serra da Estrela (Beira Alta, south-west of Guarda)	Rua I de Maio 2, Valazedo, 6260 Manteigas (☎ 075-98 23 82)
Parque Natural da Serra de São Mamede (north-east Alentejo, near Portalegre)	Praceta Heróis da Índia 8, 7301 Portalegre (☎ 045-236 31)
Parque Natural das Serras de Aire e Candeeiros (Estremadura, south of Batalha)	Jardim Municipal, 2040 Rio Maior (☎ 043-919 68)
Parque Natural de Sintra-Cascais (west of Lisbon)	Rua General Alves Roçadas 10, 2710 Sintra (☎ 01-923 51 16)
Parque Natural do Sudoeste Alentejano e Costa Vicentina (western Algarve and Alentejo coastline)	Rua Serpa Pinto 32, 7630 Odemira (☎ 083-227 35)
Parque Natural do Vale do Guadiana (Alentejo, around Mértola)	in planning stage
Reserva Natural da Berlenga (Estremadura, island west of Peniche)	Porto da Areia Norte, Estrada Marginal, 2520 Peniche (☎ 062-78 79 10)
Reserva Natural das Dunas de São Jacinto (Beira Litoral, near Aveiro)	Rua Padre António Vieiria 1, 3000 Coimbra (☎ 039- 221 51)
Reserva Natural do Estuário do Sado (south of Lisbon, near Setúbal)	Praça da República, 2900 Setúbal (☎ 065-52 40 32)
Reserva Natural do Estuário do Tejo (east of Lisbon, near Alcochete)	Avenida Combatentes da Grande Guerra 1, 2890 Alcochete (☎ 01-234 16 54)
Reserva Natural do Paúl de Arzila (Beiras, near Coimbra)	Rua Padre António Vieira 1, 3000 Coimbra (☎ 039-221 51)
Reserva Natural do Paúl do Boquilobo (Ribatejo, near Golega)	Apartado 27, 2350 Torres Novas (☎ 049-946 22)
Reserva Natural do Sapal de Castro Marim e Vila Real de Santo António (eastern Algarve, around Castro Marim)	Apartado 7, 8950 Castro Marim (☎ 081-53 11 41)
Reserva Natural da Serra da Malcata (Beira Alta, east of Penamacor)	Rua dos Bombeiros Voluntários, 6090 Penamacor (☎ 077-944 67)

areas cover 580,262 hectares – 6.54% of Portugal's land area.

The Instituto da Conservação da Natureza or ICN (☎ 01-352 33 17; fax 01-314 31 03), Rua Ferreira Lapa 29A, 1150 Lisbon, is the government agency responsible for overall park management, publicity and policy. It has some general information but the individual park offices are usually better equipped (and staffed) and can provide maps, brochures and information on trails and accommodation. Standards of maintenance and facilities vary tremendously, however. If you're a hopeful hiker, be prepared to be disappointed: 'trails' often turn out to be roads or nothing at all; the park 'map' a glossy leaflet for motorists; and 'park accommodation' a couple of huts geared (and priced) for huge school groups.

But the parks do feature vast areas of unspoilt mountains, forests or coastal lagoons. The reluctance of most Portuguese to go walking anywhere, let alone venture into remote areas means you can find some incredibly quiet and isolated spots in these parks. We describe the biggest and best of the parks in more detail in the respective regional chapters.

GOVERNMENT & POLITICS

Portugal has been a sovereign republic since 1910, when it overthrew its monarchy. But Western-style, multiparty democracy only came after the 1974 revolution of the Carnations, which removed the authoritarian Salazar-era government. According to the 1976 constitution (revised in 1982 to remove Marxist elements and reduce the power of the president), Portugal's chief of state is the president of the republic, directly elected by universal suffrage for a five-year term, for a maximum of two consecutive terms. The president, who is also the supreme commander in chief of the armed forces, still has wide powers, including the power to dissolve parliament and veto laws. The president also appoints the prime minister (following the results of parliamentary elections) and on the prime minister's proposal

can appoint or dismiss other members of government, principally the cabinet.

The prime minister is responsible both to the president and to the parliament. This single-chamber body has 230 members (including four representing Portuguese abroad) who are elected by popular vote for four years under a system of proportional representation. Portugal also has 25 representatives in the European Parliament: the last EP elections in 1994 saw the Socialist Party (Partido Socialista or PS) winning 10 seats, and the Social Democratic Party (Partido Social Democrata or PSD) winning nine, with the remaining seats divided between other parties. Portuguese citizens can cast their first vote when they're 18 years old. From then on men can also be called up for compulsory military service – anything from four to 18 months – although they have a right to conscientious objection.

Local tiers of government in the country's 18 districts consist of 305 municipal councils and 4209 parishes, each of which is governed by an assembly elected by popular vote under a system of proportional representation. The PS currently controls most of the municipal councils. Plans for regional devolution would add another tier of local government, with regional assemblies and executives.

Since 1976 the archipelagoes of Madeira and the Azores have been recognised as autonomous regions with their own governments, legislatures and administrations. Macau, Portugal's last overseas dependent territory, is governed by special statute and will revert to Chinese rule in 1999.

Portugal's two main political parties are the ruling left-of-centre PS and the opposition right-of-centre PSD. Other major opposition parties include the conservative Social Democratic Centre (Centro Democrática Social or CDS, now more commonly referred to as the Popular Party – Partido Popular or PP); and the United Democratic Coalition (Coligação Democrático Unitária or CDU), which links the hardline Communist Party (Partido Comunista Português) with other left-wing parties such as the

Greens (Partido Ecologista Os Verdes or PEV).

The October 1995 elections saw the dramatic return of the PS after 10 years of single-party rule by the PSD under the prime ministership of Aníbal Cavaco Silva. The new prime minister, 46-year-old António Guterres, managed this political coup by swinging his party behind free-market, pro-European policies, promising social improvements while reassuring financial markets of a continued commitment to budgetary rigour and the discipline of European monetary union. The electorate, tired of the corrupt, complacent and scandal-tainted PSD, gave the PS its biggest victory since it began fighting elections in 1974: it won 112 seats with 42.9% of the vote (compared with 72 seats and 29.1% in the election of 1991). The PSD trailed behind with 88 seats, while the Popular Party (PP) and communist-led CDU each won 15 seats.

The result doesn't give Guterres' government an outright majority but a defeat in parliament is only likely if the CDU joins with the two other right-wing opposition parties. A possible catalyst for this unlikely union is anti-European fervour: the Eurosceptic PP (which also has a young and increasingly popular leader) and the CDU may be poles apart in politics but they are united in opposition to the Maastricht treaty, which calls for increased European union. And after a decade's honeymoon with the EU – a period of new wealth, new roads and new facilities brought by EU funding – there is growing disillusionment as competition stiffens in the wake of the European single market and the GATT (General Agreement on Tariffs & Trade) agreements.

In the short term, however, Guterres is banking on continued prosperity (about 3% growth a year, with inflation tamed to about 4%) to keep him afloat. He has tough challenges ahead as he tries to match electoral promises of higher spending on education, health and welfare with the budgetary rigour needed to qualify for European monetary union in 1999, especially as he has promised not to raise taxes. But even if sceptics attack his political programme, at least his style of politics has won immediate public approval. In a significant break from tradition, Guterres has decided to forsake the elegant palace of previous prime ministers and commute to work from his Lisbon flat. He's also vowed to attend parliament regularly, something Cavaco Silva never did.

Cavaco Silva, meanwhile, cannily relinquished the leadership of the PSD eight months before the 1995 election, putting himself forward for presidential elections in January 1996 instead. But this austere 55-year-old economist, though credited for Portugal's economic success in recent years, could not match the ebullient charisma of the widely popular socialist incumbent, 70-year-old President Mário Soares, who had already served the maximum two terms as president. Nor could Cavaco Silva fight the tide of dissatisfaction with the *cavaquismo* era: the electorate continued with their swing to the left by voting not for Cavaco Silva but for Jorge Sampaio, a socialist and two-term Lisbon mayor who campaigned on the familiar Soares theme of tolerance and unity. His victory marks the first time since 1974 that the prime minister and president have come from the same party – a great advantage for Guterres as he walks the tightrope of office.

ECONOMY

Not so long ago, Portugal was among the poorest nations in Europe, its economy a shambles, its inflation and unemployment rates appalling, its trade deficit a nightmare, and its workforce thoroughly demoralised. Now its growth rate is among the highest in Europe (between 2.5% and 3.5%), its unemployment (7.1%) one of the lowest, and its inflation tamed to a mere 4% or so.

The dramatic turnaround started in 1985 when the austere economist, Aníbal Cavaco Silva and his centre-right Social Democratic Party came to power. The following year Portugal joined the EC (now the EU). Over the next decade the government introduced a wide range of structural reforms, extensively deregulating and liberalising the economy and launching an ambitious privatisation programme (now accelerated even further, despite the new socialist government). The EU pumped funds into its poor relative (an astounding US$12.8 million a day for the rest of this century) and, helped by dollar exchange rates and falling oil prices, Portugal's economy started to revive. Soon, it was showing the highest growth rate in Europe and increases in real wages of more than 2%. The gross domestic product (GDP) per capita rose from 51.4% of the EU average in 1985 to over 64% in 1995. Inflation – a crippling 19% a decade earlier – fell to a record low 1995.

This honeymoon period of EU membership coincided with political stability and sound monetary policy, resulting in increasing prosperity for many Portuguese. Between 1987 and 1994 the proportion of Portuguese homes with a telephone rose from 33% to 77%; those with running water rose from 82% to 94%; those with TVs from 83% to 96%; and those with cars from 36% to 54%. More than 1700 km of new roads were built.

But in 1992, after seven years of euphoria, with the economy expanding at a record rate, recession reared its ugly head. That was the

---

Adeus **to the Mule Cart,** *Olá* **to MPVs**
If anything is needed to show up the dismal state of Portugal's agriculture, it's the latest boast of the manufacturing industry: a massive US$3 billion joint venture by Ford and Volkswagen to manufacture 180,000 'multi-purpose vehicles' (MPVs) a year at a spanking new plant in Palmela (south-east of Lisbon) that opened in April 1995. While farmers in the Minho still eke out a meagre living with their mules and carts, or sit idly at home with no qualifications or incentive to seek work elsewhere, 3000 workers at the AutoEuropa plant (plus another 1500 at an adjacent parts component factory) are turning out Ford Galaxy and VW Sharan vehicles in a state-of-the-art factory. Agriculture still employs 12% of the workforce in Portugal but its contribution to the economy is declining year by year. The days of the mule are numbered: MPVs are the future. ∎

---

year, too, of the single European market, when all trade and employment barriers were removed, the year Portugal ratified the Maastricht Treaty on European Union. Portugal's small and medium-sized companies began to feel the effect of competition from more efficient European rivals, a competition intensified by the new GATT agreements. Financial pressure tightened as the country tried to meet the Maastricht Treaty's demands for eventual monetary union in 1999. For two years, the economy was in the doldrums and the new generation of Portuguese yuppies and financiers fell into gloom. The first signs of recovery in 1994 showed an expansion of foreign markets and a surge in exports. GDP registered an encouraging 1% growth, which jumped to 2.9% in 1995.

The economic picture for the next few years looks even more encouraging: further economic expansion is predicted, driven by export market growth and a rebound in domestic demand. Unemployment, although on the rise recently, is expected to fall below 7% and inflation to stay below 5%.

But these healthy figures also mask some dismal realities. The years of rapid growth have seen the gulf widen between rich and poor: all too obvious now is the poverty in the backstreets of Lisbon and Porto and the low standard of living in the rural areas of northern Portugal where many families still depend on their one mule and cart to make a meagre income out of farming. Education levels and facilities in these areas are still appalling (see Education in this chapter), unemployment is way above the national average and real wages are falling. And despite the new prime minister's electoral promises of improvements in health care, welfare and education, there's little chance of them being fulfilled soon. The government is under heavy pressure to maintain rigorous control of public finances so that Portugal can qualify for inclusion in the single European currency.

One of the government's biggest economic burdens is its inefficient agriculture sector. Some 12% of the workforce is still engaged in agriculture, forestry and fishing, but the contribution of this sector to the GDP has been dropping steadily since 1990. Lack of mechanisation and the fragmented land-tenure system contribute to production being well below the EU average. Agriculture's only notable success stories are in tomato paste (Portugal is the world's largest exporter of the stuff) and cork (the world's leading producer).

By contrast, the services sector (real estate, banking, financial services, wholesale and tourism) is booming: it now employs 56% of the population (compared with 35% a decade ago) and its GDP has been increasing at an average rate of 5.4% a year. The tourism sector alone accounts for 14.3% of the nation's GDP and 13.7% of direct and indirect employment. In 1994, nine million tourists (and 21.7 million day-visitors, largely from Spain) contributed US$3824 million in foreign exchange earnings.

The manufacturing sector still has important traditional industries, such as metal products and machinery, textiles and clothing, footwear, cork, wood and paper pulp. All major exports are mainly to EU countries, but the headline-grabbing action these days is in the huge new industrial parks with massive manufacturing projects funded by foreign investment. While projects such as these are welcomed for the employment they generate, the growing investment by Spain in much of the recently privatised service sector is viewed with alarm by many Portuguese who see their country's business slipping away into the hands of their least liked European neighbour.

Portugal's economic future undoubtedly lies with Spain and its other European partners. While trade with Portuguese-speaking Africa registered a mere 3% of Portuguese exports in 1994, EU countries (notably Germany, France and Spain) accounted for some 76% of exports and 72% of imports. If Portugal wants to be counted as a major player in the region, rather than the poor little cousin it has been for so long, it will have to stick to its rigorous economic course. And that means little chance of major social improvements for its poor and underprivileged. For the new prime minister, a dedicated socialist and Catholic, tough choices lie ahead.

POPULATION & PEOPLE

Portugal has a population of 10.5 million, almost a quarter of which is under 15 years of age. The vast majority (70%) live in rural areas, although the urban population has increased dramatically since the 1960s. At that time, urban population was 22% of the total; now it's 36% (still low compared to other European countries: Britain's urban population, for instance, is 89%).

Probably the major reason for the urban increase was the arrival of nearly a million refugees in 1974-75 following the independence of Portugal's African colonies – Angola, Cape Verde, Guinea-Bissau, Mozambique and São Tomé e Príncipe. These immigrants (both legal and illegal) make up Portugal's major ethnic groups (the 25,000 Cape Verdeans are the biggest single group). There is also a small resident Gypsy population.

The 1960s and 1970s were times of population change for other reasons, too. Ever since gold and diamonds were discovered in Brazil in the 17th century, the Portuguese have sought their fortunes (or simply a better chance of survival) overseas, notably during the 18th and 19th centuries (to Brazil) and in the 1950s and 1960s to Europe (especially France and Germany). According to Marion Kaplan in her book *The Portuguese*, some 1.3 million Portuguese emigrated between 1886 and 1926 and a similar number between 1926 and 1966. That later wave of émigrés included young men avoiding conscription in Portugal's wars of independence in the African colonies.

Portugal still has one of the highest emigration rates in Europe and one of its largest overseas populations: about three million Portuguese are said to live or work abroad. Brazil, South Africa, America and Canada have the largest settlements, and France the largest number of 'temporary' workers, their

Saudade

It's been described as a great nostalgia for the glorious past, a fathomless yearning, and a longing for home, but unless you're Portuguese you'll probably never really grasp the uniquely Portuguese passion of *saudade*. Its musical form is the aching sorrow expressed in *fado* songs – a melancholic submission to the twists and turns of fate. In Portuguese and Brazilian poetry it's a mystical reverence for nature, a brooding sense of loneliness that became especially popular among 19th and early 20th-century poets who cultivated a cult of *saudosismo*. In tangible form it's the return of thousands of émigrés to their home villages every August, drawn not just by family ties but by something much deeper – a longing for all that home and Portugal represents: the heroism of the past, the sorrows of the present, and wistful hopes for the future. ■

remittances home a major boost to the economy. You only have to visit villages in the rural north to see where the money mostly goes – into brash new houses, often proudly used as hay barns by elderly parents until their sons come home years later to retire. In August or at Christmas, when the émigrés return for holidays, you can see how the villages revive, how wealthy the young men appear compared with those left behind.

The northern Minho province, where most of the émigrés originate, is one of the poorest and most overpopulated areas of Portugal (other heavily populated regions include the central and eastern plains and the Algarve coast). The north as a whole is far more densely populated than the south, especially in the low-lying plains and along the developed coast. The population is increasing at a rate of 1.4% a year: the birth rate is among the highest in Europe but so, too, is the infant mortality rate (6.2 per 1000 live births).

Unlike most other European countries, the vast majority of Portugal's people are very similar in appearance, sharing typical Mediterranean features such as brown eyes, dark hair and dark brown skin. But the country's many invaders and settlers – from Celts and Carthaginians in the north and coastal areas,

to Romans and African Muslims mainly in the south – have left recognisable traits, too. You'll notice a distinctive north-south social division, as well – the northerners more obviously religious and conservative than their easy-going compatriots in the south.

The thousands of African and mixed-race immigrants who flooded Portugal in 1974-75 have integrated well into Portuguese society (among the more famous is the well-loved footballer, Eusébio, who came from Mozambique). African music is all the rage in Lisbon, with an increasing number of African nightclubs. Incidents of racism do occur, however. There have been sporadic violent attacks on blacks, mostly by skinheads. So far, Portugal's record of inter-racial harmony is better than in most other European countries, but as the new era of wealth exacerbates social divisions, immigrants may well face tougher times.

EDUCATION

The state of Portugal's education system is embarrassingly awful. According to the Organisation for Economic Co-operation and Development (OECD), Portugal's educational standards lag well behind those of other EU countries. One of the OECD's most alarming statistics in a 1995 report was that over 47% of Portuguese people between the ages of 15 and 64 have little or no ability to read or do sums. Another finding from UNESCO shows that in 1990, 15% of the population were illiterate (11% of males and 18.5% of females).

The Salazar regime is to blame for this legacy of backwardness. For four decades it invested as little as possible in education. 'I consider more urgent the creation of élites than the necessity of teaching people how to read,' Salazar was once quoted as saying. There were only four years of compulsory schooling.

Today, there's free (voluntary) preschool education for three to six-year-olds, and nine years of compulsory education (from age six to 15), provided free of charge in state schools. Private schools supplement the state schools. Secondary education, which is not compulsory, lasts for three years. Higher education is provided at the country's 18 universities and at the 98 other higher education establishments such as regional technical colleges. Figures indicate that 99% of the school-age population enrol in basic and secondary education, but the reality is that many children leave school early to find work. The OECD found that less than half of those between the ages of five and 29 are actually in full-time education. And only 8% of the relevant age group continue in education long enough to get a degree (half as many as in France, for instance). The system itself exacerbates the problems. There's a serious lack of teachers and schools (city kids have to go to schools in shifts), opportunities for vocational education are limited and the education system is excessively centralised. 'Given these features,' notes the OECD, 'Portugal's education and training systems have, until the beginning of the 1990s, turned out large numbers of people with low skills'. Many are now waiting to see whether the new socialist government can do its own sums correctly and find the money to fulfil its promises of reforms and improvements to the system.

ARTS
Music

Fundamental to Portugal's history of musical expression is its folk music, which you can hear throughout the country at almost every religious festival or folk dance gathering. It traces its roots to the troubadour singing that became popular in the Middle Ages, and it is traditionally accompanied by a band of guitars, violins, clarinets, harmonicas and various wooden percussion instruments. In fact, the instruments played by these rural folk groups are often a good deal more attractive than the singing itself, which could generously be described as a high-pitched repetitive wail. You can't argue with its traditional roots, though: the songs invariably relate to harvesting, sowing and other aspects of life on the land. If the foot-tapping rhythms start to get to you, you'll find it easy to pick up cassette recordings at local markets and weekly fairs: groups from the Alentejo and Minho are said to be the best.

Far more enigmatic is Portugal's most internationally famous style of music, fado. These bluesy, melancholic chants are also said to have their roots in troubadour songs (although African slave songs have had an influence, too), and are traditionally sung by one performer accompanied by one or two guitarists playing the 12-string Portuguese guitar. Fado first emerged in the 18th century in Lisbon's working-class districts of Alfama and Mouraria. A more academic version developed later in the university town of Coimbra.

The big name among fado performers is

Fado Uproar

There are two styles of fado music: one comes from Lisbon and the other from the university town of Coimbra. The Lisbon style is still considered by aficionados to be the most genuine, but there's something about Coimbra's roving bands of romantic, fado-singing students during their May celebration week that pulls at the heart-strings far more effectively than the Lisbon performers in their nightclubs. Indeed, in many ways, the Coimbra singers surpass their Lisbon colleagues in tradition. When singer Manuela Bravo announced in April 1996 that she was going to record a CD of Coimbra fados, there was an outcry by the fado department of Coimbra University. Why? Because Coimbra fado – which praises the beauty of women – is traditionally sung by men only. Her opponents, described by Bravo's supporters as 'Salazaristic, old-fashioned and musty', warn that the gutsy *fadista* will 'debauch' tradition. To their horror, she even won the support of one of Portugal's best fado guitarists, António Pinho Brojo. Even the Mayor of Coimbra got involved (on the side of Bravo), and the album, entitled *Intenções*, went ahead. Few things arouse such emotion in Portugal as fado, and nowhere more so than in Lisbon and Coimbra. ■

Expo '98 & the Arts

If you're in Lisbon for Expo '98 (see the Lisbon chapter for more on this major spectacle in 1998), take advantage of the cultural programme planned for this massive event to see and hear Portugal's finest performers. In addition to the world premiere of *White Raven*, an opera specially written for Expo '98 by Philip Glass, Bob Wilson and the Portuguese librettist Luísa Costa Gomes, there will be dozens of other occasions featuring Portuguese artists. Echoing the shift in official support of the arts since the Salazar era, a member of the Expo '98 board commented: 'Official bodies used to portray the traditional touristic image of sunshine, sandy beaches and sardines. Today, they are employing our best artists and scientists as flagships for the nation'. ■

Amália Rodrigues, although these days she only performs at the poshest clubs and doesn't always sing fado. Pick up a copy of her best album, *O Melhor* to hear what fado should really sound like. Unfortunately, Rodrigues no longer sings live: her 55-year singing career ended in 1995 after a lung operation. See the Lisbon chapter and Coimbra section in the Beiras chapter for where to hear live fado performances.

Both fado and traditional folk songs – and, increasingly, 'foreign' strains from Europe and Africa – have had a major influence in shaping Portugal's modern folk music scene (now generally known as *música popular*). This first began to attract notice in the 1960s when contemporary musicians such as José Afonso joined forces with modern poets to start a new musical movement, singing about social and political issues. Often censored during the Salazar years, its lyrics became overtly political after the 1974 revolution, with many singers using their performances to actively support the various revolutionary factions. Today's música popular has gone back to its traditional roots, and is increasingly popular, thanks to several outstanding singer-songwriters and instrumentalists such as Carlos Paredes. Some of the more notable groups include Brigada Victor Jara, Trovante

and the widely known Madredeus (whose blend of traditional and contemporary music has been described as a 'window into the Portuguese soul').

Another style of music that is fast becoming hot in Lisbon is contemporary African jazz and rock. Dozens of new African nightclubs now pulsate with the rhythms of Portugal's former African colonies. Cesaria Evora is the name to look for among Cape Verde performers, Guem for Angolan, and Kaba Mane from Guinea-Bissau.

Literature

Portuguese literature has been moulded by foreign influences since the 13th century; first, by the Provençal songs of the medieval troubadours, then by Castilian court poetry and Italian Renaissance poetry, and for the longest time of all, by Spain's literary styles and standards (from the 15th to 17th centuries nearly every major Portuguese writer was bilingual, writing both in Portuguese and Spanish).

Nonetheless, Portuguese literature retains a distinct temperament and individuality. Two major styles dominate: lyric poetry and realistic fiction. And no figure dominates the whole more than Luís Vaz de Camões (1524-80). This 16th-century poet enjoyed little fame or fortune during his lifetime. Only after his death in 1580 was his genius recognised, largely thanks to his epic poem, *Os Lusiadas* (The Lusiads). Ostensibly, the poem relates the historic sea voyage by Vasco da Gama to India in 1497, but it is also a superbly lyrical song of praise to the greatness of the Portuguese spirit, written at a time when Portugal was still one of the most powerful countries in the Western world. When it was first published in 1572 it received few plaudits. Over 400 years later, it is considered the national epic, its poet a national hero.

Traditional lyric poetry continued to flourish in the wake of Camões (and still does), but in the 19th century a tide of romanticism swept the Portuguese literary scene. The chief figurehead of the movement was poet, playwright and novelist Almeida Garrett (1799-1854) who devoted much of his life to stimulating political awareness in Portugal through his writings. He initially became politically active in the liberal cause, leading to his exile in 1823 to Europe where he encountered the Romantic literary movement. Garrett's most notable works include two long nationalistic romantic narrative poems, *Camões* and *Dona Branca*, and the novel, *Viagens na minha terra* (Travels in My Homeland) in which he mixes fiction and fact in a romantic episode that serves as an allegory of contemporary political events. He was also an important playwright (the best since the 16th-century court dramatist, Gil Vicente) and wrote several plays with the aim of establishing a national repertoire.

Garrett's contemporary Alexandre Herculano (also exiled for his political liberalism) was meanwhile continuing the long Portuguese tradition of historical literature (which flourished especially during the 16th-century Age of Discoveries) by creating an enormous body of work – notably his magnum opus, the *História de Portugal* – which established him as the founding father of modern Portuguese (and Spanish) history.

Towards the end of the 19th century several other notable writers emerged, among them José Maria Eça de Queirós, who introduced realism to Portuguese literature with his powerful 1876 novel, *O Crime do Padre Amaro* (The Sin of Father Amaro). His other outstanding works include the entertaining narratives of 19th-century life *Os Maias* (The Maias) and *A Illustre Casa de Ramires* (The Illustrious House of Ramires).

José Maria Ferreira de Castro continued the realism trend in the early 20th century with his novels *A Selva* (The Jungle – based on his experiences in Brazil) and *Os Emigrantes* (The Emigrants). Fernando Pessoa (1888-1935), author of the 1934 *Mensagem* (Message), is posthumously regarded as the most brilliant poet of his generation.

But the Salazar dictatorship that spanned much of this era suppressed both creativity and freedom of expression. Several notable writers suffered during this period, including the poet and storyteller Miguel Torga whose background in tough Trás-os-Montes gave a radical individualism to his writings (so much so that one of his novels was banned); and Maria Velho da Costa, one of the three authors of *Novas Cartas Portuguesas* (The Three Marias: New Portuguese Letters), whose modern feminist interpretation of the 17th-century *Letters of a Portuguese Nun* so shocked the Salazar regime that its authors were put on trial.

Today's post-Salazar literary scene is dominated by figures such as António Lobo Antunes and José Saramago. Saramago's international reputation has been based on impressive works, such as *Memorial do Convento* (Memorial of the Convent), which combines an astute realism with poetic fancy. Of the several novels of his available in English translation, the award-winning *Death of Ricardo Reis* is well worth tracking down. Another author high on the list of Portugal's best contemporary writers is José Cardoso Pires, whose finest novel is *Balada da Praia dos Cães* (Ballad of Dog's Beach), a gripping thriller based on a real political assassination in the Salazar era. In Portugal's former colonies (particularly Brazil), writers such as Jorge Amado are also making their mark on modern Portuguese-language literature.

Architecture

The earliest major architectural achievements likely to grab your attention in Portugal are the 11th and 12th-century Romanesque cathedrals. Often – as with Coimbra's dour example – these were built more like fortified castles than religious strongholds (the military relied on them heavily during their wars against the Moors). Surpassing them all both in design and atmosphere is the extraordinary 16-sided rotunda at the heart of Convento de Cristo in Tomar. This inner sanctuary for the Knights Templar (a religious-cum-military order) was built in the 12th century to the model of the Holy Sepulchre in Jerusalem. Although closed for visits, it still dominates the entire *convento* complex.

However, it is the Gothic style (spanning the 12th to 16th centuries) that graces some of the most aesthetically pleasing religious architecture, notably the dramatically austere church and cloister of the Mosteiro de Alcobaça (Alcobaça Abbey). Begun in 1178, the abbey is one of the finest examples of Cistercian architecture in Europe, with a soaring lightness and simplicity strongly influenced by the style of the French Cistercian abbey at Cîteaux. In its turn, Alcobaça served as a model to the 14th-century Cistercian cloisters of Coimbra, Lisbon and Évora cathedrals.

Meanwhile, secular architecture was also enjoying something of a Gothic boom, thanks to the need for constant fortifications against the Moors and to the castle-building fervour of the 13th-century Dom Dinis. Dozens of impressive castles (such as Almourol, Estremoz, Óbidos and Bragança) date from this time, many featuring massive double perimeter walls and an inner square tower. Even townsfolk got in on the Gothic act, adding classically simple Gothic stone doorways and windows to their plain granite houses (look for them in Castelo de Vide and Marvão).

But simplicity went right out the window with the construction of the Mosteiro de Santa Maria da Vitória (Batalha Abbey) at the end of the 14th century. Portuguese, Irish and French architects all worked on Batalha over the following two centuries (the final chapels were left unfinished). The combination of their different skills and the changing architectural fashions of their times – from Flamboyant Gothic to Gothic Renaissance to Manueline – makes this the most impressive and stimulating Gothic building in Portugal.

Manueline is the term given to Portugal's very own style of architecture. Marking the transition from Gothic to Renaissance, it flourished during the reign of Dom Manuel I (1495-1521) when Vasco da Gama and his peers were exploring the seas as far as India and discovering new lands and new wealth for Portugal. The confidence of this Age of Discoveries was expressed in sculptural creations of extraordinary inventiveness, drawing heavily on nautical themes: ropes, coral and anchors in twisted stone topped by ubiquitous armillary spheres (Dom Manuel's emblem) and the Cross of the Order of Christ (the former Knights Templar organisation, which largely financed and inspired Portugal's explorations). In cathedrals, architectural styles soared up like ocean waves amid a plethora of spiral decoration (aptly described by the eccentric 18th-century English novelist William Beckford as 'scollops and twistifications'). Outstanding Manueline masterpieces worth going out of your way to see are the Mosteiro dos Jerónimos at Belém (masterminded largely by architects Diogo de Boitaca and João de Castilho) and Diogo de Arruda's fantastically sculpted window in the Chapter House in the Convento de Cristo. Diogo and his brother Francisco were also responsible for creating another unique style at this time – Luso-Moorish architecture, which mixed Gothic and Moorish styles with Manueline adornment, typified in lovely horseshoe arches.

Nothing could possibly match the Manueline's imaginative flourish but, in terms of flamboyance, the baroque style surpassed it. After a brief flirtation in the early 17th century with classical and Renaissance art – notably by resident Spanish and Italian architects, including Diogo de Torralva and Filippo Terzi (the latter was responsible for Lisbon's Igreja de São Vicente de Fora) – Portuguese architects enthusiastically embraced the baroque style (named, incidentally, after the Portuguese word *barroco* for a rough pearl).

Financed by the 17th-century gold and diamond discoveries in Brazil, and encouraged by the extravagant and liberal Dom João V, local and foreign artists created baroque masterpieces of mind-boggling opulence. The Convento do Mafra was so immense it took 13 years and 15,000 workers every day to complete. A hallmark of the architecture at this time was the awesome use of *talha dourada* (gilded woodwork), which was lavished on church interiors throughout the land, particularly in Aveiro's Convento de Jesus, Lisbon's Igreja de São Roque and Porto's Igreja de São Francisco. Some of the most refined baroque architecture, however, is found in the north – the Solar de Mateus in Vila Real (by the Italian architect Nicolau Nasoni) and the monumental staircase of Braga's Bom Jesus de Monte.

Only when the gold ran out did the baroque fad fade. At the end of the 18th century, architects quietly returned to the classical style (exemplified by Mateus Vicente's Queluz Palace). And after Lisbon suffered its devastating earthquake in 1755, even more simplicity followed. The Marquês de Pombal invited architect Eugenio dos Santos to rebuild the city in a revolutionary new 'Pombal' style marked by plain houses and wide avenues. A similar opportunity has recently been given to Portugal's leading architect, Alvaro Siza Vieira, who is restoring the historic Chiado shopping district of central Lisbon following a major fire in 1988.

Contemporary Portuguese architecture can hardly hope to match the Manueline style in terms of inspiration. But among the more impressive modern creations are the Palace of Justice and the startling 'post-

Azulejos

There's no question which decorative art is Portugal's finest: painted tiles, known as *azulejos* (probably after the Arabic *al zulaycha*, which means 'polished stone'), cover everything from church interiors to train stations, house façades to fountains, all over Portugal. While the Portuguese can't claim to have invented the technique – they learnt about it from the Moors, who picked it up from the Persians – they have certainly used azulejos more imaginatively and consistently than any other nation.

Some of the earliest 16th-century tiles to be found in Portugal (for instance, at Sintra's Pálacio Nacional) are of Moorish origin and are geometric in style. But after the Portuguese captured Ceuta in 1415, they began to investigate the art more thoroughly for themselves. The invention of the majolica technique by the Italians in the 16th century, enabling colours to be painted directly onto the wet clay, over a layer of white enamel, gave the Portuguese the impetus they needed, and the azulejo craze began.

The first truly Portuguese tiles started to appear in the 1580s, gracing churches such as Lisbon's Igreja de São Roque and Santarém's Igreja de Marvila. Initially, these azulejos were multicoloured and mostly geometric, reflecting carpet or tapestry patterns, but in the late 17th century a fashion began for huge azulejo panels in churches and cloisters and on houses and public buildings, illustrating everything from cherubs to picnics, saints to bucolic landscapes. Every nobleman had to have his azulejo hunting panel or poetic allegory (as in Lisbon's Pálacio dos Marquês da Fronteira), every church its life of Christ or the saints (as in Lisbon's Igreja São Vicente de Fora). Indeed, such was the growing azulejo craze that the quality of production and colouring eventually suffered and the blue-and-white tiles produced by the Dutch Delft company were able to take over the market.

But with the 18th century arrived the great Portuguese azulejo masters António de Oliveira Bernardes and his son Policarpo, who revived the use of both blue-and-white and polychrome Portuguese tiles, producing brilliant panels that perfectly complemented their surroundings. Rococo themes and flavours also appeared, decorating fountains, stairways (Lamego's Igreja de Nossa Senhora dos Remédios) and sacristies (Lisbon's Convento da Madre de Deus). Only towards the end of the century did a simpler style and colour scheme emerge, reflecting the neoclassical movement in architecture. By then, the industrial manufacture of azulejos had started to cause another decline in quality, as did the rapid need for huge quantities of azulejos after the 1755 Lisbon earthquake.

New, imaginative uses of azulejos still appeared in the 19th century – among them, the large azulejo figures in restaurants such as Lisbon's popular Cervejaria da Trindade. The Art Nouveau and Art Deco movements took the art of azulejo even further into the public domain, with some fantastic façades and interiors for shops and restaurants, kiosks and residential buildings created by Rafael Bordalo Pinheiro, Jorge Colaço and others. Azulejos still have their place in contemporary Portuguese life: Maria Keil and Júlio de Resende are two of the leading artists, responsible for creating some stunning wall mosaics and murals.

For the complete history of this uniquely Portuguese art, visit the Museu Nacional do Azulejo in Lisbon's Convento da Madre de Deus. ∎

modern' Amoreiras shopping complex in Lisbon, and several monumental steel bridges across the Douro, Tejo and Guadiana rivers, including two designed by Gustave Eiffel (at Porto and at Viana do Castelo). Portugal's most prominent contemporary architect is Alvaro Siza, winner of the prestigious Pritzger Prize.

A relatively unsung aspect of architecture is so-called 'vernacular architecture', the shapes and forms that arise naturally over the centuries in a region's common buildings in response to climate, land use and other constraints. A fine book on the vernacular architecture of Portugal and Spain is Norman F Carver Jr's *Iberian Villages*, published in 1988.

Visual & Decorative Arts

Painting The earliest examples of visual art in Portugal are several treasure-troves of 20,000-year-old Palaeolithic paintings and carvings, especially those along the Rio Côa near Vila Nova de Foz Côa in Beira Alta. This is perhaps the first truly 'original' Portuguese art (see the boxed aside).

The cave dwellers' modern successors have been heavily influenced by French, Italian and Flemish styles. The first major exception was the 15th-century primitive painter Nuno Gonçalves, whose polyptych of the *Adoration of St Vincent* (now in Lisbon's Museu Nacional de Arte Antiga) is a unique tapestry-style revelation of 15th-century Portuguese society.

The Manueline school of the 16th century also produced some uniquely Portuguese paintings, remarkable for their delicacy, realism and luminous colours. The big names in the school are Vasco Fernandes (known as Grão Vasco) and Gaspar Vaz, who both worked from Viseu (their best works can be seen in Viseu's excellent Museu de Grão Vasco). In Lisbon, other outstanding Manueline artists were Jorge Afonso (painter to Dom Manuel I), Cristóvão de Figueiredo and Gregório Lopes.

The Renaissance era produced more notable sculpture than painting (see below) but the 17th century saw a female artist, Josefa de Óbidos, make waves with her rich still lifes. In the late 18th century, Domingos António de Sequeira produced wonderful portraits. The 19th century saw an artistic echo of the Naturalist and Romantic movements, expressed particularly strongly in the works of Silva Porto and Marquês de Oliveira, while Sousa Pinto excelled in the early 20th century as a pastel artist.

Naturalism continued to be the dominant trend this century, although Amadeo de Souza Cardoso struck out on his own impressive path of Cubism and Expressionism, and Maria Helena Vieria da Silva became noted as the country's finest abstract painter (although she lived and worked in Paris most of her life). Other eminent artists in the contemporary art world include Almada Negreiros (often called the father of Portugal's modern art movement) and Guilherme Santa-Rita. Their works and many others can best be seen in Lisbon's Centro de Arte Moderna and Porto's Museu Nacional Soares dos Reis.

Sculpture Sculptors excelled in many periods of Portugal's history. Among the first memorable creations are the carved tombs of the 12th to 14th centuries, such as the beautifully ornate limestone tombs of Inês de Castro and Dom Pedro in Alcobaça Abbey, where the detailed friezes are still impressive, despite vandalism by French soldiers in 1811. During the Manueline era, sculptors including Diogo de Boitaca (see Architecture, above) went wild with uniquely Portuguese sea-faring fantasies and exuberant decoration. At the same time, foreign influences were seeping in: first, a Flemish style (thanks to resident Flemish masters Olivier de Gand and Jean d'Ypres), followed in the 16th century by Flamboyant Gothic and Plateresque styles (named after the ornate Spanish work of silversmiths or *plateros)* from Spanish Galicia and Biscay. The Biscayan artists João and Diogo de Castilho created the most outstanding work during this time, often combining their native styles with Manueline.

During the Renaissance period, it was the

turn of the French: several French artists who had settled in Coimbra, including Nicolas Chanterène and Jean de Rouen, excelled in sculpting doorways, pulpits, altarpieces and low reliefs. The ornate pulpit in Coimbra's Igreja de Santa Cruz is regarded as Chanterène's masterpiece. Foreign schools continued to influence Portuguese sculptors in the 18th-century baroque era, when Dom João V took advantage of all the foreign artists helping with the construction of the Convento do Mafra to found a school of sculpture. Its first principal was the Italian, Alexander Giusti, but its most famous Portuguese teacher was Joaquim Machado de Castro (the museum named after him in Coimbra contains some of the country's finest sculptures and paintings). Castro's work inevitably shows strong influences from the Classical and Romantic traditions of France and Italy, especially in the terracotta figures of his baroque manger scenes.

A century later, the work of António Soares dos Reis reflects similar influences, although Soares also tried to create something uniquely Portuguese (and impossibly intangible) by attempting to portray in sculpture the melancholic feeling of saudade (see the boxed aside, Saudade, earlier in this chapter). At the turn of the 20th century, two names were prominent: Francisco Franco, and the prolific sculptor António Teixeira Lopes (Soares dos Reis' pupil), whose most famous works are his series of children's heads.

Performing Arts, Cinema & Puppetry

Although a few film directors such as Manual de Oliveira have made an international reputation for themselves (his latest film stars Catherine Deneuve and John Malkovich), Portugal's film industry is basically non-existent. Even classic theatre is still finding its feet after the repressive Salazar years, though many small theatres in Lisbon and the provinces are now flourishing, thanks largely to the support of the generous Gulbenkian Foundation.

Far more exciting are the 'fringe' performing arts, such as the puppet theatres of Porto

and Évora (Porto even has an international puppet festival in March) and the circus school in Lisbon. Further information is given in the relevant Porto, Alentejo, and Lisbon chapters.

Handicrafts & Indigenous Arts

You only have to visit the big weekly markets in Portugal to see the astounding range of handicrafts available – from ceramics, embroidery and lacework to baskets, painted furniture and carved ox yokes. The Algarve, Alentejo and Minho produce some of the finest work, although nearly every region has its speciality. In addition to the artesenato shops where these handicrafts are for sale, you can also often find items not available elsewhere at turismos and rural museums (eg in Estremoz in the Alentejo, and São Bras de Alportel in the Algarve). Porto's CRAT arts centre is another good source. For detailed information about the crafts and artisans of the Algarve and Alentejo region, check out John and Madge Measures' book, Southern Portugal.

The ceramics are perhaps the most impressive (and most frustratingly inconvenient to cart around, though the major artesenato shops can offer a packing and shipping service). The most famous pottery centres are São Pedro do Corval and Estremoz (both in the Alentejo), where the pottery is often encrusted with marble chips; Barcelos in the Minho (brightly coloured pots and cockerel; Coimbra in the Beiras (predominantly green and geometric wares); and Caldas da Rainha in Estremadura (cabbage leaf designs). Despite Caldas da Rainha's tendency to frivolity in ceramics (disgusting phallic ornaments), the town holds an important Feira Nacional da Cerâmica every year. The Algarve, too, is packed with great pottery, especially huge, Roman-style amphora jugs. Two of Portugal's most famous ceramic artists, Ernesto Silva and his wife Zabel Moita are also from the Algarve, creating stylised animals and figures from their workshop in Aljezur.

Another widely available handicraft is

baskets made from rush, willow, cane or rye straw, for both practical use and decoration. The Algarve, Alentejo and Minho are all major areas for basketry, while Trás-os-Montes has traditionally been known for its basket packsaddles. Another rural necessity still being fashioned for practical use (although increasingly for tourist souvenirs as well) are the fabulous painted wooden furniture of the Alentejo (which is made in miniature sizes, too) and the carved wooden ox yokes of the Minho region. Cleverly crafted wooden toys and miniature boats are other carved wooden specialities, and tiny straw figures dressed in traditional rural costume are widely made for decoration or souvenirs.

Hand-embroidered linen, especially tablecloths and place mats, is a flourishing handicraft throughout Portugal. Weaving (especially woollen blankets) is also a long-established tradition, particularly in the Algarve and southern Alentejo, where the craft has recently been revived and boosted by women's cooperatives and initiatives such as LEADER (established by the EU to assist rural development projects) and IN LOCO (aimed at revitalising the Serra do Caldeirão region of the Algarve). There are several weaving strongholds in the Algarve, including Mértola, Odemira and Alté (which is also famous for its crochet work) where individual women take great pride in their work.

Lace and filigree jewellery are less widespread. Although filigree jewellery has been famous in Portugal since the 18th century, its crafting is now limited mainly to the Porto area and Minho province, where the women's traditional costume (seen at folk dances and festivals) includes a lavish adornment of intricate filigree jewellery.

Lace is traditionally found only along the coast ('where there are nets, there is lace,' goes the popular saying), although there are several inland places that are famous for lace, including Loulé and Silves in the Algarve. Silves is also one of the few places in Portugal where children are actually taught the art of bobbin lace (from the age of six). Another important lace-making school is in Vila do Conde in the Minho, renowned for its lace for centuries. The town also hosts an annual crafts fair every July, which is well worth visiting if you want to track down some of the best northern handicrafts.

SOCIETY & CONDUCT
Traditional Culture
Thanks to a strong Catholic influence and decades of repression under Salazar, Portugal remains a traditional and conservative country. *Romarias* (religious festivals in honour of a patron saint) are taken seriously everywhere, especially in the northern Minho province where they can last for several days. Solemn processions are a hallmark of these events, with a candle or banner carried to a sanctuary where the devotees kiss the feet of the saint's statue. Sometimes there's a long pilgrimage to a hill-top chapel attended by participants from all over the region. And nearly always there's a finale of lay festivities, featuring a fairground atmosphere of family picnics, dances and fireworks.

More lively occasions are the festivals where folk dancing is the central attraction. They take place all over Portugal, mainly during the spring and summer, but again the north features the most flamboyant versions with each local village sending its best dance team, all boasting brilliantly embroidered costumes, the women draped in gold chains and necklaces, the children clad from top to toe in identical versions of their parents' outfits.

You get the impression at these events that nothing much has changed for centuries. In some areas (for instance, the Algarve) it's true that tourism has introduced an inevitable element of commercialism but elsewhere (such as the Minho) the extra attention has convinced local authorities to finance ever bigger displays of fabulous (but costly) floral decorations, floats or fireworks.

The only modern activity to rival the popularity of the folk dance is football: customers in bars and restaurants are glued to TV sets when a big match is being played (see Spectator Sports in the Facts for the Visitor chapter) and almost every village and town boasts its own enthusiastic team. Some traditional activities that date back centuries and require a dedicated team of participants, for instance the *pauliteiros* or stick dancers of Miranda do Douro in Trás-os-Montes, are finding it hard to compete with this relatively new obsession.

One cultural activity that seems impervious to the changing times is the lingering fondness among the male community for cafes and squares. As in most Mediterranean countries, men of all ages seem to spend hours in their local cafe gossiping over coffee or wine, or gathering in the cobbled squares to watch the world go by. City women often have their own afternoon *tête-a-têtes* in a *salão de chá* (tea room) or *pastelaria* (cake shop), but they aren't nearly so dedicated to this national pastime as their menfolk.

Dos & Don'ts

Portuguese politeness is delightful, because it is by no means purely artificial, but flows in a great measure from a natural kindness of feeling.
Lord Carnarvon, 1827

Portuguese everywhere share characteristics of friendliness and an unhurried approach to life: in other words, expect smiles and warmth (especially if you speak some Portuguese) but don't expect punctuality or brisk efficiency. This lassitude can drive business travellers and tourists mad with frustration at times, particularly in banks and post office queues, but, as in Asia, displays of anger are unlikely to get you anywhere.

Travellers may also experience another face-saving technique when Portuguese offer information: if you're asking directions (or even for information in a turismo) you'll rarely hear the simple answer, 'I don't know.' Portuguese people like to appear confident, which means their answers may not always be correct. Get a second judgement if the answer required is important.

Portuguese pride comes into play with language, too: they may be neighbours with

Spain but, after centuries of rivalry and hostility, the last thing they want to hear spoken to them is Spanish. Try English, French, or even German instead. Best of all, of course, is an attempt (however clumsy) at Portuguese. Politeness is so highly valued in this society that simply addressing someone in Portuguese (*senhor* for men and *senhora* for women, or *senhora dona* followed by the Christian name for an elderly or respected woman) will earn you lots of Brownie points.

So, too, will the presence of children (single women travellers will invariably be asked when they're going to get married and have kids). In fact, you may well be overlooked altogether in favour of your tot and you'll certainly be subjected to a frank interrogation about the child's age and health. Conservative attitudes to women (especially in the north) can also prove uncomfortable to the solo female traveller (see Women Travellers in the Facts for the Visitor chapter) but attention can be considerably reduced if you dress conservatively, particularly if you're roaming through traditionally minded rural areas.

In fact, dress can be a sensitive issue all over Portugal. While beachwear (and even nudity on some beaches) is acceptable in coastal tourist resorts, if you're visiting a church, you'll find that shorts and skimpy tops are definitely frowned upon. One way to avoid having to dress like a choirboy all day is to keep a shirt and sarong or long trousers handy as a quick cover-up for church forays. And if you're visiting the authorities (eg police or immigration office), you'll stand a far better chance of cooperation if you're well dressed.

You'll probably know if you've upset a Portuguese in any way – they're not shy of showing their emotions, whether it's anger at an obnoxious motorist, sadness at a farewell or simply grumpiness at the rainy weather. But none of this is as extreme as you may encounter in Spain or Italy. Indeed, compared with their Mediterranean neighbours, the Portuguese could even be said to be reserved – unless they're at a football match or festival. At times like this, the *joie de vivre* is infectious and the only rule of conduct for visitors is to soak up the atmosphere and enjoy.

RELIGION

As freedom of religion is part of the constitution there is no state religion in Portugal, but Roman Catholicism is the dominant faith and is adhered to by roughly 95% of the population. Other Christian denominations represented include Anglicans, Evangelists, Baptists, Congregationalists, Methodists, Jehovah's Witnesses and Mormons. There are also some 15,000 Muslims and a small community of about 2000 Jews.

Christianity has been a major force in shaping Portugal's history. The religion first reached Portugal's shores in the 1st century AD, thriving even among pagan invaders. By the third century, bishoprics had been established in Braga, Évora, Faro and Lisbon. After the Muslims invaded in 711, Christians (and Jews) were initially allowed freedom of worship, but with the arrival of the more fanatical Almoravids in the early 11th century, the Christian Reconquista

(Reconquest) picked up speed. Christian crusaders en route to the Holy Land from England, France, Germany and Holland frequently helped the kings of Portugal boot out the Moors – notably at Lisbon in 1147 and Silves in 1189.

Other Christian forces that influenced Portugal's development at this time were the Cistercians (responsible for the introduction of agriculture and architecture around Alcobaça) and powerful Christian military orders such as the Knights Templar, later reorganised into the Order of Christ. It was the wealth and vast resources of this organisation that largely financed Portugal's overseas explorations in the 15th century. The riches that ensued from the new empire went into the building of some of the most magnificent churches and monuments in Europe.

But Christianity has also been responsible for some of Portugal's darkest moments, notably the Inquisition, which was started in the 1530s by João III and his strictly Catholic Spanish wife. Thousands of victims, including many Jews, were tortured, imprisoned or burnt at the stake at public sentencing cere-

---

The Jews of Portugal

Communities of Jews first became prominent in Portugal in medieval times. They wielded power and influence as bankers, financiers, court doctors, tax collectors, astronomers and map makers. Although the Afonsine Ordinance of 1446 decreed that they must live in segregated Jewish quarters, called judiaria, they faced relatively little harassment. Indeed, when Spain's zealous Catholic rulers Ferdinand and Isabella expelled Jews from their country in 1492, Portugal's João II offered temporary refuge to an estimated 60,000 of them. Many settled in Guarda, Belmonte, Bragança, Tomar and Viana do Castelo.

But five years later, Portugal's new king, Manuel I, was forced to show his anti-Semitic credentials as a condition of marrying the Spanish rulers' daughter, Isabella. He offered the Jews a choice: 'conversion' to Christianity (with no enquiry made into their beliefs for 20 years) or emigration. Not surprisingly, many scorned the offer and left (Holland was a popular destination).

Those who remained – now known as 'New Christians' or *marranos* – faced the horrors of the Inquisition, launched by João III in 1540. Thousands were tortured, imprisoned or burnt at the stake. In 1989, President Soares offered a public apology to the Jews for this horrific period of persecution.

Today, some 2000 Jews live in Portugal, with the largest community in Belmonte, in Beira Alta. Traces of judiarias can still be found in many towns. Castelo de Vide has the country's oldest synagogue (dating from the 13th century) – a tiny and discreet little house, tucked into a cobbled lane. Tomar's former synagogue, used by the Jewish community for only a few years before Manuel's conversion order, now serves as a major Luso-Hebraic Museum, displaying gifts from Jewish visitors from all over the world. ∎

monies known as autos-da-fé. The terror was only really suppressed in 1820.

Today's Catholic Church is still powerful and highly respected. Sunday masses are widely attended (though less so in the south), as are the many religious festivals held in honour of a local patron saint. One of Europe's most important centres of pilgrimage is at Fátima (see the Estremadura & Ribatejo chapter), where up to 100,000 pilgrims congregate every May 12th to 13th and October 12th to 13th, many walking for miles or creeping towards the sanctuary on bended knees.

Northern Portugal has always been the most religious part of the country, though certain festivals (eg the celebrations in June for St Anthony, St John and St Peter: Os Santos Populares) are celebrated with fervour throughout the land. And it's in the north, too, that you're most likely to see evidence of more unusual forms of faith, some even bordering on paganism. On a hilltop above Ponte de Lima, for instance, is a tiny chapel dedicated to Saint Ovido, the patron saint of ears. The walls are covered with votive offerings of wax ears, given by devotees in hope of, or in thanks for a cured ear affliction. Similar chapels (adorned with wax limbs of all kinds) can be found tucked away even inside churches, revealing a willingness by the Catholic Church to accept some bizarre expressions of faith.

LANGUAGE

Like French, Italian, Spanish and Romanian, Portuguese is a Romance language, that is, one closely derived from Latin. It is spoken by over 10 million people in Portugal, 130 million in Brazil, and it is also the official language of five African nations (Angola, Mozambique, Guinea-Bissau, Cape Verde and São Tomé e Príncipe). In Asia it is still spoken in the former Portuguese territory of East Timor, and in enclaves around Malacca, Goa, Damão and Diu. Visitors to Portugal are often struck by the strangeness of the language, which some say sounds like Arabic. However, those who understand French or Spanish are often surprised to see how similar written Portuguese is to the other Romance languages.

The indigenous people who inhabited the Iberian Peninsula before the arrival of the Romans are considered responsible for the most striking traits of the Portuguese language. The vulgar Latin of the Roman soldiers and merchants, who were well established by 27 BC, gradually took over the indigenous languages, and a strong neo-Latin character evolved.

After the Arab invasion in 711 AD, Arabic quickly became the prestige cultural language in the Iberian Peninsula. The Arabic influence on the formation of the Portuguese language ended with the expulsion of the Moors in 1249.

During the Middle Ages, Portuguese underwent mostly French and Provençal-influenced changes. In the 16th and 17th centuries, Italian and Spanish were responsible for innovations in vocabulary.

The most useful language to speak in Portugal (after Portuguese, of course) is French. English and Spanish follow, and are about equally useful, at least in the more touristed areas. German occasionally comes in handy too.

Pronunciation

Pronunciation of Portuguese is difficult; like English, vowels and consonants have more than one possible sound depending on position and stress. Moreover, there are nasal vowels and diphthongs in Portuguese with no equivalent in English.

Vowels Single vowels should present relatively few problems:

a	short, like the 'u' sound in 'cut'; or long like the 'ur' sound in 'hurt'
e	short, as in 'bet', or longer, as in French *été* and Scottish 'laird'
é	short, as in 'bet'
ê	long, like the 'a' sound in 'gate'
e	silent final 'e', like the final 'e' in English 'these'; also silent in unstressed syllables
i	long, as in 'see', or short, as in 'ring'

o   short, as in 'pot'; long, as in 'note'; or like 'oo', as in 'good'
ô   long, as in 'note'
u   'oo', as in 'good'

Nasal Vowels Nasalisation is represented by an 'n' or an 'm' after the vowel, or by a tilde (~) over it. The nasal 'i' exists in English as the 'ing' in 'sing'. For other nasal vowels, try to pronounce a long 'a', 'ah', 'e' or 'eh' while holding your nose, so that you sound as if you have a cold.

Diphthongs Double vowels are relatively straightforward:

au   as in 'now'
ai   as in 'pie'
ei   as in 'day'
eu   pronounced together
oi   similar to 'boy'

Nasal Diphthongs Try the same technique as for nasal vowels. To say *não*, pronounce 'now' through your nose.

ão   nasal 'now' (owng)
ãe   nasal 'day' (eing)
õe   nasal 'boy' (oing)
ui   similar to the 'uing' in 'ensuing'

Consonants The following consonants are specific to Portuguese:

c   hard, as in 'cat', before **a**, **o** or **u**
c   soft as in 'see', before **e** or **i**
ç   as in 'see'
g   hard, as in 'garden', before **a**, **o** or **u**
g   soft, as in 'treasure', before **e** or **i**
g   hard, as in 'get', before **e** or **i**
h   never pronounced at the beginning of a word
nh   like the 'ni' sound in 'onion'
lh   like the 'll' sound in 'million'
j   as in 'treasure'
m   in final position is not pronounced, it simply nasalises the previous vowel: *um* (oong), *bom* (bõ)
qu   like the 'k' in 'key' before **e** or **i**
qu   like the 'q' in 'quad' before **a** or **o**
r   at the beginning of a word, or **rr** in the middle of a word, is a harsh, guttural sound similar to the French *rue*, Scottish loch, or German Bach; in some areas of Portugal this **r** is not guttural, but strongly rolled.
r   in the middle or at the end of a word is a rolled sound stronger than the English 'r'
s   like the 's' in 'see' (at the beginning of a word)

The Commonwealth of Lusophone Nations

After years of hesitation and disagreement, Portugal and six former colonies finally put their differences behind them to form the Community of Portuguese Language Countries (CPLP) in July 1996.

Taking the British Commonwealth and French-speaking equivalent, La Francophonie, as models, the CPLP groups more than 170 million Portuguese speakers from Brazil, Angola, the Cape Verde Islands, Guinea-Bissau, Mozambique and São Tomé e Principe in an alliance aimed at protecting their common language and culture and promoting political and diplomatic cooperation. One example where Portuguese language and culture are already seen as being under threat is Mozambique, which recently joined the British Commonwealth. Another area where the CPLP hopes to wield its newly united front is at the United Nations (UN): the CPLP is calling for a general reform of UN operations, and proposing that Brazil become a permanent member of the UN Security Council.

But doubts remain about the CPLP's real usefulness, especially among the African member countries. 'Will it head the same way as countless alliances that…only really exist when political leaders gather for meetings?' asked the president of Guinea-Bissau soon after the charter was signed. Practical help to solve economic problems is at the head of the list of CPLP aims, although Portugal and Brazil are adamant that the CPLP is not meant to be an economic pact. They may all speak the same language, but the honeymoon period of togetherness already looks decidedly rocky. ■

ss	like the 's' in 'see' (in the middle of a word)
s	like the 'z' in 'zeal' (between vowels)
s	like the 'sh' in 'ship' (before another consonant, or at the end of a word)
x	like the 'sh' in 'ship', the 'z' in 'zeal', or the 'ks' sound in 'taxi'

Word Stress Word stress is important in Portuguese, as it can change the meaning of the word. Many Portuguese words have a written accent and the stress must fall on that syllable when you pronounce the word.

Basics
Yes/No.	*Sim/Não.*
Maybe.	*Talvez.*
Please.	*Se faz favor/por favor.*
Thank you.	*Obrigado/a.*
That's fine/ You're welcome.	*De nada.*
Excuse me.	*Desculpe/Com licença.*
Sorry/Forgive me.	*Desculpe.*

Greetings
Hello.	*Bom dia/Olá/Chao.*
Good morning.	*Bom dia.*
Good evening.	*Boa tarde.*
Goodbye.	*Adeus/Chao.*
See you later.	*Até logo.*

Small Talk
How are you?	*Como está?*
I'm fine, thanks.	*Bem, obrigado/a.*
What is your name?	*Como se chama?*
My name is…	*Chamo-me…*
Where are you from?	*De onde é?*
I am from…	*Sou de…*
Australia	*Austrália*
Japan	*Japão*
the UK	*os Reino Unido*
the USA	*os Estados Unidos*
How old are you?	*Quantos anos tem?*
I am…years old.	*Tenho…anos.*
Are you married?	*É casado/a?*
Not yet.	*Aindo não.*

How many children do you have?	*Quantos filhos tem?*
daughter	*filha*
son	*filho*

Language Difficulties
I understand.	*Percebo/Entendo.*
I don't understand.	*Não percebo/ entendo.*
Do you speak English?	*Fala inglês?*
Could you write it down?	*Pode escrever isso por favor?*

Getting Around
I want to go to…	*Quero ir a…*
What time does the next…leave/ arrive?	*A que horas parte/chega o próximo…?*
boat	*barco*
bus (city)	*autocarro*
bus (intercity)	*camioneta*
metro	*metro*
train	*combóio*
tram	*eléctrico*

How long does it take?	*Quanto tempo leva isso?*
Where is…?	*Onde é…?*
the bus stop	*a paragem de autocarro*
the metro station	*a estação de metro*
the train station	*a estação ferroviária*
the tram stop	*a paragém de eléctrico*
Is this the bus/train to…?	*E este o autocarro/ combóio para…?*
I'd like a one-way ticket.	*Queria um bilhete simples/de ida.*
I'd like a return ticket.	*Queria um bilhete de ida e volta.*

1st class	*primeira classe*
2nd class	*segunda classe*
left-luggage office	*o depósito de bagagem*
platform	*cais*
timetable	*horário*

I'd like to hire...   *Queria alugar...*
  a car   *um carro*
  a motorcycle/   *uma motocicleta/*
  bicycle   *bicicleta*
  a tour guide   *uma guia*
        intérprete

Fill it up (ie the   *Encha a depósito,*
  tank, with petrol).   *por favor.*

Directions
How do I get to...?   *Como vou para...?*
Is it near/far?   *É perto/longe?*

What...is this?   *O que...é isto/ista?*
  street/road   *rua/estrada*
  suburb   *subúrbia*
  town   *cidade/vila*

Go straight ahead.   *Siga sempre a*
        direito/sempre
        em frente.
Turn left/right...   *Vire à esquerda/*
        direita...
  at the traffic lights   *no semáforo/nos*
        sinais de trânsito
  at the next corner   *na próxima*
        esquina

north   *norte*
south   *sul*
east   *leste/este*
west   *oeste*

Around Town
Where is...?   *Onde é...?*
  a bank/   *um banco/câmbio*
    exchange office
  the city centre   *o centro da*
        cidade/
        da baixa
  the...embassy   *a embaixada de...*
  the hospital   *o hospital*
  my hotel   *do meu hotel*
  the market   *do mercado*
  the post office   *dos correios*
  the public toilet   *sanitários/casa*
        de banho
        pública

Useful Signs	
Camping Ground	*Parque de Campismo*
Entrance	*Entrada*
Exit	*Saĺda*
Free Admission	*Entrada Grátis*
Information	*Informações*
Toilets	*WC*
Men's	*H (for homems)*
Women's	*S (for senhoras)*
Open/Closed	*Aberto/Encerrado (or Fechado)*
Police	*Polícia*
Police Station	*Esquadra Da Polícia*
Prohibited	*Proíbido*
Rooms Available	*Quartos Livres*
Train Station	*Estação*
Departures	*Partidas*
Arrivals	*Chegadas*

  the telephone centre   *da central de*
        telefones
  the tourist office   *do turismo/posta*
        de turismo/
        junta de
        turismo

What time does it open/close?
  A que horas abre/fecha?
I'd like to make a telephone call.
  Quero usar o telefone.
I'd like to change some money/travellers cheques.
  Queria trocar dinheiro/uns cheques de viagem.

Accommodation
I'm looking for ...
  procuro...
    a camping ground
      um parque de campismo
    a youth hostel
      uma pousada de juventude/
      albergue de juventude
    a guesthouse
      uma pensão (pl. *pensões*)
    a hotel
      uma hotel (pl. *hotéis*)

Do you have any rooms available?
Tem quartos livres?
I'd like to book...
Quero fazer una reserva para...
a bed
uma cama
a cheap room
um quarto barato
a single room
um quarto individual
a double room/with twin beds
um quarto de casal/duplo
a room with a bathroom
um quarto com casa de banho
a dormitory bed
cama de dormitório

for one night/two nights
para uma noite/duas noites
How much is it per night/per person?
Quanto é por noite/por pessoa?
Is breakfast included?
O pequeno almoço está incluído?
Can I see the room?
Posso ver o quarto?
Where is the toilet?
Onde ficam os lavabos (as casas de banho)?
It is very dirty/noisy/expensive.
É muito sujo/ruidoso/caro.

Food

breakfast	*pequeno almoço*
lunch	*almoço*
dinner	*jantar*
dish of the day	*prato do dia*
food stall	*quiosque de comida/uma bancada*
grocery store	*mercearia*
market	*mercado*
restaurant	*restaurante*
supermarket	*supermercado*

Is service included in the bill?
O serviço está incluído na conta?
I am a vegetarian.
Sou vegeteriano/a.

Shopping

How much is it?	*Quanto custa?*
Can I look at it?	*Posso ver?*
It's too expensive.	*É muito caro.*
bookshop	*livraria*
chemist/pharmacy	*farmácia*
clothing store	*boutique/ confecções*
laundrette	*lavandaria*
market	*mercado*
newsagency	*papelaria*
department store	*hipermercado*

Time & Dates

What time is it?	*Que horas são?*
When?	*Quando?*
today	*hoje*
tonight	*hoje à noite*
tomorrow	*amanhã*
yesterday	*ontem*
morning/afternoon	*manhã/tarde*
Monday	*segunda-feira*
Tuesday	*terça-feira*
Wednesday	*quarta-feira*
Thursday	*quinta-feira*
Friday	*sexta-feira*
Saturday	*sábado*
Sunday	*domingo*

Numbers

1	*um/uma*
2	*dois/duas*
3	*três*
4	*quatro*
5	*cinco*
6	*seis*
7	*sete*
8	*oito*
9	*nove*
10	*dez*
100	*cem*
1000	*mil*
one million	*um milhão (de)*

Health

I need a doctor.
Preciso um médico.

Where is a hospital/medical clinic?
Onde é um hospital/um centro de saúde?
I'm diabetic/epileptic/asthmatic.
Sou diabético/a; epiléptico/a; asmático/a.
I'm allergic to antibiotics/penicillin.
Sou alérgico/a a antibióticos/penicilina.
I'm pregnant.
Estou grávida.

antiseptic	*antiséptico*
aspirin	*aspirina*
condoms	*preservativo*
constipation	*constpaçao*
contraceptive	*anticoncepcional*
diarrhoea	*diarreia*
dizzy	*vertiginoso*
medicine	*remédio/ medicamento*
nausea	*náusea*
sanitary napkins	*pensos higiénicos*
tampons	*tampões*

Emergencies

Help!	*Socorro!*
Call a doctor!	*Chame um médico!*
Call the police!	*Chame a polícia!*
Go away!	*Deixe-me em paz!*
I've been robbed.	*Fui roubado/a.*
I've been raped.	*Fui violada/ Violarem-me.*
I'm lost.	*Estou perdido/a.*

Further Reading

We recommend Lonely Planet's *Western Europe phrasebook* for the basics. If you want more detail, the Chambers *Portuguese Travelmate* is a useful hybrid of phrasebook and pocket dictionary. For each English word it provides not only the usual literal translation but a variety of possible English-language contexts and phrases for this word, and the corresponding Portuguese translations of these idioms. A pocket dictionary may also be useful.

Facts for the Visitor

PLANNING
When to Go

Portugal's climate is temperate, and you'll find agreeable weather just about everywhere from April through September or October, and nearly year-round in the Algarve. Spring (late March and April) and early autumn (late September and October) bring spectacular foliage. July and August are essentially dry except in the far north, though the Algarve, the Alentejo and the upper Douro valley can get ferociously hot then.

Higher areas such as the Serra da Estrela and Peneda-Gerês ranges, and much of the Minho and Trás-os-Montes, tend to be a bit showery in summer and uncomfortably cold and wet in winter. Overall, the wettest season is from November through March, and the wettest regions are the Minho and the Serra da Estrela. Snowfall is substantial only in the Serra da Estrela, where skiers will find basic facilities. The ski season is from January to March, and February is best.

For more about the weather, see Climate in the Facts about the Country chapter.

If you're going for the beaches, remember that Portugal faces the blustery Atlantic, not the Mediterranean. The further north you go, the colder the water and the bigger the waves. Only in sheltered, shallow areas of the eastern Algarve, in summer, could you call the water warm.

Certain local festivals and celebrations are worth going out of your way for. Carnival (the three days leading up to Ash Wednesday) and Easter are two holidays celebrated with gusto all over the country; dates for these vary from year to year. See Public Holidays & Special Events in this chapter.

The peak tourist season is roughly from mid-June through August or September (and *pensões* and hotels tend to charge peak-season prices during Carnival and Easter week as well). For these times, you'll probably have to prebook middle or top-end accommodation anywhere from a few days to a few weeks ahead. Outside the peak season, crowds thin out, rooms are plentiful, and room and admission prices may drop by as much as 50% (prices in this book are for peak season). The Algarve is the exception:

Government Travel Advice

The US State Department's Bureau of Consular Affairs, Washington, DC 20520, USA, issues periodically updated Consular Information Sheets, which include entry requirements, medical facilities, crime information and other topics. It also has recorded travel information on ☎ 202-647 5225.

If you're on the Internet, you can subscribe to a mailing list for all current State Department travel advisories by sending a message containing the word 'subscribe' to travel-advisories-request@stolaf.edu (St Olaf College, Northfield, MN, USA). You can check out current and past sheets or search by key words via St Olaf's gopher server, gopher.stolaf.edu, in directory Internet Resources/US-State-Department-Travel-Advisories. St Olaf's World Wide Web URL is http://www.stolaf.edu/network/travel-advisories.html.

Get British Foreign Office travel advisories from the Travel Advice Unit, Foreign & Commonwealth Office, Room 605 Clive House, Petty France, London SW1H 9HD, UK (☎ 0171-270 4129; fax 0171-270 4228). Regularly updated Foreign Office travel advice is also displayed on BBC2 Ceefax, pp 564 ff.

Australians can ring the Department of Foreign Affairs advice line in Canberra on ☎ 02-6261 3305 for advisories on specific countries, or check them out at URL http://www.dfat.gov.ad/dfat/home.html. Also, any travel agent hooked up to the Apollo, Fantasia or Galileo networks can access these advisories directly. ■

'peak season' here runs for much of the year, from late February through November.

What Kind of Trip?

Take a tour if you have very little time or want guaranteed comfort every night, but there's enough cheap long-distance transport, lower-end accommodation and helpful tourist offices in most places to make unstructured travel entirely feasible.

Despite its small size, Portugal is so different from one end to the other that you cannot get an accurate feel for it in any one place. Nevertheless, you could easily fill a fortnight just with Lisbon, or Porto and the Douro valley, or beaches, or walking/cycling around the Minho or Trás-os-Montes.

There's plenty of nightlife in the larger towns, so solo travellers needn't be lonely. Portugal is wonderfully child-friendly too, making it a very happy place for family travel. Don't count on finding work if you want to stay for a long spell.

Maps

Road & Tourist Maps The best road map available abroad is Michelin's *Portugal*, No 440, at 1:400,000. Even more up-to-date (but without Michelin's Lisbon enlargement and its index of towns) is the 1:350,000 *Mapa das Estradas*, published and sold by Automóvel Club de Portugal (☎ 01-356 39 31; fax 01-357 47 32), Rua Rosa Araújo 24, Lisbon, and at ACP offices in Aveiro, Braga, Bragança, Coimbra, Évora, Faro, Porto, Vila Real and elsewhere. And keep an eye out for Lonely Planet's upcoming *Portugal Travel Atlas*.

Foto-Vista publishes a few good, clear tourist maps showing major roads and attractions, eg Lisbon (1:13,400) and the Algarve (1:176,000). Some tourist offices dispense an adequate 1:600,000 *Carta Turística* of the entire country, published by Guia Turístico do Norte, though some roads shown as major highways are not completed yet! The handsomest tourist map we found anywhere was Edicões Livro Branco's bilingual foldout of the entire Rio Douro valley, *Rio Douro: Porto-Barca d'Alva*, available for about

1000$00 from major bookshops, especially in Porto.

The Instituto Geográfico do Exército (see the next section) also publishes a 1:10,000 Lisbon map.

Topographic Maps Cyclists and trekkers will want topographic maps. IGeoE, the Instituto Geográfico do Exército (Army Geographic Institute) publishes 1:25,000 topographic maps of the entire country, the best for detail that includes traditional tracks and footpaths. They date from 1945-50, though there are updated versions. Some map dealers in Portugal suggested that the army was fobbing off stocks of the older ones, which include some now-abandoned routes and omit later features such as motorways and reservoirs. IGeoE also publishes a set of 1:250,000 topographic maps covering the whole country.

The civilian IPCC or Instituto Português de Cartográfia e Cadastro (Portuguese Institute of Cartography & Registry) publishes 1:50,000 topographic maps, titled *Carta Corográfica*. Some of these are more current than the military maps but lack their detail and precision. IPCC also has older 1:100,000 topographic maps.

Both the IGeoE and the IPCC have outlets in Lisbon (see Lisbon – Information). IPCC sheets are around 1000$00 each.

Map Sources A variety of road maps and army and civilian topographic maps is available from mail-order map shops abroad. Probably the widest range of Portugal maps of every sort is at GeoCenter ILH (☎ 0711-788 93 40; fax 0711-788 93 54; e-mail geocenterilh@t-online.de), Schockenriedstrasse 44, D-70565 Stuttgart, Germany. Other reliable mail-order firms are:

Stanfords, 12-14 Long Acre, Covent Garden, London WC2E 9LP, UK (☎ 0171-836 1321)

Michael Chessler Books, PO Box 2436, Evergreen, CO 80439, USA (toll-free ☎ 800-654-8502, ☎ 303-670-0093)

The Travel Bookshop, 6 Bridge St, Sydney 2000, NSW, Australia (☎ 02-9241 3554; fax 02-9241 3159)

Omni Resources (☎ 910-227-8300; fax 910-227-3748; complete catalogue on the World Wide Web at http://www.omnimap.com), 1004 S Mebane St, PO Box 2096, Burlington, NC 27216-2096, USA

A Portuguese bookshop with a good map department (military and civilian topographic maps, road maps etc) is Livraria Porto Editora (☎ 02-200 76 69), at Rua da Fábrica 90 in Porto. A few local outfits stock those topographic maps which cover nearby national and natural parks; see the sections on the various parks for convenient sources.

Municipal and regional tourist offices *(turismos)* in larger towns have street maps of varying utility. National and natural park information offices, in designated towns in or near the parks, usually have a simple, often schematic park map that is of little use for trekking or cycling.

What to Bring

Of course, bring as little as you can; get it to a bare minimum and then cut it in half! This is Europe, not Central Asia, and you can find most of the comforts you need in small-town *supermercados* or big-city *hipermercados* – bottled water, toilet paper, soap, toothpaste, shampoo, aspirin, insect repellent, razor blades, tampons, nappies, batteries etc. *Preservativos* (condoms) are available in most pharmacies and sometimes in supermarkets as well. You hardly even have to worry about clothes: the weekly markets in most sizeable towns have at least a few Gypsy dealers selling cheap clothing, and shoes are a bargain everywhere.

Seasoned travellers will already have a secure money belt. Other helpful items are a lightweight day pack, penknife, universal sink plug, sunscreen lotion, lip salve, sunhat, sunglasses, small torch, compass, a length of cord as a washing-line, a few stuff-sacks or plastic bags, a small sewing kit, and foot powder.

The Portuguese are fairly conservative about dress, and except for on beaches and in coastal Algarve towns, it's rare to see shorts and short sleeves, except on tourists.

You might want down vests or sweaters in the Algarve as late as March, and in the Serra da Estrela even in early May, but you'll probably hardly use them elsewhere (of course you'll need many more layers of clothing in the mountains in winter). If you plan to spend much time outside July and August in the showery north, a collapsible umbrella can be more comfortable than a raincoat or mac, though all of these items are available in local shops too.

For suggested documents to take along, see the Visas & Documents section of this chapter. For a suggested medical kit see the Health section of this chapter.

SUGGESTED ITINERARIES

The following suggested itineraries cover most of Portugal's worthy destinations, leaving you to work out local excursions. They assume that one day each week is spent in transit.

One week

Lisbon area
    Lisbon, Belém and Sintra (4 days); Óbidos and Nazaré (2 days).
Porto and the Douro
    Porto, and Vila Nova de Gaia (3 days); Amarante and Lamego (3 days)
The Algarve
    Sagres and Cabo São Vicente (2 days); Lagos (2 days); Tavira and Ilha de Tavira (2 days)

Two weeks

Lisbon to the Algarve
    Lisbon, Belém and Sintra (4 days); the Costa Vicentina (the west-coast Alentejo and Algarve from Cabo São Vicente up to Odemira and beyond), Sagres and Cabo São Vicente (3 days); Lagos (2 days); Tavira and the Ilha de Tavira (3 days); depart Faro
Lisbon to the Spanish border
    Lisbon, Belém and Sintra (5 days); Évora and Monsaraz (3 days); Estremoz and Elvas (2 days); Castelo de Vide and Marvão (2 days)
Lisbon to Porto
    Lisbon, Belém and Sintra (4 days); Óbidos and Nazaré (2 days); Coimbra and Luso (2 days); Lamego (1 day); from Peso da Régua head for Porto by train or by cruise boat down the Douro; Porto and Vila Nova de Gaia (3 days)

Porto, the Douro and the Minho
Porto and Vila Nova de Gaia (3 days); Viana do Castelo and Ponte de Lima (3 days); Braga and Guimarães (3 days); Parque Nacional da Peneda-Gerês (3 days); return to Porto by train or by cruise boat down the Rio Douro from Peso da Régua

One month
Central Portugal
Lisbon, Belém and Sintra (6 days); Évora, Estremoz and Elvas (4 days); Marvão and Castelo de Vide (2 days); Parque Natural da Serra da Estrela (3 days); Coimbra and Luso (3 days); Lamego, Amarante and Mondim de Basto (4 days); from Peso da Régua head for Porto by train or by cruise boat down the Douro; Porto and Vila Nova de Gaia (4 days); depart Porto

Lisbon and southern Portugal
Lisbon, Belém and Sintra (6 days); Óbidos, Nazaré, Batalha and Tomar (3 days); Évora, Monsaraz and Elvas (4 days); Beja, Serpa and Mértola (3 days); Tavira, Ilha de Tavira and Parque Natural da Ria Formosa (4 days); Lagos (3 days); Sagres and Cabo São Vicente (3 days); depart Faro or Lisbon

Lisbon and northern Portugal
Lisbon, Belém and Sintra (5 days); Coimbra (2 days); Parque Natural da Serra da Estrela (3 days); Lamego, Amarante and Mondim de Basto (4 days); take a train from Peso da Régua or cruise down the Rio Douro; Porto and Vila Nova de Gaia (4 days); Braga (2 days); Parque Nacional da Peneda-Gerês (3 days); Bragança and Parque Natural de Montesinho (3 days); return to Porto

Two months
Two months is probably enough to see most of the country without too much strain: Lisbon, Belém and Sintra (6 days); Óbidos, Nazaré, Batalha and Tomar (3 days); Costa Vicentina, Sagres and Cabo São Vicente (3 days); Lagos (2 days); Tavira, Ilha de Tavira and Parque Natural da Ria Formosa (3 days); Beja and Serpa (2 days); Évora, Monsaraz and Elvas (4 days); Marvão and Castelo de Vide (2 days); Parque Natural da Serra da Estrela (3 days); Coimbra and Luso (4 days); Porto and Vila Nova de Gaia (5 days); cruise along the Douro to Peso da Régua or take a train down the valley; Lamego, Amarante and Mondim de Basto (3 days); Viana do Castelo (2 days); Braga (2 days); Parque Nacional da Peneda-Gerês (4 days); Chaves (1 day); Bragança and Parque Natural da Montesinho (3 days); return and depart Porto

HIGHLIGHTS
Following is a list to help you find the best of everything, from a quiet beach to a rowdy festival.

Fortresses, castles & walled towns
Valença do Minho (Minho); Bragança (Trás-os-Montes); Monsanto and Sortelha (Beiras); Óbidos (Estremadura); Marvão, Elvas, Monsaraz and Mértola (Alentejo)

Other beautiful towns of historical interest
Guimarães (Minho); Coimbra (Beiras); Évora (Alentejo)

Architecture
Jerónimos monastery at Belém (Lisbon); Mosteiro de Santa Maria da Vitória at Batalha, and Mosteiro de Alcobaça (Estremadura); Convento de Cristo, Tomar (Ribatejo); the monumental baroque stairways of Nossa Senhora dos Remédios, Lamego (Douro), and Bom Jesus do Monte, Braga (Minho)

Museums
Fundação Calouste Gulbenkian, Lisbon; Museu Soares dos Reis, Porto; Museu do Abade de Baçal, Bragança; Museu Martins Sarmento, Guimarães; Museu Machado de Castro, Coimbra

Azulejos
Igreja do Carmo, Porto; São Bento station, Porto; stairway of Nossa Senhora dos Remédios, Lamego (Douro); Museu Nacional do Azulejo, Lisbon; Igreja de São João Evangelista, Évora (Alentejo); Igreja São Lourenço, Almancil (Algarve)

Roman ruins
Conimbriga, near Coimbra (Beiras); Roamn temple at Évora (Alentejo)

Pre-Roman remains
Celtic Citânia de Briteiros near Guimarães (Minho); menhirs and dolmens (standing stones) in the Évora region (Alentejo)

Markets
Barcelos (Minho); Caldas de Rainha (Estremadura); Ponte de Lima (Minho); Feira da Ladra, Lisbon

Festivals
Easter week, Braga (Minho); Festa de São João, 16 to 24 June, Porto; Festa dos Tabuleiros (Feast of Trays), first Sunday in July every four years, Tomar (Ribatejo); Romaria da Nossa Senhora da Agonia, weekend of third Sunday in August, Viana do Castelo (Minho); Feiras Novas, mid-September, Ponte de Lima (Minho)

Hill and mountain treks
Parque Nacional da Peneda-Gerês (Minho); Parque Natural da Serra da Estrela (Beiras); Parque Natural de Montesinho (Trás-os-Montes); Sintra (near Lisbon).

Quiet, relatively unspoilt beaches
    Barril on the Ilha de Tavira (Algarve); Praia de Odeceixe (north-west Algarve); São Martinho do Porto, south of Nazaré (Estremadura); São Jacinto, north of Aveiro (Beiras)
Surfing & windsurfing
    Praia do Guincho and Praia das Maçãs, west of Sintra (near Lisbon); Praia da Ribeira de Ilhas at Ericeira (Estremadura); Figueira da Foz (Beira Litoral)
Trams
    The No 28 through Lisbon's Bairro Alto, Alfama and Castelo districts
Coffee
    Everywhere except Alcoutim (Algarve)!
Watch-the-world-go-by spot
    Twin turn-of-the-century cafés, the Vianna and the Astória, facing Praça da República in Braga (Minho)
Children's parks
    Gouveia (Beiras); Castelo São Jorge, Lisbon; riverside adventure playground at Viana do Castelo (Minho)
Miscellaneous
    Espigueiros (granaries) at Lindoso and Soajo (Minho); the Iron-Age *berrões* (stone pigs) of Trás-os-Montes; ossuaries (bone chapels) in the Igreja de São Francisco, Évora (Alentejo), and Igreja do Carmo, Faro (Algarve); Europe's most south-westerly corner at Cabo São Vicente (Algarve)

TOURIST OFFICES
Local Tourist Offices

The state's umbrella organisation for tourism is ICEP (Investimentos, Comércio e Turismo de Portugal), with its headquarters at Avenida 5 de Outubro 101, Lisbon (☎ 01-793 01 03; fax 01-794 08 26).

Locally managed *postos de turismo* (tourist offices) are found throughout the country, and will provide brochures and varying degrees of help with sights and accommodation. In this book we call them turismos, as this is how they are usually signposted.

ICEP also divides Portugal into a score of semi-autonomous *regiões de turismo*, each with a headquarters town. In these towns, instead of, or in addition to, the local turismo, you might find a regional office, with information about the region as a whole. We mention these under individual towns or regions.

Lisbon's turismo appears to be run directly by ICEP, while Porto has both municipal and ICEP regional offices. ICEP also has information desks at Lisbon, Porto and Faro airports. The ICEP-run offices have information covering most of the country.

Tourist Offices Abroad

ICEP-affiliated trade-and-tourism offices abroad include the following:

Brazil
    Avenida Paulista 2001, Suite 901, 01311-300 São Paulo (☎ 011-288 87 44; fax 011-288 28 77)
Canada
    60 Bloor St West, Suite 1005, Toronto, Ontario M4W 3B8 (☎ 416-921 7376; fax 416-921 1353)
    500 Sherbrooke St West, Suite 940, Montreal, Quebec H3A 3C6 (☎ 514-282 1264; fax 514-499 1450)
France
    7 Rue Scribe, 75009 Paris (☎ 01 47 42 55 57; fax 01 42 66 06 89)
Germany
    Schäfergasse 17, 60313 Frankfurt-am-Main (☎ 069-23 40 94; fax 069-23 14 33)
Japan
    Regency Shinsaka, Suite 201, Akasaka, 8-5-8 Minato-ku, Tokyo 107 (☎ 03-54 74 44 00; fax 03-34 70 71 64)
Netherlands
    Paul Gabriëlstraat 70, 2596 VG, The Hague (☎ 070-326 4371; fax 070-328 0025)
Spain
    Gran Via 27, 1st floor, 28013 Madrid (☎ 91-522 9354; fax 91-522 2382)
South Africa
    4th floor, Sunnyside Ridge, Sunnyside Drive, PO Box 2473 Houghton, 2041 Johannesburg (☎ 011-484 3487; fax 011-484 5416)
UK
    22-25a Sackville St, London W1X 1DE (☎ 0171-494 1441; fax 0171-494 1868)
USA
    590 Fifth Ave, 4th floor, New York, NY 10036-4704 (☎ 212-354-4403 or toll-free in the USA ☎ 800-PORTUGAL; fax 212-764-6137)
    1900 L St, Suite 310, Washington, DC 20036 (☎ 202-331-8222; fax 212-331-8236)

VISAS & DOCUMENTS
Passport

Check your passport's date of expiry – you may have trouble getting a visa if it expires during or soon after your proposed visit.

Also, make sure there are still some blank pages left in your passport. Most passport offices and overseas embassies can provide you with a new passport, or insert new pages in your present one, fairly quickly.

Police in Portugal are empowered to check your ID papers at any time, so you should always carry your passport with you.

Visas

The general requirements for entry to Portugal also apply to the other signatories of the 1990 Schengen Convention on the abolition of mutual border controls – at least those who have put the agreement into effect (Belgium, France, Germany, Luxembourg, Netherlands and Spain). In fact, you can apply for visas for more than one of these countries on the same form, though a visa for one does not automatically grant you entry to the others.

Visa Extensions To extend a visa after arriving in Portugal, contact the foreigners' registration office, called Serviço de Estrangeiros e Fronteiras (☎ 01-346 61 41, ☎ 01-352 31 12), at Avenida António Augusto de Aguiar 20 in Lisbon. It's open from 9 am to 3 pm on weekdays only. Major tourist towns also have branch Serviço de Estrangeiros e Fronteiras offices. As entry regulations are already liberal, you'll need convincing proof of employment or financial independence, or a pretty good story, if you're asking to stay longer.

In theory a simpler option might be to leave Portugal, re-enter and get a new entry permit, though at present the only entry points where you'll find anybody to give you one are at Lisbon, Porto and Faro airport arrivals!

Photocopies

It's wise to carry photocopies of the data pages of your passport and visa, to ease the paperwork headaches should they be lost or stolen. Other copies you might want to carry are of your credit card and travellers cheque numbers (plus the telephone numbers for cancelling or replacing them), airline tickets, travel insurance policy, birth certificate and any documents related to possible employment.

Keep the copies in a separate place from the originals. If you're travelling with someone, you could swap copies with them. To be doubly secure, leave copies with someone at home too.

Travel Insurance

However you're travelling, it's worth taking out travel insurance. See Predeparture Planning under Health in this chapter for advice about getting travel insurance.

Driving Licence

Nationals of EU countries need only their home driving licences to be allowed to drive in Portugal. Others should consider getting an International Driving Permit as well, through an automobile licensing department in their home country. For more information see the Car & Motorcycle section in the Getting There & Away chapter.

Vehicle Registration & Insurance

If you're driving your own car into Portugal, in addition to your passport and driving licence you must carry vehicle registration and insurance documents. It's also a good idea (though not a legal requirement) to get a Green Card from your home automobile insurer, which confirms that you have comprehensive coverage. See Car & Motorcycle in the Getting There & Away chapter for details.

If you're stopped by the police, you probably won't be allowed to go back to your hotel to fetch these documents. Carry them with you whenever you're driving. If you hire a car, the hiring firm will furnish you with registration and insurance papers, plus a rental contract.

Hostel Card

Portugal's network of *pousadas de juventude* (youth hostels) are part of the Hostelling International (HI) network, and an HI card from your hostelling association at home entitles you to the standard cheap rates (refer to Accommodation in this chapter).

Student, Youth & Seniors' Cards

Numerous discounts – eg for domestic and international transport, museum admission, accommodation and in some cases restaurant meals – are available to full-time students and to those who are under 26 years of age or 60 and over. Refer to Money in this chapter for more information.

Camping Card International

Formerly known as a Camping Carnet, the Camping Card International (CCI) serves as an ID card which can be presented instead of your passport when you register at camping grounds affiliated with the Federation International de Camping at de Caravanning (FICC). It provides third-party insurance for any damage you may cause, and is sometimes good for discounts. Refer to Camping, under Accommodation in this chapter, for more information on the CCI and how to get one.

Bicycle Information

If you're cycling around Portugal on your own machine, seasoned bicycle tourists suggest carrying a written description and a photograph of it (to help police in case it's stolen), and proof of ownership.

EMBASSIES
Portuguese Embassies Abroad

Portuguese embassies abroad include the following. Where they are known, we list consular offices rather than ambassadorial headquarters:

Australia
23 Culgoa Circuit, O'Malley, ACT 2606 (☎ 02-6290 1733; fax 02-6290 1957)
Argentina
Avenida Cordobe 315, 1023 Buenos Aires (☎ 01-312 3524)
Brazil
Avenida das Nações, lote 2-CP, 70402 Brasilia (☎ 061-321 3434)
Canada
645 Island Park Dve, Ottawa, Ontario K1Y OB8 (☎ 613-729 0883; fax 613-729 4236), plus consulates in other cities

France
3 Rue de Noisiel, 75116 Paris (☎ 01 47 27 35 29; fax 01 44 05 94 02)
Germany
Ubierstrasse 78, 5300 Bonn 2 (☎ 0228-36 30 11; fax 0228-35 28 64)
Ireland
Knock Sinna House, Knock Sinna, Fox Rock, Dublin 18 (☎ 01-289 4416; fax 01-289 2849)
Israel
Beit Asia, 4 Veizman St, 64239 Tel Aviv (☎ 03-695 6361; fax 03-695 6366)
Japan
Olympia Annex, apt 304, 31-21 Jingumae, 6-chome, Shibuya-ku, Tokyo (☎ 03-34 00 79 07; fax 03-34 00 79 09)
Netherlands
Bazarstraat 21, 2518 AG, The Hague (☎ 070-363 0217; fax 070-361 5589)
New Zealand
85 Forte St, Remuera, Auckland 5 (☎ 09-309 1454; fax 09-308 9061)
South Africa
599 Leyds Street, Muckleneuk, 0002 Pretoria (☎ 012-341 2340; fax 012-443071)
Spain
Calle del Pinar 1, 28046 Madrid (☎ 91-261 7808; fax 91-411 0172)
UK
62 Brompton Road, London SW3 1BJ (☎ 0171-581 3598, premium-rate recorded message 0891-600202; fax 0171-581 3085)
USA
2125 Kalorama Rd NW, Washington, DC 20008 (☎ 202-328 8610; fax 202-462-3726), plus numerous consulates in other cities.

Foreign Embassies in Portugal

Your embassy or consulate in Portugal is the best first stop in any emergency, but there are some things it cannot do for you. These include getting local laws or regulations waived because you're a foreigner, investigating a crime, providing legal advice or representation in civil or criminal cases, getting you out of jail, and lending you money. A consul can, however, issue emergency passports, contact relatives and friends, advise on how to transfer funds, provide lists of reliable local doctors, lawyers and interpreters, and visit you if you've been arrested or jailed.

Foreign embassies and consulates in Lisbon include the following. Consulates in other cities are listed under those cities.

Argentina
  embassy: Avenida João Crisóstomo 8 (☎ 01-797 73 11)
  consulate: Rua dos Açores 59 (☎ 01-353 17 57)
Austria
  embassy: Rua das Amoreiras 70, Rato (☎ 01-387 41 61)
Belgium
  embassy: Praça Marquês de Pombal 14 (☎ 01-354 92 63)
Brazil
  embassy: Estrada das Laranjeiras 144 (☎ 01-726 77 77)
  consulate: Praça Luís de Camões 22 (☎ 01-347 35 65)
Canada
  embassy: Edifício MCB, Avenida da Liberdade 144 (☎ 01-347 48 92)
Denmark
  embassy: Rua Castilho 14-C (☎ 01-354 50 99)
Finland
  embassy: Rua Miguel Lupi 12 (☎ 01-60 75 51)
  consulate: Cais do Sodré 8 (☎ 01-347 35 01)
France
  embassy: Rua Santos-o-Velho 5 (☎ 01-60 81 21)
  consulate: Calçada Marquês de Abrantes (☎ 01-395 60 56)
Germany
  embassy: Campo dos Mártires da Pátria 38 (☎ 01-352 39 61)
Greece
  embassy: Rua Alto do Duque 13 (Belém) (☎ 01-301 69 91)
Ireland
  embassy: Rua da Imprensa à Estrela 1 (☎ 01-396 15 69)
Israel
  embassy: Rua António Enes 16 (☎ 01-357 02 51)
Italy
  embassy & consulate: Largo Conde de Pombeiro 6 (embassy ☎ 01-354 61 44, consulate ☎ 01-352 08 62)
Japan
  embassy: Rua Mouzinho da Silveira 11 (☎ 01-352 34 85)
Luxembourg
  embassy, Rua das Janelas Verdes 43 (☎ 01-396 27 81)
Netherlands
  embassy, Rua do Sacramento à Lapa 6 (☎ 01-396 11 63)
Norway
  embassy: Avenida Dom Vasco da Gama 1, Belém (☎ 01-301 53 44)
South Africa
  embassy: Avenida Luís Bívar 10 (☎ 01-353 50 41)
Spain
  embassy & consulate: Rua do Salitre 1 (embassy ☎ 01-347 23 81, consulate ☎ 01-342 26 54)

Sweden
  embassy: Rua Miguel Lupi 12 (☎ 01-395 52 24)
Switzerland
  embassy: Travessa do Patrocínio 1 (☎ 01-397 31 21)
Turkey
  embassy: Avenida das Descobertas 22 (Belém) (☎ 01-301 42 75)
UK
  embassy: Rua de São Domingos à Lapa 37 (☎ 01-396 11 91)
  Consulate, Rua da Estrela 4 (☎ 01-395 40 82)
USA
  embassy & consulate: Avenida das Forças Armadas (embassy ☎ 01-726 66 00, consulate ☎ 01-726 55 62)

There are no embassies for Australia or New Zealand in Portugal, but both countries have honorary consuls in Lisbon. Australian citizens can call ☎ 01-353 07 50 on weekdays between 1 and 2 pm; the nearest Australian embassy is in Paris. New Zealand citizens should call ☎ 01-357 41 34 during business hours; the nearest New Zealand embassy is in Rome.

CUSTOMS

There's no limit on the amount of foreign currency you can bring into Portugal. Customs regulations say visitors (at least those who need a visa) must bring in a minimum of 10,000$00 plus 2000$00 per day of their stay, but this isn't stringently enforced. If you leave with more than 100,000$00 in escudos or 500,000$00 in foreign currency you may have to prove that you brought in at least this much.

Travellers over 17 years of age from non-EU countries can bring in, duty-free, 200 cigarettes (or 100 cigarillos or 50 cigars or 250g of tobacco); one litre of alcohol which is over 22% alcohol by volume, or two litres of wine or beer. EU citizens can stagger in with considerably more, including up to 800 cigarettes (400 cigarillos, 200 cigars or one kg of tobacco) and either 10 litres of spirits, 20 litres of fortified wine, 60 litres of sparkling wine or a mind-boggling 90 litres of still wine or 110 litres of beer!

You can bring in enough coffee, tea etc for

personal use. You cannot bring fresh meat into the country.

MONEY
Costs

Although costs are beginning to rise as Portugal falls into fiscal step with the EU, this is still one of the cheapest places to travel in Europe. On a rock-bottom budget – using hostels or camping grounds, and mostly self-catering – you could squeeze by on about 3900$00 (US$25) a day per person in the high season. With bottom-end accommoda-

tion and the occasional inexpensive restau-. rant meal, daily costs would hover around 4600$00 (US$30). Travelling with a companion and timing your trip to take advantage of off-season discounts, you could eat and sleep in relative style for about 10800$00 (US$70) for two. Outside major tourist areas, prices dip appreciably.

Discounts Numerous discounts are available to full-time students and to travellers under 26 years of age or over 60.

The international student identity card

How Much in Portugal?
Following are some typical unit costs in Portugal. Prices for food and accommodation tend to vary according to the season.

Bed in a youth hostel dormitory*	about 1500$00	(US$10)
Small tent and two people at a camp site	1200$00 to 1800$00	(US$8 to US$12)
Double in a lower-end *pensão* *	3100$00 to 4600$00	(US$20 to US$30)
Double in a mid-range hotel*	6100$00 to 12300$00	(US$40 to US$80)
Double in a pousada*	14600$00 to 27600$00	(US$95 to US$180)
Meal in a medium-grade restaurant*	1200$00 to 1500$00	(US$8 to US$10)
Big Mac	440$00	(US$2.85)
Ordinary espresso coffee *(bica)*	70$00	(US$0.45)
Portuguese beer (300 ml)		
draught	200$00	(US$1.30)
bottle from supermarket	140$00	(US$0.90)
Portuguese wine (one litre)	500$00 to 1200$00	(US$3 to US$8)
Pack of Portuguese cigarettes	about 300$00	(US$2)
Local phone call (depending on the time of day)	20$00	(US$0.15)
Daily Portuguese newspaper	120$00 to 140$00	(US$0.80 to US$0.90)
Daily overseas newspaper	230$00 to 380$00	(US$1.50 to US$2.50)
Slide film (36 exp)	about 1500$00	(US$10)
Print film (36 exp)	about 900$00	(US$6)
Video cassette (90 min)	about 1100$00	(US$7)
10 kg of washing at a laundrette	1200$00 to 1500$00	(US$8 to US$10)
Cinema ticket	460$00 to 770$00	(US$3 to US$5)
Theatre ticket	770$00 to 2000$00	(US$5 to US$13)
Ballet ticket	1500$00 to 3100$00	(US$10 to US$20)
Opera ticket	6100$00 to 10,000$00	(US$40 to US$65)
Museum admission	110$00 to 610$00	(US$0.70 to US$4)
Train, 2nd-class *intercidade*, per 100 km		
(depending on the distance)	690$00 to 840$00	(US$4.50 to US$5.50),
Coach, long-distance, per 100 km		
(depending on the distance)	490$00 to 920$00	(US$3.20 to US$6)
Petrol, one litre of 95 octane unleaded	160$00 (US$1.05)	

* = high season

(ISIC) is specifically aimed at travel-related costs (reductions on airline fares, cheap or free admission to museums etc). Good for a year, it's available from youth-oriented travel agencies such as Campus Travel, STA Travel, Council Travel and Travel CUTS, from the Portuguese youth-travel agencies Tagus Travel and Jumbo Expresso, and directly from ISIC Mail Order, Bleaklow House, Howard Town Mills, Mill Street, Glossop SK13 8PT, UK.

Various 'under-26' and other youth-card schemes (including Euro<26, Go 25 and Portugal's own Cartão Jovem) provide more general discounts, such as in shops and theatres, but fewer specific travel benefits. Also good for a year, these are available for about UK£6 from most youth-travel agencies, or directly from Under 26 Mail Order, 52 Grosvenor Gardens, London SW1W 0AG, UK. More information about the ISIC and Go 25, and application forms can be sourced at URL http://www.ciee.org/idcards.htm.

Only residents of Portugal are eligible to buy the widely used Portuguese under-26 card, Cartão Jovem (eg at Movijovem, the Portugal youth hostel booking centre in Lisbon, for 1100$00). There are reciprocity agreements among many of these schemes anyway.

The various cards, particularly youth and student cards, don't automatically entitle you to discounts everywhere as some companies and institutions refuse to recognise them, but you won't know until you ask.

Many of the same kinds of discounts are available in Portugal to travellers over 60 too. The Rail Europ Senior (RES) Card gives you about 30% discount for international journeys or internal journeys connecting with an international service, such as Eurostar or Trenhotel. In order to be eligible for an RES Card you must have a local senior citizens' railcard; availability of these to visitors varies between participating countries. In Britain, visitors can purchase a Senior Card (£16) and an RES Card (£5) from accredited British Rail International travel agencies and from main-line stations.

Children under the age of eight are entitled to a discount of 50% in hotels, if they share their parents' room. Children from four to 12 years old get 50% off on Portuguese Railways, and those under four travel for free.

Currency

The unit of Portuguese currency is the *escudo*, further divided into 100 *centavos*. Prices are usually denoted with a $ sign between escudos and centavos, eg 25 escudos 50 centavos is written 25$50.

Portuguese notes currently in circulation are 10,000$00, 5000$00, 2000$00, 1000$00 and 500$00. There are 200$00, 100$00, 50$00, 20$00, 10$00, 5$00, 2$50 and 1$00 coins, though coins smaller than 5$00 are rarely used. Nowadays market prices tend to be rounded to the nearest 10$00.

Portuguese frequently refer to 1000$00 as *um conto*.

Currency Exchange

Following are approximate cash exchange rates in effect at the time of going to press.

Australia	A$1	=	125$90
Canada	C$1	=	115$10
France	1FF	=	29$70
Germany	DM1	=	100$90
Ireland	I£	=	261$40
Japan	¥100	=	136$50
Spain	100 ptas	=	120$00
United Kingdom	UK£1	=	261$20
United States	US$1	=	155$00

What to Carry & Where to Exchange It

Portuguese banks and private exchange bureaus accept most foreign currencies, but they're free to set their own fees and exchange rates. Thus an exchange bureau's low commission may be more than offset by an unfavourable exchange rate. If you need to watch every penny, you'll have to shop around, calculator in hand.

Though travellers cheques are easily exchanged, and at rates about 1% better than for cash, they are very poor value in Portugal because additional fees are so high. A bank may charge 2000$00 or more (in addition to government taxes of about 140$00) for each cheque or transaction of any size. For a US$100 travellers cheque that's over 13%! Even a US$1000 cheque costs more to exchange than the same amount of cash. You can do marginally better at certain private exchange bureaus and even some travel agencies.

The exception is American Express travellers cheques, which can be exchanged commission-free at Top Tours, Portugal's American Express representative, in Lisbon, Porto, Praia da Rocha (Portimão) and Quarteira (Algarve). Eurocheques draw low fees, typically 500$00 or less per transaction, though for these and the accompanying card you also pay an annual subscription fee of about US$15.

A more sensible alternative is a Visa, Access/MasterCard, American Express or similar card. Most sizeable tourist centres have several 24-hour automatic-teller machines (ATMs), widely known as 'Multibanco', at which you can use your card to get a cash advance in escudos. All you need is your PIN number from home. There is a handling charge of about 1½% per transaction, and exchange rates are reasonable. These cards are also accepted by many shops, hotels, and a small but increasing number of pensões and restaurants.

A small stash of cash pounds sterling or US dollars is also useful for when the Multibancos refuse to accept your card (Caixa Geral de Depositos banks seem to have the most consistently friendly machines). Foreign cash can also be changed (for higher commissions) in automatic 24-hour cash exchange machines, plentiful in the Algarve, available in Lisbon, Porto and Évora, but scarce elsewhere.

Crime against foreigners is only significant in heavily touristed areas like the Algarve, and specific neighbourhoods of Lisbon and Porto. As it usually involves pickpocketing, purse-snatching or pilfering from rental cars or camping grounds, keeping your money secure is largely a matter of common sense: don't carry a wallet, cash or credit cards in your back pocket or an open purse; use a money belt

for large sums; and don't leave money in your car, tent, hotel room or unattended backpack.

Tipping & Bargaining

If you're not unhappy with the service, a reasonable restaurant tip is about 10%. For a snack at a *cervejaria*, *pastelaria* or café, a bit of loose change is enough. Taxi drivers appreciate about 10% of the fare, and petrol station attendants 50$00 or so.

Good-humoured bargaining is acceptable in markets but you'll find the Portuguese tough opponents! Off season, you can sometimes even bargain down the price of accommodation.

Taxes & Refunds

A 17% sales tax (13% in the Azores and Madeira), called IVA, is levied on hotel and other accommodation, restaurant, car rental and some other bills. If you are a tourist who resides outside the EU, you can claim an IVA refund on goods from shops that are members of the Europe Tax-Free Shopping Portugal scheme.

At the time of research the minimum purchase eligible for a refund was 11,700$00 in any one shop. The shop assistant fills in a cheque for the amount of the refund (minus an administration fee). When you leave Portugal you present the goods, the cheque and your passport at the Tax-Free Shopping refund counter at customs for cash or a postal-note or credit-card refund.

At present this service is available only at Lisbon, Porto and Faro airports and Lisbon harbour. If you leave overland, talk to customs at your final EU border point. Further information, including a list of participating shops, is available from Europe Tax-Free Shopping Portugal (☎ 01-840 88 13) in the international departures concourse of Lisbon airport, open daily from 7 am to 1.30 am.

Items *not* covered by this refund scheme include food, books, prescription lenses, hotel costs and car rental. Don't confuse this with the totally unrelated Duty-Free Shoppers shops at these airports!

POST & COMMUNICATIONS
Sending Mail
Correio normal refers to ordinary post, including air mail, while *correio azul* ('blue mail') refers to priority or express post. Ordinary postcards and letters up to 20g cost 140$00 to destinations outside Europe, 98$00 to non-EU European destinations and 78$00 to EU destinations (except within Portugal and to Spain: 48$00). International correio azul costs a minimum of 350$00 for a 20g letter.

Stamps are sold not only at post offices but at numerous kiosks and shops with a red *Correios – selos* sign, as well as from coin-operated vending machines. 'By airmail' is *por avião* in Portuguese; 'by surface mail' is *via superfície*. For delivery to the USA or Australia, allow eight to 10 days; delivery times for Europe are four to six days.

A four to five-kg parcel sent surface mail to the UK would cost 4650$00 (about US$30). 'Economy air' (or surface airlift, SAL) costs about a third less than ordinary air mail, but usually arrives a week or so later. Printed matter is cheapest (and simplest) to send in batches of under two kg.

Don't post anything important or valuable if you can't afford to lose it. Use registered mail for important documents.

Receiving Mail
Most towns have a *posta restante* service at the central post office; if a letter doesn't specify the post office street address or postal code, that's where it goes. Best bets are the central post offices on Praça Comércio in Lisbon and on Praça General Humberto Delgado in Porto. Letters should be addressed with the family name first, capitalised and underlined, c/o posta restante, central post office, with the town name.

To collect mail, you must show your passport. A charge of 60$00 is levied for each item of mail collected. Unclaimed letters are normally returned after a month.

Addresses
Addresses in Portugal are written with the street name followed by the building number. An alphabetical tag on the number, eg 2-A, indicates an adjacent entrance or building. Floor numbers may be included, with a degree symbol, eg 15-3° means entrance No 15, 3rd floor. The further abbreviations D, dir or Dta (for *direita*, right), or E, esq or Esqa (for *esquerda*, left), tell you which door to go to. Floor numbering is by European convention, ie the 1st floor is one flight up from the ground floor. R/C *(rés do chão)* means ground floor.

Telephone
Local Calls The price of a local call depends both on its duration and on the time of day. Coin calls are charged at the rate of 20$00 per 'unit' or 'beep' *(impulso)*, card calls (see the following section) at 17$50 per unit. For local calls a unit varies from three minutes at peak times (10 am to 1 pm and 2 to 6 pm) to 12 minutes between 10 pm and 8 am. Cafés often allow customers to use their phones if there isn't a public one nearby.

Long-Distance & International Calls The largest coin accepted by standard coin telephones is 100$00, making them impractical for long-distance and international calls. Much more useful are the increasingly common Portugal Telecom 'Credifone' telephones, which accept *(cartões telefónicos)* (plastic phonecards) widely available from newsagents, tobacconists and telephone offices. A separate TLP (Telefones de Lisboa e Porto) phonecard system is in use, along with Credifone, in Lisbon and Porto. Neither card works in the other system. Both cards are sold in 875$00 (50 unit) and 2100$00 (120 unit) denominations. A youth or student card should get you a 10% discount on these cards.

Calls can be made from public telephones as well as booths in Portugal Telecom offices and post offices. International calls to Europe average about 300$00 per minute; to Australia and the USA, they're about 600$00 per minute at peak times and 450$00 off-peak. Charges from private telephones are about a third less than from public ones.

Handwritten at top: ✗ Nationwide # change - +2💲: (including area/cod...) 70 F:

Country-Direct Service

For an extra charge you can dial direct from Portugal to operators in at least 38 countries. Among these are:

Australia	☎ 05017 61 10
Austria	☎ 0505 00 43
Belgium	☎ 0505 00 32
Brazil	☎ 05017 55 10
Canada	☎ 05017 12 26
Denmark	☎ 0505 00 45
Finland	☎ 0505 03 58
France	☎ 0505 00 33
Germany	☎ 0505 00 49
Ireland	☎ 0505 03 53
Israel	☎ 05017 97 20
Italy	☎ 0505 00 39
Japan	☎ 05017 81 10
Luxembourg	☎ 0505 03 52
Netherlands	☎ 0505 00 31
New Zealand	☎ 05017 64 00
Norway	☎ 0505 00 47
Singapore	☎ 05017 65 10
Spain	☎ 0505 00 34
Sweden	☎ 0505 00 46
Turkey	☎ 0505 00 90
UK	☎ 0505 00 44
USA (AT&T)	☎ 05017 12 88
(MCI)	☎ 05017 12 34
(Sprint)	☎ 05017 18 77
(TRT)	☎ 05017 18 78

Handwritten: ➔ (21) 800800128

It's cheapest if you phone between 9 pm and 8 am, and on weekends and public holidays.

Portugal's international enquiries number is ☎ 118. From Portugal, the international access code is ☎ 00. For operator assistance or to make a reverse-charges (collect) call *(pago no destino)*, dial ☎ 099 (for Europe, Algeria, Morocco and Tunisia) or ☎ 098 (for other overseas destinations).

Hotel Calls Calls from hotels are almost double the standard rate. Any hotel or pensão with a telephone in the room is likely to have a gizmo somewhere that either prints out the number of units in each call or displays a cumulative total. If in doubt about your hotel telephone bill, ask to see the print-out.

Calls to Portugal To call Portugal from abroad, dial the international access code

☎ 351 (Portugal's country cod... phone or area code (minus its ... and the number. Important Po... phone codes include ☎ 01 (Lisbon ...u u 02 (Porto); others are noted under specific destinations.

Handwritten: ➔ eg: Lisbon - 21 + #

Fax

Post offices now operate a domestic and international fax service called Corfax, costing an unconscionable 1350$00 for the first page to Europe, North America or Australia, and more to some other points. On top of that, only half the post office form is available for your message. And to *collect* a fax at the post office you pay 240$00 per page. A friendly private travel agency or guesthouse with a fax is almost certain to be cheaper.

Handwritten: Freephone 0800's now 800 w/o 1st '0'

E-mail

Telepac, Portugal's biggest Internet provider, has a public users' centre called Quiosque Internet (☎ 01-314 2527; e-mail email@telepac.pt), where you can plug into the net or send e-mail (but not receive it) for 125$00 per quarter-hour. It's in the Forum Picoas building beside Picoas metro station in Lisbon and it's open weekdays from 9 am to 5 pm. Technical help is available and some English is spoken. An alternative is to befriend a university student or someone else with their own e-mail account.

BOOKS

Most books are published in different editions by different publishers in different countries. As a result, a book might be a hardcover rarity in one country while it's readily available in paperback in another. Fortunately, bookshops and libraries search by title or author, so your local bookshop or library is best placed to advise you on the availability of the following recommendations.

Lonely Planet

If you're planning a wider journey than just Portugal, consider taking one of LP's comprehensive 'on a shoestring' guides that include Portugal: *Western Europe* or *Mediterranean Europe*. Is your Portuguese not what it ought to be? LP can help there too, with its *Western Europe phrasebook*.

Other Guidebooks

A good book for serious footwork is Bethan Davies & Ben Cole's *Walking in Portugal*, with routes around Lisbon, Porto, Coimbra, Parque Nacional da Peneda-Gerês and the Serra da Estrela, Montesinho and Serra de São Mamede natural parks. Less single-minded pedestrians will like Brian & Eileen Anderson's small-format *Landscapes of Portugal* series, featuring both car tours and walks in separate books on the Algarve; Sintra, Cascais and Estoril; and Costa Verde, Minho and Peneda-Gerês.

Among many regional guidebooks, one of the best we found was expatriate residents John & Madge Measures' *Southern Portugal: Its People, Traditions & Wildlife*, with loving detail on the archaeology, landscapes, agriculture, flora, fauna and local products of scores of places you've probably never heard of in the Algarve and southern Alentejo. Another nice perspective is that of *Exploring Rural Portugal*, by Joe Staines & Lia Duarte.

If you'll be taking a lot of trains around the Iberian Peninsula, pick up Norman Renouf's exhaustive *Spain & Portugal by Rail*, full of network maps and charts (see the introduction to the Train section in the Getting There & Away chapter for how to order this book). If you've got the wherewithal to stay in Portugal's converted manor houses, palaces and castles, Sam & Jane Ballard's *Pousadas of Portugal* will tell you about every room and how to cross the country without staying anywhere else.

Travel

Rose Macaulay's entertaining and by now well-known collections, *They Went to Portugal* and *They Went to Portugal Too*, follow the experiences of a wide variety of English visitors from medieval times through the 19th century. These are recommended 'companion' books, easy to enjoy in small doses.

Travels in My Homeland (Viagens na Minha Terra) by Almeida Garrett, one of Portugal's best known Romantic writers and public figures, is a philosophical tour of 19th-century Portugal, an early home-grown travelogue.

History & Politics

Small and useful enough to tote along is David Birmingham's *A Concise History of Portugal*, modestly illustrated, academic but very readable, and covering events up to its 1993 publication. Too big to take along, but one of the best English-language general histories, is AH de Oliveira Marques' *History of Portugal*.

Good specific references on the discoveries are *Prince Henry the Navigator* by John Ure, and CR Boxer's *The Portuguese Seaborne Empire, 1415-1825*. For insights into the Salazar years, have a look at António de Figueiredo's *Portugal: Fifty Years of Dictatorship*. Another good reference, on the events of 1974, is *Revolution & Counter-Revolution in Portugal* by Martin Kayman.

Portugal is just one player in Daniel J Boorstin's classic *The Discoverers*, an original and panoramic look at nothing less than the way humans keep discovering their world. Boorstin is one of the most respected and readable of modern historians. Chapters on Portugal include the discovery of a sea route to India, Portugal's rivalry with Spain, and the slave trade.

Food & Drink

Edite Vieira's *The Taste of Portugal* is more than a cookbook: its selected recipes from all of Portugal's regions are spiced with cultural background information and lively anecdotes. There is also a section on wines, and an appendix on the sort of vegetarian dishes you wish you could find in Portuguese restaurants. Another good cookbook is Maite Manjon's *The Home Book of Portuguese Cookery*.

Richard Mayson's brisk, readable *Portugal's Wines &Wine-Makers: Port, Madeira &*

Regional Wines is a good introduction to the country's favourite product, and includes a history of Portuguese wine-making over the centuries. Another good resource is Jan Read's *The Wines of Portugal*. Sarah Bradford's *The Englishman's Wine*, revised in 1978 as *The Story of Port*, is the definitive history of the port-wine trade and of the British colony in Porto.

Art & Architecture
'Vernacular architecture' refers to the forms and functions shared by ordinary buildings – such as homes – that arise naturally over the centuries in response to climate, land use and other constraints. An appealing book on the region's vernacular architecture, full of fine black & white photographs, is Norman F Carver Jr's *Iberian Villages*, published in 1988. Though it's heavy on Spain, the Portuguese towns of Albufeira, Calcadinha, Guarda, Lindosa, Loulé, Monsanto, Monsaraz and Mértola get loving attention. The author is an architect and Yale professor with a passion for the subject. Unfortunately the book appears to be out of print.

Among many coffee-table books featuring Portugal's idiosyncratic architecture are two handsome ones published in Portugal with text by Júlio Gil: *The Finest Castles in Portugal* (photos by Augusto Cabrita) and *The Finest Churches in Portugal* (photos by Nuno Calvet). Another is *Country Manors of Portugal*, with text by Marcus Binney and fine photos by Nicolas Sapieha and Franceso Venturi.

Living & Working in Portugal
How to Live & Work in Portugal by Sue Tyson-Ward is a fine little tome for those planning to stay a long time or even settle down in Portugal, with sections on accommodation (and even buying a house), domestic life, work, money, driving, education, health services and, of course, travel.

General
One of the best all-round books about the Portuguese is Marion Kaplan's perceptive *The Portuguese: The Land & Its People*, published in 1991. Ranging knowledgeably all over the landscape, from literature to the Church, from agriculture to *emigrantes*, its generous feminine perspective seems most appropriate for a country whose men so often seem to be abroad.

An excellent and accessible work on anthropology and folklore is *Portugal: A Book of Folk-Ways* by Rodney Gallop.

ONLINE SERVICES
For general Portugal information, check out these web sites:

Excite City.Net (http://city.net/countries/portugal): search engine for links to cities of the world, including maps, practical information and sights

ICEP (http://www.portugal.org): marginally interesting site operated by the Portuguese tourism office, with links on doing business, tourism etc

The Portugal Traveller's Handbook (http://www. demon.co.uk/peth/index.html): index to practical information such as weather, money, transport and communications

And of course, be sure to have a look at LP's own Portugal 'destinations' page at http://www.lonelyplanet.com/dest/eur/por.htm.

Other sites, with links to home pages across Portugal, include:

A Collection of Home Pages about Portugal (http://www.well.com/user/ideamen/portugal.html): links to special-interest sites (mainly in English) about Portugal, eg news, education, literature, sports, media

EUnet Portugal (http://www.eunet.pt/portugal/portugal.html): index to sites around Portugal, including culture/media, education, politics; see especially their Virtual Travel page, with links to home pages (some with English versions) on Lisbon, Porto, the Algarve and other places

Portuguese WWW Resources (http://maui.net/makule/port.html): a miscellaneous index (in English) of web sites on topics such as language, recipes, Portuguese living abroad

SAPO or Servidor de Apontades Portugueses (http://www.sapo.pt): directory of web sites in Portugal, by topics such as news, education, entertainment, information (in Portuguese)

At the time of research the newsgroup soc.culture.portuguese was heavy with English and Portuguese exchanges (and quite a few screaming matches) about East Timor.

To access government travel tips on the Internet, see the boxed aside called Government Travel Advice earlier in this chapter. For information on access to e-mail, see the Post & Communications section, also in this chapter.

FILMS

Wim Wenders' film *A Lisbon Story* had its world première in Lisbon in 1994, the year the capital was named European City of Culture. Originally conceived as a documentary, it acquired a story line as it went along: a movie sound man wanders the streets trying to salvage a film that its director has abandoned, recording the sounds of the city. In the process he falls in love, has a close call with some gangsters, and is followed by a pack of school children. In the film Wenders pays tribute to many cinema greats, including Federico Fellini, Charlie Chaplin and the Portuguese director Manuel do Oliveira.

NEWSPAPERS & MAGAZINES
Portuguese-Language Press

Major Portuguese-language daily newspapers include *Diário de Notícias*, *Público*, *Jornal de Notícias* and the gossip tabloid *Correio da Manhã*, which licks all the others for circulation. Popular weeklies include the *O Independente* newspaper and *Expresso* magazine. On the web you can find *Público* at http://www.publico.pt and *Jornal de Notícias* at http://www.dn.pt.

Newsstands groan under numerous sports-only newspapers. For entertainment listings, check the local dailies. A monthly or seasonal calendar of regional events is also available from the turismos in tourist centres such as Lisbon, Porto and the Algarve. *Público's* Lisbon and Porto editions have classified sections with big what's-on listings.

Foreign-Language Press

Several English-language newspapers are published in Portugal by and for its expatriate population, especially in the Algarve. In addition to regional and limited international news and features, these can be good sources of information on long-term accommodation, regional events, Gypsy fairs, cheap flights, repair services, language and other courses, and even work. Best known are *APN* (Anglo-Portuguese News), published every Thursday, and the *News*, published fortnightly in regional editions. Another one is the weekly *Algarve Resident*.

It's easy to find transnational papers, including the *European*, the *International Herald Tribune* and *USA Today* and national papers from all over Europe, at big-city and tourist-centre newsstands for the equivalent of US$1.50 to US$3. Most are a day or two old. You can also find French-language newspapers such as *Le Monde* and *Le Figaro*, and a surprisingly wide selection of other foreign publications.

RADIO

Portuguese domestic radio is represented by the state-owned stations Antena 1 on MW and FM, Antena 2 on FM and Antena 3 on FM; the private Rádio Renascença (RR) and a clutch of local stations.

Rádio Difusão Portuguesa (RDP) transmits daily programmes of national and international news and other information of interest to visitors in English, French and German during the summer. In Lisbon look for it at MW 666 kHz, FM 99.4 MHz or FM 95.7 MHz; in Porto try MW 1377 kHz or FM 96.7 MHz; in the Algarve try MW 720 kHz, FM 97.6 MHz or FM 88.9 MHz.

English-language broadcasts of the BBC World Service, Voice of America (VOA) and Radio Australia can be picked up on various short-wave frequencies in Portugal. For current BBC frequency and schedule information, contact the BBC at PO Box 76, Bush House, London WC2B 4PH, UK (fax 0171-257 8258) or at its web site, http://bbc.co.uk/worldservice. Contact VOA Europe at 330 Independence Ave SW, Washington, DC 20547, USA (fax 202-619-0916; e-mail voa-europe@voa.gov) or via the VOA web site, http://www.voa.gov. You can contact Radio Australia at GPO Box 428G, Melbourne,

Victoria 3001, Australia (fax 03-9626 1899; e-mail ratx@radioaus.abc.net.au) or at its web site, http://www.abc.net.au/ra.

TV

Portuguese TV consists of channels from the state-run Telivisão Portuguesa, Canal 1 (on VHF) and TV2 (on UHF), plus two private channels, Sociedade Independente de Communicação (SIC) and TV Independente (TVI). The country also has at least 14 cable-TV companies. Portuguese and Brazilian soap operas *(telenovelas)* appear to take up the bulk of TV airtime. There are also lots of subtitled foreign movies.

At least a dozen international channels, heavy on sports, music and movies, also come in via satellite.

VIDEO SYSTEMS

If you want to record or buy video tapes to play back home, you won't get a picture if the image registration systems are different. Portugal uses PAL, which is incompatible with the French SECAM system, and the North American and Japanese NTSC system. Australia and most of Europe use PAL.

PHOTOGRAPHY & VIDEO
Film & Equipment

It's best to take film and camera equipment with you, especially if you hanker after Kodachrome, which is generally either unavailable or very expensive.

Other brands of E6-process slide film, such as Ektachrome and Fujichrome, as well as print film and 8-mm video cassettes, are widely available at franchise photo shops in tourist centres and larger towns. Prices are not outrageously higher than elsewhere in Europe: 1500$00 (US$9.50) for 36 frames of Ektachrome 400 or Fujichrome Sensia; 870$00 (US$5.50) for 36 frames of Kodak Gold 100; and 1000$00 (US$6.50) for a 90-minute TDK 8-mm video cassette.

Print film processing is as fast and cheap as anywhere in Europe. Slide and video processing are rare.

Imported 'quick-shoot' cameras are also available in franchise shops and elsewhere, though at significantly marked up prices.

Photography

Except for the occasional indoor shot with something like 400 ASA/ISO film, you'll rarely need anything faster than about 100 ASA/ISO. Strong summer sunlight can bleach out shots, so travellers who are serious about their photography should pack the relevant filters. Contrast between light and shadow is harshest at high noon; try to get out in the early morning or just before sunset for the gentlest light.

Video

Properly used, a video camera can give a fascinating record of your holiday. Unlike still photography, video 'flows' – so, for example, you can shoot scenes of countryside rolling past the train window, to give an overall impression that isn't possible with ordinary photos.

Video cameras these days have amazingly sensitive microphones. This can be a problem if there is a lot of ambient noise – filming by the side of a busy road might seem OK when you do it, but viewing it back home might simply give you a deafening cacophony of traffic noise. One good rule to follow for beginners is to try to film in long takes and not move the camera around too much. If your camera has a stabiliser, you can use it to obtain good footage while travelling on various means of transport, even on bumpy roads.

Make sure you keep the batteries charged, and have the necessary charger, plugs and transformer for the country you are visiting. In most countries, it is possible to obtain video cartridges easily in large towns and cities, but make sure you buy the correct format. It is usually worth buying at least a few cartridges duty free to start off your trip.

Finally, remember to follow the same rules regarding people's sensitivities as for still photography. Always ask permission first.

Restrictions

There are no customs limits on equipment for personal use. There are no significant restrictions on what you can shoot in Portugal, though military sites aren't a very good idea. Some museums and galleries forbid flash photography.

Photographing People

Older Portuguese often become serious and frustratingly uncandid when you take their photos, but few will object to it, and many will be delighted. Everybody seems to like having their children photographed! Nevertheless, the courtesy of asking beforehand is always appreciated. 'May I take a photograph' is *Posse tirar uma fotografia, por favor?* in Portuguese.

Airport Security

One or two doses of airport x-rays won't harm ordinary slow or medium-speed films. If you're carrying very fast film or if you'll be going through lots of airports on a long trip, lead 'film-safe' pouches help, but the best solution is hand inspection. Officials may take you for it but most will do it if you persist. Having all your film in one or two clear plastic bags makes it easier.

TIME

Portugal recently jumped time zones and is now on 'British' time, ie at GMT/UTC in winter and GMT/UTC plus one hour in summer. This puts it an hour later than Spain all year round. Madeira is the same as the rest of Portugal, while the Azores are at GMT minus one hour in winter and GMT in summer. Clocks are set forward by an hour on the last Sunday in March and back an hour on the last Sunday in October.

ELECTRICITY

Electricity is 220V, 50 Hz. Plugs are normally of the two-round-pin variety.

WEIGHTS & MEASURES

Portugal uses the metric system. Decimals are indicated with commas, and thousands with points.

LAUNDRY

You'll find *lavandarias* providing laundry services at a reasonable cost all over the place, though the work may take a day or two. Genuine self-service places are rare; there are some in Lisbon and Porto, but they'll do your wash for you in a few hours for the same price you'd pay to do it yourself. Figure 1000$00 to 1500$00 for a 10-kg load. 'Wash and dry' in Portuguese is *limpeza e seco*.

TOILETS

Public toilets (*sanitários* or *casas de banho*) are fairly common in heavily touristed areas, but elsewhere they may be scarce. The men's side is usually marked 'H' (for *homens*), and the women's side 'S' (for *senhoras*). Toilets are usually sit-down style, though we've come across a very few squat-style places. They're generally clean and usually free. Most people, however, go to the nearest café for a drink or pastry and take advantage of the facilities there; look for the 'WC' sign.

HEALTH

Portugal, like the rest of Europe, presents no serious health risks to the sensible traveller. Your main risks are likely to be sunburn, foot blisters, insect bites, dangerous ocean currents, or an upset stomach from overeating. Some people routinely experience a day or two of 'travellers' diarrhoea' upon arriving in any new country.

Every Portuguese town of any size has its own *centro de saúde* (state-administered medical centre), typically open from 8 am to 8 pm. Big cities have full-scale hospitals and clinics, with 24-hour emergency services. There are also numerous – and pricier – English-speaking private physicians, and in Lisbon even the Hospital Británico (British Hospital). The local turismo will usually be able to recommend a private clinic for speedy treatment.

Predeparture Planning

Health Insurance A travel insurance policy to cover theft, loss and medical problems is important. You may not want to insure that old backpack, but you should cover yourself for the worst case, ie an accident or illness requiring hospitalisation and a flight home. If you can't afford that, you certainly can't afford to deal with a medical emergency abroad.

A wide variety of policies is available; your travel agent will have recommendations. The international policies handled by STA Travel and other youth/student travel agencies are good value. Check the small print: some policies specifically exclude 'dangerous activities' such as scuba diving, motorcycling, hot-air ballooning, even trekking. If these are on your agenda, get another policy or ask about an amendment (for an extra premium) that includes them.

You may prefer a policy that pays doctors or hospitals directly rather than one that requires you to pay and claim later, though in Portugal you'll usually find immediate cash payment is expected. If you have to claim later, make sure you keep all documentation. Some policies ask you to call back (reverse charges) to a centre in your home country, where an immediate assessment of your problem is made. Check that the policy covers ambulances or an emergency flight home. If you have to stretch out, you'll need two seats and somebody has to pay for them!

Citizens of EU countries are covered for *emergency* medical treatment throughout the EU on presentation of an E111 certificate, though charges are likely for medications, dental work and secondary examinations including x-rays and laboratory tests. Ask about the E111 at your national health service or travel agent at least a few weeks before you go. In some countries you can get an E111 by post (in the UK we got ours *at* the post office). But even with an E111, a travel insurance policy is a good backup.

Medical Kit It's sensible to carry a small, straightforward medical kit. A possible kit list includes:

- aspirin or paracetamol (acetaminophen in the US), for pain or fever
- antihistamine (such as Benadryl), useful as a

decongestant for colds and allergies, to ease the itch from insect bites or stings, and to help prevent motion sickness; antihistamines may cause drowsiness and/or interact with alcohol, so know what you're taking
- kaolin preparation, loperamide (eg Imodium) or diphenoxylate (Lomotil) to stop up diarrhoea when you absolutely *must* travel; note that antidiarrhoea medication should not be given to children under the age of 12
- antiseptic such as povidone-iodine (eg Betadine), for cuts and grazes
- calamine lotion, to ease irritation from bites or stings
- a selection of bandages and plasters (Band-aids), for minor injuries
- scissors, tweezers and a thermometer (note that mercury thermometers are prohibited on airlines)
- insect repellent, sunscreen and lip salve (chapstick)

Health Preparations If you wear glasses take a spare pair and your prescription. You can usually get new spectacles made up quickly, cheaply and competently.

If you need a particular medication, take an adequate supply with you, as it may not always be available in pharmacies (though most pharmacies in Portugal are remarkably well equipped). It's wise to carry a legible prescription to show that you legally use the medication – it's surprising how often drugs that are over-the-counter in one place are illegal without a prescription elsewhere. Should you need to get more, you're better off knowing the medication's generic name rather than its brand name (which may not be the same locally).

Dental care is available in Portugal, but it's not a bad idea to have a routine dental checkup before you leave home.

Immunisations No vaccinations are required for entry into Portugal unless you're coming from an infected area and are destined for the Azores or Madeira, in which case you may be asked for proof of vaccination against yellow fever. But if you'll be arriving in Portugal from anywhere in Asia, Africa or Latin America, it might be worth checking with your health service or a competent travel agency before you leave home.

There are a few routine vaccinations that

are recommended whether you're travelling or not, and this Health section assumes you've had those: polio (usually administered during childhood), diphtheria and tetanus (usually administered together in childhood, with a booster every 10 years) and sometimes measles. See your physician or nearest health agency about these.

All vaccinations should be recorded on an International Health Certificate, which is available from your physician or government health department. Don't leave jabs until the last minute, as they may have to be spread over some weeks. Some are contraindicated if you're pregnant.

Contraception In Portugal the most widely available form of contraception is condoms *(preservativos)*. These are available in all pharmacies (though you may have to ask for them in smaller towns), and sometimes in supermarkets as well. If you're taking the contraceptive pill, it's safest to bring a supply from home.

Basic Rules

Many health problems can be avoided simply by taking good care of yourself, eg washing your hands often, brushing your teeth, keeping out of the sun when it's very hot, covering up or using repellent when insects are around. Care in what you eat and drink is also important, though the worst you can expect in Portugal is temporary stomach upset.

Water Tap water is almost always safe to drink in Portugal, and bottled water is sold almost everywhere. Be careful about those rustic-looking roadside springs in rural areas unless you're sure they really are springs and not just surface streams through populated areas or pastureland.

If you're planning any long hikes where you'll depend on natural water, you should know how to purify it. The simplest way is to boil it vigorously; five minutes should be enough at altitudes typical of Portugal. Iodine treatment, available in tablet form (eg Potable Aqua or Globaline), is very effective

and is safe for short-term use unless you're pregnant or have thyroid problems. A flavoured powder will disguise the taste of treated water – a good idea if you're travelling with children. Chlorine tablets (eg Puritabs or Steritabs) kill many but not all pathogens. The only commercial water filters that stop all pathogens are combined charcoal and iodine-resin filters.

Food Salads and fruit are safe anywhere in Portugal. Ice cream is usually OK, but beware of ice cream that has melted and been refrozen. Take care with shellfish (eg cooked mussels that haven't opened properly can be dangerous), and avoid undercooked meat, particularly minced meat. Be careful with food that has been cooked and then left to go cold.

If a place looks clean and well run and if the vendor also looks clean and healthy, then the food is probably OK. In general, places packed with travellers or locals are fine.

Nutrition If your diet is limited or unvarying, if you're travelling hard and fast and therefore missing meals, or if you simply lose your appetite, you can soon start to lose weight and place your health at risk.

Fruits and vegetables are good vitamin sources. If you depend on fast foods, you'll get plenty of fat and carbohydrates but little else. Remember that overcooked food loses much of its nutritional value. If your diet isn't well balanced, it's a good idea to take a multivitamin and mineral supplement including iron, especially for women, who lose a lot of iron during menstruation.

In hot climates make sure you drink enough – don't rely on thirst to remind you to drink. Not needing to urinate or very dark yellow urine is a danger sign. Carry a water bottle on long trips. Excessive sweating can lead to loss of salt and therefore muscle cramping; to avoid it, just salt your food a bit more than usual.

Medical Problems & Treatment

For minor health problems you can pop into a pharmacy *(farmácia)*; these are abundant in larger towns and often have English-speaking staff. Typical daily opening hours are from 9 am to 1 pm and 3 to 7 pm. One local pharmacy (on a rotating basis) stays open after hours; the address of the late-night one is usually posted on the window of the others. Another option is the local medical centre (centro de saúde), though you're less likely to find any English speakers.

Hospital casualty wards will help with more serious problems; we have included major hospitals in the text and maps of this book. Your embassy or the local turismo can refer you to the nearest hospital or English-speaking private doctor. So can five-star hotels, although they often recommend doctors with five-star prices.

Sun Damage In Portugal, especially on water, sand or snow, you can get sunburnt surprisingly quickly, even through cloud. Use a sunscreen and take extra care to cover areas that don't normally see sun, eg your feet. A hat provides added protection, and 15-plus sunblock cream is a good idea for nose and lips. Calamine lotion is good for soothing mild sunburn.

Remember that too much sunlight, whether it's direct or reflected (glare) can damage your eyes. If your plans include being near water, sand or snow, then good sunglasses are doubly important. Good-quality sunglasses are treated to filter out ultraviolet radiation, but poor-quality sunglasses provide limited filtering, allowing more ultraviolet light to be absorbed than if no sunglasses are worn at all. Excessive ultraviolet light will damage the surface structures and lens of the eye.

Prickly Heat Prickly heat is an itchy rash caused by excessive perspiration trapped under the skin. It usually strikes people who have just arrived in a hot climate and whose pores have not yet opened sufficiently to cope with greater sweating. Keeping cool and bathing often, using a mild talcum powder or even resorting to air-conditioning may help until you acclimatise.

Vital Signs
Normal body temperature is 37°C (98.6°F); more than 2°C (4°F) higher indicates a 'high' fever. The normal adult pulse rate is 60 to 100 per minute (children 80 to 100, babies 100 to 140). You should know how to take a temperature and a pulse rate. As a general rule the pulse increases about 20 beats per minute for each °C (2°F) rise in fever.

Breathing rate is also an indicator of illness. Count the number of breaths per minute: between 12 and 20 is normal for adults and older children (up to 30 for younger children, 40 for babies). People with a high fever or serious respiratory illness (eg pneumonia) breathe more quickly than normal. More than 40 shallow breaths a minute may indicate pneumonia. ∎

Heat Exhaustion Dehydration or salt deficiency can cause heat exhaustion. Take time to acclimatise to high temperatures and make sure you get sufficient liquids. Wear loose clothing and a broad-brimmed hat. Don't do anything too physically demanding.
Salt deficiency is characterised by fatigue, lethargy, headaches, giddiness and muscle cramps; in this case salt tablets may help. Vomiting or diarrhoea can deplete your liquid and salt levels.

Anhydrotic heat exhaustion, caused by an inability to sweat, is quite rare. Unlike other forms of heat exhaustion it's likely to strike people who have been in a hot climate for some time, rather than newcomers.

Heatstroke This serious, and sometimes fatal, condition can occur if the body's heat-regulating mechanism breaks down and the body temperature rises to dangerous levels. Long, continuous periods of exposure to high temperatures can leave you vulnerable to heatstroke. You should avoid excessive alcohol or strenuous activity when you first arrive in a hot climate.

Symptoms include feeling unwell, not sweating very much or at all, and high body temperature (39°C to 41°C or 102°F to 106°F). Where sweating has ceased, the skin becomes flushed and red. Severe, throbbing headaches and lack of coordination will also occur, and the sufferer may be confused or aggressive. Eventually the victim will become delirious or convulse. Hospitalisation is essential, but meanwhile get victims out of the sun, remove their clothing, cover them with a wet sheet or towel and fan them continually.

Fungal Infections Fungal infections, which occur with greater frequency in hot weather, are most likely to occur on the scalp, between the toes or fingers (athlete's foot), in the groin (jock itch or crotch rot) and on the body (ringworm). You get ringworm (which is a fungal infection, not a worm) from infected animals or by walking on damp areas such as shower floors.

To prevent fungal infections wear loose, comfortable clothes, avoid artificial fibres, wash frequently and dry carefully. If you get an infection, wash the infected area daily with a disinfectant or medicated soap, and rinse and dry well. Apply an antifungal cream or powder (eg Tinaderm). Try to expose the infected area to air or sunlight as much as possible, change all towels and underwear often and wash them in hot water.

Hypothermia Too much cold is just as dangerous as too much heat, particularly if it leads to hypothermia. Cold combined with wind and moisture (eg excessive sweat or a soaking rain) is especially risky. If you're trekking at high altitudes or in a cool, wet place, be prepared.

Hypothermia occurs when the body loses heat faster than it can produce it and the core temperature of the body falls. It is surprisingly easy to progress from being very cold to dangerously cold as a result of a combination of wind, wet clothing, fatigue and hunger, even if the air temperature is above freezing. It is best to dress in layers; silk, wool and some newer artificial fibres are all good insulating materials. A hat is important because a lot of heat is lost through the head. A strong, waterproof outer layer is essential, as keeping dry is vital. Carry basic supplies,

including food containing simple sugars to generate heat quickly, and lots of fluid to drink.

Symptoms of hypothermia are exhaustion, numb skin (particularly toes and fingers), shivering, slurred speech, irrational or violent behaviour, lethargy, stumbling, dizzy spells, muscle cramps and violent bursts of energy. Impaired judgement means you're much less likely to recognise it in yourself than in others.

To treat mild hypothermia, first get the sufferer out of the wind/rain, remove their clothing if it's wet and replace it with dry, warm clothing. Give them hot liquids (*not* alcohol) and some high-energy, easily digestible food. Do not rub victims, but allow them to slowly warm themselves. The early recognition and treatment of mild hypothermia is the only way to prevent severe hypothermia, which is a critical condition.

Motion Sickness Eating lightly before and during a trip will reduce the chances of motion sickness. If you are prone to motion sickness, try to find a place that minimises disturbance – near the wing on an aircraft, close to midships on a boat, near the centre on a bus. Fresh air usually helps – reading and cigarette smoke don't. Commercial motion-sickness preparations (which can cause drowsiness) must be taken before the trip starts; when you're feeling sick it's too late. Ginger (available in capsule form) and peppermint (including mint-flavoured sweets) are natural preventatives.

Bites & Stings Bee and wasp stings are usually painful rather than dangerous. Calamine lotion will provide relief and ice packs will reduce the pain and swelling. Mosquitoes are only a minor nuisance in Portugal, and mosquito-borne diseases are virtually unknown in Europe.

Snakes are probably more afraid of humans than the other way round. To minimise your chances of being bitten, wear boots, socks and long trousers when walking through undergrowth where snakes may be present, and tramp heavily to give them time to flee from you. Don't put your hands into holes and crevices. Campers should be careful when collecting firewood.

Contrary to some people's fears, snake bites do not cause instantaneous death, and antivenenes are usually available. Keep the victim calm and still, wrap the bitten limb tightly, as you would for a sprained ankle, and attach a splint to immobilise it. Then seek medical help, if possible with the dead snake for identification (but don't attempt to catch the snake if there is even a remote possibility of being bitten again). Tourniquets and sucking out the poison are now comprehensively discredited.

Lice cause itching and discomfort but present no serious risk. They make themselves at home in your hair (head lice), your clothing (body lice) or in your pubic hair (crabs). You catch lice through direct contact with infected people or by sharing combs, clothing and the like. Powder or shampoo treatment will kill the lice, and infected clothing should then be washed in very hot water.

Diarrhoea You may have a mild bout of travellers' diarrhoea on arrival in a new place, but a few dashes to the loo with no other symptoms is not serious. Moderate diarrhoea, involving half a dozen loose movements in a day, is more of a nuisance. Dehydration is the main danger, particularly for children, and fluid replacement is the main treatment. Soda water, soft drinks allowed to go flat and diluted 50% with water, or weak black tea with a little sugar, are all good. Keep your diet bland for a few days. With any diarrhoea more severe than this, get yourself straight to a hospital or doctor.

Lomotil or Imodium can stop you up but they don't cure the problem. Use them only when absolutely necessary, eg if you *must* travel. They are not recommended for children under 12 years old. Do not use them if the person has a high fever or is severely dehydrated.

Viral Gastroenteritis This is caused not by bacteria but, as the name suggests, by a virus. It is characterised by stomach cramps, diarrhoea, and sometimes by vomiting and/or a slight fever. All you can do is rest and drink lots of fluids.

Hepatitis B Hepatitis is a general term for an inflammation of the liver. Hepatitis B, also called serum hepatitis, is spread by contact with infected blood, blood products or bodily fluids – eg through sexual contact, unsterilised needles and blood transfusions, or via small breaks in the skin. Other risk situations are tattooing and body piercing. Symptoms include fever, chills, headache and fatigue, followed by vomiting, abdominal pain, dark urine and jaundiced (yellow) skin. Hepatitis B can lead to irreparable liver damage or even liver cancer.

There is no treatment for hepatitis B other than rest, drinking lots of fluids and eating lightly. A vaccine is available, although for long-lasting cover you need a six-month course.

Sexually Transmitted Diseases Sexual contact with an infected partner spreads these diseases. While abstinence is the only 100% preventative, using condoms is also effective.

Gonorrhoea, herpes and syphilis are the most common of these diseases; sores, blisters or rashes around the genitals, and discharges or pain when urinating are common symptoms. Symptoms may be less marked or absent in women. Syphilis symptoms eventually disappear completely but the disease continues and can cause severe problems in later years. The treatment of gonorrhoea and syphilis is with antibiotics. Herpes recurs but antiviral treatment helps to settle an episode.

There are numerous other sexually transmitted diseases, for most of which effective treatment is available. However, there is no cure for herpes or AIDS, Acquired Immune Deficiency Syndrome (see the following section).

HIV & AIDS HIV, the Human Immunodeficiency Virus, may develop into the usually fatal AIDS, Acquired Immune Deficiency Syndrome. Any exposure to blood, blood products or bodily fluids may put an individual at risk. Although HIV is now a major problem worldwide (including in Portugal), according to the US Centers for Disease Control the risk of infection via vaccination or transfusion is essentially nil in Portugal and the rest of Western Europe.

The major route of HIV transmission is via unprotected sex. Apart from abstinence, the most effective preventative is always to practise safe sex using condoms. HIV can also be spread by dirty needles, so acupuncture, tattooing and body piercing are potentially as dangerous as intravenous drug use if the equipment is not clean. It is impossible to detect the HIV-positive status of an otherwise healthy-looking person without a blood test.

Women's Health

Some women experience an irregular menstrual cycle on the road because of the upset in routine. Your physician can give you advice about this.

If you are taking the contraceptive pill and are crossing time zones, make sure you take a pill every 24 hours, at the same time every day. If this is difficult because it would mean you would have to take it in the middle of the night, take a pill earlier, before you go to bed, rather than later when you get up. Also, be careful if you have been sick or have had diarrhoea, as absorption of the pill may be reduced. Be prepared to use alternative methods of contraception should this occur.

Poor diet, and lowered resistance due to the use of antibiotics and even contraceptive pills, can lead to vaginal infections when travelling in hot climates. Maintaining good personal hygiene and wearing skirts or loose-fitting trousers and cotton underwear will help to prevent infections. Yeast infections (thrush), characterised by a rash, itch and discharge, can be treated with a vinegar or lemon-juice douche, or with yoghurt.

Nystatin suppositories are the usual medical prescription.

Trichomoniasis and gardnerella are more serious infections; symptoms are a smelly discharge and sometimes a burning sensation when urinating. Male sexual partners must also be treated, and if a vinegar-water douche is not effective medical attention should be sought. Metronidazole (Flagyl) is the prescribed drug.

Pregnancy Most miscarriages occur during the first three months of pregnancy, so this is the riskiest time to travel as far as your own health is concerned. Miscarriage is not uncommon and can occasionally lead to severe bleeding. The last three months should also be spent within reasonable distance of good medical care. A baby born as early as 24 weeks stands a chance of survival, but only in a good modern hospital. Pregnant women should avoid all unnecessary medication. Additional care should be taken to prevent illness and particular attention should be paid to diet and nutrition. Alcohol and nicotine, for example, should be avoided.

WOMEN TRAVELLERS

Despite the official reversal of many traditional attitudes towards women after the 1974 revolution, Portugal remains, at least on the face of it, a man's world. It is amazing how many able-bodied Portuguese men hang idly and contentedly around the central *praças* of virtually every town. While well over half of Portuguese university graduates are women, and women are increasing their representation in universities, business, science, government and the professions, there are still few women in positions of public trust.

An official organisation called the Commission for the Equality & Rights of Women (Comissão para a Igualdade e para os Direitos das Mulheres) was founded in 1976 to alter public perceptions on women's social status and is a leading advocate of women's rights. According to women's groups in Portugal (and to a 1994 report by the US State

Department, *Portugal Human Rights Practises)*, domestic violence against women is a persistent problem. There are no centres for battered women or rape victims, nor are there reliable statistics on either. Sexual harassment in the workplace is fairly common.

In traditionally minded Portugal, except perhaps in Lisbon or Porto, an unaccompanied foreign woman is considered an oddity. Older people, especially in rural areas, often ask women visitors where their husbands are, and may fuss over them as if they were in need of protection. Never mind that these same rural areas often seem populated entirely by unaccompanied Portuguese women whose husbands are either working in the fields, gossiping in the bars, employed abroad (often for years at a time), or long dead.

In restaurants a couple may receive only one menu, on the Portuguese assumption that decisions, though often made by women, are announced by men! Nobody will mind if you ask for another menu. Especially in the more conservative north, unmarried couples in search of accommodation will save themselves frequent hassles by saying they are married.

But women travelling on their own in Portugal report few serious hassles. Portuguese machismo, when it manifests at all, is irritating rather than dangerous, mainly taking the form of hissing, clucking or whistling by clusters of post-adolescent men. A bigger risk may be the stoked-up male tourists in Algarve resorts.

Nevertheless, machismo aside, Lisbon is still a big city, and women should therefore be cautious about where they go after dark, in particular the Alfama, Bairro Alto and Cais do Sodré districts, and on the metro. Hitching is not recommended for solo women anywhere in Portugal.

Organisations

The Comissão para a Igualdade e para os Direitos das Mulheres or Commission on the Equality & Rights of Women (other sources refer to the Comissão da Condição Feminina or Commission on the Status of Women) is at Avenida da República 32, 1093 Lisbon.

GAY & LESBIAN TRAVELLERS

Attitudes towards gay male lifestyles range from overall public tolerance in Lisbon (and to a limited extent in Porto and the Algarve) to bafflement in remoter parts of the country. Lesbians appear to be more or less ignored. There are many public figures who, though closeted, are generally known to be homosexual.

That's the public picture. In fact, few Portuguese homosexuals come out, fearing discovery by families or employers. In overwhelmingly Catholic Portugal, there is little understanding of homosexuality, negligible tolerance of it within families, and no public structures to support homosexuals. Although gay-bashing (homophobic violence) is relatively unknown, there is a steady stream of reported discrimination in schools, workplaces etc.

Lisbon is the only city in Portugal with a substantial range of places for gay/lesbian socialising – restaurants, bars, discos, saunas, beaches and cruising areas (but parks after dark are not a good idea). There are some places to socialise in Porto and the Algarve but few elsewhere. There are tentative plans to hold Portugal's first-ever Gay Pride Celebration in June 1997 in Lisbon.

Legal Situation

Though it has no constitutional protection, homosexuality is not illegal in Portugal. According to *Spartacus* magazine, Article 71 of the Portuguese penal code, which prohibits 'acts against nature', has been used against gays, but only rarely. Article 1915 states that gays and lesbians can lose custody of their children, and this has been used against divorced lesbians.

According to *Spartacus*, Article 31 of the penal code prohibits gays and lesbians from serving in the armed forces, although ILGA-Portugal (see the following section) claims that the military does not discriminate on the basis of sexual preference and that openly gay officers are not unknown.

Organisations

At present, Portugal's homosexual community has no united voice. The country's only advocacy organisation is ILGA-Portugal, a member of the International Lesbian & Gay Association (ILGA). Founded in 1995 and only registered in Portugal in April 1996, ILGA-Portugal is still finding its feet. A major aim is to add sexual orientation to the 'equal-rights-irrespective-of' list in Article 13 of the Portuguese constitution. ILGA-Portugal can be contacted at Apartado 21281, 1131 Lisboa Codex, Portugal (e-mail ilga@mail.telepac.pt). Its good web site, including pages on Portuguese gay news, organisations, gay life, and a big bar guide, is at http://www5.servtech.com/ilga.

A small discussion group called GTH (Grupo de Trabalho Homossexual, or Homosexual Work Group) is connected with the Revolutionary Socialist Party. The address is Rua da Palma 268, 1100 Lisboa, Portugal (☎ 01-888 27 36). A bimonthly gay newspaper, *Trivia*, was launched in January 1996; it's at Apartado 21221, 1131 Lisboa Codex, Portugal (☎ 01-362 63 16). A new lesbian-oriented periodical is *Lilas*, Apartado 6104, 2700 Amadora, Portugal.

DISABLED TRAVELLERS

Portuguese law requires public offices and agencies to provide access and facilities for disabled people. But it does not cover private businesses, and relatively few places in Portugal have special facilities for disabled travellers yet. Lisbon airport is wheelchair-accessible, and all three international airports (Lisbon, Porto and Faro) and most major train stations (particularly international terminals) have wheelchair-accessible toilets.

Carris, Lisbon's public transport agency, offers a 7 am to midnight minibus 'dial-a-ride' service (☎ 01-758 56 76) for disabled people, at a cost roughly comparable to taxis. They usually need two days notice. A similar system in Porto is operated jointly by STCP (the public-transport agency), the local Red Cross (Cruz Vermelha de Portugal or CVP) and the regional social-security agency

(Centro Regional de Segurança Social or CRSS), daily from 7 am to 9 pm; call CRSS at ☎ 02-606 66 46 or CVP at ☎ 02-606 68 72 (or fax 02-606 71 18). Coimbra's municipal transport agency, SMTUC (☎ 039-44 14 41), also runs such a service, weekdays from 6.30 am to 10 pm.

Carris (☎ 01-363 92 26) in Lisbon and the Algarve coach line Frota Azul (☎ 01-795 14 47; fax 01-937 70 85) have some adapted coaches for hire.

The UK's 'Orange Badge' scheme entitles people with severe walking difficulties to certain on-street parking concessions, and there are reciprocal arrangements with other EU countries. While some have specific concessions, Portugal's are rather vague: 'Parking spaces are reserved for badge holders' vehicles…indicated by signs with the international [wheelchair] symbol. Badge holders are not allowed to park…where parking is prohibited by a general regulation or a specific sign'. We saw very few 'disabled' parking spaces around Portugal, and then only in major towns. Orange badges are issued in the UK by local-council social services departments, and the UK Department of Transport publishes an explanatory booklet.

The Royal Association for Disability & Rehabilitation (RADAR) publishes a guidebook, updated every two years or so, called *European Holidays &Travel Abroad: A Guide for Disabled People*. Its Portugal section includes transport help and selected accommodation, especially in the Algarve. RADAR is at 12 City Forum, 250 City Road, London EC1V 8AF, UK (☎ 0171-250 3222; fax 0171-250 0212).

ICEP offices abroad can also furnish some information on barrier-free accommodation around the country; for ICEP addresses see Tourist Offices earlier in this chapter. It's mainly the upper-end hotels that have the capital to spend modifying their doors, toilets and other facilities. For local barrier-free hotels, camping grounds and other facilities, ask at the local turismo.

Organisations

The Secretariado Nacional de Reabilitação

(National Rehabilitation Secretariat; ☎ 01-793 65 17; fax 01-796 51 82), Avenida Conde de Valbom 63, Lisbon, publishes a guide in Portuguese, *Guia de Turismo para Pessoas com Deficiências* (Tourist Guide for Disabled People), updated every few years, with sections on barrier-free accommodation (including camping), transport, general information (including shops, restaurants and sights), and help numbers throughout Portugal. It's only available at their (barrier-free) offices, open weekdays from 10 am to noon and 2 to 7 pm.

A private agency that keeps a more up-to-date eye on developments and arranges holidays for disabled travellers is Turintegra (☎ & fax 01-859 53 32, contact Ms Luisa Diogo), Praça Dr Fernando Amado, Lote 566-E, 1900 Lisbon. This is also known as APTTO (Associação Portuguesa de Turismo Para Todos, or Portuguese Association for Tourism for All).

The Portuguese Handicapped Persons' Association (☎ 01-388 98 83; fax 01-387 10 95) is at Largo do Rato, 1250 Lisbon. Other organisations that might provide additional information are ACAPO, the Association of the Blind & Partially Sighted of Portugal (☎ 01-342 20 01; fax 01-342 85 18), Rua de São José 86-1, 1500 Lisbon; and APS, the Portuguese Association for the Deaf (☎ & fax 01-355 72 44).

TRAVEL WITH CHILDREN

Portugal is a splendidly child-friendly place. As Marion Kaplan observes in *The Portuguese: The Land & Its People*, 'To the Portuguese, small children, no matter how noisy and ill-behaved, are angels to be adored and worshipped, overdressed and underdisciplined'. Shopkeepers pass sweets over the counter. Waiters (or waiters' kids) scoop up your bundle of joy to play behind the counter. Even teenage boys seem to have a soft spot for toddlers. Whenever our two-year-old decided to shriek with glee or boredom in a restaurant, the only sour faces were those of other (but child-free) tourists.

Following are some tips for making a trip with kids easier. For more detailed and wide-ranging suggestions (not all of them necessary in Portugal), pick up the current edition of Lonely Planet's *Travel with Children*.

Discounts & Children's Rates

No restaurant we ate in ever objected to providing child-sized portions at child-sized prices. Children under the age of eight are entitled to a 50% discount in hotels and pensões if they share their parents' room. Lower-end places may charge nothing extra at all. Preschool children usually get into museums and other sights free.

Supplies

Basic supplies are no problem, unless perhaps you want to settle down in a remote hamlet in Trás-os-Montes. Most *mini-mercados* have at least one or two brands of disposable nappies. Pharmacies are a handy source of baby supplies of all kinds, from bottles and nappies to food supplements. The big chain supermercados stock toys and children's clothes as well. Larger cities have numerous shops devoted to kids' clothes, toys and shoes.

Health

Portugal presents no significant health risks for kids other than hot beaches and cold mountains. Restaurant food is quite safe except at obviously cheap and grotty places in bigger cities. For more information refer to the Health section in this chapter.

Accommodation

The best bets are simple pensões, which are accustomed to families with young children and are casual enough to actually enjoy them. Camping grounds are excellent places to meet other children from all over the world, and youth hostels (nearly all of which have private rooms as well as dormitories) are good for meeting older kids. Most hotels and pensões can come up with a baby cot, especially if you request it when you book the room.

Every Portuguese town from Lisbon on down seems to have its squadron of dirt-bike night-riders, so unless your child sleeps like a log, go for hotel rooms that don't face any streets.

Food

Most minimercados, and many pharmacies, have various Portuguese and imported brands of tinned baby food, and markets abound in fresh fruit and vegetables.

All but the stuffiest restaurants tolerate kids well. But a constant problem with eating out is the late hour at which restaurants open for the evening meal – 7 pm at the earliest. Most bars and snack bars can produce plain cheese sandwiches or toasted sandwiches throughout the day. Some restaurants may let you in before regular hours and cook up something simple for a child. Keep an eye out for places with children playing between meal hours – a clue that staff themselves have kids there. Lucky you if your child likes soup, as there is often at least a pot of that ready to be served as soon as you walk in the door.

Entertainment

Lisbon and Porto may look like pretty stuffy places to a child. But Lisbon's *elevadores* are great fun, Sintra's horse and cart rides are a 40-minute train ride away, and the Lisbon district of Belém has two visually appealing museums, the Museu de Marinha (Naval Museum) and Museu Nacional dos Coches (Coach Museum). The tram ride to Belém is half the fun. Porto's trams have all but disappeared, but its Tram Museum is a treat for children of all ages.

Portugal dos Pequenitos is a Coimbra theme park built especially for children, full of kid-sized miniatures of architectural monuments from all over the old empire. And the full-sized castles of Óbidos, Marvão, Castelo de Vide, Valença, Elvas and elsewhere are great for letting old and young imaginations loose (but keep hold of your toddler on those sheer-drop battlements).

From a child's perspective, the best part of Portugal is probably the Algarve, with its warmer, calmer beaches, organised water-sports (such as water-skiing, sailing, diving, windsurfing) and casual beachside cafés; a marine park (Zoomarine) with dolphin and seal shows, near Albufeira; a night-time theme park (Planeta Aventura) near Quarteira; and no fewer than three huge water parks along the main N125 highway. Bicycle rental outfits are more plentiful in the Algarve than anywhere else in the country. Some larger Algarve resorts have children's clubs for three to 11-year-olds, which can be booked through some UK tour operators.

Beaches from one end of the country to the other are an obvious source of fun and exercise, but beware of the Atlantic Ocean's undertow, and of Portugal's midday sun without sunblock cream and covering clothes.

Few towns have decent playgrounds or children's parks. We found many playgrounds so bashed up and rusty as to be dangerous. Good *parques infantil* approved by our toddler were in Gouveia (Serra da Estrela), on the riverfront at Viana do Castelo (this one is great for older kids, too), and especially in Lisbon's Castelo São Jorge. Larger towns may also have puppet theatres; Évora has a good one. Every sizeable festival comes complete with parades, fireworks, music, dancing and food. In rural areas, especially up north, friendly farmers may offer tractor or donkey rides.

For older children, see local references in this book to horse-riding centres, especially in the Algarve, the Alentejo and the Minho (Parque Nacional da Peneda-Gerês).

Childcare

Babysitters Of course you're going there to travel with the kids, but you may long for the occasional few hours on your own. A few turismos have lists of local babysitters; we had remarkable luck at some turismos, but got blank looks at others. Figure on at least 500$00 per hour for anyone with experience.

You may do better at an upper-end hotel, resort or self-catering apartment complex, some of which have their own childcare facilities staffed by trained nursery nurses. Here you might find a staff member willing to babysit after hours or able to recommend someone else who can.

Infantários Most sizeable towns have one or more private *infantários* that provide daycare for children from three months to six years of age. They usually seem to be full, and in any case aren't meant for tourists (children are typically enrolled by the month or longer), but you might find one with a place for a few weeks in the summer when some families go away. They aren't cheap – typically 14,000$00 to 18,000$00 per month – partly because they serve hot lunches.

Turismos can help you find these. We learned of one from a pensão housekeeper whose child was there, and they welcomed our two-year-old for a week. They may refuse payment; if they do, consider buying or donating toys or art supplies totalling what you otherwise would have paid in babysitting fees.

Ludoteca Ludoteca is the name of a string of privately funded kindergartens staffed by professional nursery nurses and equipped with games, toys, art supplies etc. We found them in the Algarve at Albufeira and Fuzeta (between Faro and Tavira), and in Évora, and there are probably others. They're primarily for Portuguese kids (the staff usually speak little English), although open to visiting children too. Hours vary, at a minimum from Monday to Saturday from 2 to 5 or 6 pm. Signs in Albufeira point to the *centro infantil*.

DANGERS & ANNOYANCES
Crime
Portugal has a low crime rate among European countries, but it's on the rise. Though the occasional armed robbery has been reported, crime against foreigners usually involves pickpocketing or purse-snatching, break-ins and theft from cars (especially rental cars), and pilfering from camping grounds. Crime rates are highest in heavily touristed regions such as the Algarve, and specific areas of Lisbon and Porto (refer to Dangers & Annoyances under those cities).

With the usual precautions (don't carry your wallet, cash or credit cards in your back pocket or an open purse, use a money belt for large sums, don't leave valuables in your car, tent, hotel room or unattended backpack, and use common sense about going out at night in cities), there is little cause for worry. For peace of mind, take out travel insurance. And if you *are* robbed, do not under any circumstances put up a fight! Refer also to the following section, Emergencies.

Embassy Help Your embassy or consulate is the best first stop in any emergency. For a list of consular offices and services they can provide in Portugal, see Embassies in this chapter. A consul *cannot* get local laws or regulations waived because you're a foreigner, investigate a crime, provide legal advice or representation in civil or criminal cases, get you out of jail, or (normally) lend you money.

Police If you've had anything robbed or stolen, you should visit the local police (we identify the appropriate office under each major town) – not necessarily for help in solving the crime, but for a police report, which you'll need if you hope to make an insurance claim. Except in the larger cities, you won't find much English spoken, and the police report may be in Portuguese too.

In major towns you'll probably deal with the blue-uniformed local constabulary, the Polícia de Segurança Pública (PSP). In rural areas and smaller towns it's more likely to be the nearest post of the leather-booted Guarda Nacional Republicana (GNR). Many older officers of both were part of the state security apparatus under Salazar and tend to retain a mentality of control and a dislike of visitors. Younger officers are usually easier to talk to.

Portuguese Drivers
Driving in Portugal can be a terrifying experience. Normally gentle, peace-loving Portuguese men and women can become irascible, deranged speed-freaks behind the wheel. Tailgating on the motorway at 120 km/h and passing on blind curves are the norm. Solid lines between streams of opposing traffic seem to have little meaning. Not

surprisingly, Portugal has one of the highest per capita road-accident rates in Europe.

Motorcycles

Young Portuguese men love motorcycles, in particular unmuffled dirt-bikes, though most of them probably wouldn't know a moto-cross if it bit them on the leg. In even the remotest villages, these vile machines snarl up and down quiet streets at every hour of the day and night, sundering dreams and setting teeth on edge.

Pedestrian Safety

Walking in towns can be hairy, Portuguese drivers being what they are. The country seems to have evolved without the notion of special areas for pedestrians. Until the 1970s, few people owned vehicles privately, and the roads were probably pretty safe for everybody. Even in today's car-clogged cities, pedestrianised areas and vehicle areas are often indistinguishable. In some older walled towns, narrow lanes may have little room for a single car, let alone a car *and* an absent-minded person on foot.

Ocean Currents

Atlantic Ocean currents in some coastal areas are notoriously dangerous. Be very careful about swimming on beaches that are not signposted or otherwise identified as safe.

Smoking

Three-quarters of the Portuguese population seems to smoke, and small-town restaurants rarely have no-smoking areas. There is little you can do but move upwind, outdoors, or on. Portugal does not have a high-profile antismoking lobby.

Hunting Season

Some of the Portuguese countryside (especially parts of the inland Algarve and the Alentejo) is open for hunting on certain days of the week, mainly from October through January. If you're planning any long country walks, check with the local turismo about places and days to avoid.

EMERGENCIES
Staying in Contact

In an emergency the simplest way for someone to reach you from outside Portugal is with a telephone call, fax or telegram, care of your hotel. Of course this depends on that someone knowing where you're staying!

Most foreign offices maintain 24-hour emergency operators – eg the British Foreign Office (☎ 0171-270 3000), the US State Department Citizens Center (☎ 202-647 5225; ☎ 202-647 4000 after hours), and the Australian Department of Foreign Affairs & Trade (☎ 06-261 3331). If you haven't kept someone at home informed of your where-abouts, the emergency operator can contact your embassy in Portugal. Embassies naturally prefer that other means have been exhausted before they're contacted.

National Emergency Numbers

The nationwide emergency telephone number is ☎ 112 (this was changed from the old 115 number in 1997 to bring it into line with European practice), for fire and other emergencies as well as for the police, though you're unlikely to reach an English speaker. For more routine police matters (and direct access to the fire brigade) there are also telephone numbers for each town or district, as noted.

The number for problems relating to poisoning and snake bites is ☎ 01-795 01 43.

LEGAL MATTERS

Foreigners here, as elsewhere, are subject to the laws of the host country. Penalties for dealing in, possessing and using illegal drugs are stiff in Portugal, and may include heavy fines or even jail terms.

BUSINESS HOURS

Don't plan on getting much business or shopping done anywhere between the hours of 1 and 3 pm, when the Portuguese give lunch serious and lingering attention.

Most shops are open from 9 or 9.30 am to 1 pm and from 3 to 7 pm; many close at noon. Most are closed on Saturday afternoons (except in December) and Sundays. Shopping centres are usually open every day of the week, from 10 am to 10 or 11 pm or later.

Offices normally operate on weekdays only from 9 am to 1 pm and from 3 to 5 pm. Most banks are open for public business on weekdays only from 8.30 am to 2.30 or 3 pm. Typical post office hours on weekdays are 9 am to 12.30 pm and 2.30 to 6 pm, although the post office at Restauradores in Lisbon and the main post office in Porto are open into the evening and on weekends.

Museums are typically open Tuesday to Saturday from 10 am to 12.30 pm and 2 to 5 pm. If the Monday is a holiday, museums are usually closed on the following day as well.

PUBLIC HOLIDAYS & SPECIAL EVENTS

The following are public holidays in Portugal, when banks, offices, department stores and some shops close and workers get the day off; restaurants, museums and tourist attractions tend to stay open, though public transport services are reduced.

1 January
    New Year's Day
February/March (variable)
    Carnival Tuesday (Shrove Tuesday, about six weeks before Easter)
March/April (variable)
    Good Friday
25 April
    Liberty Day (celebrating the 1974 revolution)
1 May
    Labour Day
May/June (variable)
    Corpus Christi
10 June
    Portugal Day, or Camões & the Communities Day
15 August
    Feast of the Assumption
5 October
    Republic Day (commemorating the declaration of the Portuguese Republic in 1910)
1 November
    All Saints' Day
1 December
    Independence Day (commemorating the restoration of independence from Spain in 1640)
8 December
    Feast of the Immaculate Conception
25 December
    Christmas Day

Portugal also abounds with *romarias* (religious pilgrimages), *festas* (festivals) and *feiras* (fairs), which bring whole towns or regions to a standstill. At the core of many are religious processions. The further north you go, the more traditional and less touristy these celebrations get. Some are well worth going out of your way to see (though accommodation is often solidly booked out).

Local turismos can tell you what's coming up, and some regional tourist offices (eg in the Minho) publish annual timetables of all their events. Bigger turismos may have the countrywide booklet *Fairs, Festivals & Folk Pilgrimages* or the more general and descriptive *Religious Festivals*. Following are only a handful of the biggest ones.

February/March (variable)
    Carnival, the last few days before the start of Lent (about six weeks before Easter), was traditionally an occasion for people to let off steam and thumb their noses at public decorum. Things often got out of hand, with mayhem and even murder between feuding families, but since police powers were boosted in the 1970s it seems to consist mainly of parades, and a lot of weirdly made-up kids out begging for sweets. The biggest celebrations are said to be in Loulé (Algarve), Nazaré (Estremadura) and Ovar (Beiras).

Woman in festival dress

Easter Week (March/April, variable)

Braga's Easter or Holy Week Festival is the grandest of its kind in the country, featuring a series of vast and colourful processions of which the most famous is Senhor Ecce Homo on Maundy Thursday, led by barefoot, torch-bearing penitents.

7-8 May

The Festa das Cruzes (Festival of the Crosses) in Barcelos is noted for its processions, folk performances and regional handicrafts exhibits.

12-13 May and 12-13 October

Two annual pilgrimages to Fátima (Estremadura) celebrate the first and last apparitions of the Virgin Mary to three shepherd children here in 1917; these are strictly religious events, with hundreds of thousands of pilgrims from around the world visiting one of the Catholic world's major holy sites.

First week in June

Santarém's (Ribatejo) grand farming and livestock fair, the Feira Nacional da Agricultura, also includes bullfighting, folk singing and dancing.

12-13 June

The Festa de Santo António (Festival of St Anthony) is an all-night street fair with dancing, food and parades in the Alfama and Mouraria districts of Lisbon, and the 13th is a municipal holiday there. Other communities also celebrate St Anthony's day at this time.

23-24 June

Many communities celebrate the Festa de São João (St John's Festival), but Porto parties for nearly a week beforehand, and the night of the 23rd sees everybody out on the streets cheerfully bashing each other with leeks or plastic hammers. The 24th is a municipal holiday in Porto.

Week preceding the first Sunday in July

The Festa dos Tabuleiros (Feast of Trays) in Tomar (Ribatejo), held only every four years or so, features a procession of girls and boys bearing trays laden with huge loaves of bread. The last one was held in 1995.

Weekend of the third Sunday in August

The Romaria e Festa da Nossa Senhora da Agonia (Our Lady of Suffering Pilgrimage and Festival) in Viana do Castelo (Minho) is famed for its parades, fireworks, folk art and handicrafts fair.

Mid-September

The Feiras Novas of Ponte de Lima (Minho), which date back to the 12th century, feature a vast market set up on the banks of the Rio Lima, plus folk music, funfairs and processions.

12-13 October

See 12-13 May above.

3-11 November

The Feira de São Martinho or National Horse Fair in Golegã (Ribatejo) features horse parades, riding competitions and bullfights, and a final feast of roast chestnuts and young wine.

ACTIVITIES
Walking & Trekking

Despite some magnificent rambling country, walking ranks low among Portuguese passions. There are no national walking clubs and no official cross-country trails, though some parks, including Parque Nacional da Peneda-Gerês and Parque Natural da Serra da Estrela, are starting to establish walking trails. Armed with good maps (see Planning in this chapter for map sources) you can turn this to your advantage and have remoter parts of Portugal, especially its one national and 10 natural parks, almost to yourself.

Camping is usually restricted to established camping grounds, but most trails pass close enough to villages or towns for you to find accommodation there.

Most of the good walking is in the north. Most challenging is the Serra da Estrela, which includes Portugal's tallest peak, 1993m Torre. Less taxing, but at least as beautiful, are Parque Nacional da Peneda-Gerês in the Minho and the lovely but little-visited Parque Natural de Montesinho in Trás-os-Montes. You might also consider some of the country's lesser known parks, such as tiny Parque Natural do Alvão near Vila Real. For more on Portugal's peak, see National Parks under Flora & Fauna in the Facts about the Country chapter.

Under specific parks in the regional chapters we list information offices, as well as outfits that organise pony-trekking and hiking trips and hire out gear and horses. A Lisbon agency that organises weekend walks to remoter places all over Portugal is Rotas do Vento (see Travel Agencies in the Lisbon chapter).

Good paperback books on walking in Portugal include Bethan Davies & Ben Cole's *Walking in Portugal* (Footprint Guides), and Brian & Eileen Anderson's *Landscapes of Portugal* series (Sunflower Books), with separate books on the Algarve; Sintra, Cascais and Estoril; and Costa Verde, Minho and Peneda-Gerês.

A kindred activity, especially popular in Peneda-Gerês, is orienteering.

Water Sports

Portugal's 800-plus km of coastline offers some fine surfing and windsurfing, as well as water-skiing, sailing and scuba diving. The northern beaches tend to have bigger waves, and colder water. Prime surfing and windsurfing venues are Praia do Guincho and Praia das Maçãs on the Estoril coast, and Ericeira in the Estremadura, with good conditions in the Algarve too. Only the Algarve and the Estoril coast have appreciable support facilities such as equipment rental.

Inland water sports include a limited amount of white-water boating and plenty of motorised and nonmotorised flat-water (eg reservoir) boating, particularly in Parque Nacional da Peneda-Gerês.

Cycling

Most Portuguese are bemused by the idea of cycling for pleasure. The rental of mountain bikes (BTT or *bicyclete tudo terrano*) – for anywhere from 1500$00 to 3500$00 a day – is catching on in the Algarve, around Parque Nacional da Peneda-Gerês and in some other touristed areas, but elsewhere, rental outfits are scarce. We note them wherever we have found them.

For an introduction to cycling, not as an activity but as a way of getting around Portugal, see the Bicycle section of the Getting Around chapter.

Horse Riding

There are many centres for pony and horse riding – some of which do organised trips – especially in the coastal Algarve and Alentejo, but also northwards in the Lisbon area, Ribatejo, the Beira Litoral, the Minho and Trás-os-Montes. Typical high-season rates are 1300$00 to 1900$00 per hour or about 8000$00 per day.

Canyoning & Hydrospeed

Canyoning is a relatively new adventure sport, tackling all the challenges offered by a canyon: trekking, swimming, abseiling and rock climbing. Hydrospeed is a version of white-water boating, with individual boards and helmets instead of a boat. The only agencies we know of that offer programmes for visitors in these high-adrenalin activities are Inatel and Trilhos (see the following section on Multiactivity Programmes).

Fishing

The best river fishing is in the north – for salmon, trout and barbel in the Minho, Moura, Castro, Laboreiro and Douro rivers. A fishing licence is required, and is good throughout the country; contact the Instituto Florestal, Avenida João Crisostomo 26 in Lisbon, or ask at the *câmara municipal* (town hall) closest to where you plan to fish. You can bring your own tackle into Portugal.

No licence is required for big-game fishing, a popular pastime especially in the Algarve, where deep-sea fishing parties are commonplace (eg for swordfish, tuna, shark). Marlin and other species can be fished in the cooler waters off the north coast.

Golf

Southern Portugal is full of championship-standard golf courses, with a few up north too. The Algarve west of Faro has no fewer than 17 courses and the Estoril coast (Costa de Lisboa) has 10. There are two in the Estremadura, two just south of Porto, one near Barcelos (Minho) and one at Chaves (Trás-os-Montes). ICEP, the Portuguese tourist authority, produces a glossy booklet with loving descriptions of every one of them.

Tennis

Most upper-end hotels in the Algarve have tennis courts. There are clubs, with professional instructors, at Vilamoura, Vale do Lobo (near Quarteira) and Carvoeiro (all in the Algarve), Lisbon and the Tróia Peninsula (south-east of Lisbon), and a complete tennis-holiday centre at Estoril.

Athletics

Portugal shines in track and field athletics, especially long-distance events. In 1984 Carlos Lopes won the Olympic gold medal in the men's marathon (and his time still stands as an Olympic 'best'). In the 1988 Olympics Rosa Mota took gold in the women's marathon. In 1996 Manuela Machado did it again, while Fernanda Ribeiro nosed out China's *wunderkind*, Wang Junxia, to win the women's 10,000m race.

Not surprisingly, Lisbon hosts its own international marathon, the Discoveries Marathon, held annually in late November, as well as an annual half-marathon in early March. For more information on both races, contact the marathon organisers – Xistarca (☎ 01-363 36 05; fax 01-362 07 34), Travessa Paulo Martins 9, 1300 Lisbon, Portugal – or the Federação Portuguesa de Atletismo (☎ 01-414 60 20), Largo da Lagoa 15-B, 2795 Linda-a-Velha, Portugal.

Skiing

The only place where you can be sure of snow is around Torre in the Parque Natural da Serra Estrela. Facilities (lifts, equipment rental etc) there are pretty basic. Penhas de Saúde is the major accommodation base. The season is January through March, with reliably good snow only in February.

Multiactivity Programmes

Movijovem in Lisbon, Portugal's central Hostelling International booking office, organises adventure holidays for 16 to 26-year-olds, including rafting, hiking and horse riding. From across the Rio Tejo in Barreiro, Turnatur (☎ 01-207 68 86; fax 01-207 76 75) arranges nature walks, jeep safaris, canoeing and canyoning expeditions. TurAventur (☎ & fax 066-74 31 34) in Évora does walking, biking and jeep trips across the Alentejo plains. Montes d'Aventura and Trote-Gerês (see Parque Nacional da Peneda-Gerês) can arrange trekking, horse riding, canoeing, cycling and combination trips in Peneda-Gerês. Trilhos in Porto claims to organise hydrospeed, can-

yoning, hiking and climbing trips, but it's pretty hard to get hold of anyone there.

Inatel (Instituto Nacional para Aproveitamento do Tempos Livres dos Trabalhadores) is a Portuguese workers' organisation with hotels, camping grounds and sports/leisure programmes including walking, mountaineering, paragliding, mountain biking, white-water boating, hydrospeed and canyoning. These are presently open only to members, with the apparent exception of hydrospeed, canyoning and some mountainbike trips. Contact Inatel's Departmento Desportiva in Lisbon, or its Vila Real office (see Information under Lisbon or Vila Real).

COURSES

Language

For a two-hour crash course in the basics at 3500$00 per person, contact Interlingua in Portimão (☎ 082-41 60 30; fax 082-276 90), Lagos (also called Centro de Linguas; ☎ & fax 082-76 10 70) or Lagoa (☎ 082-34 14 91). The Cambridge School offers intensive four-week group courses for foreigners from about 76,000$00, plus shorter courses and pricey private lessons; it has branches in Lisbon (☎ 01-352 74 74; fax 01-353 47 29), Porto (☎ 02-56 03 80; fax 02-510 26 52) and Coimbra (☎ 039-349 69; fax 039-339 16). Some universities, including those at Lisbon and Coimbra, offer summer courses in Portuguese language and culture for foreigners.

Other Courses

Among other things you can learn while in Portugal are:

- dance, singing, juggling, circus techniques, TV acting: evening courses from the Collectividade Cultural e Recreativa de Santa Catarina (☎ 01-887 82 25), Costa de Castelo 1, Lisbon
- Zen meditation: Centro de Alimentação e Saúde Natural (☎ 01-315 08 98), Rua Mouzinho da Silveira 25, Lisbon
- riding Portugal's famous Lusitano horses: Escola de Equitacao de Alcaiṇça (☎ 061-966 21 22), Rua de São Miguel, Alcaiṇça (near Mafra)
- arts and crafts: summer courses at the Escola da Tecnologia e Artes de Coimbra (☎ 039-259 69), Rua Venacio Rodrigues 7, Coimbra

- skydiving: weekend courses from the Centro de Paraquedismo (☎ 053-62 29 53), Braga

For information on US universities with exchange programmes in Portugal, check out this URL on the World Wide Web: http://www.studyabroad.com.

WORK

EU nationals can compete for any job in Portugal without a work permit. Non-EU citizens who want to work in Portugal are expected to get a Portuguese work permit before they arrive, with the help of their prospective employer.

Several organisations can help you search for a job in Portugal before you go, and even arrange your work permit. One of the best known is the Work Abroad Program of CIEE, the Council on International Educational Exchange (☎ 212-822 2600; fax 212-822 2699; e-mail info@ciee.org; URL http://www.ciee.org), 205 East 42nd St, New York, NY 10017-5706. Another useful resource is the Directory of Summer Jobs Abroad (☎ 01865-241 978; fax 01865-790 885; URL http://www.youthnet.org.uk/natorgs/d/dirsjbab.html), care of Vacation Work Publications, 9 Park End St, Oxford OX1 1HJ, UK. An index on the World Wide Web of library resources on overseas jobs is at http://www.lib.calpoly.edu/retriever/current/overseas.html.

As a traveller, you're more likely to decide after arriving that you need some dosh to help extend your travels, though the prospects of on-the-spot work in Portugal are limited unless you have a skill that's scarce. The search will be easier if you've brought along a curriculum vitae, references and certified diplomas or certified copies of relevant diplomas or certificates. The odds also improve if you speak passable Portuguese. Except for work where you're paid in kind or in petty cash, you'll probably have to sign a work contract.

The most realistic option is English teaching, but only if you're prepared to stay in one place for at least a few months. A TEFL certificate is a big help, though you may find work without one. See the *Páginas Amarelas* (Yellow Pages) under Escolas de Línguas for the names of schools in your chosen area. Check out the classified ads in Portugal's English-language press or, if your Portuguese is good enough, in dailies such as *Diário de Notícias* or *Público* (see Newspapers & Magazines in this chapter).

The English-language newspapers may be interested in writers or reporters. There are rare jobs in Algarve bars. In summer you can sometimes pick up day-to-day cash passing out leaflets for bars and discos in the streets of Lagos or other Algarve towns.

If you plan to stay more than three months, you'll also need a residence permit, from the local Serviço de Estrangeiros e Fronteiras (Foreigners' Registration Service) office (see Visas & Documents earlier in this chapter). We have listed some in this book, or you can ask at the local turismo.

A somewhat dated but comprehensive reference for the serious long-term job seeker is Sue Tyson-Ward's paperback, *How to Live & Work in Portugal*.

ACCOMMODATION

Most local turismos have lists of accommodation to suit a wide range of budgets, and can help you locate and even book somewhere to stay. Some turismos scrupulously avoid making recommendations, while others are happy to offer their opinions. The government grades most accommodation with a bewildering and not very useful system of one to five stars.

Prices for most places are seasonal, as noted in the following sections. Typically, the high season is mid-June or July through August or September; middle season is April

---

Oops!
Hotels and pensões often collect your passport when you check in so they can register you, as required of them by the state. But they may not always remember to return it – don't you forget! ∎

to the middle or end of June, plus September or October; and low season is the rest of the year. Prices also jump during Carnival and Easter week (dates for these are variable; see Public Holidays & Special Events in this chapter). Children under eight years old usually get 50% off. Many places will, if asked, give discounts for stays of four or more days, and bigger discounts for a week or more.

In this book we use the following price categories for an establishment's most basic double with toilet and shower or bath: bottom end (up to 4000$00); middle (4000$00 to 8000$00); top end (over 8000$00). You'll have to prebook most middle and top-end accommodation for the high season, anywhere from a few days to a few weeks ahead. The Algarve's busy season runs for most of the year, from late February through November; accommodation is even tighter than in the rest of the country, and Algarve prices run noticeably higher than the typical values quoted in this section.

For a room with a double bed, ask for a *quarto de casal*; for twin beds, ask for a *duplo*; and for a single room, ask for a *quarto individual*.

Camping

Camping is widespread and popular in Portugal, and easily the cheapest option. Depending on facilities and the season, prices per night run from about 500$00 to 600$00 per adult (or child over 10 years old), plus 400$00 to 500$00 for a car and the same again for a small tent. Considerably lower prices apply in less touristed regions and in the low season. Even in the high season, backpackers with their own small tents can always find a spot, at least at the larger grounds.

Consistently the best equipped, biggest (but priciest) camping grounds in the country are run by Orbitur. These can be prebooked through Orbitur's central booking office in Lisbon on ☎ 01-815 48 71; fax 01-814 80 45. Throughout the book we have indicated which are Orbitur sites.

The *Roteiro Campista* (1500$00), which is published annually in March and sold in most large Portuguese bookshops, is an excellent multilingual guide with details of nearly every camping ground in the country, plus regulations for camping outside these sites.

A handy campers' document is the Camping Card International (CCI) issued by the Federation Internationale de Camping et de Caravanning (FICC). Formerly known as a Camping Carnet, the CCI can be presented instead of your passport when you register at FICC-affiliated camping grounds. It provides third-party insurance for any damage you may cause, and is sometimes good for discounts. Certain camping grounds run by local camping clubs may be used by foreigners *only* if they have a CCI.

The CCI is available to members of most national automobile clubs, except in the USA; the RAC in the UK charges £4 for one. It's also issued by FICC-affiliated camping clubs such as the Camping & Caravanning Club (☎ 01203-694995) in the UK and the Federação Portuguesa de Campismo e Caravanismo or FPCC (☎ 01-812 68 90; fax 01-812 69 18) at Avenida Coronel Eduardo Galhardo 24-C, 1170 Lisbon.

Hostels

Pousadas de Juventude Portugal has a network of 20 pousadas de juventude or youth hostels (plus two in the Azores), which are part of the Hostelling International (HI) system. Rates vary, being higher for popular hostels such as Lisbon's, but in most of them a dorm bed is 1200$00 to 1400$00 in the low season and 1450$00 to 1600$00 in the high season. Most also have at least a few double rooms from 2200$00 to 3700$00 per room. One at Vilarinho das Furnas has bungalows for three (7000$00 to 9000$00) or four people (8500$00 to 11,000$00). The hostel at Mira consists mainly of a young people's camping ground. Continental breakfast is included in the price. Five hostels (Braga, Vila Nova de Cerveira, Leiria, Sines and Lagos) have kitchens where you can do your own cooking. The others offer prepared lunch or dinner for 950$00.

Five hostels (Fóz do Cávado, Ovar, Lisbon, Catalazete and Lagos) are open 24 hours a day. The rest have curfews, typically opening only from 8 am to noon and 6 pm to midnight or later, though you can usually stash your bags at any hour and come back at opening time to book in.

Demand is high, so advance reservations are essential. You can book ahead from any hostel to any other in Portugal free of charge, or pay 1000$00 per set of bookings (not per hostel) at Movijovem (☎ 01-355 90 81; fax 01-352 86 21), Avenida Duque d'Ávila 137, 1000 Lisbon – Portugal's central HI reservations office (where you can also book hostels abroad). You can book some of Portugal's hostels directly from abroad and you can even have a look at them at Movijovem's web site, http//www.telepac.pt/cartaojovem/movijovem.html.

Age doesn't matter in Portugal: rates are the same for anyone with membership. If you don't already have a card from your national hostelling association, you can get HI membership (valid anywhere except at home) by paying an extra 400$00 (and having a 'guest card' stamped) at each of the first six hostels you stay at.

At the time of research there were pousadas de juventude at:

Alentejo
    Sines
Algarve
    Alcoutim, Lagos, Portimão, Vila Real de Santo António
Azores
    Ponta Delgada, Angra do Heroísmo
Beiras
    Coimbra, Mira, Ovar, Penhas da Saúde (Covilhã)
Douro
    Porto
Estremadura
    Areia Branca (Lourinha), Leiria, São Martinho
Lisbon area
    Catalazete (Oeiras), Lisbon, Sintra
Minho
    Braga, Fóz do Cávado (Esposende), Vila Nova de Cerveira, Vilarinho das Furnas

Centros de Juventude Don't confuse the HI pousadas de juventude with Portugal's *centros de juventude* – state-funded youth activity centres which sometimes have lodgings. No HI membership is required. Anyone is welcome but on a first-come-first-served basis, and you cannot book in advance. There is no breakfast and not all of the centres have cooking facilities. But they're cheap: 1300$00 to 1500$00 a bed, if any are free. By mutual agreement, there is no centro de juventude in town if there is a pousada de juventude there. The are centros at Faro, Portalegre, Setúbal, Aveiro and Vila Real.

Cheap Rooms

Another cheap option, especially in coastal towns, is a *quarto particular* (or simply *quarto*, meaning room), usually just a room in a private house. These are easiest to find in summer. Home owners may approach you in the street or at the bus or train station; otherwise watch for 'quartos' signs. Some turismos have lists of private rooms, though most avoid the subject. The rooms are usually clean, cheap (about 3500$00 a double) and free from the restrictions of hostels, and the owners can be interesting characters. A more commercial variant is a *dormida* or rooming house, where doubles are about 4000$00 in the high season. Prices don't usually vary between seasons, but you may have some success bargaining them down in the low season.

In the smallest rural villages, where public accommodation is full or nonexistent, you might find a *casa de povos* (common house) where you can crash with the permission of the mayor or other local bigwig.

Guesthouses

The most common types of guesthouses, the Portuguese equivalent of bed and breakfasts (B&Bs), are the *residencial* and the pensão (plural, pensões). Both are graded from one to three stars, and the top-rated establishments are often cheaper and better run than some hotels clinging to their last star. High-season rates for a double with attached bath in the cheapest pensão start at about 4500$00; expect to pay slightly more for a residencial, where breakfast is usually included. There are often cheaper rooms with shared bathrooms.

These are probably Portugal's most popular form of tourist accommodation, and they tend to fill up in summer. Try to book at least a week ahead in the high season, even two or three weeks ahead in touristed areas or for good-value places. During the low season, rates drop by at least a third.

A step down from these are boarding houses, called *hospedarias* or *casas de hóspedes*, where prices are lower and showers and toilets are usually shared.

Hotels

Hotels (*hotel*, plural *hotéis*) are graded from one to five stars. For a double in the high season you'll pay about 9000$00 to 12,000$00 at the lower end and between 15,000$00 and 30,000$00 at the top end. In the same category, but more like up-market inns, are the *albergarias* and the pricier *estalagens*. In the low season, prices drop spectacularly, with a double in a spiffy four-star hotel for as little as 8000$00. Breakfast is usually included.

In some towns you may find 'apartment-hotels' – whole blocks of self-contained apartments for rent to tourists.

Room Service (☎ 0171-439 3949) is a UK hotel booking service that claims to be able to get up to 50% off the price of upper-end hotels and resorts in Lisbon, Porto, Algarve towns and elsewhere in Portugal.

Turismo de Habitação

Under a private (but government-monitored) scheme called Turismo de Habitação or 'Turihab', and smaller schemes known as Turismo Rural and Agroturismo, you can stay in anything from a farmhouse to a mansion as the guest of the owner. Some also have self-contained cottages, though owners prefer stays of at least three or four days in these. Prices for a double in the high season start at 11,500$00; in low season they may drop by as much as 50%, and you can literally stay in a palace for the price of an average B&B elsewhere in Europe.

A hefty book, *Turismo no Espaço Rural*, describing most of them, is available for about 2800$00 from Turismo de Habitação (☎ 058-74 16 72; fax 058-74 14 44), Praça da República 4990, Ponte de Lima; from the Lisbon turismo; or from ICEP offices abroad. You can book these places through the Ponte de Lima office, though you'll save a bit by dealing directly with Turihab proprietors; many places are well signposted in their towns.

Pousadas de Portugal

These are deluxe, government-run former castles, monasteries or palaces (plus some new establishments), over 60 in all, usually in areas of natural beauty or historical significance. Doubles in these run from 14,500$00 to 28,000$00 in the high season, and 10,000$00 to 23,000$00 in the low season. For more information contact ICEP offices abroad or Pousadas de Portugal (☎ 01-848 12 21; fax 01-840 58 46), Avenida Santa Joana Princesa 10, 1700 Lisbon.

FOOD

Without a shadow of doubt the Portuguese is the most refined, the most voluptuous and succulent cuisine in the world...We did acquire – thanks to the spices from the Orient, the tangy bits from Brazil and the art of using sugar from sweet-toothed countries, Turkey, India and the Moors of northern Africa – culinary skills, foods, delicacies, recipes, which turned us into a foremost gastronomic people. There is no other country that can boast such an array of national dishes...

(Fialho de Almeida, *Os Gatos*, 1893)

'Olive oil, wine and friendship, the older the better.'
(Portuguese proverb)

Eating and drinking get serious attention in Portugal, where hearty portions and excellent value for money are the norm. The only meal that may fail to fill your stomach is *pequeno almoço* (breakfast), which is traditionally just coffee and a bread roll (often taken in a café). *Almoço* (lunch) is a far bigger affair, lasting at least two hours (usually 1 to 3 pm) and, like the *jantar* (evening dinner), features three courses, including a hot main dish, invariably served with potatoes (and sometimes rice as well). As most main dishes in the cheaper eateries cost less than 1000$00 each, you'll find it easy to gorge yourself on a full three-course meal for under 1500$00 (about US$10, or US$13 with wine).

Although restaurants open at about 7 pm for dinner (with last orders at around 10.30 pm in cities), most locals don't eat until at least 8 or 9 pm. Restaurants are usually closed for service between 4 and 7 pm, even if they say they're open all day. But you'll always be able to find something to eat somewhere. In addition to the *restaurantes*, hordes of places serve snacks throughout the day: a café, café-bar or snack-bar sells sandwiches and cakes as well as coffee, tea and alcoholic drinks; some may even serve simple meals at lunch time, often at the bar counter as well as at tables. Several packed-out lunch eateries in Lisbon are almost entirely stand-up. (Nonsmokers should avoid these rush hours: Portuguese restaurants rarely have nonsmoking sections.)

Another popular place, especially at lunch times, is a *casa de pasto*, a casual eatery with cheap, simple meals. Slightly more up-market and popular with locals for both lunch and dinner is a *tasca*, a simple tavern, often with rustic décor. A *cervejaria*, literally 'beer house', serves snacks as well as drinks, while a *marisqueira* specialises in seafood (and is therefore often expensive).

Traditional Portuguese cuisine is far from fancy (it's basically the honest fare of farmers and fisherfolk) but it's always filling. If you can't face the huge servings (rice and chips with at least two pieces of meat or fish is considered quite normal for an ordinary portion), you can ask for a *meia*

Caldo Verde

This is the most typical of Portugal's soups and is made with kale or cabbage. The stalk and tough parts of the kale are removed and the rest is shredded finely so that it resembles grass. In Portugal the soup is served with a slice of maize bread and a side dish of small black olives.

Serves 4

500g (1 lb) floury potatoes, peeled and cut into quarters
4 cups (1 litre) water
salt
3 tablespoons olive oil
1 onion, finely chopped
250g (8 oz) kale or cabbage leaves, very finely shredded
1 small clove of garlic (optional)
freshly ground black pepper
4 thin slices of chouriço (optional)

Cook the potatoes in salted water until they are soft enough for mashing. Remove, mash and return to the water, along with the oil, onion and shredded cabbage, and boil for three to four minutes (the cabbage should not be overcooked or mushy). Season and serve hot. Place a slice of chouriço (a Portuguese spicy pork sausage) in each soup bowl if desired. ∎

---

dose (half-portion). This is standard practice in many restaurants, though the cost usually works out to be about two-thirds of a *dose*, not one-half. A better bargain is the *prato do dia* (dish of the day), often an excellent deal at about 700$00.

Many restaurants also advertise a tourist menu *(ementa turística)*, a set meal of the day with a choice of dishes and a glass of beer or half-bottle of wine. Sometimes these can be genuine bargains (popular with locals, too); often, however, they offer miserable portions.

Beware, too, of those tempting little titbits of olives and cheese spread or plain bread and butter, which are put on the table at the start of your meal; if you start nibbling them, you'll be charged for them (they're usually listed as a *couvert* or cover charge on the bill,

An Order of Bull, Please

Be careful not to get *uma torrada* and *uma tourada* mixed up: the first means a piece of toast; the second, a bullfight! ∎

A Portuguese Food Glossary

Entradas (Starters)

cocktail de gambas	prawn cocktail	omeleta de marisco/	shellfish/smoked ham/
salada de atum	tuna salad	presunto/cogumelos	mushroom omelette

Sopa (Soup)

caldo verde	potato and shredded-cabbage broth	sopa à alentejana	bread soup with garlic and poached egg
gazpacho	refreshing cold vegetable soup	sopa de legumes	vegetable soup
canja de galinha	chicken broth and rice	sopa de feijão verde	green-bean soup

Peixe e Mariscos (Fish & Shellfish)

ameijoas	clams ✎	lampreia	lamprey (like eel)
atum	tuna	linguada	sole
camarões	shrimp	lulas	squid ✎
carapau	mackerel	pargo	sea bream
chocos	cuttlefish	peixe espada	scabbard fish
caldeirada	fish stew with onions, potatoes and tomatoes	pescada	hake
		polvo	octopus ✎
enguia	eel ✎	robalo	sea bass
espadarte	scabbard fish	salmão	salmon
gambas	prawns	sardinhas	sardines
lagostins	crayfish	savel	shad
		truta	trout

Carne e Aves (Meat & Poultry)

borrego	lamb ✎	frango	young chicken
bife	steak	galinha	chicken
cabrito	kid	leitão	suckling pig
carne de vaca (assada)	(roast) beef	lombo	fillet of pork ✎
carneiro	mutton ✎	pato	duck
chouriço	spicy sausage	perú	turkey
coelho	rabbit	presunto	smoked ham ✎
costeleta	chop	salsicha	sausage
entrecosto	rump steak	tripas	tripe
fiambre	ham ✎	vaca	beef
fígado	liver	vitela	veal ✎

or as *pão e manteiga*, bread and butter). If you don't want them, play it safe and send them back at the outset.

To order the bill, ask for *a conta, se faz favor*. Cafés don't usually charge for service (a tip of small change is acceptable). In other establishments it's invariably included in the bill; if not, it's customary to leave about 10% (a 17% IVA tax may also be added in up-market restaurants).

Snacks

Snacks include *sandes* (sandwiches), typically with *queijo* (cheese) or *fiambre* (ham); *prego no pão* (a slab of meat sandwiched in a roll, often with a fried egg as well); *pastéis de bacalhau* (cod fishcakes); and *tosta mista* (toasted cheese-and-ham sandwich). Prices start at about 250$00. Soups are also cheap (about 200$00) and delicious; see the following section. Keep an eye out for cafés advertising *combinados*: these tasty little bargains, costing about 600$00, are miniature portions of a regular meat or fish dish, invariably served with chips (and sometimes salad).

Legumes (Vegetables)

alface	lettuce	ervilhas	green peas
alho	garlic	espargos	asparagus
arroz	rice	espinafres	spinach
batatas	potatoes	favas	broad beans
batatas fritas	fried potatoes (chips)	feijão	beans
cebolas	onions	lentilhas	lentils
cenouras	carrots	pepino	cucumber
cogumelos	mushrooms	pimentos	peppers
couve	cabbage	salada	salad
couve-flor	cauliflower	salada mista	mixed salad

Frutas (Fruit)

alperces	apricots	limões	lemons
ameixas	plums	maças	apples
amêndoas	almonds	melões	melons
ananás	pineapple	morangos	strawberries
bananas	bananas	pêras	pears
figos	figs	pêssegos	peaches
framboesas	raspberries	uvas	grapes
laranjas	oranges		

Condiments, Sauces & Appetisers

azeite	olive oil	pimenta	pepper
azeitonas	olives	piri piri	chilli sauce
manteiga	butter	sal	salt

Ovos (Eggs)

cozido	hard boiled	mexido	scrambled
escalfado	poached	omeleta	omelette
estrelado	fried	quente	boiled

Cooking Methods

assado	roasted	grelhado	grilled
cozido	boiled	na brasa	braised/charcoal grilled
ensopada de...	stew of...	no espeto	on the spit
estufado	stewed	no forno	in the oven (baked)
frito	fried		

Main Meals

Before delving into the menu (*a ementa* or *a lista*) it's always worth asking if there's a prato do dia (dish of the day) or *especialidade da casa/região* (speciality of the house or region). Greedy tourist-geared eateries may simply suggest the expensive *arroz de marisco* – a rich seafood and rice stew, usually for a minimum of two – but elsewhere you could well end up with some unusual dish that's far more exciting than the standard menu items.

Among *entradas* or starters, of best value are the excellent home-made soups. Especially popular is caldo verde, a jade-green potato and cabbage soup. In areas such as the Serra de Estrela, where local cheeses are famous, you may well find these on the entrada menu, as well as the occasional *queijo fresco* (fresh goat's cheese).

For main meals, *peixe* (fish) and seafood are exceptional value, especially at seaside resorts, though you'll find fish on the menu even in the remotest corner of the land. There's an amazing variety available, from favourites such as *linguada* and *lulas*

'Bacalhau, The Faithful Friend'

The Portuguese have been obsessed with bacalhau – salted cod – since the early 16th century. It was at this time that Portuguese fishing boats started to fish for cod around Newfoundland (claimed by the Corte Real brothers in 1500). The sailors salted and sun-dried their catch to make it last the long journey home, thereby discovering the perfect convenience food both for their compatriot sea-faring explorers (who were sailing as far as India at the time) and for their fish-loving but fridgeless folk back home. Indeed, so popular did bacalhau become throughout Portugal that it soon became known as *fiel amigo*, the faithful friend.

Most of today's cod is imported from Norway and is fairly expensive, but as it more than doubles in volume after soaking, keeps well and is extremely nourishing, it's still widely popular. If you join the fan club, you're in for a treat – there's said to be a different bacalhau recipe for every day of the year.

It takes a few centuries to get addicted: try the *bacalhau à Gomes de Sá*, a tastier version than most of the 364 other recipes (this one features flaked cod baked with potatoes, onions, hard-boiled eggs and black olives). ■

Carne (meat) and *aves* (poultry) are often hit-and-miss in Portugal: strike it lucky and you'll find delicious specialities such as *leitão assado* (roast suckling pig), best around Coimbra, *borrego* (lamb), famous in the Alentejo, and *presunto* (smoked ham), delicious in Chaves and Lamego. One of Portugal's rare culinary coups is the widely available *carne de porco à alentejana*, an inspired combination of pork and clams.

Even the cheapest menus invariably feature *vitela* (veal) and *bife* (beef steak), while *coelho* (rabbit) and *cabrito* (kid) are unexpected delights. Most popular of all poultry dishes is *frango*, widely available grilled on outdoor spits *(frango assado)*, and perfect for a takeaway meal.

Strike it unlucky, however, and you'll end up with *tripas* (tripe), most famous in Porto; the stomach-sticking *migas alentejanas*, a bread and fatty pork stodge; the unbelievably meaty *cozido à Portuguesa* stew; or worst of all, a bloody bread-based slop called *papas de sarrabulho*.

Desserts & Pastries

Sobremesas (desserts) are a surprising disappointment in restaurants, though you're in for a treat if a home-cooked *doce* (sweet pudding) such as a *leite creme* (custard) or *mousse de chocolate* is available. More often than not, however, you'll be offered the same old *pudim* (crème caramel), *arroz doce* (sweet rice) or *gelado* (ice cream) – often the expensive Ola or Motta commercial varieties. But fresh fruit is usually available, as well as cheese (the best and most expensive is *queijo da serra* from the Serra da Estrela region, a Brie-like cheese made from pure ewe's milk).

If you're hankering for some really effective tooth-decaying desserts, head for the nearest pastelaria or *casa de chá* where you can find the sweetest concoctions imaginable, invariably made from egg yolks and sugar. Nuns of the 18th century created many of the recipes, bestowing tongue-in-cheek names on the results, such as *papos de anjo* (angel's breasts) or *barriga de freira* (nun's belly). Regional specialities in this depart-

grelhado (grilled sole and squid) and *pescada* (hake) to *bife de atúm* (tuna steak), often served in the Algarve smothered in onions, and *espadarte* (scabbard fish) – not to be confused with *peixe espada* (swordfish).

The cheapest and most ubiquitous fish are *sardinhas assadas* (charcoal-grilled sardines), a delicious feast when eaten with salad and chilled white port. And you won't get far in Portugal before discovering its favourite fish dish: *bacalhau* or salted cod, which has been a Portuguese culinary obsession for 400 years.

For more exotic fish specialities, there's the popular but expensive arroz de marisco (seafood paella); *caldeirada* (fish stew) or *açorda de marisco* if it's bread-based; *cataplana*, a combination of shellfish and ham cooked in a sealed wok-style pan and typical of the Algarve region; and all the varieties of shellfish, from *amêijoas* (clams) and *camarões* (shrimps) to *lagostins* (crayfish) and *chocos* (cuttlefish).

ment include the egg-based *doces de ovos* from Aveiro and cheesecakes from Sintra *(queijadas de Sintra)*.

Vegetarian Food

Vegetarians can have a miserable time in carnivorous Portugal, where meat and offal are consumed with relish. Servings of vegetables just don't figure in traditional cuisine here. And although many restaurants (especially in tourist resort areas) now include a token few vegetarian dishes on their menus, exclusively vegetarian restaurants are few and far between.

The most easily available but utterly boring choices of unadulterated vegetarian fare are omeleta (omelettes) and batatas fritas (chips), *salada mista* (mixed salad), and *sandes do queijo* (cheese sandwiches). But there are some delicious vegetable soups on nearly every menu – from sopa de legumes, the good old vegetable purée standby to the more uniquely Portuguese sopa à alentejana, a bread, garlic and poached egg soup (better than it sounds). Even here, however, something that should be reliably vegetarian (the popular green cabbage caldo verde soup, for instance) can often be tainted with slices of chouriço (spicy smoked sausage) or bits of fatty pork, and there's no knowing whether the stock is made with meat.

Among more filling dishes, Portuguese specialities that avoid meat are some of the simple peasant migas (bread soup) dishes, notably migas do Ribatejo and migas à moda da Beira Litoral. They look disgusting (their main ingredient is soaked maize bread, with lots of olive oil and garlic to taste) and to many people, they are. Keep an eye out instead for *arroz de tomate* (tomato rice) or *favas com azeite* (broad beans with olive oil).

Or head for the markets and do your own vegetarian shopping: in addition to excellent fruit and vegetable stalls (along with the fish and meat), you'll nearly always find freshly baked bread and local cheeses – the soft handmade ewe's milk or goat's milk cheeses are well worth trying, and perfect for a picnic. Markets are best on Saturdays, worst

on Mondays and closed on Sundays. They are open from early morning to about 6 pm.

DRINKS
Nonalcoholic Drinks

Surprisingly, *sumo de fruta* (fresh fruit juice) is rare, although the local Tri Naranjus bottled varieties are a reasonable substitute. But Portuguese *água mineral* (mineral water) is excellent and widely available, either *com gás* (carbonated) or *sem gás* (still).

Coffee drinkers are in for a high time: it's freshly brewed, even in the humblest rural café (in only one place – Alcoutim in the Algarve – were we served with a disgusting English-style cuppa). It comes in all varieties with its own convoluted nomenclature.

For a small black espresso (the most popular form) simply ask for um café (or *uma bica* to be more precise: many waiters don't believe foreigners want the real thing – strong, black and punchy). You may soon graduate to a double dose, *um café duplo*, or retreat to something weaker, *um carioca*. If you want milk, ask for *um garoto* (small size) or *um café com leite*. Popular at breakfast time is the caffè latte-style *um galão*, a large milky coffee served in a glass (usually with a good deal more milk than coffee). For equal portions (in a cup) ask for *um meia de leite*.

Countless cups of coffee during the day can add up. *Uma bica* usually costs about 70$00 but it depends where you drink it: a typical Lisbon pastelaria might charge 80$00 if you drink your coffee standing up by the *balcão* (counter), 120$00 at the *mesa* (table) or as much as 200$00 outside at the *esplanada* (street tables).

Chá (tea) is usually served rather weak, in the style of Catherine of Bragança, who is best remembered not for being the wife of Charles II but for starting England on its long love affair with tea (and toast). You can ask for it *com leite* (with milk) or *com limão* (lemon), but if you ask for *um chá de limão*, you'll get a glass of hot water with a lemon rind (which is actually quite refreshing).

Also available in cafés and teahouses is

quente, hot chocolate, or *o de leite*, a glass of milk.

inks

Portuguese people like their tipple: you can pick up anything from a glass of beer or wine to a shot of *aguardente* (firewater) at cafés, restaurants and bars throughout the day (and most of the night). And bartenders aren't stingy with their tots, either: most of them don't even bother with spirit measures. A single brandy here often contains the equivalent of a double in the UK or USA.

In most places you pay when you're ready to leave (as in a restaurant) but in some foreign-owned bars there's a pay-as-you-order system *(pronto pagamento)*.

Wines Portuguese wine offers great value in all its varieties – red, white, or rosé; mature or young (and semisparkling). You can find decent *vinho da casa* (house wine) everywhere, for as little as 250$00 for a 350-ml bottle or jug. And for less than 800$00 you can buy a bottle to please the most discerning taste buds. In shops and supermarkets wine is available by the bottle, box or five-litre container (and you can leave your empty bottles at the ubiquitous bottle banks, or at supermarket checkouts).

A Glossary of Wines & Their Labels

adega	winery or cellar
ano	year
branco	white
bruto	extra dry
colheita	a single-harvest vintage tawny port, aged for at least seven years
doce	sweet
engarrafado por...	bottled by...
espumante	sparkling
garrafeira	wines of an outstanding vintage, at least three years old for reds and one year for whites
generoso	fortified wine
LBV	late-bottled vintage; a vintage port aged for four to six years in oak casks before bottling
licoroso	sweet fortified wine
meio seco	medium dry
quinta	a country property or wine estate
região demarcada	officially demarcated wine region
reserva	wine from a year of outstanding quality
ruby port	the cheapest and sweetest port wine
seco	dry
tawny port	a sweet or semisweet port, the best of which has been aged for at least 10 years; less likely than a vintage port to give you a hangover
tinto	red
velho	old
vinho branco/tinto	white/red wine
vinho da casa	house wine
vinho do Porto	port wine
vinho maduro	wine matured for more than a year
vinho regionão	a new classification for superior country wines, similar to the French *vins de pays*
vinho verde	young (literally 'green') wine, slightly sparkling and available in red, white and rosé varieties
vintage character port	a cheap version of a vintage port, blended and aged for about four years
vintage port	the unblended product of a single harvest of outstanding or rare quality, bottled after two years and then aged in the bottle for up to two decades, sometimes more
white port	usually dry, crisp and fresh; popular as an apéritif

Restaurant wine lists differentiate not only between tinto (red) and branco (white), but between *maduros* (mature wines) and vinhos verdes (semisparkling young wines). As there are over a dozen major regional wines (usually produced by cooperatives), with new ones coming onto the market all the time, you're spoilt for choice.

The most famous of the maduro wines are probably the red *Dão* table wines produced from an area just north of the Serra da Estrela. Sweet and velvety, they resemble a Burgundy. Other maduros worth trying are the increasingly popular wines from the Alentejo (the reds from Reguengos are excellent); the reds and whites of Buçaco, near Coimbra; the dry, straw-coloured whites of Bucelas in Estremadura; the table wines of Ribatejo, especially the reds of Torres Vedras and whites from Chamusca; and the expensive but very traditional-style red Colares wines (famous since the 13th century) from near Sintra – where the vines, grown on sand dunes, have never been touched by phylloxera (a fungus that has ravaged many a European wine region over the years).

The vinho verde (literally 'green wine') of the northern Minho and lower Douro valley area is also very popular: young (hence its name) and slightly sparkling, it has a low alcoholic content and comes in red, white and rosé varieties, though the white is undoubtedly the best (try it with shellfish). The best known vinho verde label is Casal Garcia, but well worth the extra escudos are the Alvarinho whites, especially those from Quinta da Brejoeira, the reds from Ponte da Barca, and whites from Ponte de Lima.

Portugal's most internationally famous rosé wine is, of course, the too-sweet, semi-sparkling Mateus rosé. The Portuguese themselves prefer their bubbles either in vinho verde form or as *espumantes naturais* (sparkling wines). The best of these are from the Bairrada region near Coimbra (try some with the local speciality, roast suckling pig) and the Raposeira wines from Lamego. Sweet dessert wines are rare – the *moscatel* from Setúbal and Favaíos and the Carcavelos wine from Estremadura offer the fruitiest flavours.

Port & Madeira Vinho do Porto (port) is Portugal's most famous export, a fortified wine made exclusively from grapes grown in the Douro valley, fortified by the addition of grape brandy, and matured in casks or large oak vats, traditionally at Vila Nova de Gaia, across the Douro river from Porto, from which it took its name. (See the Douro chapter for details of visits to the port wine lodges, the history of port and information about the Porto port wine institute, and see the Lisbon chapter for information on its port wine institute.)

Port can be red or white, dry, medium or sweet. The main difference in price and quality is between blended ports taken from a number of different harvests, and vintage port from a single high-quality harvest. All genuine ports carry the Port Wine Institute's seal. You don't need to shell out for a whole bottle just to try some port (though a cheap white or ruby only costs about 700$00 a bottle): any café, bar or restaurant can serve you a glass of port for about 150$00. For the better quality vintage brews, be prepared to pay at least 2500$00 a bottle.

Cheapest and sweetest are the ruby and red ports, made from a blend of lesser wines, bottled early and drunk young (after about three years). Also blended are semisweet or sweet tawny ports, named after the mahogany colour they gain after years aged in wooden oak casks, and very popular as an apéritif (especially with the French, who drink several million cases of the stuff every year). Check out the label ('10 Years Old', '20 Years Old' etc) for an indication of the best-quality tawnies. Vintage character port is a cheap version of a vintage (but with similar characteristics), blended and aged for about four years.

The single harvest ports range from the colheita port, a tawny made from high-quality wines and aged for at least seven years before bottling, to late-bottled vintage (LBV) ports, which are produced from an excellent harvest and aged for four to six years before bottling. The most sublime (and most expensive) port of all – vintage port – is produced in a year of outstanding quality, bottled within two years and aged for up to two decades, sometimes more. This is your ultimate after-dinner drink, always served from a decanter (not because it's classy but because there's always sediment in the bottle). Little known outside Portugal but well worth trying are white ports, ranging from dry to rich and sweet. The dry variety is served chilled with a twist of lemon.

Vinho da Madeira (Madeira) is one of the oldest fortified wines of all: vines were first introduced to this Atlantic Ocean island province of Portugal soon after it was claimed by Portuguese explorers in 1419. The English (who called the sweet version of the wine 'malmsey') became particularly partial to it (the Duke of Clarence drowned in a butt of the stuff). In addition to the malmsey dessert wine, there's a dry apéritif version called *sercial* and a semisweet *verdelho*.

Absinthe without Leave

I was hurrying through the centre of Lisbon recently, just glancing in the shop windows, when I saw a bottle of absinthe. Here I was in the capital city of a European nation that's just been presiding over the stodgy old European Union, and there was a drink for sale I thought had been banned about the time they invented light bulbs.

Portugal's like that. It wants us to think it's folksy – all fishing boats, lace and pastel-coloured palaces – when, deep down, it's mad and bad and dangerous to know. Byron liked Portugal, remember.

It's the poverty that does it. Portugal has always been too poor to be good. I've seen black magicians advertising their services in the papers in Portugal and watched teenage prostitutes besieging the exit to a fashionable nightclub.

But absinthe? In 1995? I mean, wasn't this the stuff that made Toulouse-Lautrec feel five feet tall? Wasn't absinthe what made poets want to sleep in purple and orange bedrooms? With other poets?

Anyone, I thought, who drinks the stuff has got to be stark, raving crazy. I had to get some. A trawl of the Baixa and the cafés fringing the Rossio Square yielded nothing. In the more respectable establishments, they even seemed insulted by the inquiry.

But on a cobbled back street, I came across a tiny bar in which a man was serving nips of liquor across an unvarnished wooden counter to a weather-beaten clientele. The man – one of nature's rugby forwards – actually took a step backwards when I asked for absinthe. But he had some, and it came in a truly Baudelairean bottle with electric blue foil round the neck and a cork held in place by hardened sealing wax. He wrapped it in cheap brown paper, as if it were pornography. Absinthe was first manufactured commercially by Henry-Louis Pernod in 1797. The active component, so to speak, was wormwood. The first to ban it were the Swiss in 1908. Others followed suit on the grounds that absinthe, in the words of Encyclopaedia Britannica, caused 'hallucination, mental deterioration and sterility.' Some blamed the high alcohol content. But most thought it was the wormwood. Pastis, anis, ouzo and raki are all wormwood-free absinthe substitutes.

Perhaps, I thought, the Portuguese had kept the name but not the herb. But no. The label said it was made from extract of absinto. And the dictionary translated absinto as 'common wormwood'. It also gave the following meanings for the adjective absintado: '(1) Containing absinthe (2) Bitter (3) Tormented or afflicted.' And it listed a noun, absintismo, which was an 'Illness, caused by the abuse of absinthe.'

I am thinking hard about this right now as I pour out the lime green liquid. I am also thinking about the hallucinations, the mental deterioration, the sterility, and the way foreign correspondents are not paid enough for the risks we run.

Now that I have drunk my first glass, what do I think of it? Well, the simple answer is that it tastes like a pungent variety of toothpaste. But I am noticing that the headache I had has vanished and been replaced by some unexplained tinglings and a distinct feeling of abstraction. And I am reminded that I know only two other things about wormwood.

One is that it crops up in some ominous context in the Book of Revelation. The other is that the Ukrainian word for it is 'Chernobyl'.

John Hooper
(Reprinted with permission of the *Guardian*)

Spirits Portuguese gin, whisky and brandy are all much cheaper than elsewhere in Europe, although the quality isn't as good. If you fancy something with a more unique taste and punch, try some of the aguardente firewaters: *medronho* (made from arbutus berries), *figo* (figs), *ginginha* (cherries) and *licor beirão* (aromatic plants) are all delicious – and safe in small doses. For some rough stuff that tries hard to destroy your throat, ask for a *bagaço* (made from grape husks).

Beer Stronger and cheaper than in the UK or the USA, Portugal's *cerveja* (beer) comes in three main brands of lager: Sagres and Cristal mainly in the south, and Super Bock in the north. There's little difference among them. Empty bottles can be exchanged at supermarket checkouts for a refund.

You can order beer in bars by the bottle or on draught – *um imperial* or *um fino* for a quarter-litre, *uma caneca* for a half-litre, *um girafe* for a litre. A 300-ml glass of draught costs about 200$00 (equivalent to about 150$00 for a half-pint). Bars in tourist resorts often have popular foreign brews such as bitter or stout, pricey at 400$00 for 400 ml.

ENTERTAINMENT

Perhaps the commonest forms of entertainment in all of Portugal are its many municipal and regional festas (festivals) and feiras (fairs). Many are centred on local saints' days and associated religious processions, or are part of a romaria or pilgrimage. Whole towns or regions may down tools for several days and revel in music, dance, fireworks, colourful parades, handicraft fairs or vast animal markets. For more on these events, see Public Holidays & Special Events in this chapter.

Another venerable, and uniquely Portuguese, tradition is *fado*, the haunting, melancholy Portuguese equivalent of the blues (see Arts in the Facts about the Country chapter for more on fado). Tourists get stylised versions in the *casas de fado* of Lisbon's Bairro Alto district, while shelling out minimum charges of 2000$00 to 3000$00. Locals will tell you where to find the real thing, in little cafés that may stay open most of the night. The two cities with the most distinctive fado traditions and styles are Lisbon (fado's home) and Coimbra.

More conventional bars, pubs and discos abound in Lisbon, Porto and the Algarve (where Albufeira apparently has a reputation as Portugal's disco hot spot), and smaller towns often have a disco or two on the outskirts. Many of them go right through until morning.

A number of Portugal's towns sponsor summer cultural programmes, especially music (classical, rock, jazz or folk) and dance (classical, traditional or modern). Probably the best known international music festival is Sintra's in July-August; Sintra also hosts a jazz festival in June. Others of interest include an international festival of Celtic music in Porto in March; a festival of classical music in Portimão in late May; and a folk music festival in Portimão and an international film festival in Figueira da Foz in early September. Ask at local turismos about what's coming up, or for the city's monthly or seasonal what's-on bulletin, or check out the entertainment listings in the newspapers.

European and American films (most of them thankfully subtitled, not dubbed) seem to edge out local competition in the country's cinemas. Tickets are fairly cheap, typically 500$00 to 700$00; prices are often further reduced one day a week in an effort to lure audiences away from their home videos.

SPECTATOR SPORTS
Football

Football (soccer) is a national obsession, and life – male life, at any rate, and quite possibly the national economy – comes nearly to a standstill when there's a big match on. TVs in bars and restaurants show nothing else, and old men wander distractedly through the streets with their ears to transistor radios. The season lasts from September through May, and almost every village and town finds enough players to field a team. The three major national teams are Benfica and Sporting in Lisbon, and FC Porto in Porto. Tickets are fairly cheap; check the papers or ask at local turismos about upcoming matches and venues.

Bullfighting

Bullfighting is still popular in Portugal, despite pressure from international animal-rights activists. The season runs from late April to October.

A typical tourada (bullfight) starts with a huge bull charging into the ring towards a *cavaleiro*, a horseman dressed in elaborate 18th-century-style costume and plumed tricorn hat. The 500-kg bull has his horns capped in metal balls or leather, but he's still an awesome adversary. The cavaleiro sizes him up as his backup team of *peões de brega* (footmen) distract and provoke the bull with capes. Then, with incredible horsemanship, he gallops within inches of the bull's horns and plants a number of short, barbed *bandarilha* spears into the bull's neck.

The next phase of the fight, the *pega*, features a team of eight young, volunteer *forcados* dressed in breeches, white stockings and short jackets, who face the bull barehanded, in a single line. The leader swaggers towards the bull from across the ring, provoking it to charge. Bearing the brunt of the attack, he throws himself onto the animal's head and grabs the horns while his mates rush in behind him to try and immobilise the beast, often being tossed in all directions in the process. Their success marks the end of the contest and the bull is led out of the pen among a herd of steers. Though the rules for Portuguese bullfighting prohibit a public kill, the hapless animal is usually dispatched in private afterwards.

Another style of performance (often the final contest in a day-long tourada) is similar to the Spanish version, with a *toureiro* challenging the bull – its horns uncapped – with cape and bandarilhas. Unlike in Spain, however, there's no *picador* on horseback to weaken the bull with lances. It's man against beast. And unlike in Spain, the kill is symbolic, a short bandarilha feigning the thrust of a sword.

The most traditional bullfights are held in the bull-breeding Ribatejo province, especially in Santarém during the agricultural fair in June and in Vila Franca de Xira during the town's July and October festivals (which even feature bull running in the streets). There are also more tourist-oriented touradas in the Algarve as well as in Lisbon.

The fights usually last at least two hours. Tickets (available from agents in advance or from outside the *praça de touros*, or bullring) range from 2500$00 to 4000$00, depending on where you sit: the cheapest are *sol* seats

The History of Bullfighting

The first recorded mention of bullfighting in Portugal is from the Roman historian Strabo, who wrote in the 1st century that 'the peoples inhabiting the coastal regions of the Peninsula like to challenge isolated bulls which in Hispania are very wild'.

Developing their hunting into a sport, the Celtiberian people used to hold games in Baetica (later known as Andalusia), where wild animals were killed with axes or lances. Combats with bulls were common, too, in ancient Crete, Thessaly and imperial Rome: several amphitheatres were rebuilt for bullfights in the dying days of the Roman Empire.

Portugal's modern version of the bullfight was originally conceived in the 12th century, when the tourada was developed as a method to maintain military fitness and prepare kings and nobles on horseback for battle. By the 16th century, the increasing popularity of the bloody spectacle had aroused such indignation in the Vatican that Pope Pius V decreed in 1567 that 'exhibitions of tortured beasts or bulls are contrary to Christian duty and piety'. The penalty for violating this decree (which has never been repealed) is excommunication. Only the gory death of a Portuguese nobleman, Count dos Arcos, in 1799, resulted in a less blatantly cruel version of the *tourada* in Portugal: from then on, public slaughter of the bulls was prohibited. Today's *cavaleiro* still wears a black handkerchief around his neck in remembrance of the count. ∎

(in the sun). The *sol e sombra* seats provide some shade as the sun moves around, while the most expensive tickets are for the always-shady *sombra* seats.

See Cruelty to Animals under Ecology & Environment in the Facts about the Country chapter for the more details on the unpleasant side of the sport.

THINGS TO BUY
Gourmet Products
Port wine, Portugal's best known export, is also one of the most accessible purchases for visitors. To pick up some at the source, visit one or two of the port-wine lodges in Vila Nova de Gaia, across the river from Porto.

Other worthy consumables are olive oil, numerous varieties of fresh olives, and a mouth-watering range of honeys from all over the country.

Linen, Cotton & Lace
Among modestly priced items you'll see on sale everywhere, but especially in Minho resorts including Viana do Castelo, are hand-embroidered linen and cotton; traditional costumes (in children's sizes too); and lace-work, traditionally a speciality of coastal fishing towns. Castelo Branco (Beiras) is known for embroidered bed covers. Embroidered tablecloths are a common item at the Gypsy markets that materialise regularly on the outskirts of most Portuguese towns – but bargain hard. The home of Portuguese-style bobbin lace is Vila do Conde, north of Porto, though quality work also comes from the eastern Algarve.

Ceramics
Another affordable purchase is ceramics, and not just the trademark Barcelos cockerel that appears *ad nauseam* in every gift shop in the country. Among quality pottery, both practical and decorative, are the famous black pots of Trás-os-Montes, the unique cabbage-leaf crockery of Caldas da Rainha (Estremadura), the earthenware jugs of Estremoz (Alentejo), and some interesting work from Barcelos itself. At São Pedro do

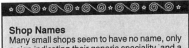

Corval, near Monsaraz (Alentejo), is one of Portugal's largest pottery centres.

Factories in Lisbon and the Algarve turn out fine azulejos, including made-to-order versions, though these aren't cheap.

Rugs, Jewellery & Leather
Those with more money to spend should consider the hand-stitched carpets of Arraiolos (now made under contract in many parts of the country), earlier versions of which graced manor houses and castles for centuries. Traditional woollen blankets are a speciality of the lower Alentejo, around Castro Verde and Mértola.

Another good-value but pricey purchase is the gold and silver filigree jewellery of the Porto area. Leather goods, especially shoes and bags, are good value; Porto is full of leather and shoe shops, though the leather-workers of Loulé and Almodôvar in the Algarve count themselves among the best.

Other Handicrafts
Within range for those on a budget is rush, palm or wicker basketwork, available throughout the country and best tracked down in municipal markets. Trás-os-Montes in general is a good place for woven goods and tapestries, and Trás-os-Montes, Beira Alta and Beira Baixa are good for wrought-iron work. Around Nazaré (Estremadura) look for inexpensive, woollen pullovers.

The Alentejo is known for its simple hand-painted wooden furniture; a large handicraft centre for this and other crafts is at Reguengos de Monsaraz. Alentejo also abounds in cheap souvenirs of native cork.

Artesanatos

Finally, even if you won't be travelling widely, keep in mind that certain quality handicraft shops (artesanatos) in Lisbon (eg Santos Ofícios in the Baixa) and Porto (eg CRAT in the Ribeira) showcase excellent work from all around the country. You'll also come across good local shops selling regional crafts and other specialities. An example is Casa da Serra in Salir, north of Loulé (itself an important centre for handicrafts of many sorts). For more on the crafts of the Algarve and Alentejo in particular, see the excellent regional guide by John & Madge Measures, *Southern Portugal: Its People, Traditions & Wildlife*.

Tax Refunds

Visitors resident outside the EU can, under certain circumstances, claim refunds on IVA, Portugal's 17% sales tax. See Taxes & Refunds under Money in this chapter for more about how and when to do this.

Getting There & Away

The only air gateways in and out of mainland Portugal are at Lisbon, Porto and Faro. Madeira's international airport is at Funchal, and the Azores' is at Ponta Delgada.

All overland connections to Portugal go through Spain, of course. The two main rail crossings are at Vilar Formoso (the Paris to Lisbon line) and Marvão-Beirã (the Madrid to Lisbon line). Two other important crossings are at Valença do Minho (Vigo in Spain to Porto) and Elvas (Badajoz in Spain to Lisbon).

Of the dozens of highway crossings, the ones with fast, high-capacity roads on both sides are at Valença do Minho, Feces de Abajo (Chaves), Vilar Formoso (Guarda), Elvas, Vila Verde de Ficalho (Serpa) and Vila Real de Santo António. Land border controls between the two countries have virtually disappeared.

AIR

The information in this section is particularly vulnerable to change: international airfares are volatile, schedules mutate, deals come and go, visa requirements change. Governments and airlines seem to take perverse pleasure in making regulations and price structures as complicated as possible.

Airports & Airlines

Portugal's international airports are at Lisbon, Porto and Faro. International carriers with scheduled services to/from *all three* airports include TAP (Air Portugal, the country's flagship carrier), Portugália (Portugal's main domestic airline, which also has some European connections), British Airways (BA), Lufthansa, Luxair and Air Liberté.

Other airlines that serve Lisbon and Porto only are Alitalia, Iberia, KLM, Sabena, Swissair, Varig and Viasa. Those that fly only to/from Lisbon include Aeroflot, Air France, Air Malta, Condor, Delta, Lauda Air, Royal Air Maroc, SAS, TAAG (Angola Airlines), Transavia, Tunis Air and TWA.

Funchal, Madeira's international airport, is served by TAP, BA, Condor and Transavia; Ponta Delgada, the Azores' international airport, is only served by TAP.

Buying Tickets

Some travel agencies just handle tours, whereas a good full-service agency can arrange everything from tours and tickets to car rental and hotel bookings. But if all you want is a cheap flight, then you need an agency specialising in discounted tickets.

Though the airlines' own best fares will give you a point of reference, they're rarely the lowest. Various types of discounted tickets can save you a lot and/or increase the scope of your travel at marginal extra cost. Shop around, and start early – some cheap tickets must be purchased months in advance. Check the travel ads in major newspapers.

Some good deals are offered by London's 'bucket shops' (see the boxed aside), but not all of them are straight shooters. Increasingly, however, these outfits are going respectable as 'consolidators' – that is, official outlets for the airlines' discounted and last-minute tickets. If you have a preferred airline, this may be your best bet for a cheap ticket. Call and ask the airline who its consolidators are.

You're safest if an agency is a member of the International Air Transport Association (IATA) or a national association such as the American Society of Travel Agents (ASTA) in the USA, the Association of British Travel Agents (ABTA) in the UK or the Australian Federation of Travel Agents (AFTA) in Australia. If you've bought your ticket from a member agency which then goes out of business, the association will guarantee a refund or an alternative. Member agencies must also have professional indemnity insurance (which functions as a secondary safety net).

Airfares

Destination	Cost	Airline	Validity
London-Lisbon*	£260	TAP	one month
London-Porto*	£260	TAP	one month
London-Faro*	£260	TAP	one month
Frankfurt-Lisbon	DM715	–	–
Paris-Lisbon	1290FF	Air Liberté	–
Brussels-Lisbon	Bf 13,710	Portugália	one month
New York-Lisbon	US$785	TWA	–
Sydney-Lisbon	A$2240	KLM	–
Melbourne-Lisbon	A$1959	Thai/Alitalia	–

* £228; valid for one year for students and those under 26

Recommended are the youth-oriented agencies, including Trailfinders and Campus Travel (UK), Council Travel (USA), Travel CUTS (Canada) and STA Travel (worldwide), which specialise in finding low airfares. Most offer the best deals to students and under-26s but they are open to all, and they won't play tricks on you. All are members of their national travel-agent associations.

Portugal Airfares

The table above gives the best nonstudent discounted airfares we found. It is meant to be indicative only, and does not include all possible points of origin. Fares quoted in this section are approximate discounted, economy, *return* fares during peak air-travel season, based on advertised rates at the time of writing. None of them constitutes a recommendation for any airline.

Fares tend to be 40% to 50% lower outside of peak season (in North America and Europe, peak season is roughly June to mid-September plus Christmas, and 'shoulder season' is April-May and mid-September to October; peak season is roughly December-January in Australia and New Zealand).

Travellers with Special Needs

If you have special requirements – eg you're in a wheelchair, taking the baby, terrified of flying, vegetarian – let the airline know when you book. Restate your needs when you reconfirm, and again when you check in at the airport. It may also be worth ringing round the airlines before you book to find out how each one would handle your particular needs.

Airports and airlines can be surprisingly helpful, but they do need advance warning. Most international airports can provide escorts from check-in to the plane, and most have ramps, lifts, accessible toilets and telephones. Aircraft toilets, on the other hand, present problems for wheelchair travellers, who should discuss this early on with the airline and/or their doctor.

Guide dogs for the blind will often have to travel in a specially pressurised baggage compartment with other animals, away from their owner, though smaller guide dogs may be admitted to the cabin. Guide dogs are subject to the same stiff quarantine laws as any other animal entering or returning to rabies-free countries, such as Britain or Australia.

Deaf travellers can ask for airport and in-flight announcements to be written down for them.

Flying with Children

Children under two travel for 10% of the standard fare (or free, on some airlines), as long as they don't occupy a seat. They don't get a baggage allowance. Bassinets or 'skycots' – for children weighing up to about 10 kg – can usually be provided by the airline if requested in advance. Children between two and 12 can usually occupy a seat for half to two-thirds the full fare, and do get a baggage allowance. Pushchairs (strollers) can often be taken as hand luggage.

The USA & Canada

The Los Angeles *Times*, San Francisco *Examiner*, Chicago *Tribune*, New York *Times*, Toronto *Globe & Mail* and Vancouver *Sun* have big weekly travel sections with lots of travel-agent ads.

Council Travel and STA Travel are reliable sources of cheap tickets in the USA. Each has offices all over the country. Council's toll-free number in the USA and Canada is ☎ 800-223-7402; STA's is ☎ 800-777-0112, and http://www.statravel.com is its Internet address. Canada's best bargain-ticket agency is Travel CUTS, with some 50 offices in major cities. The parent office (☎ 416-979-2406) is at 187 College St, Toronto M5T 1P7.

TWA, Delta and TAP have daily direct flights from New York to Lisbon in summer; Sabena also flies New York-Lisbon. Non-direct connections to Lisbon include: Iberia daily from New York and Los Angeles and three times a week from Montreal, via Madrid; KLM daily from New York via Amsterdam; TWA daily from Los Angeles and San Francisco via New York; and BA daily from Los Angeles, San Francisco and Vancouver via London.

The UK

The Saturday *Independent* and Sunday *Times* have good travel sections, and advertisements for scores of bucket shops. Also see the Travel Classifieds in London's weekly *Time Out* entertainment magazine.

The UK's best known bargain-ticket agencies are Trailfinders (☎ 0171-937 5400) at 42-48 Earl's Court Rd, Kensington, London W8 6EJ; Campus Travel (☎ 0171-730 3402) at 52 Grosvenor Gardens, London SW1W 0AG; and STA (☎ 0171-938 4711) at Priory House, 6 Wrights Lane, London W8 6TA.

All have branches throughout London and the UK, and Campus Travel is also in many Hostelling International (HI) shops.

Among Portugal-specialist agencies in London are Abreu (☎ 0171-229 9905) and Latitude 40 (☎ 0171-229 3164). ICEP, the Portuguese national tourist office (☎ 0171-494 1441; fax 0171-494 1868), can provide an exhaustive list of cooperating UK travel agencies, called *Tour Operators' Guide: Portugal.*

In summer, both TAP (☎ 0171-828 0262) and BA (☎ 0181-897 4000) fly from London (Heathrow), three times a day to Lisbon and daily to Porto. To Faro, TAP departs daily from London (Heathrow), BA once or twice a day from London (Gatwick). To Funchal (Madeira), TAP flies twice a week from Heathrow and BA three times a week from Gatwick. Both airlines offer youth and student fares.

Cheap package deals or flight-only arrangements on charter flights offer the possibility of even better deals. Most of these are London-Faro, for as little as £100 to £150 return. Combined with a Faro-Lisbon coach ride, this could be the cheapest way to get to Lisbon. Check with your own travel agency

---

Bucket Shops

In London (and certain Asian capitals, notably Delhi and Bangkok) you'll find that the lowest fares are offered by obscure, unbonded agencies taking advantage of last-minute airline discounts and other deals. Many are honest and solvent, but not all. Don't part with even a deposit until you know the date and time of the flights, the name of the airline (both outward and return), airports of departure and destination, long layovers and any restrictions. If the agent won't give this information, go elsewhere.

Watch for 'surcharges'; booking fees should not be necessary as agents get commissions from the airlines. Ask whether all your money will be refunded if the flight is cancelled or changed to a date that is unacceptable to you. Once you have the ticket, ring the airline yourself to confirm that you're actually booked on the flight. ∎

or see the newspaper travel sections. Bear in mind that charter flights have fixed dates and involve high withdrawal penalties.

France

Since France, and Paris in particular, has a huge population of Portuguese immigrants, there are frequent scheduled flights at reasonable prices to/from Paris. Summer flights from Paris (Orly) to Lisbon include four a day by TAP and one a day each by Air France, Air Liberté and Air Inter Europe;

Air Travel Glossary

Apex Apex, or 'advance purchase excursion' is a discounted ticket that must be paid for in advance. If you have to cancel or change an Apex ticket there are often heavy penalties; insurance can sometimes be taken out against these penalties.

Baggage Allowance This will be written on your ticket: usually one 20-kg item to go in the hold, plus one item of hand luggage.

Bucket Shop An unbonded travel agency specialising in discounted airline tickets.

Check In Airlines ask you to check in a certain time ahead of the flight departure (usually 1½ hours on international flights). If you fail to check in on time and the flight is overbooked, the airline can cancel your booking and give your seat to someone else.

Confirmation Having a ticket showing the flight and date you want doesn't mean you have a seat until the travel agent has checked with the airline that your status is 'OK' or confirmed. Meanwhile you could just be 'on request'.

Consolidator An air ticket broker which sells discounted tickets by agreement with selected airline companies.

Discounted Tickets There are two types of discounted fares: officially discounted (see Promotional Fares) and unofficially discounted. The lowest prices often impose drawbacks such as flying with unpopular airlines, inconvenient schedules, or unpleasant routes and connections. A discounted ticket can save you things other than money – you may be able to pay Apex prices without the associated Apex advance booking and other requirements. Discounted tickets only exist where there is fierce competition.

Full Fares Airlines traditionally offer 1st-class (coded F), business class (coded J) and economy-class (coded Y) tickets. These days there are so many promotional and discounted fares available from the regular economy class that few passengers pay full economy fare.

Lost Tickets If you lose your airline ticket, an airline will usually treat it like a travellers cheque and, after enquiries, issue you with another one. Legally, however, an airline is entitled to treat it like cash, which means that if you lose it, it's gone forever. Take good care of your tickets.

On Request An unconfirmed booking for a flight; see Confirmation.

Open Jaws A return ticket where you fly out to one place but return from another. This can save you backtracking to your arrival point.

Overbooking Airlines hate to fly with empty seats and since every flight has some passengers who fail to show up, airlines often book more passengers than they have seats. Usually the excess passengers balance those who fail to show up but occasionally somebody gets 'bumped' from the flight. If this happens, guess who it's most likely to be? The passengers who check in late.

Promotional Fares Officially discounted fares such as Apex fares, available from travel agents or directly from the airline.

Reconfirmation At least 72 hours prior to departure time of an onward or return flight you must contact the airline and 'reconfirm' that you intend to be on the flight. If you don't do this, the airline can delete your name from the passenger list and you could lose your seat. You don't have to reconfirm the first flight on your itinerary, nor any others following stopovers of less than 72 hours.

Transferred Tickets Airline tickets cannot be transferred from one person to another. Travellers sometimes try to sell the return half of their ticket, but officials can ask you to prove that you are the person named on the ticket. This is unlikely to happen on domestic flights, but on an international flight tickets may be compared with passports.

Travel Periods Some officially discounted fares, Apex fares in particular, vary with the time of year. There is often a low (off-peak) season and a high (peak) season. Sometimes there's an intermediate or shoulder season as well. At peak times, when everyone wants to fly, not only will the officially discounted fares be higher but so will unofficially discounted fares. Usually the total fare depends on the time of your outward flight – if you depart in the high season and return in the low season, you pay the high-season fare. ■

from Paris (de Gaulle), Air France and Air Inter Europe each fly at least two or three times a day.

From Orly to Porto, TAP goes at least three times a day, and Air Liberté and Air Inter Europe approximately daily. Flights from Orly to Faro go twice a week with TAP and once a week with Air Liberté. TAP goes nonstop from Orly to Funchal twice a week. On most days of the week Portugália flies from Bordeaux, Lyon and Toulouse to Porto (via Madrid).

STA Travel has offices in Paris; the main one is at CTS Voyages (☎ 01 43 25 00 76), 20 Rue des Carmes, 75005 Paris.

Air France is at ☎ 01 44 08 24 24 (or ☎ 01 44 08 22 22 for reservations), and TAP is at ☎ 01 44 86 89 89. Both offer discounted youth/student prices.

The Rest of Europe

A reliable source of bargain tickets within the Netherlands is NBBS Reizen, at Schilphoweg 101, 2300 AJ Leiden (☎ 071-523 2020; fax 071-522 6475), with over 50 'travelshops' and 'Budgetair' counters in post offices around the country.

There are abundant summer flights to Portugal from Germany. The major scheduled carriers are Lufthansa, TAP, Portugália and Iberia, and the major corridors Frankfurt-Lisbon and Frankfurt-Porto, with several daily flights on each. But there are also daily connections to Lisbon from Berlin, Dresden, Hamburg and Munich, and to Porto from Dresden and Nuremburg. At least three flights a week go to Faro from Frankfurt, Düsseldorf, Hamburg, Munich and Stuttgart. Other cities with Portugal connections are Cologne and Hanover.

Other major European departure points are Amsterdam, Brussels and Madrid. KLM flies direct from Amsterdam to both Lisbon and Porto daily, and TAP does so nearly every day. From Brussels, TAP and Sabena have at least two direct flights a day to Lisbon and Sabena goes daily to Porto. Portugália flies from Brussels to Lisbon and Porto daily except Saturday. From Madrid, TAP goes to Lisbon four to six times a day;

Portugália and Iberia go to both Lisbon and Porto several times a day.

Portugália flies from Turin, Basel, Copenhagen and Stockholm to Lisbon, Porto and Faro at least four or five times a week, via Madrid. TAP has a weekly Zürich-Geneva-Faro connection.

Among TAP's international connections to Funchal (Madeira) in summer are two a week from Madrid and weekly from Zürich. Transavia flies twice a week from Amsterdam, and Condor weekly from Düsseldorf, Frankfurt, Hamburg, Munich and Stuttgart. To Ponta Delgada (Azores), TAP flies once a week from Frankfurt.

Australia & New Zealand

STA Travel and Flight Centres International are major dealers in cheap airfares, each with dozens of offices. STA's headquarters are at 1st Floor, 224 Faraday St, Carlton, Victoria 3053, Australia (☎ 03-9347 6911; fax 03-9347 0608), and 10 High St, PO Box 4156, Auckland, New Zealand (☎ 09-309 9995; fax 09-309 9829). Flight Centre's main offices in Australia are at 19 Bourke St, Melbourne, Victoria 3000 (☎ 03-9650 2899; fax 03-9550 3751), and 82 Elizabeth St, Sydney, NSW 2000 (☎ 02-9235 3522; fax 02-9235 2871).

BUS

The cheapest way to travel around Europe is by coach, and the easiest way to arrange it is through Eurolines, a consortium of coach operators with offices all over Europe. A coach trip from the UK to Portugal can be pretty tedious, though Eurolines' coaches are fairly comfortable, with on-board toilets reclining seats, and sometimes air-con. They stop frequently for meals, though you'll save a bit by packing your own munchies (along with plenty of reading).

Discounts depend on the route, but children from four to 12 years old typically get 30% to 40% off; youth/student and senior discounts are rare or minimal. Fares given here are adult fares. You can usually get away with booking even long-distance journeys a few days ahead, though earlier booking is a good idea in summer.

Among some 200 Eurolines offices in Europe are the following:

Amsterdam
    Eurolines, Rokin 10 (☎ 020-627 5151; fax 020-627 5167)
Frankfurt
    Deutsche Touring, Am Romerhof 17 (☎ 069-790 353; fax 069-706 059)
London
    Eurolines, 52 Grosvenor Gardens, London SW1 (bookings ☎ 0990-143 219, information ☎ 0171-730 8235; fax 0171-730 8721)
Madrid
    SAIA, Estación Sur de Autobuses (☎ 91-530 76 00; fax 91-327 13 29)
Paris
    Eurolines, Gare Routière Internationale de Paris, Avenue de Général de Gaulle, Bagnolet (☎ 01 49 72 51 51; fax 01 49 72 51 61)

Portugal's main Eurolines affiliates are Internorte, Intercentro and EVA/Intersul which, as the names suggest, are based in northern, central and southern Portugal:

Internorte
    Praça da Galiza 96, Porto (☎ 02-609 32 20; fax 02-609 95 70)
Intercentro
    Rua Actor Taborda 55, a block from the main bus station in Lisbon (☎ 01-357 17 45; fax 01-357 00 39)
EVA/Intersul
    Avenida da República Guinée Bissau, Setúbal (☎ 065-520 17 20; fax 065-520 17 29)

The UK

Intercentro/Eurolines has a year-round London-Lisbon service (via Coimbra and Fátima) departing from Victoria Coach Station five times a week. It also has separate coaches to Faro and Lagos twice a week, with additional weekend services in summer. All involve a three-hour lay over and a change of coach in Paris. The adult one-way/return fare to any of these destinations is £112/142. Allow about 40 hours for London-Lisbon.

A separate direct London-Porto service (via Guarda, Viseu and other points) with Internorte/Eurolines departs on Saturday during summer and Christmas-New Year seasons only, for £79/141.

Spain

Internorte/Eurolines runs coaches between Madrid and Porto (via Salamanca) four times a week for about 5200/9800 ptas (6300$00/11,900$00) one way/return. The regional line Rodonorte links Valladolid to Porto on weekdays for 3200 ptas (3900$00).

Intercentro/Eurolines operates services three times a week between Madrid and Lisbon, an 11-hour trip costing about 5900/9400 ptas (7100$00/11,300$00); from April through September this starts at Barcelona. SAIA Eurolines has a Salamanca-Lisbon service three times a week for 3900/7000 ptas (4700$00/8500$00). All of these stop at major intermediate towns as well.

The Algarve coach line EVA runs express buses twice a day between Seville and Faro (via Vila Real de Santo António), a four-hour trip for about 1650/2970 ptas (2000$00/3600$00). Between April and November, Intersul/Eurolines runs from Seville to Lagos four times a week for about 2400/4300 ptas (2900$00/5200$00).

The Rest of Europe

Eurolines France offers a range of Portugal connections, including Paris to Lisbon (a 26½-hour jaunt, or 24 hours by express service) five times a week, for 695/995FF (one way/return) and Paris-Braga five times a week for 680/995FF.

The private line IASA (☎ 01 43 53 90 82, fax 01 43 53 49 57 in Paris; ☎ 01-793 64 51, fax 01-793 62 76 in Lisbon; ☎ 02-208 43 38, fax 02-31 01 91 in Porto) runs deluxe coaches five times a week, between Paris and Porto (via Braga) for 450FF, and between Paris and Lisbon (via Coimbra) for 480FF.

From Hamburg and Hanover, the German Eurolines affiliate runs twice a week to Lisbon for about DM260/410, twice a week to Porto for DM250/400 and once a week to Faro and Lagos for DM280/460. Fares from Cologne and Düsseldorf are slightly lower.

TRAIN

Trains are a popular way to get around Europe – comfortable, frequent and generally on time – and a good place to meet other travellers. They're cheaper than flying (except in the case of charter flights from the UK; see Air in this chapter), but still expensive unless you have one of several available rail passes (see the following section).

Tickets cannot be purchased on the train, only from departure stations or from a travel agent. You'll have little problem buying a long-distance ticket as little as a day or two ahead, even in summer. Paris, Amsterdam, Munich and Vienna are major western European rail hubs, and convenient points of departure or arrival.

If you intend to do a lot of rail travel, consider getting a copy of the *Thomas Cook European Timetable*, updated monthly with a complete listing of train schedules, plus information on reservations and supplements. Single issues are about £10 from Thomas Cook Publishing, PO Box 227, Peterborough PE3 8BQ, UK. Thomas Cook also publishes *Spain & Portugal by Rail* (see Books in the Facts for the Visitor chapter).

International trains are a favourite target for thieves, so always carry your valuables around with you, keep your bags in sight (or at least chained to the luggage rack), and make sure your compartment is securely locked at night.

Routes into Portugal

There are two standard long-distance rail journeys into Portugal. One takes the TGV Atlantique from Paris to Irún in Spain (where you must change trains), then the *Rápido Sud-Expresso* across Spain via Vilar Formoso in Portugal to Pampilhosa (where you can change for Porto), and south to Lisbon. The other route runs from Paris to Madrid, where you can catch the Talgo *Lusitânia Express* via Marvão-Beirã in Portugal to Encontramento (with connections for Porto), and on to Lisbon. Change at Lisbon for the Algarve.

Two well-used routes originating in Spain are Vigo-Porto, crossing at Valença do Minho in Portugal, and Badajoz-Elvas-Lisbon, crossing at Caia in Portugal. In the south you can ride the train west from Seville to Huelva, but for Algarve destinations you must change for Ayamonte and then bus across the border to pick up a Portuguese train at Vila Real de Santo António.

Rail Passes

Unless you're planning only very limited rail travel, it makes financial sense to get a rail pass. In addition to the following passes, others are available only in certain countries – eg Billets Internationaux de Jeunesse (BIJ) in France. Even with one of these you'll still have to pay for seat and couchette reservations, and other supplements.

Inter-Rail Inter-Rail passes are available only to residents of European countries (eg in the UK you must prove that you have been resident for at least six months). You can make no claims if your Inter-Rail card is lost or stolen.

The Inter-Rail pass for those under 26 is by zone: zone A is Ireland and the UK; zone E is France, Belgium, the Netherlands and Luxembourg; zone F is Spain, Portugal and Morocco, etc. A one-zone pass is good for 15 specified, consecutive days travel; the 2nd-class price is UK£185. Multizone passes are good for one month's travel and are better value, eg two zones is UK£220 (53,000$00), three zones UK£245 (59,000$00) and all zones UK£275 (66,400$00). Fare reductions are minimal, if at all, in the country where you buy the pass.

Although there is an Inter-Rail pass for those over 26, it's not valid for travel in Portugal.

Rail Europ Senior Card This card, which is available to women over 60 and men over 65, can bring you discounts of around 30% on international tickets, including to Portugal. To be eligible for this card you must have a local senior citizens' railcard. In Britain you can get a Senior Card and a Rail Europ Senior Card from accredited British Rail

International travel agencies, and from main-line stations.

Eurailpass Eurail pass is the Inter-Rail counterpart for non-European residents, though it's not as good a bargain. A Eurail pass is valid for unlimited rail travel in certain European countries, including Portugal (plus France, Germany and a dozen others, but not the UK). The one for under-26ers is called a Eurail pass Youth Flexi-Pass, and there are numerous options; eg any 10 days travel within two months is about US$550, and any 15 days within one month is about US$760. There is also an over-26 version, as well as passes for couples and for children.

Eurail passes are meant to be purchased before you get to Europe, although you can buy them at a few European locations for a higher price, provided your passport shows you've been in Europe for less than six months. For example, in the UK you can get them from the SNCF (French railways; ☎ 0171-803 3030) in London.

Portuguese Pass Caminos de Ferro Portugueses (CP), the Portuguese national railway, sells youth-oriented, discounted *bilhetes de grupo* for international connections from Portugal to other EU countries, for groups of two to five people aged 16 or younger.

One-Country Pass Some passes are only for travel within a single country. Under-26 travellers can buy a Euro-Domino Pass (called a Freedom Pass in the UK), good for 2nd-class travel only, for a selected number of consecutive days within a specified month. For Portugal, the cost (if purchased in the UK) is £79 (19,000$00) for three days, £99 (23,000$00) for five days or £139 (35,000$00) for 10 days.

Eurotrain in the UK (see the following section) and Tagus Travel in Portugal offer the still cheaper Explorer Pass, for a chosen number of consecutive days travel within the validity period of the pass, which is from the date of purchase until the following 31 October.

For 2nd-class travel in Portugal this is £48 (11,600$00) for seven days, £81 (19,500$00) for 14 days or £120 (28,900$00) for 21 days; there are also 1st-class options.

As with Inter-Rail tickets, these passes are only available to residents of European countries.

The UK

The Channel Tunnel can shorten a London-Lisbon rail journey by about six hours, but at present it's more expensive than flying. For more information on the Eurostar train service through the tunnel from London (Waterloo) to Paris (Nord), contact Eurostar at ☎ 01233-617 575 in the UK, or the SNCF (French railways) at ☎ 01 45 82 50 50 in Paris (they also have a web site at http://web.sncf.fr).

The normal cheap route is still from London's Victoria Station via UK-France ferries – usually Dover-Calais, sometimes Newhaven-Dieppe – a change of trains at Paris (and a change of stations, from Nord to Austerlitz or Montparnasse; fairly straightforward via the Paris metro), plus another change at either the Spanish border (Irún) or in Madrid.

There are daily departures from London (Victoria Station). If you're headed for Irún you must spend the night and half the next day in Paris. In this case, the quickest time for London to Lisbon is about 50 hours. It's possible on most days to make a tight connection right out of Paris to Madrid, but then you'll have to spend the day in Madrid instead, with a total London-Lisbon time of just two or three hours less. The return trip either way requires an overnight in Paris.

A one-way, 2nd-class adult fare for London-Lisbon is £127 (30,600$00). The corresponding under-26 fare is £107 (25,800$00); the price for seniors is £95 (22,900$00). In all cases a sleeper would cost an additional £32 (7700$00). Tickets are valid for two months, and you can break the journey en route.

For 26-&-over information and tickets, contact British Rail's 'International Rail' division (☎ 0171-834 2345; fax 0171-922

9874). A good source of under-26 bargains is Eurotrain, a service of Campus Travel (☎ 0171-730 3402), 52 Grosvenor Gardens, London SW1W 0AG.

France

The daily train journey from Paris (Montparnasse) takes 21 hours to Lisbon, a little less to Porto. A 2nd-class reserved seat to Lisbon is about 730FF (22,080$00), a six-person sleeper *(beliche)* about 810FF (24,250$00) per person, and a double sleeper 980FF (29,510$00).

Spain

The main rail route is from Madrid to Lisbon via Marvão-Beirã. The nightly journey on the Talgo *Lusitânia Express* takes 10½ hours; a 2nd-class seat is 6650 ptas (8070$00) one way, while a berth in a *turista* (four-person) sleeper is 8940 ptas (10,840$00).

The daily Paris to Lisbon/Porto train (see the preceding section) goes via San Sebastián, Vitória, Burgos, Valladolid and Salamanca in Spain; a 2nd-class reserved seat from Salamanca to Porto, for example, would be about 3670 ptas (4450$00), a sleeper 5750 ptas (6980$00). Expresses run on the Vigo to Porto route three times a day.

Connections are tedious on the Badajoz to Lisbon route (two trains a day, mostly slow regional services, with a possible train change at Entroncamento), but the scenery through the Serra de Marvão is grand. Connections are equally tedious from Seville into the Algarve (change at Huelva for Ayamonte, then take a bus across the border from there to Vila Real de Santo António), though there are four daily Seville-Ayamonte trains, and on the Portugal side four fast interregional trains to Faro, two of them continuing to Lagos.

CAR & MOTORCYCLE

Roads cross the Portugal-Spain border in at least 30 places. The easiest crossings (ie the best and biggest roads) are at Valença do Minho, Feces de Abajo (Chaves), Vilar Formoso, Elvas, Vila Verde de Ficalho (Serpa) and Vila Real de Santo António.

Portugal's national auto club, the Automóvel Club de Portugal, says that virtually all cross-border roads are now open 24 hours a day, usually with no-one even in sight at the border.

Insurance & Documents

If you're driving your own car into Portugal, in addition to your passport and driving licence you must carry vehicle registration (proof of ownership) and insurance documents. If these are in order, you should be able to keep the car in the country for up to six months.

Nationals of EU countries need only their home driving licences. Others should consider getting an International Driving Permit as well, through the automobile licensing department in your home country (you can't usually obtain one in a country other than your own). Some travel agents suggest that the international permits seem to be of diminishing interest to traffic police in Portugal.

If people other than the registered owner are to drive the car, they'll need written authorisation from the owner. For guidance on how to prepare such a document and validate it, contact your national automobile licensing department or auto club, or the nearest Portuguese consular office.

Motor vehicle insurance with at least third-party coverage is compulsory throughout the EU. Your home policy may or may not be extendable to Portugal, and the coverage of some European comprehensive policies is automatically reduced to third-party-only outside your home country, unless the insurer is notified. It's a good idea (though not a legal requirement) to get a 'Green Card' from your home insurer before you leave home; this confirms that you have comprehensive coverage.

If you're stopped by the Portuguese police, you probably won't be allowed to go back to your hotel to fetch these documents. Carry them with you whenever you're driving. If you hire a car, the hiring firm will furnish you with registration and insurance documentation, plus a rental contract.

The UK & France

The quickest route to Portugal from the UK is by ferry to northern Spain – from Plymouth to Santander with Brittany Ferries (☎ 0990-360 360) or from Portsmouth to Bilbao with P&O Ferries (information ☎ 0990-980 111; bookings ☎ 0990-980 222).

Both lines do the crossing twice a week in summer, taking about 28 hours. Peak fares (eg, about £400 for a car, driver and one passenger, and accommodation in a basic two-berth cabin) apply from mid-July to mid-August, tapering to their cheapest levels (about £250 for the same example) from October (Brittany) or November (P&O) through March. From Santander it's roughly 1000 km to Lisbon, 800 km to Porto or 1300 km to Faro.

An alternative is to take a ferry or the Channel Tunnel to France and motor down the coast via Bordeaux, through Spain (via Burgos and Salamanca) into Portugal. From the channel ports of France it's roughly 1900 km to Lisbon, 1800 km to Porto or 2200 km to Faro.

One option to reduce driving time for those using this route, or starting in France, is to use motorail (car transport by rail) for all or part of the trip through France. For information in the UK call the SNCF (French railways; information ☎ 0171-803 3030; bookings ☎ 0345-300 003; URL http://web.sncf.fr). In France, the SNCF has a nationwide telephone number (☎ 08 36 35 35 35 in French, ☎ 08 36 35 35 39 in English) for all rail enquiries and reservations.

There is also said to be a motorail service between Madrid and Lisbon.

BICYCLE

Before you leave home, go over your bike with a fine-toothed comb and fill your repair kit with every imaginable spare. You probably won't be able to buy that crucial gizmo for your machine when it breaks down somewhere in the back of beyond as the sun sets.

For information on cycling around Portugal, see Activities in the Facts for the Visitor chapter, and the Bicycle section in the Getting Around chapter.

Documents

As a 'driver' in Portugal, you're expected to have a driving licence; see Car & Motorcycle in the preceding section about licences. Like cars, bicycles are registered in Portugal, and it's a good idea to pack some sort of document showing you to be the owner of your vehicle, in the unlikely event that the police stop you. Some cyclists also carry a photograph and written description of their bicycles, to assist the police in the event that it's stolen.

Getting Your Bicycle to Portugal

Bicycles can travel by air. You *can* take yours to pieces and put it in a bag or box, but it's much easier to simply wheel it to the check-in desk, where it should be treated as baggage. Check this with the airline well in advance, preferably before you pay for your ticket.

You may have to remove the pedals, turn the handlebars sideways and drop the saddle down so that the bike takes up less space in the aircraft's hold. It's also not a bad idea to protect scratchable surfaces with plastic bubble-wrap. Let much (but not all) of the air out of the tyres to prevent them from bursting in the low-pressure baggage hold.

If you're getting to Portugal by train, your bike may be registered and sent separately to your destination, or may accompany you, usually for an extra charge.

BOAT

The only passenger ships that call at Portuguese ports nowadays are cruise ships. Once there were scheduled connections between Faro (and other Algarve ports) and North Africa, but no more. Ferries can be a part of a journey by car from the UK, however; see Car & Motorcycle in this chapter.

Car ferries crisscross the Rio Guadiana between Vila Real de Santo António (Portugal) and Ayamonte (Spain), for 165$00 per person or 950$00 per car and driver.

LEAVING PORTUGAL

For air, bus or train fares *out* of Portugal, try the youth travel agencies Tagus Travel (☎ 01-352 55 09) or Jumbo Expresso (☎ 01-793 92 64), or the Top Tours agency (☎ 01-315 58 85), all in Lisbon. Tagus also has offices in Porto, Coimbra and Braga.

Direct airline booking numbers are listed under Lisbon, Porto and Faro; in addition, country-wide numbers are available for TAP (☎ 0808-21 31 41, at local rates from anywhere in Portugal) and BA (☎ 0500-1251, toll-free from anywhere in Portugal).

Departure Taxes

Portugal's departure tax for any international flight is 1950$00. This is included in the price of any ticket from a scheduled carrier, but payable at check-in in the case of a charter flight.

Domestic departure tax depends on your destination; eg 780$00 for a Faro-Lisbon flight. This is also included in the ticket price.

WARNING

The information in this chapter is particularly vulnerable to change: prices for international travel are volatile, routes are introduced and cancelled, schedules change, special deals come and go, and rules and visa requirements are amended. Airlines and governments seem to take a perverse pleasure in making price structures and regulations as complicated as possible. You should check directly with the airline or a travel agent to make sure you understand how a fare (and ticket you may buy) works. In addition, the travel industry is highly competitive and there are many lurks and perks.

The upshot of this is that you should get opinions, quotes and advice from as many airlines and travel agents as possible before you part with your hard-earned cash. The details given in this chapter should be regarded as pointers and are not a substitute for your own careful, up-to-date research.

Getting Around

AIR

Flights within mainland Portugal are expensive. For the short distances involved they're hardly worth considering – unless you have an under-26 card, which gets you a 50% discount with Portugália, the country's main domestic carrier (Lisbon ☎ 01-840 8999), plus limited discounts from TAP. Convenient places to get under-26 cards *and* book internal flights from Lisbon are Tagus Travel (☎ 01-352 55 09) and Jumbo Expresso (☎ 01-793 92 64); Tagus also has offices in Porto, Coimbra and Braga.

Portugália and TAP both have multiple daily Lisbon-Porto and Lisbon-Faro flights (taking under an hour), year-round. TAP has an evening Lisbon-Faro flight and a morning Faro-Lisbon service connecting with all their international arrivals and departures at Lisbon, plus additional Faro links from April through October. Oddly, there's almost no way to fly Porto-Faro directly. Portugália has one flight from Porto each week, in summer only, and none in the other direction.

Without an under-26 card, a high-season one-way fare (including taxes) with Portugália is about 15,200$00 for Lisbon-Porto and 14,300$00 for Lisbon-Faro. There are no discounts on return tickets.

Only TAP has domestic services to Madeira and the Azores: to Funchal (Madeira) daily from Lisbon and Porto; to Porto Santo (Madeira) every few days from Lisbon and once a week from Porto; to Ponta Delgada (Azores) daily from Lisbon and about every other day from Porto; and daily to Terceira (Azores) and almost-daily to Horta (Azores) from Lisbon. The Azores also have their own airline, SATA Air Açores. From Lisbon, an ordinary return fare to Madeira would be about 32,600$00, and to the Azores about 46,500$00.

BUS

The demise of the state-run Rodoviário Nacional (RN) bus company spawned a host of private local firms, most of them amalgamated into regional companies which together operate a dense network of bus services. The services are of three general types: *expressos*, comfortable, fast, direct coaches between major cities; *rápidas*, fast regional buses; and *carreiras*, which stop at every crossroad. The Algarve line EVA also offers a de luxe category of coaches called *alta qualidade*.

Expressos are generally the best cheap way to get around Portugal (particularly for long trips where the cost per km is lowest), and even in summer you'll have little problem booking a ticket for the next or even the same day. An express coach from Lisbon to Faro takes just under five hours and costs about 2000$00 (2500$00 for the luxury four-hour EVA express); Lisbon-Porto takes 3½ hours for about 1800$00. By contrast the local services, especially up north, can thin out to almost nothing on weekends, especially in summer when school is out.

An under-26 card should get you a discount of about 25%, at least on long-distance services.

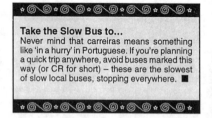

Take the Slow Bus to...
Never mind that carreiras means something like 'in a hurry' in Portuguese. If you're planning a quick trip anywhere, avoid buses marked this way (or CR for short) – these are the slowest of slow local buses, stopping everywhere. ■

TRAIN

If you can match your itinerary and pace to a regional service, travel with Caminhos de Ferro Portugueses (CP), the state railway company, is cheaper than by bus, thanks in part to state subsidies. Trains are generally slower than long-distance buses, though

Timetable Gobbledegook

One thing that will drive bus travellers up the wall is bus timetables *(horários)*. Schedules change frequently (eg between school term and summer holidays, between summer and winter), and may be conditional on religious celebrations and holidays. They often differ for each day of the week (work day, work day after a holiday, market day, Tuesday after a Monday holiday, school days that aren't Saturdays etc). While non-Portuguese speakers will have little trouble with the schedules themselves, the footnotes – which reveal whether a scheduled bus actually departs on the day you want – can be baffling.

Following are some common footnote phrases and their English meanings. Refer to the Language section in the Facts about the Country chapter for the names of months and the days of the week. Sometimes weekdays, instead of being named, are numbered and followed by the *feiras* tag common to all weekday names; thus *2as. feiras (segundas feiras)* means Mondays etc.

a partir de...	beginning on...
aos (Sábados)	on Saturdays
chegada	arrival
de (segunda) a (sexta)	from (Monday) to (Friday)
diariamente or *diário*	daily
dias úteis	working days
efectua(m)-se or *em vigôr*	in force
excepto or *exc* or *não se efectua(m)*	except
feriados nacionais/oficiais	national holidays
ligação de ou para...	connection from/to...
no período de aulas/escolas or nos dias escolares	during school term (ie from early September to late June, except around Easter and Christmas)
partida	departure
se a dia fôr feriado (or *se feriado*)	if it is a holiday
se a dia seguinte a feriado	if it follows a holiday
se vespera de feriado	if it precedes a holiday
só	only
todos os dias	every day

Now you can figure out that *de 16 Set a 30 Jun, aos Sábados (ou 6as. feiras se feriado) e 2as. feiras (ou 3as. feiras se dia seguinte a feriado)* means 'from 16 September to 30 June, on Saturdays (or Friday if the Friday is a holiday) and Mondays (or Tuesday if the Tuesday follows a holiday)'!

Incidentally, timetables are a rare commodity in rural areas; stock up on information at tourist offices or bus stations in major towns. ■

railway lovers consider the pokey pace an additional plus.

Types of Service

CP operates three main levels of service: *regional* trains (marked R on timetables), which stop everywhere and will drive you crazy; reasonably fast *interregional* trains (marked IR); and express trains, called *rápido* or *intercidade* (marked IC). *Alfa* is a special, marginally faster IC service that operates between northern cities (eg Lisbon and Porto). CP's long-distance international connections are marked IN on timetables.

Most trains have both 1st and 2nd-class carriages. Long-distance trains all have restaurant cars, and some have bars.

CP has motorail service (car transport by rail) on most major lines, including Lisbon-Porto and Lisbon-Faro. Fifteen days notice at the departure station is required, and return tickets are valid for two months.

Three of Portugal's most appealing train journeys, on narrow-gauge track climbing up out of the Douro valley, have been emasculated. The Linha da Tâmega, which once ran up from Livração to Mondim de Basto, now goes only as far as Amarante; the Linha da Tua from Tua to Bragança now ends at Mirandela; and the Linha da Corgo, which

Portugal's Railways

0   50   100 km

+++++ Railway
– – – CP Bus Line

once stretched from Peso da Régua to Chaves, has been truncated at Vila Real and the track widened to standard gauge. CP still runs buses on the old Mirandela-Bragança route, and you can use rail passes and train tickets on these.

Tickets, Reservations & Costs

Tickets cannot be purchased on the train, only from the departure station or a travel agent. Discounted and other special tickets can be purchased only at certain 'main-line' stations. There's little point in buying domestic tickets before you arrive in Portugal, but it's possible – eg in the UK from Wasteels (☎ 0171-834 7066; fax 0171-630 7628), 121 Wilton Rd (beside Victoria Station), London SW1V 1JT.

You can book tickets up to 20 days ahead, though in most cases you'll have little problem booking one for the next or even the same day, even in summer. Seat reservations are usually mandatory on IC and Alfa trains. For this, everyone – even rail-pass holders – pays an additional booking charge: 300$00 for IC, variable for Alfa (eg 790$00 for Lisbon-Porto).

Some sample 2nd-class fares from Lisbon are as follows: to Porto – 2950$00 Alfa, 2250$00 IC, 1820$00 IR; to Coimbra – 2150$00 Alfa, 1600$00 IC, 1270$00 IR; to Beja – 1150$00 IC, 980$00 IR; to Faro – 1850$00 IC, 1650$00 IR. The IC and Alfa fares include seat-reservation charges.

All connections from Lisbon southwards (eg to the Algarve) involve a ferry crossing of the Rio Tejo to/from the actual train terminus at Barreiro. This is no longer included in the train fare but in Lisbon you can purchase the 170$00 ferry tickets at the train ticket counter.

Frequent train travellers may want to buy a copy of the *Guia Horário Oficial* (360$00), with CP's complete domestic and international timetables, available from the *bilheteiras* (ticket windows) at major stations, at least in Lisbon.

Discounts Children under the age of four travel free; those from four to 12 years old

travel at half-price. Youth card-holders get 30% off R and IR services only. Travellers over 65 can get a *cartão dourado* (senior card) at ticket counters, entitling them to half-price travel on weekdays, except on suburban commuter trains at rush hour.

Bilhetes turísticos (tourist tickets) valid for seven (17,500$00), 14 (28,300$00) or 21 (40,000$00) days are available, but these are only worthwhile if you plan to spend a great deal of time moving around. There is also a special ticket *(cartão de família)* for parents and one or more children under 18 travelling together on domestic journeys over 150 km at off-peak times. Youth and senior discounts also apply to these special tickets.

See the Train section of the Getting There & Away chapter for information on other rail passes, including some that can be used only within Portugal but must be purchased before you arrive.

CAR & MOTORCYCLE

Driving allows you to go easily into the furthest corners of Portugal, though without the kind of direct contact and familiarity that public transport offers. Thanks to EU subsidies the country's road system is being steadily upgraded; there are now numerous long stretches of highway, including toll roads. Main roads are sealed and generally in good condition. Minor roads in the countryside have surprisingly little traffic, which allows you some space to watch for the frequent potholes.

The real downside of driving here is your road-mates. Courtesy is almost nonexistent. Portuguese drivers, men and women alike, seem guided by two principles: take the

---

Drinking & Driving
The maximum legal blood-alcohol level for anyone behind the wheel is a mere 0.05%. If you drink and drive and are caught, you can expect to spend the night in a lockup, and the next morning in a courtroom. ■

Highways & Toll-Roads

Portugal's modest network of *estradas* (highways) is gradually spreading across the country. Top of the line are *auto-estradas* or motorways, all of them *portagens* (toll-roads). The longest of these is the 304-km Lisbon-Porto road, the shortest the northbound lanes of the two-km Ponte de Abril 25 over the Tejo at Lisbon. Other stretches include Porto-Braga, Porto-Amarante and Lisbon-Cascais. The present total of 575 km of toll-roads charges cars and motorcycles about 9$00 per km (2690$00 for Lisbon-Porto, for example).

Highway nomenclature can be baffling. Motorway numbers prefixed with an E are Europe-wide designations. Portugal's toll-roads are prefixed with an A. Highways in its *rede fundamental* (main network) are prefixed IP, and subsidiary ones in the *rede complementare* IC. Some highways have several designations, and numbers that change in mid-flow; eg the Lisbon-Porto road is variously called E80, E01, A1 and IP1.

Numbers for the main two-lane *estradas nacionais* or national roads have no prefix letter on some road maps (eg the one published by the Automóvel Club de Portugal), while they're prefixed N on others (eg the Michelin No 440 map). ■

fastest route between here and there, and look mortality in the eye as you do so. Portugal's annual per capita death rate from road accidents is Europe's highest. The coastal roads of the Algarve and the Lisbon-Cascais axis are especially dangerous.

City driving tends to be hectic, not least in Portugal's many small old walled towns, where roads can taper down to donkey-cart size before you know it. Fiendish one-way systems (usually the only way for towns to cope with cars in their narrow lanes) can trap you for hours and force you far out of your way. Municipal parking is usually very limited, and in small towns may be restricted to the outskirts. Lisbon and Porto can hardly cope with their traffic at all.

A common sight in larger towns is the down-and-outers who hang around parking lots, wave you into spaces you'd have found for yourself anyway, and ask you for payment for this 'service'. Of course there's no need to give them anything, although 50$00 or 100$00 can't hurt, and the resulting goodwill might keep your car out of trouble.

For information on what to bring in the way of documents, refer to the Car & Motorcycle section of the Getting There & Away chapter.

Assistance

Automóvel Club de Portugal (ACP), Portu-

gal's national auto club, provides medical, legal and car-breakdown assistance for its members. But anyone can get good road information and maps from its head office (☎ 01-356 39 31; fax 01-357 47 32) at Rua Rosa Araújo 24, Lisbon; branch offices in Aveiro, Braga, Bragança, Coimbra, Évora, Faro, Porto, Vila Real and elsewhere can also help.

If you can prove that you belong to an affiliated national auto club, you can also use the emergency services (and get discounts on maps etc). ACP's emergency help numbers are ☎ 01-942 50 95 (Lisbon) for southern Portugal, and ☎ 02-830 11 27 (Porto) for northern Portugal.

Refer to Planning in the Facts for the Visitor chapter for advice on the best road-maps to carry.

Road Rules

You may not believe it after seeing what Portuguese drivers can do, but there are indeed rules. To begin with, as with the rest of continental Europe, driving is on the right. Most signs use international symbols, and lanes are marked with solid and dashed lines according to international conventions (though solid white lines do not deter Portugal's highway maniacs).

Except as marked otherwise, speed limits for cars (without a trailer) and motorcycles

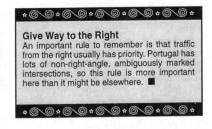

Give Way to the Right
An important rule to remember is that traffic from the right usually has priority. Portugal has lots of non-right-angle, ambiguously marked intersections, so this rule is more important here than it might be elsewhere. ■

are 60 km/h in built-up areas, 90 km/h outside towns and villages, and 120 km/h on motorways. If your driving licence is less than a year old you're restricted to 90 km/h even on motorways, and your car must display a '90' disk, available from any ACP office.

Safety belts must be worn in front and back seats, and children under 12 years old may not travel in the front seat. Motorcyclists and their passengers must wear helmets.

The legal limit for alcohol in the blood is a minuscule 0.05%, so don't even think about drinking and driving. You're not allowed to use your horn in built-up areas after dark except in an emergency.

Police are authorised to impose on-the-spot fines (in escudos), and must issue a receipt. If you prefer to slug it out in a Portuguese courtroom, you must still pay a deposit big enough to cover the maximum possible fine!

Fuel

Petrol is pricey, eg 156$00 and up for a litre of 95-octane *sem chumbo* (unleaded petrol), 159$00 for 98-octane unleaded and 110$00 for *gasóleo* (diesel). Unleaded petrol is readily available in most parts of the country. There are plenty of self-service stations, and major credit cards are readily accepted at many, but not all, stations.

Theft & Damage

Rental cars are especially at risk of break-ins in larger towns; do not leave anything of value visible in your car. In case of a theft or break-in, get a police report if you hope to claim on your insurance.

Car Rental

To rent a car in Portugal you must be at least 23 and have held your licence for over a year. There are dozens of local car-rental firms in the country, from international outfits such as Avis, Hertz, Budget and Europcar down to cheap local dealers. The biggest selections are at Lisbon, Porto and Faro airports. Because of the competition, everybody's rates in the Algarve are lower than elsewhere.

The best deals are often arranged from abroad, either as part of a package with your flight, or through an international car-rental firm. From the UK, for example, for the smallest car expect to pay about UK£130 (about 31,000$00) for seven days in the high season or UK£65 (about 16,000$00) in the low season; renting in Portugal, figure around 39,000$00 in the high season or 31,000$00 in the low season (including tax, insurance and unlimited km).

Rental companies usually insist on payment up front. For a modest additional fee you can purchase insurance from the rental company, unless you're confident of coverage by an auto policy from your home country (see the Car & Motorcycle section of the Getting There & Away chapter). A minimum of third-party coverage is compulsory throughout the EU.

BICYCLE

Cycling is a cheap, healthy, environmentally sound and, above all, enjoyable way to get around Portugal. With a mountain bike (BTT or *bicyclete tudo terrano* in Portuguese) you can probably see more (and especially more remote) places than most visitors would dream of. Although Portugal has no dedicated bicycle lanes or paths, mountain bikes seem to have the same rights of access to rural trails and tracks as do walkers.

Most Portuguese appear to think that visitors cycle around the country because they can't afford to do it any other way, so cyclists are frequently offered the cheapest accommodation or invited in to dinner with the family. On back roads you may be a source of wonderment: drivers often toot their horns, more from courtesy than anger, and delighted passengers often wave and shout. You may be put off by this the first few times, but on those long and lonely stretches you may find yourself looking forward to the next passing car!

Of course there's a downside. Especially in the north, you may encounter rain for days on end. And while there are bike shops in most larger cities, you probably won't be able to find that spare widget you need. The two biggest problems are Portuguese drivers, who are among Europe's rudest and craziest, and Portuguese back roads, a few of which are still paved with little stone blocks that can shake your teeth loose, and some have potholes that can swallow you whole (this is another good reason to bring a mountain bike).

Where to Go

Possible itineraries are numerous – in the north's mountainous national/natural parks, along the coast or across the Alentejo plains. Veteran cyclists all recommend Peneda-Gerês, especially the less visited Peneda section. More demanding is the Serra da Estrela (which serves as the Tour de Portugal's 'mountain run'). Another favourite is the Serra do Marão range between Amarante and Vila Real, which is also close to the port-wine region of the Douro valley.

Safety

Always assume you're vulnerable on a road in Portugal. When traffic is light, Portuguese drivers simply drive more recklessly. Dress colourfully so you can be spotted from a distance. Your bike should have red reflectors on the back, the wheels and the pedals, and a white or yellow light in front if you plan to ride at night.

Portuguese cyclists say that at unregulated crossroads, motorised vehicles have right of way over unmotorised ones. This may not be in the law books, but we don't recommend testing it out!

Police seem to ignore cyclists, more or less equating them with pedestrians. On the other hand, dogs who can ignore the arrival of a 50-tonne truck will chase a bicycle. If dogs make you nervous, carry a dog whistle or a dog-repellent spray.

Transporting Your Bicycle

You can take your bike on any regional (R) or interregional (IR) train as accompanying baggage for 1200$00, regardless of the distance you're going. Arrange this with the *bagagem* (baggage office) at the departure station, preferably a few days in advance. They'll give you a receipt, which you present to the bagagem at your destination. Apparently you cannot unload a bike at just any old station, so check on this too. Note that if there's no room for the bike on your train, it might go on the next train!

For a small surcharge, regional coach lines might take your bike along, but big ones such as Internorte and Intercentro probably won't. It's up to the driver, so ask first. Agreement may be more likely if you first remove the pedals, turn the handlebars sideways, drop the saddle down and perhaps take off the front wheel, so that the bike looks as small as possible. You should get some kind of written acknowledgment from the ticket seller or baggage official that the bike is on board.

Rental

The rental of BTTs – at anywhere from 1500$00 to 3500$00 a day – is catching on in the Algarve, around Parque Nacional Peneda-Gerês in the Minho, and in some other touristed areas. Elsewhere, rental outfits are scarce. In this book we note them wherever we have found them.

Other Resources

A Portuguese cycling club that may respond to visitors' queries is the Federação Portuguesa de Cicloturismo e Utilizadores de Bicicleta, or Portuguese Federation for Bicycle Touring & Cyclists (☎ 01-315 60 86;

fax 01-356 12 53), PO Box 4031, 1501 Lisbon.

For its members, the Cyclists' Touring Club in the UK publishes a useful, free information booklet on cycling in Portugal, as well as suggested route information for the Coimbra-Porto region and for the Algarve and Alentejo. Contact the club for membership details at Cotterell House, 69 Meadrow, Godalming, Surrey GU7 3HS (☎ 01483-417217; fax 01483-426994; e-mail cycling @ctc.org.uk; URL http://www.cycling.org.uk).

For information on maps, see Planning in the Facts for the Visitor chapter. For information on getting your machine into the country, and what documents to bring along, see the Bicycle section in the Getting There & Away chapter. Some specialist travel agencies offering cycling tours are listed under Organised Tours in this chapter.

HITCHING

Hitching is never entirely safe anywhere, and we don't recommend it. Travellers who decide to hitch should understand that they are taking a small but potentially serious risk. In any case, it doesn't look like an easy way to get around Portugal, and it may take considerable time and patience. We saw few hitch-hikers, even in good weather. Almost nobody stops on major highways, and on smaller roads drivers tend to be going short distances. You can meet some interesting characters, but you may only advance from one field to the next!

BOAT

Other than river cruises along the Rio Douro from Porto (see the Douro chapter) and along the Rio Tejo from Lisbon, the only important surviving waterborne transport in Portugal is cross-river ferries. The longest of these are the Transtejo commuter ferries across the Rio Tejo between Lisbon and Cacilhas, Montijo and Seixal; and the Transado ferries that make the half-hour trip across the mouth of the Rio Sado between Setúbal and Tróia (see the Lisbon chapter).

LOCAL TRANSPORT
Bus

Except in big cities such as Lisbon there's little reason to take a municipal bus, since most attractions tend to be within walking distance. Most areas have regional bus services, for better or worse (for more on these see the Bus section in this chapter).

Underground

Lisbon's underground system, the Metro, is handy for the city core, and by 1998 it will extend much further. See the Lisbon chapter for more details.

Taxi

Taxis offer good value over short distances, especially for two or more people, and are usually plentiful in larger towns. Ordinary taxis are usually marked A for *aluguer* (for hire) on the door or the number plate or elsewhere. These taxis use meters and are available on the street or in taxi ranks. The older green-topped taxis are gradually being replaced in many towns by rather spiffy cream-coloured ones. In many towns you can book a taxi by telephone, for a surcharge of a few hundred escudos above standard rates.

The fare on weekdays during daylight hours is 250$00 flag fall, plus a complex formula depending on distance and elapsed time. A fare of 500$00 is usually enough to get you across town. Once a taxi leaves the town or city limits, you pay a higher fare, and possibly the cost of a return trip (whether you take it or not). Rates are also higher at night, and on weekends and holidays. It's best to insist on the meter, although it's possible to negotiate a flat fare. If you have a sizeable load of baggage you'll pay a further 300$00.

Except for those who lurk at the international airports, drivers are, on the whole, quite honest, even in Lisbon and the Algarve.

In larger cities, including Lisbon, you'll also see meterless taxis marked T (for *turismo*), for hire from private companies for excursions. Rates for these are higher (but standardised), and the drivers are honest and polite, and speak foreign languages.

Street Names

All over Portugal the same street names crop up time and time again. Their significance is as follows:

Rua/Avenida

25 de Abril	the date when the 1974 Revolution of the Carnations began
5 de Outubro	the date in 1910 when the monarchy was overthrown and a republic established
1 de Dezembro	the date in 1640 when Portuguese independence was restored after Spanish rule
da Liberdade	referring to the freedom established by the 1974 revolution
dos Restauradores	the restorers of independence after Spanish rule
Afonso de Albuquerque	the viceroy of India who expanded Portugal's empire; he conquered Goa in 1510, Malacca in 1511 and Hormuz in 1515
Pedro Álvares Cabral	the 'discoverer' of Brazil (in 1500)
Manuel Cardoso	a 17th-century composer
Luís de Camões	Portugal's most famous 16th-century poet
João de Deus	a 19th-century lyric poet
Almeida Garrett	a 19th-century poet, playwright and novelist
Alexandre Herculano	a 19th-century historian
Alexandre Serpa Pinto	a late 19th-century African explorer

Other Transport

Enthusiasts for stately progress should not miss the trams of Lisbon and Porto, an endangered species. Also worth trying are the *elevadores* (funiculars and elevators) in Lisbon, Bom Jesus (Braga), Nazaré and elsewhere.

ORGANISED TOURS

Following are some reliable tour operators, both domestic and overseas, that offer complete packages or can arrange made-to-order tours to Portugal.

For a rundown of many of the UK's most reliable and interesting specialist tour operators, get hold of the free *AITO Directory of Real Holidays*, an annual index of member companies of the Association of Independent Tour Operators. It's available from AITO (☎ 0181-744 9280; fax 0181-744 3187), 133A St Margaret's Rd, Twickenham, Middlesex TW1 1RG, UK.

The London office of ICEP, the Portuguese state tourism organisation, publishes its own directory of cooperating travel agencies in the UK, the *Portugal Tour Operators Guide*. ICEP is at 22-25a Sackville St, London W1X 1DE, UK (☎ 0171-494 1441; fax 0171-494 1868).

City & Regional Coach Tours

Gray Line (☎ 01-352 25 94; fax 01-316 04 04), Avenida Praia da Vitória 12-B, Lisbon, organises three to seven-day coach tours to selected regions of Portugal, usually through travel agents or upper-end tourist hotels in Portugal. The AVIC coach company (☎ 058-82 97 05), Avenida Combatentes 206, Viana do Castelo, does short tours of the Douro and Lima valleys.

Miltours (☎ 089-890 46 00), Verissimo de Almeida 20, Faro, gives you a choice of day trips not only in the Algarve but all over Portugal. It also has offices in Lisbon (Rua Conde de Redondo 21, ☎ 01-352 41 66) and Porto (Rua J Simão Bolivar 209, ☎ 02-941 46 71).

Cycling Tours

Easy Rider Tours (☎ 508-463-6955, toll-free 800-488-8332; fax 508-463-6988; e-mail ezrider@shore.net; http://www.cyclery.com/easyrider), PO Box 228-STI, Newburyport, MA 01950, USA, has what looks like the biggest selection of small-group Portugal itineraries (all with one American and one Portuguese guide), including Alentejo, Minho and Costa Azul (Sesimbra to Lagos).

Guided tours by Blue Marble Travel

(☎ 201-326-9533; fax 201-326-8939) at 31 South St, Morristown, NJ 07960, USA, include a four-week Trans-Iberian (southwest France, northern Spain and northern Portugal) tour and several two-week trips around Spain and Portugal.

Progressive Travels (☎ 206-285-1987, toll-free 800-245-2229; fax 206-285-1988; e-mail progtrav@aol.com), 224 West Galer, Seattle, WA 98119, USA, offers a week-long self-guided Algarve journey, plus guided tours of the Algarve; coastal Algarve/Alentejo; central Portugal; and a Lisbon to Lagos trip for the truly fit.

Other outfits with Portugal itineraries are Butterfield & Robinson (☎ 416-864-1354, toll-free ☎ 800-678-1147; fax 416-864-0541), 70 Bond St, Toronto, Ontario M5B 1X3, Canada; and Backroads (☎ 510-527-1555, toll-free ☎ 800-462-2848; fax 510-527-1444; e-mail goactive@backroads.com; http://www.back-roads.com.biking), 801 Cedar St, Berkeley, CA 94710-1800, USA.

Walking Tours

Rotas do Vento (☎ 01-364 98 52; fax 01-364 98 43; e-mail: rotasdovento@mail.telepac.pt), Rua dos Lusíadas 5, PO Box 3010, 1301 Lisbon, organises weekend walks to more remote places all over Portugal. Per-person prices range from 5000$00 to 19,000$00, depending on the distance from Lisbon.

The Alternative Travel Group (☎ 01865-513 333; fax 01865-310 299), 69-71 Banbury Rd, Oxford OX2 6PE, UK, offers well-researched walking tours (guided or self-guided, off-the-shelf or tailor-made) with deluxe bed and board. Other UK hiking specialists with escorted small-group packages to Portugal are Ramblers Holidays (☎ 01707-331 133; fax 01707-333 276), Box 43, Welwyn Garden, Hertfordshire AL8 6PQ; Exodus (☎ 0181-675 5550; fax 0181-673 0779), 9 Weir Rd, London SW12 0LT; and Explore Worldwide (☎ 01252-319 448; fax 01252-343 170), 1 Frederick St, Aldershot, Hampshire GU11 1LQ.

Explore Worldwide's agent in Australia and New Zealand is Adventure World. The Australian office (☎ 02-9956 7766; fax 02-9956 7707) is at 3rd floor, 73 Walker St, North Sydney, NSW 2059. The New Zealand offfice (☎ 09-524 5118, toll-free ☎ 0800-652 954; fax 09-520 6629; e-mail discover@adventureworld.co.nz) is at 101 Great South Rd, Remeura, Auckland.

Progressive Travels in the USA (see Cycling Tours) runs one-week guided walking tours of the Algarve, and of the Costa Verde (Minho).

For those who are very fit (and good at reading topographic maps), Sherpa Expeditions (☎ 0181-577 2717; fax 0181-572 9788; e-mail sales.sherpa@dial.pipex.com), 131a Heston Rd, Hounslow, Middlesex TW5 0RD, UK, runs rugged one-week hiking trips in the Parque Nacional Peneda-Gerês, with modestly priced accommodation.

Nature Walks & Birdwatching

Lanius (☎ & fax 01-225 77 76), Rua de 25 Abril 35, Paivas, 2840 Amora (across the Rio Tejo from Lisbon), organises specialist nature tours up to several weeks long in the Bragança region, the Rio Tejo valley, the Alentejo and the Algarve.

Two birdwatching and botanical tour specialists in the UK are Naturetrek (☎ 01962-733 051; fax 01962-733 368), Bighton, Alresford, Hampshire SO24 9RB; and Limosa Holidays (☎ 01263-578 143; fax 01263-579 251), Suffield House, Northrepps, Norfolk NR27 0LZ.

Adventure Travel

TurAventur (☎ & fax 066-74 31 34), Rua João de Deus 21, Évora, can arrange walking, biking and jeep trips across the plains of the Alentejo, including to its mysterious megaliths. Turnatur (☎ 01-207 68 86; fax 01-207 76 75), Rua Almirante Reis 60, 2830 Barreiro (across the river from Lisbon), organises jeep safaris, canoeing, and canyoning expeditions around Portugal (see Activities in the Facts for the Visitor chapter for more about canyoning).

Movijovem (☎ 01-355 90 81; fax 01-352 86 21), Avenida Duque de Ávila 137, 1000 Lisbon – the country's central booking office for Hostelling International – organises adventure holidays in Portugal for 16 to 26-year-olds, including rafting, potholing (caving) and horse riding.

Jeep Safaris

Numerous outfits in the Algarve offer day-long jeep safaris into the foothills. Shop around: some are little more than off-road scrabbles. Perhaps the most environmentally responsible of the lot is Horizonte in Salema, with low-key trips into the Parque Natural de Sudoeste Alentejano e Costa Vicentina, including a look at the disappearing rural scene as well as wild landscapes and remote west-coast beaches. Other reliable safari agencies include Naturinfo in Sagres, and Riosul and Mega Tur in Faro (see these towns for contact details).

Other Specialist Tours

For wine tours in the Alentejo and the Douro, contact Arblaster & Clarke Wine Tours (☎ 01730-893 344; fax 01730-892 888), Farnham Rd, West Liss, Hampshire GU33 6JQ, UK.

Martin Randall Travel (☎ 0181-742 3355; fax 0181-742 1066), 10 Barley Mow Passage, Chiswick, London W4 4PH, UK, offers high-quality art, archaeology and music tours of Portugal.

Among reliable Portugal-specialist tour operators in France are Lusitania (☎ 01 44 69 75 06; fax 01 44 69 75 15), 19 Rue de la Pépinière, Paris; and Atout Portugal (call ☎ 01 43 20 78 78 or fax 01 43 22 97 20 for a list of cooperating travel agencies around France).

Transport & Accommodation Only

Perhaps all you want to do is relax in style in a few of Portugal's elegantly restored castles and manor houses, or in rural farmhouses (for more on these places, see Accommodation in the Facts for the Visitor chapter). Several agencies in the UK can get you there and make all the arrangements, including Individual Travellers Spain & Portugal (☎ 01798-869 485; fax 01798-869 343), Bignor, Pulborough, West Sussex RH20 1QD; Kingsland Holidays (☎ 01752-251 688; fax 01752-251 699), Brunswick House, Harbour Ave, Plymouth, Devon PL4 0BN; and Vintage Travel (☎ 01954-261 431; fax 01954-260 819), 13 Short Lane, Willingham, Cambridge CB4 5LG.

For those who want to assemble their own holidays, an up-market Portugal-specialist travel agency called Witney Travel, operating under the name Destination Portugal (☎ 01993-773 269; fax 01993-771 910), Madeira House, 37 Corn St, Witney, Oxfordshire OX8 7BW, UK, publishes a series of brochures about upper-end hotel, *pousada* and manor house accommodation, and one on air (scheduled and charter) and car-hire prices.

People

Lisbon

Left:	Vintage tram in the Baixa district
Centre:	A Brasileira café, Rua Garrett
Right:	Postboxes
Bottom:	Torre de Belém

Lisbon

LISBON

• pop 650,000 • postcode 1100 • area code ☎ 01

Lisbon is an enticing tangle of times past and present. It's funky and old-fashioned, unpretentious and quirky, and booming with new money and new confidence. Its position on seven low hills beside the Rio Tejo (River Tagus) was the main attraction for traders and settlers in centuries past, and it's still a stunning site. Add to that today's cultural diversity, its laid-back ambience and a time-warp of architecture, and you've got one of the most enjoyable cities in Europe. And, despite recently rising prices, it's still an economical destination, worth considering as a base for several nearby day trips after you've meandered around Lisbon itself.

Apart from its muscle-aching hills – tackled by a bevy of funiculars and half a dozen cranky old trams that hiss and zing through the streets – Lisbon is a manageable city that's small enough to explore on foot (don't even try to drive: the traffic jams and one-way streets are a nightmare). At its heart are wide, tree-lined avenues graced by Art Nouveau buildings, mosaic pavements and sidewalk cafés, while the Alfama district below Castelo de São Jorge is a warren of narrow old streets redolent of Lisbon's Moorish and medieval past. Seen from the river – one of the city's many great viewpoints – Lisbon is an impressionist picture of low-rise ochre and pastel, punctuated by church towers and domes.

But Lisbon has also been hit by massive redevelopment in recent years. Although the Alfama and Chiado districts have seen some sensitive restoration projects, many fine old buildings have been destroyed in commercial areas where office blocks are in demand. Sleepy old Lisbon is no more: it's now on a helter-skelter ride towards modernisation as it experiences new wealth and tarts up for Expo '98 (see the boxed aside).

The resulting contrasts can be startling: among the jackhammers and new high-rises are still the seedy backstreets of Alfama and

HIGHLIGHTS

Though it's a pretty subjective call, our pick of Lisbon's highlights is:

- Mosteiro dos Jerónimos at Belém
- wander (in daylight) through the Alfama district, following its lanes to the riverside and up to the views from Castelo São Jorge
- a ride on tram No 28 from Rua da Conceição (Baixa), east into the Alfama and west into the Bairro Alto
- bar-hopping through the Bairro Alto, with a stop somewhere for a taste of *vinho tinto* and fado
- the very fine Museu Calouste Gulbenkian, the Museu Nacional de Arte Antiga and the Museu do Azulejo
- the over-the-top Capela de São João Baptista in the Igreja de São Roque
- the grand mansions and lush gardens of Sintra

Cais do Sodré where you'd be wise not to wander alone at night. And though the traffic is increasingly frenzied, the main squares still maintain a caravanserai character, with lingering lottery ticket-sellers, shoe-shiners, itinerant hawkers and pavement artists.

Such contrasts give a buzz to 1990s Lisbon. You'll still find plenty of history and culture, from the magnificent Manueline masterpieces at Belém to the world-class Calouste Gulbenkian Museum. But there are pulsating new rhythms too, most noticeably in the African clubs popping up everywhere as the refugees who flooded into Portugal from the country's former African colonies in 1974-75 respond to a growing demand for their music. Nothing could be further from the soul-searing strains of the uniquely Portuguese *fado* songs (which originated here,

129

LISBON

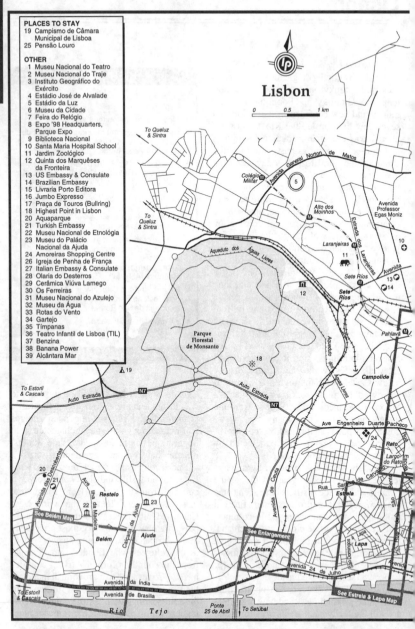

PLACES TO STAY
19 Campismo de Câmara
   Municipal de Lisboa
25 Pensão Louro

OTHER
1 Museu Nacional do Teatro
2 Museu Nacional do Traje
3 Instituto Geográfico do
  Exército
4 Estádio José de Alvalade
5 Estádio da Luz
6 Museu da Cidade
7 Feira do Relógio
8 Expo '98 Headquarters,
  Parque Expo
9 Biblioteca Nacional
10 Santa Maria Hospital School
11 Jardim Zoológico
12 Quinta dos Marquêses
   da Fronteira
13 US Embassy & Consulate
14 Brazilian Embassy
15 Livraria Porto Editora
16 Jumbo Expresso
17 Praça de Touros (Bullring)
18 Highest Point in Lisbon
20 Aquaparque
21 Turkish Embassy
22 Museu Nacional de Etnológia
23 Museu do Palácio
   Nacional da Ajuda
24 Amoreiras Shopping Centre
26 Igreja de Penha de França
27 Italian Embassy & Consulate
28 Olaria do Desterros
29 Cerâmica Viúva Lamego
30 Os Ferreiras
31 Museu Nacional do Azulejo
32 Museu da Água
33 Rotas do Vento
34 Gartejo
35 Tímpanas
36 Teatro Infantil de Lisboa (TIL)
37 Benzina
38 Banana Power
39 Alcântara Mar

Lisbon

0   0.5   1 km

To Torres Vedras

To Vila Franca de Xira & Porto

To Porto & Spain

Ave Padre Cruz

Avenida Cidade do Porto

Ave Dr Alfredo Bensaúde

Aeroporto de Lisboa

Campo Grande

Olivais Norte

Avenida Marechal Craveiro Lopez

Universidade de Lisboa

Alvalade

Avenida Marechal Gomes da Costa

Avenida Almirante Gago Coutinho

Campo Grande

Cidade Universitária

Expo '98 Site

Roma

das Forças Armadas

Ave Estados Unidos da América

Entre Campos

Avenida do Santo Contestável

Campo Pequeno

See Rato & Saldanha Map

Ave de Berna

Avenida João XXI

Praça de Londres

Saldanha

Ave da República

Avenida Almirante Reis

Areeiro

Saldanha

Alameda

Casa Saldanha

São Sebastião

Picoas

Arroios

Rua Morais Soares

Parque

Praça Marquês de Pombal

Rotunda

Anjos

Xabregas

See Bairro Alto, Baixa & Chiado Map

Intendente

Politécnico

Avenida

Restauradores

Socorro

See Alfama, Castelo & Graça Map

Rossio Train Station

Bairro Alto

Rossio

Graça

Avenida Infante Dom Henrique

Baixa

Castelo

Alfama

Calçada dos Barbadinhos

Santa Apolónia Train Station

24 de Julho

Cais do Sodré Train Station

Santo

Rio Tejo

To Montijo & Seixal

To Cacilhas

To Cacilhas

To Barreiro

Alcântara

Praça General Domingos de Oliveira

Acesso à Ponte

Alcântara Station

Avenida da Ponte

Rua dos Lusíadas

Rua da Moeda

Gilberto Rola

Avenida 24 de Julho

Largo do Calvário

Caminho Económico

0   100 m

Ave da Índia

in the Alfama district). Traditionalists may be disappointed, but this is a city on the move.

When you're ready to get off, you have the option of day trips to the massive monastery at Mafra or the rococo palace at Queluz, seaside frolics in Sesimbra or Cascais, or walks in the wooded hills of Sintra.

HISTORY

Legend has it that Lisbon was founded by Ulysses but it was probably the Phoenicians who first settled here some 3000 years ago, attracted by the fine harbour and strategic hill of São Jorge. They called the city Alis Ubbo ('delightful shore'). Others soon saw its delightful qualities too: the Greeks kicked out the Phoenicians and were in turn booted out by the Carthaginians.

In 205 BC the Romans arrived in the city known then as Olisipo, managing to hold on to the place for the next two centuries. Julius Caesar raised its rank (and changed its name to Felicitas Julia), making it the most important city in Lusitania. After the Romans, a succession of northern tribes – Alans, Suevi and Visigoths – occupied Lisbon, but in 714 the powerful Moors arrived from Morocco. They fortified the city they called Lissabona

and fought off occasional attacks by Christian forces for the next 400 years.

Finally, in 1147, after a four-month siege, the Christians under Dom Afonso Henriques recaptured the city with the help of a ruffian bunch of Anglo-Norman crusaders. It was just over a century later, in 1255, that Afonso III asserted Lisbon's pre-eminence by making it the country's capital in place of Coimbra.

Since then, Lisbon has had more than its fair share of glory and tragedy: in the 15th and 16th centuries it became the opulent seat of a vast empire after Vasco da Gama discovered a sea route to India. In the 17th century, gold was discovered in Brazil, further boosting Lisbon's importance. Merchants flocked to the city from all over the world, trading in gold and spices, silks and precious stones. Under Dom Manuel I, the extravagant style of architecture that came to be called Manueline – typified by the Mosteiro dos Jerónimos at Belém – complemented Lisbon's role as the world's most prosperous trading centre. But it was an extravagance that crumbled into rubble in the massive earthquake of 1755.

Lisbon never regained its power and prestige after the earthquake. After Napoleon's

Lisbon's Great Earthquake

It was 9.30 am on All Saints' Day, 1 November, in 1755 when the Great Earthquake struck. Many residents were caught inside churches, celebrating High Mass, as three major tremors hit in quick succession. So strong was the earthquake that its effects were felt as far away as Scotland and Jamaica. In its wake came an even more devastating fire – helped on its way by the flickering church candles – and a tidal wave that submerged the quay and destroyed the lower town.

At least 13,000 of the city's 270,000 people perished (some estimates put it at three times as many) and much of the city was devastated. Although Lisbon had suffered previous earthquakes – notably in 1531 and 1597 – there had been nothing on this scale.

Portugal's European neighbours immediately offered aid and commiseration. England sent food and pickaxes. In France there arose a lively exchange between Voltaire and Rousseau on the doctrine of providence: Voltaire's *Poème sur le désastre de Lisbonne* was followed by an account of the earthquake in his philosophical novel *Candide*, published in 1759. Dom João I's minister, the redoubtable Marquês de Pombal, proved to be the man of the moment, efficiently handling the catastrophe (though it was actually the Marquês de Alorna who uttered the famous words 'we must bury the dead, and feed the living') and rebuilding the city in a revolutionary new 'Pombal' style.

Lisbon recovered, but many of its glorious monuments and artworks had gone. It lost its role as Europe's leading port and finest city. Once revered by Luís de Camões as 'the princess of the world...before whom even the ocean bows', the city had finally bowed before the sea, and its power no longer shone. ■

forces occupied the city in November 1807 (they were finally repulsed from Portugal in 1811 by a joint British and Portuguese force), Lisbon declined with the country into political chaos and military insurrectionism. In 1908, at the height of the turbulent republican movement, Dom Carlos and his eldest son were assassinated as they rode in a carriage through the streets of Lisbon. Over the next 16 years there were 45 changes of government, another high-profile assassination (President Sidónio Pais, at Rossio station in 1918), and a cloak-and-dagger period during WWII when Lisbon (which was officially neutral) developed a reputation as a nest of spies.

Two bloodless coups (in 1926 and 1974) later rocked the city but it was the massive influx of refugees from the former African colonies in 1974-75 that had the most radical effect on Lisbon, straining its housing resources but also introducing an exciting new element.

The 1980s and 90s have finally seen Lisbon revitalised. Membership of the European Community in 1986 coincided with a stable, centre-right government which lasted a record 10 years. Massive EU funding has boosted redevelopment projects (especially welcome after a major fire in 1988 destroyed the Chiado district) and enabled Lisbon to stand in the limelight again as European City of Culture in 1994. Its next high-profile appearance, as host of Expo '98, will confirm its re-emergence on the world stage, albeit in a less glorious role than in Vasco da Gama's day.

ORIENTATION

Lisbon nestles against seven hills on the northern side of Portugal's finest natural harbour, the wide mouth of the Rio Tejo. The hills – Estrela, Santa Catarina, São Pedro de Alcântara, São Jorge, Graça, Senhora do Monte and Penha de França – are fine places for bird's-eye views of this photogenic city. São Jorge is topped by Lisbon's famous *castelo*, and each of the others by a church or a *miradouro* (lookout).

Other places to get your bearings and shoot off film are the Elevador de Santa Justa and Parque Eduardo VII. The city's highest point (at 230.5m) is within the military fortress in the huge Parque Florestal de Monsanto, west of the centre.

At the river's edge is the grand Praça do Comércio, the traditional gateway to the city. Behind it march the latticework streets of the Baixa ('lower') district, up to the twin squares of Praça da Figueira and Praça Dom Pedro IV – the latter known to virtually everybody as Rossio or Largo Rossio.

Here the city forks along two main arteries. Lisbon's splendid 'main street', Avenida da Liberdade – more a long park than a boulevard – reaches 1.5 km north-west from Rossio and the adjacent Praça dos Restauradores to Praça Marquês de Pombal and the huge Parque Eduardo VII. The other fork is the commercial artery of Avenida Almirante Reis (which becomes Avenida Almirante Gago Coutinho), running arrow-straight north for almost six km from Praça da Figueira (where it's called Rua da Palma) to the airport.

From the Baixa it's a steep climb west, through a wedge of up-market shopping streets called the Chiado, and over Rua da Misericórdia, into the pastel-coloured mini-canyons of the Bairro Alto, Lisbon's centre for food, traditional entertainment and antique shops. Eastward from the Baixa it's another climb to the Castelo de São Jorge and the ancient, maze-like Alfama district around it.

River ferries depart from Praça do Comércio and Cais do Sodré to the west. Lisbon's four long-haul train stations are Cais do Sodré (for Cascais and the Estoril coast); Santa Apolónia, 1.5 km east of Praça do Comércio (for northern Portugal and all international links); Rossio (for Sintra and Estremadura); and Barreiro (for southern Portugal), reached by ferry across the Tejo.

The city's main long-distance bus terminal is on Avenida Casal Ribeiro, near Picoas and Saldanha metro stations. A cluster of other bus companies runs from Rua dos Bacalhoeiros, a few blocks east of Praça do Comércio.

In addition to the metro and a network of city bus lines, ageing trams clank picturesquely around the hills, and spiffy new ones run six km west from Praça da Figueira, past the port district of Alcântara, to the waterfront suburb of Belém.

With the exception of Belém, Lisbon's main attractions are all within walking distance of one another, and public transport (when you need it at all) works well. Streets are generally well marked and buildings clearly numbered. Note, however, that the names of many smaller streets, and some big ones, change every few blocks.

Lisbon is connected across the Tejo to the Costa de Caparica and Setúbal Peninsula by the immense Ponte 25 de Abril, Europe's longest suspension bridge. Were you only permitted to stop and look from its 70m-high deck, the bridge would provide the finest panoramic view of the city from anywhere except the Cristo Rei monument on the other side of the Tejo (see Cacilhas under Around Lisbon).

Maps

Along with their microscopic city map, the main *turismo* (tourist office) at Praça dos Restauradores sometimes has a good free 1:15,000 *Lisboa* map. For map junkies and long-term residents there's the 230-page *Guia Urbano* city atlas, which noses into

Expo '98

For several years *lisboêtas* and visitors have been aware of something more than the usual level of civic maintenance. All across the city a frenzy of construction and reconstruction has made urban travel a misery, with traffic diversions, bus route changes, heavy machinery, big holes in the ground and lots of dust.

Lisbon has been getting ready for Expo '98, the last major world exposition of the millennium, to be held here from May through September of 1998. That year is not only the United Nations' International Year of the Oceans; it also marks the 500th anniversary of Vasco da Gama's historic discovery of a sea route to India. The theme of Portugal's big fair will be oceanic: recognition of the oceans' essential value to humanity, and preservation of marine ecosystems.

Sixty hectares of land, stretching for five km along the city's north-eastern riverfront, will be the site of several high-tech, interactive pavilions with displays about the world's seas; a performance centre called the Utopia Pavilion, hosting a live, multimedia show dedicated to the oceans; and displays from scores of countries and international organisations, including the United Nations and the EU. The highlight of the exposition is likely to be the Ocean Pavilion, housing a vast central aquarium, plus four smaller ones representing the ecosystems of Antarctica, the Indian Ocean coral reef system, the Atlantic and the Pacific. Eight million visitors are expected.

Expo '98 should give Lisbon a boost in its quest to be the home of one or more newly proposed international organisations devoted to marine resources. The exposition will also be preceded by a 100-day arts festival, culminating in the world premiere of an opera called *White Raven*, written for the event by Philip Glass, Bob Wilson and the Portuguese librettist Luísa Costa Gomes, on the theme of the world's loss of environmental innocence. Organisers clearly hope that the event will give Lisbon, and Portugal, a higher scientific and cultural profile in Europe.

Expo '98's other face is Expo Urbe, a local mega-project that aims to regenerate Lisbon's entire, decaying north-eastern waterfront. A 3.3-sq-km area of run-down docks, warehouses and factories around the exposition site is to be developed by the year 2015 into a new integrated commercial, residential and recreational hub for Lisbon. The exposition's international area will be developed as the city's new exhibition centre, and the Ocean Pavilion will remain as Europe's biggest oceanarium.

In fact the whole city is getting the biggest facelift since the 1755 earthquake. The metro (underground railway) is being expanded in every direction, including to the exposition site, where a vast multimodal station will accommodate the metro, buses, new high-speed trams, taxis, international rail links and a dedicated passenger line to the airport. Port improvements are underway as far down as Santa Apolónia station, hotel construction is in high gear, and a new 17-km bridge, named after Vasco da Gama, will cross the Tejo estuary.

Headquarters for Expo's planning and management, Parque Expo '98, are at Avenida Marechal Gomes da Costa 37 (☎ 831 98 98; fax 837 00 22), but until all those new transport links are in place it's a long trip; take bus No 19 from Areeiro metro station. ■

every corner of the city at about 1:5300; it's 2800$00 from the turismo at Restauradores. The detailed, oblique-perspective *Lisbon City Map – Vista Aérea Geral*, available for about 1100$00 from kiosks and bookshops, is great for spotting landmarks.

The Instituto Português de Cartográfia e Cadastro, or Portuguese Institute of Cartography & Registry (☎ 381 96 00; fax 381 96 99), Rua Artilharia Um 107 (postcode 1070), sells topographic maps of Portugal; take almost any bus west from Rotunda metro station on Avenida António Augusto de Aguiar. The institute is open weekdays from 9 am to 4 pm.

The Instituto Geográfico do Exército, or Army Geographic Institute (☎ 852 00 63 or 852 02 71; fax 853 21 19; e-mail igeoe @igeoe.pt; URL http://www.igeoe.pt), sells military topographic maps at their headquarters on Avenida Dr Alfredo Bensaúde in the far north-eastern Olivais Norte district. To get there take a taxi, or bus No 25A or 81 from Praça do Comércio. The institute is open weekdays from 9 am to noon and 1.30 to 4.30 pm.

See Planning in the Facts for the Visitor chapter for more on these topographic maps.

INFORMATION
Tourist Offices
ICEP has a large turismo (☎ 346 63 07) in the Palácio Foz on Praça dos Restauradores (a block north of Rossio train station). It's open daily from 9 am to 8 pm. The information supplied here is not 100% reliable, so get a second opinion if your query involves a long trip across town. The staff can advise on accommodation and will call about availability, but they won't make bookings.

There is also a turismo (☎ 849 43 23, ☎ 849 36 89) at the airport; it's open daily from 6 am to 2 am.

Lisboa Card Lisbon's municipal tourism department has a polite, switched-on office (☎ 343 36 72) at Rua Jardim do Regedor 50, across Praça dos Restauradores from the turismo; it's open daily from 9 am to 6 pm. Here you can buy a Lisboa Card, which

provides free travel on nearly all city transport, including the metro; free admission to most of the city's museums and monuments; and discounts of 15% to 50% at more museums, on bus and tram tours and river cruises. There are 24, 48 and 72-hour versions for 1200$00, 2000$00 or 2600$00 (500$00, 750$00 or 1000$00 for children from five to 11 years old) respectively – excellent value if you plan on cramming lots of sights into a short stay.

You can also buy the Lisboa Card at several other outlets, including the central post office on Praça do Comércio, and in Belém at the Mosteiro dos Jerónimos and the Museu Nacional dos Coches.

Foreign Embassies
For the addresses of foreign consular offices in Lisbon, see Embassies in the Facts for the Visitor chapter.

Visa Extensions
The place to extend a visa, or to replace a lost or stolen one, is the sweaty little office of Serviço de Estrangeiros e Fronteiras (Foreigners' Registration Service; ☎ 346 61 41, hotline ☎ 352 31 12) at Avenida António Augusto de Aguiar 20, near Parque metro station. It's open on weekdays only, from 9 am to 3 pm.

Money
Multibanco automatic-teller machines (ATMs) are everywhere around Rossio and the Baixa. You can exchange foreign banknotes for escudos at several 24-hour exchange machines – eg opposite Rossio train station at Rua 1 de Dezembro 118-A, and near Praça do Comércio at Rua Augusta 24. Be careful about using these after dark. There are also others at the airport and at Santa Apolónia station.

The best bet for exchanging cash or travellers cheques is the private Cota Câmbios exchange at Rua Áurea 283 (also known as Rua do Ouro), open weekdays from 9 am to 8 pm and Saturdays from 9 am to 6 pm; it even buys foreign coins from 3 to 5 pm on weekdays.

General banking hours are roughly 8.30 am to 3 pm on weekdays only, although the Banco Borges e Irmão (☎ 342 10 68) at Avenida da Liberdade 9-A exchanges money until 7.30 pm on weekdays and alternate Saturdays.

Top Tours (see Travel Agencies in this section) is Lisbon's American Express representative. Here, Amex travellers cheques can be cashed for no commission, and Amex cards can be used for cash advances at back-home rates.

Among French banks in Lisbon are Banque National de Paris (☎ 343 08 04) at Avenida Liberdade 16; Crédit Lyonnais (☎ 347 58 00) at Rua da Conceição 92 in the Baixa; and Société Générale (☎ 383 34 73) at Avenida Engenheiro Duarte Pacheco.

Post

The most convenient post office (☎ 347 11 22) around Rossio is in the pink building opposite the turismo on Praça dos Restauradores. It's open weekdays from 8 am to at least 10 pm and on weekends and holidays from 9 am to 6 pm.

The not-so-central central post office on Praça do Comércio, open weekdays only from 8.30 am to 6.30 pm, is the place for poste restante; mail addressed to Posta Restante, Central Correios, Terreiro do Paço, 1100 Lisboa, will go to counter 13 or 14 here. There is also a 24-hour post office at the airport.

American Express credit card and travellers cheque holders can have mail sent to the American Express representative, Top Tours (see Travel Agencies in this section).

Telephone & Fax

The best place for long-distance calls is the Portugal Telecom office at Rossio 68, open daily from 8 am to 11 pm. Here you can also buy Lisbon and Porto's own TLP telephone cards, as well as Portugal-wide Credifone cards (prices are the same); ask for a *telecard* or *cartão*. TLP telephones are more common than Credifones in Lisbon. You can also place IDD telephone calls from larger post offices. Faxes can be sent from post offices.

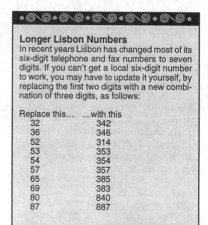

Longer Lisbon Numbers
In recent years Lisbon has changed most of its six-digit telephone and fax numbers to seven digits. If you can't get a local six-digit number to work, you may have to update it yourself, by replacing the first two digits with a new combination of three digits, as follows:

Replace this...	...with this
32	342
36	346
52	314
53	353
54	354
57	357
65	385
69	383
80	840
87	887

Operators at Lisbon's telephone enquiries number (☎ 118) will search by address as well as by name. You can find operators who speak English (ask *fala inglês?*), as well as French and Spanish speakers. At the front of the *páginas amarelas* (yellow pages) in the telephone directory is a list of headings, in English and other languages, useful to visitors. There is also a privately operated 'talking yellow pages' at ☎ 795 22 22.

E-Mail

Telepac, Portugal's biggest Internet provider, has a public user's centre called Quiosque Internet (☎ 314 25 27; e-mail email@telepac.pt) on the ground floor of the giant Forum Picoas building beside Picoas metro station (take the north-west exit from the metro). You can plug into the web or send e-mail (but not receive it) for 125$00 per quarter-hour. Some technical help is available, including in English. It's open weekdays from 9 am to 5 pm.

Travel Agencies

The city's youth-oriented travel agencies are Tagus Travel and Jumbo Expresso. Tagus (☎ 352 55 09 for air tickets or 352 59 86 for other services; fax 352 06 00) is at Rua

Camilo Castelo Branco 20 (metro: Rotunda) and is open weekdays from 9 am to 6 pm, Saturdays from 10 am to 1.30 pm. Another Tagus office (☎ 849 15 31) is at Praça de Londres, near Areeiro metro station. Jumbo Expresso (☎ 793 92 64; fax 793 92 67) is at Avenida da República 97, near Entre Campos metro station (Rua da Entrecampos exit) and also on the Aero-Bus line from the airport. Both Tagus and Jumbo offer budget-minded hotel, bus, train and air bookings (and Tagus can book some overseas hostels). They also sell ISIC and Cartão Jovem cards.

Movijovem (☎ 355 90 81; fax 352 86 21), Avenida Duque de Ávila 137 (metro: Saldanha) – Portugal's central Hostelling International booking office – has an arrangement with Tagus to sell Inter-Rail passes and airline tickets at Tagus' low rates. It also arranges adventure holiday packages for 16 to 26-year-olds, including rafting, hiking and horse riding. It's open on weekdays only, from 9.30 am to 6 pm.

Among competent mainstream travel agencies, the easiest to deal with is Top Tours (☎ 315 58 85; fax 315 58 73), Avenida Duque de Loulé 108 (metro: Rotunda). It is also Lisbon's American Express representative, so holders of American Express cards or travellers cheques can get commission-free currency exchange and cash advances, help with lost cards or cheques, and can have mail and faxes held or forwarded (the Lisbon postcode to use is 1050). It's open weekdays only, from 9.30 am to 1 pm and 2.30 to 6.30 pm.

Rotas do Vento (☎ 364 98 52, ☎ 364 98 59; fax 364 98 43), Rua dos Lusíadas 5, organises weekend guided walks (in Portuguese, with some English) for groups of six to 18, to both nearby and remote corners of Portugal; book two weeks or more ahead. It's on the 4th floor, around the block from Largo do Calvário (on the No 15 tram line from Praça da Figueira or Praça do Comércio, or the No 18 tram from Praça do Comércio), and stays open until 7 pm on weekdays.

Two other able outdoor specialists are just across the Tejo. Lanius (☎ & fax 225 77 76), Rua de 25 Abril 35, Paivas, 2840 Amora,

organises specialist nature tours in the Rio Tejo valley, the Alentejo and Algarve, and the Bragança region. Turnatur (☎ 207 68 86; fax 207 76 75), Rua Almirante Reis 60 in Barreiro, organises nature walks, jeep safaris, canoeing and canyoning trips.

The Instituto Nacional para Aproveitamento do Tempos Livres dos Trabalhadores (Inatel) is a Portuguese workers' organisation that runs its own hotels, camping grounds and a range of sports and leisure programmes. The only programmes open to nonmembers appear to be hydrospeed, canyoning and some mountain bike trips (see Activities in the Facts for the Visitor chapter for more on Inatel and on these sports). To sign up, visit the Departmento Desportiva (☎ 885 22 75, ☎ 885 31 05; fax 885 15 61), open from 9 am to 6 pm on weekdays only, at Calçada de Santa Ana 180. The best way up is on the Elevador de Lavra, or take the stairs behind the Palácio dos Condes de Almada. Take the lift to the 3rd floor, turn left and go to the end of the corridor.

Guidebooks

The Real Lisbon is an English-language version of a popular Portuguese guide to Lisbon's food, entertainment, shops etc; it's sold in city bookshops and at the turismo on Praça dos Restauradores.

ANA (Aeroportos e Navegação Aérea), the airport authority, publishes and regularly updates the free *Your Guide: Lisboa*, which has a slightly muddled walking tour and lists of food, upper-end hotels and nightlife; pick one up at the ANA counter at airport arrivals or at the airport turismo.

Bookshops

Few of Lisbon's bookshops *(livrarias)* offer much of interest in English, aside from guidebooks. The city's biggest bookseller is Livraria Bertrand, with at least half a dozen shops, the original and biggest of which (☎ 342 19 41) is at Rua Garrett 73 in Chiado. There are others in the Amoreiras shopping centre and the Centro Cultural de Belém. The closest bookshop to the Rossio is Livraria

Diário de Notícias at Rossio 11, with a modest range of guides and maps.

The only shop devoted entirely to Lisbon is the elegant Livraria Municipal at Avenida da República 21-A (metro: Saldanha), with books on city history, art and architecture (including a few titles in English), and easy chairs. Nearby, at Avenida Marquês de Tomar 38, is Lisbon's only exclusively French bookshop, Librairie Française. Livraria Buchholz, at Rua Duque de Palmela 4 (metro: Rotunda), has a huge literature collection in Portuguese, English, French and German.

For second-hand books, there are two or three dusty shops along Calçada do Carmo as it climbs up behind Rossio train station.

Libraries

Among Lisbon's best *bibliotecas* are the General Arts Library of the Fundação Calouste Gulbenkian (☎ 793 51 31; fax 793 51 39; e-mail apg@gulbenkian.puug.pt) at Avenida de Berna 56 (metro: Pahlavã); and the Biblioteca Nacional (☎ 795 01 30, ☎ 797 47 41) at Campo Grande 83 (metro: Entre Campos). The central municipal library (☎ 797 13 26) is in the Palácio das Galveias (metro: Campo Pequeno).

Campuses

The vast Universidade de Lisboa campus, five km north-west of Rossio, has its own metro station, Cidade Universitária.

Cultural Centres

The reading room of the USA's Abraham Lincoln Center (☎ 357 01 02), Avenida Duque de Loulé 22-B (two blocks from Picoas metro station), with a massive stock of American books and magazines, is open weekdays from 2 to 5.30 pm.

The British Council (☎ 347 61 41, ☎ 347 95 18), at Rua de São Marçal 174, also has a good reading room. It's open Tuesday through Friday from noon to 6 pm. Take bus No 15 or 58 from Rua da Misericórdia.

At Avenida Luís Bívar 91 are the Institut Franco-Portugais de Lisbonne (☎ 311 14 00) and the Alliance Française (☎ 315 88 06).

There is also a reading room (☎ 352 01 49) at the German Embassy, at Campo dos Mártires da Pátria 37.

Laundry

The friendly Lavandaria Sous'ana (☎ 888 08 20) in shop No 423 of the Centro Comércial da Mouraria, Largo Martim Moniz (metro: Socorro), is self-service but they'll do your wash for you in a few hours for the same price (4.5 kg for 1000$00). It's open Monday to Saturday from 9.30 am to 8.30 pm.

The Texas Lavandaria, at Rua da Alegria 7, is open weekdays, with rather slow dry-cleaning, washing and ironing services.

Medical Services

Farmácias (pharmacies) are plentiful in Lisbon. They are typically open weekdays from 9 am to 6 or 7 pm, except at lunch time, and Saturdays from 9 am to 1 pm. The closed ones sometimes post a list of others that are open. Operators at the general telephone enquiries number (☎ 118) can tell you where to find an open farmácia at any hour of the day or night. A competent pharmacy near the city centre is Farmácia Estácio at Rossio 62.

The Hospital Britânico or British Hospital (☎ 395 50 67, ☎ 397 63 29 after hours), at Rua Saraiva de Carvalho 49, has English-speaking staff and doctors. Other large hospitals include São José (☎ 886 01 31) on Rua José António Serrano, and Santa Maria Hospital School (☎ 352 94 40, ☎ 797 51 71) on Avenida Professor Egas Moniz.

Emergency

There is a 24-hour, English-speaking, tourist-oriented police subsection (Subsecção de Turismo) inside the courtyard at the SPS section office at Rua Capelo 13 in Chiado. Call ☎ 346 61 41, ext 279, or the country-wide emergency number (☎ 112).

Dangers & Annoyances

There is metro and other construction literally everywhere in Lisbon in preparation for Expo '98, but it should run itself out by then. Meanwhile, cranes stab the photogenic skyline, the pavements are full of excavations, and dust blows everywhere.

Urban crime against foreigners usually involves pickpocketing, purse-snatching or car break-ins. There's no need to be paranoid, but try to avoid wandering after dark in the back streets around Alfama and Cais do Sodré. The Bairro Alto is fairly safe, and is in fact the place to be for nightlife and good food. Use a money belt, and keep cameras and other tourist indicators out of sight when not in use.

THE BAIXA & THE RIVERFRONT

Following the catastrophic earthquake of 1755, one of the few people who kept their heads was the autocratic Marquês de Pombal. He put Lisbon on the road to recovery, and took the opportunity to rebuild the city centre as quickly as possible, in a severe and simple, low-cost, easily managed style.

The entire area from the riverside to the Rossio, with a stream meandering through it, was reborn as a rectangular grid of wide, pavement-lined commercial streets, each dedicated to a trade. The memory of these districts lives on in the district's north-south street names – Áurea (formerly Ouro, gold), Sapateiros (shoemakers), Correeiros (saddlers), Prata (silver), Douradores (gilders) and Fanqueiros (cutlers).

This 'lower town' remains the de facto heart of Lisbon. Down the middle runs pedestrianised Rua Augusta, the old street of the cloth merchants, now overflowing with cafés, restaurants, shops and banks. A fair fraction of the city's bus and tram lines funnel through Praça do Comércio at the Baixa's riverside end, or Rossio and Praça da Figueira at its upper end.

From Praça do Comércio to Cais do Sodré

Before the earthquake, Praça do Comércio was called Terreiro do Paço (Palace Square), after the royal Palácio da Ribeira that overlooked it until the morning of 1 November 1755. Despite its present demeaning role as a parking lot, the huge square, open to the river, still feels like the entrance to the city,

thanks to Joaquim Machado de Castro's bronze **equestrian statue** of Dom José I at the centre; the 18th-century, arcaded **government ministries** along three sides; and Verissimo da Costa's **Arco da Victória**, the arch opening onto Rua Augusta.

In fact most visitors coming by river or sea in bygone days would have arrived here. It was also from here that Dom João VI and his massive entourage fled to Brazil in 1807.

At the north-western corner of the square, by the central post office, is the spot where Dom Carlos and his eldest son, Luís Filipe, were assassinated in 1908. Just west of here is a smaller square, **Praça do Município**, dominated by Lisbon's 1874 town hall on the eastern side, the former marine arsenal on the southern side, and a finely carved, 18th-century *pelourinho* (pillory) at the centre.

Continuing west for another 400m along Rua do Arsenal, you arrive at Lisbon's other main riverfront plaza, Praça do Duque da Terceira, better known by its riverfront name, **Cais do Sodré**. Here are more government offices, a few consulates, the Transtejo car ferry, and the Cais do Sodré train station (from where electric trains speed off to Cascais and the Estoril coast).

A few short blocks west of the square is the city's kinetic main market, the domed **Mercado da Ribeira** – officially the Mercado Municipal 24 de Julho. Get here early in the morning to see feisty vendors hawking vegetables, fruit, seafood and more.

From here, Avenida 24 de Julho runs for three km along the river to the Port of Lisbon and the warehouse district of **Alcântara**. This strip is also a major axis of Lisbon's nightlife (see Entertainment). A pleasant way to return to Praça do Comércio is along the breezy riverfront promenade.

Eastward from Praça do Comércio

About 250m east of the Arco da Victória, on the northern side of Rua da Alfândega (see the Alfama, Castelo & Graça map), is the **Igreja da Conceição Velha**. Its finely carved Manueline façade was rebuilt and reattached to this church after the earthquake. A bit further along, where Rua dos

Rato

Rua do Salitre

Casino

Avenida

Avenida da Liberdade

Jardim Botânico

Rua da Escola Politécnica

Pr. da Alegria

Rua da Alegria

Rua da Mãe d'Água

Rua de Santo António da Glória

Rua da Glória

Praça do Príncipe Real

Rua Dom Pedro V

Rua da Rosa

Rua de São Pedro

Rua da

Praça dos Restauradores

Restauradores Metro

Rossio Train Station

Largo Trindade Coelho

Bairro Alto

Alcântara

Duque

Tv. da Queimada

Rua da Atalaia

Rua da Barroca

Rua do Diário de Notícias

Rua do Norte

Rua das Gáveas

Rua da Misericórdia

Rua Nova da Trindade

Calçada da Estrela

Rua Miguel Lupi

Rua de São Bento

Largo de São Bento

Rua dos Poiais de São Bento

Calçada do Combro

Santa Catarina

Rua da Rosa

Rua do Loreto

Largo do Chiado

Rua Serra Pinto

Rua António Maria Cardoso

Avenida Dom Carlos I

Rua do Alecrim

Calçada Marquês de Abrantes

Rua de São Paulo

Rua Vítor

Rua de Dom Luís I

Rua da Moeda

Avenida 24 de Julho

R Remolares

R Bernardino Costa

Cais do Sodré

Praça do Duque da Terceira

Cais do Sodré Train Station

Avenida da Brasília

Cais do Sodré Ferry Terminal

Rio Tejo

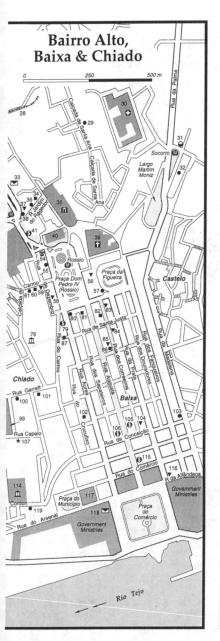

Bairro Alto,
Baixa & Chiado

0   250   500 m

PLACES TO STAY
7	Residencial Nova Avenida
8	Hotel Botânico
10	Casa de São Mamede
24	Pensão Monumental
25	Hotel Suiço-Atlântico
34	Residencial Campos
44	Pensão Londres
47	Pensão Globo
60	Pensão Estação Central
61	Residencial Estrêla do Mondego
68	Pensão Duque
69	Pensão Estrêla de Ouro
81	Pensão Arco da Bandeira
82	Pensão Moderna
86	Pensão Insulana
101	Pensão Estrêla do Chiado
102	Pensão Galicia
119	Residencial Nova Silva

PLACES TO EAT
2	Restaurante Os Tibetanos
13	Confeitaria Císter
23	Restaurante O Brunhal
37	Pinóquio
49	Cafetaria Brasil
52	Restaurante O Tacão Pequeno
56	Casa Suiça
58	Café Nicola
59	Celeiro
67	Casa Transmontana
72	Pap'Açorda
77	Cervejaria da Trindade
83	Restaurante João do Grão
84	Restaurante Ena Pái
85	Lagosta Vermelha
90	Tasca do Manel
98	Café A Brasileira
104	Restaurante Yin-Yang
116	Martinho da Arcada
122	Restaurante Porto de Abrigo
124	Pastelaria & Snack Bar Brasilia
125	Caneças

OTHER
1	Danish Embassy
3	Canadian Embassy
4	Spanish Embassy & Consulate
6	Texas Lavandaria
9	Universidade Internacional
14	Casa Achilles
16	British Council
26	Banco Borges e Irmão
27	Banque National de Paris
28	Elevador de Lavra
29	Inatel
30	São José Hospital
31	Mafrense Bus Terminal
32	Lavandaria Sous'ana
33	Post Office
35	Palácio dos Condes de Almada
36	Lisboa Card Office
38	ABEP Ticket Agency

Continued on next page

39	Igreja de São Domingos	117	Town Hall
40	Teatro Nacional de Dona Maria II	118	Central Post Office
41	Multibanco ATM	121	Mercado da Ribeira
42	Turismo	126	Finnish Consulate
45	Miradouro de São Pedro de Alcântara		
46	Elevador da Glória		**ENTERTAINMENT**
53	Solar do Vinho do Porto	5	Hot Clube de Portugal
54	Portugal Telecom	11	Memorial
55	Farmácia Estácio	12	Trumps
57	Carris Ticket Kiosk	15	Brica Bar
62	Museu de Arte Sacra	17	Xeque-Mate
63	Igreja de São Roque & Capela de São	18	Tatoo
	João Baptista	19	Discoteca A Lontra
78	Museu Arqueológico do Carmo & Con-	20	Bar 106
	vento do Carmo Ruins	21	Finalmente
79	Cota Câmbios	22	Ritz Clube
80	Livraria Diário de Notícias	43	Pavilhão Chinês
87	Elevador de Santa Justa	48	Nova
92	Igreja de Santa Catarina	50	O Forcado
93	Palácio da Assembleia da República	51	Primas
94	Finnish Embassy	64	Frágil
95	Swedish Embassy	65	Arroz Doce
97	Brazilian Consulate	66	Café Luso
99	Basílica da Nossa Senhora dos Mártires	70	Adega Mesquita
100	Livraria Bertrand	71	Três Pastorinhos
103	Santos Ofícios	73	A Capela
105	Banco Comércial Portuguesa	74	Tertúlia
106	Crédit Lyonnais	75	Adega do Machado
107	Police Subsection for Tourists	76	Lisboa à Noite
108	Teatro Nacional de São Carlos	88	Nono
109	Teatro Municipal de São Luís	89	Adega do Ribatejo
110	Fábrica Sant'Ana	91	Ma Jong
111	Elevador da Bica	96	Incógnito
112	Miradouro de Santa Catarina	113	Álcool Puro
114	Museu do Chiado	120	Absoluto
115	Multibanco ATM	123	Ó Gilíns Irish Pub

Bacalhoeiros merges with Rua da Alfândega, is the startling early 16th-century **Casa dos Bicos** (House of Facets), with a prickly façade (restored and reconstructed in the early 1980s) that was a folly of Afonso de Albuquerque, a former viceroy of India.

Various alleys and gloomy staircases climb up from Rua da Alfândega into the Alfama district and the Castelo de São Jorge.

Central Baixa
Under the streets of the Baixa is a series of tunnels, believed to be the remnants of a **Roman spa** (or waterworks) and probably dating from the 1st century AD. You can descend into the mouldy depths – by way of the offices of Banco Comércial Portuguesa at Rua Augusta 62-74 – only on regular group tours organised by the Museu da Cidade (see the Museums & Other Attractions section).

Alternatively you can rise above the Baixa at a stately pace. At the eastern end of Rua da Conceição you can catch a clanking **No 28 tram** up past the Sé into the old Alfama and Graça districts. At the other end of the Baixa, the **Elevador de Santa Justa**, an incongruously huge but charming wrought-iron lift designed by one Raul Mésnier (not Gustave Eiffel as some sources insist) and completed in 1902, will hoist you above the café tables of Rua de Santa Justa to a viewing platform at eye level with the Convento do Carmo ruins in the Chiado district.

Rossio & Praça da Figueira
This pair of plazas form the gritty heart of the Baixa, with transport to everywhere, lots

Rolling Motion Square

This was the nickname given to the Rossio by early English visitors because of the undulating mosaic pattern of the pavements here (and elsewhere in the city). The mosaics were first installed by prison labour gangs in the 19th century and are now mostly in evidence around the fountains.

They may make you seasick, but they're more sensible than they look. Hand-cut white limestone and grey basalt cubes are pounded into a bed of sand, making a hard surface which nevertheless lets the rainwater through. In the course of street works such as the Rossio's pre-Expo '98 disruptions, they're simply dug up and reused. ■

of cafés from which to watch a cross-section of Lisbon's multicultural population, and thousands of pigeons. You'll also find hustlers and hawkers preying cheerfully on visitors. You're bound to pass through here every day you're in Lisbon, on your way to more interesting neighbourhoods.

In the middle of the Rossio is a **statue**, allegedly of Dom Pedro IV, for whom the square is formally named. The story goes that the statue is actually of Emperor Maximilian of Mexico and was abandoned in Lisbon en route from France to Mexico after news arrived of Maximilian's assassination. On the northern side of the square is the restored 1846 **Teatro Nacional de Dona Maria II**, with a façade topped by a statue of 16th-century playwright Gil Vicente.

In less orderly times the Rossio was the scene of animal markets, fairs and bullfights. The theatre was built on the site of a palace in which the unholiest excesses of the Portuguese Inquisition took place in the 16th to 19th centuries. Around the corner, just to the north of Praça da Figueira, is the vast **Igreja de São Domingos**. In this church's pre-earthquake incarnation the Inquisition's judgements or autos-da-fé were handed down.

Across Largo de São Domingos from the church is the **Palácio dos Condes de Almada**, also called the Palácio da Indepen-

déncia or Palácio da Restauração, where the *restauradores* met for the last time in 1640 before rising against the Spanish occupation.

West of the theatre is Rossio train station (from where trains tunnel out to the Campolide district before zipping on to Sintra), and a bit to the north is the busy Praça dos Restauradores.

CHIADO & BAIRRO ALTO

These two districts, lying above the Baixa to the west, make a perfect pair for day-and-night exploration. The Chiado, a wedge of wide streets roughly between Rua da Misericórdia and Rua do Crucifixo, is the posh place for shopping and for loitering in elegant cafés. The Bairro Alto, a fashionable residential district in the 17th century (and still boasting some fine mansions), is now better known as the raffish heartland of Lisbon's nightlife.

The best way to start exploring the Chiado is on the extraordinary **Elevador Santa Justa**, a macho wrought-iron lift rising from the junction of Rua Santa Justa and Rua Áurea in the Baixa, almost to the doorway of the Convento do Carmo.

The Chiado is also the place to gape at the destruction wrought by fire and earthquake: the ruined **Convento do Carmo**, uphill from Rua Garrett, stands as a stunning testimony to the 1755 earthquake. Only the Gothic arches, walls and flying buttresses remain of what was once one of Lisbon's largest churches. It was built in 1423 by Dom Nuno Álvares Pereira, Dom João I's military commander, who turned religious after a life of fighting, and spent the last eight years of his life in complete obscurity in this Carmelite convent. Now its ruins serve as an atmospheric open-air home for the small **Museu Arqueológico do Carmo** (see Museums & Other Attractions).

In contrast to the convent, the gutted buildings that have pockmarked the Chiado since a massive fire in 1988 are now being rapidly rebuilt and restored in time for Expo '98 by architect Alvaro Siza Vieira, who is largely maintaining the Chiado's old style. The fire caused irreparable damage to many elegant buildings (especially in Rua do Crucifixo) but one survivor is the **Teatro Nacional de São Carlos** in Rua Serpa Pinto. Lisbon's opera house and its largest, handsomest theatre, it was built in the 1790s in imitation of the San Carlos theatre in Naples. It stands opposite the smaller Teatro Municipal de São Luís.

Two more *elevadors* – the funicular **Elevador da Glória** and **Elevador da Bica** – provide stately entrance to the Bairro Alto, and are worth the ride in any case. The Elevador da Glória climbs from near the turismo on Praça dos Restauradores, up to gardens and a superb viewpoint atop one of Lisbon's seven hills, **São Pedro de Alcântara**. Across the road is the **Solar do Vinho do Porto** (see the boxed aside in the Entertainment section), where you can sample up to 300 different varieties of port in a suitably salubrious setting.

DAMIEN SIMONIS

Traditional liquor shop in the Baixa district

A short walk downhill to Largo Trindade Coelho brings you to the Bairro Alto's most famous cultural asset, the **Igreja de São Roque**. The dull façade of this Jesuit church, built in the late 16th century, largely by architect Felipe Terzi, is one of Lisbon's biggest deceptions: inside, the side chapels are crammed with gold and glitter, mosaics of marble and ornate azulejos in Florentine style. The custodian leads visitors from one chapel to the next, switching on the lights and saying proudly, 'Portuguese! Portuguese!' as if he can't believe it himself.

Just when you think you've seen everything, you arrive at the *pièce de résistance*, the **Capela de São João Baptista**, the chapel to the left of the altar. Commissioned in 1742 by Portugal's most extravagant king, Dom João V, it was designed and built in Rome by the Italian architect Luigi Vanvitelli using the most expensive materials possible, including amethyst, alabaster, agate, lapis lazuli and Carrara marble. After its consecration by Pope Benedict XIV it was dismantled and shipped to Lisbon for what was then a staggering £225,000. Check out the intricate marble mosaics, which from a modest distance look just like paintings. It's all completely over the top, of course, but extraordinary nonetheless.

If you still haven't seen enough gilded artwork and liturgical extravaganza, pop into the **Museu de Arte Sacra** next door (described in Museums & Other Attractions).

From the southern end of the Bairro Alto (at the junction of Rua da Moeda and Rua de São Paulo, walking distance from Cais do Sodré) the **Elevador da Bica** creeps up to Rua do Loreto, a few blocks west of Praça de Luís Camões. Riding this gives you a chance to explore the unsung neighbourhood of **Santa Catarina**, the south-westerly arm of the Bairro Alto. This compact, maze-like district couldn't be less like the Chiado. It's bright with hanging laundry, and alive with the sound of balcony gossip, chattering kids and caged songbirds. The district's name comes from the 17th-century **Igreja de Santa Catarina** in Calçada do Combro, largely rebuilt after the 1755 earthquake but still full of pre-earthquake gilded woodwork and with a gloriously ornate baroque organ. Downhill, at the end of Rua Marechal Saldanha, on another of Lisbon's seven hills, is the **Miradouro de Santa Catarina**, with a bird's-eye view of the river and the Ponte 25 de Abril.

ALFAMA, CASTELO & GRAÇA

This area east and north-east of the Baixa, hurtling all the way down to the river's edge, is Lisbon's oldest and most historically interesting district. It's also one of the most rewarding areas for walkers and photographers, thanks to the warren of medieval streets in the Alfama district and the outstanding views from three of Lisbon's seven hills – São Jorge, Graça and Senhora do Monte.

The Alfama area was inhabited by the Visigoths as far back as the 5th century. Though remnants of a Visigothic town wall still remain, it was the Moors who gave the district much of its distinctive appearance and atmosphere, as well as its name: the Arabic *alhama* means springs or bath, probably in reference to the hot springs found near Largo das Alcáçarias. In Moorish times the Alfama was an upper-class residential area, but after various earthquakes destroyed most of the fine mansions (and the churches which the Christians later built) it reverted to a working-class quarter inhabited mainly by fisherfolk. It was one of the few districts to be saved from the ravages of the 1755 earthquake, thanks to its steep layers of stone.

Today, its bewildering maze of alleys and lanes (called *becos* and *travessas*) and steep stairways is in sharp contrast to the Baixa's prim, straight streets. Tumbling downhill from the castle to the river, with streets often narrow enough to shake hands across, the Alfama has a village atmosphere – you can quickly feel like an intruder if you take a wrong turn into someone's back yard. At night, it's probably not wise to wander around alone, not only because it's so easy to get lost (maps are little use in this clustered neighbourhood) but also because the area

still maintains a somewhat unruly reputation.

By day, the Alfama is a jovial, lively enclave of taverns and tiny grocery stores, sizzling sardine smells and squawking budgies. In the early mornings, fisherwomen sell fresh fish from their doorways and hang flapping laundry from their windows to dry. Not so long ago, they would have congregated at the public open-air laundries too, but in recent years many of their houses have been modernised under the Reabilitação Urbana d'Alfama project. This scheme has inevitably led to some gentrification and commercialisation in the main streets. For real rough-and-tumble atmosphere, delve into the back alleys, or visit during the Festas dos Santos Populares in June (see Special Events) when the whole quarter buzzes.

From the Baixa, it's an easy stroll from Rua da Conceição up to the Alfama's most important religious monument, the **Sé**. This Romanesque cathedral was built in 1150, soon after the city had been recaptured from the Moors by Afonso Henriques. He was wary enough of his enemy to want the church built like a fortress (the French architects designed a very similar fortress-cathedral for Coimbra). It's been extensively restored following Lisbon's various earthquakes and is now rather dull. While you're here, though, it's worth checking out the baroque organs and intricate baroque crib by Machado de Castro in a chapel off the north aisle. The Gothic cloister is open daily, except Mondays, from 10 am to 1 pm and 2 to 6 pm; entry is 100$00 (free on Sunday). The sacristy (same hours, 300$00) contains various religious paraphernalia, including São Vicente relics in a mother-of-pearl casket.

From here you can strike uphill for the castle, along Rua Augusto Rosa to Largo das Portas do Sol (which is also the route of the No 28 tram), or downhill along Rua de São João da Praça into the guts of the Alfama. If you don't fancy the uphill walk, bus No 37, departing from Praça da Figueira, goes directly to the castle.

Following the lower route from the cathedral will take you past the Largo de São

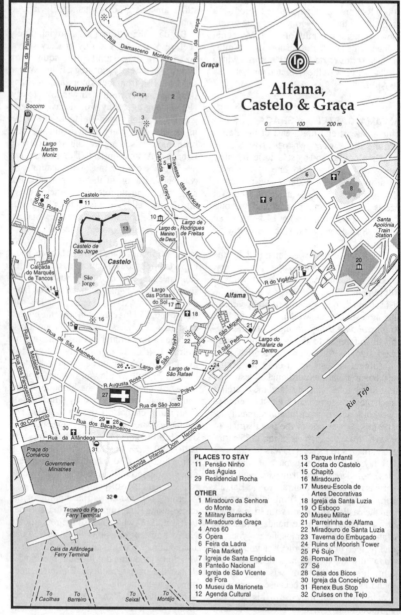

Alfama, Castelo & Graça

0   100   200 m

PLACES TO STAY
11 Pensão Ninho
    das Águias
29 Residencial Rocha

OTHER
1   Miradouro da Senhora
    do Monte
2   Military Barracks
3   Miradouro da Graça
4   Anos 60
5   Ópera
6   Feira da Ladra
    (Flea Market)
7   Igreja de Santa Engrácia
8   Panteão Nacional
9   Igreja de São Vicente
    de Fora
10 Museu da Marioneta
12 Agenda Cultural

13 Parque Infantil
14 Costa do Castelo
15 Chapitô
16 Miradouro
17 Museu-Escola de
    Artes Decorativas
18 Igreja de Santa Luzia
19 O Esboço
20 Museu Militar
21 Parreirinha de Alfama
22 Miradouro de Santa Luzia
23 Taverna do Embuçado
24 Ruins of Moorish Tower
25 Pé Sujo
26 Roman Theatre
27 Sé
28 Casa dos Bicos
30 Igreja da Conceição Velha
31 Renex Bus Stop
32 Cruises on the Tejo

Rafael, with its ruined **Moorish tower** (part of the Moors' original town wall) and nearby **old Jewish quarter** (marked by the tiny Rua da Judiaria), into the Alfama's liveliest street, **Rua de São Pedro**. All along here, to the Largo do Chafariz de Dentro ('fountain within the walls') at the bottom of the street, is where you'll find most of the Alfama's busiest shops, market stalls, taverns and cafés; these are especially boisterous in the morning and at lunch times.

If your legs are up to it, you can then follow the alleys and stairways up from Largo do Chafariz de Dentro to Largo das Portas do Sol. En route, check out another bustling street, **Rua de São Miguel**, parallel to the lower Rua de São Pedro (and accessible via the connecting Beco do Mexias, a tiny alley crammed with shops). The picturesque Beco da Cardosa (uphill again from Rua de São Miguel) is also worth exploring for its 16th and 18th-century houses.

Following the uphill route from the cathedral along Rua Augusto Rosa you'll pass the uninteresting ruins of a **Roman theatre** (apparently consecrated by Nero in 57 BC) off to the left in Rua de São Mamede, before reaching two of the area's most stunning viewpoints: the **Miradouro de Santa Luzia** and, a little further on, the **Largo das Portas do Sol** (the 'sun gateway', originally one of the seven gates into the Moors' city). Other worthwhile sights here include the **Igreja da Santa Luzia**, with wall panels of azulejos depicting the capture of the castelo from the Moors, and the nearby **Museu-Escola de Artes Decorativas** (see the Museums & Other Attractions section).

Downhill from the Largo das Portas do Sol, take the first turn-off on the right and stagger up the last stretch for the **Castelo de São Jorge**. There are other routes into the castle, but this is the easiest to follow (and some entrances, eg the one by Largo do Menino de Deus, may be closed).

From its Visigoth beginnings in the 5th century, the castelo has had quite a history: fortified by the Moors in the 9th century, sacked by the Christians in the 12th century (see the boxed aside), used as a royal residence from the 14th to 16th centuries and as a prison in every century, what's left has now been tarted up for tourists. Within its massive battlements you'll find everything from a posh restaurant and open-air café to caged birds and strutting peacocks, buskers and craft hawkers and a superb wooden *parque infantil* (children's playground). Best of all, the castelo's 10 towers and shady paths and terraces offer great panoramas over the city and river.

There's little left of the former palace, Paço de Alcáçova, built in the southern corner of the castelo by Dom Dinis on the site of a Moorish palace (it was already in ruins by the 17th century), but the nearby medieval quarter of Bairro de São Jorge still retains some of its original flavour.

North of the castle is the run-down old **Mouraria** quarter, where the Moors lived after the Christian conquest of Lisbon.

North-east of the castelo lies the **Graça** district. If you follow Rua de São Tomé up from Largo das Portas do Sol, you'll first pass the small Largo de Rodrigues de Freitas (see Museums & Other Attractions for details on the intriguing Museu da Marioneta here) before reaching Calçada da Graça. The former Augustinian convent at the end of this road now serves as a barracks but climb up to the left and you'll come to a splendid viewpoint, the **Miradouro da Graça**, atop one of Lisbon's seven hills.

Another 700m beyond the convent (turn left off Rua da Graça into Rua Damasceno Monteiro) is the third major viewpoint in the area, from yet another of Lisbon's hills, the **Miradouro da Senhora do Monte**, the best place in town for views of the castelo and Mouraria district.

A couple of cultural eye-openers lie within walking distance to the east of Largo de Rodrigues de Freitas (tram No 28 also passes close by): the Igreja de Santa Engrácia and the Igreja de São Vicente de Fora. If you come here any time on a Saturday or on Tuesday morning, you'll also find Lisbon's **Feira da Ladra** flea market in full swing in the nearby Campo de Santa Clara (see Things to Buy). Dominating the scene is the

The Siege of Lisbon

The reconquest of Lisbon from the Moors in 1147 is one of the more unsavoury chapters in Portugal's early history. Afonso Henriques, Count of Porto, had already thrashed the Moors at Ourique in 1139 (and started calling himself King of Portugal) and now he set his sights on Lisbon. Short of experienced troops, he persuaded a ruffian band of English, Flemish, French and German adventure-crusaders on their way to Palestine to give him a hand. 'Do not be seduced by the desire to press on with your journey,' begged the Bishop of Porto on the king's behalf, 'for the praiseworthy thing is not to have been to Jerusalem, but to have lived a good life while on the way.'

It sounded an attractive idea (they were offered all the enemy's loot if the city were taken) and in June 1147 the siege of the Castelo de São Jorge began. The Moors were at first contemptuous – 'How many times within your memory have you come hither with pilgrims and barbarians to drive us hence?' – and managed to hold out for 17 weeks. But in October the castelo's defences finally gave way and the 'Christian' forces (described more correctly by a contemporary reporter as 'plunderers, drunkards and rapists...men not seasoned with the honey of piety') showed their true colours by raping and pillaging their way through the city, despite assurances of leniency for the losers from Afonso himself. The only good man among them appears to have been one Gilbert of Hastings, an English priest who later became Bishop of Lisbon. ■

huge dome of the **Igreja de Santa Engrácia**. When work began on the church in 1682, it was planned to be one of the grandest in Lisbon. After 284 years of neglect and bureaucratic cock-ups (at one point it was even used as a warehouse for artillery), it was finally inaugurated in 1966 as the Panteão Nacional (National Pantheon). Its six marble cenotaphs, dedicated to the memory of historic figures including Vasco da Gama and Luís de Camões, and its tombs of former Portuguese presidents and literary figures such as Almeida Garrett are all very sombre. The best thing about the place is the view from the dome (the guide can usually be persuaded to take visitors to the top in the elevator). It's open daily from 9 am to 1 pm and 3 to 7 pm.

Far more impressive is the nearby **Igreja de São Vicente de Fora** (*fora* refers to the church being 'outside' the old city wall). Built by the master of the Italian Renaissance style, Felipe Terzi, between 1582 and 1627, its wide nave and coffered vault are striking in their simplicity. Check out the cloisters, too, for their 18th-century azulejo panels on La Fontaine's Fables. The former refectory (open daily from 10 am to 1 pm and 2 to 5 pm; entry is 200$00) is now a mausoleum containing the black marble tombs of the entire Bragança dynasty – everyone from

João IV (who died in 1656) to Manuel II (who died in exile in England in 1932). The dark rooms can feel bizarre and spooky, especially with the sounds of the flea market resonating through one wall and Mass through the other.

ESTRELA & LAPA

Those with the stamina to go beyond the Bairro Alto can ascend another of Lisbon's seven hills, Estrela, and explore the surrounding district of the same name. The attractions are limited but the view from the hill is fine.

The easiest way to get there is on westbound tram No 28 from Rua da Conceição (Baixa), tram No 25 from Cais do Sodré, or bus No 13 from Praça do Comércio. The most interesting way to get there is through Santa Catarina (see the Chiado & Bairro Alto section) – a two to 2.5-km walk from the Baixa via Largo do Chiado, Calçada do Combro and Calçada da Estrela, up to the Basílica da Estrela.

As you leave Santa Catarina, head north on the arterial Avenida Dom Carlos I to Largo de São Bento and the imposing **Palácio da Assembleia da República** (or Palácio da Assembleia Nacional), Portugal's houses of parliament, the nucleus of which is the 17th-century former convent of São

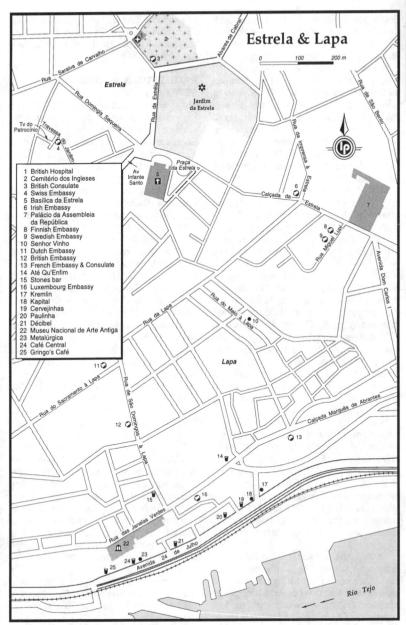

Estrela & Lapa

0   100   200 m

1 British Hospital
2 Cemitério dos Ingleses
3 British Consulate
4 Swiss Embassy
5 Basílica da Estrela
6 Irish Embassy
7 Palácio da Assembleia
   da República
8 Finnish Embassy
9 Swedish Embassy
10 Senhor Vinho
11 Dutch Embassy
12 British Embassy
13 French Embassy & Consulate
14 Até Qu'Enfim
15 Stones bar
16 Luxembourg Embassy
17 Kremlin
18 Kapital
19 Cervejinhas
20 Paulinha
21 Décibel
22 Museu Nacional de Arte Antiga
23 Metalúrgica
24 Café Central
25 Gringo's Café

Bento. The Assembleia has convened here since 1833. At the rear is a vast public park, and several other buildings including the official residence of the prime minister.

At the top of Calçada da Estrela are the massive dome and belfries of the **Basílica da Estrela**. Completed in 1790 by order of Dona Maria I (whose tomb is here) in gratitude for bearing a male heir, the church is all elegant neoclassicism outside and chilly, echoing baroque inside. Its best feature is the view across Lisbon from the dome, the weight of which was ingeniously spread over three concentric structures by architect Mateus Vicente de Oliveira. Also check out the life-size Christmas manger, with figures carved by Joaquim Machado de Castro (better known for the statue of Dom José I in Praça do Comércio). The church is open daily from 7.30 am to 7 pm, except at lunch time.

Across the road is a well-tended, big yet cosy public park, the **Jardim da Estrela**. Beyond this lies a patch of heresy in this Catholic land, the Protestant **Cemitério dos Ingleses** (English Cemetery), founded in 1717 under the terms of the Treaty of 1654 with England. Among expatriates at rest here are novelist Henry Fielding (author of *Tom Jones*), who died in the course of a visit to Lisbon for his health in 1754. At the far corner is all that remains of Lisbon's old Jewish cemetery.

You can lose yourself for a few hours in the **jardim botânico** (botanical garden), a welcoming little hillside park with paths diving down past forests of shrubs to clusters of cacti and palms. It's a great place for a picnic and is open on weekdays from 9 am to 8 pm (weekends from 10 am, and in winter until 6 pm only); entry is 200\$00. The main entrance, on Rua da Escola Politécnica, is also accessible on Bus No 100 from Praça da Figueira.

To the south of Estrela is Lapa, Lisbon's diplomatic quarter. The main attractions for visitors are on its river-facing side: the first-class **Museu Nacional de Arte Antiga** (see Museums & Other Attractions), and the bars and discos of Avenida de 24 Julho (see Enter-

tainment). To reach the museum from Estrela, take tram No 25 from in front of the basilica to Rua das Janelas Verdes and walk two blocks west.

RATO, SALDANHA, CAMPOLIDE & SETE RÍOS

These northern and north-western areas of Lisbon have a hotchpotch of attractions ranging from hothouses to high culture. Energetic walkers can reach the nearest of them by following Avenida da Liberdade, but metro and bus connections are also available.

Saldanha's one must-see is the **Fundação Calouste Gulbenkian** museum complex, described fully under Museums & Other Attractions, and best reached by metro to Pahlavã station.

When you need a breather, the **Parque Eduardo VII** is just down the road (and at the top of Avenida da Liberdade). Although increasingly sacrificed to development, the park – named after England's Edward VII who visited Lisbon in 1903 – is still a delightful escape from the city, especially in its so-called **estufas** (greenhouses) in the north-western corner of the park. The estufa *fria* (cool) and estufa *quente* (hot) contain an exotic collection of tropical and subtropical plants, bursting up among palm trees and cacti, ferns and flamingo pools. They're open daily from 9 am to 6 pm; entry is 75\$00. Take the metro to Parque or Rotunda, or bus No 31, 41 or 46 from Rossio.

You'd think the **jardim zoológico** (zoo) would be top of the list for kids, but it's better enjoyed as a hilltop garden than a zoo. Most of the animals are housed in very depressing conditions (with more attention paid to sponsors' corporate logos than to the animals' comfort) and made to perform senseless tricks for the public. The dolphin show is more professional but still heavy on talk and slapstick humour. The zoo (☎ 726 93 49), close to Sete Ríos metro station, is open daily in summer from 9 am to 8 pm (in winter until 6 pm). Admission is 800\$00 for adults and 600\$00 for children, plus 500\$00 for the dolphin show.

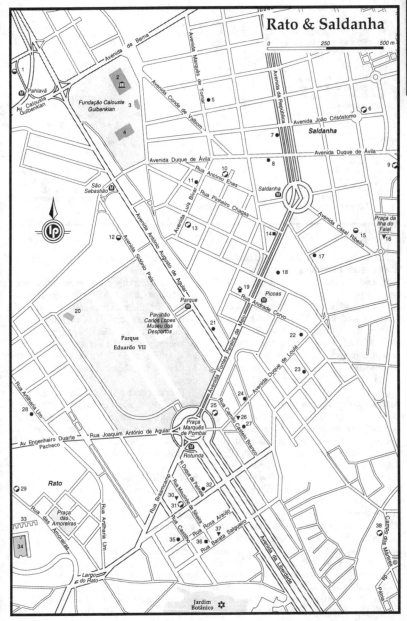

Rato & Saldanha

0   250   500 m

Avenida de Berna

Avenida Marquês de Tomar

Avenida Conde de Valbom

Avenida da República

Av Calouste Gulbenkian

Pahlavã

Fundação Calouste Gulbenkian

São Sebastião

Avenida João Crisóstomo

Saldanha

Avenida Duque de Ávila

Rua António Enes

Rua Pinheiro Chagas

Saldanha

Avenida Luís Bívar

Avenida António Augusto de Aguiar

Avenida Sidónio Pais

Avenida Cesar Ribeiro

Praça da Ilha do Faial

Parque

Pavilhão Carlos Lopes Museu dos Desportos

Rua Andrade Corvo

Picoas

Parque Eduardo VII

Avenida Fontes Pereira de Melo

Avenida Duque de Loulé

Rua Artilharia Um

Rua Joaquim António de Aguiar

Rua Castilho C Coelho Branco

Praça Marquês de Pombal

Av Engenheiro Duarte Pacheco

Rotunda

Rato

Rua Braamcamp

R. Duque de Palmela

Rua das Amoreiras

Praça das Amoreiras

Rua Artilharia Um

Rua Mouzinho de Silveira

Rua Castilho

Rua Rosa Araújo

Rua Barata Salgueiro

Campo dos Mártires

Avenida da Liberdade

Campo dos Mártires da Pátria

Largo do Rato

Jardim Botânico

Far more uplifting is the **Quinta dos Marquêses da Fronteira**, at Largo de São Domingos de Benfica 1, a 10-minute walk west of the zoo. This 17th-century mansion, which is still inhabited, is known for its fabulous gardens with manicured box trees, and for its abundant azulejos. The *quinta* (☎ 778 20 23) is open for guided tours daily, except Sundays, from 10.30 am to noon. Admission is 1000$00 (for quinta and gardens) or 300$00 (gardens only).

Aqueduto dos Águas Livres

Once one of Lisbon's major attractions, but curiously overlooked by visitors nowadays, is Lisbon's extraordinary Aqueduct of Free Waters, with 109 grey stone arches that lope south across the hills into Lisbon from Caneças, over 18 km away. It was built to bring the city its first clean drinking water, by order of Dom João V, who laid the inaugural stone at Mãe d'Água (Mother of Water), the city's main reservoir at Praça das Amoreiras. Its cost was borne by the citizenry through a tax on meat, olive oil and wine. Most of the work was done between 1728 and 1748, under the gaze of engineer Manuel da Maia and architect Custódio Vieira. Its construction was interrupted by the 1755 earthquake (but apparently little

was damaged) and it was not completed until 1835.

For considerably more information about the aqueduct, check out the Museu da Água. In summer, the museum and the municipal water company jointly run walking tours of the aqueduct and Mãe d'Água, as well as another reservoir, the Reservatório de Patriarcal in Praça do Principe Real. See the Museums & Other Attractions section for details.

The aqueduct is at its most impressive at Campolide, where the tallest arch is about 65m high. Take any train from Rossio station to the first stop, or bus No 2 from Rossio, or bus No 15 from Cais do Sodré. For Mãe d'Água, take bus No 9 from Rossio.

NORTHERN LISBON

Among the few attractions in Lisbon's northern suburbs is its Moorish-style **praça de touros** (bullring), across Avenida da República from Campo Pequeno metro station. See Spectator Sports in this chapter for information on the action there.

Further out are three museums in 18th-century palaces: the interesting Museu da Cidade in the Palácio Pimenta (metro: Campo Grande); and the side-by-side Museu Nacional do Traje and Museu Nacional de

Teatro, on the grounds of the Quinta de Monteiro-Mór (take bus No 7 from Praça da Figueira, or bus No 3 from Campo Grande metro station). See Museums & Other Attractions in this chapter.

BELÉM

The district of Belém, about six km west of Rossio, was the launch pad for Portugal's Age of Discoveries. Perhaps most famously, it is the place from which Vasco da Gama set sail on 8 July 1497 for the two-year voyage in which he discovered a sea route to India, setting in motion a fundamental shift in the world's balance of power.

Upon Vasco da Gama's safe return, Dom Manuel I ordered the construction of a monastery on the site of the riverside chapel (founded by Henry the Navigator) in which da Gama and his officers had kept an all-night vigil before departing on their historic voyage. The monastery, like its predecessor, was dedicated to the Virgin Mary, St Mary of Bethlehem (in Portuguese, Santa Maria de Belém) – hence the district's name.

The monastery, and an offshore watch-tower also commissioned by Manuel I, are essential viewing for every visitor to Lisbon – don't miss them. Jointly designated a UNESCO World Cultural Heritage Site in 1984, they are among the finest remaining examples of the exuberant Portuguese brand of Renaissance-Gothic architecture called Manueline (for more on the Manueline style, see Arts in the Facts about the Country chapter). They are also among the few structures in Lisbon to have survived the 1755 earthquake undamaged.

This peaceful suburb, which also boasts several other historical monuments and a clutch of worthy museums, makes a good full-day outing from central Lisbon.

In the summer a mobile turismo sets up in the Praça do Império, the huge square in front of the monastery.

Transportation is straightforward, but *don't* go on a Monday, when nearly everything in Belém is closed.

The most interesting way to get there is on the No 15 tram, which takes about 20 minutes from Praça do Comércio or 25 minutes from Praça da Figueira. Alternatively, take bus No 43 from Praça da Figueira or bus No 28 from Praça do Comércio. Get off at Largo dos Jerónimos, opposite the monastery.

Trains depart from Cais do Sodré station three to five times an hour on weekdays, slightly less frequently on weekends and holidays, and take seven minutes to get to Belém. You can take any train; tickets are 110$00. From Belém station the monastery is a few hundred metres west along the riverfront.

The railway line and the Estoril motorway cut the riverfront off from the rest of Belém, but pedestrian bridges and tunnels cross them in three places.

Mosteiro dos Jerónimos

Manuel I ordered this monastery to be built in memory of Vasco da Gama's discovery of a sea route to India and, while he was at it, arranged that its church be made a pantheon for himself and his royal descendants (many of whom are now entombed in its chancel and side chapels).

Huge sums were funnelled into the project, including so-called 'pepper money', a 5% tax levied on all income from the spice trade with Portugal's expanding African and Far Eastern colonies.

Work began in about 1502, following a Gothic design by architect Diogo de Boitac, considered one of the originators of the Manueline style. After his death in 1517, building resumed with a Renaissance flavour under Spaniard João de Castilho and, later, with classical overtones under Diogo de Torralva and Jérome de Rouen (Jerónimo de Ruão). The monastery was only completed towards the end of the century. The huge neo-Manueline western wing and the domed bell tower, which date from the 19th century, seem out of keeping with the rest.

The monastery was populated by monks of the Order of St Jerome, whose spiritual job was to give comfort and guidance to sailors

– and, of course, to pray for the king's soul. When the order was dissolved in 1833, the monastery was used as a school and orphanage until about 1940.

The façade of the **church** is dominated by João de Castilho's fantastic south portal, dense with sculptures in Renaissance style by Nicolas Chanterène. You enter through the west portal, now obscured by a modern connecting passage. In contrast to the extravagant exterior, the interior is sparsely adorned, spacious and lofty beneath an unsupported baroque transept vault 25m high. Vasco da Gama is interred in the lower chancel, in a place of honour opposite the revered poet Luís de Camões.

The central courtyard of the **cloisters** is an unnervingly peaceful place, even when it's crowded; perhaps it's the fundamental harmony of its proportions that makes many visitors just sit down on the steps or lean against its columns, as soon as they walk in.

In the old refectory an azulejo panel depicts the Biblical story of Joseph. The sarcophagus in the echoing chapter house on the north-eastern corner belongs to the 19th-century Portuguese historian Alexandre Herculano.

The monastery and church are open daily, except Mondays and holidays, from 10 am to 6.30 pm (to 5 pm in winter). Admission to the cloisters is 400$00. There is no charge to see the church, although entry is discouraged when there are weddings (Saturdays around 11 am and 3 pm, and Sundays around 1 and 3 pm) or Mass is being held (weekdays at 8 and 9.30 am and 7 pm, and Sundays at 8, 9 and 10.30 am, noon, and 7 pm).

In the monastery's western wing is the Museu Nacional de Arqueologia. Just across a small plaza is the Museu de Marinha, and at the rear of the plaza is the Planetário Calouste Gulbenkian; see Museums & Other Attractions for more information.

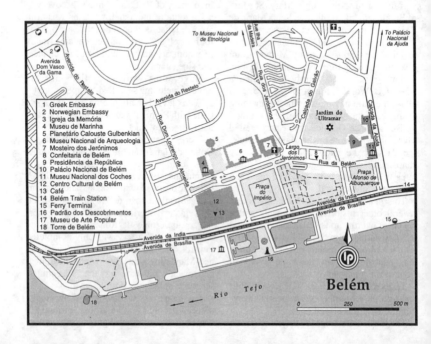

1 Greek Embassy
2 Norwegian Embassy
3 Igreja da Memória
4 Museu de Marinha
5 Planetário Calouste Gulbenkian
6 Museu Nacional de Arqueologia
7 Mosteiro dos Jerónimos
8 Confeitaria de Belém
9 Presidência da República
10 Palácio Nacional de Belém
11 Museu Nacional dos Coches
12 Centro Cultural de Belém
13 Café
14 Belém Train Station
15 Ferry Terminal
16 Padrão dos Descobrimentos
17 Museu de Arte Popular
18 Torre de Belém

Belém

Torre de Belém

Ten minutes on foot from the monastery, the Tower of Belém sits obligingly in the river. This hexagonal chesspiece has come to symbolise Lisbon and the Age of Discoveries and is perhaps Portugal's most photographed monument. Manuel I intended it as a fortress to guard the entrance to Lisbon's harbour. Before the shoreline slowly shifted south, the tower sat right out in midstream (and the monastery sat on the riverbank). Designed by Francisco Arruda, the tower is an arresting mixture of early Gothic, Byzantine and Manueline styles. Admission price and opening times are the same as for the monastery, though there's little inside that you can't see from the outside.

Padrão dos Descobrimentos

After admiring the tower, walk upriver to a modern memorial to Portuguese sea power. The huge limestone Discoveries Monument, inaugurated in 1960 on the 500th anniversary of the death of Prince Henry the Navigator, is shaped like a stylised caravel and crowded with important Portuguese figures. At the prow is Henry the Navigator;

Padrão dos Descobrimentos

behind him are explorers Vasco da Gama, Diogo Cão and Fernão de Magalhães, poet Luís de Camões, painter Nuno Gonçalves and 27 others. Opposite the entrance is a wind rose. Inside are exhibition rooms, and a lift and stairs to the top, which offers a bird's-eye view of the monastery and the river. It's open daily, except Mondays, from 9.30 am to 6 pm, and admission is 310$00 (half-price for students, and free for kids under 12).

Centro Cultural de Belém

The massive, squat Belém Cultural Centre, on the western side of Praça do Império and opened to the public in 1993, competes visually with the monastery as a moose would with a unicorn. But it's one of Lisbon's main cultural venues, with a full programme of its own. The interior plaza also gets lots of unofficial use as a roller-blade arena.

Ajuda

Ajuda is a former royal quarter on a hilltop above Belém. A 10-minute walk (or take bus No 27) up Calçada do Galvão from Largo dos Jerónimos is a little marble basilica, the Igreja da Memória, built by Dom José I on the site of an unsuccessful attempt on his life, and now the resting place of his chief minister, the formidable Marquês de Pombal.

If you bear right at the church and left up Calçada da Ajuda (or take bus No 14 or 73 directly from Praça Afonso de Albuquerque in Belém) you'll come to the oversize Palácio da Ajuda. Begun in the late 18th century, left in limbo when the royal family fled to Brazil, used as a royal residence from 1861 to 1905, but never quite finished, it's now the marginally worthwhile Museu do Palácio Nacional da Ajuda and full of royal kitsch; see Museums & Other Attractions.

Other Attractions in Belém

Other worthy museums in and around Belém are the Museu Nacional dos Coches (on Praça Afonso de Albuquerque), the Museu de Arte Popular (on Avenida de Brasília by the Centro Cultural de Belém) and the Museu Nacional de Etnológia (on Avenida

Ilha da Madeira in the Restelo district, a relatively easy walk up Rua dos Jerónimos and Avenida da Ilha da Madeira, past Restelo stadium). For more information refer to Museums & Other Attractions, below.

The present official National Palace (Palácio Nacional de Belém) and the Presidential Palace (Presidência da República) are on Calçada da Ajuda just beyond the Museu Nacional dos Coches.

MUSEUMS & OTHER ATTRACTIONS

Lisbon has 40 or 50 museums, ranging from obscure house-museums to the world-class Gulbenkian. The city's best are the Museu Calouste Gulbenkian and its sibling Centro de Arte Moderna, the Museu Nacional de Arte Antiga, the Museu do Azulejo, and the Museu-Escola de Artes Decorativas. Other good ones are the Museu Nacional de Etnológia, Museu da Cidade and Museu da Água.

Museum hours change like quicksilver, so if you're making a long trip to visit one, it's worth calling ahead. Most museums are closed on Mondays. A few have free admission on Sundays and national holidays, at least until 2 pm. Palaces tend to have free admission on Sundays until 1 pm, and are closed Tuesdays. Specific hours and charges are noted for each point of interest. Youth and student discounts are available.

Fundação Calouste Gulbenkian

Meticulously designed and set in a peaceful, landscaped garden at Avenida de Berna 45-A, the **Museu Calouste Gulbenkian** (☎ 793 51 31) is without a doubt Portugal's finest museum and one of Europe's unsung treasures. The collection spans every major epoch of Western art and much Eastern art, with hardly an unappealing item in it. Spend at least a full day here if you can.

The foundation's adjacent **Centro de Arte Moderna** (Modern Art Centre) boasts the country's best collection of 20th-century Portuguese art, including works by Amadeo de Souza Cardoso, Almada Negreiros and Maria Helena Vieira da Silva. Also here is ACARTE (Serviço de Animação, Criação Artística e Educação pela Arte), the Department of Animation, Artistic Creation & Education through Art, which promotes contemporary Portuguese performance and other arts. ACARTE runs the **Children's Art Centre** in the complex; though designed for

---

Calouste Gulbenkian

Calouste Sarkis Gulbenkian, born to Armenian parents in Istanbul in 1869, was one of the 20th century's wealthiest men and best known philanthropists, and an astute and generous patron of the arts years before he struck it rich in Iraqi oil. His great artistic coup was the purchase of works from Leningrad's Hermitage in 1928-30, when the young Soviet Union desperately needed hard currency.

In his later years he adopted Portugal as his home and bequeathed to it his entire, stupendous art collection – snubbing Britain (though he had British citizenship) after it foolishly labelled him a 'technical enemy' for working as an economic adviser in Paris at the time of the Vichy government. He lived in Portugal from 1942 until his death in 1955. In 1969 his art collection was moved into its own purpose-built quarters, Lisbon's Museu Calouste Gulbenkian.

Gulbenkian also bestowed on Portugal an extraordinary artistic, educational, scientific and charitable foundation that has become Portugal's main cultural life force. The Fundação Calouste Gulbenkian, with assets now exceeding a billion US dollars and a budget bigger than some Portuguese ministries, funds architectural restoration and the construction of libraries, museums, schools, hospitals, clinics, and centres for disabled people all over the country. In Lisbon it runs the Museu Calouste Gulbenkian and has endowed the adjacent Centro de Arte Moderna, built concert halls and galleries, and gathered together its own Orquestra Gulbenkian, Coro (Choir) Gulbenkian and a contemporary dance ensemble called Ballet Gulbenkian.

The foundation's main offices (☎ 793 51 31; fax 793 51 39; e-mail apg@gulbenkian.puug.pt) are at Avenida de Berna 45-A, 1067 Lisbon. ∎

Portuguese-speaking children, its exhibitions and related activities may also be of interest to visitors.

The Museu Calouste Gulbenkian and the Centro de Arte Moderna also host changing exhibitions and an entire programme of live music and other performances. In summer both are open Tuesdays, Thursdays, Fridays

Museu Calouste Gulbenkian Highlights

Among the classical and oriental art collections, some of the most memorable items are in the small Egyptian Room: an exquisite 2700-year-old alabaster bowl, small female statuettes (each with a different hairstyle), the extraordinarily modern-looking sculpture of a priest's head, and a superb series of bronze cats. In the adjoining Greek and Roman section, don't miss the outstanding 2400-year-old Attic vase, Roman glassware in magical colours, and an absorbing collection of Hellenic coins, etched with finely carved heads and figures. Moving on to Oriental Islamic art, Gulbenkian's eye picked out only the best in 16th and 17th-century Persian carpets (note the Portuguese influence in one, illustrating black-hatted Portuguese explorers in their boats), and illuminated Armenian manuscripts and books from the 16th to 18th centuries. Turkish faïence and azulejos from the same era glow with brilliant greens and blues, rust-reds and turquoise feather patterns, while 14th-century mosque lamps from Syria have strikingly sensuous shapes. The Chinese and Japanese collection features an inevitably rich display of porcelain, lacquer, jade and celadon – especially lovely are the 19th-century Japanese prints of flowers and birds by Sugakudo.

The huge European art section is arranged in chronological order, from medieval ivories and manuscripts to paintings from the 15th to 18th centuries. You'll recognise plenty of big names including Rembrandt (check out his sad *Figure of an Old Man*), Van Dyck (a much spookier version of an old man), Rubens (the painting of his second wife, Hélène Fourment, shows more than his usual passion) and 15th-century Ghirlandaio (his *Portrait of a Girl* is perhaps the loveliest portrait of all here). Other delightful artworks from this era include a white marble *Diana* by Houdon and a trio of 16th-century Italian tapestries portraying naughty, chubby cherubs in a cherry orchard.

Applied art of the 18th century is comprehensively represented with Aubusson tapestries,

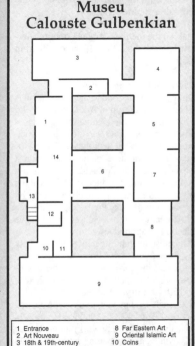

Museu Calouste Gulbenkian

1 Entrance	8 Far Eastern Art
2 Art Nouveau	9 Oriental Islamic Art
3 18th & 19th-century	10 Coins
European Art	11 Greek & Roman Art
4 Silverware	12 Egyptian Art
5 18th-century French Art	13 Upstairs to Temporary
6 Middle Ages to	Exhibits
17th Century	14 Foyer
7 Renaissance Art	

fabulous if often fussy furniture (including items from Versailles), Sèvres porcelain, silverware and intricate clocks (all in working order, naturally). Some of the most outstanding paintings in the collection are Gainsborough's *Mrs Lowndes* (her cute spaniel trotting beside her), two wonderfully atmospheric La Tour portraits, and some typically turbulent Turners. There's a whole room of works by Francesco Guardi and a passionate *Spring Kiss* by Rodin. Finally, Art Nouveau fans will be delighted with a superb collection of magical jewellery by French designer René Lalique, who created fantasies in the form of coronets and hair combs, brooches and necklaces. ∎

and Sundays from 10 am to 5 pm, and Wednesdays and Saturdays from 2 to 7.30 pm (in winter, Tuesday to Sunday from 10 am to 5 pm). Entry is 500$00 for each museum (but free on Sunday mornings). The Children's Art Centre is open weekdays only – in summer from 9 am to 1 pm and 2.30 to 5.30 pm. There is a snack bar in the main museum building and a restaurant in the Centro de Arte Moderna.

The most convenient way to get there is by taking the metro to Pahlavã station; alternatively, take bus No 31, 41 or 46 from Rossio.

Museu Nacional de Arte Antiga

Running a close second to the Gulbenkian is the National Museum of Ancient Art (☎ 396 41 51), housed in a 17th-century palace at Rua das Janelas Verdes 9 in the Lapa district. Here is the official national collection of works by Portuguese painters, the largest such collection in Portugal. The museum also features other European paintings of the 14th to 20th centuries, including works by Hieronymous Bosch, Piero della Francesca and Albrecht Dürer, as well as an extensive collection of applied art.

The most outstanding item is undoubtedly the *Panels of São Vicente* by Nuno Gonçalves, the most brilliant of the Portuguese school of painters who flourished in the 15th century, influenced by Flemish artists such as Jan van Eyck (who visited Portugal in 1428). These six panels (Gonçalves' only extant work) show a crowd of Lisbon's citizens paying homage to São Vicente, Portugal's patron saint. It's an extraordinarily detailed and revealing work, portraying every class of citizen, from beggars to fishermen, monks to Moorish knights, Jews, priests and nobles (including the Duke of Bragança and his family). The two stunning central panels feature a kneeling Dom Afonso V and Dona Isabel, Prince Henry the Navigator (with his distinctive floppy hat) and the young prince João, the future Dom João II. Gonçalves himself is thought to be the figure in the far left corner of the central left panel.

Few contemporary Portuguese works in the rest of the museum come close to this masterpiece, but the *Annunciation* by the Flemish artist-monk, Frei Carlos, is a lovely work of luminous colour. Among the European paintings, the *Temptation of St Anthony* by Bosch is stunningly horrible: in this vision of Apocalypse, skeletons play harps, men are rats, fish fly and villages burn (and St Anthony piously ignores it all). After this, it's a relief to look at the gentle works by Dürer, Holbein, della Robia and Van Dyck. Also note the delightfully prim and proper family portrait of the Viscount of Santarém by the 18th-century Portuguese artist, António de Sequeira.

There are several gifts from Calouste Gulbenkian featured in the museum's applied art collection, including an Apollo torso from the 5th century BC, but the *namban* screens by Japanese artists are the most fascinating items in the museum's new wing. Namban (literally 'barbarians from the south') is the name the Japanese gave to the Portuguese when they landed on Tanegaxima island in southern Japan in 1543, and it has come to refer to all the Japanese arts inspired by this encounter. The 16th-century screens show the Portuguese arrival in intriguing detail.

Other items from this empire-building era include Indo-Portuguese chests inlaid with mother-of-pearl and Afro-Portuguese carved tusks. Interesting, too, are the examples of Chinese porcelain shipped to Lisbon, and 18th-century Portuguese attempts at copying these imports.

Finally, don't overlook the incredible silverware collection, which includes dozens of masterpieces by the French silversmith Thomas Germain and his son François-Thomas. Made in the late 18th century for the Portuguese court and royal family, they feature fantastic flights of fancy and whimsical flourishes.

The museum is open Tuesdays from 2 to 6 pm and Wednesday to Sunday from 10 am to 6 pm; it is closed Mondays. Admission is 500$00. Take bus No 40 or 60 from Praça da Figueira, or tram No 15 or 18 west from Praça do Comércio.

Museu Nacional do Azulejo

Perhaps the city's most attractive museum is the National Azulejos Museum (☎ 814 77 47) in the Xabregas district, north-east of Santa Apolónia station. A splendid array of tiles from as early as the 15th century (plus displays on how they're made) is integrated into the elegant buildings of the former convent of Nossa Senhora da Madre de Deus Church. Among highlights are a 36m-long panel depicting pre-earthquake Lisbon, upstairs in the large cloister, and a lovely mural, *Our Lady of Life* by Marçal de Matos (dating from about 1580). There are also some charming 20th-century azulejos.

The church itself, with its beautiful tiles (and walls and ceiling crowded with paintings depicting the life of St Francis); the Manueline cloister; and the stupendous baroque chapel and adjacent rooms of carved, gilded wood are highlights in their own right. The complex was founded for the Poor Clare order of nuns in 1509 by Dona Leonor, wife of Dom João II.

The museum also boasts an excellent restaurant in a fine garden setting (see Places to Eat). Take bus No 104 from Praça do Comércio or No 105 from Praça da Figueira. The museum is open Tuesdays from 2 to 6 pm and Wednesday to Sunday from 10 am to 6 pm (closed Mondays); give yourself at least an hour. Entry is 350$00. Reproduction tiles, coffee-table books and other items are for sale in the lobby.

For more information about azulejos, see the aside under Visual & Decorative Arts in the Facts about the Country chapter.

Museu-Escola de Artes Decorativas

The Museum-School of Decorative Arts (☎ 886 21 83) is owned and operated by the private Fundação Ricardo do Espírito Santo Silva, founded in 1953 to showcase banker Espírito Santo Silva's striking collection of 16th to 19th-century furniture and other decorative articles, ranging from a silver picnic set to beautiful Arraiolos rugs. The foundation has also set up educational projects to encourage traditional crafts, and provides adjacent workshop space to cabinet-makers, silversmiths, bookbinders and others working with traditional methods.

All of this, plus a book and souvenir shop, coffee shop, restaurant, library and temporary exhibitions, are housed on several floors of the elegant 18th-century Palácio Azurara (which itself sports some fine original azulejos), at Largo das Portas do Sol 2. It's open daily, except Mondays, from 10 am to 5 pm (to 8 pm on Tuesdays and Thursdays in summer). Admission is 500$00, and half-hour tours can be arranged.

The *largo* (square) itself, reached from the Baixa by tram No 28, or from Praça da Figueira on bus No 37, offers grand views over Alfama and the river.

Museu da Água

Lisbon only got a dependable water supply in the 18th century. The system, ordered by Dom João V, included the huge Aqueduto dos Águas Livres or Aqueduct of Free Waters (described in the Rato, Saldanha, Campolide & Sete Ríos section earlier in this chapter) and several reservoirs, including the main Mãe d'Água (Mother of Water) at Praça das Amoreiras, and the smaller Reservatório de Patriarcal at Praça do Principe Real, by the botanical garden.

The Water Museum (☎ 813 55 22), devoted to Lisbon's water supply down the centuries, won the Council of Europe's Museum Prize in 1990. It's located in the former Barbadinhos pumping station on Rua do Alviela (built in 1880 to provide water to higher parts of Lisbon), and is open daily, except Sundays and Mondays, from 10 am to 12.30 pm and 2 to 5 pm. Admission is 200$00. Take bus No 104 from Praça do Comércio or No 105 from Praça da Figueira, and get off four stops after Santa Apolónia station. Walk up Calçada dos Barbadinhos, turn right into Rua do Alviela and walk to the end.

The city's water company and the museum jointly run guided walking tours of the aqueduct (usually in Portuguese) every Thursday and Saturday in summer, starting at Mãe d'Água (get there on bus No 9 from Rossio). For meeting times, ask at the museum. There are also tours of the Reservatório de Patriarcal, and occasional exhibitions at both reservoirs.

Museu da Cidade

The City Museum (☎ 759 16 17) provides a telescopic view of Lisbon's history. Its highlights include an enormous model of pre-earthquake Lisbon, numerous old maps and prints from before and after the quake, and azulejo panels of city scenes. Almada Negreiros' portrait of the poet Fernando Pessoa is also here, as well as the shoes and shawl of Amália Rodrigues, Portugal's foremost fado singer.

The museum is housed in the fine 18th-century Palácio Pimenta (said to have been built by Dom João V for one of his mistresses), at Campo Grande 245. It's open daily, except Mondays, from 10.30 am to 1 pm and 2 to 6 pm. Admission is 320$00 (but free on Sunday mornings). Take the metro to Campo Grande station, or bus No 1 or 36 from Rossio.

The museum also organises group tours of the ruins of a Roman spa beneath the streets of the lower Baixa district (described in the Baixa section earlier in this chapter). Tours run at 3, 4 and 5 pm every Thursday afternoon in summer.

Museu de Arte Sacra

The Religious Art Museum (☎ 346 03 61), also known as the Museu de São Roque, is housed in the former convent of the Igreja de São Roque on Largo Trindade Coelho. Inside is a mind-boggling array of liturgical accessories – gold-threaded vestments, bookstands of carved bronze, gem-encrusted chalices, bejewelled mitres – in particular those from the church's Capela de São João Baptista, a stupefyingly expensive folly of Dom João V described in the Bairro Alto & Chiado section earlier. The museum is open daily, except Mondays, from 10 am to 5 pm. Admission is 150$00, but free on Sundays.

Museu Nacional dos Coches

Though its focus is narrow – royal, aristocratic and church coaches of the 17th to 19th century – the National Coach Museum is one of Lisbon's most eye-popping (and popular) sights, and has one of the best such collections in the world. The museum was founded in 1905 to preserve the monarchy's many horse-drawn carriages, and subsequently beefed up with more from the patriarchate and various noble families. There are enough gilded, painted and truly over-the-top vehicles to numb the senses and, like the Museu de Arte Sacra, they illustrate the ostentation and staggering wealth of the old Portuguese élite. The museum (☎ 363 80 22) is in the former royal riding school on Praça Afonso de Albuquerque in Belém. It's open daily, except Mondays, from 10 am to 5.30 or 6 pm. Admission is 450$00.

Museu Nacional de Etnológia

The National Ethnological Museum (☎ 301 52 64-5) mounts excellent temporary exhibitions, changing several times a year, from its collection of some 26,000 items. Exhibits include audio-visual displays (including music) on Portugal's former colonies in Africa and Asia, and a wide-ranging display of traditional textiles and weaving techniques from all over the world, notably Indonesia.

The museum is on Avenida Ilha da Madeira in the Restelo district, a relatively easy walk up from Belém (or take bus No 32 directly from Praça da Figueira). It's open Tuesdays from 2 to 6 pm and Wednesday through Sunday from 10 am to 6 pm (closed Mondays). Admission is 350$00.

Museu Nacional de Arqueologia

First opened in 1893, the National Archaeological Museum (☎ 362 00 00), in the west wing of the Mosteiro dos Jerónimos in Belém, includes ceramics, sculpture, tiles, glass and coins from prehistory through Moorish times, and a large collection of antique gold jewellery from the Bronze Age through Roman times. It's open Tuesdays from 2 to 6 pm and Wednesday through Sunday from 10 am to 6 pm (closed Mondays). Admission is 180$00.

Lisbon

Top Left:	Art Nouveau doorway
Top Right:	Houses in the Alfama district
Bottom Left:	Casa del Pica, Bairro Alto district
Bottom Right:	Elevador da Bica, Bairro Alto district

BETHUNE CARMICHAEL

BETHUNE CARMICHAEL

JULIA WILKINSON

Around Lisbon

Left: Palácio Nacional da Pena, Sintra
Right: Sintra
Bottom: Cabo da Roca

Museu Arqueológico do Carmo

The photogenically ruined arches of the Convento do Carmo, on Largo do Carmo in the Chiado district, are an effective setting for a rambling collection of artefacts called the Carmo Archaeological Museum. Among the items scattered around the open-air nave are Luso-Romano statuary, a huge carved tomb of Ançã limestone containing the bones of Ferdinand I, and a 3500-year-old Egyptian mummy clasping its knees beside gruesome preserved Peruvian skulls complete with hair.

Implicitly this is also a museum of the 1755 earthquake that brought down the church and convent (discussed further in the Bairro Alto & Chiado section earlier). The exhibits are open daily, except Sundays and Mondays, from 10 am to 6 pm during April through September, and from 10 am to 1 pm and 2 to 5 pm the rest of the year. Admission is 300$00. From the Baixa it's a steep walk, or an easy ride on the Elevador de Santa Justa.

Museu do Chiado

The Chiado Museum (☎ 343 21 48), known until 1994 as the Museu Nacional de Arte Contemporânea, in the former Convento de São Francisco at Rua Serpa Pinto 4 in the Chiado, is a respectable collection of contemporary Portuguese paintings, drawings and sculpture from approximately 1850 to 1950. Among painters represented are Rafael Bordalo Pinheiro, José de Almada Negreiros, Amadeo de Souza Cardoso and Maria Helena Vieira da Silva. The museum is open Tuesdays from 2 to 6 pm and Wednesday through Sunday from 10 am to 6 pm (closed Mondays). Admission is 400$00.

Museu da Marioneta

Lisbon's Puppet Museum (☎ 887 86 96) is for puppet aficionados of all ages, not just for kids. It's crammed with every kind of puppet imaginable, from finger puppets to life-size creations. Especially interesting are the traditional Portuguese puppets from the 19th century and an Asian collection (including elephant puppets from Burma). There's also a tiny theatre where performances for children are often held at weekends.

The museum is at Largo Rodrigues de Freitas 13, on the eastern side of the Castelo São Jorge and not far from the No 28 tram line. It's open daily, except Mondays, from 10 am to 1 pm and 2 to 6 pm; admission is 300$00.

Museu Nacional do Traje & Museu Nacional do Teatro

The National Costume Museum (☎ 759 03 18) and National Theatre Museum (☎ 757 25 47) both occupy 18th-century palaces in the grounds of the lush Parque Monteiro-Mór in the far north of the city. The Museu Nacional do Traje features changing exhibits of court and common dress from the Middle Ages to the present, and the Museu Nacional do Teatro has theatrical costumes, props, posters and lots of photos of actors. Both are open Tuesdays from 2 to 6 pm and Wednesday to Sunday from 10 am to 6 pm (closed Mondays) – though they're a little too far away to be worth a trip (take bus No 7 from Praça da Figueira, or bus No 3 from Campo Grande metro station).

Museu Militar

The Military Museum's main claim to fame is its artillery collection, said to be the world's biggest. War freaks can also look at other heavy and light arms, medals and patriotic paintings. The museum (☎ 888 21 31) opened in 1842 in a palace at the site of a former military arsenal and foundry on Largo do Museu da Artilharia. It's open daily, except Sundays and Mondays, from 11 am to 6 pm (in winter from 10 am to 4 or 5 pm). Take bus No 104 from Praça do Comércio or No 105 from Praça da Figueira.

Museu de Arte Popular

The Folk Art Museum (☎ 301 12 82), a collection of clothing, fabrics, ceramics, furniture, tools, toys and more from around the country, organised by region, is as good a one-stop look as you can get of Portugal's charming and diverse folk arts. Among items you're unlikely to spot anywhere else are bagpipes from Mirando do Douro, toby jugs from Aveiro and huge spiked dog collars for the beasts of Castelo Branco. The museum is on Avenida de Brasília by the Centro Cultural de Belém, and is open daily, except Mondays, from 10 am to 12.30 pm and 2 to 5.30 pm. Admission is 200$00.

Museu de Marinha

Beside Mosteiro dos Jerónimos in Belém is the Naval Museum (☎ 362 00 10), with model ships from the Age of Discoveries to the present, several small boats including an 18th-century brigantine, a turn-of-the-century royal cabin from the yacht *Amélia*, complete with fireplace and pianola, the seaplane *Santa Cruz* that made the first crossing of the south Atlantic in 1922, and cases full of astrolabes and navy uniforms.

This place is great fun if you happen to be in a school group, of which there are always many here. Admission is free for children under 10, and half-price for those from 10 to 19 years of age; adults pay 300$00. It's open daily, except Mondays, from 10 am to 5 pm (to 6 pm on Sundays).

Museu do Palácio Nacional da Ajuda

This endless museum of royal belongings, in the never-quite-completed Ajuda National Palace (official royal residence from 1861 until 1905) is dominated by the furnishings of Dona Maria II and her husband Dom Ferdinand, whose lack of taste will be familiar to visitors to Sintra's Pena Palace, their summer retreat. Also on the grounds is the Galeria de Pintura do Rei Dom Luís (Dom Luís Art Gallery), open from 10 am to 6 pm except Mondays, with changing exhibitions.

The palace is in the Ajuda district, a 20-minute walk above Belém on Calçada da Ajuda (or hop on bus No 14 or 73 at Praça Afonso de Albuquerque). You can also get there directly on tram No 18 from Praça do Comércio. It's open daily, except Wednesdays, from 10 am to 5 pm, and admission is 200$00.

Other Galleries & Exhibition Centres

Beside those mentioned above, at least two other venues host changing art exhibitions and sometimes music and other performances. The Sala de Exposições da Caixa Geral de Depósitos, in the Caixa Geral de Depósitos building on Rua Arco do Cego, is open weekdays, except Tuesdays, from 10 am to 5 pm, and weekends from 3 to 7 pm.

Planetarium & Aquaparque

The Planetário Calouste Gulbenkian (☎ 362 00 02), on Praça do Império beside Mosteiro dos Jerónimos in Belém, has a 40-minute show for 400$00. Far away in Caselas (north of Belém) is the Aquaparque (☎ 301 50 17); take bus No 43 from Belém (or directly from Praça da Figueira).

ORGANISED TOURS
Bus & Tram Tours

Carris, the municipal transport company, has a 1½-hour Hills Tour by tram, up to four or five times a day, up and around the hills on both sides of the Baixa, for 2800$00. It also has a 2000$00 open-top bus Tagus Tour of the city and Belém, six or seven times a day, arranged so you can get off, explore, and pick up the next bus an hour later. Both tours are in English. They depart from Praça do Comércio and there is no need to book ahead.

From offices next door to one another, Gray Line (☎ 352 25 94), Cityrama (☎ 355 85 69) and Portugal Tours (☎ 316 03 99) run more or less identical sightseeing bus tours of Lisbon and the surrounding region, for identical prices. Typical Lisbon offerings include a three-hour city tour for 4900$00; Lisbon by night (four hours), with a restaurant meal, for 11,900$00; and Lisbon plus the Estoril coast or Lisbon plus the Costa Azul (full day) for 11,900$00. All buses depart from a terminal on Avenida Sidónio Pais, a block south of São Sebastião metro station, and pick up passengers at selected hotels. The easiest place to book a seat is through a travel agent or up-market hotel, but if there's a space you can usually hop aboard the daytime trips without a booking.

River Cruises

For a relaxed look at the city from a unique point of view, Gray Line (☎ 887 50 58) runs two-hour, multilingual cruises on the Tejo (Cruzeiros no Tejo). They depart daily (at least from April through October) at 3 pm from the eastern end of the Terreiro do Paço ferry terminal by Praça do Comércio. The boats go down as far as Belém, cross the river and return, with no stops. The price is 3000$00 if you buy a ticket at the terminal, more if you book it through a hotel (in which case you get picked up from – but not returned to – the hotel). In summer tickets are also sold from a kiosk at the bottom of Rua do Carmo. For student-card holders, children under six and adults over 65, the price is 1500$00.

SPECIAL EVENTS
Expo '98

From May through September of 1998, Lisbon will play host to the last big world's fair of the millennium, called Expo '98. For more information refer to the boxed aside earlier in this chapter.

Festas dos Santos Populares

In June the city lets its hair down with its Festos dos Santos Populares (Festivals of the Popular Saints), Christianised versions of traditional summer solstice celebrations. Lisbon is the birthplace of Santo António (known elsewhere as St Anthony of Padua), and the city's biggest bash of the year is the Festa de Santo António on 12-13 June. The Alfama district (and to some extent Mouraria and Bairro Alto) parties through the night of the 12th, with little *tronos* (thrones) for Santo António in every square, plus parades, music, dancing, fireworks and, of course, lots of wine and grilled sardines. On the 13th, a municipal holiday, revellers rest and the devout go to church.

The city then goes on buzzing for the rest of June, with city-sponsored concerts, exhibitions and street theatre. Along with many communities across Portugal, Lisbon also celebrates the Festa de São João (St John) on the 23-24 June, and the Festa de São Pedro

(St Peter) on the 28th and 29th. Across the Rio Tejo at Montijo, the Festa de São Pedro is a fisherfolk celebration that dates from the Middle Ages, with a blessing of the boats, as well as bullfights and a running of the bulls.

Music Festivals

The Fundação Gulbenkian (see Museums & Other Attractions) organises several annual international music festivals in Lisbon. These include Jornadas de Música Contemporânea (Journeys in Contemporary Music) at venues around the city in May; Jazz em Agosto (Jazz in August) in the foundation's gardens in early August; and Jornadas de Música Antiga (Journeys in Ancient Music) at various historical sites around Lisbon in October.

Athletic Events

Lisbon hosts an international marathon, the Maratona de Lisboa (known in English as the Discoveries Marathon), every year in late November, and an annual half-marathon in early March. If this sounds like a nice way to see the city, contact the Federação Portuguesa de Atletismo (☎ 414 60 20), Largo da Lagoa 15-B, 2795 Linda-a-Velha.

PLACES TO STAY

During high season, advance bookings are imperative for any accommodation near the city centre. The turismo at Praça dos Restauradores will make enquiries about accommodation, but no reservations. There appear to be very few private rooms for short-term rental in Lisbon.

PLACES TO STAY – BOTTOM END
Camping

Six km west of Rossio on the far side of Parque Florestal de Monsanto is the big (1400 sites), well-equipped *Campismo de Câmara Municipal de Lisboa* (☎ 760 20 61; fax 760 74 74). It's open year-round. Rates from May through September are 405$00 per person over 10 years old, 265$00 per car, 345$00 to 770$00 per tent or caravan; these drop by 60% or more in low season. Youth-card holders get 50% off in low season. To get there take bus No 14 or 43 from Praça da Figueira.

The next nearest camping ground is a pricey one run by Clube de Campismo de Lisboa, about 20 km north-west at Almornos. There are half a dozen more across the Tejo along the Costa de Caparica, and others to the west at Sintra, Praia Grande and Praia do Guincho (see Around Lisbon).

Hostels

Lisbon's big pousada de juventude (☎ 353 26 96) is close to the centre at Rua Andrade Corvo 46, just off Avenida Fontes Pereira de Melo. The closest metro station is Picoas.

You can also take bus No 46 from Santa Apolónia or the Rossio, bus No 44 or 45 from Cais do Sodré, or bus No 44, 45 or the Aero-Bus from the airport. Even if you don't stay, the hostel's bulletin board is a good place for messages, tips and suggestions for places to eat.

The next nearest hostel is the beachside *Pousada de Juventude de Catalazete* (☎ 443 06 38) on Estrada Marginal in Oeiras, 12 km west of Lisbon. From Cais do Sodré station, take an Oeiras or Cascais train to Oeiras, a 20 to 25-minute trip; there are four to six departures hourly.

Both these hostels are open 24 hours a day. They are very popular so reservations are essential – in summer, preferably at least a month ahead. There's also a hostel at Sintra, 45 minutes from Lisbon by train from Rossio station (see Around Lisbon).

Movijovem (☎ 355 90 81; fax 352 86 21), Avenida Duque de Ávila 137 (near Saldanha metro station), is the central booking office for all of Portugal's Hostelling International youth hostels. It's open from 9.30 am to 6 pm on weekdays only.

Pensões & Residencials – Rossio & Praça dos Restauradores

Residencial Campos (☎ 346 28 64, ☎ 346 28 53), on the 3rd floor at Rua Jardim do Regedor 24, offers simple, good-value doubles with a shower for 4000$00, or with a bath from 4500$00. The same people run *Residencial Estrela do Mondego* (☎ 346 71

09) at Calçada do Carmo 25, up behind Rossio station, where rooms are bigger but rates are the same.

Further up, at No 53 in pedestrian-only Calçada do Duque, *Pensão Duque* (☎ 346 34 44) has good vibes and clean singles/doubles with shared shower and toilet for about 2500$00/3500$00. At the top of the hill at Largo Trindade Coelho 6, the noisier *Pensão Estrela de Ouro* (☎ 346 51 10) has similar prices.

Residencial Nova Avenida (☎ 342 36 89), on quiet Rua de Santo António da Glória 87 near Praça da Alegria, has old but well-kept doubles with shower for 3000$00.

Pensões & Residencials – Baixa

We didn't find anything appealing in this price range in the Baixa. Indeed, some cheapos looked like borderline firetraps.

Pensões & Residencials – Chiado

It's a long climb to the 4th floor, but plain, comfortable doubles/triples with shower at *Pensão Estrela do Chiado* (☎ 342 61 10), Rua Garrett 29, are reasonable at 4000$00/ 5000$00.

Pensões & Residencials – elsewhere

Pensão Louro (☎ 813 34 22), at Rua Morais Soares 76, three blocks east of Arroios metro station, is a student hostelry during the school year but in July and August some spartan multi-bed rooms with showers are available, including doubles for about 3000$00.

Residencial Rocha (☎ 887 06 18) is in a slightly depressing corner of the city, at Rua dos Bacalhoeiros 12, in the Alfama district opposite the Renex bus stand, but doubles with toilet and shower are cheap at 4000$00.

PLACES TO STAY – MIDDLE
Rossio & Praça dos Restauradores

Near the bottom of the Elevador da Glória at Rua da Glória 21, the *Pensão Monumental* (☎ 346 98 07) has functional singles/doubles (noisy on the street side) from 5000$00/ 6000$00. Adequate doubles at *Pensão Estação Central* (☎ 342 33 08), Calçada do Carmo 17, behind Rossio station, are overpriced at 5000$00 without shower, 6500$00 with.

Baixa

Many mid-range places in the Baixa are in old residential flats – chipped and fading, but warm and welcoming. A good one is the bright *Pensão Arco da Bandeira* (☎ 342 34 78), just inside the arch of the same name, at Rua dos Sapateiros 226. It has plain, clean doubles with shared facilities for under 4500$00. If you don't mind climbing four flights of grotty stairs, another cheerful place with similar prices is *Pensão Moderna* (☎ 346 08 18) at Rua dos Coreeiros 205; it's surrounded by good, modestly priced eateries. Another with a long climb is *Pensão Galicia* (☎ 342 84 30) at Rua do Crucifixo 50, where doubles with shared toilet are 3500$00 and up, or 4500$00 with shower and a little balcony.

Pensão Insulana (☎ 342 31 31), Rua da Assunção 52, has simple, pleasant doubles with bath for 7700$00. A couple wrote to say their backpack full of valuables disappeared at *Pensão Aljubarrota*, across the road at No 53; give it a miss.

Bairro Alto & Chiado

The best value in this neighbourhood and price bracket is *Pensão Londres* (☎ 346 22 03; fax 346 56 82) at Rua Dom Pedro V 53. Singles/doubles on the upper floors, with fine views across the city, run from 4000$00/5300$00 with shared shower to 7000$00/9300$00 with attached bath, all with breakfast; downstairs rooms are a little cheaper. This popular place gets booked out a month ahead in summer. Nearby at Rua do Teixeira 37, the pleasant *Pensão Globo* (☎ 346 22 79) has doubles without shower from 3500$00, or with shower for 4500$00. From Praça dos Restauradores, both places are easy to reach on the Elevador da Glória.

Good value at the southern end of the Chiado is the *Residencial Nova Silva* (☎ 342 43 71; fax 342 77 70), at Rua Vitor Cordon 11, where plain singles/doubles with toilet, shower and river views are 4000$00/5000$00.

Elsewhere

The *Residencial Lisbonense* (☎ 354 46 28, ☎ 354 48 99), on four upper storeys at Rua Pinheiro Chagas 1 in the Saldanha district (metro: Saldanha), has pleasant, bright singles/doubles with bath, telephone and air-conditioning from 4000$00/7000$00, with breakfast.

PLACES TO STAY – TOP END
Rossio & Praça dos Restauradores

Hotel Suiço-Atlântico (☎ 346 17 13; fax 346 90 13), close to the turismo at Rua da Glória 3, has well-maintained singles/doubles with bath for 7500$00/9500$00.

At Rua Mãe d'Água 16-20, a few steps from the botanical garden, is the bland but pleasant *Hotel Botânico* (☎ 342 03 92; fax 342 01 25), where doubles with TV, telephone, air-con and minibar are 12,000$00 with shower or 13,000$00 with bath, all with breakfast.

Major credit cards are accepted at both places.

Castelo de São Jorge

Lofty in every sense is *Pensão Ninho das Águias* (☎ 886 70 08), just below the castle but a long climb above the street at Costa do Castelo 74. With a flower garden, stunning views over the city and 14 elegant rooms, this place gets booked up a month ahead in summer and reservations are essential. Doubles/triples are about 6500$00/7500$00 with shared toilet and shower and 7500$00/8500$00 with their own.

Elsewhere

Casa de São Mamede (☎ 396 31 66) is a small hotel in an elegant townhouse at Rua Escola Politécnica 159. Doubles/triples with bath, TV and telephone start at 10,000$00/12,000$00, including breakfast. It's a long climb from Rossio, or you can take bus No 15 from Cais do Sodré and get off a couple of blocks past the Universidade Internacional.

Just off Avenida da Liberdade at Rua Mouzinho da Silveira 3, the well-run *Hotel Jorge V* (☎ 356 25 25) has singles/doubles with shower, TV and telephone for 8000$00/ 10,000$00, with breakfast. It's midway between Avenida and Rotunda metro stations.

PLACES TO EAT

Lisbon is not a gastronomic paradise, but you can fill up and enjoy without spending a lot of money.

Restaurants & Cafés

Good (and good-value) restaurants and cafés are concentrated in the Baixa and Bairro Alto districts. With a few exceptions noted here, places off Rossio and Praça dos Restauradores, while sometimes very good, tend to be poorer value for money. Avoid the dinnertime rush and sit down to eat before about 7.30 pm; better yet, go for lunch.

Rossio & Praça dos Restauradores Not

for vegetarians is a good little casa de pasto called *Casa Transmontana* (☎ 342 03 00) at Calçada do Duque 39. It serves one or more strong-tasting northern Portuguese specialities, eg chicken or rabbit cooked in its own blood, at a modest 700$00 to 1100$00 per plate. Also recommended is the sweet pudim de castanhas (chestnut pudding). It's open daily from noon to 3 pm and 7.30 to 11.30 pm (but on Sundays in the evening only); on weekends, book ahead or arrive early.

For a coffee or a meal, the handsome Art Deco *Café Nicola*, at Rua 1 de Dezembro 16-26 and around the block at Rossio 24, is the grande dame of Lisbon's turn-of-the-century cafés, its maroon walls lined with paintings. We found it closed because of metro expansion, and had to settle for pricey coffee and a fraction of the atmosphere at *Nicola Gourmet*, Rua 1 de Dezembro 10. It's closed on Sundays.

A good spot close to the turismo is the unpretentious *Restaurante O Brunhal* (☎ 347 86 34) at Rua da Glória 27. It has well-prepared standard pratos do dia for 600$00 to 700$00 and service beyond the call of duty.

Opposite the turismo at Praça dos Restauradores 79 is *Pinóquio* (☎ 346 51 06),

with pricey but tasty seafood specials. A block back, along Rua das Portas de Santo Antão, a string of restaurants offers good but seriously overpriced seafood at sunny outdoor tables for tourists who cannot find their way out of the centre.

Baixa The Baixa has plenty of burgers and beer if that suits you, but also some of the best modestly priced food in Lisbon. Our favourite is *Restaurante João do Grão* (☎ 342 47 57) at Rua dos Coreeiros 228, open daily from noon to 4 pm and 7 to 11 pm (closing earlier in winter). Don't confuse the decades-old 'Inglish Menu Trnsletion' (sic) with the real thing, which has a long list of salads, soups and fish and meat standards, helpfully arranged in order of price. You can eat well here for under 2000$00. Two other good-value places on the same street are *Restaurante Ena Pãi* (☎ 342 17 59) at No 180 and the casual casa de pasto *Lagosta Vermelha* (☎ 342 48 32) at No 155 (closed Sunday).

Down at Praça do Comércio 3, *Martinho da Arcada* (☎ 887 92 59) makes much of the fact that it has been in business since 1782. It was once a haunt of the literary set, including Fernando Pessoa, though renovation has altered its clientele from literati to tourists. The café, good value for a stand-up or sit-down lunch (daily specials are about 700$00), is open from 7 am to 9 pm; the very much pricier restaurant closes at 10 pm, and both are closed on Sundays.

Bairro Alto & Chiado Mention Bairro Alto and most tourists think 'fado', although most casas de fado are better known for their music than their menus. See the Entertainment section for several tourist-friendly fado houses with adequate food, most of them in the Bairro Alto.

The informal, family-run *Tasca do Manel* (☎ 346 38 13) at Rua da Barroca 24 serves plain, tasty Portuguese standards that are good value at 1000$00 to 1800$00 per dish. Cavernous *Cervejaria da Trindade* (☎ 342 35 06) at Rua Nova da Trindade 20-C is a former convent building with arched ceilings, gorgeous 19th-century tilework and a robust, busy atmosphere. They've been serving food here for over 150 years. It's a bit pricey (beef and seafood specialities from the grill start at 1200$00) but it makes a great lunch stop. It's open daily, except holidays, from noon to 1 am.

Pap'Açorda (☎ 346 48 11), at Rua da Atalaia 57, features startling décor and excellent, expensive açorda (bread and shellfish mush served in a clay pot). It's popular with celebrities and celebrity-watchers, so advance bookings are essential. It's open from noon to 2 pm and 7.30 to 10.30 pm.

Short on atmosphere but with daily specials modestly priced from 600$00 is the bright, plain *Cafetaria Brasil* at Rua de São Pedro de Alcântara 51. Check out the unusual décor at *Restaurante O Tacão Pequeno* (☎ 347 28 48), around the corner at Travessa da Carra 3-A.

Near Cais do Sodré station, *Restaurante Porto de Abrigo* (☎ 346 08 73), Rua dos Remolares 18, has good fish and seafood dishes for 800$00 to 1700$00. One of several basic cheapies in the same area is *Pastelaria & Snack Bar Brasilia* (☎ 346 69 02) at Praça do Duque da Terceira 10, with daily specials for about 800$00. These and most other places in this neighbourhood are closed on Sundays and holidays.

Elsewhere A pastelaria and café crammed with Portuguese at lunch is *Balcão do Marquês* (☎ 354 50 86) at Avenida Duque de Loulé 119, two blocks from Rotunda metro station. Eating is mainly stand-up (balcão means counter) and there are stacks of sandwiches or a large daily menu of meaty plates for under 800$00, plus soups, salads and sweets. Take an ordering ticket when you enter; service is crisp and cheerful. It's open weekdays from 7 am to 9 pm and Saturdays from 7 am to 3 pm.

One of the finest settings for a light lunch is the restaurant of the *Museu Nacional do Azulejo*, in the old convent of Nossa Senhora da Madre de Deus Church; take bus No 104 from Praça do Comércio or No 105 from Praça da Figueira. Choose from a small menu of salads, crêpes or meat and fish dishes for 1000$00 to 1300$00, and eat in the bright, traditional kitchen (tiled with azulejos, of course) or the plant-filled garden.

If you're nostalgic for pizzas and burgers, try the cheerful *Big Apple Restaurante*, at the rear of a shopping arcade at Rua Barata Salgueiro 28, a block off Avenida da Liberdade. It's open from noon to 3.30 pm on weekdays, and Friday and Saturday nights from 7 to 11 pm; fuel up here for the Ad Lib disco upstairs (see Entertainment).

In Belém there is a good café in the Centro Cultural on the western side of Praça do Império, and lots of small restaurants and pastelarias on Rua de Belém, just east of the monastery.

Vegetarian Thankfully, in this country that so loves its meat, the capital has a few good, modestly priced vegetarian eateries.

Our choice for best value is *Restaurante Os Tibetanos* (☎ 314 20 38), part of a school of Tibetan Buddhism in an old house topped with prayer flags at Rua do Salitre 117, on the northern side of the botanical garden (metro: Avenida). It offers a changing 750$00 rice and vegetable prato simples, plus soups, salads and pastries in a fresh, peaceful atmosphere. It's open for meals from noon to 2.30 pm and 7.30 to 10 pm on weekdays, and to 10.30 pm on Saturdays. It serves teas, coffee and munchies from 4.30 to 7 pm.

Also recommended is the *Restaurante Espiral* (☎ 357 35 85) at Praça Ilha do Faial 14-A in the Estefânia district (metro: Saldanha). It's open daily from 10 am to 10 pm with macrobiotic rice and vegetable dishes, Chinese-style vegetables and light meals for less than 600$00 per course, plus lots of sweet snacks and desserts – and sometimes live music. Next door at No 14-B is a food shop and snack bar with soups, salads and sandwiches for under 300$00; it's open from 10 am to 8.30 pm.

The *Centro de Alimentação e Saúde Natural* (☎ 315 08 98) is a small restaurant with a weedy, meditative courtyard at Rua Mouzinho da Silveira 25 in Rato (between

Avenida and Rotunda metro stations). On weekdays from noon to 9 pm and Saturdays from noon to 2 pm it has a small selection of vegetarian and macrobiotic plates for under 1000$00, plus soups and desserts. Next door is a health-food shop, and courses in massage and Zen meditation are offered upstairs.

At Rua 1 de Dezembro 65, by Rossio train station, is a health-food shop called *Celeiro*, open weekdays from 8.30 am to 8 pm and Saturdays to 7 pm. A macrobiotic restaurant upstairs was either abandoned or under serious renovation when we were there. On the next block is a good small supermarket, also called Celeiro.

Restaurante Yin-Yang, a vegetarian place upstairs at Rua dos Coreeiros 14 in the Baixa, was closed when we visited.

Pastelarias & Confeitarias

Lisbon has enough pastry shops and coffee shops to keep you buzzing all day, and the Portuguese love 'em. Many restaurants also have a separate area devoted to this excellent Portuguese pastime. You'll often pay less to have your snack at the balção (counter), and quite a lot more to have it at a table out on the esplanada.

Our favourite spot around the Rossio is a big pastelaria called *Casa Suiça* (☎ 342 80 92) at Rossio 96-101 (through to Praça da Figueira 3-A). It has good coffee and a dizzying array of pastries and sweets available daily from 7 am to 10 pm.

With strong literary associations and art all over the walls, *Café A Brasileira* (☎ 346 95 47), open daily from 8 am to 2 am at Rua Garrett 120 (soon to be directly above a new metro station) in the Chiado, is a very elegant setting for a snack.

Beloved of students and old dears from the neighbourhood, for its pastries and big coffees, is cheerful *Confeitaria Císter*, at Rua da Escola Politécnica 107.

At Rua Bernardino Costa 34-36 in Cais do Sodré is a fine little bakery and pastelaria called *Caneças*, with hot fresh bread, croissants, cakes and light snacks. It's open weekdays from 6 am to 7.30 pm and Saturdays from 8 am to 2 pm.

Finally, when you go to Belém, don't miss the *Confeitaria de Belém*, opposite the tram stop on Rua de Belém, where the traditional custard tarts called pastéis de Belém are made on the premises and consumed (for about 100$00 each) in vast quantities.

ENTERTAINMENT

Lisbon's main concert halls are at the Fundação Calouste Gulbenkian (☎ 795 02 36) and the Centro Cultural de Belém (☎ 301 96 06). In the Chiado, Lisbon's opera house, the Teatro Nacional de São Carlos (☎ 346 59 14) at Rua Serpa Pinto 9, and the neighbouring Teatro Municipal de São Luís (☎ 342 71 72) at Rua António Maria Cardoso 54, have their own concert, opera and theatre seasons.

Free concerts are often held on weekends

Chapitô

If you pop into the *Chapitô* bar (☎ 887 82 25), below Castelo São Jorge at Costa do Castelo 7, you'll discover that it's more than an open-air pub with a great view. It's actually part of a school of circus arts and show business run by the Collectividade Cultural e Recreativa de Santa Catarina (Santa Catarina Cultural & Recreation Collective), founded in the mid-1980s.

Next door at No 1 are the collective's office, library, theatre, gallery, recording studios, classrooms and a day-care centre. On the patio you may see street-theatre or juggling workshops; in the bar you may hear live music, poetry readings or other late-evening entertainment. The collective runs evening courses in dance, music, singing, juggling, circus techniques and TV acting, and presents performances, films and exhibitions – all listed in its own monthly programme (in Portuguese), and also usually in the newspapers, in the *Agenda Cultural* and at the turismo.

There is also a small restaurant, *Gargalhada Geral*, which serves salads, soups and sandwiches; it's open from 7.30 pm to 2 am. The bar is open from 9.30 pm to 2 am. Both are closed on Sundays. ∎

– and almost daily during the Festas dos Santos Populares in June (see Special Events in this chapter) – at several city churches and former churches, including the Basílica da Estrela (Estrela), Igreja de São Roque (Bairro Alto), Convento do Carmo (Chiado), Basílica da Nossa Senhora dos Mártires (Chiado) and the Sé (Alfama).

If you're visiting with children, check out Teatro Infantil de Lisboa or TIL (☎ 363 99 74) at Rua Leão Oliveira 1, just off Largo do Calvário in the Alcântara district.

For current listings, pick up the free monthly *Agenda Cultural* from the turismo, the Lisboa Card office at Rua Jardim do Regedor 50, or Agenda Cultural's office at Largo da Rosa 5 in the Alfama – or see the listings in the daily *Público* newspaper. The Gulbenkian and the Centro Cultural de Belém publish their own schedules as well. The city operates a 24-hour 'what's on' hotline (☎ 790 10 62) with information about theatre, dance, classical music, rock concerts, cinema, galleries, exhibitions and so on in Portuguese.

The ABEP ticket agency, on Praça dos Restauradores opposite the turismo, is fine for bullfights, cinemas, football and stadium concerts, but you're better off buying concert tickets at the venues.

Serious nightlifers who can read a little Portuguese should pick up the latest edition of the paperback *Guia da Noite de Lisboa*, which lists hundreds of clubs. *The Real Lisbon* is a somewhat dated but good English-language version of a popular guide to Lisbon's food, entertainment and other attractions. Both are sold in city bookshops, and the latter also at the turismo.

But bear in mind that clubs come and go like the wind; those listed here are only a drop in the bucket. Your best bet may be to do what everybody else does: trawl the neighbourhoods mentioned in the following sections – mainly the Alfama, Bairro Alto, Avenida 24 de Julho or Alcântara – depending on what's of interest to you.

Cinemas

There are something like 60 cinemas in Lisbon, usually with a few lightweight English-language films on hand, either dubbed or subtitled. Among at least seven multiscreen theatres, the biggest is the 10-screen *Amoreiras* (☎ 383 12 75) at the Amoreiras shopping centre on Avenida Engenheiro Duarte Pacheco. For listings (and critiques), see the 'PubliPúblico' classifieds in *Público*. Tickets at Amoreiras are 700$00 (500$00 on Mondays).

Discos

Lisbon has scores of discos, though they boom and bust at lightning speed. Some have occasional live bands.

Bairro Alto

Frágil (☎ 346 95 78), Rua da Atalaia 126-128; open 10 pm to 4 am (closed Sundays); well established but still trendy

Três Pastorinhos (☎ 346 43 01), Rua da Barroca 111-113; open 11 pm to 4 am

Incógnito (☎ 60 87 55), an unmarked door at Rua dos Poiais de São Bento 37; open 11 pm to at least 4 am (3 to 7 am Tuesdays; closed Sundays)

Avenida 24 de Julho

Absoluto (☎ 395 50 09), Rua Dom Luís I 5 (24 de Julho); open to 4 am, Thursday to Saturday only; restaurant and bar, too

Kapital (☎ 395 59 63), Avenida 24 de Julho 68; open 11.30 pm to 4 am (closed Mondays and Wednesdays); hypertrendy; disco, bar and roof terrace

Kremlin (☎ 60 87 68), Escadinhas da Praia 5; open 1 am to 7 am (to 8 am Fridays and Saturdays; closed Sundays and Mondays); acid and techno; young and very trendy

Metalúrgica (☎ 397 14 88), Avenida 24 de Julho 110; open 10 pm to 4 am; blues, rock and pop; all ages; good vibes

Alcântara

Alcântara Mar (☎ 363 64 32), Rua da Cozinha Económica 11; open 11.30 pm to 6 am (closed Mondays and Tuesdays); rock on Wednesdays and Thursdays, funk on weekends; also a café (☎ 363 71 76); outside is the 'Souk de Alcântara', a row of trailers dishing up munchies all night

Benzina (☎ 363 39 59), Travessa de Teixeira Júnior 6; open midnight to 6 am; soul, funk, acid jazz, rock and pop in good ship *Titanic* décor

Gartejo (☎ 395 59 77), Rua João de Oliveira Miguens 38; open 10 pm to at least 4 am (closed Sundays); young and very trendy, some live bands

Rato

Ad Lib (☎ 356 17 17), Rua Barata Salgueiro 28, 7th floor; open 11 pm to whenever (closed Sundays and Mondays); yuppies and business types

Rock & Pop

Fancy some good old baby-boomer boogie? Here are a few suggestions.

Álcool Puro (☎ 396 74 67), Avenida Dom Carlos I 59 (24 de Julho); open 11 pm to 4 am (closed Sundays); live rock and dancing

Anos 60 (☎ 887 34 44), Largo do Terreirinho 21 (Mouraria); open 9.30 pm to 3 am (closed Sundays), live 60s music on Fridays and Saturdays

Até Qu'Enfim (☎ 396 59 39), Rua das Janelas Verdes 2, Lapa; open 10 pm to 2 am daily

Jazz

The Fundação Calouste Gulbenkian and Hot Clube de Portugal organise an excellent international jazz festival at the fundação's open-air amphitheatre (see Museums & Other Attractions) each year in early August. The box office (☎ 793 51 31, ext 3402; fax 795 52 06) is open Tuesday through Saturday from 1 to 7 pm, and before each show. Tickets are 1500$00 and there are discounts for young people, over-65s, musicians and actors.

Hot Clube de Portugal (☎ 346 73 69), Praça da Alegria 39 (metro: Avenida); open 10 pm to 2 am (closed Sundays and Mondays), the centre of the jazz scene; live music at least three or four nights a week, with sessions at 11 pm and 1.30 am

Café Luso (☎ 342 22 81), Travessa da Queimada 10, Bairro Alto; open 8 pm to 3.30 am (closed Mondays); casa de fado with jazz on weekends

Tertúlia (☎ 346 27 04), Rua do Diário de Notícias 60, Bairro Alto; open 10.30 pm to 2 am (closed Sundays); some live jazz; easy-going; all ages

Fado

Listening to Portugal's 'blues' in its authentic form is a wonderfully melancholy way to drink your way through the night (for more about fado, see the Arts section in the Facts about the Country chapter), and the Alfama district is said to be its true home.

But every tourist wants to say they've heard it, and the sad truth is that many of Lisbon's casas de fado now offer pale imitations – 'tour-bus meets Greek taverna', as one travel writer put it – and often at prices to make you moan along with the fadista. Nearly all are restaurants, and insist that you spend a minimum (consumo mínimo) of 2000$00 to 3500$00 on their food and drinks in order to stay and hear the music; you're likely to spend twice that if you have dinner.

Following are many of Lisbon's better known fado houses, with an indication of minimum charges.

Adega do Machado (☎ 342 87 13), Rua do Norte 91, Bairro Alto; music from 9.30 pm to 3 am (closed Mondays); minimum 2500$00

Adega do Ribatejo (☎ 346 83 43), Rua Diário de Notícias 23, Bairro Alto; music 8.30 pm to midnight (closed Sundays); minimum 1800$00, reasonable food prices, better value than most

Adega Mesquita (☎ 346 20 77), Rua Diário de Notícias 107, Bairro Alto; 8 pm to 3.30 am; minimum 2000$00

Café Luso (☎ 342 22 81), Travessa da Queimada 10; open 8 pm to 3.30 am (closed Mondays), minimum 2000$00; jazz on weekends

Lisboa à Noite (☎ 346 26 03), Rua das Gáveas 69, Bairro Alto; open 8 pm to 3 am (closed Sundays); minimum 2750$00

Nono (☎ 346 86 25), Rua do Norte 47, Bairro Alto; open 8 pm to 3.30 am (closed Sundays); minimum 1500$00

Os Ferreiras (☎ 885 08 51), Rua de São Lázaro 150, near Largo Martim Moniz (metro: Socorro); open midnight to 2 am; minimum 1500$00

O Forcado (☎ 346 85 79), Rua da Rosa 219, Bairro Alto; open 8 pm to 2 am (closed Wednesdays); minimum 2500$00

Parreirinha de Alfama (☎ 886 82 09), Beco do Espírito Santo 1, Alfama; open 8 pm to 3 am; minimum 2000$00

Senhor Vinho (☎ 397 26 81), Rua do Meio à Lapa 18, Lapa; open 8.30 pm to 3 am (closed Sundays); minimum 3000$00

Taverna do Embuçado (☎ 886 50 88), Beco dos Cortumes 10, Alfama; open 9 pm to 2.30 am (closed Sundays); no minimum

Tímpanas (☎ 397 24 31), Rua Gilberto Rola 24, Alcântara; open 8 pm to 2 am (closed Wednesdays); minimum 2000$00

African Music

The African music scene (with its roots predominantly in Cape Verde, but also

Mozambique, Guinea Bissau and Angola) bops in bars all over town.

Discoteca A Lontra (☎ 369 10 83), Rua de São Bento 155, Bairro Alto; music starts after midnight (closed Mondays); one of the best known venues in town

Banana Power (☎ 363 18 15), Rua de Cascais 51-53, 2nd floor, Alcântara

Ritz Clube (☎ 346 59 98), Rua da Glória 57, just off Avenida da Liberdade; open 10 pm to 4 am (closed Sundays); mainly Cape Verdean; late meals

Brazilian Music
For live Brazilian rhythms, ring the bell at Largo de São Martinho 6, Alfama for the *Pé Sujo* bar (☎ 886 56 29); it's closed on Mondays.

Irish Music
Homesick Dubliners should head down to *Ó Gilíns Irish Pub* (☎ 342 18 99) at Rua dos Remolares 8-10 (Cais do Sodré), where Conor Gillen will fill your glass with draft Guinness daily from 11 am to 2 am; there is also live traditional Irish music on most Saturday nights and live jazz with brunch on Sundays.

Bars
This section is for people who are mainly looking for watering holes. Many places also have music (sometimes live) and dancing, so if that's what you're after, see the sections on discos and live music too. Avenida 24 de Julho is the strip with the heaviest concentration of discos and bars. Midnight traffic jams here are not revellers going home, but trendy young things arriving.

Alfama
Chapitô (☎ 887 82 25), Costa do Castelo 7

Costa do Castelo, corner of Costa do Castelo and Calçada do Marquês de Tancos; open 10 pm to 2 am (closed Mondays); bar-restaurant with city views

O Esboço (☎ 887 78 93), Rua do Vigário 10; open 11 pm to 2 am (closed Sundays); cheap meals

Ópera (☎ 886 23 18), Travessa das Mónicas 65; open 10 pm to 2 am (Friday and Saturday nights to 3.30 am); cheap meals; occasional art exhibits

---

Solar do Vinho do Porto
The Instituto do Vinho do Porto (Port Wine Institute) is an autonomous agency, based in Porto, with the job of maintaining the reputation of the port wine appellation by controlling its quality and output and promoting it generically. Among other things, it operates the *Solar do Vinho do Porto* (☎ 342 33 07) in an old palace at Rua de São Pedro de Alcântara 45, right at the top of the Elevador da Glória in the Bairro Alto. Here you can sample various port wines, from about 150$00 a glass, in a subdued, living-room-like setting, and peruse (or buy) books and other information on port wine. It's open weekdays from 10 am to 11.45 pm and Saturdays from 11 am to 10.45 pm. There's another solar in Porto. ∎

Bairro Alto & Chiado
A Capela, in a former chapel at Rua da Atalaia 45; open 10 pm to 2 am (Fridays and Saturdays to 4 am); sometimes live jazz

Arroz Doce (☎ 346 26 01), Rua da Atalaia 117; open 6 pm to 2 am (closed Sundays); cheerful and unpretentious

Ma Jong (☎ 342 10 39), Rua da Atalaia 3; open 11 pm to 2.30 am; lots of artists

Nova (☎ 346 28 34), Rua da Rosa 261; open 10 pm to 2 am (Fridays and Saturdays to 2.30 am); trendy

Pavilhão Chinês (☎ 342 47 29), Rua Dom Pedro V 89; open 6 pm to 2 am (from 9 pm Sundays); idiosyncratic turn-of-the-century décor; pool tables

Primas (☎ 342 59 25), Rua da Atalaia 154; open 9.30 pm to 2 or 3 am; noisy local pub with pinball machines

Avenida 24 de Julho
Café Central (☎ 395 61 11), Avenida 24 de Julho 112; open 10 pm to 4 am; rock and blues

Cervejinhas (☎ 60 80 50), Avenida 24 de Julho 78-B

Décibel (☎ 396 17 29), Avenida 24 de Julho 90-B/C; open 11 pm to 3.30 am; psychedelic rock for all ages

Gringo's Café (☎ 396 09 11), Avenida 24 de Julho 116; open until 2 am (closed Sundays); Tex-Mex café-bar with food to 1 am; margarita-land

Paulinha (☎ 396 47 83), Avenida 24 de Julho 82-A; open 10.30 pm to 4 am (closed Sundays and Mondays); all ages

Lapa
Stones (☎ 396 45 45), Rua do Olival 1; open to 4 am (closed Mondays); 60s and 70s rock

Gay & Lesbian Bars Many gay bars are clustered in the hilly streets of Rato and northern Bairro Alto.

Bar 106 (☎ 342 73 73), Rua de São Marçal 106; open 9 pm to 2 am; one of the best and busiest

Brica Bar (or *O Brica*; ☎ 342 89 71), Rua Cecilio de Sousa 84; open 9 pm to 4 am

Finalmente (☎ 347 26 52), Rua da Palmeira 38; closed Mondays; weekend drag shows

Memorial (☎ 66 88 91), Rua da Gustavo de Matos Sequeira 42-A; open 10 pm to 3.30 am (closed Mondays); very popular; gay and lesbian

Tatoo (☎ 67 07 26), Rua de São Marçal 15; open 8.30 pm to 2 am (closed Sundays)

Trumps (☎ 67 10 59), Rua da Imprensa Nacional 104-B; open 11 pm to 4 am (closed Mondays); huge dance floor

Xeque-Mate (☎ 37 28 30), Rua de São Marçal 170; open 10 pm to 2.30 am

SPECTATOR SPORTS
Football

Lisboêtas are as obsessed as anybody with football (soccer). Of Portugal's three good national teams, two – Benfica and Sporting – are based in Lisbon. The two have been rivals ever since Sporting beat Benfica, 2-1, on 1 December 1907.

The season runs from September through May, and most league matches are on Sundays; check the papers or ask at the turismo about upcoming contests. Tickets are fairly cheap and are sold at the stadium on match day, or you can buy them, for slightly inflated prices, at the ABEP ticket agency on Praça dos Restauradores, opposite the turismo.

Benfica (properly Sport Lisboa e Benfica) plays at Estádio da Luz in the north-west Benfica district (nearest metro station Colégio Militar, or take bus No 41 from Rossio). For ticket information call ☎ 726 60 53, or contact Benfica's enquiries office (☎ 726 61 29; fax 726 47 61).

Sporting (properly Sporting Clube de Portugal) plays at Estádio José de Alvalade, just north of the university. The nearest metro station is Campo Grande, or take bus No 1 or 36 from Rossio. For information, call ☎ 758 90 21 (or fax 759 93 91).

Bullfighting

Between April and October, bullfights are staged at the Moorish-style praça de touros (bullring) across Avenida da República from Campo Pequeno metro station (or take bus No 1, 21, 36, 44, 45 or 83 from Rossio). The season runs from May through October, with fights usually on Thursdays or Sundays. Tickets, on sale outside the bullring, range from 2500$00 to 4000$00, depending on whether you want a *sol* (sunny), *sol e sombra* (sunny and shady) or *sombra* (shady) seat. You can also buy tickets for a bit more from the ABEP ticket agency on Praça dos Restauradores, opposite the turismo.

You can see more traditional bullfights in bull-breeding Ribatejo province, especially in Santarém during its June agricultural fair and in Vila Franca de Xira during the town's July and October festivals. See Spectator Sports in the Facts for the Visitor chapter for more about bullfights, and Flora & Fauna in the Facts about the Country chapter for a discussion of the associated cruelty-to-animals issue.

THINGS TO BUY
Azulejos & Ceramics

Lisbon has many azulejos factories and showrooms. One of the finest (and priciest) is Fábrica Sant'Ana, the pink building at Rua do Alecrim 95. The street-level showroom is open weekdays from 9 am to 7 pm and Saturdays from 10 am to 2 pm. The factory is upstairs, along with what look like the offices of azulejo-makers' guilds.

Another good showroom for azulejos (including made-to-order items) and other ceramic ware is Cerâmica Viúva Lamego (☎ 885 24 02) at Largo do Intendente Pina Manique 25 (metro: Intendente). Pottery fanatics will also like the venerable, family-run Olaria do Desterros (☎ 885 03 29), which is a few blocks away in a neighbourhood of warehouses and hospitals. The factory (there's no obvious showroom) is at entry F in an alley, seemingly within the grounds of the Hospital do Desterro, at Rua Nova do Desterro 14.

The attractive Museu dos Azulejos (see

Museums & Other Attractions) has a small shop, which also includes more affordable azulejo souvenirs.

Wine

Portuguese wine of any variety – red, white or rosé; *maduro* (mature) or semisparkling young *vinho verde* – offers very good value. And you needn't hunt for specialist shops: good stuff is available in supermarkets, and 800$00 to 900$00 (US$5 to US$6) will buy something to please the snobbiest taste buds.

If it's port wine you're interested in, have a taste at the Solar do Vinho do Porto, Rua de São Pedro de Alcântara 45 in the Bairro Alto, and then head for the supermarket. Failing that, the Instituto do Vinho do Porto runs a shop in the international departures concourse at the airport.

Refer to Drinks in the Facts for the Visitor chapter to learn more about Portuguese wines.

Handicrafts

A fascinating (if rather overpublicised) *artesanato* is Santos Ofícios, Rua da Madalena 87, at the edge of the Baixa district, with an eclectic range of folk art from all around Portugal. It's open daily, except Sundays, from 10 am to 8 pm. For bronzeware, check out Casa Achilles, at Rua de São Marçal 194 in Rato.

For something decidedly down-market, but more entertainment than bargain basement, browse the sprawling Feira da Ladra (literally 'Thieves' Market'), which materialises every Tuesday morning and all day Saturday at Campo de Santa Clara, beside the Igreja de São Vincent de Fora in the Alfama district. In addition to cheap clothes and old books, you'll find a motley array of junk, from nuts and bolts to old buttons and brassware, second-hand spectacles and old 78-rpm records.

Another regular Lisbon market is the Feira do Relógio, held on Sundays on Rua Pardal Monteiro in the Bairro de Relógio district (take bus No 59 from Praça da Figueira or bus No 103 from Areeiro metro station).

Shoes

These are a bargain all over Portugal, and Lisbon abounds in *sapaterias* (shoe shops).

Amoreiras

Check out the trendy Complexo das Amoreiras, Portugal's biggest shopping centre, looming on a hilltop north-west of the city centre. There are some 300 boutiques, restaurants, snack bars and cinemas, and the colossal, chrome-plated complex designed by architect Tomás Taveira is startling. It's on Avenida Engenheiro Duarte Pacheco; take almost any bus west from Rotunda metro station on Rua Joaquim António de Aguiar.

GETTING THERE & AWAY

Air

From Lisbon, both Portugália and TAP have multiple flights daily to/from Porto and Faro, year-round. TAP has a daily evening flight to Faro and a morning one back, scheduled to connect with all its international arrivals and departures in Lisbon.

Over two dozen carriers have scheduled international services to Lisbon, including daily links in summer with London, Paris, Frankfurt, Berlin, Dresden, Hamburg, Munich, Amsterdam, Brussels, Madrid and New York, and less frequent connections to other cities. For more on Lisbon's international and domestic air links and fares, see

---

Arriving in Lisbon by Air
As you exit from the arrivals concourse at the airport, you'll find a helpful turismo (☎ 849 43 23, 849 36 89), which is open daily from 6 am to 2 am. Further on is a desk maintained by ANA, the city airport authority, with arrivals and departures information, its own handy mini-guidebook to the city called *Your Guide: Lisboa*, and a very useful *Taxi Information* pamphlet to help you avoid getting stung by the less-than-scrupulous drivers who hang out here. See the Lisbon Getting Around section for how to get from the airport to the city centre. ■

the Getting There & Away and Getting Around chapters.

Among useful airline booking numbers in Lisbon are the following:

TAP	☎ 841 69 90
	or toll-free ☎ 0808-21 31 41
Portugália	☎ 842 55 59
Air France	☎ 790 02 02
Alitalia	☎ 353 61 41
British Airways	☎ 346 43 53
	or toll-free ☎ 0500-1251
Iberia	☎ 355 81 19
Delta	☎ 353 76 10
KLM	☎ 847 63 54
Lufthansa	☎ 357 38 52
Sabena	☎ 346 55 72
SAS	☎ 347 30 61
SATA Air Açores	☎ 353 95 11
Swissair	☎ 347 11 11
TAAG Air Angola	☎ 357 58 99
TWA	☎ 314 71 41
Varig	☎ 353 91 53
	or toll-free ☎ 0500-1234

Lisbon Airport is 20 minutes from the city centre when there's no traffic, but 45 minutes or more in rush hour; see the Getting Around section for airport transport information.

For flight arrival and departure information, call ☎ 840 20 60.

Bus

Express coaches connect Lisbon with nearly all of Portugal's major towns on a daily basis. Some sample one-way fares are: Porto (at least seven buses daily, 5½ hours) 1800\$00; Coimbra (at least 11 daily) 1250\$00; Évora (five daily) 1250\$00; Faro (six daily) 2000\$00; Viano do Castelo 1900\$00. For help translating baffling timetable footnotes, see the Getting Around chapter.

Lisbon is also linked to London and Paris at least four times a week in summer, and less often to Cologne, Düsseldorf, Hamburg, Hanover, Madrid, Barcelona and other European cities. For more on international coach links, see the Getting There & Away chapter.

Rede Expressos and its affiliates, a few other descendants of the now-privatised Rodoviário Nacional (RN) line such as EVA (from the Algarve), and all international coaches, operate from the long-distance bus terminal (☎ 354 54 39) at Avenida Casal Ribeiro 18 (metro: Saldanha). This is the best bet for almost any destination within Portugal.

Renex (☎ 887 48 71, ☎ 888 28 29), which includes local lines Resende, Caima and Frota Azul, operates from Rua dos Bacalhoeiros, a few blocks east of Praça do Comércio. Buses run to Mafra every few hours from the little Mafrense bus company terminal at Rua Fernandos da Fonseca 18 (on Largo Martim Moniz by Socorro metro station), via Avenida Casal Ribeiro.

Train

For information on the Caminhos de Ferro Portugueses (CP) domestic rail network and services – *regional* (R), *interregional* (IR), *intercidade* (IC) and Alfa – see the Getting Around chapter. Some sample IC/IR 2nd-class fares from Lisbon are 2250\$00/1820\$00 to Porto (four IC, four IR trains a day), 1600\$00/1270\$00 to Coimbra (six IC, four IR a day) and 1850\$00/1650\$00 to Faro (two IC, two IR a day). There is also extra-fast Alfa service to some points, eg four a day to Porto (2950\$00) and three a day to Coimbra (2150\$00). These Alfa and IC fares include required seat reservation charges.

Lisbon is linked to London and Paris by a daily service (the *rápido Sud-Expresso*) through northern Spain, and to Madrid by the nightly Talgo *Lusitânia Express*. For more on international train links and some fares to/from Lisbon, see the Getting There & Away chapter.

Lisbon has four major train stations. Santa Apolónia is the terminus for trains from northern and central Portugal and for all international services. Cais do Sodré serves trains to Cascais and Estoril, while Rossio serves Sintra and Estremadura. Barreiro, on the other side of the river, is the terminus for *suburbano* services to Setúbal and all long-distance services to the south of Portugal, including the Algarve; connecting ferries leave frequently from the pier at Terreiro do Paço, by Praça do Comércio.

Santa Apolónia station has a helpful CP information desk (☎ 888 40 25, ☎ 888 50 92) at door No 8; the desk is open from 8 am to 10 pm, the telephones until 11 pm. The international section at door No 47 includes an international ticket desk (and machines for buying certain domestic IC and Alfa tickets with credit cards); a bank, cash exchange machine and credit-card ATM machine; a snack bar and restaurant (open 7 am to 11 pm); and car-rental agencies. The baggage office is at door No 25.

Rossio station also has an information office, open from 9 am to 8 pm. All four stations have luggage lockers. At the Terreiro do Paço pier, travellers bound for southern Portugal buy two tickets: a 160$00 ferry ticket to Barreiro plus their onward train ticket.

Car & Motorcycle

The best unlimited-mileage car-rental rate we found was from City Tour (☎ 847 85 13; fax 847 85 18) at the airport: 4200$00 per day for a week or more. The best one-day rate we found, 6600$00, was from Nova Rent (☎ 387 08 08; fax 387 31 30). Other home-grown companies with low multiday rates include Olivauto (☎ 847 30 06; fax 848 01 78), Solcar (☎ 356 05 00; fax 356 05 04) and AA Castanheira (☎ 357 00 60).

Multinational car-rental firms in Lisbon include Avis (☎ 356 11 76, or ☎ 0500-1002 toll-free in Portugal), Hertz (☎ 0500-1231 toll-free in Portugal), Alamo (☎ 383 03 91; fax 387 33 17), Europcar (☎ 353 51 15; fax 353 67 57) and Tupi (Budget; ☎ 797 13 77). Typical minimum rates are about 11,500$00 per day, 55,500$00 per week, and 8000$00 per day for over a week.

You can rent a motorcycle from Gesrent (☎ 385 27 22), Rua Nova de São Mamede 29-31. Prices per day for a Yamaha 50 are about 3300$00 for up to three days, 3000$00 for up to a week, and 2800$00 for more than a week.

Ferry

The Transtejo ferry line has several riverfront terminals. Two are adjacent to Praça do Comércio: Terreiro do Paço terminal, from where passenger ferries cross the Rio Tejo to

Returning Rental Cars to Lisbon Airport

If you return a car to the airport, watch for signs directing you into the *rental car* lot. If you go into the regular car park instead, you'll have to pay to get out! ■

Montijo (270$00), Seixal (200$00) every hour or so (fewer at weekends), and Barreiro; and, next to it, Cais da Alfândega terminal, from where passenger ferries go every 10 minutes, all day, to Cacilhas (90$00). Car ferries go to Cacilhas from a pier at Cais do Sodré. The ferry line serving the Barreiro train terminus is called Soflusa.

GETTING AROUND
The Airport

Bus No 91, called the Aero-Bus, is a special service departing from outside the arrivals hall about every 20 minutes from 7 am to 9 pm. It takes 20 to 45 minutes (depending on traffic) between the airport and the city centre, including a stop right outside the turismo on Praça dos Restauradores. The price is 430$00/1000$00 for a Bilhete Turístico that you can continue to use on all city buses, trams and funiculars for one or three days. Note that the Passe Turístico (see the Bus, Tram & Funicular section) is for some obscure reason *not* good for this bus. For outbound TAP passengers who show their air tickets, the ride to the airport is free.

Local bus Nos 8, 44, 45 and 83 also run right past the turismo, but you have to walk further at the airport to board them, and they're a nightmare in rush hour if you have baggage.

For a taxi, figure on about 1500$00, plus an extra 300$00 if your luggage needs to go in the boot.

Bus, Tram & Funicular

Companhia Carris de Ferro de Lisboa, or Carris, is the municipal transport service (for all but the metro). Its buses and trams run from about 5 or 6 am to 1 am, with some night bus and tram services. Lisboêtas are surprisingly orderly in bus queues.

You can get a transport map, *Planta dos Transportes Públicas da Carris* (including a welcome map of night-time services) from the turismo and sometimes from Carris kiosks, though during the city's pre-Expo '98 building frenzy, route changes were so frequent that the map was not always reliable.

Individual tickets are 150$00 on board, or half that if purchased beforehand. Prepaid tickets are sold at Carris kiosks, open daily from 9 am to 8 pm, at Praça da Figueira, at the foot of the Elevador de Santa Justa, and in front of Cais do Sodré station. From these kiosks you can also get a one-day (430$00) or three-day (1000$00) Bilhete Turístico good for all buses, trams and funiculars. From these kiosks and most metro stations you can also get a four-day (1550$00) or seven-day Passe Turístico, which is good for buses (except the Aero-Bus), trams, funiculars *and* the metro. You must show your passport to get the (non-transferable) Passe Turístico.

But none of these is a particularly great bargain unless you plan to do a lot of riding far from the centre. A better deal is the Lisboa Card (see Lisbon Information), which is good for most tourist sights as well as bus, tram, funicular and metro travel.

Buses Useful bus routes include: Nos 32, 44 and 45 (Praça dos Restauradores, Praça do Comércio, Cais do Sodré); Nos 35 and 107 (Cais do Sodré, Santa Apolónia); Nos 9, 39 and 46 (Praça dos Restauradores, Santa Apolónia); and No 37 (Praça da Figueiro, Castelo do São Jorge).

Trams The clattering, antediluvian trams *(eléctricos* or *tranvías)* are an endearing component of Lisbon. Don't leave Lisbon without riding tram No 28 through the narrow streets of the Alfama district, and back around to Largo Martim Moniz; the best place to catch it is east-bound on Rua da

Conceiçao in the Baixa. West-bound from Rua da Conceição, it clanks through Bairro Alto to Estrela peak.

Two other useful lines are the No 15 from Praça da Figueira and Praça do Comércio, via Alcântara to Belém; and the No 18 from Praça do Comércio via Alcântara to Ajuda. The No 15 line has, in addition to the old trams, some posh new articulated ones, which also have machines on board for tickets and one and three-day passes. Tram stops are usually marked by a small *paragem* sign hanging from a lamppost or the overhead wires.

Funiculars The city has three funiculars (elevadores or *ascensors* in Portuguese), which labour up and down the steepest hills around Praça dos Restauradores, plus the extraordinary Elevador de Santa Justa, a huge wrought-iron lift that raises you from the Baixa straight up to eyelevel with the Convento do Carmo ruins.

Santa Justa is most popular with tourists, but the most charming ride is on the Elevador da Bica through the Santa Catarina district, at the south-western corner of Bairro Alto.

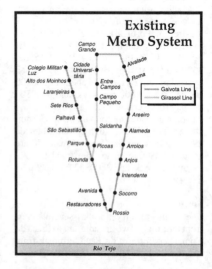

Existing Metro System

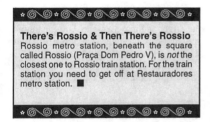

There's Rossio & Then There's Rossio
Rossio metro station, beneath the square called Rossio (Praça Dom Pedro V), is *not* the closest one to Rossio train station. For the train station you need to get off at Restauradores metro station. ■

The other two funiculars are the Elevador da Glória, from Restauradores up to the São Pedro de Alcântara viewpoint, and the Elevador do Lavra from Largo de Anunciada, on the eastern side of Restauradores.

All operate daily from 7 am to 11 pm (on Sundays and holidays from 9 am to 11 pm) except the Elevador da Glória, which runs from 7 am to 1 am daily. They're not for anyone in a hurry!

Transport for Disabled Travellers

For disabled people, Carris operates a 24-hour dial-a-ride service (☎ 363 20 44 or 758 56 76) at a cost comparable to taxis. Try to book your rides a day or two in advance. Carris

apparently also has a[...] wheelchair space for h[...]

Metro

The modest *metropolitano* (und[...] system, with 19 km of track and 25 stations, is useful only for short hops across the centre. But a huge pre-Expo '98 expansion is pushing it out in all directions, including to Cais do Sodré, Alcântara and the Expo site. By the year 2000 there will be 37 km of track and 47 stations. Rossio is by far the busiest station, with some 63,000 passengers a day.

Individual tickets cost 70$00 and it's 500$00 for a *caderneta* of 10 tickets. Tickets can be purchased from windows or automatic dispensers. Single tickets should be validated in the little machine at the entrance to the trains (there *are* ticket inspectors). A one-day metro pass is 200$00, and both the Passe Turístico and the Lisboa Card are good for free travel.

The system operates from 6.30 am to 1 am. Entrances are marked by a big red M. Travel is quite straightforward. Useful signs include *correspondência* (transfer between

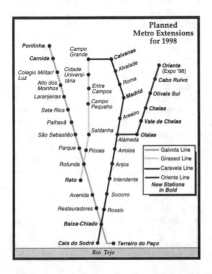

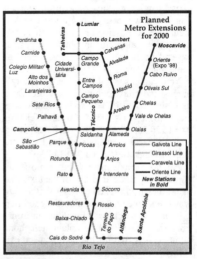

and *saída* (exit to the street). Pick-
ets can be a nuisance in rush-hour
owds.

Car & Motorcycle

Lisbon has two ring roads, both of which are
useful for staying *out* of the centre. On maps
the inner one is marked CRIL (Cintura
Regional Interna de Lisboa), the outer one
CREL (Cintura Regional Externa de
Lisboa).

The city has a few permit-only spaces for
disabled drivers, but so far, visitors have no
special access to them. A pilot project is
apparently on the cards for an EU-wide
permit, however.

Portugal's national auto club, Automóvel
Club de Portugal or ACP (☎ 356 39 31; fax
357 47 32), is at Rua Rosa Araújo 24 (metro:
Avenida or Rotunda). It's open weekdays
from 9 am to 5.30 pm, with maps, guidebooks and camping information on the
ground floor, and a helpful information
office on the 2nd floor. For more about ACP
services, see the Car & Motorcycle section
of the Getting Around chapter.

Taxi

Compared with the rest of Europe, Lisbon's
táxis are quick, cheap and plentiful. You can
flag one down, or pick one up at a rank –
including at Rossio, Praça dos Restauradores, near all train and bus stations, at
top-end hotels, and at the intersections of
some major roads.

You can also call for one. The city's
biggest radio-taxi company is Rádio Táxis
de Lisboa (☎ 815 50 61); other reliable ones
are Autocoope (☎ 793 27 56) and Teletáxis
(☎ 815 20 76, ☎ 815 20 16). A reliable tourist-
taxi outfit (for excursions, at fixed standard
rates) is Unidos de Lisboa (☎ 814 73 53).

All taxis have meters, but rip-offs do
happen. In particular, a few of the taxis that
haunt the airport take new arrivals the long
way round to their destinations. A good *Taxi
Information* brochure – including information about rates and complaint telephone
numbers – is free for the taking at the exit
from the arrivals concourse. If you think you

may have been cheated, get a receipt from
the driver and make a claim with the tourist
subsection of the police (☎ 346 61 41, ext
279).

See Local Transport in the Getting Around
chapter for more about taxis and taxi fares.

Bicycle

Lisbon traffic is a horror for cyclists. You're
better off stashing your bike with left-
luggage at the train station or airport and
seeing the city by public transport. Better
hotels and pensões may have a storage room.
See the Getting Around chapter for information on putting your machine on a bus or
train.

Nova Rent (☎ 387 08 08; fax 387 31 30)
rents out mountain bicycles as well as cars.
Prices are 3900$00 for the weekend,
1700$00 per day for up to seven days, or
8400$00 for a week.

Around Lisbon

SINTRA

• *pop 20,000* • *postcode 2710* • *area code* ☎ *01*

If you make only one side trip from Lisbon,
Sintra should receive top priority. Cool and
verdant, and just 28 km north-west of
Lisbon, Sintra is one of the most enchanting
day trips from the city and a worthwhile
destination in its own right for several days
exploration or relaxation.

Situated on the northern slopes of the
craggy Serra de Sintra, its lush vegetation
and spectacular mountaintop views towards
the coast have lured admirers since the times
of the early Iberians: they found the ridge so
mystical they called it the Mountain of the
Moon and made it a centre of cult worship.
The Romans and Moors were equally capti-
vated (the remains of a Moorish castle
overlook the town). And for 500 years the
kings of Portugal chose Sintra as their
summer resort, and the nobility built extravagant villas and surrealist palaces on its
wooded hillsides. Poets – especially the
romantic English – were enraptured by its

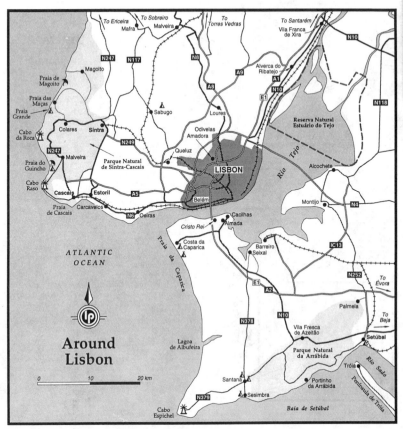

Around
Lisbon

ATLANTIC
OCEAN

0   10   20 km

natural beauty. Even Lord Byron (who had few nice things to say about Portugal) managed to be charmed: 'Lo! Cintra's glorious Eden intervenes, in variegated maze of mount and glen,' he wrote in his famous travel epic, *Childe Harold*.

Despite hordes of summer tourists, especially in July when the town hosts a major music festival, Sintra still has a bewitching atmosphere and offers some fantastic walks and day trips: the **Parque Natural de Sintra-Cascais** encompasses both the Serra de Sintra and nearby coastal attractions (including Cabo da Roca, Europe's most westerly

point). Try to avoid weekends and public holidays when the narrow, winding roads groan with tour buses.

And if it's the Byronic, romantic aspect you're after, plan a visit soon: designated a UNESCO World Heritage Site in 1995, Sintra now faces grandiose 'revival' plans by local authorities with ambitions to make it 'the cultural capital of Portugal.'

Orientation & Information

Arriving at Sintra by train or bus you'll find yourself in Sintra's new town, Estefânia, where most of the cheap accommodation is

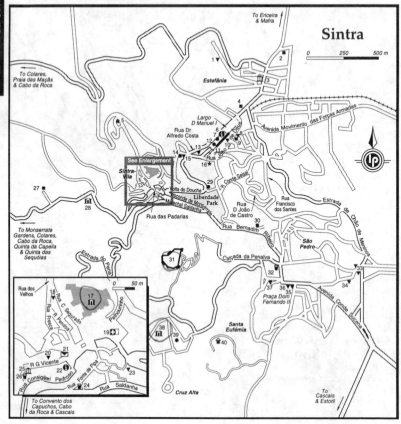

located. It's 1.5 km (about 15 minutes walk) away from the heart of Sintra's cultural attractions at Sintra-Vila (also called Vila Velha, 'old town'). A couple of km south-east of Sintra-Vila is the São Pedro district: you'll only need to go here if you're heading for the pousada de juventude nearby, want to visit the big fortnightly market (held on the second and fourth Sunday of the month), or if you'd like to sample some of São Pedro's excellent restaurants.

If you're arriving by car, note that driving and parking in Sintra-Vila can be murder on weekends and public holidays: it's often

easier to park near the station and walk. Be sure to lock up well and keep valuables with you when you park at the Pena National Palace, Castelo dos Mouros and Monserrate Gardens.

There are two turismos, one at the train station (☎ 924 16 23), and the main one (☎ 923 11 57; fax 923 51 76) at 23 Praça da República in Sintra-Vila, near the Palácio Nacional de Sintra (Sintra National Palace). This memorably polite and well-run office is open daily from 9 am to 7 pm (until 8 pm from June to September). It provides a free map (packed with information), as well as

PLACES TO STAY		PLACES TO EAT		OTHER	
2	Villa das Rosas	1	Orixás	6	Turismo
3	Museu de Arte	8	O Tunel	11	Train & Bus Stations
	Moderna	9	Piela's Café	12	Lavandaria Teclava
4	Pensão Nova Sintra	10	Restaurante	16	Police Station
5	Casa Miradouro		Parreirinha	17	Palácio Nacional de
7	Monte da Lua	13	Topico Bar &		Sintra
9	Piela's		Restaurant	19	Centro de Saúde
14	Casa de Hóspedes	15	A Tasca do Manel	21	Turismo (Main Office)
	Adelaide	20	Tulhas Bar &	22	Post Office
18	Hotel Tivoli		Restaurant	24	Fonte da Pipa
27	Hotel Palácio de	23	Casa da Avó	25	Museu do Brinquedo
	Seteais	33	Adega do Saloio	26	Estrada Velha
30	Residencial Sintra	34	Toca do Javali	28	Quinta da Regaleira
40	Pousada de	35	Solar de São Pedro	29	Horse & Carriage
	Juventude de Sintra	36	Restaurante Pic Nic		Rides
		37	Taverna dos	31	Castelo dos Mouros
			Trovadores	32	Mourisca Bar
				38	Palácio Nacional da
					Pena
				39	Pena Park

help with accommodation. Walkers might also be interested in the *Walking in Sintra* booklet (its poor maps are due for an update) and botanists in the detailed *Sintra: A Borough in the Wild*, both usually available at the turismo.

There are several laundrettes; the most convenient is Lavandaria Teclava (☎ 923 03 37), opposite the train station at 27D Avenida Miguel Bombarda. It's open weekdays from 8 am to 7.30 pm, and to noon on Saturdays.

The post office (open weekdays from 8 am to 6 pm) and banks are in Sintra-Vila, near the turismo. The *centro de saúde*, or medical centre, (☎ 923 34 00) is at Rua Visconde de Monserrate 2, but for medical emergencies it's advisable to head for Cascais Hospital (☎ 01-484 40 71). The police station (☎ 923 07 61) is at Rua João de Deus 6.

Palácio Nacional de Sintra

Recently repainted a shocking bright white, the Sintra National Palace (also known as the Paço Real or Palácio da Vila) dominates the town with its two huge, conical chimneys. Of Moorish origins, the palace was greatly enlarged by João I in the early 15th century, adorned with Manueline additions by Manuel I the following century, and repeatedly restored and redecorated right up to the present day.

Historically, it's connected with a treasury of notable occasions: João I planned his 1415 Ceuta campaign here; the three-year-old Sebastião was crowned king in the palace in 1557; and the paralytic Afonso VI, who was effectively imprisoned here by his brother Pedro II for six years, died of apoplexy in 1683 while listening to Mass in the chapel gallery.

As for the palace's aesthetic appeal, the mixed styles create a muddled architectural result but there are some fascinating decorations inside. The highlights are the palace's unrivalled display of 15th and 16th-century azulejos (especially in the Sala dos Árabes or Arab Room), which are some of the oldest in Portugal; the Sala das Armas (Armoury Room, also called the Sala dos Brasões or Coat of Arms Room), with the heraldic shields of 74 leading 16th-century families on its wooden coffered ceiling; and the delightful Sala dos Cisnes (Swan Room), which has a polychrome ceiling adorned with 27 gold-collared swans.

Most memorable of all is the ground-floor Sala das Pêgas (Magpie Room), with a ceiling thick with painted magpies (*pêgas*), each holding in its beak a scroll with the words *por bem* ('in honour'). The story goes that João I commissioned the cheeky decoration to represent all the court gossip about his advances toward one of the ladies-in-waiting. Caught red-handed by his queen, 'por bem' was the king's allegedly innocent response.

The palace is open daily, except Wednesdays, from 10 am to 1 pm and 2 to 5 pm; entry is 400$00. Beware of getting stuck in a tedious log jam: the 20-minute guided tours get overloaded with tour groups during the summer and on weekends and holidays.

Castelo dos Mouros

A steep three-km climb from Sintra-Vila leads to the ruins of this castle, which has battlements that snake over the craggy mountainside. First built by the Moors, the castelo was captured by Christian forces under Afonso Henriques in 1147. Much restored in the 19th century, it offers some wonderful panoramas: as long as Sintra's famous sea mists aren't rolling around, you should be able to see as far as Cabo da Roca. Late afternoon is best for taking some spectacular photographs of the nearby Pena Palace. The castelo is open daily from 10 am to 6 pm (5 pm from October to May); admission is free.

Palácio Nacional da Pena

Another 20-minute walk up from the castelo is the most bizarre building in Sintra, the Pena National Palace. This extraordinary architectural confection, which rivals the best Disneyland castle, was cooked up in the fertile imagination of Ferdinand of Saxe Coburg-Gotha (artist-husband of Queen Maria II) and Prussian architect Ludwig von Eschwege. Commissioned in 1840 to build a 'romantic' or 'Gothick' baronial castle from the ruins of a 16th-century Jeronimite monastery that still stood on the site, Eschwege delivered a Bavarian-Manueline fantasy of embellishments, turrets and battlements (and a statue of himself in armour, overlooking the palace from a nearby peak).

The interior is just as mind-boggling: the rooms have been left just as they were when the royal family fled on the eve of revolution in 1910. There's Eiffel-designed furniture, Ferdinand-designed china, and a whole

room of naughty nude paintings. More serious artwork includes a 16th-century carved alabaster altarpiece by Nicolas Chanterène in the original monastery's chapel.

The palace is open daily, except Mondays, from 10 am to 1 pm and from 2 to 5 pm; entry is 400$00.

Below the palace (en route from the castelo if you're walking) is the enchanting **Pena Park**, open daily from 10 am to 6 pm (5 pm from October to May); free admission. It's packed with lakes and exotic plants, huge redwoods and fern trees, camellias and rhododendrons. Among the follies and cottages is a chalet built for Ferdinand's mistress, a German opera singer he titled Condessa d'Edla.

Convento dos Capuchos

For the biggest contrast in styles imaginable, take the first left as you descend from Pena Palace, head five km along the main road that snakes south-west along the ridge and then turn right into the woods to reach this atmospheric Capuchin monastery.

A tiny troglodyte hermitage, buttressed by huge boulders and darkened by surrounding trees, the *convento* was built in 1560 to house 12 monks. Their dwarf-size cells (some little more than hollows in the rock) are lined with cork; hence the convento's popular name, Cork Convent. Visiting the place is an Alice-in-Wonderland experience as you squeeze through low, narrow doorways to explore the warren of cells, chapels, kitchen, and cavern where one recluse, Honorius, spent an astonishing but obviously healthy 36 years (he was 95 when he died in 1596). Hermits hid away here right up until 1834 when the monastery was finally abandoned. It's now open daily for visits from 10 am to 6 pm (5 pm from October to May); entry is 200$00.

Monserrate Gardens

Down from the ridge and four km west of Sintra-Vila (about 50 minutes on foot) is another must-see spot: the Monserrate Gardens. Rambling and romantic, they cover 30 hectares of wooded hillside and feature everything from roses to conifers, tropical tree ferns to eucalypts, Himalayan rhododendrons to at least 24 species of palms.

The gardens were first laid out in the 1850s by the painter William Stockdale (with help from London's Kew Gardens), who imported many of the plants from Australasia and Mexico. Neglected for many years (the site was sold to the Portuguese government in 1949 and practically forgotten), its tangled pathways and aura of wild abandon are immensely appealing.

Recent EU funding can scarcely keep up with the garden's demands, although the local Amigos de Monserrate (Friends of Monserrate) group keeps pressure on for continued maintenance, as well as for restoration of the garden's **quinta**. This bizarre Moorish-looking building – described by Rose Macauley in *They Went to Portugal* as a place of 'barbarous orientalism' – was constructed in the late 1850s by James Knowles for the wealthy merchant Englishman Sir Francis Cook. The quinta's previous incarnation was as a Gothic-style villa rented by the rich and infamous British writer William Beckford in 1794 after he fled Britain in the wake of a homosexual scandal. Beckford, who loved the 'beautiful Claude-like place', added his own touch of landscaping and even imported a flock of sheep from his estate in England. Today, there are various plans for restoring and opening it to the public: one of the most tasteful ideas is to turn it into a teahouse.

The gardens are open daily from 10 am to 6 pm (5 pm from October to May); entry is 200$00.

Museu do Brinquedo

Sintra has several art museums of rather specialist interest, but this toy museum is a delightful collection of lead soldiers, clockwork trains, Dinky toys and porcelain dolls. It's currently at Largo Latino Coelho and open daily, except Mondays, from 10 am to 12.30 pm and 2 to 6 pm; entry is 250$00. There are plans to move it to a new Museu Infantil Technológico Lúdico (Children's Technology Museum) due to open in late 1997 in the renovated former fire station on the corner of Volta do Duche and Rua Visconde de Monserrate.

Museu de Arte Moderna

Sintra is putting itself on the international art map with this new museum, which opened in spring 1997. Housed in Sintra's ornate former casino in Estefânia, its collection of some of the world's best postwar art (with a particularly strong selection of pop art) is funded by business tycoon José Berardo. Among the 350 or so pieces are works by Warhol, Lichtenstein and Kossoff.

Check with the turismo for admission times and fees.

Other Attractions

Between the gardens and Sintra-Vila you'll pass the brazenly luxurious **Hotel Palácio de Seteais**. Originally built in 1787 for the Dutch consul in Lisbon, its name (Palace of Seven Sighs) is said to refer to the Portuguese reaction to the 1808 Convention of Sintra (despatched from here), which gave the French reprehensibly lenient terms after their invasion. The interior has some fantastic murals (even piano lids are painted) but unless you can fork out for a room or a meal you probably won't get a foot past the snobby reception.

There's a string of lavish private villas on the way back to Sintra, notably the fairytale **Quinta da Regaleira**, known locally as Quinta dos Milhões because it cost so many millions to build. Built at the turn of the century for Carvalho da Silva, a Brazilian mining millionaire, this quinta was designed in pseudo-Manueline style by a stage designer. It now belongs to Japanese businessman Jorge Nichimura, though he rarely stays here.

Activities

The Sintra region is increasingly popular for mountain-biking and hiking trips run by tour operators.

Sintraventura, an operation run by the Sintra town council's sporting division (☎ 920 76 53; fax 924 35 81; contact Carlos Pereira) offers occasional day-long mountain biking or walking trips for a mere

Parque Natural de Sintra-Cascais

The Sintra-Cascais Natural Park (14,583 hectares) is one of the most delightful areas in Portugal. Easily accessible from Lisbon, its terrain ranges from the verdant lushness of Sintra itself to the crashing coastline of Guincho (a champion site for modern surfers). Other coastal attractions include the lively coastal resort of Cascais and the wild and rugged Cabo da Roca, Europe's most westerly point. Sintra's mountains have exceptional climatic conditions enjoyed by dozens of plant and tree species; a large number of exotic species were also introduced to Pena Park and Monserrate Gardens during the 18th and 19th centuries. There are no official park trails but there are plenty of walking routes in the parks and to the main points of interest. ∎

300$00 per person, but you need to contact the office in advance for exact dates and booking details.

Wild Side Expedições e Excursões (☎ & fax 443 37 44; mornings only) organises day-long hiking trips (4000$00 per person), mountain biking in the Peninha region of Sintra, Cabo da Roca or Guincho (6000$00) and even cliff-climbing near Castelo dos Mouros or Capo da Roca (7000$00). Half-day outings cost 40% less. If you want to bike it alone, head to Cascais to rent a bike.

Wild Side is also planning one-week activity courses that include horse riding, but meanwhile you can trot in the tamer grounds of Centro Hípico Penha Longa Country Club (☎ 924 90 33) for 3500$00 an hour. The club is about five km south of Sintra-Vila.

Organised Tours

Guided tours to Sintra's major sites usually operate in summer only (check with the turismo) and cost about 6000$00 per person. Most of the Lisbon regional bus tours (see Lisbon – Organised Tours) include Sintra in their itineraries, though usually only a visit to the Pena or Sintra National Palace. The new Cascais-based Stagecoach bus company (☎ 01-486 76 81) also has plans for Sintra tours.

Special Events

Sintra's big annual event is a classical music festival, the Festival de Música, held from around mid-June to mid-July. It features international performers playing in the palaces and other suitably posh venues. It's followed by the equally international Noites de Bailado, a classical and contemporary dance festival that lasts until the end of August. For more details contact the turismo.

Places to Stay

Camping Praia Grande (see West of Sintra) is on the coast 12 km from Sintra.

The youth hostel, *Pousada de Juventude de Sintra* (☎ 924 12 10), is at Santa Eufémia, four km from Sintra-Vila and two km southwest of São Pedro, which is the closest you'll get by bus. Along with dormitory beds, it has double rooms, which are good value at 3300$00. Advance bookings are essential.

Some of the cheapest accommodation in Sintra itself is in the 80 or so private quartos (rooms) that go for about 3500$00 a double (without bath) or 5000$00 (with bath). Ask at the turismo for details. Most budget guesthouses are near the train station. *Casa de Hóspedes Adelaide* (☎ 923 08 73), Rua Guilherme Gomes Fernandes 11, a 10-minute walk from the station, is the kind of place where rooms are rented by the hour, but don't let that put you off: clean, simple doubles (without bath) go for 3500$00 per night.

Closer to the station, at Largo Afonso d'Albuquerque 25, *Pensão Nova Sintra* (☎ 923 02 20) is a cosy old house with doubles at 5000$00 (without private bath but including breakfast) and a pleasant outdoor patio. Immediately across the railway, at Rua João de Deus 70, *Piela's* (☎ 924 16 91) is justifiably popular as much for its hospitable and informative proprietor as for its immaculate doubles (5000$00 without bath and 6000$00 with). The rooms are above Piela's café and snooker room. The charming *Monte da Lua* (☎ & fax 924 10 29), right opposite the station at Avenida Miguel Bombarda 51, has tastefully decorated doubles with TV and bath for 7000$00 or

6000$00 without bath. Try to get one of the quieter rooms at the back which overlook the wooded valley.

In an enviably picturesque position on the high road between Sintra-Vila and São Pedro, *Residencial Sintra* (☎ 923 07 38) is a big old mansion at Travessa dos Avelares 12, with 10 high-ceilinged and spacious rooms that go for 12,000$00. Perfect for families, there's an outdoor patio, rambling garden, swimming pool and children's swings and slides. Advance bookings are essential.

Among several Turihab properties in the area, the 19th-century *Villa das Rosas* (☎ & fax 923 42 16) at Rua António Cunha 2-4 in Estefânia, boasts some splendid décor, with azulejos in the hall and dining room. There's also a tennis court in the grounds. Doubles with breakfast cost 15,000$00. The candy-striped 19th-century *Casa Miradouro* (☎ 923 59 00; fax 924 18 36), perched above Sintra-Vila at Rua Sotto Mayor 55, has grand views and six doubles at 17,500$00, including breakfast.

Top-end accommodation includes the modern *Hotel Tivoli* (☎ 923 35 05; fax 923 15 72), right in the centre of Sintra-Vila at Praça da República, where deluxe doubles will set you back 18,000$00. But if you've got it, it's worth splashing out 4000$00 more for the atmosphere and antiques in *Quinta das Sequóias* (☎ 924 38 21; fax 923 03 42), a superb manor house just beyond the Hotel Palácio de Seteais. Nearby, in the wooded valley below Monserrate Gardens, is a 16th-century former farmhouse, *Quinta da Capella* (☎ 929 01 70; fax 929 34 25), where gorgeous rooms cost just 24,000$00 a double.

Over-the-top luxury can be found at *Hotel Palácio de Seteais* (☎ 923 32 00; fax 923 42 77), Rua Barbosa du Bocage 8, where the privilege of staying in this 18th-century palace will cost you a mind-boggling 40,000$00 per night. Finally, if you're in a Byronic mood, ask about the place where he apparently stayed, the *Lawrence Hotel*. Built in 1786 and closed for the last 50 years, it's now being restored into a 17-room hotel and is due to open in late 1997.

Places to Eat

Estefânia Head for Rua João de Deus, on the other side of the railway line: in addition to *Piela's* café (see Places to Stay) there are three restaurants, including the *Restaurante Parreirinha* (☎ 923 12 07), a smoky locals' den at No 45, which has great grilled fish and chicken (try the succulent grilled garoupa); and the smarter *O Tunel* (☎ 923 13 86), at No 86, where dishes such as arroz de pato no forno (roast duck and rice) are good value at about 950$00.

The unpretentious *A Tasca do Manel* (☎ 923 02 15), next to the ornate câmara municipal (town hall) at Largo Dr Vergílio Horta 5 has pratos do dia for an appetising 800$00 a dish. Nearby, at Rua Dr Alfredo Costa 8, the *Topico Bar & Restaurant* (☎ 923 48 25) is more expensive but offers live music (Portuguese or Afro-Brazilian) on Wednesdays, Fridays and Saturdays. For an up-market splurge in artistic surroundings, *Orixás* (☎ 924 16 72), at Avenida Adriano Julio Coelho 7, is an interesting Brazilian restaurant-cum-art gallery stuffed with wooden sculptures of nubile women. Dishes are exotic and expensive (at least 2000$00 each).

Sintra-Vila Many of the cafés and restaurants here are geared for the passing tourist trade, ie they are overpriced and soulless. But *Tulhas Bar & Restaurante* (☎ 923 23 78), a converted grain warehouse at Rua Gil Vicente 4, has maintained its character and quality. Specialities include an excellent bacalhau com natas (bacalhau in a cream sauce) for 1100$00, but expect to pay about 1500$00 for most other dishes. It's closed on Wednesdays. Cheaper and simpler is *Casa da Avó* (☎ 923 12 80), at Rua Visconde de Monserrate 46, which serves basic dishes daily except Mondays for under 1000$00.

For Sintra's famous queijadas (sweet cheese cakes), head for the popular *Casa da Piriquita* pastelaria at Rua das Padarias 1-5.

São Pedro In this area of town is a cluster of restaurants for meat-lovers, notably *Toca do Javali* (☎ 923 35 03; closed Wednesdays) at Rua 1 de Dezembro 12, where you can get your teeth into a chunk of javali (wild boar) for about 2000$00. Go early to get one of the few outdoor tables in the garden. Down the road, at Travessa Chão de Meninos, two outlets of *Adega do Saloio* (☎ 923 14 22; closed Tuesdays) have skinned goats on display, ready for grilling, as well as other standard grilled offerings. Dishes cost from 1400$00 to 2000$00 but some cheaper half-portions are also available.

Overlooking the huge cobbled Praça Dom Fernando II at the heart of São Pedro is the popular French restaurant *Solar de São Pedro* (☎ 923 18 60; closed Wednesdays), where you can find everything from frogs' legs Provençal (2500$00) to roast duck with orange (1900$00). The adjacent *Restaurante Pic Nic* (☎ 923 08 60), at Praça Dom Fernando II 10, offers cheaper, humbler fare with the added bonus of outdoor tables.

Entertainment

Fonte da Pipa (☎ 923 44 37), Rua Fonte da Pipa 11-13, is a cosy bar with snacks and inexpensive drinks; it's open nightly from around 9 pm. The central *Estrada Velha* (☎ 923 43 55) at Rua Consiglieri Pedroso 16 is another popular bar, usually open until around 2 am.

São Pedro also has a lively bunch of bars: just off the square, *Taverna dos Trovadores* (☎ 923 35 48) is an up-market tavern with fado on Fridays (minimum charge 1500$00) and other types of live music on Thursdays. A more casual dive popular with locals is *Mourisca Bar* (☎ 923 52 53), at Calçada de São Pedro 56, where you can play snooker, darts or chess.

Getting There & Away

Trains run every 15 minutes between Lisbon (Rossio station) and Sintra (the last train back to Lisbon is at 1.23 am). The 45-minute journey costs 180$00. Buses leave from Sintra's train station regularly for popular destinations such as Cascais (direct or via Cabo da Roca, 540$00; via Estoril, 330$00), Mafra (370$00), Ericeira (410$00), and the nearby beach of Praia Grande (280$00) via Colares. Services are reduced on Sundays and public holidays. There's a regular service to Sintra-Vila and São Pedro.

The tram service (July to August only) from Banzão, near Colares, to Praia das Maçãs, about 12 km to the west, has recently been taken over by Stagecoach Tours. Originally used for transporting wine and other goods from Colares, the tram line is now the focus of ambitious revival plans: a new section of the line to Ribeira de Sintra (1.5 km from the centre of Sintra) was due for completion by the end of 1996 and will eventually run to the centre itself.

Getting Around

Bus A privately run bus to the Palácio Nacional da Pena (500$00 per person) departs from the town centre; the turismo has the timetable.

Car The nearest car-rental outfits are in Cascais, but the turismo can arrange to have a car delivered to Sintra without extra charge.

Taxi Taxis are expensive but useful for one-way trips to the start of a walk or for quick one-day tours. Available at the train station and outside the Palácio Nacional de Sintra, they aren't metered so check first what the fare should be with the turismo (which has a comprehensive price list). For a return trip to Pena Palace, the Castle or Monserrate, figure on about 2000$00 (including one hour waiting time). There's a 20% supplement on weekends and holidays.

Horse & Carriage Getting around by horse and carriage is the most romantic option. Operated by Sintratur (☎ 924 12 38) they clip-clop all over the place, even as far as Monserrate (7000$00 return). The cheapest quick clop is to Estefânia (5000$00 return). The turismo has a full list of prices; or ask the drivers, who wait for customers at the entrance to Liberdade Park on the main Volta do Duche road to Estefânia.

Walking Walkers will get itchy feet just sniffing Sintra. The most popular walking route is from Sintra-Vila to the ruined Castelo dos Mouros above town, a relatively easy 50-minute hike (the turismo staff will point you in the right direction). The energetic can continue to Palácio Nacional de Pena (another 20 minutes) and up to the Serra de Sintra's highest point, the 529m Cruz Alta, with its spectacular views.

Less well trodden (and harder to follow) is the three-km path from Monserrate Gardens to the forest hideaway of Convento dos Capuchos (also accessible by walking five km along the road from Pena Palace). Beware of getting stranded at any of these destinations late in the day: there's no public transport back to Sintra. And walking the roads (especially to Monserrate) can be nerve-wracking on a busy weekend when mammoth tour buses squeeze close to the roadside to get past each other.

Pick up a copy of the *Landscapes of Portugal: Sintra, Cascais, Estoril* by Brian & Eileen Anderson for more detailed descriptions of off-road walks (and car tours). See Activities for information on organised walks.

WEST OF SINTRA

The most alluring day-trip destinations out of Sintra are to the **beaches** of Praia das Maçãs and Praia Grande, about 12 km to the west. Praia Grande, as its name suggests, is a big sandy beach with ripping breakers, backed by ugly apartments and a few cafés. Praia das Maçãs is more popular with Sintra's youth for its late-night revelries.

En route to the beaches, eight km west of Sintra, is the ancient ridge-top village of **Colares** (not to be confused with traffic-clogged Várzea de Colares on the main road below). It's a laid-back spot with spectacular views and has been famous for its wines since the 13th century: these were the only vines in Europe to survive the 19th-century phylloxera plague, thanks to their deep roots and the local sandy soil. Call in advance to visit the Adega Regional de Colares (☎ 929 12 10) and taste some of the velvety reds.

Attracting all the tour buses, however, is **Cabo da Roca** (Rock Cape), about 18 km west of Sintra. This sheer cliff plunging 150m to the roaring sea below is Europe's westernmost point. A wild and rugged spot, it's surprisingly uncommercialised, perhaps because it feels too uncomfortably remote: there are only a couple of stalls, a café and a tourist office where you can buy a certificate (500$00, or 800$00 for the deluxe version) to show you've been here.

Places to Stay & Eat

Praia Grande has one camping ground, *Camping Praia Grande* (☎ 929 05 81). Otherwise accommodation in this area is expensive: it costs at least 8000$00 a double to stay at the *Residencial Oceano* (☎ 929 23 99), *Residencial Real* (☎ 929 20 02) – both in Praia das Maçãs – or *Casa de Hóspedes de Piscina* (☎ 929 21 45) in Praia Grande. For other alternatives, check out the private quartos signs on the road to Praia das Maçãs.

You'll have better luck with food, especially at Praia das Maçãs, where seafood restaurants such as *Buzio* (☎ 929 21 72) and *Cai Ao Mar* (☎ 928 23 74) are popular; both are on the main street above the beach.

Entertainment

At last count, there were three discos at Praia das Maçãs: *Concha* (☎ 929 20 67), on the left by the GALP station; *Casino Monumental* (☎ 929 20 24) in the centre; and *Quivuvi* (☎ 929 12 17) further along on the right, in a modern shopping mall. They can keep you bopping till 4 am on weekends.

Getting There & Away

Buses from Sintra train station run directly to Praia Grande in summer, or you can take any bus heading for Fontanelas or Azenhas do Mar via Praia das Maçãs and get off at the Ponte Rodizio turn-off (about three km beyond Várzea de Colares); Praia Grande beach is about 400m away. There's also a summer-only (July to September) tram service between Banzão (500m beyond Várzea de Colares) and Praia das Maçãs.

Check with Sintra's turismo on the tram's planned extension to Sintra.

You can reach Cabo da Roca from Sintra or Cascais: a regular bus service connecting the two towns goes via the cape (as well as Colares). Services are far fewer on Sundays and public holidays.

ESTORIL
• postcode 2765 • area code ☎ 01

This beach resort 26 km west of Lisbon along the Costa do Estoril has long been a favoured haunt of the rich and famous. It has Europe's biggest casino, a mild climate and a genteel ambience that smothers any hint of unruly excitement (for that, as well as cheaper accommodation and a wider range of bars and restaurants, head to Cascais, a couple of km further west along the coast). But if you fancy a quiet break gambling away the escudos, or playing golf on one of half a dozen top-notch courses near Estoril, there's accommodation to suit most pockets (the deeper the better).

Orientation & Information

Arriving by train, you'll be on Avenida Marginal right across from Estoril's central attraction: the pleasantly shady Parque do Estoril, with the casino at the top. Buses also stop at the train station.

The turismo (☎ 466 38 13; fax 467 22 80) is at Arcadas do Parque, on the left side of the park opposite the train station. It's open daily from 9 am to 7 pm (Sundays 10 am to 6 pm).

Things to See & Do

The **casino** is open daily from 3 pm to 3 am. In addition to the gaming rooms (everything from roulette to baccarat, slot machines to blackjack, 21 and the popular dice game of French bank), there's a vast restaurant where you can have dinner before watching the international floor show (nightly at 11 pm, 9000$00 per person including dinner, 4500$00 without dinner). If you don't fancy forking out for this or the gambling (there's a minimum bet of 1000$00 and you'll need your passport to enter), or can't find an outfit respectable enough to get past the bouncers, at least try to get a look at the lobby, which doubles as an art gallery.

Estoril's attempt at a beach is behind the train station (accessible from the turismo via an underpass).

Organised Tours

Regional bus tours such as Grayline's (see Lisbon – Getting Around) include a quick visit to Estoril's casino. Cityrama (☎ 355 85 69) in Lisbon organises an evening outing (11,900$00 per person) with time to visit the floor show and gambling rooms.

Special Events

Racing fanatics may prefer to put their bets on the Grand Prix Formula 1 World & Euro-

---

Golf on the Estoril Coast

As far as beach resorts go, Estoril is one of the dullest places west of Lisbon. But if you're a gambler or golfer (and preferably rich) you'll be in seventh heaven: Estoril not only has Europe's biggest casino, it's also got half a dozen spectacular golf courses within 25 km.

The closest is just two km north: Golf do Estoril has two courses overlooking the sea – one 18-hole, 69 par, and the second 9 holes and par 34. The Quinta da Marinha course, nine km west, was designed by Robert Trent Jones to give both high handicappers and scratch golfers a challenge, with the course rolling over wind-blown dunes and rocky outcrops.

Ten km north-west is the 18-hole, 72-par Penha Longa golf club, a well-equipped Trent Jones Jr creation with superb views of the Serra de Sintra and Atlantic Ocean. Nearby are Golf Estoril-Sol, designed by John Harris and Ron Fream, and the 18-hole Quinta da Beloura, designed by Rocky Roquemore who's also responsible for the newest course in the region, the 18-hole Belas Clube de Campo, 22 km north-east of Estoril in the Carregueira hills. Estoril's turismo has full details. ■

pean Championships, held in late September or early October at the Autodromo do Estoril, nine km north of town.

Places to Stay

The nearest pousada de juventude (youth hostel) is at Oeiras, nine km east of Estoril (see Lisbon – Places to Stay).

The pick of the pensões is *Pensão Smart* (☎ 468 21 64), at Rua José Viana 3 (entrance on Rua Maestro Lacerda 6) in a quiet residential area 10 minutes walk from the station. Doubles with breakfast start at 6500$00. Cheaper digs can be found nearby at *Casa de Hóspedes Paula Castro* (☎ 468 06 99), on Rua da Escola 4, where basic doubles without bath go for about 5000$00.

More up-market residencials can be found along the busy Avenida Marginal a few minutes walk east of the station (turn right when you exit): *Residencial São Mamede* (☎ 467 10 74; fax 467 14 18) has comfortable doubles with breakfast for 7500$00. A good 20-minute walk north of the centre, at Rua de São Pedro, Porta B, Bairro de Santo António, is the popular *Toca dos Grilos* guesthouse (☎ 467 47 03; fax 467 46 92), a modern seven-room house with garden and swimming pool. Doubles are 9000$00. For a grand old seaside hotel that fits Estoril's ambience to a tee, head for *Hotel Inglaterra* (☎ 468 44 61; fax 468 21 08) at Rua do Porto 1. Its value-for-money doubles (11,000$00) are quickly booked up in high season.

Places to Eat

Restaurants here are pricey: you're better off heading for Cascais. *Casabranca* (☎ 467 29 98) is a trendy place in an elegant old house at Avenida Biarritz 8, but the *English Bar* (☎ 468 04 13), at Avenida Sabóia 9, near Monte Estoril train station (15 minutes walk along the seafront towards Cascais), is more popular, especially for its excellent but expensive seafood. Cheaper snacks in more casual surroundings can be found at *Frolic*, by the Hotel Palácio on Avenida Clotilde, on the eastern side of the park.

Getting There & Away

From Cais do Sodré train station in Lisbon it's a half-hour trundle on the Linha de Cascais to Estoril (180$00). There are frequent buses between Sintra and Estoril. For Cascais you can hop on the train or, more pleasantly, walk along the seafront for about an hour.

CASCAIS

• *pop 19,000* • *postcode 2750* • *area code* ☎ *01*

This former fishing village has been tuned into tourism since 1870 when the royal court first came here for the summer, bringing a train of nobility in its wake. It's now the liveliest beach resort on the Estoril Coast, attracting a young and international crowd, especially Brits (all year) and French and Italians in August. If you like your home comforts (John Bull pubs, McDonald's, even Marks & Spencer), you'll be happy in the touristy pedestrianised centre or on the three small beaches nearby. But there's a surprisingly unspoilt old town area, which provides a pleasant afternoon's meander, and some remnants of traditional fishing activity that carries on regardless of the tourists.

Orientation & Information

Everything of interest is within easy walking distance. The train station (where buses for nearby destinations also congregate) is on Avenida Marginal, a 10-minute walk north of the pedestrianised Rua Frederico Arouca, where you'll find most of the tourist-oriented shops and restaurants. Near the western end of this street is the informative turismo (☎ 486 82 04), at Rua Visconde de Luz 14. It's open daily from 9 am to 8 pm (to 7 pm from October to May; Sundays from 10 am to 6 pm).

Most banks in town have Multibanco facilities for credit card cash advances. For the best exchange rates on travellers cheques, go to Cambitur (☎ 486 75 28) at Rua Frederico Arouca 73a. This travel agency also rents cars and organises sightseeing trips. It's open Monday to Saturday from 9.30 am to 7 pm and on Sundays from 2 to 7 pm.

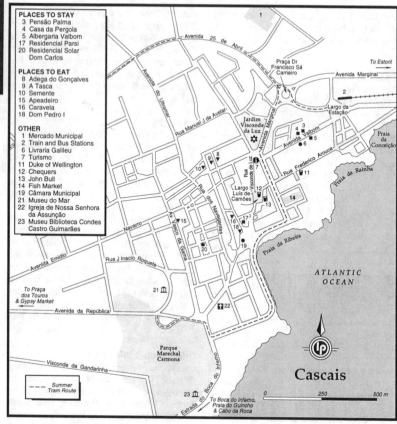

PLACES TO STAY
3 Pensão Palma
4 Casa da Pergola
5 Albergaria Valbom
17 Residencial Parsi
20 Residencial Solar
   Dom Carlos

PLACES TO EAT
8 Adega do Gonçalves
9 A Tasca
10 Semente
15 Apeadeiro
16 Caravela
18 Dom Pedro I

OTHER
1 Mercado Municipal
2 Train and Bus Stations
6 Livraria Galileu
7 Turismo
11 Duke of Wellington
12 Chequers
13 John Bull
14 Fish Market
19 Câmara Municipal
21 Museu do Mar
22 Igreja de Nossa Senhora
   da Assunção
23 Museu Biblioteca Condes
   Castro Guimarães

Cascais

A good source of second-hand books in English, Spanish, Italian, French and German is Livraria Galileu, at Avenida Valbom 24a.

Old Cascais

To catch a hint of Cascais' former life as a fishing village, head for the **fish market** between Praia da Ribeira and Praia da Rainha at about 6 pm every day (except Sunday) when an auctioneer sells off the daily catch in an unintelligible rapid-fire lingo.

The atmospheric back lanes and alleys to the west of the câmara municipal (town hall)

are also well worth exploring. In a shady square just south-west of the town hall is the **Igreja de Nossa Senhora da Assunção** with azulejos that predate the 1755 earthquake that destroyed most of the town.

The large and leafy Parque Marechal Carmona nearby contains the **Museu Biblioteca Condes Castro Guimarães**. This late 19th-century mansion of the Counts of Castro Guimarães is now a museum displaying the family's furnishings (especially pretty Indo-Portuguese furniture), paintings and books, as well as archaeological finds from the area. It's open daily, except

Mondays, from 11 am to 12.30 pm and 2 to 5 pm; entry is 250$00.

More intriguing is the **Museu do Mar**, north of the park on the other side of the Avenida da República, which has a small, quality collection of model boats and marine artefacts. It's open daily, except Mondays, from 10 am to 4.30 pm for 200$00.

Markets

The town's **municipal market**, off Avenida 25 de Abril on the northern outskirts of town, takes place on Wednesday and Saturday mornings (Wednesdays are best), while a **Gypsy market** fills the area next to the praça de touros (bullring) a couple of km west of town on the first and third Sunday of the month. Market junkies might also want to take the train five stops back down on the line to Lisbon for the Thursday morning market at Carcavelos, famous for its cheap t-shirts and clothes (especially kids' stuff).

Beaches

Most of the activity in Cascais centres around its restaurants and bars but there are beaches if you want them: three sandy stretches (Praia da Ribeira is the largest and closest) tucked into little bays just a few minutes walk south of the main drag, Rua Frederico Arouca. They're nothing to write home about (nor is the water quality) but they make pleasant suntraps if you can find an empty patch.

Cascais' most famous tourist attraction is **Boca do Inferno** (literally, 'mouth of hell'), a couple of km west of the centre, where the sea roars into an abyss in the coast. You can walk there in about 20 minutes and join the crowds pouring out of their tour buses, but don't expect anything dramatic unless there's a storm raging.

Far more exciting waves are made at **Praia do Guincho**, nine km north-west of Cascais. This long, wild beach is a surfer's and windsurfer's paradise (the 1991 World Surfing Championships were held here), with massive crashing rollers. But there's a strong undertow which can be dangerous for swimmers and novice surfers.

Horse Riding

If you prefer to keep your feet on (or just above) the ground, check out the horse-riding facilities at the Centro Hípico da Quinta da Marinha (☎ 487 14 03), a couple of km inland from Praia do Guincho, where you can rent horses for 4000$00 an hour.

Bullfighting

Cascais boasts Portugal's largest praça de touros (bullring) where bullfights take place regularly (at least every weekend during summer). Check with the turismo for dates and times.

Special Events

Summertime musical events include a popular international jazz festival in June. In mid-August, Cascais honours the patron saint of its fisherfolk, the Senhora dos Navegantes, with a day-long procession through the streets.

Places to Stay

Camping Orbitur do Guincho (☎ 487 10 14; fax 487 21 67) is in Areia, about a km inland from Praia do Guincho and nine km from Cascais. Hourly buses run to Guincho from Cascais train station.

Accommodation prices in Cascais soar in summer, and in August you'll be hard pushed to find a place at all without advance reservations. The best budget bets are private rooms (quartos), usually available for about 5000$00 a double. The turismo can help you locate them.

The *Residencial Parsi* (☎ 484 57 44; fax 483 71 50), Rua Afonso Sanches 8, is a crumbling old building overlooking the waterfront that has doubles (without private bath) from 5000$00. Closer to the station is the *Pensão Palma* (☎ 483 77 97; fax 483 79 22), at Avenida Valbom 13. It's one of a pair of dainty town villas and is as pretty as a doll's house, with a fragrant flower garden out the front. Doubles range from 6500$00 (no bath) to 11,500$00 (with bath and breakfast). Next door, *Casa da Pergola* (☎ 484 00 40; fax 483 47 91) is a much more up-market Turihab establishment with an ornate façade

LISBON

decorated with hand-painted tiles. Rooms with bath and balcony in the house are a steep 17,000$00 a double but only 9000$00 in the garden annexe. More modern and less inspired accommodation can be found across the road at *Albergaria Valbom* (☎ 486 58 01; fax 486 58 05) at No 14, where comfortable doubles go for 11,500$00.

In a quiet part of the old town, at Rua Latino Coelho 8, *Residencial Solar Dom Carlos* (☎ 486 84 63; fax 486 51 55) is a 16th-century former royal residence that features a chapel where Dom Carlos used to pray. Rooms are 20th century (all with private bath) and cost 10,000$00.

Places to Eat

There are plenty of restaurants serving unmemorable tourist-oriented stodge and overpriced seafood in the town centre. It's worth heading away from the crowds for something better. *Dom Pedro I* (☎ 483 37 34), tucked into a backstreet corner of the old town at Beco dos Invalides 5, serves tasty and reasonably priced dishes from 800$00; go early to grab one of the few prized outdoor tables on the cobbled steps.

Further west, *Apeadeiro* (☎ 483 27 31), at Avenida Vasco da Gama 32, is locally famous for its grilled fish. Another popular haunt is the more up-market *Adega do Goncalves* (☎ 483 02 87), at Rua Afonso Sanches 54, where hearty servings cost around 1200$00 a dish. Simpler and cheaper is *A Tasca*, opposite at No 61; try the delicious fish kebabs. Seafood splurges are best had at *Caravela* (☎ 483 02 80), Rua Afonso Sanches 19, where you can indulge in crab, lobster or prawns. Expect to pay at least 1300$00 a dish.

The only vegetarian restaurant in town is the modest *Semente* snack bar (☎ 483 23 92), at Rua Poco Novo 65, where you can find tofu pies, quiches, millet salads and fresh fruit juices. It's open daily except Sundays.

Entertainment

There's no lack of bars to keep the nights buzzing, especially in Rua Frederico Arouca and the Largo Luís de Camões area, just down the road from the turismo, where the bars triple as cafés, restaurants and discos. For British-style establishments with imported beers and bopping music, check out *John Bull* on Praça Costa Pinto 32, *Chequers* (☎ 483 09 26) in Largo Luís de Camões, and the *Duke of Wellington* at Rua Frederico Arouca 32.

Getting There & Away

Trains from Lisbon's Cais do Sodré station run every 20 minutes (from 5 am to 2.30 am) for the 25-minute trip to Cascais (180$00). Buses run regularly throughout the day from outside Cascais train station to Sintra and Cabo de Roca, and every hour to Praia do Guincho and Mafra. Cascais is also included in most regional bus tours from Lisbon (see Lisbon – Organised Tours).

Getting Around

From May to October a free tourist tram normally runs between the train station and the Parque Marechal Carmona and up to the Hotel Citadela on the north-western outskirts of town. There's also one solitary horse and carriage which does half-hour trips for about 3000$00 (5000$00 for a grand circuit), starting just down the road (towards the waterfront) from the turismo.

In addition to Cambitur (see Information), there are several other car-rental agencies, including Auto Jardim (☎ 483 10 73) and Automix (☎ 482 12 91) with all-inclusive rates from around 5000$00 per day. To rent bikes or motorcycles contact Gesrent (☎ 486 45 66) at Centro Comercial Cisne, Loja 15, Avenida Marginal; or AA Castanheira (☎ 483 42 59) at Edificio Sol de Cascais, Loja 11, Avenida 25 de Abril. Prices range from about 1500$00 per day for a mountain bike to 5300$00 for a Yamaha 125. You have to be at least 21 to rent a motorcycle (25 for bikes over 500 cc) and to have had a motorcycle licence for at least a year.

QUELUZ

• *pop 42,900* • *postcode 2745* • *area code* ☎ *01*
The only reason to stop at this dull town five km north-west of Lisbon, en route to Sintra,

is to see the pink-hued **Palácio de Queluz**, which was converted in the late 18th century from a hunting lodge to a summer residence for the royal family. It's the most elegant example of rococo architecture in Portugal, a miniature Versailles with feminine charm and formal gardens of whimsical fancy. One wing of the palace is often used to accommodate state guests and visiting dignitaries but the rest is open to the public daily, except Tuesdays, from 10 am to 1 pm and 2 to 5 pm; entry is 400$00.

The palace has witnessed some extraordinary royal scenes. Built for Prince Dom Pedro between 1747 and 1752 and designed by the Portuguese architect Mateus Vicente de Oliveira and French artist Jean-Baptiste Robillon, it was Dom Pedro's niece and wife, Queen Maria I, who inspired the most scintillating gossip about the place: she lived here for most of her reign, going increasingly mad. Her fierce, scheming daughter-in-law, the Spanish Carlota Joaquina, supplied even more bizarre material for the wealthy British visitor William Beckford to write about – most famously, an occasion when she insisted that Beckford run a race with her maid in the garden and then dance a bolero (which he did, he relates, 'in a delirium of romantic delight').

Today the interior still has hints of its owners' eccentric characters, though the furnishings are typical of the time, including English and French-style furniture, Arriaolos carpets, porcelain chinoiserie and floors inlaid with exotic woods. Highlights are the mirror-lined Throne Room, a wood-panelled Music Room (still used for concerts), the Ambassador's Room with a floor of chequered marble and ceiling painting of the royal family attending a concert, and Pedro IV's 'circular' bedroom (actually a circular ceiling over a square room) with scenes from *Don Quixote* on the walls. The palace's vast kitchens have been converted into an expensive restaurant, *Cozinha Velha*.

The garden is a delightful medley of box hedges, fountains and lead statues, and features an azulejo-lined canal where the royal family went boating.

Getting There & Away

It's a 20-minute train ride (150$00) on the Sintra line from Lisbon's Rossio station to Queluz-Belas, followed by a 15-minute walk downhill (follow the signs) to the palace.

MAFRA

• *postcode 2640* • *area code* ☎ *061*

The unremarkable town of Mafra, 39 km north-west of Lisbon, is famous for its massive Palácio-Convento de Mafra, the most awesome of the many extravagant monuments created in the 18th-century reign of Dom João V, when money was no problem. There's nothing else of interest in town, so it's best to come here on a day trip from Lisbon, Sintra or Ericeira.

Orientation & Information

You can't miss the palace: its huge grey façade dominates the town. The poorly signposted turismo (☎ 81 20 23; fax 521 04) is on Avenida 25 de Abril, five minutes walk north down the main street from the palace, beside the Auditorio Municipal Beatrix Costa. It's open weekdays from 9.30 am to 7 pm and on weekends from 9.30 am to 1 pm and 2.30 to 7.30 pm (to 6 pm in winter). The turismo has a decent map of the Mafra area (300$00) and useful information on nearby attractions.

Palácio Nacional de Mafra

The Mafra National Palace is a combination of palace, monastery and basilica – a huge baroque and neoclassical monument covering 10 hectares. It was begun in 1717, to fulfil a vow by Dom João V upon granting of a male heir. As the king's coffers filled with newly discovered gold from Brazil, the initial design – meant for 13 monks – was expanded to house 280 monks and 140 novices, and to incorporate two royal wings. No expense was spared to build its 880 halls and rooms, 5200 doorways, 2500 windows and two bell towers boasting the world's largest collection of bells (57 in each). Indeed, when the Flemish bell-founders queried the extravagant order for a carillon of bells, Dom João is said to have doubled the order and to have sent the money in advance.

Under the supervision of the German architect Friedrich Ludwig, up to 20,000 artisans (including Italian masons and carpenters) worked on the monument. That figure rose to a mind-boggling 45,000 workers in the last two years of construction, all of them kept in order by 7000 soldiers. The presence of so many outstanding artists spurred João V to establish a school of sculpture in the palace; this functioned from 1753 to 1770 and employed many of Portugal's most important sculptors. Though the building may have been an artistic coup, the expense of its construction and the use of such a large workforce helped destroy the country's economy.

It was only briefly used as a palace – in 1799, as the French prepared to invade Portugal, Dom João VI and the royal family fled to Brazil, taking most of Mafra's furniture with them. In 1807, General Junot put his troops in the monastery, followed by Wellington and his men. From then on, the palace became a favourite military haven. Even today, most of it is used as a military academy.

One-hour tours (excluding the basilica) take you through innumerable galleries of polished wooden floors, down 230m-long corridors, through interminable salons and apartments and up dozens of flights of stairs – and this is only a fraction of the place.

It's easy to get dazed by it all, but a few things stand out, including some amusing 18th-century pinball machines in the games room; grotesque hunting décor in the dining room, where chandeliers are made of antlers' horns and chairs are upholstered in deerskin; and the monastery's infirmary where insane monks were locked away. Most impressive is the magnificent barrel-vaulted baroque library, housing nearly 40,000 books from the 15th to 18th centuries. At 88m it's the longest room in the building. According to the original plan its ceiling was to have been gilded, but at this point the money ran out.

The central basilica, with its two bell towers, is wonderfully restrained by comparison with the rest of the palace, featuring multihued marble floors and panelling and Carrara marble statues.

The palace-monastery is open daily, except Tuesdays and public holidays, from 9.30 am to 5 pm (closed from 1 to 2 pm in winter); entry is 300$00. The one-hour guided tours are actually little more than an 'escort' by a (Portuguese-speaking) guard; tours in English, French or German have to be booked in advance.

Tapada de Mafra

The palace's park and hunting ground, Tapada de Mafra, originally enclosed by a perimeter wall 20 km long, is also open for guided tours. The tours take place at 10 am, 11 am, 3 pm and 4 pm on Fridays, Saturdays and Sundays (at 10 am and 3 pm on Saturdays and Sundays in winter). The 90-minute tours (call ☎ 511 00 a day ahead to reserve a place) take visitors to see the park's deer and wild boar and its falcon-recuperation centre (the former royal hunting lodge is currently being converted into a pousada and tearoom). The tours are a combination of bus transport and walking and cost 950$00 for adults and 500$00 for children under 10.

Sobreiro

Another unusual excursion from Mafra is to the village of Sobreiro, about four km northwest (take any bus heading to Ericeira), where sculptor José Franco has created a craft village with a traditional bakery and cobbler's and clockmaker's shops, as well as several small windmills and watermills. Kids love it here; so do adults, especially when they discover the rustic *adega* (bar) with good red wine, snacks and meals.

Horse Riding

There are plans to run horse-riding trips in the Tapada de Mafra. Meanwhile horse-lovers can go to the Escola de Equitação de Alcainça (☎ 966 21 22) about five km southeast of Mafra at Rua de São Miguel, Alcainça, where you can rent horses for 3000$00 an hour. You can also take an intensive four-day riding course on Lusitanos

Wolf Recovery Centre

Some ten km north-east of Mafra is the Centro de Recuperação de Lobo Ibérico (Iberian Wolf Recovery Centre), established in 1988 to provide a home for wolves that have been trapped, snared or kept in dire conditions and are unable to function in the wild any longer. Kept 'in the most naturalistic surroundings possible', there are now some 22 wolves at the centre, all from the north of the country where Portugal's last 300 Iberian wolves roam. You can visit the centre if you call in advance (mobile ☎ 061-0931-532312); the best time to visit is around 5 pm when the wolves emerge in the cool of the dusk. To support the centre's activities you can 'adopt' a wolf for about 5000$00 a year. See Endangered Species under Flora & Fauna in the Facts about the Country chapter for more on the Iberian wolf.

To reach the centre, take a bus from Mafra to Malveira, then pick up any Torres Vedras-bound bus and get off at Vale de Guarda (about four km from Malveira). ■

horses for 18,500$00 per day (including meals and accommodation).

Getting There & Away

There are regular buses to Mafra from Ericeira (20 minutes) and Sintra (45 minutes, 370$00). Hourly buses from Lisbon take 1½ hours (530$00) and leave from the minuscule Mafrense bus company terminus at Rua Fernandos da Fonseca 18 (right by the Socorro metro station), going via the main bus station on Avenida Casal Ribeiro.

SETÚBAL PENINSULA

The Setúbal Peninsula – the northern spur of the region the tourist board calls the Costa Azul – is an easy hop from Lisbon by ferry across the Tejo river, with regular bus connections to all the major points of interest. You can laze on the vast beaches of Costa da Caparica, join trendy lisboêtas in Sesimbra's beach resort further south or eat great seafood in nearby Setúbal. Setúbal's express bus connections make it a convenient stopover if you're heading south or east. There are two major nature reserves as well – the Reserve Natural do Estuário do Sado and Parque Natural da Arrábida, both worth exploring if you have your own transport.

Cacilhas

This suburb across the Rio Tejo from Lisbon is notable mainly for its fish restaurants and the **Cristo Rei**, the immense statue of Christ with outstretched hands visible from almost everywhere in Lisbon. The 28m-high statue (a small version of the one in Rio de Janeiro) was built in 1959 and partly paid for by Portuguese women grateful for the country having been spared the horrors of WWII. A lift (operating from 9 am to 7 pm in summer) takes you right to the top from where you can gasp at the panoramic views.

Getting There & Away Ferries to Cacilhas (90$00) run every 10 minutes from Lisbon's Cais da Alfândega river terminal by Praça do Comércio. The trip takes about 10 minutes, with the last boat leaving at around 10.30 pm. A car ferry also runs every 20 minutes from Cais do Sodré (this one runs all night). To reach the statue, take the bus from stand No 9 at the bus station opposite Cacilhas' ferry terminal. Or you can take bus No 52 or 53 directly from Lisbon's Praça de Espanha (get off just after the bridge).

Costa da Caparica

This eight-km stretch of beach on the west coast of the peninsula is Lisbon's favourite weekend escape, with cafés, restaurants and bars catering to every age group. During the summer a narrow-gauge railway runs along the entire length of the beach, giving you the option of jumping off at any one of 20 stops; earlier stops attract families, later ones gays and nudists. The turismo (☎ 01-290 00 71) at Praça da Liberdade can fill you in on accommodation options (including several camping grounds) but these are expensive.

Getting There & Away Buses run to the Costa da Caparica regularly from Lisbon's Praça de Espanha (taking about an hour) and from Cacilhas' bus terminal (stand No 17 or 25).

Setúbal

• *pop 80,000* • *postcode 2900* • *area code* ☎ *065*

Once an important Roman settlement, Setúbal is now the largest town on the Setúbal Peninsula and Portugal's third-largest port (after Lisbon and Porto). Situated on the north bank of the Sado estuary, some 50 km south of Lisbon, it's refreshingly untouristy, concentrating more on its fishing, commercial port and industries (sardine-canning, cement and salt) than on visitors. But with its easy-going atmosphere, nearby beaches and good cheap restaurants, it makes an ideal weekend escape from Lisbon. It's also a suitable base for exploring the Parque Natural da Arrábida, though you'll need your own transport unless you take one of the adventure trips mentioned below.

Orientation & Information There are two train stations. The one opposite Praça do Brasil, 700m north of the city centre, serves trains from Lisbon, while the local station is centrally located at the eastern end of Avenida 5 de Outubro. The main bus station is also on this avenida, five minutes walk from the municipal turismo (☎ 53 42 22) on Praça do Quebedo. The turismo is open weekdays only from 9 am to 12.30 pm and 2 to 5.30 pm.

For more comprehensive information head for the regional turismo (☎ 52 42 84; fax 367 45). It's at Travessa Frei Gaspar 10, near the town's pedestrianised shopping centre (around 10 minutes walk south of the bus station). It's open from 9 am to 7 pm daily (closed 12.30 to 2 pm on Mondays and Saturdays, and on Sunday afternoons). Brisk and efficient, the office has stacks of publications about the Setúbal region and a touch-screen information terminal outside.

Banks and shops are plentiful in the pedestrian area near the regional turismo office.

The main post office is further north, on Avenida 22 de Dezembro, a few minutes walk from the Igreja de Jesus.

Igreja de Jesus There's only one major cultural site in Setúbal: the Igreja de Jesus in Praça Miguel Bombarda (at the western end of Avenida 5 de Outubro). Constructed in 1491, it was designed by Diogo de Boitac, better known for his later work on Belém's Mosteiro dos Jerónimos. The small church itself is late Gothic in style but walk inside and you'll see the earliest examples of Manueline decoration – extraordinary twisted pillars, like writhing snakes, made from delicately coloured Arrábida marble. The walls of the nave and chancel are more conservative, decorated with fine 18th-century azulejos on the life of the Virgin. The church is open Tuesday to Saturday from 9 am to 12.30 pm and 2 to 5.30 pm.

Museu de Setúbal Around the corner from the Igreja de Jesus, on Rua Balneários Dr Paula Borba, is the town's major museum. It houses a renowned collection of 15th and 16th-century Portuguese paintings, azulejos, and ecclesiastic gold and silver. It's open Monday to Friday from 9 am to 12.30 pm and 2 to 5.30 pm.

Museu de Arqueologia e Etnografia The Archaeological & Ethnographic Museum, at Avenida Luísa Todi 162, houses an impressive collection of Roman remains. Setúbal was founded by the Romans at the beginning of the 5th century after their fishing port of Cetobriga (now Tróia), on the opposite side of the river mouth, was destroyed by an earthquake in 412. The museum opens its doors Tuesday to Saturday from 9.30 am to 12.30 pm and 2 to 5 pm, and Sundays from 9.30 am to 12.30 pm.

Castelo São Filipe Worth the half-hour stroll to the west of town is this castle built by Filipe I in 1590 to fend off an English attack on the invincible Armada. Converted into a pousada in the 1960s, its ramparts are still huge and impressive and its chapel

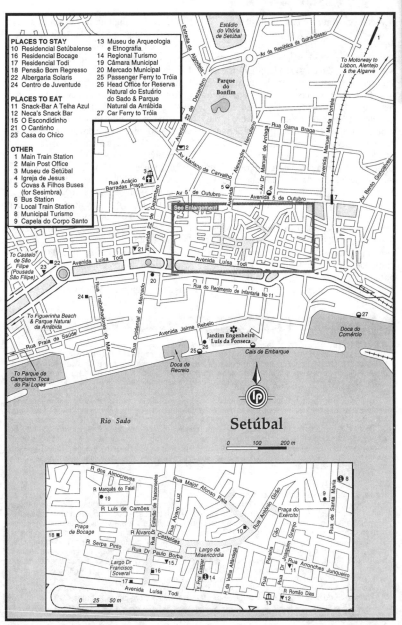

PLACES TO STAY
10 Residencial Setúbalense
16 Residencial Bocage
17 Residencial Todi
18 Pensão Bom Regresso
22 Albergaria Solaris
24 Centro de Juventude

PLACES TO EAT
11 Snack-Bar A Telha Azul
12 Neca's Snack Bar
15 O Escondidinho
21 O Cantinho
23 Casa do Chico

OTHER
1 Main Train Station
2 Main Post Office
3 Museu de Setúbal
4 Igreja de Jesus
5 Covas & Filhos Buses
  (for Sesimbra)
6 Bus Station
7 Local Train Station
8 Municipal Turismo
9 Capela do Corpo Santo

13 Museu de Arqueologia
   e Etnografia
14 Regional Turismo
19 Câmara Municipal
20 Mercado Municipal
25 Passenger Ferry to Tróia
26 Head Office for Reserva
   Natural do Estuário
   do Sado & Parque
   Natural da Arrábida
27 Car Ferry to Tróia

Estádio
do Vitória
de Setúbal

To Motorway to
Lisbon, Alentejo
& the Algarve

Parque
do
Bonfim

See Enlargement

To Castelo
de São
Filipe
(Pousada
São Filipe)

To Figuerinha Beach
& Parque Natural
da Arrábida

To Parque de
Campismo Toca
do Pai Lopes

Doca do
Comércio

Doca de
Recreio

Cais de Embarque

Jardim Engenheiro
Luís da Fonseca

Rio Sado

Setúbal

0   100   200 m

Praça
de Bocage

Praça do
Exército

Largo da
Misericórdia

Largo Dr
Francisco
Soveral

Avenida Luísa Todi

0   25   50 m

boasts 18th-century azulejos on the life of São Filipe.

Beaches For good beaches, head west of Setúbal along the coast road until you reach Figuerinha, Galapos or Portinho da Arrábida – all fine beaches, accessible by buses from Setúbal in summer. More crowded are the beaches of Sesimbra, and Tróia (across the mouth of the Sado estuary), which has become hideously developed.

Organised Tours For active exploration of the Parque Natural da Arrábida and Reserva Natural do Estuário do Sado, contact Safari Azul (π & fax 55 24 47), Rua Cidade de Leiria 3-5, which organises everything from horse riding (3000$00 an hour) and mountain biking (7000$00 per person per day) to climbing, canoeing (8000$00 per person per day), kayaking and helicopter tours. US-based Easy Rider Tours (see Organised Tours in the Getting Around chapter) has a

Costa Azul biking tour that includes a day's biking through the Serra da Arrábida.

Another unusual way to experience the area is aboard a modern galleon, the *Riquitum*, which sails along the Sado Estuary on four-hour trips (2500$00 per person) leaving every Friday at 9 am from the Cais de Embarque, just west of the Doca do Comércio (commercial dock). The trips are organised by Troiacruze (π 222 77 40; fax 222 77 55), which also offers short scuba-diving courses.

Four-wheel-drive tours in the Tróia Peninsula (3500$00 for a half-day tour on weekends only) and Setúbal Peninsula (8000$00 for a full-day tour daily except weekends) are offered by Novas Fronteiras (π 53 29 96; fax 396 63), Avenida 22 de Dezembro 46.

Wine buffs may be interested in the free wine-cellar tours of the José Maria da Fonseca adega (π 218 02 27) at Rua José Augusto Coelho 11, Vila Fresca de Azeitão,

---

Parque Natural da Arrábida

The Arrábida Natural Park stretches along the south-east coast of the Setúbal Peninsula, from Setúbal to Sesimbra. Covering the 35-km-long Serra da Arrábida mountain ridge, with its sweeping views of the Atlantic, this is an area rich in Mediterranean thickets and plants (over a thousand different species), butterflies, beetles and birds (especially birds of prey). Even seaweed comes in 70 different varieties here.

The variety of flora makes for great local honey, especially in the gardens of the Convento da Arrábida, a 16th-century former convent overlooking the sea just north of Portinho. Cheese and wine are other famous local products (see Setúbal – Organised Tours for details of wine-cellar tours).

There's little public transport through the park (buses between Setúbal and Sesimbra mostly skirt its northern boundary), so your best option is to rent a car or motorcycle and walk. For ideas of where to go, see the *Walking Guide to Arrábida and Sado* (no maps), published by the Região de Turismo da Costa Azul. It's available at the regional turismo in Setúbal and from park headquarters (π 52 40 32) at Praça da República, Setúbal.

Reserva Natural do Estuário do Sado

The Sado Estuary Natural Reserve encompasses a vast coastal area (23,160 hectares) around the Sado river and estuary, stretching from Setúbal in the north to near Alcácer do Sal in the south-east. Its mud banks and marshes, lagoons, dunes and former salt pans are a vitally important habitat for mammals, molluscs and migrating birds. The mammal species that attracts the most attention is *Tursiops truncatus*, a species of dolphin (known in Portuguese as Roaz-Corvineiro) often found in coastal waters. There are thought to be only about 50 dolphins left in this area, fighting for survival as the mouth of the estuary becomes increasingly developed. Among the 100 or so bird species worth looking out for are flamingoes (over a thousand of the birds usually winter here), white storks (spring and summertime) and resident marsh harriers and little egrets.

Without your own transport, explorations of the park are inevitably limited. The *Walking Guide to Arrábida & Sado* details several hikes but they start several km from any bus routes. ∎

where the famous *moscatel* of Setúbal is made. Catch any Sesimbra-bound bus from Setúbal to reach Vila Fresca de Azeitão. The adega is open on weekdays from 9 am to noon and 2 to 5 pm, with tours several times daily.

Places to Stay The adequate *Toca do Pai Lopes* (☎ 52 24 75) municipal camping ground is 1.5 km west of the town centre on Rua Praia da Saúde (near the shipyards). During the summer, there's a regular bus going to Figuerinha beach which passes close by both this camping ground and the one a couple of km further along the coast at Outão (☎ 383 18).

In Setúbal itself, the centro de juventude in Largo José Afonso has dorm beds for 1300$00 (although they're often booked out by youth groups).

There are several other reasonably priced options: the friendly *Residencial Todi* (☎ 205 92), at Avenida Luísa Todi 244, has tatty but clean doubles without/with bath from 2500$00/3500$00; a triple here is good value at 4000$00. Another attractive bargain is the central *Pensão Bom Regresso* (☎ 298 12) overlooking the pleasant Praça de Bocage. It offers doubles with bath from 3000$00. Similarly priced is the *Residencial O Cantinho* (☎ 52 38 99) at Beco do Carmo 1 (its restaurant is signposted but not the residencial).

Up several notches is the comfortable *Residencial Bocage* (☎ 215 98; fax 218 09), on the pedestrianised Rua São Cristovão at No 14, where doubles with breakfast are 5800$00. The smart, pretentious *Residencial Setúbalense* (☎ 52 57 90; fax 52 57 89), in another central pedestrianised lane at Rua Major Afonso Pala 17, offers air-con rooms with TV, international direct-dial phone and room service for 9000$00. A more attractive choice in this bracket is the four-star *Albergaria Solaris* (☎ 52 21 89; fax 52 20 70) on Praça Marquês de Pombal 12, where doubles with all the frills cost 10,000$00.

Most luxurious of all is the *Pousada de São Filipe* (☎ 52 38 44; fax 53 25 38), within the walls of the town's hilltop castle (some of the rooms are in the old dungeons). Doubles will set you back a tidy 28,000$00.

Places to Eat There are lots of cheap little eateries in the lanes just east of the regional turismo office: *Neca's Snack Bar* (☎ 377 13), at Rua Dr António Joaquim Granjo 10, is a welcoming little place which (despite its name) serves regular meals including bargain pratos do dia (eg, a dozen sardines) for 650$00 and special titbits such as a delicious queijo de ovelha (sheep's cheese). In the nearby Rua Arronches Junqueiro, locals cram into the *Snack-Bar A Telha Azul* (☎ 373 71) at lunch time for its cheap, filling meals.

A more mainstream restaurant in the pedestrian area is *O Escondidinho* (☎ 52 34 08; closed Sundays), at Rua José António Januario da Silva 4-6, which has several tables outside and meia doses (half-portions) from 850$00. For excellent seafood and fish dishes, head for the western end of Avenida Luísa Todi, where there's a string of seafood restaurants. *Casa do Chico* (☎ 395 02; closed Mondays) at No 490 is small and friendly and offers weekend specialities such as arroz de tamboril (monkfish with rice) and caldeirada à Setúbalense (Setúbal-style seafood stew).

Getting There & Away From Lisbon, train connections are complicated since you must first cross the Rio Tejo to Barreiro. Far easier are the buses that leave every hour from Praça de Espanha, or from Cacilhas (stand No 13), a quick ferry-hop from Lisbon's Cais de Alfândega terminal.

For buses from Setúbal to Sesimbra, go to the stop outside the office of Covas & Filhos bus company on Avenida Alexandre Herculano 5a (five minutes walk from the main bus station), where buses leave around nine times a day. This is also the place to get Solexpresso bus tickets to the Algarve, Elvas, Peniche and Portalegre.

Ferries to the Tróia Peninsula depart every 30 to 45 minutes daily. The fare is 120$00 per person (520$00 for a car).

Car-rental agencies include Avis (☎ 52 69 46) at Avenida Luísa Todi 96 and Alucar

(☎ 53 32 85; fax 52 54 05) at Avenida Combatentes da Grande Guerra 60.

Sesimbra
• *pop 7300* • *postcode 2970* • *area code* ☎ *01*

This former fishing village sheltering under the Serra da Arrábida, at the western edge of the Arrábida Natural Park, some 30 km west of Setúbal, has become a favourite seaside resort with lisboêtas (it's only about an hour and a half away from the city). At weekends and in high season, the traffic, jet skis and bar music hardly provide a tonic of tranquillity but if you like your beaches to buzz, this little resort may fit the bill.

Orientation & Information The bus station is on Avenida da Liberdade, five minutes walk up from the seafront. Turn right when you reach the bottom of the avenida, pass the small 17th-century Forte de Santiago (not open to the public) and you'll reach the turismo (☎ 223 57 43) at Largo da Marinho, just off the main Avenida dos Náfragos. It's open daily from 9 am to 8 pm in summer (from 10 am to 12.30 pm and 2 to 5.30 pm in winter) and can help with accommodation.

Things to See & Do Eating and drinking seem to be the main activities in Sesimbra, though **water sports** attract a few sober souls during the day: windsurfers and paddle boats can be rented along the beach in summer, and swimming is good on either side of the Forte do Santiago.

The unusually energetic can hike up to the ruined Moorish **castelo** (allow at least an hour), which was taken from the Moors by Dom Afonso Henriques in the 12th century, retaken by the Moors, and finally snatched back by the Christians under Dom Sancho I in the following century. Perched 200m above the town, it's a great spot for coastal panoramas.

To see the last vestiges of Sesimbra's traditional fishing lifestyle, head for the **Porto de Abrigo** a km or so west of the town centre, where fishermen auction off their catch in the late afternoon.

Places to Stay The nearest camping ground is at Forte de Cavalo (☎ 223 36 97), just a km west of town, but it's often packed out in summer. The next nearest options are the municipal site at Maçã (☎ 268 53 85), four km north (take any Lisbon or Setúbal bus) or the better equipped Valbom site (☎ 268 75 45) at Cotovia, only a km further north.

Although accommodation here is generally expensive, it's always worth enquiring at the turismo about private rooms (quartos), which are often available in summer for around 5500$00 a double. Some of the most obvious are the well-signposted rooms of *Senhora Garcia* (☎ 223 32 27) at Travessa Xavier da Silva 1; these are pricey at 7000$00 a double (with bath) but spacious and clean. Alternatively, try *Residencial Chic* (☎ 223 31 10) at No 6, opposite, where adequate doubles (without bath and with noisy night-time music from the downstairs café) are about 4000$00.

In the upper price bracket, there's the comfortable *Residencial Nautico* (☎ 223 32 33), a 10-minute walk uphill from the waterfront, at Bairro Infante Dom Henrique 3, which has doubles with breakfast for 9000$00. For 500$00 more you can be right by the sea at the weather-worn 1950s *Pensão Espadarte* (☎ 223 31 84; fax 223 32 94) at Avenida 25 de Abril 11, east of the Forte do Santiago. More attractive is the *Casa da Terrina* (☎ 268 02 64), a 19th-century converted farmhouse about three km from Sesimbra at Quintola de Santana (take the bus to Cabo Espichel). There are five doubles here for 10,000$00, and a swimming pool in the grounds.

Places to Eat You're spoilt for choice with fish restaurants, especially along Avenida 25 de Abril, east of the Forte do Santiago. Prices aren't cheap, though, and can often escalate alarmingly if you make anything other than a run-of-the-mill choice. Along the waterfront in the other direction, a pleasant option is *Restaurant Baia* (☎ 223 20 12) at No 45 next to the Hotel do Mar. For cheaper fare, head for the backstreets around the bus station.

Entertainment Among the many bars and cafés on the waterfront, *Sereia* (☎ 223 20 90), at Avenida dos Náufragos 20, attracts a lively crowd and is open until at least 2 am.

Getting There & Away Buses to Sesimbra depart from Lisbon's Praça de Espanha three to four times a day and about nine times a day from Setúbal and Cacilhas (bus stand No 11).

The Algarve

Loud, boisterous and full of foreigners, the Algarve is about as far from quintessential Portugal as you can get. It's been the country's major tourist resort area since the 1960s, when Faro's airport opened, leading to a flood of package tours from Britain and, increasingly, Germany and France. The big attraction? Almost year-round sun, great beaches and low prices.

Those are still the Algarve's big drawcards, though rampant development during the late 1970s between Lagos and Faro destroyed much of the coastline's picturesque qualities and polluted inland and offshore areas. In recent years tourism has gone increasingly up-market, with more environmentally conscious developers and a clutch of luxurious villa resorts complete with designer golf courses and marinas.

Not all of the Algarve's 270 km of coastline is a built-up disaster zone. West of Lagos are wild and almost deserted beaches. The coast east of Faro hosts many unspoilt towns and villages, and a string of sandy offshore islands making up the Parque Natural da Ria Formosa, which is favoured by wildlife and beach bums alike.

And for those who've filled up on seascapes and the packed resorts of Lagos and Albufeira, there are the forested slopes of the Serra de Monchique with its old spa village of Caldas de Monchique; the fortified village of Silves; and the market town of Loulé tucked away in the hills. Less accessible and wilder still are the Algarve's fringes – the west coast from Sagres to Odeceixe, and in the east the inland road wriggling north near the Rio Guadiana, which forms the border with Spain.

History

The Algarve's sunny disposition and long, warm coastline has attracted foreigners since the time of the Phoenicians, some 3000 years ago. The Phoenicians, who made their mark

HIGHLIGHTS

- the dramatic coastline at Sagres
- the offshore islands of the Parque Natural da Ria Formosa
- the unspoilt town of Tavira
- a jeep safari in Parque Natural de Sudoeste Alentejano e Costa Vicentina
- Silves, the former Moorish capital of the Algarve

by establishing trading posts along the coast, were followed by the Carthaginians, who founded several major entrepôts, including Portus Hannibalis (Portimão) in 550 BC.

But as in the rest of Portugal, the Romans were the most serious and influential early settlers. During their 400-year presence they introduced wheat, barley and grapes; built roads and luxurious palaces (check out the remains at Milreu, near Faro); and gave the Portuguese language its Latin foundations.

In the wake of the Romans came the Visigoths, and then in 711 the first wave of Moors from North Africa. The Algarve was to remain their stronghold for 500 years. Silves (called Xelb by the Moors) became their opulent capital, boasting 'attractive buildings and well-furnished bazaars', according to Idrisi, the 12th-century Arab chronicler.

The Algarve Moors were a mixed ethnic bunch: around Faro they were mostly Egyptians but elsewhere they included Syrians, Persians, and Berbers from Morocco. Among them were notable historians, philosophers, astronomers and poets, including two outstanding female poets, Xílbia and Mariam. By the mid-9th century the power-

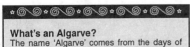

What's an Algarve?

The name 'Algarve' comes from the days of Moorish occupation. While most of the new arrivals to the area around Beja and Faro came from Egypt, the territory east of Faro to Seville (in present-day Spain) was settled largely by Syrians, who called it *al-Gharb al-Andalus* (western Andalusia). ■

ful, prosperous Algarve had become quite independent of the larger Muslim emirate to the east, around what is now Seville and Córdoba in Spain.

As the Christian Reconquista got underway in the early 12th century, the Algarve became the ultimate goal for a succession of crusaders and kings. Though Dom Sancho I captured Silves and territories to the west in 1189, the Moors staged a comeback in the Algarve and it wasn't until the first half of the 13th century that the Portuguese finally wrested this last part of the country back for keeps.

Two centuries later came the Algarve's age of importance when Prince Henry the Navigator chose windswept Sagres, the furthest south-west corner of Europe, as the base (or at any rate as a point of inspiration) for a pioneering effort to push the limits of cartography, navigation and ship design. He had his ships built, equipped and staffed in Lagos for the daring expeditions that soon followed to Africa and Asia, raising Portugal to the status of a major imperial power.

Nothing since then has put Portugal so firmly on the world map. Today the Algarve has a far more modest place on this map as a premier sun-and-surf destination and expatriate haven.

Geography

The Algarve divides neatly into five regions: the leeward coast or Barlavento, from Vila Real de Santo António to Faro; the central coast, from Faro to Portimão; the windward coast or Sotavento, from Lagos to Sagres; the

Costa Vicentina, facing west into the teeth of Atlantic gales; and the interior.

Much of the leeward coast is fronted by a chain of sandy or boggy offshore *ilhas*, most of them now part of the wildlife-rich Parque Natural da Ria Formosa. The beach, golf, disco and nightclub scene – and the heaviest resort development – are concentrated along the central coast. West of Lagos, the shore grows increasingly steep and rocky, culminating in the wind-scoured grandeur of the Cabo de São Vicente, Europe's southwestern corner.

The interior, along the border with the Alentejo, is surprisingly hilly and verdant, rising to two high-elevation clusters. Best known to visitors is the Serra de Monchique, north of Portimão, topping out at 902m-high Fóia. Less visited is the Serra do Caldeirão, running north from Faro into the Alentejo.

The Algarve's capital and largest town is Faro. Its easternmost town, Vila Real de Santo António, is a border crossing to Ayamonte in Spain, to which it is linked by car ferry and the nearby E1 motorway bridge across the Rio Guadiana.

Information

Tourist Offices Every town of any size has a *turismo* (tourist office) dispensing leaflets, maps and information. Faro has an extraordinarily helpful municipal turismo, which makes a worthwhile early stop even if you aren't interested in the town. Also notable in its own way is one of the country's rudest and least helpful turismos, at Lagos.

Among useful material from better turismos are town maps, guides to accommodation and camping sites, and a monthly *Events* pamphlet. Keep an eye open at the airport, and some turismos, for a useful free booklet called *Algarve Tips*, which has up-to-date emergency numbers and information on banks and ATMs, petrol stations, restaurants, nightlife, handicraft shops, and sports. *Discover* is a free what's-on bulletin for the windward coast, from Lagos to Sagres.

Consular Offices Among foreign consulates in the Algarve are Canadian, Dutch,

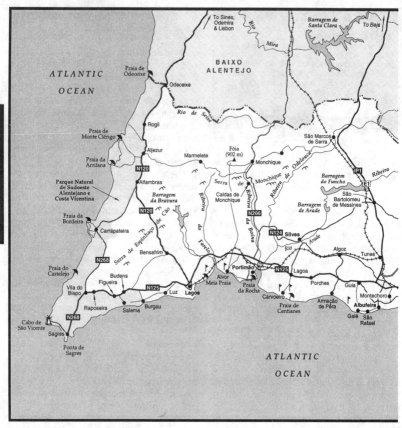

Danish, Belgian and German offices at Faro; British, Austrian and Swedish offices at Portimão; a French office at Quarteira; and a Spanish one at Vila Real de Santo António.

Newspapers & Magazines

A number of English-language newspapers, including *APN*, *The News* and *The Algarve Resident*, aimed primarily at the expatriate community, provide entertainment listings and information on regional attractions, markets, Gypsy fairs and coming events – not to mention long-term accommodation, cheap flights, language courses and even work.

Dangers & Annoyances

The Algarve has one of Portugal's higher levels of petty crime, mainly theft. Paranoia is unwarranted, but don't leave anything of value in your vehicle or unattended on the beach. Also annoying are the apartment-timeshare salespeople of Albufeira, Portimão and elsewhere.

Swimmers should beware of dangerous ocean currents, especially on the west coast. Beaches are marked by coloured flags: red means the beach is closed to bathing, yellow means swimming is prohibited but wading is fine, green means anything goes.

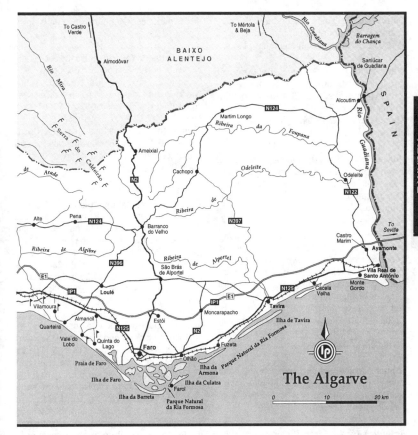

The Algarve

0   10   20 km

Activities

Walking Walkers can pick up the handy *Algarve: Guide to Walks* (250$00) from the Faro tourist office. The booklet details 20 rural walks from 0.7 to 12 km, of varying difficulty, and has information on trailhead access by bus, taxi or car.

Portimão-based Tempo Passa (☎ 082-41 71 10, evenings ☎ 082-47 12 41) offers a dozen different guided walks in the Algarve. Algarve Walkers (☎ 082-35 88 04) is an informal club that convenes every month or so for a trek around some interesting part of the region.

Cycling BTT Aventura (☎ 089-54 18 34, ☎ 58 89 79) in Albufeira runs guided day trips using its own mountain bikes, as well as longer trips in the Algarve and Alentejo.

Sailing & Deep-Sea Fishing Numerous outfits (including resort hotels) offer half-day or full-day sailing trips along the central coast, many of them starting from the big marina at Vilamoura. Other points of embarkation include Lagos, Alvor, Portimão and Armação de Pêra. Deep-sea fishing trips depart during the summer from Alvor, Portimão and Vilamoura.

Scuba Diving There are organised diving centres at Vilamoura, Albufeira, Armação de Pêra, Luz and Sagres, among other places.

Water-Skiing Jaunts are easily arranged through resorts around Vilamoura, Albufeira, Armação de Pêra and Portimão, or with outfits in Quarteira, Alvor, Luz and Sagres. There is an *escola de ski* at Meia Praia, east of Lagos.

Horse Riding The Algarve has more than a dozen *centros hípicos* (riding centres) and *centros de equitação* (equestrian centres), concentrated mainly between Faro and Albufeira.

Golf There are at least nine seaside courses between Faro and Albufeira, four in the Portimão area and others scattered elsewhere along the central coast. Top of the line are probably Quinta do Alto (Alvor), Vilamoura I, II and II (Vilamoura), Vila Sol (Vilamoura) and the deluxe Quinta do Lago (Almancil). At the Faro turismo you might be able to bag a copy of the ICEP's glossy booklet on Portugal's golf courses.

Tennis Most upper-end resort hotels here have tennis courts, and there are clubs, with professional instructors, at Vilamoura, Vale do Lobo and Carvoeiro.

Activities for Children Programmes at the Zoomarine aquatic park (☎ 089-56 11 04) at Guia include a good half-hour dolphin show three times a day, plus less captivating seal and parrot 'performances'; there are also two public swimming pools. The park is open daily from 10 am to 8 pm from May through mid-October (to 6 pm the rest of the year). Admission is 1950$00 for adults and 1200$00 for children aged three to 10.

The Algarve has at least three huge waterslide parks along the N125 road – Slide & Splash west of Lagoa, The Big One near Guia, and Atlântico Parque between Almancil and Faro. Parcolândia or Planeta Aventura (☎ 089-39 58 03) is a night-time

theme park near Quarteira, open daily from 7 pm to 2 am.

River Cruises You can cruise the Rio Arade between Portimão and Silves, or the Rio Guadiana between Vila Real de Santo António and Odeleite. For Rio Arade trips, contact Tempo Passa (☎ 082-41 71 10, evenings 082-47 12 41) in Portimão. A reliable agency for Rio Guadiana trips is Riosul (☎ 089-80 72 59) in Faro, which also does a combined jeep safari and river cruise day trip for 8600$00.

Special Events

The Algarve's most important religious festival is at Loulé: the Romaria da Nossa Senhora da Piedade, held on the second Sunday after Easter, when the image of Our Lady of Pity (or Piety) is returned to its shrine atop the Monte da Piedade on a massive float carried up the mountain at a trot by devotees. One of Portugal's biggest carnival celebrations is also held at Loulé in late February/early March, with parades, mask competitions and dancing.

On the first or second weekend in September, the Algarve Folk Music & Dance Festival takes place in over a dozen towns in the region, culminating on Sunday evening with a big show at Praia da Rocha (Portimão).

Rather tourist-oriented bullfights are staged at Lagos, Albufeira and Vila Real de Santo António during the summer, though the real ones are all up north, especially in the Ribatejo (see Spectator Sports in the Facts for the Visitor chapter for more on bullfighting).

Things to Buy

Although Algarve factories turn out fine azulejos, and the leatherworkers of Loulé consider themselves among the country's best, the Algarve is chiefly a booming outlet for souvenirs produced elsewhere. Moorish-influenced ceramics and local woollens (cardigans and fishing pullovers) are good value.

The region's main handicrafts centre is around Loulé. For more on the crafts of the

Wines of the Algarve

The Algarve has long been an important wine-making area: the Mediterranean climate, rich soil and high-quality vines produce full-bodied wines with low acidity and a high alcohol content. The whites are traditionally very dry, the reds light and young. Although 20th-century development has erased many vineyards, there are still about 40,000 acres of them in the Lagoa area, producing the Algarve's best known wines. Other major wine-producing areas are Lagos, Tavira, and Portimão. ■

Algarve, see the excellent guide by John & Madge Measures, *Southern Portugal: Its People, Traditions & Wildlife*, available in bookshops in Faro and elsewhere.

Lagoa is the centre of the Algarve's modest wine-growing region (see the boxed aside). You may also want to try Algarviana, a local bitter almond liqueur, or the salubrious bottled waters of Monchique, which are on sale everywhere.

Markets Though municipal markets are open more or less daily, most sizeable towns also have regular weekly farmers' markets, and many have big, usually monthly, Gypsy markets featuring itinerant hawkers of everything from souvenirs to cheap clothes to kitchenware. The Algarve's Gypsy markets tend to be fairly touristy.

Among good weekly markets are those at Tavira, Olhão and Loulé (Saturdays), and Quarteira (Wednesdays). Popular Gypsy markets include those at Lagos (first Saturday of the month), Alvor (every other Tuesday) and Portimão (first Monday of the month). Check out the what's-on pages of the English-language papers, or the turismo's monthly *Events* pamphlet, for complete listings.

Getting There & Away

Air Faro is one of Portugal's three international airports, and the only place in the Algarve that has scheduled flights, including daily direct ones from Lisbon and from London. Scheduled international carriers serving Faro are TAP, Lufthansa, British Airways and Portugália. For more information see the Faro section, the Getting There & Away chapter (for international connections), or the Getting Around chapter (for domestic connections).

Bus Several companies, including Renex and EVA, operate regular and express services to the Algarve's major towns from elsewhere in Portugal. By express coach, Faro is about five hours from Lisbon; the fare is 2000$00.

EVA runs coaches twice a day, year-round, between Faro and Huelva (in Spain), with immediate connections to/from Seville; the journey from Faro to Seville (five hours) costs 1990$00. In summer, Intersul runs direct express coaches between Lagos and Seville, departing four times a week in April and May and six times a week from June through October; the six-hour trip, via Portimão, Albufeira, Faro, Tavira and Vila Real de Santo António, costs about 3000$00.

Train From Lisbon (via Barreiro) there are at least five fast trains a day to Lagos and Faro; *interregional* services take five to 5½ hours, *intercidade* services four to 4½ hours. A once-a-week fast service links Porto directly to Lagos via Coimbra and Santarém.

From Spain, four trains a day go west as far as Huelva, where you must change for Ayamonte and then bus across the Rio Guadiana (or walk a km or so to the river and ferry across) to pick up a Portuguese train at Vila Real de Santo António.

Car The most direct route from Lisbon to Faro takes about five hours. For motorists arriving via Ayamonte in Spain, the E1 motorway bridge, four km north of Vila Real de Santo António, now bypasses the old ferry crossing of the Rio Guadiana.

ALGARVE

Getting Around
Bus The Algarve's two main coach lines are EVA and Froto Azul. Between them they cover most useful destinations, fairly frequently, all year round. EVA's Linha Litoral (Coastal Line) links Lagos, Portimão and Albufeira eight times a day; it goes as far east as Faro twice a day, and to Vila Real de Santo António and Ayamonte (Spain) once a day.

If you plan to bus around the Algarve a lot, consider the Passe Turístico, good for either 3 or 7 days of unlimited travel on most main routes (but not everywhere) on both lines, and available from most ticket offices.

Car By car you can blast your way west from Vila Real de Santo António as far as Albufeira on the Via Infante, the high-speed E1/IP1 motorway which will eventually run the length of the south coast – or you can poke along through every coastal town on the two-lane N125. Several roads wiggle slowly and scenically through the interior, in particular the N266 through the Serra de Monchique, the N124 across the Serra do Caldeirão and the N122 along the Spanish border.

Heavy competition has pushed average car-rental rates in the Algarve below those elsewhere in Portugal. The cheapest deal in summer is 8500$00 for three days, from Florentina in Lagos; more typical rates are about 12,000$00/24,000$00 for 3/7 days.

Motorcycle & Bicycle Mountain bikes, scooters and motorcycles can be rented all over, especially on the central coast; see individual town listings. Typical 3/7-day charges start at about 3500$00/7000$00 for a mountain bike, 5000$00/10,000$00 for a motor scooter, or 13,000$00/28,000$00 for a motorcycle.

Organised Tours The Algarve's veteran coach-tour agency is Miltours (☎ 089-890 46 00) in Faro. Others include MB Tours (☎ 082-260 45, toll-free ☎ 0500-2369) and Pandatours (☎ 082-41 55 41) in Portimão, and Mega Tur (☎ 089-80 76 48; fax 089-80 74 89) in Faro. Regional trips include the leeward coast as far as Ayamonte in Spain; Silves and the Serra de Monchique; Lagos and Sagres; the Saturday market at Loulé and the Wednesday market at Quarteira. Typical prices are 3000$00 to 4000$00 for a half-day tour or 5000$00 to 7000$00 for a full-day tour, depending on pick-up point. The turismos at Faro and elsewhere have brochures with details.

Several outfits run all-day jeep trips into the hills or along the west coast. The best of them take time to show you what is a fast-disappearing rural way of life, along with surprisingly wild scenery. Most environmentally conscientious of the lot is probably Horizonte (☎ 082-658 55; fax 022-659 20) in Salema, specialising in the Parque Natural Sudoeste Alentejano e Costa Vicentina. Other reliable ones are Naturinfo (☎ 082-645 20, ☎ 645 51; fax 082-645 39) in Sagres, and Riosul (☎ 089-80 72 59; fax 089-80 72 58) and Mega Tur (☎ 089-80 76 48; fax 089-80 74 89) in Faro. A full-day safari with Riosul is about 7200$00 per person.

Faro & the Leeward Coast

FARO
• pop 51,540 • postcode 8000 • area code ☎ 089
Faro is the Algarve's capital and main transport hub, and a thriving commercial centre – but surprisingly pleasant for all that. With the region's best turismo, it's also a useful place to get your bearings. The main sights of historical interest are within its compact old town centre.

History
The Phoenicians and Carthaginians maintained a trading post here on the site of an older fishing village. The Romans in turn built this into a major port and administrative centre, which they called Ossonoba. When the Christian Visigoths built a cathedral dedicated to St Mary the town became known as Santa Maria or Santa Maria de Ossónoba.

But the town's maturation came under the Moors. Santa Maria became the cultured capital of a short-lived 11th-century principality founded by a prince, Mohammed ben Said ben Hárun, from whose name 'Faro' is said to have evolved. Afonso III took the town in 1249 (it was the last major Portuguese town to be recaptured from the Moors), walled it and gave it a charter a few years later.

The first works produced on a printing press in Portugal came from Faro in 1487 – books in Hebrew made by a Jewish printer named Samuel Gacon.

A brief golden age – heralded by a city charter in 1544 and an episcopal seat transplanted from Silves in 1577 – was brought to an abrupt end in 1596 during Spanish rule when troops under the Earl of Essex, en route back to England from Cadiz in Spain, plundered the city, burned most of it to the ground, and carried off hundreds of volumes of priceless theological works from the bishop's palace.

A rebuilt Faro was shattered by an earthquake in 1722 and, aside from its sturdy old centre, flattened by the big one in 1755. Its present form dates largely from post-quake rebuilding.

Orientation

The town's hub is Praça de Dom Francisco Gomes, with a traffic roundabout, a tidy marina and a vest-pocket park called Jardim Manuel Bívar, or just 'Jardim'. From here the town's main shopping and restaurant zone extends eastward, centred on pedestrianised Rua Dom Francisco Gomes and Rua de Santo António; what remains of the old town is just to the south.

The bus and train stations are an easy walk from Praça de Dom Francisco Gomes, about 250m and 500m north-west on Avenida da República respectively. The airport is about six km west of the centre, off the N125 highway.

Offshore is the widest stretch of the Parque Natural da Ria Formosa. While many of the near-shore sandbars along here simply disappear at high tide, two of the bigger

sea-facing islands – Ilha de Faro to the south-west and Ilha da Culatra to the south-east – have lighthouses, small summer settlements and good beaches. In between them, on Ilha da Barreta, is wind-blasted Cabo de Santa Maria, Portugal's southernmost point.

Information

Tourist Offices The very good municipal turismo (☎ 80 36 04) is beside the Arco da Vila gate to the old town, at the southern end of the Jardim Manuel Bívar. It's open every day from 9.30 am to at least 7 pm. There is also a turismo, usually open from 8 am to midnight, at the airport.

A separate, regional turismo administrative office (Região de Turismo do Algarve; ☎ 80 04 00) is in a flashy new building at Avenida 5 de Outubro 18. There is also an information desk here, dispensing advice and regional brochures from 9 am to 6 pm on weekdays only, but it's of minimal use.

Foreign Consulates Canada and the Netherlands have consulates in adjacent high-rise blocks on Rua Frei Lourenço de Santa Maria, behind the Igreja de Nossa Senhora do Carmo. Canada's (☎ 80 37 57) is at No 1 and is open weekdays from 9 am to 12.30 pm and 2 to 5 pm; the Dutch one (☎ 209 03) at No 2 showed no signs of life when we were there. There is a Danish consulate at Rua Conselheiro de Bívar 10. The Belgian consular office (☎ 82 30 99) is at Rua de Santo António 68 and Germany's (☎ 80 31 48) is at Avenida da República 166.

Money Faro has around 20 Multibanco ATMs, the most central of which are in the Banco Nacional Ultramarino on Rua de Santo António, and the nearby Banco Espírito Santo and Banco Português do Atlântico.

Post & Communications The main post office, including an office for calls, faxes and telegrams, is on Largo do Carmo, nearly half a km from the centre. It's open weekdays from 8.30 am to 6.30 pm and Saturdays from

ALGARVE

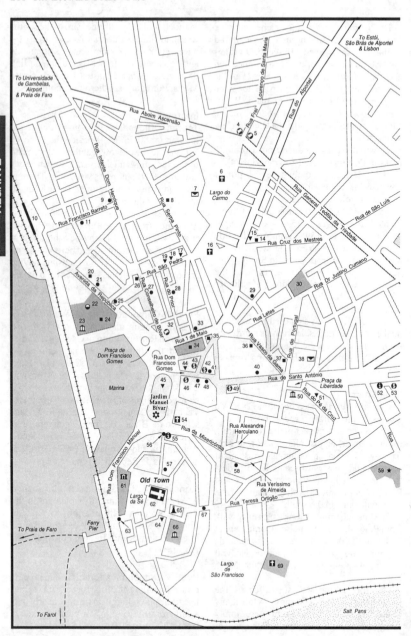

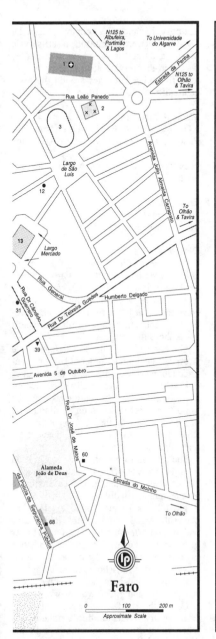

ALGARVE

PLACES TO STAY
8	Apartmentos Vitória
14	Casa de Hóspedes Adelaide
20	Residencial Avenida
24	Hotel Eva
26	Residencial Madalena
34	Hotel Faro
35	Residencial Oceano
36	Vasco da Gama
37	Hotel Santa Maria
60	Residencial Alameda
68	Centro de Juventude

PLACES TO EAT
13	Mercado Municipal
15	Restaurante A Taska
17	Casa de Pasto
18	A Garrafeira do Vilaça
19	Restaurante Queda d'Água
39	Supermarket
44	Café Aliança
45	Cafés
51	Restaurante Green
64	Taverna da Sé

OTHER
1	Faro District Hospital
2	Old Jewish Cemetery
3	Stadium
4	Canadian Consulate
5	Dutch Consulate
6	Igreja de Nossa Senhora do Carmo & Capela dos Ossos
7	Main Post Office
9	Riosul
10	Train Station
11	Automóvel Club de Portugal (ACP)
12	Laundry
16	Igreja de São Pedro
21	Abreu Tours
22	EVA Bus Station
23	Museu Marítimo
25	Frota Azul, Caima & Renex Bus Ticket Office
27	Mega Tur
28	Kream
29	Laundry
30	Teatro Lethes
31	Lavandaria Modelo
32	Danish Consulate
33	Alliance Française
38	Post Office
40	Arty's
41	Livraria Bertrand
42	Multibanco ATM & Bank
43	Multibanco ATM & Bank
46	Bank
47	TAP
48	Livraria Rés do Chão
49	Multibanco ATM & Bank
50	Museu Etnográfico
52	Regional Turismo
53	Bank

Continued on next page

54	Misericórdia de Faro
55	Municipal Turismo
56	Arco da Vila
57	Town Hall
58	Miltours
59	Police
61	Bishop's Palace
62	Sé (Cathedral)
63	Arco da Porta Nova
65	Statue of Dom Afonso III
66	Museu Arqueologica
67	Arco de Repouso & Old Town Walls
69	Igreja de São Francisco

9 am to 12.30 pm. Closer to the centre is a smaller post office on Rua Dr João Lúcio.

Travel Agencies The venerable Algarve travel agency Miltours (☎ 890 46 00) is at Rua Veríssimo de Almeida 20. Another reliable tour agency is Mega Tur (☎ 80 76 48; fax 80 74 89) at Rua Conselheiro de Bívar 80, though it generally takes bookings through other agencies and hotels. Riosul (☎ 80 72 59; fax 80 72 58), at Rua Infante Dom Henrique 63, does jeep safaris and Rio Guadiana boat trips. Abreu Tours (☎ 80 53 35; fax 80 54 70) is at Avenida de República 124.

Bookshops Two big shops with a few English-language books on the Algarve are Arty's on Rua de Santo António and Livraria Bertrand on Rua Dom Francisco Gomes. Opposite the latter is the small Livraria Rés do Chão.

Campuses Faro has two universities: the Universidade do Algarve (Penha campus), beyond the hospital on Estrada da Penha, and the Universidade de Gambelas, out on the road to the airport. An unnumbered municipal bus route serves both, departing from Jardim Manuel Bívar every half-hour on weekdays from October through June. In addition, bus No 15 goes to Gambelas from Jardim every hour or two.

Cultural Centres The closest thing to a French cultural centre is Alliance Française (☎ 288 81), on Rua 1 de Maio.

Laundry Lavandaria Modelo, at Rua Dr Cândido Guerrero 23, calls itself self-service but isn't, though it does have a same-day wash-and-dry service at normal prices. At least five other laundries around the town centre offer next-day service.

Medical Services The Faro District Hospital (☎ 80 34 11, ☎ 80 34 20) is on Rua Leão Penedo, over two km north-east of the centre, beside the N125 highway. Bus No 15 goes there every hour or two from Jardim, taking 15 to 20 minutes.

Emergency The main police station (☎ 82 20 22) is east of the centre at Rua da Polícia de Segurança Pública 32.

Old Town

Within the medieval walls of the small *cidade velha* is what little of Faro survived the Earl of Essex and two big earthquakes, most of it renovated in a jumble of styles. Nevertheless it has a pleasantly dog-eared, lived-in feel, and plenty of gift and handicrafts shops to browse in.

You enter through the Renaissance-style **Arco da Vila**, built by order of Bishop Francisco Gomes, Faro's answer to the Marquês de Pombal, who saw to the city's brisk reconstruction after the 1755 earthquake. At the top of the street is Largo da Sé, lined with orange trees, with the *câmara municipal* (town hall) on the left and the ancient **Sé** (cathedral) in front of you.

The cathedral was completed in 1251, on the probable site of a Moorish mosque, an earlier Visigoth cathedral and, before that, a Roman temple. Badly damaged in 1755, its original Romanesque-Gothic exterior has been submerged in subsequent Gothic renovations and extensions, except for its tower gate and two chapels. The stubby sandstone tower was probably taller before the earthquake. The interior, a hotch-potch of Gothic, Renaissance and baroque styles, has some fine azulejos and gilded woodwork.

Off to the right of the cathedral is the 18th-century former **bishop's palace**, finished in multicoloured azulejos. At the southern end of the largo is a little 15th-century town gate, the **Arco da Porta Nova**, facing the sea. Around to the left of the cathedral is a bronze **statue** of Dom Afonso III, the king who recaptured the Algarve from the Moors, in a small square of the same name. Facing the square is the 16th-century **Convento de Nossa Senhora da Assunção**. Its cloisters now house the town's archaeological museum (see Museums).

From here you can leave the old town through the medieval **Arco de Repouso** or Gate of Rest, named in reference to the story that Afonso III, after taking Faro from the Moors, rested and heard Mass in a nearby chapel. Here are some of the oldest sections of the town walls, Afonso III's improvements on Moorish defenses.

Misericórdia de Faro
The main attraction of the 16th-century Misericórdia church is its striking Manueline portico, the only part of an earlier chapel that withstood the 1755 earthquake. When we were there a family of storks had set up house atop the façade.

Igreja de Nossa Senhora do Carmo
The twin-towered, vanilla and butterscotch Church of Our Lady of Carmel was completed in 1719 under João V and paid for with (and spectacularly gilded inside with) Brazilian gold. Many visitors overlook this in favour of a more ghoulish attraction in the cemetery behind the church – the **Capela dos Ossos**, a 19th-century ossuary-chapel built from the bones and skulls of over a thousand monks as a pointed reminder of earthly impermanence (Évora's Igreja de São Francisco has a similar chapel).

Other Churches
If you haven't seen enough gilded woodwork yet, have a look at the dazzling 18th-century baroque interior of the Igreja de São Francisco, which also includes azulejo panels depicting the life of St Francis. Its old cloisters now serve as barracks for the Faro Infantry.

At the bottom of Largo do Carmo is the 16th-century Igreja de São Pedro. Its interior is filled with 18th-century azulejos and carved woodwork.

Museums
The municipal **Museu Arqueológica** (Archaeological Museum), in the Convento de Nossa Senhora da Assunção in the old town, features Phoenician and Carthaginian relics, Roman mosaics (including a huge panel found in 1968 on a Faro building site) and, upstairs, a splendid collection of azulejos from every period since the 15th century. The museum is open, on weekdays only, from 9.30 am to noon and 2 to 5 pm; entry is 110$00.

In the left entrance of the district assembly building at Praça da Liberdade is the **Museu Etnográfico** (Ethnographic Museum). It houses ceramics, fabrics, lots of baskets and straw mats, photos and little dioramas of 20th-century home life – with not a word anywhere, in Portuguese or any other language, about what, when or who. With a 300$00 entry fee it's a poor bargain. The museum is open on weekdays from 10 am to 6 pm.

In the harbourmaster's building at the northern end of the marina is the modest **Museu Marítimo** (Maritime Museum) full of maps, model ships, fish and nautical gear. It's open weekdays from 9 am to 12.30 pm and 2 to 5.30 pm; entry is 100$00.

Teatro Lethes
This little Italianate theatre is Faro's most charming cultural venue; it hosts drama, music and dance programmes. Built in 1874, it was once the Jesuit Colégio de Santiago Maior and is now the property of the Portuguese Cruz Vermelha (Red Cross).

Old Jewish Cemetery
What remains of Faro's old Jewish cemetery is opposite the hospital on Rua Leão Penedo.

Beaches
The town's beach, Praia de Faro, with miles

of sand, windsurfing and half a dozen cafés, is out on the Ilha de Faro. Take bus No 14 or 16 from Jardim (25 minutes; buses depart about every quarter-hour in summer; 150$00) or, between June and September, a ferry from near the Arco da Porta Nova. There are also ferries out to the settlement of Farol and several long beaches on the Ilha da Culatra. See Getting Around for ferry information.

Horse Riding

Among horse-riding centres in the region are Centro Hípico Quinta do Lago (☎ 089-39 43 69) and Paraíso dos Cavalos (☎ 089-39 68 64), both in Quinta do Lago, and Quinta dos Amigos (☎ 089-39 52 69) in Escanxinas, outside Almancil.

Special Events

Faro's two big fairs are the Festa e Feira da Senhora do Carmo (Our Lady of Carmel) in mid-July, with a religious procession on the first day, and the Feira de Santa Iria in mid-October. Neither is particularly true to its roots: the former has evolved into a big agricultural fair, the latter into a modest craft fair. Faro's main fairground is the big Largo de São Francisco on the eastern side of the old town.

Faro also hosts an international summer music festival, O Verão Músical do Algarve (Algarve Musical Summer), in July and August.

Places to Stay

Camping, pensão and hotel rates are very seasonal; we give midsummer rates here.

Camping There is a big, cheap municipal camping ground (☎ 81 78 76) at Praia de Faro. It is open year-round, and sample summer fees are 75$00 per person, 25$00 for a shower, 75$00 to 120$00 for a tent and 50$00 per car. There's a restaurant on the site. Take bus No 14 or 16 from Jardim.

Hostels The centro de juventude (☎ 200 71), at Rua da Polícia de Segurança Pública 1, is a state-funded youth resource centre with four or five dozen beds, available to all (HI/IYHA membership not required). Dorm beds are 1500$00 and cannot be booked. There are also a few basic double rooms for 3200$00 with shared shower and toilet, or 4000$00 with their own, which can be booked. The staff prefer that you check in after 6 pm.

Private Rooms & Boarding Houses Faro has two universities (see Information), but most students stay in private rooms. So, in summer (when they go home) there's little in the way of empty dormitory beds, but private rooms are fairly plentiful. Watch for 'quartos' signs. The municipal turismo can also help.

Upstairs at Rua Vasco da Gama 37, right in the town centre, is a spartan old rooming house called *Vasco da Gama* (☎ 82 38 41), with doubles with shared shower and toilet for just 2500$00. Singles/doubles at the cheerful *Casa de Hóspedes Adelaide* (☎ 80 23 83), Rua Cruz dos Mestres 7, are 2000$00/3000$00 with shared shower and loo, or 2500$00/4000$00 with their own. There are also four-bed rooms for 4000$00.

Residencials Faro has about 15 residencials, and the municipal turismo can call them and make recommendations. Among better value ones, all with singles for about 5000$00, doubles at 6000$00 to 7000$00, and attached shower or bath, are the following. Close to the centre is the friendly *Residencial Oceano* (☎ 82 33 49), upstairs at Travessa Ivens 21 on the corner of Rua 1 de Maio. *Residencial Madalena* (☎ 80 58 06), at Rua Conselheiro de Bívar 109, also has a few cheaper rooms without bath, and a TV room and bar. Away from the centre but recommended is the small *Residencial Alameda* (☎ 80 19 62) at Rua Dr José de Matos 31.

Up a notch is *Residencial Avenida* (☎ 82 33 47), opposite the bus station at Avenida da República 150, where doubles are 5000$00 without attached bath and toilet, or 7000$00 with.

Hotels As central as you can get is the boxy *Hotel Faro* (☎ 80 32 76; fax 80 35 46) at Praça de Dom Francisco Gomes 2, overlooking the marina; singles/doubles with bath, satellite TV and air-con are 7500$00/ 10,500$00, with breakfast. The ageing *Hotel Santa Maria* (☎ 82 40 64; fax 82 40 65) at Rua de Portugal 17 has earnest service and comfortable rooms for 7500$00/ 9000$00 with toilet and shower or 9600$00/ 10,800$00 with bath (less outside peak season), though rooms facing the street are noisy. Under reconstruction when we were there was the *Hotel Eva*, adjacent to the bus station.

Apartments If you want to hunker down in a flat for a week, try *Apartamentos Vitória* (☎ 80 65 83; fax 80 58 83) at Rua Serpa Pinto 60, where a furnished studio/apartment for two, with kitchenette, linen and cleaning service, is 33,000$00/44,000$00 a week.

Places to Eat

Restaurants Our favourite eatery in town is the popular self-service *Restaurante Queda d'Água* (☎ 82 45 24) at Rua de São Pedro 31. It's open for lunch from noon to 2 or 3 pm on weekdays, and for dinner from 7 to about 11 pm daily, with good fish, seafood and other specials at mid-range prices (1000$00 to 2000$00 per course).

Those on a tight budget can check out *A Garrafeira do Vilaça* (☎ 80 21 50) next door at No 33, or the cheap casa de pasto a few doors away. Also recommended is the modest *Restaurante A Taska* at Rua do Alportel 38. The atmosphere and simple food are very popular with local people, so go early or late.

At the upper end, *Restaurante Green* (☎ 213 03), Rua do Pé da Cruz 9, offers various good seafood specialities at 1200$00 to 3600$00 per course, and arroz de marisco for two for 3450$00; reservations are essential. It's closed on Sundays.

Cafés A fine place to linger over coffee and pastries or breakfast is the wood-panelled, turn-of-the-century *Café Aliança* on Rua

Dom Francisco Gomes. Service is snappy, and it also has sandwiches, salads, crêpes, juices and shakes. Slightly down-market, but also good for people-watching, are the plain cafés in the Jardim Manuel Bívar.

Self-Catering Check out Faro's big mercado municipal (town market) in Largo Mercado; it's especially lively in the early morning. There's also a decent little supermarket a couple of blocks down Rua Dr Cândido Guerrero.

Entertainment

Kream (☎ 204 59) is a disco at Rua do Prior 38, a block or so from the Hotel Faro, open Wednesday through Saturday from 8 pm to 3 am. In the old town, nose in for a beer or a bica at the little *Taverna da Sé*, just west off Praça Afonso III.

Getting There & Away

Air Both Portugália and TAP have daily flights to/from Lisbon, year-round. TAP's daily 9.35 pm Lisbon-Faro flight and 7 am Faro-Lisbon one connect with all its international arrivals and departures at Lisbon. Portugália has just one direct Porto-Faro flight each week, in summer only.

In summer there are flights daily from London with TAP and British Airways; three times a week from Frankfurt and weekly from Düsseldorf with Lufthansa; and twice a week from Paris, Zürich and Geneva with TAP. Most charter flights into Portugal come to Faro.

For flight enquiries, call the airport on ☎ 81 89 82. TAP also has a booking office in the town centre, on Rua Dom Francisco Gomes.

Among useful airline booking numbers in Faro are the following:

British Airways	☎ 81 84 76
	or toll-free ☎ 0500-1251
KLM	☎ 81 89 10 (but no flights to Faro)
Lufthansa	☎ 80 07 50
Portugália	☎ 80 08 52
TAP	☎ 81 83 59
	or toll-free ☎ 0808-21 31 41

Bus At Avenida da República 106, across the street from the big EVA bus station (☎ 80 37 92), is a small ticket office (☎ 81 29 80) for the Frota Azul, Caima and Renex lines.

From Lisbon to Faro, EVA has at least six express coaches (2000$00) daily, including a night run, plus four quicker *alta qualidade* services (2400$00). Renex also runs three coaches a day from Lisbon. EVA coaches for Huelva (1900$00), with connections for Seville in Spain, depart at 9 am and 5 pm daily.

Eastward, there are at least seven coaches a day to Tavira (400$00) and Vila Real de Santo António (590$00); and westward, there are three to Portimão (710$00) and one to Lagos (950$00), with more on weekdays. For Sagres, change at Lagos.

Train There are at least five fast trains a day to Faro from Lisbon; interregional (IR) services take five hours, intercidade (IC) four hours. The 2nd-class IR/IC fare is 1650$00/ 1850$00. A once-a-week fast service links Faro directly to Porto (9½ hours) departing Faro on Friday afternoons and Porto on Sunday evenings.

From Faro there are five fast trains a day to Vila Real de Santo António, seven to Albufeira and two to Lagos. Additional fast services to Lagos involve a change at Tunes junction.

For timetable information, call the train station on ☎ 80 17 26. The information kiosk at the station is open daily from 9 am to 1 pm and 2 to 7 pm.

Getting Around

The Airport Buses No 14 and 16 make the 18-minute trip between the airport (150$00) and Jardim every quarter-hour until about 9 pm in summer. A taxi will cost about 1100$00 during the day.

Car & Motorcycle Portugal's national auto club, Automóvel Club de Portugal or ACP, has a branch office (☎ 80 57 53) at Rua Francisco Barreto 26-A; it's open weekdays from 9 am to 12.45 pm and 2 to 4.30 pm.

Taxi Taxi fares jump up 20% from 10 pm to 6 am and on weekends and holidays, though fares vary according to the current price of petrol. To call a taxi, dial ☎ 80 16 89 or ☎ 80 17 47.

Ferry From June through September, ferries depart from the pier next to Arco da Porta Nova and head for Praia de Faro on the Ilha de Faro. The trip takes 20 minutes, and ferries depart at 9 and 11.30 am, and 3.30 and 6 pm (the last boat back is at 7 pm).

There are also ferries to Farol on Ilha da Culatra. It's a 45-minute trip, with ferries departing Faro in July and August at 8.15 and 10.15 am, and 2.30, 5 and 7.15 pm, with fewer departures in June and September. In winter they depart Faro only at 6 pm on Fridays and holidays, and at 9 am and 4 pm on weekends. Other ferries depart from Olhão (see Olhão).

Ferry timetables are fickle; for current information call the owner, Senhor Roque, on ☎ 81 71 84.

AROUND FARO
São Brás de Alportel
• postcode 8150 • area code ☎ 089

Few visitors think of staying overnight in this friendly little town 17 km north of Faro but, if you've got the time, it makes a pleasantly untouristed base for visiting Estói seven km to the south. You can also explore the surrounding countryside, part of the so-called Barrocal region, a fertile limestone belt between the mountains and the sea, which stretches all the way from Cabo de São Vicente and is characterised by an abundance of olive, carob, fig and almond trees.

Orientation & Information The ugly new town area is centred on Largo de São Sebastião, where buses stop and where you'll find the helpful turismo (☎ 84 22 11) in a kiosk at the corner of Rua Luís Bívar, the road to Loulé. The turismo is open weekdays from 9.30 am to 12.30 pm and 2 to 5.30 pm, and Saturdays from 9.30 am to noon.

Museu Etnográfico do Trajo Algarvio This
unexpectedly delightful museum (☎ 84 34
44) is 10 minutes walk east of the turismo, at
Rua Dr José Dias Sancho 61. A rambling
collection of local costumes, handicrafts,
agricultural implements and household
goods (with occasional special exhibitions)
is displayed in an old mansion with lots of
dark and musty corners. It's open Tuesday to
Friday from 10 am to 1 pm and 2 to 5 pm,
and weekends from 2 to 5 pm; entry is
100$00. Check out the miniature handmade
Algarvian figures for sale at the entrance.

Old Town Another surprise is the peaceful
old town area south of the turismo. Follow
Rua Gago Coutinho from Largo de São
Sebastião to the 16th-century Igreja Matriz,
which has breezy views of orange groves
from its doorstep. Nearby, below what used
to be a bishop's palace (now a nursery
school), is a pleasantly landscaped municipal swimming pool (open in summer daily
from 10 am to 7 pm; entry is 100$00) and
children's play area.

Special Events The town's biggest religious festival is Easter Sunday, when a
procession of torch-bearing townsfolk run
through the streets shouting 'Hallelujah!'.

Places to Stay Residencial São Brás (☎ &
fax 84 22 13), at Rua Luís Bívar 27, is the
cheapest option, with doubles from 5000$00
(including breakfast). The modern Estalagem Sequeira (☎ 84 34 44; fax 84 37 92)
next to the turismo at Rua Dr Evaristo Gago
9, has similar doubles for 6000$00. The
Pousada de São Brás is currently being renovated.

Places to Eat There are several restaurants
along the Estrada de Tavira, notably Luís dos
Frangos (☎ 84 26 35), also called Rei da
Brasa, at No 134. It's an unpretentious
churrasqueira with great grilled chicken and
turkey (bife de peru) from 600$00. It's
closed on Mondays.

For something more special, head 1.5 km
in the opposite direction, along the Loulé

road, for the Restaurante Lena (☎ 84 24 94).
This small casa tipica, decorated in traditional rustic style, is packed out at lunch
time; try the excellent cabrito a casa (roast
kid). It's closed on Sundays.

In Mesquita Baixa, just off the Tavira road
2.5 km east of São Brás de Alportel, is the
unusual Lagar de Mesquita (☎ 84 18 88).
Run by an Estonian woman with support
from LEADER (an organisation promoting
rural tourism), it offers a weekend-only
buffet of Portuguese dishes with live music
(everything from big bands to classical
piano, and flamenco to Afro-Brazilian). The
concert tickets cost 2500$00, and the buffet
2000$00.

Getting There & Away During the week
there are nine buses a day to São Brás de
Alportel from Faro (via Estói) and three a
day from Loulé. Services are reduced on
weekends and holidays.

Estói

A most rewarding day trip from Faro is to the
enchantingly derelict palace at Estói, 11 km
north of Faro, and on to the nearby Roman
ruins at Milreu.

Palácio do Visconde de Estói This 18th-
century palace (now owned by the Faro
municipal council) is a short walk from
Estói's village square, where buses from
Faro stop. Down a palm-shaded avenue, past
abandoned stables and outhouses, are the
overgrown gardens fronting the palace. The
pink rococo palace, a smaller version of
Queluz palace, is under restoration (as it has
been for years) and closed to the public. But
the intimate gardens are a delight, featuring
busts of poets, 19th-century azulejos depicting naked mythological ladies, and an
ornamental pool with equally voluptuous
statues. The gardens (free admission) are
open Tuesday to Saturday from 9 am to 12.30
pm and 2 to 5 pm.

Milreu Some 800m down the main road from
Estói's square are the ruins of Milreu, a
Roman equivalent of the Estói palace.

Dating from the 1st century AD, the ruins show the characteristic form of a peristyle villa, with a gallery of columns around a courtyard. In the surrounding rooms geometric motifs and friezes of fish were found, although these have now been removed for restoration. The most tantalising glimpses left of the villa's former glory are the fish mosaics in the suite of bathing chambers to the west of the villa's courtyard.

The bathing rooms include the *apodyterium* or changing-room (note the arched niches and benches for clothes and post-bath massage), and the *frigidarium*, which had a marble basin to hold cold water for cooling off after the bath. Other luxuries included underground heating and marble sculptures (now in the museums of Faro and Lagos).

The most interesting aspect of the site is its *nymphaerium* or water sanctuary, a temple devoted to the cult of water, to the right of the entrance. Its interior was once decorated with polychrome marble slabs and its exterior with fish mosaics (some are still visible). In the 3rd century the Visigoths converted it into a church, adding a baptismal font and a small mausoleum.

The site is open Tuesday to Sunday from 10 am to 12.30 pm and 2 to 5 pm (free admission). An information sheet describing it (in English, French or German) is available at the entrance.

Getting There & Away During the week, nine buses a day make the 20-minute run from Faro to Estói (continuing on to São Brás de Alportel). The last bus back to Faro is at 7 pm.

OLHÃO
• *pop 37,000* • *postcode 8700* • *area code ☎ 089*
Olhão, Algarve's biggest fishing port, is a clamorous, sprawling town beside a vast precinct of docks, canning factories and the Sopursal salt works. So why come? Buried at the historical centre, at the water's edge, is an appealing little kernel of town, surprisingly well preserved and untouristy, which could still stand alone as the fishing village

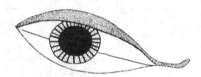

Some fishing boats have a protective eye painted on the prow.

it once was. Not surprisingly, there's also plenty of good, cheap seafood.

Offshore are the numerous sandy islands of the Parque Natural da Ria Formosa. There are good beaches on Ilha da Culatra and Ilha da Armona, both of which can be reached by boat. Ria Formosa's headquarters and a small visitors centre are just east of town.

Central Olhão seems to have more funeral parlours per sq km than any other Portuguese town – perhaps owing to the funerals-only Capela de Nossa Senhora da Soledade, right behind the parish church.

Orientation
Olhão has few streets running at right angles to one another. From the small EVA bus station on Rua General Humberto Delgado, turn right (or from the train station, turn left), ie east, and it's one block to the inner town's main avenue, Avenida da República. Turn right and look for the clock tower of the parish church, two or three blocks along, at the edge of the central, pedestrianised shopping zone.

At the far side of this zone, Avenida 5 de Outubro runs along the waterfront. Across it are the twin domed brick buildings of the fish market, and just to the left (east) is the town park, Jardim Patrão Joaquim Lopes.

Information
Olhão's eager turismo (☎ 71 39 36) is in the centre of the pedestrian zone: at the prominent fork beside the parish church, bear right along Rua de Comércio and follow it round to the right; the turismo is on the first corner.

There are at least three banks along Avenida da República with Multibanco ATMs.

The post, telegraph and telephone office is on Avenida da República, a block north of the parish church. The police can be reached on ☎ 70 21 44. To make an appointment at the local *centro de saúde* (medical centre) call ☎ 70 20 55.

One of two Ludoteca private kindergartens in the Algarve is at Fuzeta, 10 km to the east of Olhão (the other is in Albufeira). It's in the town hall (Junta de Freguesia da Fuzeta), right across Avenida 25 de Abril from the camping ground. It's open Monday to Saturday from 2 to 7 pm. Little English is spoken.

Bairro dos Pescadores
Just back from the market and park, in the city's historical heart, is the so-called Fishermen's Quarter, a knot of compact, cubical houses decorated with flower boxes, caged canaries and fading pastel whitewash or tile fronts. The bairro is threaded by roughly cobbled lanes too narrow for cars and is all (so far) mercifully ungentrified. From a distance it looks charmingly North African, although the Moors left in the 13th century and none of these houses is more than a few hundred years old. Nobody seems to have a good explanation for this style, found elsewhere in the Algarve only at Fuzeta.

Mercado Municipal
The biggest day for the colourful fish market on Avenida 5 de Outubro is Saturday, while the slowest day is Monday.

Beaches
Good beaches nearby include Farol (said to be the best of the lot) and Hangares on Ilha da Culatra, and Armona and Fuzeta on Ilha da Armona. Ilha da Culatra also has its own year-round fishing community. There are ferries to both islands from the pier just east of Jardim Patrão Joaquim Lopes; see Getting Around.

Special Events
Olhão hosts a seafood festival, with food stalls and folk music, in the Jardim Patrão Joaquim Lopes during the second week of August. The town also lets down its hair for the Feira del Maio on 30 April and 1 May, and the Fiera de San Miguel at the end of September.

Places to Stay
Camping The well-equipped, 800-place *Camping Olhão* (☎ 700 13 00; fax 700 13 90) is about two km east of Olhão and 800m off the N125. It's open year-round; sample rates during June through September are 590\$00 per person, 400\$00 to 950\$00 per tent and 470\$00 per car. A bus goes there from beside Jardim Patrão Joaquim Lopes every hour or two on weekdays and on Saturday mornings, but not on Sundays or holidays.

From mid-January to mid-November, Orbitur (☎ 71 41 73; Lisbon central booking ☎ 01-815 48 71; fax 01-814 80 45) runs the basic *Camping Ilha da Armona* (7900\$00 in July-August and 3900\$00 from November through March) on Ilha da Armona, but it has four-person bungalows only and tents are not allowed. Free camping is forbidden on the beaches. See Getting Around for ferry information.

Cheapest is the small, plain municipal *Parque de Campismo de Fuzeta* (☎ 79 34 59; fax 79 40 34), right on the waterfront at the end of the main street in tiny Fuzeta, about 10 km east of Olhão. Sample summer rates are 250\$00 per person, 300\$00 to 500\$00 per tent, 500\$00 to 600\$00 per car and 130\$00 for a shower, with about 40% off these rates during the rest of the year.

Residencials There are fewer places to stay than you would expect, and they fill up in summer. The best bet is to head straight for the turismo, which can advise you on what's available. In summer most residencials here charge about 5000\$00 for a basic double, usually with attached shower.

The clean rooms with shower and balcony at *Boémia Rooms* (☎ 72 11 22, ☎ 70 33 74), at Rua da Cêrca 20, are good value and there's a communal kitchen. From the EVA bus station, turn left and left again into Rua 18 de Junho; Rua da Cêrca is the third street

ALGARVE

on the right. Nearby is *Pensão Torres* (☎ 70 26 81) at Rua Dr Paulo Nogueira 13, two blocks beyond Rua da Cêrca. Very central (around the block from the turismo) is *Pensão Bicuar* (☎ 71 48 16) at Rua Vasco da Gama 5; across the street is *Alojamentos Vasco da Gama* (☎ 70 31 46).

Hotels The town's only hotel is the two-star *Ria-Sol* (☎ 70 52 67; fax 70 52 68), half a block west along Rua General Humberto Delgado from the EVA bus stand, at No 37. Threadbare doubles with bath, TV and telephone are not great value at about 8500$00 in summer. There is a dining room for breakfast only.

Places to Eat

The pedestrian zone around Rua Vasco da Gama (the left fork by the parish church) has plenty of overpriced tourist cafés to choose from.

Those trying to keep to a budget will like the three cheap, homey casas de pasto on Praça Patrão Joaquim Lopes, a square smaller than its name, right across Avenida 5 de Outubro from the market. All have sizeable seafood menus, from which you can eat well for under 2500$00. Our favourite is

Casa de Pasto Algarve on the north-eastern corner; others are *Dionísio* on the western side, and *Santos* a block west on Avenida 5 de Outubro.

East along Avenida 5 de Outubro you'll find one upscale fish restaurant after another. Recommended are the generous portions at *Papy's* (☎ 70 71 44); also good is *Restaurante Isidro* (☎ 71 41 24). A good but pricey place away from the waterfront is *O Aquário*; from the Capela de Nossa Senhora da Soledade at the rear of the parish church, walk two blocks east on Rua Dr João Lúcio.

Getting There & Away

Bus Renex coaches to/from Lisbon (three a day) stop in front of the train station. EVA runs coaches from Faro to Olhão (a 15 to 20-minute trip) about every 20 or 30 minutes on weekdays, less often on weekends and holidays. Some of the weekday buses continue on from Olhão station to the waterfront at Bairro dos Pecadores.

Train Olhão is 10 to 15 minutes from Faro on the Faro-Vila Real de Santo António line, with trains coming through every two hours or so. Fuzeta is a further 15 minutes down the line.

Parque Natural da Ria Formosa

The Ria Formosa Natural Park is a lagoon system stretching for 60 km along the Algarve coastline from just west of Faro to Cacela Velha.

The park's string of dunes and sandbars encloses a vast area of marshlands, channels, small islands and streams, which constitute a vital habitat for migrating and nesting birds. This is the place to see curlews, ducks and warblers on their winter migration from Northern Europe, or sandpipers and sea-doves on their spring migration from Africa. The rare sultan chicken also hangs out here.

And it's not only birds who fancy the place: you'll find some of the Algarve's quietest, biggest beaches on the sandbank ilhas of Faro, Culatra, Armona and Tavira (see the Faro, Olhão and Tavira sections).

The park headquarters (☎ 70 41 34; fax 70 41 65) at Castro Marim, three km east of Olhão, has a visitors centre, open daily from 9 am to 12.30 pm and 2.30 to 5.30 pm. It provides bountiful information (in English, French and German) about the park's flora and fauna, and there is a 2.4-km nature trail across the dunes. Entry is 200$00 for adults, 50$00 for children from 13 to 18 years old, and free for younger ones.

To get to the park headquarters take any Tavira-bound bus from Olhão, get off at the Cepsa petrol station, and walk seaward for about one km (it's 200m beyond the Camping Olhão camping ground). Alternatively, a bus goes to the camping ground every hour or two on weekdays and Saturday mornings, from beside Jardim Patrão Joaquim Lopes in Olhão. ■

Salt of the South

Take plenty of sea water. Add weeks of hot sun. Let the water evaporate in specially enclosed areas. Add more water and let it evaporate. Keep the sun shining. And hey presto, you've got salt! This is the process, more or less, that has been followed in Portugal and elsewhere for thousands of years in order to make salt.

The Algarve's long coastline, vast salt marshes and long hot summers make it ideal for salt production. Near Olhão, the huge Sopursal factory uses modern mechanical methods to produce some 10,000 tonnes of salt a year (that's about half of Portugal's entire consumption). The best quality stuff is reserved for table salt; the rest is used to produce an extraordinary variety of products, from bleach to baking soda to glass.

Just outside Tavira, en route to Quatro Águas, you can see extensive salt pans – each as big as a football field – and enormous heaps of salt piled up by tractors and left to dry. Salt collection usually starts around the end of August. Here and elsewhere, salt is still collected by hand, but these days there are more economic rewards from transforming salt pans into fish farms to cultivate expensive species, such as sole and bream, for export to northern Europe. ■

Getting Around

Ferries run out to the ilhas from the pier at the eastern end of Jardim Patrão Joaquim Lopes. Boats to Ilha da Armona go every 60 to 90 minutes daily from 15 June to 15 September, slightly less often on weekdays in early June and late September, and in winter just twice a day; the last trip back from Armona in summer is at 8 pm.

For Ilha da Culatra and Farol, boats go every hour or two from 1 June to 17 September, and three times a day in winter; the last boat back in summer leaves Culatra at 8 and Farol at 8.20 pm.

TAVIRA

• pop 24,500 • postcode 8800 • area code ☎ 081

Sick and tired of the Algarve's tourist ghettos? Head 30 km east of Faro and you'll find relief in Tavira. This picturesque little town straddling the Rio Gilão three km from the coast is still remarkably unspoilt. Elegant 18th-century houses border the river; castle ruins overlook at least 37 churches in a tangle of old streets; 16th-century mansions with Manueline window flourishes line the back streets; and fishing boats bob at the quay, where a traditional market takes place daily.

You'd hardly call the place lively, though there are bars and discos for those who want them. And there's a superb, undeveloped beach (with camp site) on the nearby Ilha de Tavira. If you're looking for a quiet, relaxing base in an attractive setting, Tavira is hard to beat.

History

Tavira's origins are vague: it's likely that the area was inhabited in Neolithic times, and later by Phoenicians, Greeks and Carthaginians. The Romans left more traces – their settlement of Balsa was just down the road, near Santa Luzia (three km west). The seven-arched bridge the Romans built at Tavira (then called Tabira) was an important link in the route between Baesuris (Castro Marim) and Ossonoba (Faro).

In the 8th century, Tavira was occupied by the Moors. They built the castle (probably on the site of a Roman fortress) and two mosques. Their downfall came in 1242 when Dom Paio Peres Correia reconquered the town. Those Moors who remained were segregated into the *mouraria* neighbourhood, outside the town walls.

Tavira's importance was established during the Age of Discoveries: as the closest port to the Moroccan coast it was the base for Portuguese expeditions to North Africa, supplying provisions (especially salt, wine and dried fish) and providing a hospital for sick soldiers. Its maritime trade also expanded, with exports of salted fish, almonds, figs and wine to northern Europe. In 1520, already

ALGARVE

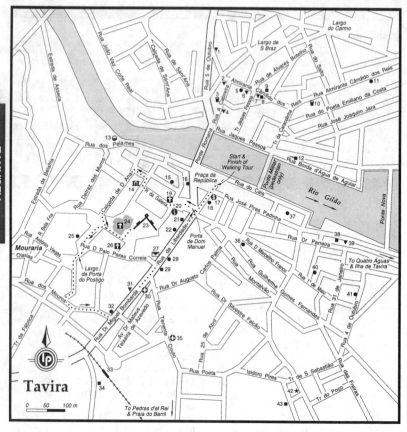

the most populated settlement in the Algarve and rich in noblemen's houses and churches, it was raised to the rank of a city.

Decline set in during the early 17th century when the North African campaign was abandoned and the Rio Gilão became so silted up that large boats couldn't enter the port. In 1645 came the devastating effects of the plague, followed by the 1755 earthquake. After a brief spell producing carpets in the late 18th century, Tavira found a more stable income from its tuna fishing and canning industry, although this too declined in the middle of this century when the tuna shoals moved elsewhere. Today it relies increasingly on tourism.

Orientation

The train station is on the southern edge of town, a km from the centre. To get to the town centre from the station, walk along Avenida Dr Mateus Teixeira de Azevedo until you reach the main street, Rua da Liberdade. The bus terminal is by the river on the western edge of town, a five-minute walk from the town centre and Praça da República. Most of the town's shops and facilities are on the southern side of the river.

ALGARVE

PLACES TO STAY		
8	Pensão Residencial Lagôas	
9	Pensão Residencial Almirante	
12	Residencial Princesa do Gilão	
21	Pensão Residencial Castelo	
29	Pensão Residencial Mirante	
34	Quinta do Caracol	
38	Mare's Residencial	
43	Convento de Santo António	

PLACES TO EAT	
1	Cantinho do Emigrante
2	Churrasqueira O Manel
4	Restaurante O Patio

6	Snack-Bar Petisqueira-Belmar	
7	Restaurante Bica	
31	Casa Pirica	
39	Casa de Pasto A Barquinha	

OTHER	
3	Patrick's
5	Lavandaria Alagoa
10	Bar Toque
11	Tavira Health Club
13	Bus Terminal
14	Palácio da Galeria
15	Lorisrent
16	Mota Rent
17	Banks
18	Câmara Municipal
19	Igreja da Misericórdia
20	Turismo

22	Kioskau
23	Castelo
24	Igreja de Santa Maria do Castelo
25	Convento da Nossa Senhora da Graça
26	Igreja de Santiago
27	Post Office
28	Capela de Nossa Senhora da Conçeicão
30	Clinica Medica
32	Integralis
33	Train Station
35	Centro de Saúde
36	Cine Teatro
37	Market
40	Azulejo Azul Artesenato
41	Passilava
42	Police Station

Information

Tourist Office The turismo (☎ 225 11) is near Praça da República at Rua da Galeria 9. Its cheerful staff can provide all kinds of regional information and can help with accommodation. In summer it's open weekdays from 9.30 am to 7 pm and weekends from 9.30 am to 5.30 pm.

Money Banks with Multibanco ATMs are plentiful around Praça da República and along Rua da Liberdade.

Post & Communications The post office (open weekdays from 8.30 am to 6 pm) is at the top of Rua da Liberdade.

Bookshops Near the post office, at Rua da Liberdade 24, is Kioskau, a well-stocked bookshop with English, French and German newspapers and local guidebooks. Recommended are the locally produced *Walking Tours of Tavira* (in English, French and German) and *Your Guide to Tavira*.

Laundry Lavandaria Alagoa (☎ 32 58 23), at Rua Almirante Cândido dos Reis 12, charges 300$00 a kg for one-day service. Passilava (☎ 32 65 89), at Rua 4 de Outubro 7, charges 320$00 a kg and also has dry-cleaning and ironing services. Passilava is

open weekdays from 9 am to 1 pm and 3 to 7 pm, and Saturdays from 9 am to 1 pm.

Medical Services The centro de saúde (☎ 320 10 00, ☎ 32 40 23) is at Rua Tenente Couto. A 24-hour private clinic, Clinica Medica (☎ 817 50), at Avenida Dr Mateus Teixeira de Azevedo 5, provides speedier (and pricier) treatment.

Emergency The main police station (☎ 220 22) is on Campo dos Máritires da Pátria, on the southern edge of town.

Walking Tour

From the Praça da República, head up the cobblestone steps of Rua da Galeria past the turismo and through one of the old town gates, the **Porta de Dom Manuel**, built in 1520 when Dom Manuel I made Tavira a city. Facing you at the end of the lane is the **Igreja da Misericórdia**. Continue along Rua da Galeria to the left of the church to the 16th-century **Palácio da Galeria**, now somewhat decrepit, though the baroque window above the main doorway remains impressive.

Circling round the back of the *palácio* on Calçada de Dona Ana brings you to the **Igreja de Santa Maria do Castelo** and, beside it, the entrance to the **castelo**. Just to the right of the castle is the whitewashed **Igreja de Santiago**; the area beside it was once the Praça da Vila, the old town square. On the other side of the square is the **Convento da Nossa Senhora da Graça**.

Downhill from here is the **Largo da Porta do Postigo**, at the site of another old town gate and the town's Moorish 'ghetto'. From here, head along Rua das Portas do Postigo to Rua dos Mouros, then turn left into Rua Dr Miguel Bombarda and on to Rua da Liberdade.

Igreja da Misericórdia

Built in the 1540s, this church is considered the Algarve's most important Renaissance monument, thanks largely to its finely carved (though now worn and weather-beaten) arched doorway, which is topped by statues of Nossa Senhora da Misericórdia, São Pedro and São Paulo.

Igreja de Santa Maria do Castelo

This 13th-century church was built on the site of a Moorish mosque (its clock tower still has some Arab-style windows). Inside, you'll find the tomb of the conqueror – Dom Paio Peres Correia – as well as those of the seven Christian knights whose murder by the Moors precipitated the final attack on the town.

Castelo de Tavira

Now more of a prim little garden than a defensive bulwark, the castle's restored octagonal tower is a great place for looking out over Tavira's attractive tiled rooftops, which probably owe their wave-like Oriental style to ideas brought back by 15th-century explorers. The castle is open daily from 9.30 am to 5.30 pm (free admission).

Convento da Nossa Senhora da Graça

Founded in 1568 on the site of the former Jewish quarter, this convent was largely rebuilt at the end of the 18th century and is now used by the military.

Around Largo da Porta do Postigo

At the largo there was once another entrance into the walled town. After the Christian Reconquista, the Moors established their neighbourhood outside the walls here. It's a quarter of typically narrow streets and small houses, still in evidence along Rua António Viegas and Rua das Olarias.

Along Rua da Liberdade

Opposite the post office is the 16th-century Capela de Nossa Senhora da Conceição, where former kings are said to have prayed. At No 60 is a 16th-century mansion with a fine 2nd-storey Renaissance window, and at No 27 an 18th-century palace with baroque door frames.

Ponte Romana

This Roman bridge near the Praça da República owes its present design to a 17th-century restoration. The latest touch-up job was in 1989, after floods knocked down one of its pillars.

Praça da República

Once you've explored Tavira's old town, the laziest thing to do is to sit by the river and watch the world go by: there are cafés on both sides of the river and a pleasant garden on the Praça da República side where the locals hang out.

Here, too, is Tavira's **market**, one of the best in the Algarve. Every morning there's a wonderful display of fresh fish, as well as superb fruits and vegetables, home-made cakes, goat's cheese and honey. On Saturday mornings, it extends outside along the quayside and is as traditional as they come, with everything from sacks of potatoes to quivering rabbits.

Quatro Águas

More energetic visitors can walk a couple of km east along the river, past the market and the salt pans (see the boxed aside) to Quatro Águas, distinguished by its abandoned tuna-canning factory. As well as the jumping-off point for Ilha de Tavira (see Around Tavira), this seaside nub has some excellent seafood restaurants and a couple of small cafés by the pier, which are popular with the motorbike brigade on summer evenings.

Sauna
To soothe aching limbs after a long bike ride, book yourself a 750$00 sauna at the Tavira Health Club (☎ 226 28), across the river on Rua Almirante Cândido dos Reis. It's open weekdays from 10 am to 8 pm.

Horse Riding
Rides are available at Colina da Rosa Country Club (☎ 97 14 69) in Santa Catarina, which is 13 km north-west of Tavira (a 20-minute bus ride).

Special Events
Tavira's biggest festival is its Festa de Cidade on 24 and 25 June. Myrtle and paper flowers decorate the entire town, free sardines are dished up by the town hall, and dancing and frolicking in the street continues until the wee hours.

Places to Stay
Camping The nearest camp site (☎ 235 05) is ideally located on Ilha de Tavira (see Around Tavira), a step away from the island's huge beach, and it's open from May through October.

Private Rooms & Apartments In the town your best bet during high season may be private rooms, which usually go for about 4000$00 a double. Self-catering flats are also available, though usually for a minimum of a week's stay. The turismo has all the contacts.

Pensões & Residencials Among budget pensões, the long-standing favourite (despite an often surly reception) is *Pensão Residencial Lagôas* (☎ 222 52), across the river at Rua Almirante Cândido dos Reis 24. Clean singles/doubles go for 2500$00/4000$00 without bath (5000$00 for a double with bath). Across the street at No 51, *Pensão Residencial Almirante* (☎ 221 63) is a dark but cosy family house full of clutter, with just

six rooms; these go for 3000$00 (without bath) or 4000$00 (with).

For central convenience, the old-style *Pensão Residencial Castelo* (☎ 239 42), at Rua da Liberdade 4, wins hands down: its rooms (some with great river views) cost about 5000$00 a double. At Rua da Liberdade 83 is *Pensão Residencial Mirante* (☎ 222 55), with an eye-catching façade of plasterwork and tiles. Prices range from 4000$00 to 6000$00 a double (the latter with breakfast).

Smarter places by the river include the dull but efficient *Residencial Princesa do Gilão* (☎ & fax 32 51 71) at Rua Borda d'Água de Aguiar 10, where singles/doubles are 5000$00/6000$00; and the posher *Mare's Residencial* (☎ 32 58 15; fax 32 58 19) at Rua José Pires Padinha 134, where high-season prices soar to 12,000$00 a double.

Turihab *Quinta do Caracol* (☎ 224 75; fax 231 75), behind the train station off the Faro road, is a converted 17th-century farmhouse in a spacious garden. Each of the seven rooms has been converted into separate quarters with typical Algarve furnishings (all but one with a kitchenette) for 14,000$00 each.

On the south-eastern edge of town opposite a new housing estate in Campo dos Martires da Pátria, the *Convento de Santo António* (☎ & fax 32 56 32) is hidden behind high walls next to its church. This former Franciscan monastery, founded in 1606, has been owned by the same family since the 1870s. Seven furnished rooms (formerly monks' cells) are set around a sunlit cloister where breakfast is served. The cosy living room was once the monks' kitchen. Room prices start at 14,000$00 and it's well worth a splurge.

Places to Eat – budget
Despite a failing tuna-fishing industry, tuna is still Tavira's speciality. It's especially good at riverside restaurants such as *Casa de Pasto A Barquinha* (☎ 228 43), Rua José Pires Padinha 142, where prices are reasonable and the service is friendly (the salads are

ALGARVE

great too). More basic (with a TV blaring) is the locals' hang-out, *Casa Pirica* at Rua Dr Miguel Bombarda 22, where dishes start as low as 700$00; it's closed on Sundays.

Another unpretentious and popular eatery is *Restaurante Bica* (☎ 238 43), across the river at Rua Almirante Cândido dos Reis 24, where you can eat well (try the rabbit or the house speciality – fried shrimps with garlic) for under 1500$00. There are several other attractive options in this neighbourhood, including *Snack-Bar Petisqueira-Belmar* (☎ 32 49 95), at Rua Almirante Cândido dos Reis 16, with rustic décor and half-portion prices from 600$00 (closed on Mondays).

The nearby *Churrasqueira O Manel* (☎ 233 43), at Rua António Cabreira 39, is the place for frango no churrasco (grilled chicken) and other grilled offerings (it has a takeaway service too). Further up at Praça Dr António Padinha 27, a tiny eight-table den, *Cantinho do Emigrante* (☎ 236 96), has a surprisingly big menu with dishes from 800$00, despite its rough-and-ready appearance.

Places to Eat – top end
For more salubrious surroundings and tourist-oriented service, head for *Restaurante O Patio* (☎ 230 08) at Rua António Cabreira 30; it has a popular rooftop terrace. Dishes aren't cheap (cataplanas from 4000$00 for two; duck with orange for 1300$00) but they're tasty. Another up-market fish restaurant is the riverside *Mare's Restaurante* (☎ 32 58 15) at Rua José Pires Padinha 134.

For the best seafood splurges – at not extravagant prices – head two km east of town to Quatro Águas to *Portas do Mar* (☎ 812 55); it has daily specials as well as excellent arroz de marisco for 1350$00.

Entertainment
There is a clutch of lively bars across the river on Rua de Poeta Emiliano da Costa and at the eastern end of Rua Almirante Cândido dos Reis. For Guinness on tap, 'flaming bomb' cocktails at 380$00 a shot, and high-quality sounds, check out *Bar Toque* (☎ 32

66 43) at Rua Almirante Cândido dos Reis 118. More cocktails and satellite TV, plus bar snacks, are on offer at *Patrick's* (☎ 32 59 98) at Rua Dr António Cabreira 25.

There's one huge disco in town – *UBI* (☎ 32 45 77) – at the far eastern end of Rua Almirante Cândido dos Reis, with an open-air bar and music until 5 am. Other discos in the vicinity include *Joy Disco* at km-post 121 en route to Faro on the N125, and the summertime *Disco de Barril* (see Around Tavira).

Things to Buy
For classy Algarve handicrafts (azulejos, woollens and basketware), check out Azulejo Azul Artesenato; it's tucked away at Rua Terreiro do Garção 27.

Getting There & Away
Running between Faro and Tavira are 15 trains a day (taking 40 to 60 minutes) and seven buses (four at weekends, taking an hour).

Getting Around
Bicycles and motorbikes can be rented from Lorisrent (☎ 32 52 03, mobile ☎ 0931-27 47 66), near the turismo at Rua Damião Augusto de Brito 4. Expect to pay around 800$00 a day for a mountain bike, or 2200$00 a day for a Suzuki automatic. Similar prices are offered by Mota Rent (☎ 32 56 47), at Praça da República 10, which also hires out cars, typically for about 18,000$00 for three days. Taxis line up in the Praça da República.

AROUND TAVIRA
Ilha de Tavira
Part of the Parque Natural da Ria Formosa, this is one of a string of similar sandy ilhas stretching along the coast from Cacela Velha to just west of Faro. The huge beach at its eastern end, opposite Tavira, has a camp site and a string of café-restaurants, as well as water-sports facilities in summer. In the off season, it feels incredibly remote and empty. Don't forget the sunscreen: the low dunes offer no shade.

Further west on the ilha is **Praia do Barril**,

ALGARVE

Now You See Me, Now You Don't...

The strictly protected *Chamaeleo chamaeleon* (Mediterranean chameleon) isn't native to Portugal. This bizarre 25-cm-long reptile, with independently moving eyes, a tongue longer than its body and a skin styled in variable colour schemes (from bright yellow to jet black), only started creeping around southern Portugal about 70 years ago; it was probably introduced from North Africa where it's common. This particular species is the only one found in Europe, and its habitat is restricted to Crete and the Iberian Peninsula. In Portugal it's got no further than the leeward Algarve, where it hides out in pine groves and coastal shrub lands.

Your best chance of coming across the slow-moving beastie is either in the Quinta de Marim area of the Parque Natural de Ria Formosa or in Monte Gordo's conifer woods (six km west of Vila Real de Santo António), which have been designated a protected area in order to preserve the species. In hibernation from December to March (the only other time it comes to ground is in October to lay its eggs), the chameleon is most commonly seen on springtime mornings, slowly clambering along branches or among shrubs. ■

---

accessible by a miniature train that trundles over the mud flats from Pedras d'el Rei, a classy chalet resort four km west of Tavira. There are a couple of café-restaurants where the train stops, and the popular summertime Disco de Barril, but the rest is just sand, sand, sand as far as the eye can see.

Getting There & Away Ferries make the five-minute hop to the ilha (160$00 return) from Quatro Águas, two km east of Tavira. They run from mid-April to October, leaving every 10 minutes from July to mid September and every half-hour the rest of the time. The last boat back leaves at about midnight or later in August, 11 pm in June and July, and 9 pm in April, May and September – but check with the ferryman! A bus goes hourly to Quatro Águas in peak season from the Tavira bus terminal, via Cine Teatro cinema on Rua Dom Marcelino Franco. A taxi to Quatro Águas is about 500$00.

In peak season there's often a direct boat to the island, departing from near Tavira's market up to six times a day. In the off season, ferries are erratic; you could try bargaining with the fishermen at the quayside for a ride to Quatro Águas or even to Ilha de Tavira.

For Barril, take a bus from Tavira for the 10-minute ride to Pedras d'el Rei, from where a little train runs regularly to the beach

from March through September; the fare is 100$00. In the off season the timetable is at the whim of the driver. Walking takes around 15 minutes.

Cacela Velha

Once completely overlooked by the Algarve's tourist invasion, and only recently discovered by the tour-bus brigade, this hamlet 12 km east of Tavira is still remarkably untouched by the 20th century. All you'll find are a clutch of cottages next to gardens, olive and orange groves, a church, an old fort, a couple of café-restaurants and a splendid view of the sea and the nearby ilha. Magically, there's nothing to do but follow a path down the scrubby hillside to the beach; or sit on the church walls, listen to the surf and watch pigeons wheel above the olive trees.

Getting There & Away There's no direct bus service from Tavira but Cacela Velha is only a km inland from the N125 (a couple of km before Vila Nova de Cacela), which is the Faro-Vila Real de Santo António bus route. Coming from Faro, there are two turn-offs to Cacela Velha; the second is the more direct.

VILA REAL DE SANTO ANTÓNIO
• *pop 8000* • *postcode 8900* • *area code* ☎ *081*
Ever since a bridge was completed over the

Rio Guadiana four km north of town in 1991, Vila Real's importance as a frontier post and ferry-crossing point for Spain has declined. Nothing attests to this better than the abandoned turismo and its indoor plants, which have been left to grow, triffid-like, to eerily huge sizes.

Spanish day-trippers still come here to buy cheap linen, towels and peculiar life-size china dogs (Dalmatians go for 6500$00 if you're interested). Tourists from the Algarve resorts come here for boat trips along the Guadiana (see the boxed aside). As a result, there are plenty of good restaurants and convenient coach links with Spain.

The town itself is architecturally impressive, thanks to the Marquês de Pombal who, in a few brisk months in 1774, stamped the town with his hallmark grid pattern of streets (just like Lisbon's Baixa district) after the original town was destroyed by floods.

Orientation
The seafront Avenida da República is one of the town's two main shopping and eating thoroughfaresi the other is pedestrianised Rua Teofilio de Braga, which leads straight up from the seafront and past the spacious main square, Praça Marquês de Pombal.

The quaint little train station is on the riverfront, just beyond the ferry terminal, about 100m east of Rua Teofilio de Braga. Buses pull into the nearby terminal on Avenida da República.

Information
The nearest turismo (☎ 444 95) is now at the tourist resort of Monte Gordo, six km west of town (a 10-minute bus ride). In summer it's open from 9.30 am to 12.30 pm and 2 to 7 pm (to 5.30 pm on weekends).

There's a Spanish consulate (☎ 448 88) at Avenida Ministro Duarte Pacheco in Vila Real, open weekdays from 9 am to 12.30 pm and 2.30 to 5.30 pm.

Places to Stay
If you're after a beach and tourist-oriented facilities, go to nearby Monte Gordo. There's

a shady municipal camping ground (☎ 425 88) there too, but it gets clogged with campers in summer.

In Vila Real itself, good budget accommodation is rare. You could try the pousada de juventude (☎ 445 65) at Rua Dr Sousa Martins 40, though it quickly fills with riotous groups in summer. At the clean, friendly *Pensão Baixa Mar* (☎ 435 11) at Rua Teofilio de Braga 3, small doubles without bath are overpriced at 5500$00.

Places to Eat
Cruise Avenida da República for plenty of tempting options (mostly with outdoor seating), including the popular (though rather pricey) *Caves do Guadiana* at No 90. Cheaper fare can be found along Rua Teofilio de Braga and adjoining streets: *Churrasqueira Arenilha*, opposite the post office on Rua Cândido dos Reis, is a good bet, with grilled fish dishes from 950$00 and pratas do dia from 650$00 (for a half-portion).

Getting There & Away
Bus The daily Linha Litoral buses to Lagos aren't any quicker than a train, but there are at least eight ordinary services a day to Tavira, Olhão and Faro, and regular runs to nearby Castro Marim and Monte Gordo. Long-haul coach services include a twice-daily 12-hour marathon to Braga, right at the other end of the country; and six runs to Lisbon (taking six hours).

If you're aiming to get further afield in Spain than Ayamonte, take the twice-daily express coach service to Huelva (1¼ hours), with connections on to Seville (just over three hours).

Train Vila Real de Santo António is the eastern terminal of the Algarve railway line, with services to/from Lagos at least seven times a day. The fastest interregional service takes 2½ hours and the slowest regional service, with changes at Faro and/or Tunes, takes an hour longer.

Cruising on the Guadiana

A great way to see Portugal and Spain at the same time is on a boat up the Rio Guadiana (which serves as the border for some 50 km). The route from Vila Real de Santo António to Odeleite passes some delightful little villages, including Castro Marim with its formidable hilltop castle.

Some tour operators, including Riosul (☎ 081-44 077 in Monte Gordo or ☎ 089-80 72 59 in Faro), arrange summertime trips daily for around 7000$00 per person (half-price for children aged four to 10) including barbecue lunch and time for a swim. ■

Ferry To hop across the border to white-washed Ayamonte, the most enjoyable route is still by ferry. It runs every 40 minutes from about 8 am to 1 am, and the fare is 140$00 per person and 650$00 per car.

CASTRO MARIM

• *postcode 8970* • *area code* ☎ *081*

This tiny village five km north of Vila Real de Santo António is entirely dominated by its huge castle. The battlements provide a ringside seat for gazing out over the surrounding fens and marshes of the **Reserva Natural do Sapal**, the bridge to Spain, and the pretty little village below.

There are few facilities in the village itself, but it makes a pleasant stopover en route north, or a day trip from Vila Real, and is especially rewarding if you're a birdwatcher – the *reserva natural* is famous for its flamingoes.

Information

The efficient little turismo (☎ 081-53 12 32), in the shadow of the castle at Praça 1 de Maio 2-4, is open weekdays from 9.30 am to 12.30 pm and 2 to 5.30 pm, and Saturdays from 9.30 am to noon.

Castelo

Castro Marim's castle was built by Dom Afonso III in the 13th century on the site of Roman and Moorish fortifications. In 1319 it became the first headquarters of the religious military order known as the Order of Christ, a revamped version of the Knights Templar. Until they moved their base to Tomar in 1334, the soldiers of the Order of Christ used this castle to keep watch over the estuary of the Rio Guadiana and the frontier with Spain – where the Moors were still in power.

But the ruins you see today date from the 17th century, when Dom João IV ordered the addition of vast ramparts. At the same time a smaller fort, the **Castelo de São Sebastião**, was built on a nearby hilltop. Much was destroyed in the 1755 earthquake, but the hilltop ruins of the main fort are still pretty awesome.

There's little to see inside the wonderfully derelict castle walls except a restored 14th-century church, the **Igreja de Santiago**,

ALGARVE

Reserva Natural do Sapal de Castro Marim e Vila Real de Santo António

Established in 1975, this nature reserve is the oldest in Portugal, covering some 2000 hectares of marshland, brackish fens and commercial salt pans bordering the Rio Guadiana just north of Vila Real. Among its most important winter visitors are the greater flamingoes, spoonbills, avocets and Caspian terns. In spring you can see dozens of white storks.

The park's head office (☎ 081-53 11 41) is due to move from Castro Marim's castle to a new base and interpretative centre in Montinho (a five-minute bus ride to the north), open weekdays from 9 am to 12.30 pm and 2 to 5.30 pm. Already in Montinho is some park accommodation (including a two-room house for 4700$00). It's popular with botanists and groups of birdwatchers so you need to book ahead. Another rewarding area for spotting the park's birdlife is around Cerro do Bufo, about two km south-west of Castro Marim, before São Bartolomeu. The park office can provide a map and more details. ■

where Henry the Navigator, who was Grand Master of the Order of Christ, is said to have prayed.

Places to Stay & Eat

There's no accommodation in the village. If you're keen to hang out to study the flora or fauna of the park, your best bet is the self-catering villas in Vista Real (☎ 081-53 15 97), a few km north of Castro Marim, which cost about 7000$00. The turismo has details. There are rumours that a pousada will soon be built inside the castle.

There are several reasonable restaurants on Rua de São Sebastião, a short walk from the turismo.

Getting There & Away

Buses from Vila Real de Santo António make the eight-minute run to Castro Marim at least six times a day. They continue to Montinho, where the park's head office is located.

The Central Coast

LOULÉ
• *pop 9000• postcode 8100 • area code* ☎ *089*

Loulé, one of the Algarve's largest inland towns, is a former Roman and Moorish settlement with an attractive old quarter and castle ruins. Just 16 km north-west of Faro and 11 km north of Quarteira, it's become a popular destination for tour groups every Saturday, thanks to its big weekly Gypsy market and its long-established reputation as a handicraft centre. Its laid-back atmosphere and good range of restaurants make it worth a stay overnight to enjoy the place once the day-trippers have gone.

Orientation

The bus station is on Rua Nossa Senhora de Fátima, on the northern edge of town, about five minutes walk from the centre. The train station is five km south-west of the centre (take any Quarteira-bound bus).

If you're arriving by car (especially on a

Saturday), try to arrive very early in the morning or you'll have some nightmare car parking problems.

Information

Inside the converted ruins of the castle in the old town area is the turismo (☎ 46 39 00), open weekdays in July and August from 9.30 am to 7 pm and weekends from 9.30 am to 12.30 pm and 2 to 7 pm. The rest of the year it's open weekdays from 9.30 am to 12.30 pm and 2 to 7 pm and Saturdays from 9.30 am to 12.30 pm.

Castelo & Museums

The restored castle ruins house the **Cozinha Tradicional Algarvia** (traditional Algarve kitchen) display (up the steps from the turismo) and the small **Museu Municipal de Arqueológica** next to the turismo. The museum's attractive displays feature some fine fragments of Bronze Age and Roman ceramics, including an eye-catching 10th-century bowl with swirling patterns. The museum is open Monday to Saturday from 9 am to 5.30 pm (free admission).

Activities

The Quinta do Azinheira (☎ 41 59 91, mobile ☎ 0676-75 71 30) at Aldeia da Tôr,

---

Where Eagle Owls Fly

Off the tourist track, in the foothills of the Serra do Caldeirão some 21 km north-west of Loulé, is the Rocha da Pena, a 479m-high limestone outcrop that was made a 'classified site' in 1993 because of its rich flora and fauna. Orchids, narcissi and native cistus cover the slopes, where red foxes and Egyptian mongooses are common. Among the many bird species to be seen are the huge eagle owl, Bonelli's eagle and buzzard.

A *centro ambiental* (environmental centre) has been established in the village of Pena, and there is a 4.7-km circular trail starting from Rocha, one km from Pena. A brochure (in Portuguese) with details of the walk should be available at the turismo or the câmara municipal (town hall) in Loulé. ■

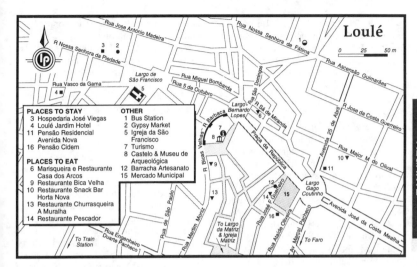

Loulé

```
PLACES TO STAY
 3  Hospedaria José Viegas
 4  Loulé Jardim Hotel
11  Pensão Residencial
    Avenida Nova
16  Pensão Cidem

PLACES TO EAT
 6  Marisqueira e Restaurante
    Casa dos Arcos
 9  Restaurante Bica Velha
10  Restaurante Snack Bar
    Horta Nova
13  Restaurante Churrasqueira
    A Muralha
14  Restaurante Pescador

OTHER
 1  Bus Station
 2  Gypsy Market
 5  Igreja da São
    Francisco
 7  Turismo
 8  Castelo & Museu de
    Arqueológica
12  Barracha Artesanato
15  Mercado Municipal
```

ALGARVE

about 12 km north, offers horse riding as well as trips combining horse riding and a jeep safari to the 'panoramic Algarve sierra'.

Special Events

Weekdays and out of high season, Loulé is a pretty dozy place. But come carnival time (late February or early March), it's livelier than almost anywhere else in the Algarve, with parades and tractor-drawn floats, dancing and singing, and lots of jolly, high-spirited behaviour.

Another major but far more sombre event in Loulé's calendar is the *romaria* (religious festival) of Nossa Senhora da Piedade. Linked to ancient maternity rites, it's probably the Algarve's most important religious festival: on Easter Sunday, a 16th-century image of Our Lady of Pity is carried down from its hilltop chapel two km north of town to the parish church (Igreja Matriz). Two weeks later, a much larger procession of devotees lines the steep route to the chapel to witness and accompany the return of the image to its home. The eye-catching new Igreja de Nossa Senhora da Piedade next to this old chapel was completed in 1995, and it now dominates the skyline.

Places to Stay

En route to the Gypsy market (see Things to Buy) you'll see a bright sign in the window of Café Viegas at Largo do São Francisco 30, advertising *Hospedaria José Viegas* (☎ 46 33 85). The hospedaria is actually 30m down the road at Rua Nossa Senhora da Piedade 64. Doubles with bath cost 3500$00 and singles without bath cost 2000$00. Check in at the Café Viegas for reservations if there's no-one at the hospedaria.

Another good budget place, next to the mercado municipal on Praça da República, is *Pensão Cidem* (☎ 41 55 53), at Travessa do Mercado 1, which has doubles without bath from 2500$00 (or 4000$00 with). If the door's closed, ask at the nearby Restaurante Pescador (see Places to Eat).

Similarly central, at Rua Maria Campina 1, is *Pensão Residencial Avenida Nova* (☎ 41 50 97, or call the motherly owner, Maria Josefina Cory, at her home on ☎ 41 64 06 from 6 to 8 pm, or 9 pm to midnight). The big, squeaky-floored rooms here are good value, especially for trios or families. Doubles with shower are 4000$00 (3000$00 without).

Top of the range is the *Loulé Jardim Hotel*

(☎ 41 30 94; fax 631 77), a turn-of-the-century building with modernised rooms in the quiet Praça Manuel d'Arriaga. Singles/doubles with all the frills (there's a small swimming pool too) will set you back 8000$00/10,000$00.

Places to Eat

Restaurante Pescador (☎ 46 28 21), in the lane right next to the mercado municipal, is the place to head for at Saturday lunch time if you like a good family hubbub. Big helpings, lots of fish dishes and reasonable prices make this a popular local choice.

For open-air dining in a walled garden, head for *Restaurante Snack Bar Horta Nova* (☎ 46 24 29, closed Wednesdays) on Rua Major Manuel do Olival, specialising in home-made pizzas (from as little as 600$00), charcoal-grilled meat and fish.

Pricier but still pleasantly unpretentious is *Marisqueira e Restaurante Casa dos Arcos* (☎ 41 67 13, closed Sundays) at Rua Sá de Miranda 23-25 (its entrance in the alley of arches off Rua São Domingos is easier to find). In simple pine and brick décor you can feast off lobster and crabs, swordfish steak or filet mignon. Expect to pay around 1200$00 a dish.

Restaurante Churrasqueira A Muralha (☎ 41 26 29), in the shadow of the castle walls at Rua Martim Moniz 41, is a tastefully decorated little nook with brick floors and azulejo-adorned niches. Grilled chicken and fish dishes are reasonably priced, ranging from 600$00 to 1000$00.

For a splurge, try the nearby *Restaurante Bica Velha* (☎ 46 33 76), at Rua Martim Moniz 17, which has the best reputation in town for typical Algarve specialities such as cataplanas.

Things to Buy

Turn right (south) out of the castle, in the direction of the parish church (Igreja Matriz) at Largo da Matriz, and you'll find yourself in a network of narrow streets where artisans in tiny workshops produce some of the Algarve's finest handicrafts, notably lace and leather goods, brass and copperware, wooden and cane furniture.

Many of the finished products are also displayed in craft shops along Rua da Barbaca (behind the castle) and in the *mercado municipal*. This Moorish-looking building on Praça da República is the centre of activity on Saturday mornings when the market is in full swing with all kinds of produce on sale, from ducks and rabbits to honey and walnuts. Loulé's biggest copperware shop, Barracha Artesanato, is here too, on the corner of Rua José F Guerreiro and Rua 9 de Abril. For real Portuguese atmosphere and produce, this municipal market is far more interesting than the tourist-geared Gypsy market the other side of town, off Rua Nossa Senhora da Piedade. This sells the same variety of cheap clothes and t-shirts, lace tablecloths and plastic junk that you'll find in all other Algarve Gypsy markets. If you need a new t-shirt wardrobe, follow the crowds or the signs along pedestrianised Rua 5 de Outubro. The market winds down at about noon.

Getting There & Away

Both Faro and Lagos-bound trains stop at Loulé station (five km to the south of town) at least eight times a day. Buses are far more convenient: there are regular connections from Faro and Quarteira, and at least seven buses a day from Albufeira and Portimão.

VILAMOURA

This 1600-hectare private development 20 km west of Faro boasts Portugal's largest marina (with berths for over 1000 boats), three golf courses (with two more to come), and 35,000 beds in various 'villages' of luxurious apartments. These are now being expanded to make Vilamoura the largest residential resort in Europe by the next century. The massive environmental blow is softened by Vilamoura's plans to be the first resort in southern Europe to apply standards set out in a worldwide environmental management programme for the tourism industry, called Green Globe.

But unless you want to mingle with the

yachting set at the marina, goggle at designer bikinis on the huge beach, or play a round of golf or roulette (there's a casino here too, of course) you wouldn't want to come anywhere near the place.

Getting There & Away
If you land here by mistake, a nice way to escape is on the *Condor de Vilamoura*, a replica of an American fishing schooner, which departs daily from the marina for a three-hour return trip (about 5500$00 per person) to São Rafael, just beyond Albufeira, or a six-hour trip (about 10,000$00 with barbecue lunch) to Galé, a little further round the coast. For more information call ☎ 089-31 40 70.

Alternatively, there are plenty of buses; see Quarteira.

QUARTEIRA
Vilamoura's poor cousin, Quarteira, just two km away, is another huge development of holiday flats, hotels and apartments. Its claim to fame is its nonstop sandy beach, stretching pretty much all the way to Faro, and its seafront promenade, the longest in the Algarve, which is packed with tourist bars, cafés and souvenir shops. It also has a popular Gypsy market every Wednesday.

If this is all you're after, you'll find Quarteira as easy a place to hang out as Albufeira, the Algarve's other major tourist resort. The turismo (☎ 089-31 22 17) on the seafront Avenida Infante de Sagres can offer accommodation options (though in high season the up-market choices are invariably booked out). It's open daily from 9.30 am to 12.30 pm and 2 to 7 pm.

There's a French consulate (☎ 31 44 75) at nearby Lusotur-Vilamoura.

Getting There & Away
There are regular bus connections from Quarteira to Vilamoura, Faro, Albufeira and Loulé, as well as three Linha Litoral services daily during the week to/from Lagos, and four daily alta qualidade express services to Lisbon (taking five hours).

ALBUFEIRA
• *pop 22,000* • *postcode 8200* • *area code* ☎ *089*
This once-pretty fishing village now epitomises the worst of Algarve tourism, catering almost entirely to the package-tour brigade with overpriced restaurants, raucous bars and discos, and ugly towers of apartment hotels and holiday flats on all the surrounding hillsides. True, the beaches are still pleasant and there is at least a little character left in the old town's steep and narrow back streets and its small fishing harbour. And there's certainly a lively resort atmosphere during the summer, with buskers and hawkers in the street by day and plenty of late-night entertainment.

If you want to forget you're in Portugal (you'll hear more British and German than Portuguese), Albufeira may be just the ticket for a hassle-free holiday with guaranteed bacon-and-egg breakfasts, beer on tap and football on TV.

Orientation
The bus station is on Avenida da Liberdade, in the north of town, 10 minutes walk from the turismo and five minutes from the town's focal point, Largo Engenheiro Duarte Pacheco, where most of the cafés, bars and restaurants are clustered. The main street is Rua 5 de Outubro. The train station is an inconvenient six km north, reached by shuttle bus from the bus station (see Getting Around).

Information
Tourist Office The surly turismo (☎ 51 21 44) is at the southern end of Rua 5 de Outubro, near the tunnel to the beach. In summer it's open daily from 9.30 am to 7 pm (in winter it closes for lunch from 12.30 pm to 2 pm on Mondays, Fridays and weekends).

Money In and around Largo Engenheiro Duarte Pacheco you'll find plenty of banks with Multibanco ATMs, and several 'no-commission' (but often low exchange rate) private exchange bureaus.

ALGARVE

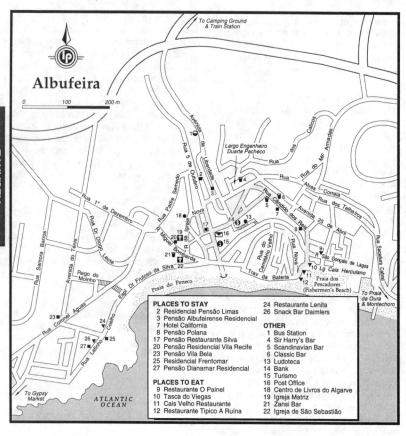

Albufeira

0   100   200 m

PLACES TO STAY
2 Residencial Pensão Limas
3 Pensão Albufeirense Residencial
7 Hotel California
8 Pensão Polana
17 Pensão Restaurante Silva
20 Pensão Residencial Vila Recife
23 Pensão Vila Bela
25 Residencial Frentomar
27 Pensão Dianamar Residencial

PLACES TO EAT
9 Restaurante O Painel
10 Tasca do Viegas
11 Cais Velho Restaurante
12 Restaurante Tipico A Ruína

24 Restaurante Lenita
26 Snack Bar Daimlers

OTHER
1 Bus Station
4 Sir Harry's Bar
5 Scandinavian Bar
6 Classic Bar
13 Ludoteca
14 Bank
15 Turismo
16 Post Office
18 Centro de Livros do Algarve
19 Igreja Matriz
21 Zansi Bar
22 Igreja de São Sebastião

Post & Communications The post office next to the turismo is open weekdays only, from 9 am to 12.30 pm and 2 to 6 pm.

Bookshops For second-hand books in languages from English to Swahili, check out Centro de Livros do Algarve (☎ 51 37 73), at Rua da Igreja Nova 6, and at Loja 16 of the Centro Commercial shopping arcade. The kiosks around Largo Engenheiro Duarte Pacheco stock a wide range of international newspapers and magazines.

Childcare There's a Ludoteca kindergarten

(see Childcare in the Facts for the Visitor chapter) on Travessa Pedro Samora, just off Largo Engenheiro Duarte Pacheco. It's open daily from 9 am to 12.30 pm and from 2 to 7 pm.

Medical Services The 24-hour centro de saúde (☎ 58 69 33) is two km north of town on the road to the train station. The nearest major hospital is in Faro.

Emergency The police station (☎ 51 54 20) is on Rua dos Caliços.

Beaches

Forget culture in Albufeira: people come here mainly to swim, sunbathe, eat and drink (and drink and drink, if the number of bars is any indication). The town's beach, **Praia do Peneco**, through the tunnel near the turismo, is pleasant enough, but for more local flavour, head five minutes east to **Praia dos Pescadores** (Fishermen's Beach, also called Praia dos Barcos). It still has a hint of Albufeira's fishing past, with fishermen mending their nets beside their high-prowed and brightly painted boats. But it's also become *the* place for some trendy bars and seafood restaurants (see Places to Eat).

Further afield – both east and west of town – are numerous beautifully rugged coves and bays, though the nearest are heavily developed and often crowded. The easiest to reach is **Praia da Oura**, a couple of km to the east (30 minutes on foot; follow Avenida 25 de Abril and climb the steps at the end to reach the road to the beach). The two-km strip of restaurants and bars along the road north of the Praia da Oura to Montechoro has become almost as lively as the centre of Albufeira itself.

Between Praia da Oura and **Praia da Falésia**, 10 km to the east, is a string of less crowded beaches, including **Balaia** and **Olhos de Água**, all accessible by local bus (a dozen every weekday to Olhos de Água, all but three of which continue to Praia da Falésia).

One of the best beaches to the west, **Praia da Galé**, about nine km away, is a centre for jet-skiing and water-skiing. There's no direct bus service to this beach or the others en route, though local buses to Portimão do run along the main road about two km above the beaches.

Activities

Summertime activities in Albufeira include tourist-oriented **bullfights** held from Easter to September every Saturday at 5 pm in the Praia da Oura bullring, and **live dance** or **music shows** every night in Largo Engenheiro Duarte Pacheco.

For more adventurous trips out of Albu-feira, ask any travel agency about **mountain-bike**, **canoe** and **jeep excursions** organised by BTT Aventura (☎ 54 18 34, ☎ 58 89 79), which can also arrange five or seven-day expeditions around the Algarve and Alentejo.

Among several local jeep safari outfits are Zebra Safari (☎ & fax 58 87 96) and Riosul (☎ 80 72 58). Riosul does a day-long 'Super Safari', which also includes a cruise down the Rio Guadiana, for 8600$00, including lunch.

Travel agents can also arrange trips to the **Zoomarine** aquatic park at Guia, eight km north-west of Albufeira on the N125 (for more on Zoomarine see Activities in this chapter's introduction).

Special Events

The major local festival is the Festa da Ourada on 15 August, honouring the fishermen's patron saint, Nossa Senhora de Ourada (Our Lady of the Oracle) with a beach procession.

Places to Stay

During the high season, accommodation in Albufeira is difficult to get without prior reservation.

Camping The nearest camping ground is the well-equipped *Parque de Campismo de Albufeira* (☎ 58 95 05; fax 58 76 33), near Alpouvar, two km north of town off the Estrada de Ferreiras (the road to the train station).

Private Rooms The turismo keeps a list of quartos, most costing 3500$00 to 5000$00 for a double.

Pensões & Residencials Budget residencials include the central *Residencial Pensão Limas* (☎ 51 40 25) at Rua da Liberdade 25 and the nearby *Pensão Albufeirense Residencial* (☎ 51 20 79) at No 18, both with doubles for about 5500$00. *Pensão Restaurante Silva* (☎ 51 26 69) at Travessa 5 de Outubro 21 (turn right out of the turismo and take the second left) also has cheap rooms but prefers that you take half-board (10,000$00) in high season.

A 10-minute walk west along the seafront brings you to several quieter residencials, including the quaintly old-fashioned *Pensão Dianamar Residencial* (☎ 51 23 79) at Rua Latino Coelho 36. With 14 simple rooms, it's a bargain at 4000$00 a double. *Residencial Frentomar* (☎ 51 20 05) at No 25 has fancier rooms (some with a sea view) for about 6000$00. *Pensão Vila Bela* (☎ 51 55 35), nearby at Rua Coronel Aguas 15, is even more popular (it's got a swimming pool), with doubles for 10,000$00.

In the same bracket is the more central *Pensão Residencial Vila Recife* (☎ 58 67 47; fax 58 71 82) at Rua Miguel Bombarda 12. It's a pretty place with a surprising 92 rooms at 10,000$00 a double, often block-booked by tour groups. *Pensão Polana* (☎ 58 71 68) at Rua Cândido dos Reis 32 is also popular with package tours – perhaps because it's only a short stagger away from a strip of nearby bars. Noisy doubles are 8500$00. The same management runs the up-market *Hotel California* (☎ 58 68 33; fax 58 68 50) at Rua Cândido dos Reis 12, where doubles soar in summer to at least 12,000$00.

Places to Eat
Spaghetti, fish and chips, pizzas, burgers, and bacon and eggs are everywhere. Finding decent alternatives at reasonable prices is more difficult, though there is a wide choice of cuisines, from standard Portuguese to Chinese, Indian, Italian and even Irish.

If you're prepared to walk 10 minutes from the centre, you'll come across little places like *Snack Bar Daimlers* at Rua Latino Coelho 24, which, despite its name, is as unpretentious as you can get, with prices from 700$00 for Portuguese favourites such as feijoada. Even the fussier *Restaurante Lenita* at No 14A has a reasonable tourist menu for 1500$00 and other dishes for under 1000$00.

Another good hunting ground is around Praia dos Pescadores (Fishermen's Beach), with some great seafood restaurants on the waterfront and less-expensive options in the backstreets. *Restaurante Típico A Ruína* (☎ 51 20 94), on Largo Cais Herculano, bags one of the best seaside spots. It isn't cheap but you get superb sea views from the rooftop terrace (or a pleasantly rustic setting inside). Nearby, *Cais Velho Restaurante* (☎ 51 40 87) offers a marginally calmer environment than its lively neighbour, *Tasca do Viegas*, and slightly cheaper prices for fresh seafood (boards outside list the daily catch).

In the street behind, Rua São Gonçalo de Lagos, check out *Restaurante O Painel* (☎ 51 36 61) for its varied menu of Italian and Portuguese dishes. *Sotavento* (☎ 51 27 19), in the same street at No 16, has reasonably priced Portuguese dishes served in a pretty azulejo-tiled restaurant.

Self-Catering The town's main fruit and vegetable market (open mornings only; closed Mondays) is on Rua dos Caliços, a 15-minute walk north of the centre.

Entertainment
Bars are a dime-a-dozen around Largo Engenheiro Duarte Pacheco and nearby Rua Cândido dos Reis. Nearly all offer happy hours (at various times of the day) and are open until at least 2 am.

For noise volume that drowns out conversation, check out *Classic Bar* and the nearby *Scandinavian Bar* on Rua Cândido dos Reis. *Zansi Bar* on Rua Miguel Bombarda (opposite Residencial Vila Recife) offers darts, snooker, satellite TV and Eurosport, as well as pizzas, hamburgers and English breakfasts. *Sir Harry's Bar* at Largo Engenheiro Duarte Pacheco 37 is one of the older British-style pubs, with the best of British brews on tap.

On Avenida Dr Francisco de Sá Carneiro (near the Vila Nova Shopping Centre) *Espelho Bar* (☎ 556 38) is said to be popular with the gay crowd, as is *Vogue* on Praia da Oura.

Things to Buy
A Gypsy market selling mostly clothes and shoes is held on the first and third Tuesday

of the month in the Orada district, about 1.5 km south-west of the centre (follow the seaside Rua Latino Coelho to its end, then turn right).

Getting There & Away

The main bus station (☎ 51 43 01, ☎ 58 97 55) is confusing and chaotic: express coaches (eg Linha Litoral services) tend to slip in and out very quickly. There are regular weekday services to Faro, Vilamoura and Quarteira (at least every hour), plus three express Linha Litoral services; about 10 buses a day to Portimão and Silves; and about seven a day to Loulé, Lagoa and Lagos. Weekend services are limited.

Long-distance coaches include five daily to Lisbon, plus four express alta qualidade services; two daily to Évora; and two daily services across the border to Huelva in Spain (with onward connections to Seville). The Huelva run (changing at Faro) takes about 3½ hours and costs 1550$00 (2640$00 to Seville).

Trains run seven times daily to Lagos (410$00) and a dozen times a day to Faro (280$00), but beware of the tedious local services. There are six trains daily to nearby Tunes, from where you can pick up connecting services to Lisbon (1755$00 in 2nd-class express).

Getting Around

To reach the train station, take the 155$00 *estação* shuttle bus, which leaves every hour or so from the main bus terminal on Avenida da Liberdade.

Among several car-rental agencies is Auto Jardim do Algarve (☎ 58 97 15; fax 58 77 80) in the Edifício 'Brisa' on Avenida da Liberdade.

CARVOEIRO

• *postcode 8400* • *area code* ☎ *082*

Flanked by cliffs, backed by hills and surrounded by an ever-expanding collection of shops, bars and restaurants, this small seaside resort five km south of Lagoa has grown in 20 years from a little-known fishing village to one of the Algarve's most

Elaborate honeycomb chimneys, dating from Moorish times, are one of the Algarve's visual trademarks.

popular self-catering holiday areas, with estates of foreign-owned villas sprawled across the hillsides. The town itself is a laid-back spot compared to resorts like Albufeira, though the summertime tourist invasion tends to suffocate the place.

Orientation & Information

Buses from Lagoa stop right by the beach, beside a small and practically useless turismo (☎ 35 77 28). The post office and several banks are on Rua dos Pescadores (the one-way road from Lagoa).

Beaches

The town's little beach, **Praia do Carvoeiro**, bordered by several cafés, is set in a picturesque cove. A km east on the coast road is **Algar Seco**, a favourite stop on the tour-bus itinerary thanks to its dramatic rock formations.

If you're looking for a decent swimming spot, it's worth continuing several km east along the main road, Estrada do Farol, to

Praia de Centianes, where the secluded cliff-wrapped beach is almost as dramatic as Algar Seco. Buses heading for Praia do Carvalho (nine a day from Lagoa, via Carvoeiro) pass nearby (ask for Colina Sol Aparthotel, the massive Moorish-style hotel on the clifftop).

Activities

For aquatic action, head for the Slide & Splash **water-slide park**, open daily from 10 am to 7 pm. It's two km west of Lagoa (though its access road from the N125 is just 300m west of Lagoa).

If you play **golf**, you have a choice of three nearby courses: the 18-hole Vale da Pinta (☎ 526 70), set in a centenarian olive grove; the neighbouring 9-hole Quinta do Gramacho (☎ 526 70), part of the Carvoeiro Club west of town; and the challenging 9-hole Clube de Golfe do Vale de Milho (☎ 35 85 02) near Praia de Centianes, east of town, with some of the Algarve's best-value play (about 2500$00 for 9 holes).

At Centro Hípico Casa Galaraz (☎ 35 80 55), just off the Estrada de Benagil a few km north-east of town, **horse riding** (including a Shetland pony for the kids) is available.

At nearby Lagoa you can visit the Adega Cooperativa **winery** for a taste of the Algarve's best wine (check opening times with the turismo).

Places to Stay

You'll be lucky to find anywhere to stay in high season. The turismo has a list of places but no prices. Among the cheapest (and best placed) private rooms are those in an attractive complex of flats on Rua da Igreja (the road climbing up east of the beach) that belong to a Canadian woman, *Brigitte Lemieux* (☎ 35 63 18). These cost 8000$00 a double (50,000$00 for a week) with sea view, fridge and toaster. Similarly priced are the five rooms at the nearby *Pensão Baselli* (☎ 35 71 59), just off Rua da Igreja. In the off season, prices in even the swishest hotels can drop 50%.

Places to Eat

There are plenty of places to choose from both in town and in the Monte Carvoeiro villa complex above the beach to the west. *Curva do Casino* (☎ 35 75 96) at Rua do Casino 36, near the post office, is a friendly little place popular for its fish dishes. Slightly more up-market is the bright white *O Chefe António* (☎ 35 89 37) on Estrada do Farol, where you can indulge yourself with dishes such as prawns flambé (1800$00) or paella (1200$00).

For something different, try the *Malaysian Inn* in Monte Carvoeiro, which serves up curries from 1000$00, as well as vegetarian dishes and delicious desserts. Its outdoor patio makes a great play area for kids.

Entertainment

Among Carvoeiro's bars, check out *Sinfonia* (☎ 356 00), in Rua dos Pescadores, for its live music (Portuguese and Brazilian) on Thursdays and Saturdays; *Sully's* (☎ 35 77 87), near the beach at Rua do Paraiso, for its British beers and breakfasts; and the *Long Bar*, on Rua dos Pescadores, for its lively young crowd.

Things to Buy

At Porches, five km east of Lagoa on the N125 (take any Albufeira-bound bus from Lagoa), you'll find some of the Algarve's best quality pottery: hand-painted ceramics with a distinctively rural style.

Getting There & Away.

Buses run to Caravoeiro at least five times a day from Portimão and almost every hour from Lagoa.

Getting Around

Taxis are available at the bottom of Estrada do Farol. You can rent bicycles, scooters and motorbikes from Motorent (☎ 35 65 51). For car hire call the Travel Shop (☎ 35 79 47).

SILVES

• pop 33,000 • postcode 8300 • area code ☎ 082
It's hard to believe now, but this dozy town beside the Rio Arade, 15 km north-east of

Portimão, was once the Moorish capital of the Algarve. Its imposing red stone castle towers above the surrounding orange and almond groves, a powerful reminder of the past.

History
From the mid-11th to mid-13th centuries, Shelb (or Xelb) as it was then known, rivalled Lisbon in prosperity and influence: according to the 12th-century Arab geographer Idrisi, there was a population of 30,000, a port and shipyards, and 'attractive buildings and well-furnished bazaars'.

Its downfall began in June 1189, when Dom Sancho I laid siege to it, supported by a horde of (mostly English) hooligan crusaders who had been persuaded (with the promise of loot) to pause in their journey to Jerusalem and give Sancho a hand. The Moors holed up inside their impregnable castle but after three hot months of harassment they finally ran out of water and were forced to surrender. Sancho was all for mercy and honour, but the crusaders would have none of it: they stripped the Moors of their possessions as they left (including the clothes on their backs), tortured those remaining and wrecked the town.

Two years later the Moors exacted their revenge by recapturing the place. It wasn't until 1249 that the Christians gained control once and for all. But by then Silves was a shadow of its former self.

Orientation & Information
Silves train station is two km south of town (a mostly downhill walk for those arriving). Long-distance buses use the riverfront road at the bottom of town, crossing the Rio Arade on a modern bridge slightly upriver from a picturesque 13th-century footbridge. It's a steep but short climb from here to the switched-on turismo (☎ 44 25 55) on Rua 25 de Abril. It's open from 9.30 am to 12.30 pm and 2 to 7 pm (to 5.30 pm at weekends), and can help with accommodation.

Castelo
The castle is, of course, the town's highlight, commanding great views over the town and surrounding countryside. Restored in 1835, its chunky red sandstone walls enclose a rather dull interior where unkempt gardens serve as a playground for hordes of visiting school kids who clamber over a statue of Afonso III (who finally recaptured Silves from the Moors in 1249). Archaeological digs are in progress to discover more of the site's Roman and pre-Roman past. The Moors' occupation is recalled by a deep well and a vaulted water cistern (still in use today). The castle is open daily from 9 am to 7.30 pm; entry is 250$00.

Sé
Just below the castle is the Sé (cathedral), built in 1189 on the site of an earlier mosque, rebuilt after the 1242 Reconquista and subsequently restored several times. The stark, fortress-like building has only a few of its original Gothic touches left, including the nave and aisles. Apart from several fine tombs (probably of 13th-century crusaders) there's little of interest inside. It's open daily from 8.30 am to 1 pm and 2.30 to 6 pm.

Museu de Arqueologia
In Rua das Portas de Loulé is an archaeological museum offering some intriguing glimpses into Silves' illustrious history. Its centrepiece is an original Moorish water cistern and well. The museum is open daily from 10 am to 6 pm, and admission is 350$00.

Special Events
In late July or early August the slightly rowdy Festival da Cerveja (beer festival) is held within the castle walls to the sound of brass bands and folk-dance groups – the closest Silves gets to recalling those unruly summer months under siege.

Places to Stay
The old-fashioned *Residencial Sousa* (☎ 44 25 02), in the heart of the old town at Rua Samoura Barros 17, has spacious singles/doubles for 3500$00/4000$00. Similarly priced but noisier is *Pensão-Restaurante*

Ladeiro on the N124 across the river. Another restaurant-cum-hotel is the eye-catching *Residencial Ponte Romana* (☎ 44 32 75) beside the old bridge, with doubles for 5000$00 to 6000$00. Right on Silves' historic doorstep, at the castle entrance, the *Estabelecimentos Dom Sancho* (☎ 44 24 37) has a few rooms (for about 6000$00) above its busy café and souvenir shop.

If you're after rural peace and quiet, head five km north-east (en route to São Bartolomeu de Messines) to Sitio São Estevão, where you'll find the Italian-run *Quinta do Rio* (☎ & fax 44 24 37), a recently restored house set among orange groves, with plenty of space for kids to romp around. Doubles range from 6000$00 to 8000$00 (including breakfast).

Places to Eat

You'll find the cheapest fare in the string of restaurants beside the mercado municipal down by the river, many specialising in grilled fish dishes and piri-piri chicken. *A Adega Snack Bar & Restaurant* (☎ 44 21 43), set back from the road opposite the old bridge, offers bargain dishes from 500$00. Across the river on the N124, *Restaurante Ladeiro* (☎ 44 28 70) packs in the locals at lunch time with hearty Portuguese standards.

Restaurants in the town itself are more geared to tourists, though *Restaurante Rio* (☎ 44 26 82), at Rua Comendador Vitarinho 23, has long been famed in the Algarve for its seafood and shellfish. This is *the* place to try arroz de marisco. *Café Inglês* (☎ 44 25 85) has its own tree-shaded terrace just below the castle entrance, a relaxing place to indulge in home-made soups, fruit juices and cakes (there's an indoor bar and restaurant too).

Getting There & Away

Seven buses a day (five at weekends) shuttle between Silves and its train station, two km to the south, timed to meet some of the dozen or so trains a day that arrive from Lagos and Vila Real de Santo António (via Faro). There are also regular bus connections from Albufeira (nine every weekday), Lagoa (11),

São Bartolomeu de Messines (nine) and Portimão (nine).

See Portimão for information on river cruises up the Rio Arade to Silves.

PORTIMÃO

• pop 40,000 • postcode 8500 • area code ☎ 082

This unattractive fishing port and sardine canning centre 16 km east of Lagos hogs the west bank of the Rio Arade three km inland from Praia da Rocha. Portimão's past sounds rather more glorious than its present: inhabited by successive settlers – Phoenicians, Greeks and Carthaginians (Hannibal himself is said to have set foot here) – it was called Portos Magnus by the Romans and fought over by Moors and Christians. In 1189 crusaders under Dom Sancho I sailed up the Rio Arade from here to besiege Silves. The 1755 earthquake practically flattened the place.

Today it's the Algarve's second most important fishing port (after Olhão) and a popular destination for day-trippers from nearby holiday resorts, who come mainly for the shopping. In addition to a clutch of quality handicraft shops in the streets around the turismo, there's also a Gypsy market, one of the Algarve's biggest and best (see Markets).

The only other reasons to come here are to take a boat trip upriver to Silves or to enjoy a slap-up sardine lunch at the riverside 'Sardine Quay' before exploring the town's small old quarter. The riverside esplanade is a cheerful place to hang out, with its cafés, gardens and ubiquitous knots of gossiping men (but beware the sleazy time-share sales-people, and con men selling amazingly cheap 'gold' rings).

It's hardly worth an overnight stay when far more attractive choices are available in nearby Praia da Rocha, Lagos and Silves.

Orientation

Two highway bridges cross the Rio Arade estuary to Portimão: one built in 1876, apparently with iron left over from the Eiffel Tower, and a dramatic modern construction completed in 1991. Drivers should be pre-

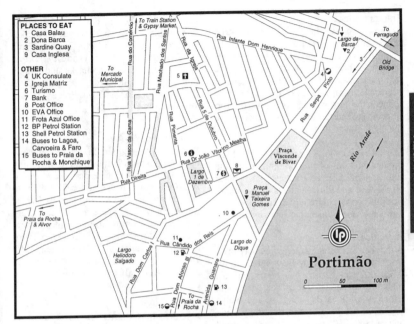

PLACES TO EAT
1 Casa Balau
2 Dona Barca
3 Sardine Quay
9 Casa Inglesa

OTHER
4 UK Consulate
5 Igreja Matriz
6 Turismo
7 Bank
8 Post Office
10 EVA Office
11 Frota Azul Office
12 BP Petrol Station
13 Shell Petrol Station
14 Buses to Lagoa, Carvoeira & Faro
15 Buses to Praia da Rocha & Monchique

Portimão

ALGARVE

pared for a devilish one-way system that shunts you all over the place.

Praça Manuel Teixeira Gomes is the main square and central rendezvous point, bordered by cafés, shops and gardens. There's no bus station, but buses stop at various points along two poorly signposted main roads running south-west from this square, parallel to the river: north-bound Avenida Guanare (look for the Shell petrol station) and south-bound Rua Dom Afonso III (look for the BP station). Information and tickets for EVA, Intersul and Eurolines services are available at the EVA office (☎ 41 81 20) just off the square at Largo do Dique 3. There is a Frota Azul bus office down the road to the west.

The train station is awkwardly located on the northern edge of town, with no connecting bus services. On foot it's 15 minutes away on mostly pedestrianised streets, including the main shopping street, Rua do Comércio.

Information

There is a marginally helpful turismo (☎ 236 95) on Rua Dr João Vitorino Mealha, opposite Largo 1 de Dezembro, which is a 10-minute walk from the nearest bus stops. It's open daily from 9.30 am to 12.30 pm and 2 to 6 pm.

There are plenty of Multibanco ATMs around this square and nearby Praça Manuel Teixeira Gomes. The post office is also by the praça, on the corner of Rua 5 de Outubro. The police can be contacted on ☎ 41 75 10.

Hungry net-surfers should check out *Casa Inglesa* (☎ 41 62 90) on Praça Manuel Teixeira Gomes, which bills itself as a cybercafé.

There are at least three consulates in or near town, including an Austrian office (☎ 41 62 02) on Rua Engenheiro José de Bívar, Praia da Rocha, and a British office (☎ 41 78 00; fax 41 78 06) at Largo Francisco A Maurício 7, which is open weekdays from 10 am to noon and 3 to 4.30 pm.

ALGARVE

Things to See
The town's parish church, the **Igreja Matriz**, stands on high ground a couple of blocks uphill from the turismo and features a 14th-century Gothic portal – all that remains of the original structure after the 1755 earthquake. More interesting echoes of the past can be found in the narrow streets of the **old fishing quarter** around Largo da Barca, just before the old highway bridge.

Markets Portimão's Gypsy market is held on the first Monday of every month behind the train station. A flea market also takes place on the first and third Sundays of the month (mornings only) in front of the new mercado municipal on Avenida São João de Deus.

Activities
A number of operators along the quay offer **boat trips** upriver to Silves for about 2500$00 per person (4½ hours return), including lunch and soft drinks. Other boat trips, as well as day-long guided walks (5000$00 per person) and safaris by mule and cart (8000$00 per person), are organised by an outfit called Tempo Passa (☎ 41 71 10 daytime, ☎ 47 12 41 evenings), which has a stall in Praça Manuel Teixeira Gomes.

Horse riding is available at Centro Hípico Vale de Ferro (☎ 964 44; fax 964 43), near Mexilhoeira Grande (turn off the N125 4.2 km west of Portimão). There's a free pick-up service from Portimão as long as there are at least two of you riding for a minimum of two hours. The centre organises day trips as well as overnight excursions into the Serra de Monchique.

Places to Stay
There is a pousada de juventude (☎ 857 04) awkwardly located in the village of Coca Maravilhas, two or three km north of Portimão. You can get at least halfway there on any bus to Monchique.

Places to Eat
The best hunting ground is in the old quarter, especially along the 'sardine quay', a river-side strip of stalls and humble restaurants which sell some of the best charcoal-grilled sardines in the Algarve. Two more up-market seafood restaurants in nearby Largo da Barca are *Casa Balau* (☎ 233 51) and *Dona Barca* (☎ 841 89). For cakes, snacks and simple Portuguese fare, head for the popular *Casa Inglesa* (☎ 41 62 90) on Praça Manuel Teixeira Gomes.

Getting There & Away
Portimão has regular bus connections to other destinations in the Algarve, including half a dozen services on weekdays to Albufeira and Faro, eight services daily to Monchique and hourly services to Lagos, Silves and Alvor. There are at least eight express buses a day to Lisbon. Some regional coach-tour operators, including the Faro-based Mega Tur (☎ 089-80 76 48) and MB Tours (☎ 082-260 45 or toll-free ☎ 0500-2369), offer half-day shopping trips to Portimão.

AROUND PORTIMÃO
Praia da Rocha
This vast stretch of sand backed by towering ochre-red cliffs and scattered with bizarre rocky outcrops was one of the first beaches in the Algarve to be patronised by overseas tourists in the 1950s and 60s. Although ugly ranks of hotels and apartments, shops, bars, casinos and discos have long since destroyed its charm and tranquillity, the beach resort still has a few old mansions and guesthouses (some dating from the 19th century) that give it a touch of class. And the beach itself is still one of the most impressive in the Algarve.

Orientation & Information The esplanade, Rua Tomás Cabreira, high above the beach and with most of the shops, hotels and restaurants, is the resort's main drag. At the eastern end is the shell of the Fortaleza da Santa Catarina, the fort built in the 16th century to stop pirates and invaders sailing up the Rio Arade to Portimão harbour.

Opposite the fort is the turismo (☎ 222 90), open daily during summer from 9.30 am to 8 pm. The post office and a taxi rank are at the centre of the esplanade, near the junction with the Portimão road, Estrada Praia da Rocha. Here, in the Hotel da Rocha, is a branch of Top Tours (☎ 41 75 52) where you can cash American Express cheques free of commission charges.

The telephone code for Praia da Rocha is ☎ 082.

Beaches Various steps along the esplanade lead down to the beach. If you don't want to join the crowds, head for the west end where a tunnel called Buraco da Avô leads through the rocks to a series of smaller, more secluded beaches.

Activities Pandatours (☎ 41 55 41), based at the Residencial São José (see Places to Stay) offers both coach tours (to as far away as Évora and Lisbon) and day-long jeep safaris for about 6500$00 per person. Fishing safaris are organised by Foley's Pub (☎ 41 40 03).

Places to Stay Not surprisingly, bargain accommodation is nonexistent here, unless you come in winter. Pensão or hotel accommodation is almost impossible to find in high season without prior reservations, though there are plenty of private quartos (ask at the turismo) at about 5500$00 a double.

Pensão Residencial Solar Penguin (☎ & fax 243 08) is an old villa, set back from the esplanade on Rua António Feu (just beyond Hotel Bela Vista), which has been run by the same Englishwoman for 30 years. It has seen better times, but the musty atmosphere and décor are redolent of Praia da Rocha's sedate early days. Double rooms (a few with sea views) cost about 8500$00 including breakfast. Cheaper (about 7000$00 a double), but with less character and more night-time disco noise, is *Pensão Toca* (☎ 240 37) on the backstreet Rua Engenheiro Francisco Bívar. On the same street is the equally simple *Residencial São José* (☎ 240 35), where doubles go for about 8000$00.

In the upper price bracket are two century-old gems. The *Albergaria Vila Lido* (☎ & fax 242 46) on Avenida Tomás Cabreira (next to the turismo) is a delightful 19th-century mansion with a dozen rooms spiralling to 16,000$00 for a double in high season. Bagging the best beach view from the middle of the esplanade is *Hotel Bela Vista* (☎ 240 55; fax 41 53 69), a whimsical turn-of-the-century creation converted to a hotel in 1936, with marvellously worked wooden ceilings and 19th-century azulejos. Only two of the 14 rooms lack a sea view. In much demand, its doubles are 23,000$00 (but in winter drop to as little as 10,000$00).

Places to Eat There are plenty of snack bars and cafés along the esplanade, as well as several on the beach. *Lena's Croissanteria*, on the esplanade opposite Hotel Bela Vista, is a pleasant spot for breakfast, vegetarian dishes, ice cream or crêpes. The *Pensão Residencial Solar Penguin* serves good crêpes too (as well as main dishes) on its well-hidden terrace halfway down the cliff to the left of the pensão.

For a change from standard Portuguese fare, try the North Indian and Balti cuisine at *Maharaja da Rocha* (☎ 41 32 68) at the turismo end of the esplanade; or the nearby *La Dolce Vita* (☎ 41 68 12) for fresh homemade pastas. Seafood restaurants are inevitably expensive, though some, such as the elegant *Serra e Mar* (☎ 26 78 10) on Rua António Feu (opposite Hotel Bela Vista), offer a reasonable tourist menu for around 2300$00.

Entertainment You won't have any trouble finding a decent bar with entertainment on tap. Often run by Irish or English people, they cater to all age groups, offering everything from darts and quiz nights to satellite TV and live music. Check out *Man of Aran* in the Hotel Atlântico at the western end of the esplanade for its Irish atmosphere and brews, or the popular *Shaker Bar* opposite Pensão Solar Penguin for some boppier beats.

Getting There & Away Praia da Rocha buses leave Portimão every quarter-hour in summer until midnight; the fare is 165$00 (85$00 if you buy a block of 10 tickets). The bus terminus in Praia da Rocha is by the fort, with another stop behind the central Hotel Rocha on Rua Engenheiro José Bívar. The last bus back to Portimão leaves around 11.30 pm.

Praia da Rocha is on the itinerary of several regional coach tours. You can also pick up day trips from here to other destinations in the Algarve, and even to Seville in Spain.

Getting Around There are several car and motorbike-rental outfits, including Motorent (☎ & fax 834 95) on Rua Caetano Feu near the Hotel da Rocha.

Alvor

Once a quiet little fishing village – with a history that goes back to Carthaginian days – Alvor and its huge beach are now a popular day-trip destination from Portimão (nine km to the north-east) and its nearby resorts: the narrow cobbled lanes at the heart of the village are chock-a-block with bars and restaurants. The large **market** held on the second Tuesday of every month is another big attraction.

Down by the harbour there's still some traditional atmosphere, with crusty old fishermen hanging around and restaurants sizzling sardines on outdoor grills for lunch – try the bright and cheerful *Tony and Ria's* for a good-value 1500$00 lunch of sardines, soup, salad and wine. The beach itself also has a string of restaurants, many of which specialise in the clams that are gathered here at low tide.

Getting There & Away From Portimão there are at least a dozen buses a day to Alvor (20 minutes). It's a five-minute walk from the bus stop to the harbour.

The Windward Coast & the Costa Vicentina

LAGOS
• *pop 22,000* • *postcode 8600* • *area code* ☎ *082*

Heaving with young people all summer, bursting with restaurants, boutiques, bars and clubs, and adjacent to some of the Algarve's best beaches and most dramatic coastline, cheerful Lagos has acquired a reputation as a good-time town.

Contrasting with this modern-day persona is its honoured history as the point of origin for most voyages during Portugal's extraordinary Age of Discoveries. Aside from sturdy town walls and the layout of the steep and narrow streets, only a few fragments of this period survived the devastating 1755 earthquake.

History

Phoenicians and Greeks appreciated this port at the mouth of the muddy Rio Bensafrim. Later, the Romans called it Lacobriga and the Moors called it Zawaia. Afonso III took it back from the Moors in 1241, and it was from here that the Portuguese carried on harassing the Muslims of North Africa. In 1415 a giant fleet set sail from Lagos under the command of the 21-year-old *infante* Prince Henry to seize Ceuta in Morocco – and set the stage for Portugal's groping exploration of the west African coast and its ambitious Age of Discoveries.

Lagos shipyards built and launched Prince Henry's caravels, and Henry split his time between his own trading company here and his school of navigation at Sagres. Local boy Gil Eanes left here in command of the first ship to round west Africa's Cape Bojador in 1434. Others continued to bring back information about the African coast – along with ivory, gold, and slaves. Lagos has the dubious distinction of having hosted (in 1444) the first sale of black Africans as slaves to Europeans, and it subsequently grew into a centre of the slave trade.

It was also from here in 1578 that Dom Sebastião, along with the cream of Portuguese nobility and an army of Portuguese, Spanish, Dutch and German buccaneers, left on his disastrous crusade to Christianise North Africa, ending in debacle at Alcácer-Quibir in Morocco. Sir Francis Drake inflicted heavy damage on the town a few years later in 1587.

Lagos served as the Algarve's high-profile capital from 1576 until the 1755 earthquake, which flattened it and brought its illustrious career to an end.

Orientation

The N125 highway comes right in along the riverfront as Avenida dos Descobrimentos. Drivers are strongly advised to leave their cars in the car park here and avoid getting trapped in the inner town's web of narrow, steep, cobbled, one-way lanes.

A breezy promenade lines the Rio Bensafrim, running north for about a km from the fortress on the Ponta da Bandeira. At the far end a pedestrian drawbridge crosses the river to the marina and the *docapesca* (fishing harbour). Meia Praia beach comes right up to the river mouth near the fishing harbour.

The administrative centre of Lagos is pedestrianised Praça Gil Eames (say 'zheel yenesh'), which is ringed by the town hall, the post office, banks and shops. At the centre is a ridiculous statue of Dom Sebastião looking like a teenage girl astronaut.

The long-distance bus station, just north of the walled centre, is an eight-minute walk from Praça Gil Eames. The train station, at the back of the marina, is a 12-minute walk from Praça Gil Eames.

Information

Tourist Offices One of Portugal's least helpful turismos (☎ 76 30 31) is on Rua Marquês de Pombal, a few steps from Praça Gil Eames. It's open on weekdays from 9.30 am to 12.30 pm and 2 to 5 pm (later in summer), and probably on weekends but with no fixed schedule.

For entertainment information you'll do

Portuguese caravels revolutionised sailing – their triangular sails could pivot around the mast, allowing the ships to reach great speeds.

better with the privately produced, frequently updated free map called *Out & About in Lagos*, available from better residencials, shops and bars. For practical help – with accommodation, car rental, babysitting, medical assistance, repairs, even flights – try the Florentina agency (☎ 76 42 86, ☎ 76 88 06) at Rua Dr Joaquim Tello 8.

Money Among other Multibanco ATMs and currency exchanges are two on Praça Gil Eames: Caixa Geral de Depósitos and Banco Nacional Ultramarino.

Post & Communications The central post and telephone office, open weekdays from 9 am to 6 pm, is on Rua das Portas de Portugal, just off Praça Gil Eames.

Bookshops The tourist-oriented Loja do Livro bookshop at Rua Dr Joaquim Tello 3 is open from 10 am to 1 pm and 3 to 7 pm, at least on weekdays.

Laundry A fairly quick laundry service is available at the youth hostel (see Places to Stay), and there is a laundry on Rua Conselheiro Joaquim Machado.

Medical & Emergency Services The Lagos District Hospital (☎ 76 30 34, ☎ 76 28 06) is on Rua do Castelo dos Governadores, just off Praça da República. The central police station (☎ 76 29 30) is opposite the town museum on Rua General Alberto Silveira.

Historic Lagos
Most sites of historical interest are clustered

at the southern end of the old town around Praça da República, also called Praça do Infante. The statue of Henry the Navigator was erected in 1960 on the 500th anniversary of his death, and to mark the opening of the Avenida dos Descobrimentos.

Igreja de Santo António & Town Museum
A block back from the Praça da República on Rua General Alberto Silveira is Lagos' main historical attraction, the little Igreja de Santo António, with an astonishing interior of gilded, carved wood, a Manueline extravaganza of ripening grapes and beaming

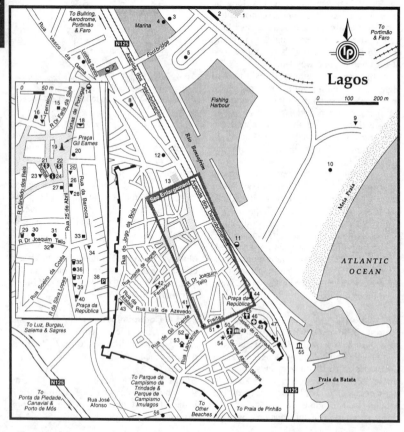

cherubs. The dome and the azulejo panels were installed after the 1755 earthquake.

Enter from the street or from the adjacent town museum (☎ 76 23 01), an odd but appealing collection of azulejos, 16th-century grave markers, pickled fetuses, coins, handicrafts and church vestments. It's open daily, except Mondays and holidays, from 9.30 am to 12.30 pm and 2 to 5 pm, for 320$00.

Slave Market The art gallery at an arcaded corner of the Praça da República is in the town's former customs house, the site (though probably not the original building) of Europe's first black slave market. You won't find any plaques or postcards – the authorities are naturally reluctant to call attention to this darker side of Portugal's golden age.

Igreja de Santa Maria The St Mary (or Misericórdia) Church facing the Praça da República is of interest mainly for its 16th-century entrance; most of the rest dates from the mid-19th century. Check out the spacey mural behind the altar.

Town Walls Just south of Praça da República is a restored section of the stout town walls, built (atop earlier versions) during the reigns of Manuel I and João III in the 16th century. In fact they extend intermittently, with at least six bastions, for about 1.5 km around the central town.

From an elaborate **Manueline window** in the wall adjacent to the present-day hospital, tradition has it that Dom Sebastião attended an open-air Mass and spoke to the assembled nobility before leading them to defeat at Alcácer-Quibir.

In the archway just to the left is a small **shrine** to the Algarve's only home-grown saint, São Gonçalo de Lagos, a 14th-century fisherman's son who, as an Augustinian monk, was known for his stirring sermons, hymns and writings.

Fortaleza da Ponta da Bandeira This little fortress at the southern end of the promenade

ALGARVE

PLACES TO STAY
15 Residencial Lagosmar
26 Residencial Marazul
27 Residencial Caravela
33 Residencial Baía & Residencial Rubi-Mar
53 Pousada de Juventude de Lagos

PLACES TO EAT
9 Linda Bar
13 Mercado Municipal
17 Bar Na Forja
23 Restaurante Kalunga
25 O Cantinho Algarvio
28 Restaurante O Miradouro
34 Barroca Jazz Bar & Restaurante
39 Bar Vitaminas
41 Mullens
42 Casa Rosa Bar
43 Restaurante A Muralha

OTHER
1 Saturday Market
2 Train Station
3 Bom Dia
4 Bluewater Sportsfishing
5 Espadarte do Sul
6 Safari Moto
7 Bus Station
8 City Tour
10 Sailboard Rentals
11 Ferry to Meia Praia
12 Avis
14 Taxi Stand
16 Laundry
18 Post & Telecom Office
19 Statue of Dom Sebastião
20 Town Hall
21 Bank
22 Bank
24 Turismo
29 Rosko's
30 Centro de Línguas
31 Florentina Agency
32 Loja do Livro Bookshop
35 Zanzibar
36 Motoride Cycle Rental
37 Stones
38 Car Park
40 Art Gallery in Old Customs House
44 Statue of Henry the Navigator
45 Igreja de Santa Maria
46 Lagos District Hospital
47 Archway & Shrine to São Gonçalo de Lagos
48 Manueline Window
49 Town Museum
50 Igreja de Santo António
51 Centro Cultural
52 Taverna Velha
54 Police
55 Fortaleza da Ponta da Bandeira & Portuguese Discoveries Museum
56 Motoride Cycle Rental

was built in the 17th century to protect the port. It now houses a museum on the Portuguese discoveries. Both are open daily, except Mondays, from 10 am to 6 pm; entry is 320$00 (half-price for youth-card holders).

Market
Lagos' big Gypsy market is held on the morning of the first Saturday of each month, behind the train station.

Beaches
Meia Praia, the vast expanse of sand to the east of town, has sailboard rentals and water-skiing lessons, plus lots of laid-back restaurants and beach bars. South of town the beaches – Batata, Pinhão, Dona Ana, Camilo and others – are smaller, more secluded, lapped by calm waters and punctuated with amazing grottoes, coves and towers of coloured sandstone.

You can walk to most of them, or visit these and others, including Canavial and Porto de Mós on the south-facing headlands, by boat (see Boat Trips). Canavial and Porto de Mós are also accessible from the road to the Atalaia headland. Further west is the fine Praia da Luz (see Lagos to Sagres).

Ponta da Piedade
Aside from the beaches, Lagos' big geophysical attraction is 'Point Piety', a dramatic wedge of headland protruding south from Lagos, with contorted, polychrome sandstone cliffs and towers, complete with lighthouse and hundreds of nesting egrets. On a clear day you can see west to Carvoeiro and east to Sagres. It's three windswept km from town, on foot or by taxi. The surrounding area is brilliant with wild orchids in spring.

Bullfights
Tourist-oriented bullfights are staged on Saturdays in April and May at the bullring just north of town on the N120 road.

Other Activities
Tiffany's (☎ 082-693 95) is a **horse-riding** centre at Vale Grifo in Almádena, about 10

km west of Lagos on the N125; if you have no wheels, they'll come and get you in Lagos. Another centre is Quinta Paraiso (☎ 672 63, ☎ 675 07) at Fronteira, about seven km north of Lagos on the N120 road.

For a unique view of the coast, fly a **microlight** over it. These are available from the Aero Club de Lagos (☎ 76 29 06, ☎ 76 76 12), open daily from 10 am to 1 pm at the aerodrome, on the N125 about two km north-east of Lagos.

Boat Trips
Bom Dia (☎ 76 46 70; mobile ☎ 0931-81 07 61) runs near-shore trips on traditional schooners, with drinks, picnic, and stops for swimming and snorkelling. Tours available include a two-hour trip to the beaches and grottoes beneath Ponta da Piedade for 2000$00, a 3½-hour bay cruise for 3500$00, or an all-day sail to Sagres with a minibus tour of Cabo São Vicente for 7500$00. The office is in the marina's commercial centre.

Espadarte do Sul (☎ 76 18 20) does similar jaunts to the grottoes, plus snorkelling and big-game fishing trips. Its office faces the fishing harbour. Bluewater Sportsfishing (☎ 76 82 46; mobile ☎ 0931-82 00 44) specialises in half-day and all-day deep-sea fishing trips. It costs 10,000$00 for a day of fishing or 6000$00 if you're just watching, plus 1000$00 for lunch. Check marina berth C3 for this outfit.

Local fishermen offering motorboat jaunts to the grottoes also trawl for customers along the seaside promenade.

Language Courses Fancy a quick Portuguese language brush-up? Contact Centro de Línguas (Interlingua; ☎ & fax 76 10 70), upstairs at Rua Dr Joaquim Tello 32.

Places to Stay
In addition to a few pensões and residencials, Lagos abounds in resort-style hotels and albergarias (at least seven), motels (at least three) and rental apartment blocks. There are more places out on Meia Praia, and even a hotel on Praia Dona Ana. Most are filled to the gunwales in summer, though you can

always track down something adequate if you're only staying for a day or two.

Prices are very seasonal; they are highest from July through August or September, 10% to 20% lower in April-June and October, and 25% to 35% less the rest of the year. We give midsummer rates here.

Camping The small *Parque de Campismo da Trindade* (☎ 76 38 93), just 200m south of the Lançarote gate in the town walls, is run by the local football club. July-August rates are 450$00 per person, 450$00 to 600$00 per tent and 300$00 to 400$00 per car.

Upscale is the huge *Parque de Campismo Imulagos* (☎ 76 00 31; fax 76 00 35). Its 60 bungalows get booked out in summer, but those who have tents or caravans should have no problem finding a spot (there are about 1400 sites). There's also a market, laundrette, bar and restaurant. Sample August rates are 890$00 per person, 500$00 to 780$00 per tent and 400$00 per car; if you get lucky, a bungalow is 8000$00 for two. It's on the road to Porto de Mós, a 10 or 15-minute walk from town. From June through September there is also a free shuttle bus from the train station once an hour.

Hostels The *Pousada de Juventude de Lagos* (☎ 76 19 70), Rua Lançarote de Freitas 50, has 62 beds, kitchen facilities and a notice board that usually has a few useful tips about food, activities etc. It's open 24 hours a day.

Private Rooms Private, unlicensed quartos are plentiful in summer and their owners will harass you to distraction all over town; anyone wearing a daypack is a target. Figure on about 5000$00 for a double, though quality varies widely.

Residencials At the bottom of the price scale, the small, glum *Residencial Baía* (☎ 76 22 92), on the ground floor at Rua da Barocca 70, has adequate doubles with shower for 2500$00. We found few other places that could be called 'bottom-end' on the basis of summer prices. Upstairs at the

same address is the more comfortable *Residencial Rubi-Mar* (☎ 76 31 65), where a basic double without bath is about 5000$00 with breakfast, and some rooms have limited sea views. Book a week or so ahead in summer.

In the central pedestrian zone at Rua 25 de Abril 8 is the *Residencial Caravela* (☎ 76 33 61), where a plain double with bath is 5800$00 with breakfast. Across the way at No 13, the bigger *Residencial Marazul* (☎ 76 97 49; fax 76 99 60) has comfortable singles/doubles with shower for 6500$00/8000$00, or with bath for 8700$00/9000$00, including breakfast.

The friendly, professionally run *Residencial Lagosmar* (☎ 76 32 22; fax 76 73 24), at Rua Dr Faria da Silva 13, has 45 rooms with bath, TV and telephone for about 7000$00/9500$00, with breakfast.

Places to Eat

There's abundant good food in town, both Portuguese and international, and including some vegetarian fare.

Restaurants Tables spill into the pedestrianised streets around Praça Gil Eanes from a dozen tourist-oriented places of uneven quality, at prices 20% to 30% higher than elsewhere in town – sardines, potatoes or salad for 600$00, bacalhau for 1400$00, meaty specials for 1400$00 to 2000$00 or more. Of these, we like *Restaurante O Miradouro* (☎ 76 37 46), formerly O Lamberto, upstairs at Rua 25 de Abril 21. On weekends the cooks prepare a good arroz de marisco (a soupy seafood and rice stew), which you can opt to enjoy on the rooftop terrace.

Just a few steps north at Rua Afonso d'Almeida 17, *O Cantinho Algarvio* (☎ 76 12 89) offers Algarve specialities at slightly more modest prices (meat courses to 2000$00 and fish courses from 1000$00 to 3000$00); it's closed on Sundays. Around the block, the *Barroca Jazz Bar & Restaurante* (☎ 76 71 62) at the southern end of Rua da Barroca has similar prices, along with a vegetarian plate for 1200$00, and special

ALGARVE

children's platters. It's open from 7 pm to 2 am with live jazz on most nights in summer.

At Rua dos Ferreiros 17, a plain and popular local restaurant called *Bar Na Forja* (☎ 629 05) dishes up good daily specials, in portions that will test your stomach's capacity, for around 1500$00.

Restaurante A Muralha (☎ 76 36 59), beneath the old city walls at Rua da Atalaia 15, is open from 7 pm to 4 am (except Mondays) with late suppers to the sound of fado; reservations are suggested. For something a little different, try the Angolan dishes at *Restaurante Kalunga* (☎ 76 07 27); it's upstairs at Rua Marquês de Pombal 26.

Café-Bars In summer the *Casa Rosa Bar* at Rua do Ferrador 22 advertises 'travellers food' from a huge menu with main meals at 800$00 to 1000$00; these are heavy on meat but include salads, vegetarian dishes, omelettes and burgers. *Bar Vitaminas* (☎ 76 04 29) at Rua 25 de Abril 103 has a similar menu. A few doors along at No 93 is *Zanzibar*, a watering hole with a salad bar, vegetarian offerings, sandwiches and all-day breakfasts to the tune of indie/alternative music.

Mullens is a wood-panelled pub with taped music and a sizeable menu of soups, salads, sandwiches, and, in the evening, full steak, chicken or seafood dinners for 1000$00 to 2000$00 per course. It's at Rua Cândido dos Reis 86. The bar is open in summer from noon to 2 am, with food from 7 to 11 pm.

Out at Meia Praia, the *Linda Bar* (☎ 76 16 51) has good pub grub and good tunes.

Self-Catering The mercado municipal, on Avenida dos Descobrimentos just north of the post office, overflows with good fruit, vegetables, fish and meat; it's open daily except Sundays.

Entertainment
Bars Lagos is chock-a-block with bars and cafés, most of them staying open to 2 or 3 am in summer. Young people make spare cash by handing out flyers about them in summer;

before you chuck these in the bin, check for the occasional good discount. Refer to Café-Bars in the Places to Eat section for some places that serve up food and music along with the drinks.

Other places to check out are *Taverna Velha* at Rua Lançarote de Freitas 54, a few steps down from the youth hostel; an Irish bar called *Rosko's* (☎ 76 39 05), a few blocks away at Rua Cândido dos Reis 79; and *Stones* at Rua 25 de Abril 101.

Jazz The *Barroca Jazz Bar & Restaurante* (☎ 76 71 62), at the southern end of Rua da Barroca, is open foam 7 pm to 2 am, with live jazz on most nights in summer and on weekends in winter.

Concerts & Exhibitions Lagos' main venue for classical recitals and performances, as well as art exhibits, is the Centro Cultural on Rua Lançarote de Freitas; it's open daily from 10 am to 8 pm.

Getting There & Away
Bus The long-distance bus station (☎ 76 29 44) is on the Rossio de São João, just north of the walled town.

Lagos is connected to the rest of the coastal Algarve by EVA's Linha Litoral services, which go hourly to Portimão, once a day to Faro (950$00) and Vila Real de Santo António (1000$00, 3½ hours), and every hour or two to Sagres (440$00). EVA runs at least half a dozen express coaches to/from Lisbon each day for 2100$00, plus four faster alta qualidade services for 2400$00.

In summer, Intersul runs express coaches between Lagos and Seville (in Spain), four to six times a week; the fare is about 3000$00.

Train Lagos is at the western end of the Algarve branch line, with three fast interregional trains a day and a host of slower ones running all the way to Vila Real de Santo António. At least five fast direct trains a day link Lagos and Lisbon; interregional (IR) services take 5½ hours (1800$00), intercidade (IC) trains take 4½ hours.

Getting Around
Car, Motorcycle & Bicycle Motoride (☎ 76 17 20) rents out bikes, scooters and motorcycles from Rua José Afonso 23, just outside the town walls, or through agents in the centre (eg one on Rua 25 de Abril). Typical three/seven-day rates are about 3400$00/ 6800$00 for a mountain bike, 8400$00/ 18,000$00 for a scooter, and 13,000$00/ 28,000$00 and up for a motorbike. Safari Moto (☎ 76 43 14) at Rua Lucinda Santos 4, just north of the bus station, also rents out scooters and bikes.

The Florentina agency (☎ 76 42 86, ☎ 76 88 06) at Rua Dr Joaquim Tello 8 has cars starting from 8500$00 for 3 days – the best deal we found in the Algarve. Typical three/seven-day rates for a car from City Tour, on Rua Vasco da Gama near the bus station, are about 12,000$00/24,000$00. Numerous hotels and travel agencies also have their own deals. Avis is just north of the mercado municipal on Rua Vasco da Gama.

Taxi There is a taxi stand at the bottom of Rua das Portas de Portugal. To call a taxi, dial ☎ 76 35 87 or % 76 32 19.

Ferry Ferries run to and fro across the estuary to the Meia Praia side in summer; they leave from a landing just north of the Praça da República.

LAGOS TO SAGRES
The steep and rugged shoreline west of Lagos is the last segment of the south coast to fall prey to developers, but you can see it happening before your eyes as the once-sleepy fishing hamlets and beach hideaways of Luz, Burgau and Salema are inexorably 'resortified'.

So far, however, they still have coarse, clean beaches; snug, whitewashed houses; a few bright *barcos da pesca* pulled up on the slipways; minimal souvenir shops; and a sense of peaceful isolation. There are a few modest hotels, pensões and private rooms; two camping grounds; plenty of stick-to-your-ribs Portuguese food and cheerful bars; and convenient local buses from Lagos.

West of Burgau the coast road enters the Parque Natural de Sudoeste Alentejano e Costa Vicentina (South-West Alentejo & Costa Vicentina Natural Park).

Luz
Praia da Luz beach is good enough, and close enough to Lagos (six km), to get an extra share of day-trippers. The Sea Sports Centre (☎ 082-78 95 38), open year-round at Avenida dos Pescadores 4, offers scuba-diving lessons, equipment rental and boat trips. At the turn-off from the coastal road, *Restaurante Dom Milhano* (☎ 082-78 98 34) serves seafood and other dishes from 600$00 up; it's open from 10 am to 4 pm and 6 pm to midnight. Around the corner the very English *Luz Tavern* has pub grub and is open daily from noon to 2 am.

Burgau
A sleepier alternative to Luz is tiny, cobbled Burgau, 12 km from Lagos. Rua 25 de Abril drops steeply to a cramped landing. The centre of the tourist traffic is the friendly *Beach Bar Burgau*, west of the landing on the gravelly beach; it's open for food until 3 am and for drinks until 5 am.

Salema
Despite the condominiums rising like mushrooms around it, Salema, set on a wide bay 17 km from Lagos, has an easy-going atmosphere and several small, secluded beaches within a few km – Praia da Salema by the village, Figueira to the west and Boca do Rio to the east. Right by the landing, *Restaurante Atlântico* dishes up decent food at a Portuguese pace, and there are other bistros and bars in the village's single, whitewashed seafront lane (try the good *Boia Bar* just east of the landing). Pick up fruit, vegetables and cheese from the trucks that park in the square each morning.

Information
There are no turismos in these hamlets, though Salema has a helpful tour and travel agency called Horizonte (☎ 082-658 55; fax 082-659 20) in a commercial arcade in front

ALGARVE

of a villa and apartment complex called the Salema Beach Club, about 300m uphill to the west from the landing. It can help with currency exchange, accommodation, moped and car rental, boat trips and bus tickets, among other things. It also runs good jeep trips within the Costa Vicentina. It's open on weekends too.

Places to Stay

Camping A well-equipped Orbitur franchise, *Valverde Camping* (☎ 082-78 92 11; Lisbon central booking ☎ 01-815 48 71; fax 01-814 80 45), is six km west of Lagos and 1.5 km east of Luz. Sample summer rates are 660$00 per person, 560$00 to 880$00 per tent and 550$00 per car; there are also some bungalows. From Avenida dos Descobrimentos in Lagos it's 10 minutes away on any Burgau or Salema-bound bus.

At Espiche, on the N125 about two km from Luz, is *Turiscampo* (☎ 082-78 94 31), with rates about 30% lower than Valverde's in summer, and 60% lower in winter. With similar rates is the comfortable *Quinta dos Carriços* camping ground (☎ 082-643 51), 1.5 km north of Salema (0.5 km off the N125).

Private Rooms While Salema's hotels, and rental apartments in all three villages, get booked out months ahead in summer, squads of residents are everywhere with offers of overpriced quartos, typically 5000$00 or more for a double with a bath.

Estalagens If money is no object, rise above it all at Salema's elegant *Estalagem Infante do Mar* (☎ 082-651 37; fax 082-650 57), which is at the top of the hill on the road out to the N125. A comfortable double with bath, TV and balcony facing the sea is 11,000$00 from mid-July to mid-September, tapering off to 6000$00 in winter. Advance booking (two or three weeks ahead in summer) is essential.

Getting There & Away

All three villages are on a slow coastal road running parallel to the N125 from the western suburbs of Lagos. At least eight or nine buses go daily in summer to Burgau via Luz, and an equal number to Salema. The direct ones to Salema take about 40 minutes. If you're driving to Salema, go via Budens or Figueira on the N125, as the Burgau-Salema road can be dicey.

SAGRES
• *pop 1500* • *postcode 8650* • *area code* ☎ *082*

Sagres is a small fishing port at the western end of the Algarve. While there are fine beaches and recreational opportunities, the main reasons to make the trip are geographical and historical.

Blasted by a steady, cutting wind and huge Atlantic waves, and with sheer cliffs facing a sea horizon on three sides, the Ponta de Sagres promontory seems the very edge of Europe. Its position and the austere landscape surely figured in Prince Henry the Navigator's choice of this place for a new, fortified town and a semimonastic school of navigation that specialised in cartography, astronomy, navigation and ship design and set Portugal on course for the Age of Discoveries.

At least that is what the current mix of history and myth says. Henry was, among other things, governor of the Algarve and had a residence in its primary port town, Lagos, from where most expeditions actually set sail. He certainly did put together a kind of nautical think-tank, though how much thinking actually went on out at Sagres is not known. He had a house somewhere near Sagres, where he died in November 1460. In any case it's easy to see why he was obsessed with the place.

In May 1587 the English privateer Sir Francis Drake, in the course of harassing supply lines to the Spanish Armada, captured and wrecked the fortifications around Sagres. The Ponta de Sagres was re-fortified after the earthquake of 1755, which had left little of verifiable antiquity standing.

Paradoxically, quirky ocean currents give Sagres some of Portugal's mildest winter weather, and Atlantic winds keep the summers cool.

ALGARVE

Orientation

Tourist brochures insist on giving their attention to the plain, whitewashed district headquarters town of Vila do Bispo at the western end of the N125. From there a 10-km gauntlet of villas along the N268 attests to the arrival of development even at this remote corner of the Algarve.

At a roundabout at the end of the N268, roads go west for six km to the Cabo de São Vicente, south for one km to the Ponta de Sagres and east for 250m to little Praça da República at the head of Sagres town, what there is of it. One km east of the praça, past age-of-tourism hotels and apartments, is the port, still a centre for boat-building and lobster-fishing.

Information

The nearest turismo is in Vila do Bispo, but on the corner of Praça da República is an efficient private tourist agency called Turinfo (☎ 645 20, ☎ 645 51; fax 645 39) where you'll find currency exchange, stamps, excursions, bicycle and car rental, and contacts for private rooms and flats. It also seems to own half the bars and eateries in town. It's open daily from 10 am to 7 pm.

There's a small currency exchange about 300m east on Rua Infante Dom Henrique. The main post office is 600m north-east of the square on Rua do Mercado. The nearest medical clinic is the centro de saúde (☎ 661 79, ☎ 660 70) in Vila do Bispo.

An excellent booklet on the history of Sagres, called *Sagres* and published by the Vila do Bispo town council, is on sale at Turinfo.

Fortaleza de Sagres

The Sagres fortress (which dates in its present form from 1793) is more impressive from outside than inside, consisting only of a massive front wall and two bastions. Apparently there were short lateral walls inside as well once – the flat promontory's

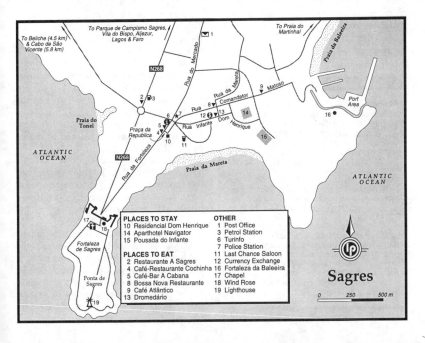

Sagres

PLACES TO STAY	OTHER
10 Residencial Dom Henrique	1 Post Office
14 Aparthotel Navigator	3 Petrol Station
15 Pousada do Infante	6 Turinfo
	7 Police Station
PLACES TO EAT	11 Last Chance Saloon
2 Restaurante A Sagres	12 Currency Exchange
4 Café-Restaurante Cochinha	16 Fortaleza da Baleeira
5 Café-Bar A Cabana	17 Chapel
8 Bossa Nova Restaurante	18 Wind Rose
9 Café Atlântico	19 Lighthouse
13 Dromedário	

0   250   500 m

sheer cliffs were protection enough around the rest.

Just inside the gate is what looks like a stone *rosa dos ventos* or wind rose (for measuring the direction of the wind), 43m in diameter. It was excavated in the 18th century and possibly built for Prince Henry. It seems unlikely that much else except the foundations dates from that time, though the oldest buildings, including a cistern tower to the east, a house and the small Igreja da Nossa Senhora da Graça to the west, and the remnants of a wall running part of the way across may have been built upon what was there before. Many of the gaps between the buildings are the result of a 1950s clearance of 17th and 18th-century ruins to make way for a reconstruction (later aborted) to co-incide with the 500th anniversary of Henry's death.

In 1992 the state pulled down an 18th-century replica of a building (adjacent to the cistern tower), apparently constructed in Henry's time, that housed one of Europe's more stunningly located youth hostels, replacing it with an ugly little museum. Near the southern end of the promontory is a modern lighthouse. Death-defying anglers with huge poles perch atop the cliffs all around, hoping to land bream or sea bass (though we never saw them catch anything).

Access to the fort is free.

Other Forts

Overlooking Sagres harbour are the ruins of the small **Fortaleza da Baleeira**, thought to have been built in the mid-16th century to protect the harbour.

The **Fortaleza de Beliche**, built in 1632 on the site of an older one, is 4.5 km from the Sagres roundabout on the way to Cabo de São Vicente. Inside is a small chapel on the site of the ruined Igreja de Santa Catarina (and possibly an old convent), as well as a restaurant and two rooms for rent.

Cabo de São Vicente

No visit to Sagres would be complete without a trip to Cape St Vincent, Europe's south-westernmost point. Awesome is the only word for this barren, throne-like headland where, in the words of the poet Luís de Camões, the land ends and the sea begins. This was the last bit of home that terrified Portuguese sailors would have seen as they headed out into the unknown sea.

The cape – a revered place even in the time of the Phoenicians and known to the Romans as Promontorium Sacrum – takes its present name from a Spanish priest martyred by the Romans (see the boxed aside). The old fortifications trashed by Sir Francis Drake in 1587 were subsequently reduced to rubble by the 1755 earthquake.

At the end of the cape is a powerful lighthouse (hundreds of ocean-going ships round this cape every day) and a former convent. Some scholars place Henry the Navigator's house in a small castle to the right of the lighthouse grounds.

The best time to come here is at sunset, when you can almost hear the hissing as the sun settles into the sea. It would make a stunning cliff-side walk from Sagres, though it's almost six km each way in a stiff wind. There are cafés or restaurants in several places along the road. There is no public transport.

St Vincent

St Vincent (São Vicente) was a Spanish preacher killed by the Romans in 304 in Valencia. Various legends say his body was either washed up at the Cabo de São Vicente, or borne here on a boat accompanied by ravens (or perhaps carrion crows, like those still common in the area). A shrine, which Muslim chronicles refer to as the 'Crow Church', was built and became an object of Christian pilgrimage even in Moorish times, though it was apparently destroyed by Muslim fanatics in the 12th century.

Afonso Henriques, Portugal's first king, quick to see the saint's symbolic value, had the remains moved to Lisbon in 1173, again by ship – and again supposedly accompanied by ravens. St Vincent was made Lisbon's patron saint (his remains now rest in the Igreja de São Vicente de Fora there) and there is a raven on the city's coat of arms. ■

ALGARVE

Parque Natural de Sudoeste Alentejano e Costa Vicentina

The South-West Alentejo & Costa Vicentina Natural Park is a strip of rugged, sparsely developed coastline with high cliffs and ragged coastal outcrops, isolated beaches, inlets and estuaries. It runs for about 120 km from Burgau to the Cabo de São Vicente and up nearly the entire western Algarve and Alentejo shore. It's rarely more than five or six km wide except where it follows the Rio Mira valley to Odemira in the Alentejo.

This is Portugal's newest natural park, amalgamated in October 1995 from several protected areas in an effort to forestall development and protect an ecosystem rich and complex enough to have been designated a 'biogenetic reserve' by the Council of Europe.

Here there are at least 48 plant species that are found only in Portugal, and a dozen or so found only within the park. Otters thrive in the river valleys, foxes roam in areas near the shore, and a few lynx and other wild cats lurk in the deeper valleys. The most visible wildlife is birds: some 200 species enjoy the coastal wetlands, salt marshes and cliffs, including Portugal's last remaining ospreys. Storks nest on coastal outcrops. This is also an important migratory stop in spring and autumn.

The N268/N120 road roller-coasters for long stretches along the inland edge of the pine-scented and silent park, passing through hills deeply etched by rivers on the way to the sea. The most picturesque stretches are north and south of Carrapateira and between Rogil and Odeceixe.

Beaches The west coast is lined with good beaches which are backed up against cliffs or sand dunes, some of which are huge and relatively empty even in summer. Among good ones that are relatively accessible in a sturdy car are Castelejo (north-west of Vila do Bispo), Bordeira (by Carrapateira), Arrifana and Monte Clérigo (near Aljezur), and Odeceixe. A great many others are only accessible if you have a 4WD or a healthy appetite for walking.

Information The park headquarters (☎ 083-22735; fax 083-228 30) are at Rua Serpa Pinto 16 in Odemira, in the Alentejo.

Guided Tours Access by jeeps and other vehicles has been limited since the area became a natural park, but there are a few good options. Horizonte (☎ 082-658 55; fax 082-659 20) in Salema runs low-impact 4WD trips (they're shy of the term 'jeep safari') around the Algarve end of the park, down to remote beaches and up to isolated villages in the Serra do Espinaço de Cão (Dog's-Back Ridge). A full-day trip with lunch costs about 7000$00.

Naturinfo (☎ 082-645 20; fax 082-645 39) in Sagres organises similar small-group jeep trips, as well as guided walks, mountain-bike trips, and donkey treks (including multiday donkey treks in summer). ■

Activities

Turinfo, under the name Naturinfo, runs **jeep trips**, **bike tours**, **donkey treks** and walks to beaches along the Costa Vicentina or into the Serra de Monchique, all-day minibus tours to Monchique and Silves, **boat trips** down the coast as far as Lagos, and **fishing trips**. Another firm operating cruises and fishing trips is Cabo de São Vicente Cruzeiros (☎ 082-641 98, mobile ☎ 0931-34 06 42).

Praia do Martinhal is the focus for **windsurfing** (the water is wetsuit-cold). At Mareta the Clube Martinhal aquatic sports centre (☎ 643 33) offers **sea-kayaking** day trips, windsurfing, **snorkelling** and, in summer, **scuba diving**. **Surfing** is possible at all beaches except Martinhal.

Beaches

There are four good beaches within a short drive or long walk from Sagres: Praia da Mareta right below; Praia do Martinhal just to the east; Praia do Tonel on the other side of the Ponta de Sagres; and isolated Praia de Beliche, on the way to the Cabo de São Vicente. The Praia da Baleeira, adjacent to the harbour, is pretty gummed up from all the boat traffic.

Places to Stay

Sagres gets crowded with backpackers and

villa types in summer, though it's marginally easier to find modest accommodation here than in the rest of the Algarve. In a criminal act in 1992, the government dismantled the area's only hostel, which was out on the Ponta de Sagres.

Camping The well-maintained *Parque de Campismo Sagres* (☎ 643 51, ☎ 643 61) is two km from town, just off the road to Vila do Bispo. Typical August rates are 500$00 per person, 500$00 to 700$00 per tent, 250$00 per car and 100$00 for a shower. About 17 km from Sagres, on the beach below Raposeira, east of Vila do Bispo, is the basic *Ingrina Camping* (☎ 662 42), with slightly lower rates and pricier showers.

Other Options Some locals in Sagres let out rooms for 3500$00 to 5000$00 a double, or flats for 7000$00 to 15,000$00 at the height of the season. On Praça da República is the *Residencial Dom Henrique*, where a double with bath is about 7000$00 with a land view or 10,000$00 with a sea view, including breakfast. Ask about all of these at Turinfo.

At the giant *Aparthotel Navigator* (☎ 643 54), just off Rua Infante Dom Henrique, a double apartment in high season is about 15,000$00. Behind this, the very elegant *Pousada do Infante* (☎ 642 22) offers posh doubles for 22,000$00 and up! For the cost of an extra bed here, you could stay elsewhere for a couple of nights. The little fortaleza at Beliche has two rooms for rent, but they're said to be booked up about three years ahead!

Except at the pousada, all prices drop by 50% or even more outside summer.

Places to Eat

Cheap, filling meals can be had at the *Restaurante A Sagres* at the roundabout as you enter the village. On Praça da República are the *Café-Bar A Cabana* and the *Café-Restaurante Cochinha*. The latter has a small restaurant upstairs and home-made pies on the menu; it's open from 7.30 am to 11 pm.

About 300m from the square on Rua Infante Dom Henrique is the *Dromedário*

bistro-bar, with fresh juices and muesli for breakfast from 10 am, pizzas during the day and drinks till 3 am. The menu at the *Bossa Nova Restaurante*, on Rua Comandante Matoso, includes pizzas, salads and vegetarian dishes; it's open from noon to midnight in summer, plus winter weekends and holidays. You could also try *Café Atlântico* – it's a bit further out, near the turn-off to the pousada.

Entertainment

A cheerful place for a drink with a sea view is the *Last Chance Saloon*, just down the hill from the square; it's open from 5 pm to 4 am.

Getting There & Away

About a dozen coaches a day run between Sagres and Lagos, with fewer on Sundays and holidays. There are at least three that go direct to/from Faro (or you can change at Lagos). There is one daily coach direct to Lisbon (4½ hours), and three to Évora (six hours). There's no bus station; just flag them down on Rua Comandator Matoso near the square.

Getting Around

Turinfo can arrange for a rental car from Lagos; expect a minimum of three days to cost around 15,000$00 in summer, or 10,000$00 in winter.

CARRAPATEIRA

The only reason to stop at this village 14 km north of Vila do Bispo is its beaches – the fine Praia da Bordeira, two km to the north, and the smaller Praia do Amado, about one km south of the village down a link road.

Private rooms are available in Carrapateira in summer and there's a pricey residencial, the *Casa Fajarra* (☎ 082-971 19) with doubles for about 9000$00 and up, on the N120 a 15-minute walk above Praia da Bordeira. There's a restaurant at Bordeira, but no facilities at Amado.

There's at least one bus daily, between Vila do Bispo and Aljezur, that stops here.

The Algarve
Top: Small cottage near Monchique
Middle: Palácio do Visconde de Estói
Bottom: Praia dos Pescadores (Fishermen's Beach), Albufeira

VICKI BEALE

JULIA WILKINSON

JULIA WILKINSON

The Coast
Top: Sagres, Algarve
Middle: São Martinho do Porto, Estremadura
Bottom: Albufeira, Algarve

ALJEZUR
• *pop 4850* • *postcode 8670* • *area code* ☎ *082*

While not worth a special trip, this tidy village presided over by a ruined 10th-century Moorish castle makes a pleasant stop if you're motoring or bussing along the coast. Accommodation is not hard to find, the castle gives you a wide panorama of the landscape, and there are several good beaches in the vicinity.

Orientation
Aljezur has two cleanly separated halves: the old Moorish settlement climbing up to the castle from the south-west side of the Ribeira de Aljezur, and Igreja Nova (New Church) on the other side, about 350m up the hill. (Why? After the 1755 earthquake the Bishop of Faro urged villagers to relocate away from the river, where malarial mosquitoes bred.) The road to Monchique turns south from below Igreja Nova.

Information
The helpful turismo (☎ 982 29) on the north-east side of the river can help with private rooms and other accommodation. It's open weekdays from 9.30 am to 12.30 pm and 2 to 7 pm (to 5 pm in winter). Beside it is the bus stop, and behind it a small morning marketplace (with a big market on the third Monday of each month). A bank and the post office are about 300m south on the road to Sagres. The local police can be contacted on ☎ 981 30.

Castelo
The view from the simple castle, slowly disintegrating under the boots of its visitors, is worth the steep 700m walk (go left at the parish church). It was captured without a fight by Christian forces in 1249; a local story says the Muslim defenders were all down at the beach.

Beaches
There are two very good beaches adjacent to Aljezur: surfable **Praia do Monte Clérigo**, with a small holiday settlement, seven km away; and the grand **Praia da Arrifana**

beside a fishing village, nine km away. Near Arrifana is an unfinished tourist 'town' called Vale da Telha. All are accessible on a bus departing Aljezur every day at 8.55 am and returning from Arrifana at 6.30 pm. If you're driving, the turn-off is one km south of town.

A turn-off for the smaller Praia da Amoreira is four km north of Aljezur on the N120.

Places to Stay
Camping *Camping-Caravaning Vale da Telha* (☎ 082-984 44) is about three km south of Praia de Monte Clérigo, not far from the beach at Vale da Telha. Rates include 360$00 per person, 360$00 to 480$00 per tent and 360$00 per car. The somewhat better equipped and wheelchair-accessible *Parque de Campismo Serrão* (☎ 082-986 12) is four km north of Aljezur and 800m down the road to Praia de Amoreira (which is 2.5 km away). Sample rates are 550$00 per person, 450$00 to 750$00 per tent and 420$00 per car; there are also bungalows. Both camping grounds are open year-round.

Other Options Private rooms are not hard to find in summer; the turismo keeps a list. *Tasca Borralho* (see Places to Eat) has three clean rooms with shared shower and toilet for about 2000$00 per person, which is good value. The *Restaurante A Lareira* (☎ 984 40), about 300m out on the road to Monchique, also has a few rooms.

In summer, a double with bath is about 6000$00 at the *Hospedaria São Sebastião* (☎ 980 52); it's on the N120, 400m south of the bridge. *Residencial Dom Sancho* (☎ 981 19), on Largo 1 de Maio at the centre of Igreja Nova, has doubles with bath, seriously overpriced at 4000$00 to 5000$00 per person. We found no one home at the *Hospedaria O Palazim* (☎ 982 49), two km north on the N120, but it looks quiet and well run, and there's a restaurant next door.

Places to Eat
Several plain cafés and restaurants are clustered around the bridge, including the

Restaurante Ponte-a-Pé (☎ 988 54) facing the riverside jardim (garden) at Largo da Liberdade, on the south-west side. The cheerful *Tasca Borralho* (☎ 99 11 58) at Rua Dom Francisco Gomes de Avelar 5, opposite the Residencial Dom Sancho in Igreja Nova, has a modest menu of good home-cooked dishes – you can eat well for 1500$00. Among restaurants on the N120 south of the bridge are the *Primavera* (☎ 982 94) and *Ruth* (☎ 985 34).

Praia da Arrifana has two seafood restaurants – the *Oceano* (☎ 99 73 00) and *Brisamar* (☎ 984 36) – and a supermarket. At Praia da Amoreira is *Restaurante Paraíso do Mar* (☎ 99 10 88).

Getting There & Away
Daily EVA buses between Vila do Bispo and Aljezur (a 45-minute trip) depart at 8.05 pm from Vila do Bispo and at 1.30 and 6.50 pm from Aljezur. EVA also runs at least three buses each weekday and one on Saturdays to/from Lagos. Lisbon is five hours away, with daily departures from Aljezur at mid-morning and mid-afternoon.

Getting Around
The local taxi service can be contacted on ☎ 981 23 or mobile ☎ 0931-57 46 30.

ODECEIXE
Tiny Odeceixe, the first/last town on the Algarve's west coast and the only other one besides Sagres and Carrapateira that feels like a summer hang-out, clings to the southern side of the Ribeira de Seixe valley right by the N120; the other side is in the Alentejo. Its main attraction is Praia de Odeceixe, a small, lovely, very sheltered beach 3.5 km down-valley. Unfortunately there are no regular buses to the beach.

Places to Stay & Eat
If you can't get one of the village's many quartos, which go for around 3000$00 per double and up, try *Hospedaria Cláudio* (☎ 941 17, ☎ 943 17) at Rua do Correia 12, opposite the post office and near the N120, which also serves as an information office.

Pensão Luar (☎ 941 94) at Rua da Várzea 28, at the rear of the village, just to the left off the road to the beach, has doubles with shower for about 6000$00 at the height of summer. There is also a pensão (☎ 945 81) at the beach.

Sample summer rates at the very well-equipped, wheelchair-accessible *Parque de Campismo São Miguel* (☎ 082-941 45, ☎ 942 45), on the N120 about two km north of the village, are 590$00 per person, 590$00 to 850$00 per tent and 550$00 per car. It's open year-round; book ahead in summer if you can. It also rents out caravans.

The *Café O Retiro do Adelino*, on the road through the village to the beach, serves plain meals.

Getting There & Away
EVA runs at least three buses each weekday and one on Saturdays to/from Aljezur and Lagos.

The Interior

MONCHIQUE
• *pop 6500* • *postcode 8550* • *area code* ☎ *082*
Up in the forested Serra de Monchique, 24 km north of Portimão, this busy little market town begins to feel like the real Portugal at last, its densely wooded hills a welcome touch of wilderness after all the holiday villas further south. There's no outstanding reason to linger here, though it makes a pleasant day trip together with Caldas de Monchique, or an ideal break on the way in or out of the Algarve.

Orientation & Information
Buses drop you right in the town centre, the Largo dos Chorões, where a reconstructed water wheel and new café with outdoor seating make a pleasant place to wait for your bus after you've finished meandering around. In the valley below is a small park and children's playground.

Monchique's Moonshine
You can find commercial brands of *medronho* (a locally made firewater) everywhere in Portugal, but according to those who have suffered enough hangovers to know, the best of all is the illicit, privately made brew from Monchique.

The Serra de Monchique is thick with medronho's raw material, the arbutus or strawberry tree. Its berries are collected in late autumn, fermented and then left for several months before being distilled in the kind of big copper stills you see for sale as tourist souvenirs all over the Algarve.

Home-made medronho is usually clear and always drunk neat, like schnapps. It's strong, of course, but as long as you don't mix it with other drinks it doesn't give you a hangover (say the connoisseurs). Early spring (when distilling is in action) is the best time to track down some of this brew in Monchique: ask around (and keep an empty bottle handy). ∎

Old Town

A series of brown walking signs starting near the bus station directs visitors up into the town's narrow old streets and major places of interest. The **Igreja Matriz** is the most notable piece of architecture, thanks to an extraordinary Manueline porch decorated with twisted columns looking like lengths of knotted rope.

Ten minutes further uphill is the ruined Franciscan monastery of **Nossa Senhora do Desterro**, built in 1632. From below, the monastery's empty shell looks sad and spooky but its hilltop position offers a great view of the town and surrounding hills.

Places to Stay

The *Residencial Estrela de Monchique* (☎ 931 11) at Rua do Porto Fundo 46, just a minute's walk up from the bus terminal, has good-value rooms with bath for 4000$00, and a casual and friendly café. Similarly priced rooms with rustic décor but less atmosphere are available at the large, modern *Residencial Miradouro* (☎ 921 63) on Rua dos Combatentes do Ultramar, a 10-minute walk in the opposite direction from the old town, up Rua Engenheiro Duarte Pacheco.

Places to Eat

The popular *A Charrete* (☎ 921 42) at Rua Dr Samora Gil 30-34 is a big family-style place with cabinets full of local pottery and other knick-knacks; you can eat well here for under 2000$00. Even more delightful is the *Restaurante Central* at Rua da Igreja 5,

where hospitality and honest food have won rave reviews from travellers for years (their scribbled recommendations cover the walls).

Entertainment

Barlefante (☎ 927 74) on Travessa da Guerreira is a popular bar. It stays open until 1 am.

Getting There & Away

Over a dozen buses daily run between Lagos and Portimão, from where eight daily services make the 45-minute run to Monchique (370$00). There's also a summertime-only express service twice a day from Albufeira via Silves.

AROUND MONCHIQUE

Fóia

If you've got your own transport (there's no bus service), you can head up the N266-3 to the 902m Fóia peak, the Algarve's highest point, eight km west of Monchique. Along the road, which climbs through eucalyptus and pines, is a string of restaurants specialising, for some reason, in piri-piri chicken. The peak itself is a disappointment, bristling with ugly telecommunication towers, but its panoramic views make it a popular destination for tour buses. On clear days you can see out to the corners of the Algarve – Cabo de São Vicente (near Sagres) to the south-west and Odeceixe to the north-west. Hikers might like to tackle the eight-km route back down to Monchique outlined in the Algarve tourist board's *Algarve: Guide to Walks* (see Activities in the chapter introduction).

ALGARVE

Caldas de Monchique

The snug hamlet of Caldas de Monchique, six km south of Monchique at the head of a delightful valley full of eucalyptus trees, has been a popular spa for over two millennia and still is. The Romans loved its 32°C, slightly sulphurous waters, which are said to be good for rheumatism and backache, asthma and other ailments. Dom João II came here for years in an unsuccessful attempt to cure the dropsy that finally finished him off.

By staying the night you can see it at its most peaceful, before and after the daily queue of tour coaches disgorges its chattering mobs.

Orientation & Information Some Portimão-Monchique buses venture off the N266 on a one-way loop road round the town centre. Others only stop on the highway, leaving you with a half-km stroll down to the centre – little more than a cluster of almost quaint, Victorian-style buildings around a miniature square. Here are Caldas' three hotels, a restaurant, several bars, and a handicraft shop in a grandiose former casino with ersatz battlements – nearly all under the same management.

The most peaceful patch is the prim, streamside garden above the square. Down the valley are the main spa buildings, open from June through October, and below these a huge, ugly bottling plant (the waters of Caldas de Monchique are on menus all over Portugal, and you can fill your own jug with them at a tap on the outbound road, just beyond the square).

There is no turismo or other reliable source of information about the place. By the parking lot is a post office. The telephone code is ☎ 082.

Places to Stay & Eat There's no need to take the waters to stay here. In any case, you should try to book a few weeks ahead. The stodgy *Central* spa-hotel (☎ 922 04; fax 939 20) offers treatment downstairs and rooms upstairs; in summer a spartan double is about 4500$00 without bath or 5500$00 with,

breakfast included. A double with TV, telephone and bath in the adjacent *Albergaria Velha* (same ☎ & fax as the Central) is 7600$00, including a big breakfast; downstairs is the posh *Restaurante 1692*. Decidedly upscale is the four-star *Albergaria Lageado*, set back from the square. Out on the main road the *Restaurante & Residencial Granifóia* (☎ 926 57) has plain doubles with shower for 5000$00 and up. Winter brings discounts of 15% (at the Central) to 50% (at the Granifóia).

Getting There & Away At least eight buses between Portimão and Monchique stop here daily, along with summer-only express coaches from Albufeira via Silves twice a day.

ALCOUTIM

• *pop 4280* • *postcode 8970* • *area code* ☎ *081*

As the N122 twists through coarse hills towards Alcoutim in the treeless valley of the Rio Guadiana (which forms the Algarve's entire eastern border), a fine hilltop stronghold comes into view. You round a final bend to discover that it's across the river in Alcoutim's mirror image, the Spanish village of Sanlúcar de Guadiana. It's hard to imagine that Alcoutim's lower, humbler fortress was ever a match for the Spanish one.

Like dozens of other fortified villages that face each other across the Rio Guadiana, these two castles and their whitewashed, vest-pocket towns are a reminder of centuries of mutual distrust. Forts have probably risen and decayed here ever since the Phoenicians made this an important river port. Dom Fernando I of Portugal and Don Henrique II of Castile signed a tentative peace treaty here in the 14th century.

Nowadays the two towns beckon to one another's visitors, and of course there's no such thing as a border post any more. There isn't really much to do, but you can wander the towns' pretty, cobbled lanes; poke about in their castles; photograph the many elaborate chimneys and the storks nesting atop Alcoutim's parish church; or ride a boat across (or along) the placid river.

Castelo

The original Portuguese castle probably dates from pre-Moorish times; what you see now is from the 14th century. Within the ruins are a handicraft shop, a snack bar, an incongruous green lawn, and excavations in progress.

River Trips

Signs advertise a 15 to 20-minute trip on the river in a small fishing boat for 500$00; ask the fishermen at the landing just below Praça da República (the small, plain central square).

Places to Stay & Eat

Accommodation is sparse. Several villagers rent out rooms; ask at one of the shops or cafés on the square. We saw some 'quartos' signs along Rua Dom Sancho.

One km north of the square, across a bridge and past the fire station, is a newish youth hostel, the *Pousada de Juventude de Alcoutim* (☎ & fax 081-460 04) – open, with military precision, from 8 am to noon and 6 pm to midnight. A dorm bed is 1450$00 and there are some doubles without bath for 3200$00.

Getting There & Away

Alcoutim is at the end of a branch road off the N122 highway between Vila Real de Santo António and Beja (Alentejo). On weekdays only, EVA buses depart Vila Real at 9 am and 5.10 pm, stopping at Alcoutim about 1¼ hours later. One bus comes from Beja via Mértola on weekday afternoons.

ALGARVE

The Alentejo

Torrid summers and rolling plains character-
ise this vast southern province, one of the
poorest and least populated parts of the
country, stretching *alem Tejo*, 'beyond the
Tejo', to cover almost a third of Portugal.
Coming from Lisbon or the Algarve, you'll
be struck by the emptiness and the austere,
mesmerising nature of the land: mile after mile
of huge agricultural estates freckled with cork
and olive trees and awash with wheat.

City folk may find it dull (and admittedly,
the lower part of the province – Baixo
Alentejo – has few big attractions) but if
you're looking for open spaces across which
to hike or ride a horse, or for a Portugal
steeped in rural traditions, here they are.

But there's culture too, especially in the
northern part of the province, Alto Alentejo.
The region's biggest attraction is the delightful Renaissance city of Évora, a UNESCO
World Heritage Site with well-preserved
16th-century mansions, churches and a
Roman temple. Nearby are the marble towns
of Estremoz, Borba and Vila Viçosa, the
heavily fortified frontier town of Elvas, and
scores of prehistoric stone monuments.

It's the lure of the land, however, that
makes the Alentejo special. Some of the
country's finest rural architecture is found
here, in particular in the medieval hilltop
outposts of Monsaraz and Marvão. Alentejan
folk dancers and singers are among the
country's best. Its cuisine is one of the most
distinctive, thanks to a history of pig and
sheep farming and entrenched poverty which
forced farmers to conjure up entire meals out
of bread. The Alentejan bread-based *açorda*
soups, the *migas à Alentejana* pork stews
(which look disgusting but taste OK if you're
ravenous) and the inspired *carne de porco à
Alentejana* (pork and clam stew) are national
favourites now but are still best savoured on
their home turf. Don't forget to try one of the
strong local *aguardente* firewaters. Even the
red table wines are punchy (the best are from
Borba and Reguengos de Monsaraz).

Coastal Alentejo – which includes part of
the Parque Natural de Sudoeste Alentejano e
Costa Vicentina (see the boxed aside in the
Algarve chapter) – maintains the wild provincial allure. If you like your swimming
rough and refreshing, you'll love the beaches
here: try the low-key resorts west of Odemira
or north of Sines.

Transport is excellent between major towns,
but in the sticks you're often down to a bus or
two a day – which suits the pace of the province. As long as you avoid the ferocious
summer heat, cycling is a great alternative for
short excursions across the plains.

History

The Alentejo's early settlers left traces everywhere in the form of scores of dolmens,
menhirs and stone circles, making the
Alentejo one of the country's richest areas of
prehistoric remains. But it was the Romans
who made the greatest impact on the land,
introducing 'foreign' crops like vines, wheat
and olives, and building dams and irrigation
schemes. Most significantly, they established huge estates called *latifúndios* (which
still exist today) to make the most of the
region's few rivers and poor soil.

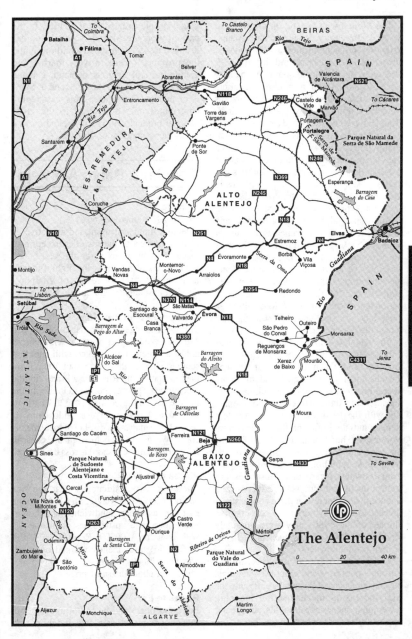

ALENTEJO

The Moors, who arrived on the scene in the early 8th century, developed the Romans' irrigation projects further and introduced new crops like citrus fruit and rice. By 1279 they were on the run to southern Spain or forced to live in special *mouraria* quarters outside town walls. Many of their citadels were later reinforced by the 'castle-king', Dom Dinis, who established a chain of frontier fortresses along the Spanish border. Continuing conflicts with Spain ensured that 'they were rebuilt and reinforced countless times so that the Alentejo now boasts some of the most spectacular hilltop fortresses in the land – Monsaraz, Estremoz and Elvas, Beja and Serpa, Marvão and Castelo de Vide.

But despite all the efforts of Romans and Moors, the Alentejo remained agriculturally poor and backward – and increasingly so as the 15th-century Age of Discoveries led to an explosive growth in maritime trade and the seaports became the focus of attention. Only Évora flourished, under the royal patronage of the House of Avis, although even this city declined once the Spanish seized the throne in 1580.

The Alentejo's low political profile was only rarely punctuated by events such as those in 1834, when the civil war between the absolutist Dom Miguel and his more liberal brother Pedro reached a climax with the defeat of Miguel's forces at Évoramonte. But with the 1974 revolution, the Alentejo stepped into the limelight: the landless rural workers who had laboured on the latifúndios for generations rose up in support of the communist rebellion and seized the land from its owners. Nearly one thousand estates were collectivised. But lack of expertise and finance meant that few of these cooperatives succeeded, and in the more conservative climate of the 1980s they were gradually reprivatised. Most are now back in the hands of their original owners.

Today the Alentejo remains among Europe's poorest – and emptiest – regions: the consequences of Portugal's entry into the EU (increasing mechanisation meaning fewer jobs), successive droughts, and greater opportunities elsewhere have led many young people to head for the cities. In the past 40 years the Alentejo's population has declined by 45% to just half a million. While the province's cork, olives, marble and granite are still in great demand, and the deep-water port and industrial zone of Sines is of national importance, this vast region contributes only a fraction to the gross national product, and is still looked on as a backwater struggling to survive.

Coastal & Baixo Alentejo

ODEMIRA
• *postcode 7630 • area code ☎ 083*

Odemira, though pleasant and attractive, is of little interest to the traveller except as a place to change buses for the coast, and perhaps as a place to stay the night if there's no room at the seaside resorts of Vila Nova de Milfontes and Zambujeira do Mar.

Orientation & Information
The town lounges on the banks of the Rio Mira. The oldest part of town, with narrow cobbled streets (now choked with cars that seem too big for them), is about 400m from the bus station, up Rua Sousa Prado (by the clock tower), past Largo Sousa Prado. In the middle of it is the *turismo* (☎ 326 21), hard to find and not much use aside from its second-rate map and a display of local handicrafts. We got more help from the cheerful *papelaria* (stationery shop) across the square.

Places to Stay
There are two residencials near the bus station. *Casa Rita* (☎ 226 28), a block to the east, serves cheap sandwiches and home-made soup, and upstairs has plain doubles with bath for 3500$00. *Residencial Idálio* (☎ 221 56), prominently marked on a hill about two blocks further on, offers a homier setting for about the same price.

Places to Eat
For atmosphere and basic Portuguese grub the choice is between two neighbouring

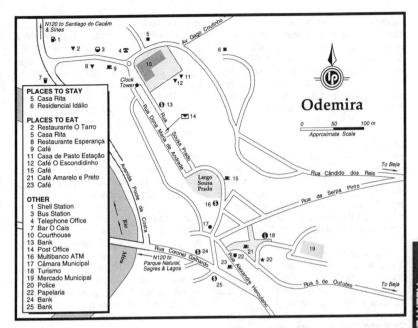

PLACES TO STAY
5 Casa Rita
6 Residencial Idálio

PLACES TO EAT
2 Restaurante O Tarro
5 Casa Rita
8 Restaurante Esperança
9 Café
11 Casa de Pasto Estação
12 Café O Escondidinho
15 Café
21 Café Amarelo e Preto
23 Café

OTHER
1 Shell Station
3 Bus Station
4 Telephone Office
7 Bar O Cais
10 Courthouse
13 Bank
14 Post Office
16 Multibanco ATM
17 Câmara Municipal
18 Turismo
19 Mercado Municipal
20 Police
22 Papelaria
24 Bank
25 Bank

Odemira

0   50   100 m
Approximate Scale

cafés spilling onto the square behind the courthouse. Our favourite is *Casa de Pasto Estação* – also enjoyed all morning by what looks like most of Odemira's unemployed men, gossiping and sipping coffee or aguardente. Next door is *Café O Escondidinho*, with upstairs dining too.

If you're in a hurry to catch a bus, grab a bite at *Casa Rita*, a block east of the bus station; the bottom-end *Restaurante Esperança* across the street from the bus station; or *Restaurante O Tarro* just around to the right. Nearly everything is wall-to-wall with high school students at lunch time.

If you manage to find the turismo, then enjoy a coffee or light meal in the square at the small *Café Amarelo e Preto*. A few steps up the hill from there is the mercado municipal.

Entertainment

Locals claim the *Bar O Cais*, opposite the Shell station near the bus station, is popular with Odemira's young people.

Getting There & Away

At least two buses a day link Odemira with Évora; two a day go to Portimão and, on weekdays, there are two to Lagos and two to Lisbon. The 2¼-hour trip from Lagos costs 960$00, and the 6½-hour trip from Lisbon costs 1400$00. Forget trains: the nearest station is 22 km east of town.

VILA NOVA DE MILFONTES

Down at the mouth of the Rio Mira, 25 km north-west of Odemira, is the small port town of Vila Nova de Milfontes. It's the Alentejo's most popular ocean resort, beloved of Portuguese as well as foreign holiday-makers for its unpretentious atmosphere and good beaches, on both sides of the estuary.

In 1486, Dom João directed that the town be made the port for the regional centre of Odemira, and the Spanish monarch Felipe I had a fort built here. The fort is today occupied by a sniffy top-end inn.

ALENTEJO

Orientation & Information

You're greeted by ugly urban sprawl on the outskirts, but it gets better as you approach the centre. The small turismo (☎ 965 99) is opposite the police station on Rua António Mantas (coming into town, this is the first right after the primary school), and open daily. The telephone code is ☎ 083, the same as Odemira's.

Beaches

The best beaches are along the coast, on either side of the Rio Mira estuary (but watch out for very strong river currents). In summer, whenever enough passengers have arrived to fill it, a ferry crosses the estuary to beaches on the other side; the ferry departs from a landing below the fort.

Places to Stay

If you're not too choosy, accommodation is not a big problem, even in summer. The turismo keeps a list of private rooms, and 'quartos' signs are common.

Camping There are three year-round camping grounds within easy reach. Closest is *Campiférias* (☎ 964 09; fax 965 81), on Rua da Praça opposite the mercado municipal, half a km from the turismo (walk west to the first intersection, Rua de São Sebastião, then north). Sample rates are 460$00 per person, 360$00 to 420$00 per tent and 250$00 per car. The shady, wheelchair-accessible *Parque de Campismo Milfontes* (☎ 961 40; fax 961 04) is a short way on, and 10% to 20% more expensive than Campiférias in peak season. Both have a pool, restaurant, and bungalows for rent as well.

The wheelchair-accessible *Parque de Campismo Sitava* (☎ 89 93 43; fax 89 95 71) is four km north of the town centre, with rates similar to those at Campiférias.

Pensões & Residencials Among modestly priced places are the following; the turismo lists others. The most central, on Largo do Rossio, is *Residencial Mil-Réis* (☎ 992 33), where a double with bath, TV and a veranda is 8500$00. Four blocks from the turismo on

Rua D at No 34 is *Residencial Golfinho Azul* (☎ 99 70 49), with doubles from 5500$00 to 6000$00. The *Pensão do Cais* (☎ 962 68), out on the road to the town pier, charges similar prices. About 700m west of the turismo on Rua António Mantas is *Pensão Eirada da Pedra*, with doubles from 7500$00, and nearby is a cheaper option, *Quinta das Varandas*, where doubles start at 5000$00.

Hotels The town's only hotel is the *Social* (☎ & fax 965 17), a short walk west of the town centre on Avenida Marginal. Doubles with bath start at 7000$00.

Places to Eat

Recommended are the grilled fish at the *Restaurante do Cais*, downstairs from the pensão of the same name – or continue down Rua do Cais to *Restaurante A Fateixa* for more of the same. Slightly up-market, with a good seafood stew and good vibes (you can eat well for 2500$00 per person), is *Restaurante Mira Mar*, opposite the fort.

Getting There & Away

Daily coaches – two in the morning, year-round, plus several more in the afternoon in summer – come down from Lisbon (4½ hours). In summer there are daily coaches from Sagres and from Portimão (at other times, change at Odemira).

ZAMBUJEIRA DO MAR

A simpler, smaller, cheaper (but equally popular) version of Vila Nova de Milfontes, with a fine Atlantic-facing beach, is Zambujeira do Mar.

Accommodation is mostly in private rooms, though there are several residencials too; the turismo (☎ 083-611 05) can help you find one. There's also a camping ground, the *Parque de Campismo Zambujeira* (☎ 083-611 72; fax 083-613 20), on the main road just east of the village; typical peak-season rates are 550$00 per person, 520$00 to 650$00 for a tent, 380$00 per car, and 50$00 for a shower; there's also a pool and restaurant.

Transport is limited to a few awkward bus connections a day from Odemira.

MÉRTOLA
• *postcode 7750* • *area code* ☎ *086*

Perched on a ridge between the serene Rio Guadiana and its tributary Ribeira de Oeiras is a Moorish castle, and wound round the hill beneath it is the delightfully flinty old heart of Mértola, a picturesque village of little houses that has hung onto its personality without becoming an open-air museum. In fact few tourists get here, partly because accommodation is limited and partly because it's a long way from anywhere – midway between Beja and Vila Real de Santo António, and 20 km from Spain.

Mértola has a long history and, for a village of its size, is serious about it. First to arrive were Phoenician traders who sailed up the Guadiana; Carthaginians followed. The settlement's strategic position led the Romans (who called it Myrtilis) to beautify it and the Moors (who called it Mertolah) to fortify it. Dom Sancho II took it in 1238. The village has several museums, and plenty of archaeological digs in progress around the castle.

Local men were, until a few decades ago, heavily dependent on work on the copper mines at Mina de São Domingos, about 15 km to the east, which are now exhausted. It's hard to see how anyone survives these days, as there's little flat land or good soil.

In contrast to the abandoned-looking landscape between here and Alcoutim, the road north towards Beja is pretty, with pasture and grain, cork oaks and eucalypts. Mértola is now within a brand-new protected area, the Parque Natural do Vale do Guadiana.

Orientation
From a roundabout at the convergence of the Serpa and Beja roads, it's about half a km south-west to the Café Guadiana and, beside it, the turn-off into the compressed old town and up to the castle. Old Mértola has few right angles or horizontal surfaces, and driving into it is asking for trouble: even a

donkey would have trouble on its skewed, cobbled, narrow lanes. Ugly 20th-century Mértola is west and north of the roundabout.

Information
The very helpful turismo (☎ 625 73), across the road from the Café Guadiana, is open daily from 9 am to 12.30 pm and 2 to 5.30 pm (weekends from 10 am). Two banks on Rua Dr Afonso Costa can exchange foreign currency. A few doors from the banks is the police station, and across the road is a turn-off to the local hospital.

Walking Tour
Walk into the old town from beside the Café Guadiana. With its cobbled lanes and sleepy atmosphere, old Mértola is like a time warp. Cats preen on the roofs and black-clad old women sit on their doorsteps chatting and knitting.

Keeping to the left at every fork in the road, you'll find yourself beside a little clock tower topped with a stork's nest overlooking the Rio Guadiana. Below and off to the left are the remains of what may have been a Moorish pier. Further south is the pretty town square, Largo Luís de Camões, which is full of orange trees. At its western end, in the cellar of the *câmara municipal* (town hall), is a small museum of Roman-era Mértola (see Museums & Galleries).

Igreja Matriz
If you enter the old town by the Café Guadiana but keep to the right at every fork, you arrive at Mértola's Igreja Matriz (parish church), which is square, flat-faced and topped with little conical decorations. It's best known for the fact that it was once a mosque, and among the few to have survived the Reconquest; it was reconsecrated in the 13th century. An unwhitewashed cavity in the wall on the right behind the altar is apparently the former mosque's *mihrab* or prayer niche. Note also the goats, lions and other figures carved around the peculiar Gothic portal.

There's no admission fee, though when we were there supplicants included one crafty old dear offering what looked like tickets in exchange for money.

Castelo

Above the Igreja Matriz looms Mértola's fortified castle, mostly dating from the 13th century but built upon Moorish foundations. It has surviving inner and outer walls and a prominent keep, and ongoing archaeological digs at its feet. If the keep isn't open you may well find a cheerful archaeology student or someone else who'll let you in for the climb up to a bird's-eye view of the entire town and the two river valleys.

Museums & Galleries

In the cellar of the câmara municipal is the modest but good **Museu Romano** (Roman Museum). Its main attraction is the foundations of the Roman house upon which the building rests, along with a small collection of pots, sculpture and other artefacts. It's open only on weekdays from 9 am to noon and 2 to 5.30 pm.

The 16th-century Igreja da Misericórdia, beyond the câmara municipal at the southern end of the old town, is said to contain a small collection of Islamic artefacts which the turismo refers to as the **Museu Islâmico**, open in summer. Though we found this closed, we did come across an exhibition of Islamic ceramics on the road up to the castle. Also here is an exhibition of traditional wool rug weaving called **Oficina de Tecelagen** ('weaving workshop').

North of the old town is yet another museum, the **Museu Paleocristão** (Archaeological Museum). It has Roman and

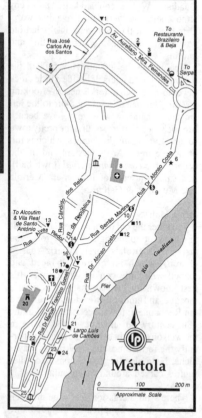

Mértola

0   100   200 m
Approximate Scale

PLACES TO STAY
3   Residencial San Remo
5   Café Campaniço
11 Oasis Pensão
12 Residencial Beira Rio
22 Casa Janelas Verdes

PLACES TO EAT
1   Restaurante Repuxo
2   Restaurante Alengarve
13 Tasca
15 Restaurante O Migas
16 Café Guadiana

OTHER
4   Bus Stand
6   Police
7   Museu Paleocristão
8   Hospital
9   Bank
10 Bank
14 Turismo
17 Oficina de Tecelagen
18 Exhibition of Islamic Ceramics
19 Igreja Matriz
20 Castelo
21 Clock Tower
23 Museu Romano
24 Tribunal
25 Museu Islâmico

Moorish pottery, jewellery and strange figurines. None of these places, except the Museu Romano, seems to have fixed hours; ask at the turismo.

Special Events
Mértola's main festival of the year, lasting for two weeks around 24 June, is the Festa de São João. The smaller Feira de São Mateus is held on the last weekend in September.

Places to Stay
Mértola has little accommodation and it fills right up in summer, so book ahead if you can. The turismo can help you find a private room, typically 3000$00 to 6000$00 for a double, though there are cheaper ones too.

True to its name, the friendly *Residencial Beira Rio* (☎ 623 40), at Rua Dr Afonso Costa 18 just below the town walls, has a fine view of the Rio Guadiana. Rooms are small and plain but very quiet on the river-facing side; a double with shared bath is 4000$00. Next door is the newer but similar *Oasis Pensão* (☎ 624 04, ☎ 627 01).

The other residencial in town is the big *Residencial San Remo* (☎ 621 32), on Avenida Aureliano Mira Fernandes in 'newer' Mértola, where three or four rooms share a bath, and a double is 3000$00. The only place offering rooms with attached bath is *Café Campaniço* (☎ 622 85) on Rua José Carlos Ary dos Santos. A double with bath and TV is 4000$00.

Top of the line is *Casa Janelas Verdes* (☎ 621 45), an old home done up in traditional style as part of the turismo Rural scheme, where a double with its own bath (but down the hall) is 6000$00, complete with a famously good breakfast. It's right in the middle of the old town, at Rua Dr Manuel Francisco Gomes 38.

Places to Eat
Food here is cheap but pretty limited. For light meals or a bica in the sunshine, try the cheerful *Café Guadiana* at the turn-off to the castle. Just up the main road is a small tasca,

open for lunch only, with main courses under 1000$00.

Just inside the old town is *Restaurante O Migas*, pronounced 'oh migash', which is what you might say about the house special – migas – a cheap, filling but rather depressing sludge of fried bread and pork chunks – an indicator of the limited options available in this hard-scrabble region. Another local item on the menu is fried hare, and there's a cheap and sizeable fish menu.

Other restaurants include the *Alengarve* and *Repuxo*, both on Avenida Aureliano Mira Fernandes, and the *Brazileiro* at the top of hill, opposite the petrol station, on the Beja road.

Getting There & Away
The bus stand is by the roundabout. A Lisbon-Vila Real de Santo António express coach passes through in each direction once a day. There is one other daily bus to Mértola from Vila Real (under two hours away), and three from Beja (less than an hour away). Lisbon is about four hours away.

BEJA
• pop 22,000 • postcode 7800 • area code ☎ 084
At its worst, Baixo Alentejo's principal town is dull and depressing, with drunks often lounging in the main pedestrianised street and budget accommodation hard to come by. But while you wouldn't want to make a special trip here, you can spend a pleasant few hours meandering through its historic old centre. Its various transport connections also make it a convenient stopover en route between Évora and the Algarve.

History
Built on the highest point of the surrounding plains, Beja was founded by the Romans, who called it Pax Julia after peace between the Romans and rebellious Lusitanians was restored by Julius Caesar. It soon became an important agricultural centre – as it still is today – flourishing principally on the trade in wheat and oil.

Little evidence remains of the 400 years

ALENTEJO

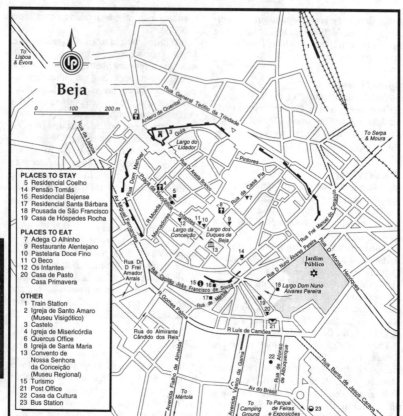

Beja

0   100   200 m

PLACES TO STAY
5   Residencial Coelho
14 Pensão Tomás
16 Residencial Bejense
17 Residencial Santa Bárbara
18 Pousada de São Francisco
19 Casa de Hóspedes Rocha

PLACES TO EAT
7   Adega O Alhinho
9   Restaurante Alentejano
10 Pastelaria Doce Fino
11 O Beco
12 Os Infantes
20 Casa de Pasto
    Casa Primavera

OTHER
1   Train Station
2   Igreja de Santo Amaro
    (Museu Visigótico)
3   Castelo
4   Igreja de Misericórdia
6   Quercus Office
8   Igreja de Santa Maria
13 Convento de
    Nossa Senhora
    da Conceição
    (Museu Regional)
15 Turismo
21 Post Office
22 Casa da Cultura
23 Bus Station

of subsequent Moorish rule, except for some distinctive 16th-century azulejos in the Convento de Nossa Senhora da Conceição (now the Museu Regional). The town was recaptured from the Moors in 1162.

Beja's fame among the Portuguese rests on a scandalous series of 17th-century love letters allegedly written by one of the convent's nuns, Mariana Alcoforado, to a French cavalry officer, Count Chamilly. She was said to have had a love affair with the count while he was stationed in Beja during the time of the Portuguese war with Spain. The passionate *Five Letters of a Portuguese Nun* first emerged in a French 'translation' in 1669 and later appeared in English, but, as the originals were never found, the letters' authenticity has been the subject of lively controversy ever since.

Orientation

Beja's historic core is circled by a ring road and surrounded by ugly modern outskirts. The train station is on the north-east edge of town and the bus terminal is on the south-east side. The main sights are all within easy walking distance of each other.

Information

Tourist Office The cheery turismo (☎ 236 93) is at No 25 on the pedestrianised Rua Capitão João Francisco de Sousa. It's open Monday to Saturday from 10 am to 8 pm (to 6 pm in winter).

Money There are Multibanco ATM near the turismo, along the adjacent pedestrianised Rua de Mértola and at the top of the street near Largo Dom Nuno Álvares Pereira.

Post & Communications The post and telephone office is just south of Largo Dom Nuno Álvares Pereira, on Rua Luís de Camões (the post office entrance is on Rua do Canal).

Quercus The local branch (☎ 32 13 26) of Portugal's major environmental organisation, Quercus, keeps irregular hours at Praça da República 29.

Emergency The main police station is on Largo Dom Nuno Álvares Pereira.

Praça da República

This attractive square with a central *pelourinho* (pillory) and an elegant Manueline arcade on the north side is the historic heart of the old city. Dominating the square is the 16th-century Igreja da Misericórdia, a hefty church with an immense porch that started life as a meat market – hence its suitably crude, hammered stonework.

Convento de Nossa Senhora da Conceição & Museu Regional

This former Franciscan convent on Largo da Conceição, founded in 1459, displays a mix of plain Gothic and fancy Manueline styles typical of the time. The interior is even more lavish, especially the rococo chapel drowning in 17th and 18th-century gilded woodwork. The cloister has some splendid 16th and 17th-century azulejos, although the earliest and most interesting examples are in the chapter house, which also sports an incredible painted ceiling and carved doorway.

The museum's collection pales by comparison with the convent itself, though it manages a bit of something on almost every era, from Roman mosaics and stone tombs to 16th-century paintings. It's open from 9.45 am to 1 pm and 2 to 5.15 pm daily except Mondays and holidays; the 100$00 admission fee includes the Igreja de Santa Amaro (same opening hours).

Castelo

The castle was built on Roman foundations by Dom Dinis in the late 13th century. There are grand views of rolling Alentejan wheat fields from the top of the Torre de Menagem (100$00 admission). The Museu Militar (Military Museum) inside the castle consists of a few scattered cannons in the grounds. In summer the castle is open Tuesday to Saturday from 10 am to 1 pm and 2 to 6 pm (in winter from 10 am to noon and 1 to 4 pm).

Igreja de Santa Amaro & Museu Visigótico

Just beyond the castle, the Igreja de Santa Amaro (or parts of it at any rate) dates from the early 6th century, when it was a Visigothic church, which would make it one of the oldest standing buildings in Portugal. Inside, some of the original columns display intriguing carvings. It now serves as a Visigothic museum and keeps the same hours as the Museu Regional.

Special Events

One of Beja's biggest annual events is its Ovibeja 'sheep fair' in mid-March. Held in the Parque de Feiras e Exposições on the south-eastern outskirts, it features cow and horse markets, sheep shows and an enthusiastic display of regional music, handicrafts and gastronomy. Other major festivals are the Festas da Cidade in May and the Festa de São Lourenço e Santa Maria, a lively affair with lots of singing and dancing, in the second week of August.

Places to Stay

Beja's municipal camping ground (☎ 243 28) is off Avenida Vasco da Gama (not far from the bus terminal) and is part of a municipal sports area that includes a swimming pool and tennis courts. Typical rates are 315$00 per person, 210$00 to 368$00 for a tent and 210$00 per car.

Some of the cheapest digs in town are at the run-down *Pensão Tomás* (☎ 32 46 13; fax 32 07 96), at Rua Alexandre Herculano 7, which has musty doubles with shower for 4500$00. At roughly the same price and standard are the old-fashioned rooms of *Casa de Hóspedes Rocha* (☎ 32 42 71), at Largo Dom Nuno Álvares Pereira 12.

A better option with bright upstairs rooms (some overlooking the square) for around 6000$00 a double is *Residencial Coelho* (☎ 32 40 31; fax 32 89 39) at Praça da República 15. Near the turismo are several similarly priced residencials: the frilly *Residencial Bejense* (☎ 32 50 01) at Rua do Capitão João Francisco de Sousa 57 (all rooms with shower), and *Residencial Santa Bárbara* (☎ 32 20 28; fax 32 12 31) at Rua de Mértola 36, whose large carpeted doubles have private baths.

Gorgeous luxury can be found in the *Pousada de São Francisco* (☎ 32 84 41; fax 32 91 43) on Largo Dom Nuno Álvares Pereira where a double room – converted from a cell of the 16th-century São Francisco Convent – will set you back 23,000$00.

Places to Eat

There are several options on or near Rua dos Infantes ranging from the cheap locals' favourite, *O Beco* (☎ 259 00) at Beco da Rua dos Infantes, with dishes from around 900$00, to the classy *Os Infantes* at Rua dos Infantes 14, which has a menu of very good Alentejan specialities from around 1300$00. *Pastelaria Doce Fino*, Rua dos Infantes 29, serves yummy regional pastries in a bright, modern setting.

Casa de Pasto Casa Primavera (☎ 259 80), opposite the post office at Rua do Canal 19, is a simple place with dishes from around 850$00. For a wider choice, head for the popular *Restaurante Alentejano* (☎ 238 49) at Largo dos Duques de Beja 6, where servings are huge and reasonably priced. It's

closed on Saturdays and packed at lunch times.

At Rua da Casa Pia 28 (opposite Red Cross headquarters) is the unmarked *Adega O Alhinho* (☎ 246 15), which is a little dive stacked with huge wine jars (your table wine comes straight from the jar!). Choose your entrance: one of the two stable doors leads into the dark, seedy bar, while the red door leads into the tiny restaurant where you'll be lucky to get a seat at lunch time. Dishes are cheap (from 700$00) and include a mouth-watering choice of desserts. It's closed on Sundays.

Getting There & Away

Bus Ordinary bus services are usually quicker and more frequent than the train for nearby destinations. On weekdays there are nine buses daily to Serpa, eight to Évora and four to Mértola (around half that number on weekends). There are also services to Faro via Albufeira three times daily, to Lisbon around four times daily, and a service to Tomar and Vila Real de Santo António once a day.

Train Beja is on the Lisbon to Funcheira (near Ourique) railway line, with trains to/from Lisbon's Barreiro station five times daily (taking two to three hours). The railway's bus service also connects Beja with Évora twice daily and with Serpa and Moura three times daily.

SERPA
• *postcode 7830* • *area code ☎ 084*

Approach Serpa on a dusky summer's evening from Beja (30 km to the north-west) and the striking outlines of the castle walls and aqueduct above the surrounding plains might lead you to believe you've arrived at an undiscovered medieval outpost. It's a pity the ugly grain elevator on the outskirts ruins the image.

A pity, too, that there are few decent budget places to stay and that transport connections are sparse: Serpa's untouristy, laid-back atmosphere and narrow lanes, cobbled in patterns and lined with white-washed houses, make it a tempting place for a stop en route to Spain or the Algarve.

Orientation

Those who are arriving by car must brave tight-fit gateways into the old town, blind corners and streets so narrow pedestrians often have to squeeze into doorways when cars pass by.

The bus station, mercado municipal and camping ground are about 700m south-west of the town centre, Praça da República. If you've arrived on the railway's shuttle bus from Beja, you'll be unceremoniously dumped by the road on the northern out-skirts, a 20-minute walk from the town centre.

Information

Right in the centre at Largo Dom Jorge de Melo 2, the friendly turismo (☎ 537 27) has maps, brochures and a display of local handi-crafts and it can help with accommodation. It's open daily from 9 am to 12.30 pm and 2 to 5.30 pm, except in peak season when afternoon hours are 4 to 7 pm.

There's a bank around the corner in Praça

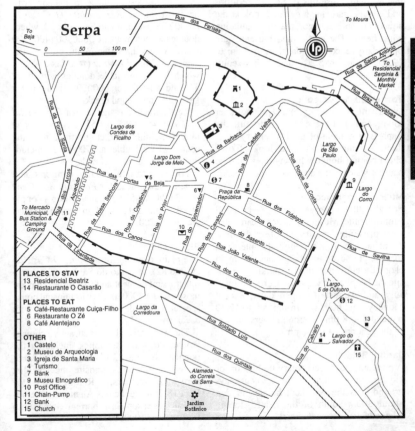

ALENTEJO

PLACES TO STAY
13 Residencial Beatriz
14 Restaurante O Casarão

PLACES TO EAT
5 Café-Restaurante Cuiça-Filho
6 Restaurante O Zé
8 Café Alentejano

OTHER
1 Castelo
2 Museu de Arqueologia
3 Igreja de Santa Maria
4 Turismo
7 Bank
9 Museu Etnográfico
10 Post Office
11 Chain-Pump
12 Bank
15 Church

da República, and another outside the walls on Largo 5 de Outubro. The post office is near the centre on Rua do Governador.

Castelo

The courtyard of the surprisingly small castle is entered beneath a precariously balanced bit of ruined wall. In the keep is the small **Museu de Arqueologia** with a life-size plaster rendition of the Last Supper and a small, poorly labelled collection of archaeological remnants revealing bits of Serpa's history, which goes back to the arrival of the Celts over 2000 years ago.

The view from the **battlements** is the best feature, with close-ups of Serpa's rooftops and cottage gardens, a detailed look at the aqueduct, and a panorama of undulating wheatfields. The castle (and museum) are open daily, except holidays, from 9 am to 12.30 pm and 2 to 5.30 pm; there is no entry fee.

Town Walls & Aqueduct

Walls still stand around most of the inner town, and along the west side run the impressive remains of an 11th-century aqueduct. At one end is what looks like a chain-pump (though why anyone would be hauling water *to* the aqueduct is not clear).

Museu Etnográfico

Serpa's other major attraction is its good Ethnographic Museum, which features a well-presented portrayal of traditional Alentejan life, from agricultural implements to olive presses to rural costumes. It's in an elegantly converted market building opposite the hospital on Largo do Corro. In June, July and August it's open daily, except Mondays and holidays, from 9 am to 12.30 pm and 4 to 8 pm (afternoon hours the rest of the year are 2 to 5.30 pm).

Jardim Botânico

A pleasant spot to rest weary limbs – or for kids to run off energy in the adjacent playground – is the well-kept botanic garden about 300m south of the centre, facing Alameda do Correia da Serra.

Monthly Market

On the last Tuesday of each month a huge country market with clothes, toys, shoes and agricultural implements sprawls outside the walls, beside Rua de Santo António on the north-east outskirts.

Places to Stay

There is an excellent municipal camping ground, *Serpa Parque de Campismo* (☎ 532 90), at Largo de São Pedro on the south-west edge of town near the bus station. It's open all year and fees include entry to the swimming pool opposite.

Budget accommodation is hard to come by. The cheapest available rooms appear to be those above *Restaurante O Casarão* (☎ 902 95), at Largo do Salvador 20, where doubles without bath are 3000$00 (4000$00 with). Across the square is the crisply efficient *Residencial Beatriz* (☎ & fax 534 23), which has comfortable doubles with bath, TV and air-con for 6000$00 (including a generous continental breakfast).

Less attractive is the newish *Residencial Serpinia* (☎ 530 55; fax 539 61) on the road to the monthly market, north-east of the centre, where doubles are 7000$00 – including disco music at weekends.

For more tasteful modern comforts, and superb views, head for *Pousada São Gens* (☎ 537 24; fax 533 37) on a hilltop a couple of km south of town. High-season doubles are 19,000$00.

Places to Eat

The plain, pleasant *Restaurante O Casarão* (☎ 906 82), at Largo do Salvador 20, has a select menu of meat and fish dishes that are mostly under 1000$00. Try its unusual house speciality, açorda (bread-based stew) with bacalhau.

There are several other attractive choices around Praça da República, including the popular, well-run *Café-Restaurante Cuica-Filho* (☎ 905 66), opposite the socialist party's headquarters, at Rua das Portas de Beja 18. It has delicious Alentejan specialities such as ensopada de borrego (lamb stew) for just over 1000$00.

At Praça da República 10, *Restaurante O Zé* (☎ 902 46) is something of a tourist magnet and its bar is lively with young locals. The overwhelmingly friendly Zé recommends his creamy queijo de Serpa cheese and it's well worth the 400$00 tag. Across the square, the Art Deco *Café Alentejano* (☎ 531 89) is a fine place to buzz up on bicas and local queijadas de Serpa pastries. The restaurant upstairs is pricey.

For self-caterers, the whitewashed mercado municipal, liveliest in the mornings, is south-west of the centre on the way to the bus station.

Getting There & Away

On weekdays nine buses run from Beja to Serpa, two of which continue to Moura. Where once there was a rail link there's now a shuttle bus service run by the railway – it travels three times daily between Beja and Moura via Serpa, although passengers are dropped off on the main road on Serpa's outskirts.

The Spanish frontier at Ficalho is 55 minutes away and is accessible by one bus daily (weekdays only).

MOURA

• *postcode 7860* • *area code* ☎ *085*

Surrounded by a soporific landscape of undulating wheatfields and olive orchards, Moura feels a bit like a ghost town. Some 60 km north-east of Beja, well off the main tourist trail, it was once patronised by the wealthy for its thermal spa (which is still in use). Now its quiet, broad streets and elegant houses seem oddly grandiose for such an out-of-the-way place.

The town's most dramatic moment in history is something of a fantasy too: legend recounts how a Moorish woman, Moura Salúquiyya, opened the gates of the town to her betrothed only to find a horde of Christians had murdered him and his escort and dressed in their victims' clothes. They sacked the town, and Moura flung herself from a tower in despair.

The Moors' 500-year occupation came to an end in 1232 with a rather less inspired takeover by Christian forces, though Moura's name lived on and her fate was inscribed in the town's coat of arms.

Today the town makes a pleasant excursion, if only to visit the immaculate Moorish quarter (one of the best preserved in Portugal) or to soak in the spa. Don't plan a long stay – unless you're scouting for romantic film settings you could die of boredom within 24 hours.

Orientation

The bus station is by the defunct railway station at the newer, southern end of town. It's a 10-minute walk from here to the old town, where you'll find all the main places of interest.

Information

It's a five-minute walk from the bus station (turn left into the first main street, Rua das Forças Armadas, and right at the end) to the turismo (☎ 249 02; fax 236 02) on Largo de Santa Clara. If you're driving from Serpa you'll pass it on your way into town. The office, open weekdays only from 9 am to 1 pm and 2 to 6 pm, can provide a list of accommodation and a fairly useless town map.

Spa

The thermal spa is at the entrance to the shady Jardim Dr Santiago at the east end of Praça Sacadura Cabral. It's open Tuesday to Saturday from 8 am to 1 pm and 3 to 6 pm; for 100$00 you can soak in a bath for 15 minutes. The bicarbonated calcium waters, said to be good for rheumatism, also burble from the richly marbled Fonte das Três Bicas (Fountain with Three Spouts) just before the entrance.

Igreja de São Baptista

Just outside the gardens you'll notice the Manueline portal of this 16th-century church. It's a flamboyant bit of decoration – carvings of knotted ropes, crowns and armillary spheres – on an otherwise dull façade. The church has little of interest inside except

---

Water Wars

The arid Alentejo is always gasping for water. One of Portugal's major agricultural regions, it has a host of irrigation schemes and reservoirs to keep its soil from cracking up. In addition, an agreement with Spain in 1968 was meant to ensure that the waters of the Rio Guadiana (which rises in Spain and flows through the Alentejo) were fairly shared.

But successive droughts have strained the agreement: Spain is accused of using more water from the Guadiana than the agreed amount, and the Alentejo is suffering. Now, after decades of delay, the Portuguese have taken matters into their own hands and have started work on a giant dam at Alqueva (near Moura) to guarantee both irrigation supplies and electricity for years to come.

The 96m-high dam will create one of the biggest reservoirs in Europe when it's finished in 2002 – so big that it could substantially reduce the average temperature of the surrounding region. One thing that's likely to heat up, on the other hand, is the dialogue with Spain, which has its own incompatible plans for making the most of the Guadiana. ■

---

for some so-so 17th-century Sevillian azulejos.

Mouraria

The old Moorish quarter lies at the west end of Praça Cabral: a tight cluster of narrow cobbled lanes bordered by white terraced cottages with eye-catching broad chimneys. Dusk is a good time to wander here – people lean out of their stable-doors for a chat and kids play hide and seek in the streets.

Castelo

Above the old town is a ruined tower, the last remnant of a Moorish fortress. Rebuilt by Dom Dinis and again by Dom Manuel I in 1510, the castle itself was largely destroyed in the 18th century, but it still sports a couple of chunky towers.

Places to Stay

Closest to the bus station, at Rua da Vitória 8, is the rude *Pensão Italiana* (☎ 223 48); if you can get a foot in the door you'll find doubles from 3500$00. A better bet is *Pensão Alentejana* (☎ 225 29), just down the road at Largo José Maria dos Santos 40. Doubles without bath in this appealing old house are 2500$00; newer rooms with private bath are on the cards.

The posh place in town is *Hotel de Moura* (☎ 25 10 90; fax 246 10), overlooking quiet Praça Gago Coutinho. The ornate façade hides a surprisingly tacky interior, but the rooms (9850$00 a double, including breakfast) have all the frills.

Places to Eat

There are plenty of cafés and restaurants around Praça Sacadura Cabral. For regional delicacies try *Restaurante Mourense O Carlos* (☎ 225 98) at Rua da República 37. *Talho Charcutaria* at No 15 has an excellent selection of regional wines, cheeses and cold meats.

The mercado municipal is in a huge glassed-in building in Praça Sacadura Cabral, a 10-minute walk from the turismo.

Getting There & Away

There are two bus services on weekdays between Beja and Moura (via Serpa), in addition to the three bus services run each day by the railway.

Alto Alentejo

ÉVORA

• *pop 54,000* • *postcode 7000* • *area code ☎ 066*
Évora, Alentejo's capital and main agricultural marketplace, is also one of Portugal's most delightful towns, with a combination of historical elegance and a lived-in feel. Its well-preserved, Moorish walled centre – with prominent remains dating back to

Roman times and a trove of other architectural and artistic treasures (not to mention plenty of good cafés and restaurants) – make it an easy spot for lingering. It boasts more official monuments and buildings of public interest than any Portuguese city except Lisbon. In 1986 UNESCO declared the entire centre a World Heritage Site.

You'll need a couple of days to make the best of it. Try not to make one of them a Monday, when most tourist attractions and many other establishments are closed.

History

Évora's history is long and rich. The Celtic settlement of Ebora was here before the Romans, who came in 59 BC, made it a military outpost and eventually an important centre of Roman-occupied Iberia. It was probably the headquarters of a rebel governor, Quintus Sertorius, who attempted unsuccessfully to detach most of the region from the Roman Empire.

After a depressing Visigothic spell, the town again flowered as a centre of trade under the Moors. In 1165 Évora's Muslim rulers were hoodwinked by a rogue Christian knight known as Giraldo Sem Pavor (Gerald the Fearless) who, according to one well-embellished story, single-handedly stormed one of the town's watchtowers by climbing up a ladder of spears driven into the walls. From there he distracted municipal sentries while his companions took the town with hardly a fight. The Moors took it back in 1192, holding on to it for another 20 years or so.

Évora's golden era came in the 14th to 16th century when it was favoured by the Alentejo's own House of Avis, along with numerous scholars and artists. It was declared an archbishopric in 1540 and got its own Jesuit university in 1559. When the cardinal-king Dom Henrique, last of the Avis line, died and Spain seized the throne in 1580, the royal court left Évora and the town began wasting away. The Marquês de Pombal's closure of the university in 1759 was the last straw. French forces plundered the town and massacred its defenders in July 1808.

Orientation

Évora climbs a gentle hill above the Alentejo plain. Around the walled centre runs a ring road from which you can enter on several 'spoke' roads. The town's focal point is Praça do Giraldo, 200m from the bus station on Rua da República. The train station is outside the walls, one km south of the square.

If you're driving, save your temper (and your wing mirrors) by staying out of the old town's narrow one-way streets. You'll be lucky to find a parking space in Praça do Giraldo.

Certain parts of Rua João de Deus and Rua 5 de Outubro near Praça do Giraldo are theoretically pedestrian-only and kerbed, but that doesn't stop delivery vehicles and others, so keep your eyes open.

Information

Tourist Office The town's very helpful turismo (☎ 226 71), right on Praça do Giraldo at No 73, is open from 9 am to 7 pm on weekdays, and 12.30 to 5.30 pm on weekends and holidays. They'll give you a poor town map with a few walking routes; a bigger, better map is the *Planta de Évora* that's for sale in a tobacco shop around the corner on Rua do Raimundo, and at the Livraria Nazareth (bookshop) across the square.

Money There are dozens of Multibanco ATMs on and around Praça do Giraldo. The town's only automatic-exchange machine is outside the turismo.

Post & Communications Phonecards are on sale at newsagents and tobacco shops and at the telephone office, north of the square on Rua do Menino Jesus. Around the block on Rua de Olivença is the main post office, where you can also place calls. The post office is open weekdays from 8.30 am to 6.30 pm and Saturdays from 9 am to 12.30 pm.

Travel Agencies TurAventur (☎ & fax 74 31 34), upstairs at Rua João de Deus 21, has adventurous walking, biking and jeep tours of the Alentejo. Bike tours include a 40-km

ALENTEJO

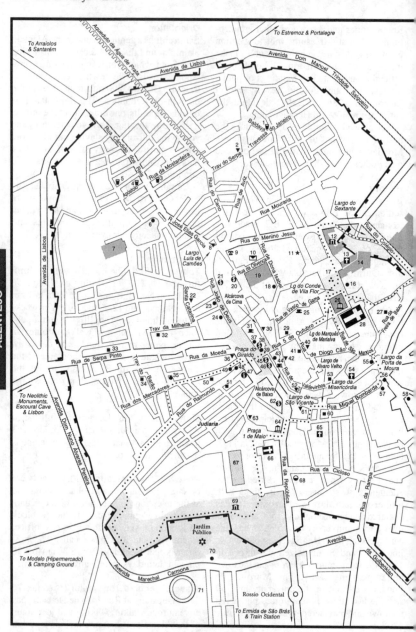

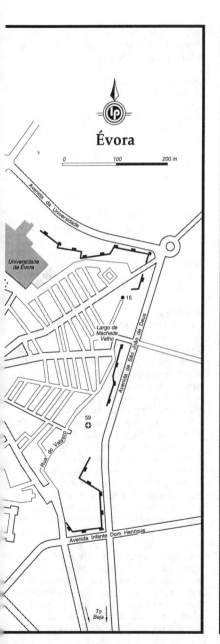

PLACES TO STAY
14 Pousada dos Lóios
27 Pensão Policarpo
29 Residencial Riviera
32 Hotel Santa Clara
33 Residencial O Alentejo
34 Pensão Portalegre
41 Residencial Diana
50 Pensão O Giraldo
51 Pensão Os Manueis
53 Residencial Solar Monfalim
60 Hotel Planície

PLACES TO EAT
2 Restaurante-Bar Molhóbico
8 Restaurante Martinho
22 Restaurante O Garfo
25 Dom João Cafetaria
30 Restaurante O Grémio
31 Café Arcada
36 Restaurante & Cafetaria Cozinha de
   Santo Humberto
40 O Contesavel
42 Restaurante Aquario
44 Cafetaria 35
52 Restaurante O Túnel
61 Gelataria Zoka
63 Café Restaurant O Cruz

OTHER
6 Évora Rent-a-Bike
9 Telephone Office
10 Post Office
11 Police Station
12 Palácio dos Duques de Cadaval
13 Igreja de São João
14 Pousada dos Lóios
16 Public Library
17 Templo Romano
18 Hertz
19 Câmara Municipal
20 Multibanco ATM
21 Multibanco ATM
23 TurAventur
24 Foto Inácio
26 Museu de Évora
28 Sé & Cloister
35 Lavandaria
37 Pharmacy
38 Multibanco ATM
39 Livraria Nazareth
43 Bookshop
45 Multibanco ATM
46 Multibanco ATM
47 Turismo & Automatic Exchange Machine
48 Tobacco Shop
49 Alliance Française
54 Igreja da Misericórdia
55 Bookshop
56 Pharmacy
57 Turalentejo
58 Casa Cordovil
59 Évora District Hospital

Continued on next page

ALENTEJO

62	Multibanco ATM
64	Museu do Artesanato
65	Igreja da Nossa Senhora da Graça
66	Igreja de São Francisco & Capela dos Ossos
67	Mercado Municipal
68	Bus Station
69	Palácio de Dom Manuel (Galeria das Damas)
70	Ludoteca de Évora (Kindergarten)
71	Bullring

ENTERTAINMENT

1	Bar Desassossego
3	Pub O Trovador
4	Diplomata Pub
5	Club Dezasseis
7	Teatro Garcia de Resende
15	Casa dos Bonecos

pedal around the region's megalithic stone monuments (see Around Évora). Its all-day jeep safari packages include a monuments tour, a castles tour and a handicrafts tour, each costing 17,500$00.

Turalentejo (☎ 227 17), Rua Miguel Bombarda 78, seems competent enough at making orthodox travel arrangements and organising car rental. It's open weekdays from 9 am to 7 pm and on Saturday mornings.

Bookshops The town's biggest bookshop, Livraria Nazareth, upstairs at Praça do Giraldo 46, has a few maps and camping guides and a limited number of books in English about Portugal. There are smaller bookshops at the north end of Alcárcova de Baixo and at Rua da Misericórdia 11.

Campuses Outside the walls to the north-east are the Italian Renaissance-style courtyards of the Universidade de Évora, a descendant (reopened in the 1970s) of the original Jesuit institution founded in the 16th century.

Cultural Centres The Alliance Française (☎ 233 39) isn't really a cultural centre but a language teaching centre, but it serves as a point of contact for French-speakers. It's at Rua dos Mercadores 3 (2nd floor), just behind the turismo.

Photography Foto Inácio, a photo shop offering three-hour developing and printing, is at Rua João de Deus 9.

Childcare In the jardim público is Ludoteca de Évora (☎ 217 89), a privately funded kindergarten for 5 to 14-year-olds. Younger children are also welcome but must be accompanied by an adult. It's open from 10 am to noon and 2 to 6 pm (to 5 pm in winter), and on weekends from 3 to 6 pm.

Laundry A cheerful *lavandaria* on Largo dos Mercadores offers next-day service.

Medical Services The Évora District Hospital (☎ 221 32) is east of the centre on Rua do Valasco.

Emergency The police headquarters (☎ 263 41) is on Rua Francisco Soares Lusitano, opposite the Templo Romano.

Walking Tour
From **Praça do Giraldo**, the hub of the old town, walk up pedestrianised Rua 5 de Outubro past cafés, restaurants, handicrafts shops and a few upper-end guesthouses; snoop into the crossing alleys for more of the same. At the top, on Largo do Marquês de Marialva, is the imposing **Sé** (cathedral).

Bearing left past the former archbishop's palace, now home to the good **Museu de Évora**, and through Largo do Conde de Vila Flor, you reach the remains of the **Templo Romano** (Roman temple), the best known of Évora's architectural monuments. Behind and beyond the temple are the public library; the **Convento dos Lóios** (now an elegant inn); its 15th-century church, the **Igreja de São João**; and the **Palácio dos Duques de Cadaval**, incorporating the towers of a 14th-century castle.

Continue round the palace and head east across Largo do Sextante, beneath some of the oldest **town walls**. Carry on along Rua do Colégio to the stately **Universidade de Évora**. From here, turn sharply right and climb past a small church and walled, private townhouses along Rua da Freiria de Cima.

Bear right at the rear of the cathedral and cross beneath an arch, back into the square in front of the museum.

Cross in front of the cathedral and down the stairs past its **cloister**, following Rua de São Manços around to the left and then bear right into **Largo da Porta de Moura**, with its globular Renaissance fountain. Turn right on Rua Miguel Bombarda, past shops and cafés, into Largo de Alvaro Velho, from where several cobbled lanes (most picturesquely Travessa da Caraça with its Moorish arches) descend to the **Igreja da Nossa Senhora da Graça**. Beware of cars in these lanes, which can press you to the wall.

From the church, head out onto Rua da República, go a block south and turn right past the **Museu do Artesanato** into Praça 1 de Maio, where you can rest your feet and have a bica or a cheap meal. Facing one another across the long square are the **Igreja de São Francisco** and the **mercado municipal**. At the far end is the peaceful **jardim público**, the **Palácio de Dom Manuel** and some photogenic 17th-century sections of the **town walls**.

Cross west through the park to Rua do Raimundo and climb up through Évora's former **judiaria** (Jewish quarter) back into Praça do Giraldo.

Praça do Giraldo & Around

This square has seen some potent moments in Portuguese history, including the 1483 execution of Fernando, Duke of Bragança, the public burning of victims of the Inquisition in the 16th century, and fiery debates on agrarian reform in the 1970s. Nowadays it harbours idle men and hungry pigeons at all hours of the day.

The narrow lanes to the south-west once defined Évora's judiaria. In the other direction, Rua 5 de Outubro climbs to the Sé and the old town's smartly restored heart. To either side of Rua 5 de Outubro, handsome townhouses feature wrought-iron balconies, and alleys pass beneath Moorish-style arches. Every other place on the way up is a handicrafts shop or a restaurant.

Sé

Évora's richly endowed, fortress-like cathedral – surely one of the most imposing churches in southern Portugal – was begun about 1186 during the rule of Sancho I, Afonso Henriques' son, probably on the site of an earlier mosque, and was completed about 60 years later. The flags of Vasco da Gama's ships bound for India were blessed here in 1497.

You enter through a portal flanked by 14th-century stone apostles, flanked in turn by massive, dissimilar granite towers with 16th-century conical hats. Stout and Romanesque at first, the cathedral gets more Gothic the closer you look, starting with the front door and continuing inside. Chandeliers hang from oversized rosary chains. The chancel, remodeled when Évora became the seat of an archdiocese, represents the only significant stylistic fiddle since the cathedral was completed.

Climb the steps in the south tower to the choir stalls and up to the **treasury**, which comprises several small galleries of grotesquely sumptuous ecclesiastical gear including vestments, statuary, chalices and paintings.

From the cathedral you can enter the cool **cloister**, an early 14th-century addition. Downstairs are the stone tombs of Évora's last four archbishops. At each corner of the cloister a dark circular staircase climbs to the top of the walls, from where there are good views across the Alentejo landscape.

The church, treasury and cloisters are open daily, except Mondays, from 9 am to noon and 2 to 5 pm. Admission is 300$00 for the whole lot.

Museu de Évora

Adjacent to the cathedral, in what used to be the archbishop's palace (built in the 16th century and frequently renovated), is the small, elegant Évora Museum. Luminous fragments of old statuary and façades from around the Alentejo – including Roman, medieval, Manueline and later styles – fill the courtyard. Upstairs are several rooms with temporary exhibits, former episcopal furnishings, and a gallery of Flemish paintings, including *Life of the Virgin*, a striking 13-panel series that was originally part of the Sé's altarpiece, done by anonymous Flemish artists, most or all of them working in Portugal around 1500.

The museum is open daily, except Mondays, from 10 am to 12.30 pm and 2 to 5 pm. Admission is 250$00.

Templo Romano

Across the Largo do Conde de Vila Flor from the museum are the startling remains of a 2nd or early 3rd-century Roman temple. It's Évora's visual trademark and the best preserved Roman monument in Portugal and probably the Iberian Peninsula. Though it's commonly referred to as the 'Temple of Diana', there's no consensus about the deity to which it was dedicated.

How did these 14 Corinthian columns, capped with Estremoz marble, manage to survive in such good shape for 18 centuries? The temple was apparently walled up in the Middle Ages to form a small fortress (and even used as the town slaughterhouse for a time), its heritage only rediscovered late in the 19th century.

Igreja de São João & Convento dos Lóios

The little Church of St John the Evangelist, facing the Templo Romano, was founded in 1485 by one Rodrigo Afonso de Melo, Count of Olivença and the first governor of Portuguese Tangier, to serve as his family's pantheon. Behind its elaborate Gothic portal is a nave lined with gorgeous azulejos produced in 1711 by one of Portugal's best known tilemakers, António de Oliveira Bernardes. Through grates in the floor you can see a cistern that predates the church, and an ossuary full of monks' bones.

Unfortunately, the church is privately owned, and open only unpredictably for tours (400$00). You might have some luck asking at the nearby Palácio do Duques de Cadaval, owned by the same family.

Though it's a national monument, the former Convento dos Lóios to the right of the church – including elegant Gothic cloisters

topped by a Renaissance gallery – was converted in 1965 into the top-end Pousada dos Lóios (see Places to Stay). They're clearly not thrilled to have tourists wandering around, so it's effectively out of bounds unless you can disguise yourself as a wealthy guest.

On the other side of the church, in a walled area that might once have been church gardens or a graveyard, is an upscale outdoor restaurant. The pousada and restaurant are reminders of how much of Évora's cultural patrimony remains in private hands.

Palácio dos Duques de Cadaval

West of the Igreja de São João is a 17th-century façade attached to a much older palace and castle, as revealed by the two powerful square towers that bracket it. The Palace of the Dukes of Cadaval was given to the governor of Évora, Martim Afonso de Melo, by Dom João I and also served from time to time as a royal residence. A section of the palace still serves as private quarters of the de Melo family; the other main occupant is the city's highway department. You can at least have a look at the inner courtyard through the open gate on weekdays. At the back the palace adjoins the town walls.

Town Walls

About a fifth of Évora's population lives within its old walls, some of them built atop 1st-century AD Roman fortifications (traces of which can be seen from the garden behind the Palácio dos Duques de Cadaval). Over three km of 14th-century walls enclose the northern part of the old town, while the bulwarks along the south side (such as those running through the jardim público) date from the 17th century. Several other ranks of walls have all but disappeared.

Largo da Porta de Moura

The so-called Moor's Gate to the inner town once stood beside what is now a pleasant square, the Largo da Porta de Moura, just south of the Sé. Among several elegant mansions around the square (and contemporary with the odd 16th-century Renaissance fountain in the middle) is Casa Cordovil, built in appealing Manueline-Moorish style, at the south-east end.

Igreja de São Francisco & Capela dos Ossos

On Praça 1 de Maio is Évora's best known church, a huge Manueline-Gothic structure completed around 1510 and dedicated to St Francis, adorned with the period's exuberant nautical motifs. Legend has it that the Portuguese navigator Gil Vicente is buried here.

But what draws the crowds through the dark interior is the Capela dos Ossos (Chapel of Bones), a small room behind the altar with walls and columns faced with the bones and skulls of some 5000 people. The bones were collected by 17th-century Franciscan monks from the overflowing graveyards of several dozen churches and monasteries. Adding to the ghoulish atmosphere is what looks like the desiccated corpse of a child, hanging off to the right as you enter. Portugal has other ossuary chapels, but this one is the creepiest. An inscription over the entrance translates roughly as 'We bones await yours'.

The chapel is open Monday to Saturday from 8.30 to 1 pm and 2.30 to 6 pm, and Sundays from 10 to 11.30 am and 2.30 to 6 pm (unless there are services in the church); admission is 50$00. The entrance is just to the right of the altar.

Jardim Público & Palácio de Dom Manuel

The pleasant public gardens straddle the 17th-century fortifications south of the Igreja de São Francisco. Inside the walls is the so-called Galeria das Damas (Ladies' Gallery) of the 16th-century Palácio de Dom Manuel (Dom Manuel's Palace), in a pastiche of Gothic, Manueline, neo-Moorish and Renaissance styles. Tradition has it that Vasco da Gama was here given command of the ships that ultimately sailed to India.

From the town walls you can see, a few blocks to the south, the crenellated, pointy-topped, 'Arabian Gothic' profile of the **Ermida de São Brás** (Chapel of St Blaise), dating from about 1490), possibly an early project of Diogo de Boitac, considered the originator of the Manueline style. There's little of interest inside.

On the park's lower level, outside the walls, is a good **parque infantil** (playground) and the Ludoteca de Évora (see Information).

Igreja da Nossa Senhora da Graça

Down an alley off Rua da República is one of Évora's more melancholy sights, the ungainly, neglected baroque façade of the Church of Our Lady of Grace topped by four uncomfortable-looking stone giants. It's mainly of interest to art historians, marking one of the first appearances (in the 17th-century cloister of the adjoining monastery) of the Renaissance style in Portugal.

Museu do Artesanato

This handicrafts museum featuring ceramics, painted furniture and other regional crafts, some of them for sale, has been closed for several years but is due to reopen in a government building at Praça 1 de Maio 7.

Aqueduto da Água de Prata

Marching into the town from the north-west is the Silver Waters Aqueduct, designed by Francisco de Arruda (better known for Lisbon's Tower of Belém) and completed in the 1530s to bring clean water to Évora. Walk up Rua do Cano to the end of the aqueduct, which is almost at street level. As the street drops the aqueduct rises, with houses, shops and cafés built right into its perfect arches. The surrounding neighbourhood, plain and unbothered by tourism, has an almost village-like feel.

Special Events

Évora's biggest annual bash, and one of the Alentejo's best country fairs, is the Feira de São João, held from approximately 22 or 23 June to 1 or 2 July. The Friday before Palm Sunday features a sizeable town fair called the Feira dos Ramos (Palm Fair).

Places to Stay

Accommodation is usually pretty tight in Évora. In summer it's wise to book ahead, though the tourist office will help you track down something to fit your budget in any case. They even post a list of places on the door when they're closed, including telephone numbers and prices. Many streets have signs directing you to the town's hotels and pensões. There are also some private rooms not listed with the turismo; watch for 'quartos' signs. Most university students stay in private rooms, so there are no cheap dormitory beds to be had.

Camping There is a well-equipped, year-round *Orbitur camping ground* (☎ 251 90; fax 298 30) about two km south-west of the town. Sample rates are 550$00 per person, 450$00 to 840$00 per tent and 470$00 per car. There are no local buses to the camping ground, but buses to Alcáçovas stop there. A taxi from the town centre is about 500$00.

Pensões & Residencials The few bottom-end beds available in Évora are mainly in the lanes behind the turismo. Cheapest is the run-down but quiet *Pensão Portalegre* (☎ 223 26), at Travessa do Barão 18, where a single/double with bath is 2000$00/3000$00. Two cordial places slightly up the scale are *Pensão Os Manueis* (☎ 228 61), upstairs at Rua do Raimundo 35, which has doubles without/with shower for 3500$00/5500$00; and *Residencial O Alentejo* (☎ 229 03), upstairs at Rua de Serpa Pinto 74, where a double is 4000$00 (with shared shower), 5000$00 (with attached shower) or 6000$00 (with bath). Similarly priced but noisier is *Pensão O Giraldo* (☎ 258 33) at Rua dos Mercadores 27.

On the other side of the square at Rua de Diogo Cão 2 is the sombre *Residencial Diana* (☎ 220 08, ☎ 74 31 13; fax 74 31 01), where doubles without/with bath go for 6500$00/9000$00, including breakfast. Better value at much the same price is *Pensão Policarpo* (☎ & fax 224 24), in a 16th-century townhouse at Rua da Freiria de Baixo 16. It's one of many older backstreet mansions with quiet courtyards behind high walls.

Another such place, at the upper end of the

scale, is the *Residencial Solar Monfalim* (☎ 220 31; fax 74 23 67), upstairs at Largo da Misericórdia 1. It has spotless singles/doubles from 10,000$00/12,000$00, with breakfast. This is due to be upgraded to an albergaria, so prices will probably rise.

Hotels Though calling itself a residencial, the professionally run *Riviera* (☎ 233 04, 251 11; fax 204 67), bang in the centre at Rua 5 de Outubro 49, is in effect a hotel. It's good value at 9000$00 for doubles with bath and TV, breakfast included. Offering plain, clean rooms at similar prices is the quiet *Hotel Santa Clara* (☎ 241 41; fax 265 44) at Travessa da Milheira 19.

The cheapest doubles (with bath and TV) at the unexceptional Best Western *Hotel Planície* (☎ 240 26; fax 298 80), Rua Miguel Bombarda 40, are a breathtaking 12,000$00.

In a class of its own is the snooty but deluxe *Pousada dos Lóios* (☎ 240 51; fax 272 48), occupying the former Convento dos Lóios beside the Templo Romano. A double in high season is 28,000$00 and in low season a mere 23,000$00.

Turihab On the plains around Évora are at least 10 converted farmhouses or quintas registered under the turismo de Habitacão or turismo Rural schemes. Recommended is *Monte da Serralheira* (☎ 74 39 57; fax 74 12 86). It's four km south of town – and possibly the only one with self-catering apartments (the smallest of which, for two, is about 7500$00 per night). They also have horses to ride. The turismo can help with this and others.

Places to Eat
Évora is awash with cafés and restaurants, many of them quite good value.

Restaurants Recommended is *Restaurante O Garfo* (☎ 292 56), Rua de Santa Catarina 13, offering healthy servings of feijoada ha alentejana (lamb and bean stew) for 950$00 and other lamb dishes at about 1100$00, in traditional surroundings. Another good place is *Restaurante Martinho* (☎ 230 57) at Largo

Luís de Camões 24. It's open daily for lunch, and for dinner until midnight, serving chargrilled fish and lamb, pork and rabbit stews.

Restaurante Aquario, Rua de Valdevinhos 7, does grilled lamb, beef and pork for under 1300$00, and has good borreguinhos de caldeirada (lamb ribs in tomato and vegetable sauce) for 1200$00. Pricier (fish and meat courses from 1300$00), but with good service and generous portions, is the small *Restaurante O Grémio* (☎ 74 29 31) at Alcárcova de Cima 10; it's open daily from noon to 3 pm, and daily, except Sundays, from 8 to 11 pm. The little *Restaurante O Túnel* (☎ 266 49), hidden away at Alcárcova de Baixo 59, has a long menu of meat courses, plus pork or lamb pratas do dia, for under 1200$00; it's closed on Sundays.

Restaurante Cozinha de Santo Humberto (☎ 242 51), at Rua da Moeda 39, is open for lunch and dinner with pricey regional specialities (and a fine dessert selection) in a traditional setting; advance bookings are suggested. A separate *cafetaria* faces Praça do Giraldo at No 85. Both are closed on Thursdays.

Cafés & Café-Restaurants The cavernous, busy *Café Arcada*, at Praça de Giraldo 10, dishes up sturdy, sensibly priced food all day – eg soups for 500$00, salads for 500$00 to 800$00, six kinds of omelettes, and various pratos do dia for 900$00 to 1350$00.

A recommended cheapo (no dish over 1200$00) is the locally popular *Café Restaurante O Cruz* (☎ 74 47 79) at Praça 1 de Maio 20, one of several places opposite the market, whose regional standards include good bacalhau in their own style and tasty carne com ameijoas (meat with clams). They're open daily from 8 am to 8 pm.

Another good-value place is *Restaurante-Bar Molhóbico* (☎ 74 43 43), at Rua de Aviz 91, which has a small dining section offering meat dishes and half a dozen versions of bacalhau (all under 1500$00) from 12.30 to 3.30 pm and 6.30 pm to at least 1.30 am.

Snacks *O Contesavel* is a comfortable, wood-panelled coffee and tea shop (salão de chá) at Rua de Diogo Cão 3, opposite the Residencial Diana. Another good coffee and snack spot is *Cafetaria 35* at Alcárcova de Baixo 35. A popular student hang-out that stays open late is *Dom João Cafetaria* at Rua de Vasco da Gama 10. Finally, if you've got a serious case of the munchies, enjoy yourself at the popular *Gelataria Zoka* ice-cream and coffee parlour at Largo de São Vicente 14 (at the west end of Rua Miguel Bombarda).

Self-Catering Pick up fruit and vegetables from the mercado municipal on Praça 1 de Maio and eat them in the adjacent jardim público. There is a Modelo hipermercado just beyond the town limits on the road to the camping ground and Alcáçovas.

Entertainment
Dance & Drama The 19th-century municipal Teatro Garcia de Resende, on Praça Joaquim António de Aguiar, has its own theatre company and drama school.

Puppet Theatre Five actors from the Teatro Garcia de Resende studied for several years with the only surviving master of a traditional rural puppet style called 'bonecos de Santo Aleixo' (puppets of Santo Aleixo). They offer performances of this and other styles, as well as hand-puppet shows for children, at a little theatre called Casa dos Bonecos (☎ 264 69, ☎ 251 99), at the end of a small beco (cul de sac) off Largo de Machede Velho, east of the university. They give shows for the general public only at weekends; tickets cost about 500$00 (300$00 for children's matinées). For current offerings, ask at the turismo.

Bars Most bars stay open until at least 2 am. Among popular student hang-outs are a cluster of bars north-west of the centre: *Club Dezasseis* (☎ 265 59) at Rua do Escrivão da Cámara 16; the *Diplomata Pub* (☎ 256 75), with frequent live music, at Rua do Apóstolo 4; and the *Pub O Trovador* (☎ 273 70) at Rua da Mostardeira 4. *Restaurante-Bar Molhóbico* (☎ 74 43 43) at Rua de Aviz 91 is open for dinner until 1.30 am (see Places to Eat) and drinks until at least 2 am. *Bar Desassossego* (☎ 264 75) at Travessa do Janeiro 15 is open daily, except Sundays, from 10 pm until (so they said) 2 pm next day.

Spectator Sports
Évora has its own bullring outside the walls near the jardim público. The bullfight season is roughly from May through October; ask the turismo about upcoming events.

Things to Buy
The lower end of Rua 5 de Outubro is a gauntlet of pricey *artesanatos*, heavy on cork knick-knacks, hand-painted furniture and pottery. There is also a shop at the Museu de Artesanato. You'll find cheaper pottery outside on the shady side of the mercado municipal.

On the second Tuesday of each month a Gypsy market sprawls across a big field called the Rossio Ocidental, just outside the walls on the road to the train station.

Getting There & Away
Bus From the claustrophobic bus station (☎ 221 21, ☎ 242 54) on Rua da República there are at least five Évora-Lisbon express coaches (2¾ hours) a day, and as many more ordinary coaches (3¾ hours), plus additional weekday-only services. Two Moura-Lisbon coaches also stop here. There are two direct Évora-Coimbra (4½ hours, via Santarém) coaches daily. Other daily long-distance express services include three to Faro (five hours, via Beja), one to Portimão and Lagos, and one to Porto.

Train Évora is on a branch line off the Lisbon-Beja railway line. The eastward service to places like Estremoz has long since been discontinued, leaving Évora effectively at the end of the line. From Évora's station (☎ 221 25) there are several express trains daily to Lisbon (three hours), plus slower services, as well as trains to the Algarve (tedious and indirect), Coimbra

(changes required), and regional chug-a-lug services to Beja.

Car Hertz (☎ 217 67) is at Rua de Dona Isabel 11. Europcar rents cars through the Turalentejo travel agency (see Information).

Getting Around
Taxi Évora's taxi drivers look pretty honest. Not all taxis have meters, so drivers may do their own fare calculations on the basis of fixed weekday, night and weekend rates. On a weekday expect to pay about 500$00 for a ride from Praça do Giraldo to the train station or the camping ground.

Bicycle Évora Rent-a-Bike (☎ 76 14 53) rents out mountain bikes for about 1500$00 a day (cheaper for three or seven days) from their own kiosk, which is part of a snack bar on Praça Joaquim António de Aguiar.

AROUND ÉVORA
The plains around Évora abound in prehistoric remains, including at least one cave decorated with Cro-Magnon art, and several dozen sizeable Neolithic stone monuments – menhirs (individual standing stones), dolmens (funereal temples or tombs) and cromlechs (circles of upright stones).

The following are among the easiest sites to find on your own; all are within a radius of about 10 km and could be visited in a single day trip. The roads are rough, more suited to 4WDs or mountain bikes than cars. Rent a bike from Évora Rent-a-Bike (and take food and water) or talk to TurAventur (see Évora – Information) about a guided trip.

A good booklet, *Guide to the Megalithic Monuments of the Évora Region*, is available from the Évora turismo. See also the boxed aside entitled Dolmens, Menhirs & Other Mysteries.

Neolithic Stone Monuments
Head west from Évora on the old Lisbon road (N114). At São Matias, 12 km out, turn south on a rough road to Guadalupe.

Four km beyond Guadalupe is Valverde,

road (N114). At São Matias, 12 km out, turn south on a rough road to Guadalupe.

Four km beyond Guadalupe is Valverde, home of the Universidade de Évora's modern School of Agriculture and the 16th-century Convento de Bom Jesus. Turn east at the convent onto a dirt track, following the signs to **Anta Grande do Zambujeiro**, the 5000-year-old Great Dolmen of Zambujeiro, the largest dolmen in Europe and now a national monument. Under a shabby sheet-metal shelter in a field of wildflowers and yellow broom, there are seven stones, six metres high, that form a huge chamber. The capstone was removed by archaeologists in the 1960s. Most of the site's relics – potshards, beads, flint tools etc – are in the Museu de Évora.

Return to Guadalupe and head west, again following signs, past the phallic **Menir dos Almendres** (Almendres Menhir) and the ruined **Anta dos Almendres** (Almendres Dolmen). About six km from Guadalupe, on a hill with a view of Évora, is the **Cromeleque dos Almendres** (Almendres Cromlech). One of Portugal's most dramatic Neolithic monuments, it's a huge oval of some 95 rounded, engraved granite monoliths – a Portuguese Stonehenge.

Carry on west for three more km to the N370 and turn left towards Santiago do Escoural, about five km away. Just after the Escoural cave (see the following section) and before the village, turn left and continue on for three km to the tiny, whitewashed **Anta Capela de São Brissos**, a 17th-century chapel with a vestibule built around several surviving stones of a dolmen.

Santiago do Escoural

Two or three km east of the village of Santiago do Escoural is a cave adorned with charcoal renditions of bison, horses and other animals, which are thought to be the work of Cro-Magnon artists.

Tours, organised at the cave, are given for groups of around 10 people, so you might have to wait around a bit. There is no charge, but tips are appreciated. The cave is open daily except Mondays and holidays. To get there from Évora take a regional bus to Santiago do Escoural and get off at *a gruta* (the grotto) before the village. From Santiago do Escoural it's about 25 km back to Évora via Valverde and the N380.

ARRAIOLOS

If you're after some superb Portuguese handicrafts (and have a few thousand dollars to spare), it's worth stopping at this pretty hilltop village 20 km north of Évora to shop for the exquisite Arraiolos hand-woven carpets which have been made here for seven centuries. Apart from the carpet shops lining Rua Alexandre Herculano there's little else to see, though there's a grand panorama from the ruined hilltop castle.

Getting There & Away

During the week, a handful of buses each day link Arraiolos with Évora (reduced to one or two at weekends).

ÉVORAMONTE

Travelling between Évora and Estremoz on the N18, you can't miss the stout white 16th-century castle of Évoramonte, 17 km from Estremoz, perched almost 500m above the plain on a spur of the Serra da Ossa.

Close up, the restored, concrete-clad monument is disappointing; its four plain round towers are distinguished only by a Manueline flourish of knotted stone, like bow ties, and interior columns with spiral carving. The one-street village is usually ghostly quiet.

Évoramonte saw fame only once, in 1834 when it hosted the battling brothers Dom Miguel and Dom Pedro: the house (No 41) where the Concession of Évoramonte was signed, sending Dom Pedro to the throne and Miguel into exile, is marked by a simple plaque.

Getting There & Away

During the week there are several buses daily between Évora and Estremoz, via Évoramonte. It's a steep climb from the new town near the main road up to the castle.

MONSARAZ
• *postcode 7200* • *area code* ☎ *066*

Arguably the most attractive fortified hilltop village in Portugal, Monsaraz is visible from miles around, towering over a somnolent landscape of ploughed fields and wild meadows dotted with cork and olive trees and Neolithic monuments.

Occupied long before the Moors arrived in the 8th century, Monsaraz was recaptured by the Christians under Giraldo Sem Pavor (Gerald the Fearless) in 1167 and subsequently given to the Knights Templar as a reward for their assistance. The castle was added in 1310.

You only need half an hour to meander from one end of the immaculate village to the other, but it's worth considering an overnight stay – a medieval aura descends over the town once the day-trippers have gone, and the panorama from the castle walls is best savoured at dusk and dawn.

Orientation

Happily there's no room for tour coaches or cars inside the walled village, so your arrival at one of the four gates will be as it should be: on foot. From the main parking lot, the Porta da Alcoba leads directly into the central Praça Dom Nuno Álvares Pereira. The main gate, Porta da Vila, is at the north end of town (the castle is at the other end) and leads directly into Rua São Tiago and the parallel Rua Direita, Monsaraz's two main streets.

Information

On Praça Dom Nuno Álvares, a half-hearted turismo (☎ 551 36) hands out lists of accommodation and bus times back to Reguengos de Monsaraz.

Igreja Matriz

The parish church (near the turismo) was rebuilt after the 1755 earthquake and again a century later. It has just one interesting possession, a 14th-century marble tomb carved with saints. An eye-catching 18th-century pelourinho, topped by a Manueline-style globe, stands outside.

Museu de Arte Sacra

Housed in a fine Gothic building (once perhaps the town's courthouse) beside the Igreja Matriz, the Museum of Sacred Art has a small collection of 14th-century wooden religious figures and 18th-century vestments and silverware. Its most famous item is a rare example of a 14th-century secular fresco (showing a good and bad judge, the latter appropriately two-faced). The museum is open from 9 am to 2 pm and 3 to 7 pm daily; entry is 200$00.

Casa da Inquisição

The now-ruined House of the Inquisition, near the castle, was established by a fanatically Catholic local aristocrat in 1536 when anti-Jewish fervour was sweeping Spain and Portugal.

Castelo

The castle at the south-west end of the village was one of many built by Dom Dinis as part of a defensive chain along the Spanish border. Now converted into a small bullring, its ramparts offer a great panorama over the Alentejan plains.

Special Events

Monsaraz gets packed out during its week-long Museu Aberto (Open Museum) music festival in July and on the second weekend of September, when bullfights and processions take place as part of the Festa de Nossa Senhora dos Passos. Unless booked well in advance, accommodation is almost impossible to find at these times.

Places to Stay

Several villagers have cashed in on the tourist era by converting their cottages into guesthouses or self-catering apartments. Some are now pricey Turihab properties. Among the least expensive – charging

BETHUNE CARMICHAEL

JULIA WILKINSON

The Alentejo
Top: Sunset over Marvão
Bottom: Cobbled street in Castelo de Vide

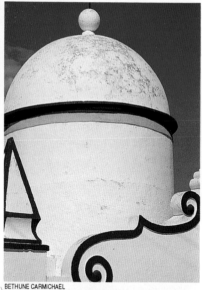

The Alentejo

Top Left: Water fountain, Telheiro, near Monsaraz
Top Right: Woman painting a house, Monsaraz
Bottom Left: Houses built into the aqueduct, Évora
Bottom Right: Templo Romano, Évora

around 5000$00 a double – are on Rua Direita: *Casa Dona Antónia* (☎ 551 42) at No 15, and *Casa do Condestável* (☎ 551 81) at No 4. At Praça Dom Nuno Álvares Pereira 10 is *Casa de António Pinto* (☎ 553 88) with five rooms; the cheapest of these (without private bath) costs around 5000$00.

Outside the walls are two posh establishments with comfortable doubles starting around 14,000$00. The *Estalagem de Monsaraz* (☎ 551 12; fax 551 01), at Largo São Bartolomeu 6, is a converted 300-year-old mansion with rustic décor, a garden and a swimming pool. They also organise jeep, bicycle and canoeing trips.

Offering even more rural pursuits (horse-riding, walking tours etc) is *Horta da Moura* (☎ 552 06; fax 552 41), a couple of km away en route to Mourão. Everything about this Alentejan quinta, set on an estate of fruit and olive trees, is on a grand scale, including its seven huge suites and six double rooms, fireplaces, furniture and, of course, the rates.

Places to Eat
There's a handful of restaurants, geared for tourists, most offering traditional Alentejan lamb dishes such as borrego assado (roast lamb) for around 1000$00 to 1200$00. For great sunset views over the plains, check out *Café Restaurante O Alcaide* (☎ 551 68) at Rua São Tiago 15. This and the *Restaurante São Tiago* (☎ 551 88), further along the same street at No 3, have their own bars too. For posh ambience and prices, head for *A Casa do Forno* (☎ 551 90) in Travessa da Sanabrosa.

Self-catering options are limited to bread and cheese from a grocer's at the Porta da Vila end of Rua São Tiago, and pastries from *Pastelaria A Cisterna* at the Porta da Vila end of Rua Direita.

Things to Buy
Near Porta da Vila a trio of handicraft shops sells hand-woven goods, miniature furniture and ceramics.

Getting There & Away
On weekdays there are at least three buses

daily between Monsaraz and Reguengos de Monsaraz (from where you can pick up connections to Évora). There's also one direct service daily from Évora (except Sundays).

REGUENGOS DE MONSARAZ
• *pop 11,000* • *postcode 7200* • *area code* ☎ *066*
This small, insignificant farming town, once famous for its sheep and wool production, is on the tourist trail today only because of its proximity and connections to Monsaraz. It's also close to the pottery centre of São Pedro do Corval (see Things to Buy) and an impressive half-dozen dolmens and menhirs out of around 150 scattered across the surrounding plains.

Useful as a one-night stopover if you don't make it to Monsaraz in time (or for dolmen fans), Reguengos also has a thriving handicrafts industry and some great local wine, Terras d'el Rei.

Orientation
The bus station is on the south-west outskirts of town, about 200m from the central Praça da Liberdade where you'll find cafés and accommodation.

Information
Near the main square, on Rua 1 de Maio, is the municipal turismo (☎ 513 15, ☎ 522 29). Staff may not speak English but they try hard and can often provide more information on Monsaraz than Monsaraz's own turismo. They also have a sketch map of nearby dolmens. The office is open weekdays from 9 am to 12.30 pm and 2 to 6 pm, and on weekends from 10 am to 12.30 pm and 2 to 5 pm.

Wineries
The Adega Cooperativa de Reguengos de Monsaraz (☎ 524 44), just outside town on the Monsaraz road, offers free group tours of its wine factory and could probably be persuaded to take individuals who sound keen enough.

Another major *adega*, with some lovely

ALENTEJO

old wine cellars, is Herdade do Esporão (☎ 517 06; call in advance for visits), a few km south of town. In operation as a winery for some 700 years, it produces mostly red wines for the domestic market.

Places to Stay & Eat

In the heart of town, on Praça da Liberdade, are a couple of decent places to stay. Cheapest is *Pensão Fialho* (☎ 51 92 66) at No 17, with seven neat little singles/doubles with bath for 2000$00/3000$00. *Pensão Gato* (☎ 523 53) nearby is a notch smarter with doubles at 4000$00 (without private bath) or 5000$00 (with).

Both pensões have restaurants; Gato's is the pricier one. Alternatively, try *Restaurante Central* (☎ 522 19), also on the praça, with a varied and imaginative menu.

Things to Buy

Mantas, hand-woven woollen blankets, are a Reguengos speciality. You can see these and other handicrafts – ceramics, wickerware and typical hand-painted Alentejan furniture – being produced in a workshop near the Adega de Cooperativa de Reguengos. The workshop (converted from an old slaughterhouse) belongs to TEAR (Portuguese for 'loom'), an association of young artisans founded to help preserve traditional local crafts.

If you're particularly interested in handwoven goods, check out the last remaining hand-loom producer of mantas Alentejanas, Fabrica Alentejana de Lanificios (☎ 521 79) – it's on the Mourão road east of town.

Serious ceramics buffs should head for São Pedro do Corval, five km east, whose 32 workshops make it one of the largest pottery centres in Portugal. Traditional Alentejan wares made here include plates, pots and floor tiles.

Getting There & Away

Reguengos is connected with Évora by a 45-minute bus service five times daily on weekdays. At least three buses daily (on weekdays only) run to Monsaraz.

ESTREMOZ

• *pop 8000* • *postcode 7100* • *area code* ☎ *068*

Dominated by its medieval hilltop castle, Estremoz is an elegant town of startling whiteness, thanks largely to its extensive use of marble. So plentiful is the supply of high-grade marble in this region that Estremoz and its neighbouring towns of Borba and Vila Viçosa are quite blasé about it, using it even for the doorsteps and window frames of its humblest cottages.

But despite appearances, Estremoz is basically a simple market town that's famous for its earthenware pottery, large Saturday markets, preserved plums and goat cheeses. One of the country's most charming rural museums is here too.

With a plentiful supply of restaurants and pensões it makes a convenient base for visiting the other marble towns or a suitable stopover en route to Évora or Portalegre. But it's hardly a hub of excitement – linger too long and you might calcify too.

Orientation

The lower, newer town, enclosed by 17th-century ramparts, is dominated by a huge square, Rossio Marquês de Pombal (known as the Rossio), where you'll find most accommodation, restaurants and shops. A 10-minute climb west of the Rossio brings you to the medieval quarter with its 13th-century castle and keep (which is now a pousada).

The bus station is on the south side of the Rossio beside the câmara municipal, although there is talk of moving it to the defunct train station on Avenida 9 de Abril, a 10-minute walk to the east.

Information

In a kiosk on the south-west corner of the Rossio is the turismo (☎ 33 20 71). Its cheerful staff can provide maps and other information, and it's open daily from 10 am to 12.30 pm and 3 to 6 pm.

Various banks around the Rossio and adjacent Largo da República have Multibanco ATMs. The post office is on Avenida 5 de Outubro. At the northern end of Avenida 9

Dolmens, Menhirs & Other Mysteries

You come across them all over the Alentejo plains, especially around Monsaraz and Évora: faintly engraved boulders, mysterious stone circles, towering fertility objects and cave-like stone tombs. They're part of a megalithic (literally, 'large stone' in Greek) style of construction found all along the European Atlantic coast and were built some five to six thousand years ago.

Nearly all are related to ritual worship of some kind. Dolmens are megalithic temples used as tombs, covered with a large flat stone and usually situated on hilltops or near water. Menhirs (tall, upright stones) and cromlechs (stone circles) were also places of worship and their construction represents a remarkable community effort.

There are half a dozen outstanding examples between Reguengos de Monsaraz and Monsaraz, including the Menhir de Bulhoa, four km north of Monsaraz off the Telheiro-Outeiro road. This phallic stone has intriguing traces of carved circles and lines. An even more impressive seven-tonne phallic monument stands as the centrepiece in the Cromleque do Xerez, a group of some 50 menhirs five km south of Monsaraz, en route to Xerez de Baixo and Mourão.

The Reguengos de Monsaraz turismo can provide a rough sketch map showing the location of these and other nearby menhirs. The excellent *Guide to the Megalithic Monuments of the Évora Region* is also available at Évora's turismo. ∎

JULIA WILKINSON

Cromeleque do Xerez

ALENTEJO

de Abril is the medical centre (*centro de saúde*; ☎ 228 69). The police station (☎ 222 89) is in the câmara municipal. There is a shady children's playground on Largo Dragões de Olivença, north-west of the Rossio.

The Lower Town

On the fringes of the Rossio are several imposing old churches, former convents and, on the north side, some monastic buildings which have been converted into an army barracks. Opposite these is an attractive marble-edged water tank called the Lago do Gadanha (Lake of the Scythe), after its scythe-wielding statue of Neptune. Some of the prettiest marble streets in town are south of the Rossio, off Largo da República.

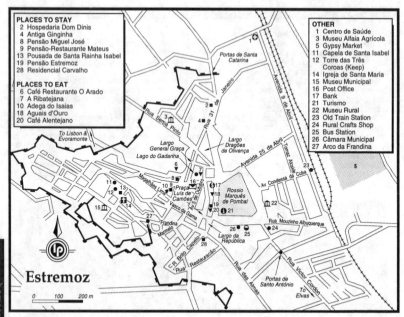

PLACES TO STAY
2 Hospedaria Dom Dinis
4 Antiga Ginginha
8 Pensão Miguel José
9 Pensão-Restaurante Mateus
13 Pousada de Santa Rainha Isabel
19 Pensão Estremoz
28 Residencial Carvalho

PLACES TO EAT
6 Café Restaurante O Arado
7 A Ribatejana
10 Adega do Isaias
18 Aguais d'Ouro
20 Café Alentejano

OTHER
1 Centro de Saúde
3 Museu Alfaia Agrícola
5 Gypsy Market
11 Capela de Santa Isabel
12 Torre das Três Coroas (Keep)
14 Igreja de Santa Maria
15 Museu Municipal
16 Post Office
17 Bank
21 Turismo
22 Museu Rural
23 Old Train Station
24 Rural Crafts Shop
25 Bus Station
26 Câmara Municipal
27 Arco da Frandina

Estremoz

0   100   200 m

Câmara Municipal Peek into this 17th-century former convent for a look at the imposing staircase decorated with azulejos of hunting scenes.

Museu Rural This delightful one-room museum at Rossio 62 portrays 1950s rural Alentejan life in miniature, with pottery and straw figures clothed in traditional costume, and model houses, carts and animals in cork and wood. Also on display is a huge wooden olive press and some typical Estremoz pottery. The museum is open daily, except Mondays, from 10 am to 1 pm and 3 to 5.30 pm; entry is 100$00.

Museu Alfaia Agrícola A museum of old agricultural and household equipment doesn't sound thrilling, but this cavernous old warehouse on Rua Serpa Pinto has some fascinating stuff on its three floors, from old

presses and threshers to huge brass pots and pans. It's open Tuesday to Friday from 9 am to noon and 2 to 5 pm; at weekends it's open in the afternoons only. Admission is 300$00.

The Upper Town
On foot you can reach the upper town by various wriggling routes but the easiest is to follow the narrow Rua da Frandina from the lower town's Praça Luís de Camões and enter the inner castle walls through the Arco da Frandina.

Palace & Keep At the top of the upper town is the stark white former royal palace, now the sumptuous Pousada de Santa Rainha Isabel. The palace was built in the 13th century by Dom Dinis for his new wife, Isabel of Aragón. After her death in 1336 (Dinis had died 11 years earlier) it became an ammunition dump. An inevitable explosion in 1698 destroyed most of it and the surrounding castle, though João V restored the palace in the 18th century for use as an armoury.

The 27m-high Torre das Três Coroas (Tower of the Three Crowns) survived and is still the dominant feature. It was supposedly built by three kings – Sancho II, Afonso III and Dinis.

Visitors are welcome to look around the public areas of the pousada and climb the keep, which offers a fantastic view of the old town and surrounding plains – though a grain elevator ruins the view to the east. Vertigo sufferers should refrain from looking down the holes intended for dumping boiling oil on invaders.

Chapel & Church The stout, square 16th-century Igreja de Santa Maria beside the pousada – more of an art gallery for some mediocre Portuguese primitive paintings than a church – keeps erratic hours. More interesting is the Capela de Santa Isabel behind the keep. This chapel was built in 1659 in honour of the queen who had died, aged 65, after a journey from Santiago de Compostela in Spain. The walls are covered with fine 18th-century azulejos portraying scenes from the life of the saintly queen.

A legend recalls how the king once demanded to see what she was carrying in her skirt (she was so generous to the poor she even gave them her own food). She let go of her apron but the bread she had been carrying had been miraculously transformed into roses.

The chapel is open to the public daily, except Mondays, from April to October only.

Museu Municipal Opposite the pousada, this museum offers another view of rural Alentejan life, though it's not as engaging as the Museu Rural. Housed in a 17th-century almshouse, it specialises in Estremoz pottery figurines. Upstairs is a reconstruction of a typical Alentejan house interior. The museum is open daily, except Mondays and holidays, from 9 am to 11.45 am and 2 to 5.45 pm; entry is 160$00.

Saturday Market

Although a shadow of its former self since the Gypsy market was moved to the eastern outskirts of town, the weekly Saturday market which hogs the Rossio still displays some fine Alentejan goodies and Estremoz specialities, especially goat and ewe's milk cheeses and a unique style of unglazed, ochre-red pottery.

Places to Stay

Some of the cheapest private rooms can be found at *Antiga Ginginha* (☎ 226 43), a private house at Rua 31 de Janeiro 4 belonging to a motherly old woman. Her two street-facing rooms are 1500$00/3000$00 for a single/double. The only drawback is occasional late-night noise from the adjacent disco-bar.

Another budget choice is the run-down *Residencial Carvalho* (☎ 227 12) at Largo da República 27, where old-fashioned doubles without bath are 4000$00 (including breakfast). Similarly priced, and packed out on Friday nights, is *Pensão Estremoz* (☎ 228 34), part of the Café Alentejano at Rossio 14. Despite its imposing marble staircase, the rooms (especially the bed springs) have seen better days.

At Travessa da Levada 8, west of the Rossio, *Pensão Miguel José* (☎ 223 26) has a warren of 13 tiny modern rooms. The owners are surly but the rooms – 3500$00/5000$00 without/with bath, breakfast included – are neat and clean. The welcome is warmer at the similarly priced *Pensão Restaurante Mateus* (☎ 222 26) at nearby Rua do Almeida 39.

The up-market choice in the lower town is *Hospedaria Dom Dinis* (☎ 33 27 17; fax 226 10) at Rua 31 de Janeiro 46, with well kitted-out doubles for 12,500$00. Surpassing everything is the *Pousada Rainha Santa Isabel* (☎ 33 20 75; fax 33 20 79), where you can stay in splendour, surrounded by antique furnishings and fine tapestries, for a mere 28,000$00.

Places to Eat

The upstairs restaurant of *Café Alentejano*

ALENTEJO

(☎ 228 34), at Rossio Marquês de Pombal 14, is *the* place to be on Saturday market days. Its various meat specialities include an English favourite, lamb with mint sauce!

You'll also need to be front of the queue for dinner at *Adega do Isaias* (☎ 223 18). This award-winning, dark and rustic tasca at Rua do Almeida 21 has outdoor grills, communal bench-tables and huge terracotta wine jars from which your house wine is served. It's not cheap – grilled meat dishes start at around 950$00 – but the atmosphere is worth the extra escudos. Get here by 7.30 pm to bag a seat. It's closed on Sundays.

Every other restaurant seems dull by comparison, but one that's popular with the locals is *A Ribatejana* (☎ 236 56) at Largo General Graça 41. It has half-portions from 500$00. Nearby, at Rua Narciso Ribeiro 7, is *Café Restaurante O Arado* (☎ 33 34 71), which specialises in frango no churrasco (roast chicken).

One of the best restaurants in town is the rather pretentious, wood-panelled *Aguais d'Ouro* (☎ 33 33 26) at Rossio Marquês de Pombal 27. If you don't mind paying upwards of 1400$00 per dish, you'll eat very well. Try the house speciality, borrego com espargos (lamb with asparagus).

Things to Buy
If you miss the Saturday market – or need some horse tackle, cowbells or baskets – there's a great handicraft and rural goods shop at Rua Victor Cordon 16, south-east of the Rossio.

Getting There & Away
On weekdays there are half a dozen buses between Estremoz and Évora including three express services (taking about an hour). Around six buses daily go to Évoramonte and Portalegre, with four to Elvas and three to Vila Viçosa. Buses to Lisbon and Faro leave three times daily.

BORBA
• *postcode 7150* • *area code* ☎ *068*
You'd think a town famous for its wine, antiques and marble would be a bit preten-

tious, but Borba keeps a pretty low profile. It has little in the way of notable monuments and has always been overlooked in favour of Vila Viçosa, six km to the south-east.

One of the three 'marble towns' (the others are Estremoz and Vila Viçosa), Borba is ringed by huge marble quarries and glows with marble whiteness. Even the public loos are made of marble. You can spend an agreeable few hours here, checking out the antique shops or visiting the wineries. Accommodation options are better at Estremoz.

The town comes to life once a year, in early November, when it hosts a huge country fair.

Orientation & Information
Borba's main square, Praça da República, with its ornate 18th-century marble fountain, the Fonte das Bicas, is the focus of town. The turismo (☎ 941 13) is in the camâra municipal on Rua do Convento das Servas.

Wineries
There are three adegas in town, all producing the famous Borba full-bodied red and white *maduro* (mature) wines, which are among the best in Portugal. Two adegas offer guided tours, probably in Portuguese. The turismo can help you arrange a visit.

The Adega Cooperativa de Borba (☎ 942 64), out on the Estremoz road, is the largest and produces over 10 million litres of wine a year. Opposite this is the Sociedade de Vinhos de Borba (☎ 942 10), whose ornately carved portal is worth a look. The adegas are usually open weekdays only, from 9 am to noon and 2 to 5.30 pm.

Getting There & Away
There are only two or three buses a day between Borba, Estremoz and Vila Viçosa.

VILA VIÇOSA
• *pop 6000* • *postcode 7160* • *area code* ☎ *068*
Vila Viçosa is a palatial but relaxing place and the finest of the three 'marble towns', with marbled streets, marble mansions, marble-adorned churches (over 20 of them) and a hilltop walled castle (alas, made only of stone). It's actually best known for its

Paço Ducal, the palatial home of the Bragança dynasty, whose kings ruled Portugal until the republic was founded in 1910. You can easily cover the sights in a day trip from Estremoz.

Orientation

Regional buses stop at the huge, sloping Praça da República. At the top is the 17th-century Igreja de São Bartolomeu; at the bottom is Avenida Bento de Jesus which leads to the castle. The ducal palace is five minutes walk north of the praça (follow Rua Dr Couto Jardim).

Information

The turismo (☎ 983 05, ☎ 88 11 01), on the right about halfway down the praça, is a useful stop if you want to find out about private accommodation.

Paço Ducal

The austere palace of the dukes of Bragança dates from the early 16th century when the fourth duke, Dom Jaime, decided to move out of his uncomfortable hilltop castle. The Bragança family had settled in Vila Viçosa in the 15th century when they were among the wealthiest nobles in the land. After the eighth duke became king in 1640, he and his successors – especially the last of the line, Manuel I – continued to visit the palace even

though it no longer hosted the banquets and festivities of Dom Jaime's time.

The interior is now pretty dull: the best furniture went to Lisbon after the eighth duke ascended the throne, and some went on to Brazil, where the royal family fled in 1807. But the private apartments have a ghostly fascination – toiletries, knick-knacks and clothes of Dom Carlos and his wife, Marie-Amélia, are laid out as if the royal couple were about to return (Dom Carlos left one morning in 1908 and was assassinated in Lisbon that afternoon).

Outside, at right angles to the palace, the Convento das Chagas de Cristo, once a mausoleum for the duchesses, is now being transformed into a pousada. The 16th-century cloisters now house an armoury museum, and the stables a coach museum.

The hour-long guided tours of the palace (usually in Portuguese), which set off daily, except Mondays, from 9.30 am to noon and 2.30 to 5 pm, are demanding on pocket and patience. The bracing fee of 1000$00 includes the armoury museum but not the coach museum – that's another 250$00.

Castelo

Dom Dinis' walled, hilltop castle, south of the palace, was where the Bragança family lived before the palace was built. A few small houses (still inhabited), a 16th-century

ALENTEJO

Skeletons in the Bragança Cupboard

The most illustrious member of the powerful Bragança family – descended from Dom João I's illegitimate son, Afonso – was the eighth duke, who in 1640 became a reluctant king, Dom João IV, sealing Portugal's liberation from Spanish rule. But there are murky corners in the dynastic history too.

The third duke, Fernando, was executed in Évora in 1483 on the orders of his brother-in-law Dom João II, who deliberately struck at the family's immense power and wealth by accusing the duke of plotting against the monarchy.

By far the nastiest episode concerns the fourth duke, Dom Jaime, who murdered his young wife Leonor de Gusmão on 2 November 1512 in a fit of jealous rage. Already suspicious that his wife was having an affair, he caught a young pageboy climbing into the window of her quarters at the Vila Viçosa palace. Despite her pleas of innocence the duke 'with five slashes ripped out her life'. Only later was it revealed that the pageboy was probably visiting one of the queen's ladies-in-waiting.

The last murderous event was the assassination on 1 February 1908 of Dom Carlos and his son in Lisbon. Two years later the monarchy was overthrown and the royal Bragança line came to an end. Today's leading Bragança noble, Dom Duarte, keeps a low, politically correct profile, supervising an experimental eco-farm in the north of the country. ■

pelourinho and the 15th-century Igreja de Nossa Senhora da Conceição are all that remain of the town that once surrounded the castle.

The castle itself has recently been transformed into the *Museu de Caça* (hunting museum) and is stuffed with gruesome trophies, many snared by the dukes on their 2000-hectare royal hunting ground north of Vila Viçosa and visible from the castle. The museum is open daily from 9.30 am to 1 pm and 2.30 to 6 pm (to 5 pm in winter); entry is 400$00.

Places to Stay
The best budget options are private rooms around the praça, typically costing 4000$00 to 5000$00 a double. Try Praça da República 27 (☎ 983 18) or nearby Rua Dr Couto Jardim 7 (☎ 981 69). For appropriate baronial ambience, there's *Casa dos Arcos* (☎ 985 18) at Praça Martim Afonso de Sousa 16. Part of the Turihab scheme, it's a converted 18th-century mansion offering self-catering suites and six doubles. Further out on the Borba road is *Casa de Peixinhos* (☎ 984 72), a 17th-century manor house with rooms furnished in tiles and antiques. Rates at both places range from 12,000$00 to 16,000$00.

Places to Eat
You'll find plenty of restaurants and cafés around Praça da República and the marketplace, including the recommended *Os Cucos* (☎ 988 06) in the gardens near the mercado municipal. The mercado itself – busiest on Wednesdays – is north of the praça at the end of Rua Dr António José da Almeida.

Getting There & Away
There are two to three buses daily from Estremoz to Vila Viçosa via Borba; the trip takes 25 minutes.

ELVAS
• *pop 15,000 • postcode 7350 • area code ☎ 068*
This massively fortified frontier town, 15 km west of Spanish Badajoz and 40 km east of Estremoz, boasts the most sophisticated 17th-century military architecture in Europe, with well-preserved moats, curtain walls, bastions, fortified gates and three forts. Inside the walls, though, it feels much like any other Alentejan market town, half-heartedly hosting Spanish day-trippers during the week and coming to a complete standstill on Sunday afternoons.

There's plenty to see here if you're fond of battlements and fortresses, and walkers will have a field day following the old aqueduct or the town walls, or clambering up the steep cobbled streets. Other than that there's little to do except to join the shoppers hunting for cheap towels, china ornaments and the locally famous sticky candied plums.

History
Elvas only really charges into the history books in 1230, when it was recaptured from the Moors after 500 years of relatively peaceful occupation. The following centuries saw interminable attacks from Spain, interrupted by occasional peace treaties. The only successful attack was in 1580, allowing Philip II of Spain (the future Felipe I of Portugal) to set up court here for a few months. The garrison's honour was redeemed during the Wars of Succession when, in 1644, it held out against a nine-day Spanish siege. In 1659, its numbers reduced by an epidemic to a mere one thousand men, it withstood an attack by a 15,000-strong Spanish army.

The massive fortifications – extended and rebuilt throughout the 17th and 18th centuries – had their last period of glory in 1811-12, when the Duke of Wellington used them as a base for attacking Badajoz during the Peninsular War.

Orientation
The town centre is surprisingly compact considering the extent of the walls. The bus station and turismo are side-by-side in the central Praça da República, and all the major sights of interest are a short walk away. Those arriving by train will find themselves at Fontaínhas, four km north of town (from where buses shuttle to the bus station). Drivers should park on the outskirts and

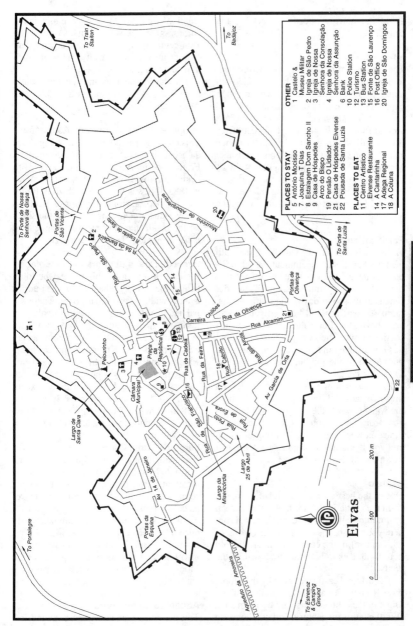

ALENTEJO

PLACES TO STAY
5 António Mocisso
7 Joaquina T Dias
8 Estalagem Dom Sancho II
9 Casa de Hóspedes
19 Pensão O Lidador
21 Casa de Hóspedes Elvense
22 Pousada de Santa Luzia

PLACES TO EAT
11 Centro Artístico
Elvense Restaurante
14 A Cantarinha
17 Adega Regional
18 A Coluna

OTHER
1 Castelo &
Museu Militar
2 Igreja de São Pedro
3 Igreja de Nossa
Senhora da Consolação
4 Arco do Bispo
Igreja de Nossa
Senhora da Assunção
6 Bank
10 Police Station
12 Turismo
13 Bus Station
15 Fonte de São Lourenço
16 Post Office
20 Igreja de São Domingos

Elvas

0   100   200 m

To Train Station
To Badajoz
To Forte de Nossa Senhora da Graça
To Forte de Nossa Senhora da Graça
Portas de São Vicente
To Forte de Santa Luzia
Portas de Olivença
To Portalegre
To Estremoz & Camping Ground
Aqueduto da Amoreira

Largo de Santa Clara
Câmara Municipal
Pelourinho
Praça da República
Rua de Cadeia
Rua da Feira
Rua de São Francisco
Rua Pinto
Rua de Évora
Largo 25 de Abril
Largo da Misericórdia
Portas da Esquina
Av 14 de Janeiro
Av Garcia de Orta
Rua Alcamim
Rua da Olivença
Carreira
Chilões
Rua de São Pedro
R Sta da Bandeira
R Espírito de Santo
Mouzinho de Albuquerque
Rua Cano

avoid the narrow one-way streets in the centre.

Information
The turismo (☎ 62 23 36), open from 9 am to 6 pm on weekdays and 9 am to 12.30 pm and 2 to 5.30 pm weekends, wins a rotten candied plum for its uselessness.

There are several Multibanco ATMs around Praça da República. The post office is downhill on Rua da Cadeia, and the police station (☎ 62 26 13) is uphill on Rua Isabel Maria Picão. The district hospital (☎ 62 21 77) is south of the centre near the pousada.

Every Monday there's a big market, just off the Lisbon road west of town, around the aqueduct.

Fortifications
Walls encircled Elvas as early as the 13th century, but it was the eminent French military engineer Vauban who extended them in the 17th century into the formidable defences you see today by adding moats, ramparts, bastions and fortified gates. Also added was the Forte de Santa Luzia, just south of town. The Forte de Nossa Senhora da Graça, three km north of town, still in use but closed to the public, was added in the following century.

For a fascinating close-up of the walls and the town, descend from the castle and follow the walls towards the Igreja de São Domingos, from where you can head back up to Praça da República. Go even further round and you'll end up in Largo 25 de Abril, just down the street from the post office.

Castelo
One of the best views of the fortifications is from the castle in the north of town, a steep 15-minute walk from the central praça. From here you can see the orange-walled barracks (still in use) in the east of town and the old houses and churches clustered within the walls.

The original castle was built by the Moors on a Roman site and later rebuilt by Dom Dinis in the 13th century and by Dom João II in the late 15th century. Today it houses a small Museu Militar whose enthusiastic curator gives personal tours. Among the 18th-century guns and old maps are the giant 19th-century keys to the city – 11 in all, each in its own box.

The castle and museum are open daily from 9 am to 12.30 pm and 2 to 5.30 pm. Admission is free.

Igreja de Nossa Senhora da Assunção
This rather dull-looking church facing Praça da República was originally designed by Francisco de Arruda in the early 16th century. Before Elvas lost its episcopal status in 1882, this was the city's cathedral. Renovated in the 17th and 18th centuries, it retains a few Manueline touches, notably the south portal. Inside, the most eye-catching feature is the sumptuous 18th-century organ.

Igreja de Nossa Senhora da Consolação
It's easy to overlook this modest building behind the former cathedral, but the interior is an Aladdin's cave of surprises. There are painted marble columns under a cupola, and fantastic 17th-century azulejos covering every surface. The unusual octagonal design was inspired by a Knights Templar chapel which stood on a nearby site some years before this church was built in the mid-16th century. The church is open daily, except Mondays, from 9.30 am to 12.30 pm and 2.30 to 7 pm (to 5.30 pm in winter). Admission is free but donations are welcome.

Largo de Santa Clara
This delightful cobbled square facing the Igreja de Nossa Senhora da Consolação is a breath of fresh air compared with the town's sombre fortifications. Its whimsical centrepiece – a polka-dotted pelourinho – wasn't meant to be fun, of course: criminals would once have been chained to the metal hooks at the top. But the fancy archway with its own loggia at the top of the square is pure Moorish artistry and a flourish in the town walls which once trailed past here.

Aqueduto da Amoreira
This massive aqueduct with huge cylindrical

buttresses and several tiers of arches runs for seven km from the west of town to bring water to the marble fountain in Largo da Misericórdia. It took about 100 years to complete and was finally finished in 1622.

The aqueduct is best seen from the Lisbon road, west of the centre.

Special Events
Elvas lets its hair down for a week in late September to celebrate the Festas do Senhor da Piedade e de São Mateus with everything from agricultural markets and bullfights to folk dancing and huge religious processions (especially on the last day). You'll need to book accommodation well in advance if you want to join in.

Places to Stay
Camping On the south-west outskirts (off the N4 Estremoz road) is the basic *Senhor Jesus da Piedade* camping ground (☎ 62 37 72), open from May to mid-September only. Typical rates are 300$00 per person, 300$00 to 400$00 for a tent and 300$00 per car.

Guesthouses The cheap and cheerful *Casa de Hóspedes Elvense* (☎ 62 31 52), just inside the city walls at Avenida Garcia de Orta 3A, has doubles without private bath for around 3000$00 (4000$00 with). Similarly priced are *Pensão O Lidador* (☎ 62 34 42) at Rua Alcamim 33, and the run-down *Casa de Hóspedes Arco do Bispo* (☎ 62 34 22) at Rua Sineiro 4.

Among comfortable private rooms are the well-signposted ones of *António Mocisso* (☎ 62 21 26) at Rua Aires Varela 5, five minutes walk from the turismo; doubles (some with air-con and TV) go for a bargain 5000$00. En route, the friendly *Joaquina T Dias* (☎ 62 47 22) at Rua João d'Olivenca 5 has three rooms for similar prices.

Hotels Mainstream accommodation can be found at *Estalagem Dom Sancho II* (☎ 62 26 84; fax 62 47 17), on Praça da República, where a comfortable double is 7500$00. The *Pousada de Santa Luzia* (☎ 62 21 94; fax 62 21 27), on Avenida de Badajoz, was the first

of Portugal's pousadas (opening in 1942), though age hasn't mellowed its stark modern appearance. It's on the south edge of town and has luxurious rooms for 16,500$00.

Places to Eat
The obvious choice for people-watching is *Centro Artistico Elvense Restaurante* (☎ 62 27 11) on the praça. It also has a small indoor dining area with main dishes from around 900$00. At Rua de São Lourenço 6E is *A Cantarinha* (☎ 62 18 39), a chic place with good pratos do dia from 650$00.

Some of the town's best restaurants are in the vicinity of the post office: *Adega Regional* (☎ 62 91 82) at Rua João Casqueiro 22 is very popular locally, as is the nearby *A Coluna* (☎ 62 37 28) at Rua do Cabrito 11, with azulejos on the walls and lots of bacalhau on the menu. Dishes are 1000$00 and up, though the tourist menu is good value at 1500$00.

Getting There & Away
Bus Coaches run to Portalegre, Évora, Estremoz and Vila Viçosa at least twice a day, with express services once a day to Faro and four times daily to Lisbon.

Twice-daily Elvas-Badajoz buses take about 20 minutes.

Train There are three services a day to Elvas via Portalegre from Lisbon's Santa Apolónia station (with changes at Abrantes and/or Entroncamento). Buses run between the town centre and the train station (four km north of town) four times daily.

The Lisbon-Elvas train service continues across the border to Badajoz twice a day.

PORTALEGRE
• *pop 15,500* • *postcode 7300* • *area code* ☎ *045*
Portalegre, Alto Alentejo's capital and commercial centre, is of interest to most travellers only as a place to change buses on the way to Castelo de Vide and Marvão. But if you have a few hours, it's worth walking around its small walled centre, which has a 16th-century cathedral, a handful of 17th and 18th-century mansions (thanks to a period of

ALENTEJO

wealth from textile manufacturing) and some striking old and new azulejos.

Orientation

Portalegre has an hourglass shape, with the new town to the north-east and the old town spreading across a hilltop to the south-west. The 'waist' is the Largo António José Lourinho traffic roundabout, better known to all as the Rossio. The bus station is half a block west of the roundabout.

The pedestrianised Rua 5 de Outubro and Rua do Comércio climb into the walled town. At the top, a right turn at the Café Alentejano takes you along Rua 19 de Junho to the cathedral, or you can carry on over the hill on Rua de Elvas to the turismo at the bottom, as awkward a location as you could ask for. Streets are surprisingly poorly marked.

Information

The turismo (☎ 218 15, ☎ 284 53) is in the headquarters of the regional tourist office at Estrada de Santana 25. Here you can get a miserable map and some help with private rooms; it's open daily from 10 am to 12.30 pm and 2 to 5.30 pm (weekends from 9 am).

At least three banks around the Rossio, plus one at the top of Rua de Elvas and one on Largo Camões, have exchange desks and/or Multibanco ATMs. The main post and telephone office is a block north of the Rossio.

There are bookshops, of marginal interest to non-Portuguese speakers, at Rua 5 de Outubro 61 and at the top of Rua do Comércio. There is a laundry on Rua 5 de Outubro. The police station is on Rua 31 de Janeiro.

Sé

In 1545 Portalegre became the seat of a new diocese and soon got its own cathedral. The sombre, twin-towered 18th-century façade, with a stork's nest and a broken clock, presides over the whitewashed Praça do Município. The sacristy is full of fine azulejos; otherwise the 16th-century interior is of minimal interest.

Museu Municipal & Mansions

Beside the cathedral, in an 18th-century mansion and former seminary, is the modest town museum, featuring the obligatory period furnishings, religious art – including, for some reason, a huge number of figures of Santo António (St Anthony) – and some handsome Arraiolos carpets. The museum is open daily, except Tuesdays, from 9.30 am to 12.30 and 2 to 6 pm; entry is 230$00.

To the east, Rua 19 de Junho sports numerous faded 17th-century baroque townhouses and mansions.

Convento do São Bernardo

A few years before Portalegre became a bishopric, this convent (also known as Convento de Nossa Senhora da Conceição) – a visual rival to the cathedral – was founded by the Bishop of Guarda, who is buried inside. It's now a military training academy. For an impromptu tour, including a look at the building's excellent 18th-century azulejos and the bishop's beautiful tomb sculpted by Nicolas Chanterène, ask politely for the *diretor* (warden). There's no charge.

Fábrica de Tapeçarias

Tapestries made Portalegre famous and wealthy in the 16th century (followed by silk in the 17th), but the bubble burst after the 1703 Treaty of Methuen led to an invasion of English textiles. The town's last remaining tapestry factory is in a former Jesuit college on Rua Gomes Fernandes, just off the Rossio. Pop into the office on the 1st floor and ask about a tour (weekdays from 9.30 to 11 am and 2.30 to 4.30 pm) of the studios and weaving room. In their showroom you can see the results – huge reproductions of classical paintings and patterns with a 250,000 knots per square metre, in a range of some 8000 colours (all on commission and not for sale).

Town Walls

Fragments of the original walls almost totally enclose the old town. Along the east side you can glimpse the ruins of a castle erected in 1290 by Dom Dinis.

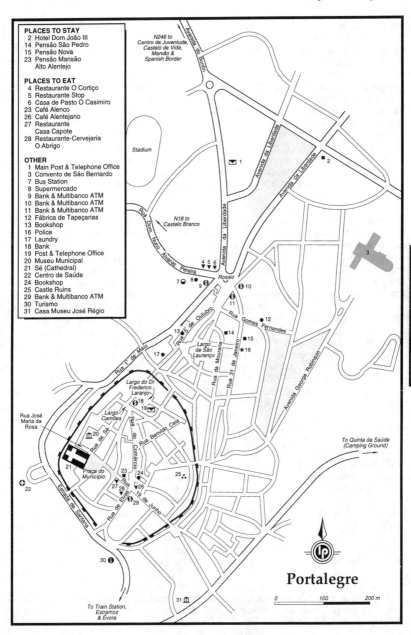

PLACES TO STAY
2 Hotel Dom João III
14 Pensão São Pedro
15 Pensão Nova
23 Pensão Mansão
   Alto Alentejo

PLACES TO EAT
4 Restaurante O Cortiço
5 Restaurante Stop
6 Casa de Pasto O Casimiro
23 Café Alenco
26 Café Alentejano
27 Restaurante
   Casa Capote
28 Restaurante-Cervejaria
   O Abrigo

OTHER
1 Main Post & Telephone Office
3 Convento de São Bernardo
7 Bus Station
8 Supermercado
9 Bank & Multibanco ATM
10 Bank & Multibanco ATM
11 Bank & Multibanco ATM
12 Fábrica de Tapeçarias
13 Bookshop
16 Police
17 Laundry
18 Bank
19 Post & Telephone Office
20 Museu Municipal
21 Sé (Cathedral)
22 Centro de Saúde
24 Bookshop
25 Castle Ruins
29 Bank & Multibanco ATM
30 Turismo
31 Casa Museu José Régio

ALENTEJO

Portalegre

0   100   200 m

Places to Stay
There are some private rooms available; see
the turismo or ask around at the town's cafés
and restaurants.

Camping At *Quinta da Saúde* (☎ 228 48),
three km north-east on the N246-2 road to
Reguengos, is an Orbitur camping ground
that's open from mid-January to mid-
November. Typical rates are 480$00 per
person, 400$00 to 720$00 for a tent and
430$00 per car; they also have some bunga-
lows. Also here is a considerably more
up-market Turihab property (ask about it at
the Portalegre turismo).

Hostels A centro de juventude (☎ 227 76)
on Avenida do Bonfin, north of the Rossio,
has dormitory-style accommodation on a
first-come-first-served basis for 1300$00 per
person (no HI/IYHF card required), plus a
few doubles. Its doors are open from 8 to 10
am and 7 pm to midnight, though someone
is usually on duty all day so you can stash
your bags and sign up for a bed.

Pensões The *Pensão Nova* (☎ 216 05, ☎ 33
12 12), at Rua 31 de Janeiro 28-30, has pokey
doubles for 3500$00 without shower,
5000$00 with shower or 6000$00 with TV
and telephone too. About the same (and
under the same management?) is the *Pensão
São Pedro*, around the block at 14 Rua da
Mouraria. Up a few notches, and better
value, is the friendly *Pensão Mansão Alto
Alentejo* (☎ 222 90), above Café Alenco at
Rua 19 de Junho 61, which has plain, clean
doubles for 4500$00 without shower or
5500$00 with.

Hotels The *Hotel Dom João III* (☎ 33 01 92;
fax 33 04 44) on Avenida da Liberdade has
big, boring singles/doubles with bath, TV
and telephone for 6300$00/10,500$00,
including breakfast.

Places to Eat
Food here is plain, sturdy and cheap. Among
locally favoured restaurants around the
Rossio are three neighbours on Rua Dom

Nuno Álvares Pereira – the basic casa de
pasto *O Casimiro* at No 7, *Restaurante Stop*
at No 13 (with fish courses under 1200$00
and meat courses under 1600$00) and the
friendly *Restaurante O Cortiço* at No 17.
Across the road is a sizeable supermarket for
self-caterers.

Café Alentejano, at the top of Rua do
Comércio, looks like the local top spot for
coffee and gossip. A stone's throw away at
Rua de Elvas 74 is the cheap and cheerful
Restaurante-Cervejaria O Abrigo (☎ 227
78); it's closed on Tuesdays. Along Rua 19
de Julho you can enjoy coffee and croissants
at *Café Alenco* at No 65, or a good-value
lunch at *Restaurante Casa Capote* (☎ 217
48) at No 60 (with fish dishes under 800$00
and caldo verde for 130$00).

Getting There & Away
Portalegre is most easily reached by bus, and
is a useful hub for getting to Castelo de Vide
and Marvão. Four express coaches daily link
it directly with Lisbon (4¼ hours, 1350$00),
and there are two buses daily linking it with
Évora (2¼ hours, 820$00), Beja and Faro.
There is also a daily through bus between
Vila Real de Santo António and Beja.

You can get to Portalegre by train three
times a day, in under an hour from Elvas or
in under four hours from Lisbon, but the
station is 12 km south of town. Shuttle buses
meet all arrivals and departures. Note that
you cannot get from here to Castelo de Vide
and Marvão by train without backtracking a
quarter of the way across the country.

CASTELO DE VIDE
• *pop 4500* • *postcode 7320* • *area code* ☎ *045*
One of the Alentejo's most appealing fortified hilltop villages, Castelo de Vide sits high
above the surrounding olive plains at the
northern tip of the Parque Natural da Serra
de São Mamede, 15 km north of Portalegre
and just west of the Spanish border.

Despite some modern development
outside the walls, this ancient spa town has
largely maintained its traditional appearance
and lifestyle, leaving the day-trippers to its
smaller and more stunning neighbour, Mar-

vão. Not that Castelo de Vide doesn't have its own attractions: below its 14th-century castle are steep narrow lanes lined with flowerbeds and an ancient judiaria.

If you're looking for a rural base with character and charm, Castelo de Vide comes up trumps. It's a no-frills market town where you can still meet farmers clopping home on their donkeys at dusk and pausing to collect water from the old marble fountain.

Orientation

The heart of town is two parallel squares backed by the Igreja de Santa Maria da Devesa. The upper one, just a wide area in Rua Bartolomeu Álvares da Santa with a pelourinho in the middle, is where you'll find the turismo and the town hall. Walk through the town hall archway to the larger Praça Dom Pedro V.

The castle, medieval quarter and judiaria lie to the north-west: dive into the lanes behind the church and follow the signs to Fonte da Vila (the old town fountain). From there it's a short, steep climb to the synagogue and castle.

Buses stop beside the turismo, while the train station is four km north-west of town.

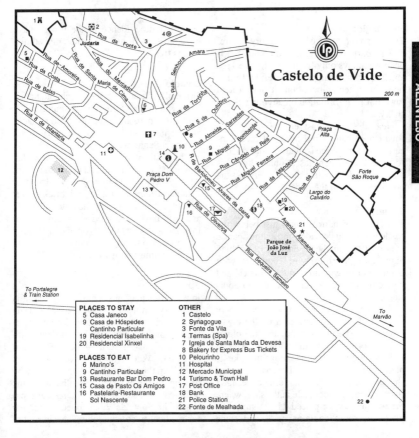

Castelo de Vide

PLACES TO STAY	OTHER
5 Casa Janeco	1 Castelo
9 Casa de Hóspedes	2 Synagogue
Cantinho Particular	3 Fonte da Vila
19 Residencial Isabelinha	4 Termas (Spa)
20 Residencial Xinxel	7 Igreja de Santa Maria da Devesa
	8 Bakery for Express Bus Tickets
PLACES TO EAT	10 Pelourinho
6 Marino's	11 Hospital
9 Cantinho Particular	12 Mercado Municipal
13 Restaurante Bar Dom Pedro	14 Turismo & Town Hall
15 Casa de Pasto Os Amigos	17 Post Office
16 Pastelaria-Restaurante	18 Bank
Sol Nascente	19 Police Station
	22 Fonte de Mealhada

ALENTEJO

Parque Natural da Serra de São Mamede

After the endless rolling plains of Baixo Alentejo, the Serra da São Mamede comes as a welcome change: four peaks (Fria, Marvão, Castelo de Vide and São Mamede) top off this mountain range along the Spanish border near Portalegre. The park includes all of them, stretching from Castelo de Vide in the north to just beyond Esperança in the south.

This 40-km-long massif helps provide the surrounding region with essential rainfall and humidity, and serves as a rich area for plants and wildlife. Its combination of Atlantic forest and Mediterranean bush make it an ideal habitat for the rare trumpet narcissus and stonecrop as well as European royal deer and dozens of bird species: more than half the species that breed in Portugal nest here. While visiting the rocky enclaves of Castelo de Vide and Marvão, keep an eye out especially for vultures and eagles, kites and black storks.

With your own transport you can delve right into the heart of the park on wriggly rural roads to traditional villages like Alegrete and Esperança. Bus transport is available from Portalegre to Castelo de Vide and Marvão.

Information

The turismo (☎ 913 61), on 'pillory square' at Rua Bartolomeu Álvares da Santa 81, is open weekdays only from 9 am to 12.30 pm and 2 to 5 pm. It can provide useful information about accommodation in and around town but its information on anything else is shaky.

Near the south-east end of the pillory square are a bank and the post office. South-east of the post office is shady Parque de João José da Luz which has a small children's playground. The police station overlooks the north-east side of the park.

Judiaria

The cluster of narrow lanes just below the castle is Castelo de Vide's most atmospheric quarter. It's a medieval enclave of cobbled paths and dazzling white cottages with Gothic doorways and window frames, and potted plants and flowers around their doorsteps.

A sizeable community of Jews settled here in the 13th century, attracted by the area's prosperity. The tiny synagogue – the oldest one in Portugal – on the corner of Rua da Judiaria and Rua da Fonte looks just like its neighbouring cottages. The bare interior shows little evidence of its former use, apart from a wooden tabernacle and a shelf where the scriptures were placed. Now a museum, its lower room contains maps and some photographic evidence of the town's past. It's open daily from 9 am to 5.30 pm; admission is free.

Castelo

Originally, Castelo de Vide's inhabitants all lived within the castle's sturdy outer walls; even now there are some occupied cottages and a small church, the 17th-century Igreja da Nossa Senhora da Alegria.

The castle itself, within the inner walls, was built by Dom Dinis and his brother Dom Afonso between 1280 and 1365. Its most notable feature is a 12m-tall brick tower which probably predates the outer defences and may have been used as an armoury or lookout post. The castle is open daily from 9 am to 12.30 pm and 2 to 8 pm (to 5.30 pm in winter); admission is free.

Spa

In a pretty square just below the judiaria is the well-worn, 16th-century marble Fonte da Vila which, along with several other fountains in the village, provides residents with the delicious mineral water for which Castelo de Vide is known (people with cars can fill up their water bottles more easily by driving to the Fonte da Mealhada on the south-east edge of town). The *termas* (spa) beside the Fonte da Vila is open in summer for medical treatments; the water is said to be good for diabetes and kidney and blood-pressure problems.

Praça Alta

If you stagger up one of the half-dozen very steep streets leading east off the pillory square, you'll come to Praça Alta at the top of the town. In the unkempt north-east corner is the ruined Forte São Roque, now little more than a few crumbled walls but still commanding fine views.

Market

There's a big market in Praça Dom Pedro V every Friday, with clothes, shoes, pottery, tools and toys for sale.

Special Events

Castelo de Vide's big bash is the Festa de São Lourenço on 15 August, when folk-dance groups from all over Portugal display their skills on the football pitch on the town's south-eastern outskirts.

Places to Stay

Probably because of the spa, there is plenty of accommodation, none of it terribly cheap. Most convenient at the lower end of the scale is *Casa de Hóspedes Cantinho Particular* (☎ 911 51) at Rua Miguel Bombarda 9, a welcoming, no-frills place with doubles from around 4500$00, including breakfast. At about the same price but loaded with atmosphere are the two rooms in *Casa Janeco* (☎ 912 11) at Rua da Costa 56A; it's a private house in one of the old lanes at the foot of the castle.

The up-market residencials are all near the Parque de João José da Luz. The friendly, fussy *Residencial Xinxel* (☎ 914 06), at Largo do Paço Novo 5, has immaculately clean doubles with bath and breakfast from 5000$00, and the sunlit inner courtyard provides a Mediterranean touch. Next door is *Residencial Isabelinha* (☎ 918 96), where modern rooms with more frills are 7000$00, with breakfast.

Places to Eat

Cantinho Particular (☎ 911 51), at Rua Miguel Bombarda 9, has decent food and an appealing family ambience. A hearty plate of meat, rice and chips costs around 900$00. Another down-to-earth spot (with a bar full of locals) is *Casa de Pasto Os Amigos* on Rua de Bartolomeu Álvares da Santa; snack on snails or tuck into a plateful of squid or roast pork for under 1000$00.

On Praça Dom Pedro V, the cheery *Pastelaria-Restaurante Sol Nascente* (☎ 917 89) serves small cheap meals from 600$00, though it's mostly a place for cake and coffee. For classier meals, head for the nearby *Restaurante Bar Dom Pedro* (☎ 912 36), which has excellent regional dishes in a rustic setting, or *Marino's*, by the Igreja de Santa Maria (just off the pillory square) at Rua Volta do Penedo 6, which specialises in Italian fare.

The mercado municipal is down the hill from Praça Dom Pedro V.

Getting There & Away

Bus On weekdays four or five buses make the half-hour run between Portalegre and Castelo de Vide. Three buses daily connect Castelo de Vide and Marvão, via Portagem (8.5 km south-east of Castelo de Vide). There are two express services daily to/from Lisbon; buy tickets for these from the little bakery at Rua 5 de Outubro, just off the pillory square.

Train There are two regional train services daily between Lisbon and Castelo de Vide, but the train station is four km north-west of town and there are no bus links; taxis charge about 500$00.

The Lisbon-Madrid Talgo *Lusitânia Express* doesn't stop at Castelo de Vide but at Marvão-Beirã, 14 km to the north-east, passing through en route to Valencia de Alcántara in Spain at 1 am.

MARVÃO

• *pop 1000* • *postcode 7330* • *area code* ☎ *045*

Like a chameleon, fading into its rocky pedestal one minute and blazing white in the midday sun the next, Marvão is one of those extraordinary places you can't quite believe. Everything seems visually perfect: enclosed

ALENTEJO

within serpentine walls are immaculate little houses with Manueline windows or Renaissance doorways; narrow cobbled streets free of traffic; and an awesome castle rising from the rock. The surrounding panorama is of wild peaks and Spanish horizons.

But as with that other hilltop gem, Monsaraz (near Évora), summertime visitors often outnumber residents. All the more reason to plan an overnight stay to make the most of this 900m-high eyrie in the silence of dawn or dusk, when kites and eagles circle overhead and the cottages sink into the castle's shadow.

History

Not surprisingly, considering its impregnable position and its proximity to the Spanish frontier (10 km away), Marvão has long been a prized possession. Even before the walls and castle existed, there was a Roman settlement in the area, and Christian Visigoths were here when the Moors arrived in 715. It was probably the Moorish Lord of Coimbra, Emir Maraun, who gave the place its present name; the Moors certainly had a hand in fortifying the village.

In 1160, Christians took control. In 1226 the town received a municipal charter, the walls were extended to encompass the whole summit and the castle was rebuilt by Dom Dinis.

Marvão's importance in the defence against the Spanish Castilians was highlighted during the 17th-century War of Restoration, when further defences were added to the castle. Two centuries later it was briefly at the centre of the tug-of-war between the liberals and royalists: in 1833 the liberals used a secret entrance to seize the town – the only time Marvão has ever been captured.

Orientation

Arriving by car or bus you'll find yourself outside one of the four village gates, Portas de Ródão, which leads directly into Rua de Cima where most shops and restaurants are. Drivers can enter this gate and park near Praça do Pelourinho (Pillory Square), which backs onto Rua de Cima. The castle is a 10-minute walk uphill from Praça do Pelourinho on Rua do Espírito Santo.

Information

The turismo (☎ 931 04) is on Rua Dr Matos Magalhães, just south of the street leading to the castle. It's open daily from 9 am to 5.30 pm. As well as providing town maps and information (in English as well as Portuguese), staff can tell you about private accommodation. A bank and the post office face one another across Rua do Espírito Santo.

Castelo

The formidable castle built into the rock at the west end of the village dates from the end of the 13th century, but most of what you see today was built in the 17th century. There's little left inside but if you walk along the walls you'll be rewarded with some astounding sheer-drop views.

Museu Municipal

Just before the castle, the Igreja de Santa Maria houses this engaging little museum with everything from Roman remains and skeletons to gruesome old medical implements. It's open daily from 9 am to 12.30 pm and 2 to 5.30 pm; admission is 150$00.

Places to Stay

The turismo has details of private accommodation options including singles/doubles for 2500$00/4000$00 and small apartments with kitchens for around 5500$00.

Within the walls, the other options are pricey: *Pensão Dom Dinis* (☎ 932 36), opposite the turismo on Rua Dr Matos Magalhães, has doubles from around 8000$00. High-season doubles in the elegant *Pousada de Santa Maria* (☎ 932 01; fax 934 40) on Rua 24 de Janeiro will set you back 18,000$00. At Santo António das Areias, six km to the north, is the chic *Pensão o Poejo* (☎ 926 40) where doubles are around 7000$00.

Places to Eat

There's a string of bar-restaurants along Rua de Cima and a couple nearby, including the

Bar do Centro de Convivio in Largo do Terreiro, which has outdoor seating, and *Bar-Restaurante Varanda do Alentejo* in Praça do Pelourinho, which serves some earthy Alentejan specialities (including sarapatel, a pork liver and blood sausage).

Getting There & Away

Bus There are one or two buses daily (weekdays only) from Portalegre to Marvão (taking 50 minutes) and two to three buses daily connecting Marvão with Castelo de Vide, usually with a change of buses at Portagem. Express buses leave twice daily for Lisbon (one only on Sunday), but you must buy your ticket the day before at Bar do Centro de Convivio in Largo do Terreiro.

Train The nearest train station, Marvão-Beirã, is nine km north of Marvão. Check with the turismo on the current time for connecting shuttle bus (usually just one a day, via Santo António das Areias).

See Castelo de Vide for information about the daily Lisbon-Madrid express train which stops at Marvão-Beirã station once a day.

BELVER

A small, proud 12th-century castle dominates this diminutive village on the north bank of the Rio Tejo seven km north of Gavião.

Once a vital Christian defence against the Moors (for a long time the Rio Tejo marked the boundary of territory reconquered by the Christians), the castle has recently been restored and has a new access road. It contains a 15th-century reliquary, but it's the commanding views that are its main attraction. Unfortunately, the Barragem de Belver (Belver Dam) five km upstream has transformed the Tejo into a silent shadow of its former self.

The village below the castle is a humble one-café place, but what it lacks in facilities it makes up for in friendliness.

Places to Stay & Eat

There's only one place: *Café-Restaurante O Castelo*. The house speciality is lampreias (lampreys) but you can get less slippery dishes too. The café rents out a few simple rooms nearby for around 2000$00.

Getting There & Away

Bus connections are few and far between – check at the café for the current timetable.

Belver is on the Lisbon-Guarda railway line, with four trains daily stopping en route from Castelo Branco and six en route from Lisbon. The station is below the village.

ALENTEJO

Estremadura & Ribatejo

These two skinny provinces surrounding and stretching north of Lisbon are full of contrasts. They boast the country's most stunning architectural masterpieces – the monasteries of Mafra, Alcobaça and Batalha, and Tomar's Convento de Cristo. There are also the beautiful *parque natural* areas of Sintra, Arrábida (see Around Lisbon in the Lisbon chapter) and Serras de Aire e Candeeiros, which are wonderful for wildlife and walking. And the Estremaduran coast, a great destination for surfers and seafood-lovers, has lively resorts interspersed with a generous sprinkling of undeveloped, empty beaches.

On the other hand, the provinces also possess a large number of dull or heavily industrialised towns. The Ribatejo (meaning 'Tejo riverbank') is worse in this respect than its neighbour: around Abrantes and Torres Novas is a nasty concentration of textile, paper and chemical factories built up around areas that were once thriving river ports. There is still plenty of countryside – the rich alluvial plains are important areas for growing wheat, olives and vegetables and, most famously, for breeding bulls and horses. Santarém, host of the Feira Nacional da Agricultura (National Agricultural Fair), which celebrates the agricultural lifestyle of the province with gusto, is one of the few attractive towns in the Ribatejo. Also worth visiting is Tomar, which is the former headquarters of the Knights Templar.

But apart from Santarém and Tomar, your time is generally better spent in Estremadura – so called because it was the 'furthest land from the Douro' *(extrema Durii)* when the Christians wrested it from the Moors. Here you can feast on culture and coastal attractions, or visit the caves of the Mira de Aire region and the cute hilltop village of Óbidos. Most places are accessible by both train and bus, and there are quick and easy connections from Lisbon.

The Setúbal peninsula, Sintra, Mafra and

HIGHLIGHTS

- the Gothic-Manueline Mosteiro de Santa Maria da Vitória at Batalha
- the 12-th century Cistercian Mosteiro de Santa Maria de Alcobaça
- Tomar, the former headquarters of the Knights Templar
- the fortified village of Óbidos

the Estoril coast are all covered in the Lisbon chapter.

ERICEIRA
• *pop 4460* • *postcode 2655* • *area code* ☎ *061*
This pretty little seaside resort of bright white houses edged in blue is fast becoming as popular with the young Lisbonite and European crowd as Cascais, 45 km to the south. Part of the reason is an abundance of reasonably priced accommodation, seafood restaurants and lively bar-discos. Another attraction is its surf – the 1995 World Surfing Championships were held at nearby Praia da Ribeira de Ilhas. Transport connections are quick and easy from Lisbon, Sintra and Mafra (which is just 10 km east).

Apart from its increasing attention to tourism, Ericeira still has a pleasant small-town atmosphere and a thriving fishing industry. There's little actually to see in town, so you can simply loll around in the sun, surf on the crashing waves or gorge on seafood for a day or so – an attractive option if you've had your fill of architecture and culture in northern Estremadura. Indeed, Ericeira is famous for hosting people on escape visits: on 5 October 1910, as the

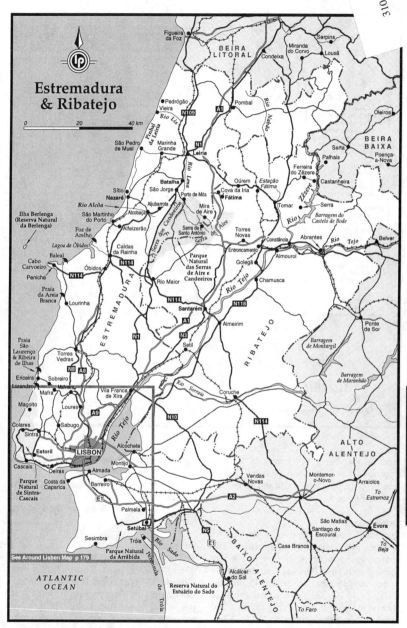

Estremadura & Ribatejo

0   20   40 km

BEIRA LITORAL

BEIRA BAIXA

Figueira da Foz

Miranda do Corvo

Serpins

Condeixa

Lousã

Pedrógão Vieira

Pombal

Oleiros

N109

A1

Rio Lis

Rio Nabão

São Pedro de Muel

Marinha Grande

Serta

Palhais

Poença-a-Nova

N1

Leiria

Rio Lena

Ferreira do Zêzere

Castanheira

Ourém

Estação Fátima

Batalha

São Jorge

Porto de Mós

Cova da Iria

Fátima

Tomar

Serra

Sítio

Nazaré

Mira de Aire

Rio Alcôa

Aljubarrota

Serra de Santo António

Barragem do Castelo de Bode

Belver

Alcobaça

Ilha Berlenga (Reserva Natural da Berlenga)

São Martinho do Porto

Alfeizerão

Torres Novas

Constância

Abrantes

Rio Tejo

Foz de Arelho

Caldas da Rainha

Entroncamento

Almourol

Lagoa de Óbidos

Parque Natural das Serras de Aire e Candeeiros

Golegã

Baleal

Cabo Carvoeiro

Óbidos

N114

Rio Maior

Rio Tejo

Chamusca

Peniche

Praia da Areia Branca

N114

Santarém

N118

Ponte de Sor

Lourinha

A1

Almeirim

Barragem de Montargil

Praia São Lourenço & Ribeira de Ilhas

Torres Vedras

N1

N3

Setil

Barragem de Maranhão

Ericeira

Sobreiro

N8

A8

Lizandro

Mafra

Malveira

Vila Franca de Xira

Rio Sorraia

Coruche

Magoito

Loures

A9

N10

N114

Colares

Sabugo

Rio Tejo

ALTO ALENTEJO

Sintra

Estoril

LISBON

Alcochete

Montemor-o-Novo

Arraiolos

Cascais

Oeiras

Montijo

Vendas Novas

To Estremoz

Parque Natural de Sintra-Cascais

Almada

Barreiro

E1

A2

Costa da Caparica

Palmela

São Matias

Évora

Setúbal

Santiago do Escoural

To Beja

Sesimbra

Tróia

N5

Casa Branca

Parque Natural da Arrábida

Rio Sado

E1

BAIXO ALENTEJO

See Around Lisbon Map p 179

Alcácer do Sal

ATLANTIC OCEAN

Reserva Natural do Estuário do Sado

To Faro

Península de Tróia

ESTREMADURA

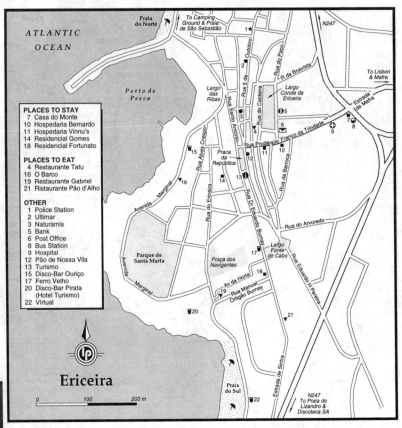

PLACES TO STAY
7 Casa do Monte
10 Hospedaria Bernardo
11 Hospedaria Vinnu's
14 Residencial Gomes
18 Residencial Fortunato

PLACES TO EAT
4 Restaurante Tatu
16 O Barco
19 Restaurante Gabriel
21 Ristaurante Pão d'Alho

OTHER
1 Police Station
2 Ultimar
3 Naturamis
5 Bank
6 Post Office
8 Bus Station
9 Hospital
12 Pão de Nossa Vila
13 Turismo
15 Disco-Bar Ouriço
17 Ferro Velho
20 Disco-Bar Pirata
   (Hotel Turismo)
22 Virtual

Ericeira

0   100   200 m

republic was being proclaimed in Lisbon, Portugal's last king, Dom Manuel II, fled here from his palace at Mafra and sailed into exile in England.

Orientation

The town sits high above the sea and its beaches are backed by steep cliffs. The central Praça da República is just a few minutes walk from Porto de Pesca bay, while three sandy beaches are within 15 minutes walk: Praia do Sul (also called Praia da Baleia) to the south, and Praia do Norte and Praia de São Sebastião to the north. A few

km further north is another good beach, the unspoilt Praia de São Lourenço.

Arriving by bus, you'll find yourself at the top end of Rua Prudéncio Franco da Trindade, 10 minutes walk east of the Praça da República.

Information

The gung-ho *turismo* (☎ 631 22; fax 86 59 09), at Rua Dr Eduardo Burnay 33A, is open a record 15 hours (from 9 am to midnight) daily during July and August. It closes at 10 pm in mid-season and 8 pm in winter. Not only is it a useful source of information, it also has several telephones which you can conveniently use without coins or cards: you pay for your calls at the desk afterwards.

There are plenty of banks with automatic-teller machines (ATMs) scattered around town, including one next to the post office which is on Largo Conde da Ericeira, just off Rua Prudéncio Franco da Trindade.

The hospital (☎ 86 45 08) is just before the bus station, at the top of Rua Prudéncio Franco da Trindade. The police station (☎ 635 33) is on Rua 5 de Outubro.

Surfing

Surfing is Ericeira's big attraction. The world championship site, Praia da Ribeira de Ilhas, is just a few km north of town, though the nearer Praia de São Sebastião is challenging enough for most amateurs.

If you've arrived boardless, you can try renting one from Ultimar (☎ 623 71), Rua 5 de Outubro 37A, for around 1500$00 a day. It's open from 9 am to 1 pm and 3 to 7 pm daily, except Sundays, and also sells fishing equipment and wetsuits.

Special Events

Ericeira's big annual fair is held from 25 to 28 July on Largo da Feira (just off Praia de São Sebastião).

Places to Stay

Camping The nearest camping ground is the excellent *Parque de Campismo Municipal de Mil Regos* (☎ 627 06), above Praia de São Sebastião. It's open from May to December and has a swimming pool. Open year-round is the *Clube Estrela* (☎ 525 25) camping ground at Sobreiro, four km east of Ericeira.

Private Rooms Although Ericeira gets packed out in summer (especially at weekends), it shouldn't be too much of a problem finding a room: if touts don't find you first at the bus station, the turismo should be able to help with private quartos (around 6000$00 a double in high season). As with the pensões, the longer you stay, the more likely you can bargain the price down.

Pensões & Residencials Cosiest of the budget guesthouses is the old-fashioned *Residencial Gomes* (☎ 636 19), right in the town centre at Rua Mendes Leal 11. Doubles without/with bath go for 4500$00/6000$00. Along Rua Prudéncio Franco Trindade are several other choices, including the spic-and-span *Hospedaria Bernardo* (☎ 623 78) at No 17 which has doubles ranging from 5000$00 to 7000$00 and a one-bedroom apartment for 8000$00. At No 25, *Hospedaria Vinnu's* (☎ 638 30) is next to a noisy disco-bar but has pleasantly bright doubles for around 6000$00. Nicest of all, at the top of this street at No 1, is *Casa do Monte* (☎ 626 65; fax 86 44 02), where all doubles have bath and TV and cost up to 8000$00. Another popular choice, at Rua Eduardo Burnay 7, is *Residencial Fortunato* (☎ & fax 628 29), where doubles with breakfast are a bargain at 6000$00.

Places to Eat

For seafood that isn't too outrageously expensive, try *Restaurante Gabriel* (☎ 633 49), on Avenida da Horta, opposite the Hotel Turismo. The restaurant itself is pretty dull but the grilled fish (halibut, scabbard or mackerel) is great. Expect to pay around 1200$00 a dish (or 1650$00 for the tourist menu). It's closed on Wednesdays.

If you're after something classier, the seaview *O Barco* (☎ 627 59), overlooking the Porto de Pesca at Avenida Marginal (also called Rua Capitão João Lopes) 14, fits the bill (an expensive one), with its range of seafood specialities. It's closed on Thursdays.

Cheaper, simpler fare (chips and salad with almost everything) is on offer at the small and friendly *Restaurante Tatu* (☎ 86 47 05) at Rua Fonte do Cabo 58, though you can splurge on more expensive local dishes – arroz de marisco (seafood rice) or açorda de marisco (bread-based shellfish stew).

Sick of fish? Head for the Italian *Ristorante Pão d'Alho*, where you can get pizzas and pastas for under 1000$00. It's in the new part of town at the southern end of Rua Dr Eduardo Burnay, on Estrada de Sintra 2.

For pastry snacks with outdoor watch-the-world-go-by seating, the pastelarias on Praça de República are perfect. The town's best bread shop, *Pão de Nossa Vila*, is here too.

Naturamis (☎ 638 17), a health-food shop at Travessa do Correio 1, stocks a reasonable range of vitamins and other supplies.

Entertainment

At last count, there were some 25 bars and discos in and around Ericeira. The biggest on the disco scene is *Discoteca SA – Sociedade Anonima* (☎ 623 25), which is housed in a cavernous former adega (winery) just off the N247 three km south of town at Foz do Lizandro. If you don't fancy the late-night walk home, a more central option is the Hotel Turismo's big *Disco-Bar Pirata*, or the locally more popular *Disco-Bar Ouriço* (☎ 621 38), which is above the Porto de Pesca at Av Marginal 10. The modern, soul-less Praça dos Navegantes (near Hotel Turismo) comes alive at night with a handful of bars open until late. One of the friendliest is the nearby *Ferro Velho* (☎ 635 63) at Rua Dr Eduardo Burnay 7C.

Several other bars are scattered on or above the beaches, especially nearby Praia do Lizandro which has a choice of three – *Limipicos* (☎ 86 41 21), *Marbar* (☎ 631 99) and *Koala Bar*. Closer to town, check out the relatively new *Virtual* on Praia do Sul.

Getting There & Away

From around 7 am to 8 pm daily there are buses to/from Mafra every 45 minutes and to/from Sintra every hour. At least seven buses daily (on weekdays) run to Lisbon, taking 1½ hours.

For the camping ground, Praia de Ribeira de Ilhas and other beaches north, buses leave regularly during the day from Praça dos Navegantes.

PENICHE

• pop 15,000 • postcode 2520 • area code ☎ 062

There are only a couple of reasons for coming to this drab town surrounded by ugly outskirts: one is to use its ferry connections to the island Reserva Natural da Berlenga, 10 km off shore; and the other is to splurge on some fantastic cheap seafood – Peniche has a flourishing fishing port and busy harbour. Once the cross-country IP6 motorway is finished, Peniche will probably also be swamped with Spaniards heading for the nearby beaches.

Once an island, which became joined to the mainland in the late 16th century when silt created a narrow isthmus, the cramped walled town now feels rather claustrophobic – or perhaps it's just the lingering atmosphere of Salazar's notorious prison, once housed in the huge and impressive 16th-century seaside fort. To see Peniche at its jolliest, you'd need to be here in early August for the Festa de Nossa Senhora de Boa Viagem, although accommodation is at a premium at this time.

Orientation

Two bridges connect Peniche to the isthmus. The northernmost, Ponte Velha, leads directly into the town's main street, Rua Alexandre Herculano. Drivers following the N114 should turn left into Avenida 25 de Abril which then feeds into Rua Alexandre Herculano. The N114 continues for three km round the Peniche peninsula to Cabo Carvoeiro and its lighthouse.

Keep following Rua Alexandre Herculano south and you'll soon reach the old town centre and fort. A few minutes walk east of the fort is the harbour, where boats leave for Ilha Berlenga. Avenida do Mar, where most of the seafood restaurants can be found, stretches north of the harbour, beside the isthmus.

From the bus station, it's a 10-15 minute walk, via Ponte Velha, to Rua Alexandre Herculano, where you'll find the turismo.

Information

The turismo (☎ 78 95 71) is tucked into a shady public garden just off Rua Alexandre Herculano. The office, open daily in summer from 9 am to 8 pm and in winter from 10 am to 1 pm and 2 to 5 pm, is pretty helpful.

Shops and banks with ATMs can be found along Rua Alexandre Herculano and Rua

José Estevão. The police station is in this area too, on Rua Marquês de Pombal; the hospital is on the town's northern outskirts, off Rua General Humberto Delgado.

Fortress

Dominating the southern end of the peninsula, this imposing 16th-century *fortaleza* was in use as late as the 1970s, when it was converted into a temporary home for refugees from the newly independent African colonies. Twenty years before, it had a grimmer role as one of Salazar's notorious jails for political prisoners.

Today it houses an archaeological and craft museum, though you can still make out some cells and solitary-confinement areas. It's open daily, except Monday, from 10 am to 7 pm (5 pm in winter); entry is 100$00.

Cabo Carvoeiro

The western cape of the peninsula, marked by a lighthouse, is a rough and breezy spot with fantastic ocean views. It's a three-km walk from the town.

Beaches

Two of the best beaches close to town are on the north coast of the peninsula (a 20-minute walk away) and at Baleal, three km to the north-east. There's little development at either place and the waters are fairly calm.

Places to Stay

Camping The year-round municipal camping ground (☎ 78 95 29) is 1.5 km east of town, off the Caldas da Rainha road, just before the Rio da Lagôa. There's also the more isolated and windy *Peniche Praia* (☎ 78 34 60) site, about 20 minutes walk from town, on the northern shore of the peninsula.

Hostels The nearest pousada de juventude (☎ & fax 061-42 21 27) is 17 km south, at Praia da Areia Branca. A bed in a bunk room costs 1450$00 per person and there are also some doubles (without private bath) for 3200$00.

Private Rooms The turismo frowns on touts offering private quartos and has its own list of approved rooms for about 5000$00 a double, though these are often booked out in August.

Pensões & Residencials Best of the centrally located pensões are *Mili Residencial* (☎ 78 39 18), at Rua José Estevão 45, which has clean, spacious double rooms for around 6000$00; the similarly priced *Residencial Vasco da Gama* (☎ 78 19 02) down the same road at No 23 (prices here include breakfast); and the slightly cheaper *Residencial Katekero* (☎ 78 71 07) at Avenida do Mar 70, which has some rooms with seaviews.

For out-of-town comforts, mini-golf, swimming, tennis and horse riding, the best option is Turihab's *Quinta das Tripas* (☎ & fax 75 97 33), three km east of town at Atouguia da Baleal. As you'd expect, rooms are pricey – 9000$00 a double – though discounts are offered for long stays.

Places to Eat

Avenida do Mar is the best trawling area for seafood restaurants: prices and standards are pretty similar at all of them but the twin restaurants *Katekero I & II* (☎ 78 14 80, ☎ 78 71 07) at No 90 have a bright and lively atmosphere. *Restaurante Beira Mar* at No 106 is also popular and serves a filling caldeirada (fish stew) for 1300$00.

For a wide range of other reasonably priced dishes in a friendly if rather dark and drab setting, there's *Taverna dos Mareantes* (☎ 78 36 26) at Travessa dos Mareantes 6. It's closed on Mondays.

Getting There & Away

There are eight express coaches daily to/from Lisbon (1¾ hours) and three to/from Coimbra, via Leiria, Nazaré and Caldas da Rainha. There are also local bus services (at least seven a day) to Caldas da Rainha, Óbidos and Torre Vedras.

RESERVA NATURAL DA BERLENGA

Just 10 km off shore from Peniche, this tiny 78-hectare island is a rocky, treeless place

ESTREMADURA

with weird rock formations and caverns. The thousands of seabirds that nest here take priority over human visitors – the only development that's been allowed are houses for a small fishing community, a lighthouse, a shop and a café. Paths are clearly marked with stones to stop day-trippers trespassing into the birds' domain.

Linked to the island by a narrow causeway is the squat 17th-century Forte de São João Baptista, now one of the country's most windswept and spartan hostels.

Places to Stay

There's a small, rocky camping ground near the harbour but you have to book in advance at the Peniche turismo (☎ 78 95 71). The charge for a two-person tent is around 800$00.

You also have to make advance reservations for the *Forte de São João Baptista hostel* (☎ 78 25 68). Facilities are pretty basic: you need to bring your own sleeping bag and cooking equipment.

Getting There & Away

Regular ferries make the 50-minute run to the island from Peniche harbour from June to mid-September (depending on the weather); the fare is 2500$00 return. During high season, there are usually three sailings, at 9 am, 11 am and 5 pm, with the return trips at 4 pm and 6 pm. Tickets tend to sell out quickly during this time. In the low season there's only one run, at 10 am, returning 6 pm. For current details, contact Residencial Avis (☎ 78 21 53) near the turismo on Praça Jacob Pereira.

Privately organised trips operated by Tur Pesca (☎ 78 99 60, mobile ☎ 0936 65 15 72; fax 78 30 13) run throughout the year, costing 3000$00 per person, as long as there is a minimum of five passengers. In summer you'll probably have to book at least two days ahead for these four to five-hour return trips. The first trip of the day usually departs at around 10 am; during summer there are at least two more sailings a day. Tickets and information are available at the Tur Pesca

kiosk in Largo da Ribeira at the Peniche harbour.

If you're prone to seasickness, choose your day carefully: the crossing to Berlenga can often be very rough!

ÓBIDOS
• *pop 830* • *postcode 2510* • *area code* ☎ *062*

Fortified hilltop villages don't come much prettier than this immaculate little place, six km south of Caldas da Rainha. Entirely enclosed by high medieval walls, Óbidos perches on its limestone ridge like a fairy-tale watchtower, overlooking a largely unspoilt landscape and a 16th-century aqueduct. Until the 15th century it overlooked the sea, but when the bay silted up, leaving only a lagoon, the town became landlocked.

In the half-dozen cobbled lanes, houses are bright white, edged with jolly strips of blue or yellow, and draped in bougainvillea or wisteria. Pots of geraniums fill window sills where cats doze in the sun.

No wonder Dom Dinis' wife, Dona Isabel, fell in love with the place when she visited in 1228. Her husband gave the village to her as a wedding gift, establishing a royal custom which continued until the 19th century. Today day-trippers flock here in their thousands during the summer. Like them, you can see Óbidos in an hour if you're pressed, but by staying overnight you can catch a hint of the town's medieval aura.

Orientation

The town's fancy main gate, Porta da Vila, leads straight into the main street, Rua Direita, where you'll find the turismo, shops and cafés. If you're arriving by train, you'll have a 20-minute climb up from the station at the northern foot of the ridge: a path leads to the Porta da Cerca at the other end of Rua Direita from Porta da Vila.

Buses stop on the main road just outside the Porta da Vila.

Information

The efficient turismo (☎ 95 92 31; fax 95 93 40), on Rua Direita, is open daily from 9.30

am to 1 pm and 2 to 6 pm, and has maps and lists of accommodation and restaurants.

There's a small local market just outside the Porta da Vila.

Castelo

Although the walls date from the time of the Moors (and were later restored), the castle is one of Dom Dinis' fine 13th-century creations: a traditional, no-nonsense affair of towers, battlements and big gates. Converted into a palace in the 16th century, it's now enjoying another life as a deluxe *pousada* (see Places to Stay).

Igreja de Santa Maria

The town's main church, at the northern end of Rua Direita, was built on the site of a Visigothic temple which was later converted into a mosque. Restored several times since, it dates mostly from the Renaissance and had its greatest moment of fame in 1444 when 10-year-old Afonso V married his eight-year-old cousin Isabel here.

The church's interior is more striking than the exterior: its ceiling is painted and its walls are covered with blue 17th-century *azulejos*. Also take a look at the fine 16th-century Renaissance tomb on the left (probably carved by the French sculptor Nicolas Chanterène) and the paintings by Josefa de Óbidos to the right of the altar.

Museu Municipal

The only real reason for trudging through this dull museum of religious paintings is to see the one outstanding portrait by Josefa de Óbidos. (It tends to go on visits elsewhere so check with the turismo beforehand.) The museum, next to the church, is open daily from 10 am to 12.30 pm and 2 to 6 pm; entry is 250$00.

Special Events

If you arrive on August 20, you're in for a treat: free sardines and wine are dished out to visitors by the town hall staff to celebrate what they call Tourist Day.

A more sophisticated annual event is the

Josefa de Óbidos

You'd hardly call her works masterpieces but the paintings by this 16th-century Spanish-born artist are certainly among the most accomplished Iberian paintings of their time.

Born in Seville in 1634, Josefa de Ayala settled in an Óbidos convent when she was young, staying until her death in 1684 – hence her nickname, Josefa de Óbidos. One of the few female Portuguese painters to win lasting recognition, she excelled in richly coloured still lifes and detailed religious works. ■

festival of ancient music held October each year. Accommodation can be tight at this time.

Places to Stay

Some of the best deals are the unofficial private rooms around town. The turismo turns a blind eye to them and has no listings, but you'll see 'quartos' signs in shop and house windows all over the place, including Rua Direita 40 and 41, at the little shop just inside Porta da Vila and next to the Café-Restaurante Conquistador in Rua Josefa Óbidos. The rooms usually cost around 4500$00 a double.

Alternatively, the cheapest guesthouse is *Residencial Martim de Freitas* (☎ 95 91 85), on the Caldas da Rainha road just outside the town walls. It obviously doesn't have the atmosphere of places inside the walls but it does have a pretty little garden and reasonable doubles from 6000$00.

Pricier, but with considerably more charm, are the several Turihab properties, including *Casa do Poço* (☎ 95 93 58), on Travessa da Rua Nova, which has four secluded rooms around an inner courtyard for 7500$00 to 9000$00; and the similarly priced *Casa do Relógio* (☎ 95 92 82), an 18th-century mansion just outside the walls at Rua da Graça.

If money's no problem, the unrivalled choice is the *Pousada do Castelo* (☎ 95 91 05; fax 95 91 48), where palatial rooms are a whopping 28,000$00.

ESTREMADURA

Places to Eat

Restaurants in Óbidos, like the accommodation, tend to be pricey, although there's plenty of choice. Among the cheaper options are the scruffy *Bar das Muralhas* outside the Porta da Vila (below the Albergaria Josefa de Óbidos), which serves snacks and simple meals; and the *Café-Restaurante 1 de Dezembro* (☎ 95 92 98), next to the Igreja de Santa Maria in Largo de São Pedro, which has pleasant outdoor seating and a standard menu of dishes from 1000$00.

Most other places have dishes for around 1200$00 and up. The much-touted *Restaurante Alcaide* (☎ 95 92 20), on Rua Direita, boasts a nice balcony dining area but its food is actually rather boring and badly prepared. A more imaginative menu (as well as outdoor seating) is on offer at *O Conquistador* (☎ 95 95 28), on Rua Josefa de Óbidos, where you can get exotic stuff like stewed river eel and wild boar escalope (cheaper and simpler daily specials are available too). More up-market still is the tastefully decorated *A Illustre Casa de Ramiro* (☎ 95 91 94), just outside the walls in Rua Porta do Vale; try the excellent house speciality, arroz de pato à Óbidense (Óbidos-style duck and rice).

Getting There & Away

There are five trains a day between Lisbon and Óbidos (all except the first requiring a change at Cacém), taking two to 2½ hours.

Buses regularly make the 20-minute hop to and from Caldas da Rainha and about eight a day run to/from Peniche.

CALDAS DA RAINHA

• *pop 20,000* • *postcode 2500* • *area code* ☎ *062*

This quaint, old-fashioned town near Óbidos is mostly famous for two things: its spa and its pottery. It owes its existence (and its name) to the queen *(rainha)* Dona Leonor, wife of Dom João II, who passed by one day in the 1480s and noticed people bathing in the steaming sulphuric waters. She decided to build a spa hospital here (raising the money herself, or so the story goes). Following its completion in 1484, a park and a church were also established.

The hot springs *(caldas)*, – said to be excellent for respiratory problems and rheumatism – drew a stream of nobility and royalty to the town, which reached its peak of popularity in the 19th century.

Today, though the hospital is still going strong, the town itself feels a bit dowdy. But with its plentiful accommodation and restaurants, a great daily market and good transport connections, it could make a relaxing stopover for a day or so.

Orientation

Ringed by sprawling new town development and highways, the central old town is compact by comparison. The train station is about 250m west of the turismo on Praça 25 de Abril, and the bus station is just over 100m south-east of it. The hospital, market square (Praça da República) and most of the hotels and restaurants are a short walk south of the bus station.

Information

The turismo (☎ 83 10 03; fax 84 23 20) is at the junction of Rua Engenheiro Duarte Pacheco and Praça 25 de Abril, and is open on weekdays from 9 am to 7 pm and on weekends and holidays from 10 am to 1 pm and 3 to 7 pm.

There are banks with ATMs around Praça 25 de Abril and Praça da República. The post office is on Rua Engenheiro Duarte Pacheco. Also on Praça da República is the police station (☎ 83 20 23). The general hospital (☎ 83 03 00) is nearby, off Rua Diário de Notícias.

In addition to the daily market in Praça da República, there's also a Gypsy market every Monday in the Santa Rita neighbourhood on the north-eastern outskirts of town.

Igreja de Nossa Senhora do Pópulo

Although you can't take a dip in the waters of the Hospital Termal without a letter from your doctor, you can visit the church behind the hospital. Commissioned by the queen, it features polychrome 17th-century azulejos which cover the walls inside.

Parque Dom Carlos I

This shady central park (also sometimes called Parque Dona Leonor) is a pleasant place to hang out. As well as a lake, tennis courts and camping ground, it also hosts the marginally interesting Museu de Pintura José Malhoa (open daily, except Mondays, from 10 am to 12.30 pm and 2 to 5 pm; entry is 250$00) which displays 19th-century paintings by Malhoa and others.

Museu da Cerâmica

The best of a trio of art museums across the Rua Visconde de Sacavém from the Parque Dom Carlos I, this one pays homage to the potter who put Caldas da Rainha on the ceramic map in the 19th century: Rafael Bordalo Pinheiro, who created lovable figures in clay. Among his more memorable works on display here is his life-size representation of the Passion. The museum is open from 10 am to noon and 2 to 5 pm daily, except Monday; entry is 250$00 (free on Sunday mornings).

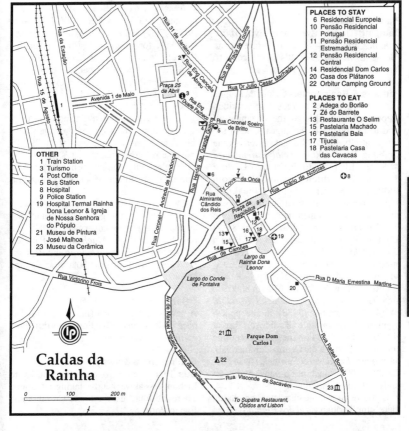

PLACES TO STAY
6 Residencial Europeia
10 Pensão Residencial Portugal
11 Pensão Residencial Estremadura
12 Pensão Residencial Central
14 Residencial Dom Carlos
20 Casa dos Plátanos
22 Orbitur Camping Ground

PLACES TO EAT
2 Adega do Borlão
7 Zé do Barrete
13 Restaurante O Selim
15 Pastelaria Machado
16 Pastelaria Baia
17 Tijuca
18 Pastelaria Casa das Cavacas

OTHER
1 Train Station
3 Turismo
4 Post Office
5 Bus Station
8 Hospital
9 Police Station
19 Hospital Termal Rainha Dona Leonor & Igreja de Nossa Senhora do Pópulo
21 Museu de Pintura José Malhoa
23 Museu da Cerâmica

Caldas da Rainha

0   100   200 m

Parque Dom Carlos I

Largo da Rainha Dona Leonor

Largo do Conde de Fontalva

To Supatra Restaurant, Óbidos and Lisbon

ESTREMADURA

Market

Surrounded by elegant houses, the skinny Praça da República makes an attractive setting for the town's traditional daily market. Mostly geared to locals, it also caters to the tourist trade with a few stalls of basketware and local pottery (Caldas da Rainha does a memorable line in cabbage-leaf pottery and phallic mugs).

Try to arrive around 9 am for the best bustle (Saturdays are busiest).

Special Events

Caldas da Rainha celebrates its role as a pottery centre by hosting the Feira Nacional da Cerâmica, usually in July.

Places to Stay

Camping There's a very attractive *Orbitur camping ground* (☎ 83 23 67) right by the Parque Dom Carlos I. It's open from 16 January to 15 November.

Pensões & Residencials Caldas da Rainha has a good range of reasonably priced accommodation, though the cheapies all tend to be fraying at the edges. One of the best centrally located budget options is the rambling *Pensão Residencial Estremadura* (☎ 83 23 13; fax 336 76), Largo Dr José Barbosa 23, which has doubles from 4000$00. The price includes breakfast, which you take at its smarter, more expensive sister establishment next door, *Pensão Residencial Central* (☎ 83 19 14; fax 84 32 82). Equally well situated is the *Residencial Dom Carlos* (☎ 83 25 51; fax 83 16 69), opposite the park at Rua de Camões 39A, which has doubles from 5500$00.

Offering doubles for 7000$00 to 8000$00 are the old *Pensão Residencial Portugal* (☎ 342 80; fax 84 13 33) in the pedestrianised Rua Almirante Cândido dos Reis at No 30; and at No 64 on the same street (the entrance is through the Centro Commercial), the modern *Residencial Europeia* (☎ 347 81; fax 83 15 09), which has a rather overbearingly helpful proprietor.

If you're after more character and charm, there's the Turihab *Casa dos Plátanos* (☎ 84 18 10; fax 84 34 17) just east of the park at Rua Bordalo Pinheiro 24. Its eight double rooms, with beautifully carved beds, are good value at 9000$00 (including breakfast).

Places to Eat

There are several cheap eateries in the lanes off Praça da República (as well as a clutch of seedy bars). The best of the bunch is *Restaurante O Selim* (☎ 84 11 22), at Rua do Parque 17, a simple little place with standard dishes from 800$00. A smarter choice nearby is *Tijuca* (☎ 242 55), at Rua Camões 89, which has some surprisingly down-to-earth items on its menu, such as stewed goat and rabbit. Another good hunting area is the Travessa da Cova da Onça, off Rua Almirante Cândido dos Reis – *Zé do Barrete* (☎ 83 27 87) is the most popular place here, especially for its grills. At Rua Engenheiro Cancela de Abreu is the *Adega do Borlão* (☎ 84 37 25), a rustic bar-restaurant with dishes from 1200$00; the daily specials (including soup, main dish and coffee) for 850$00 are good value.

If you have your own transport (or don't mind a 20-minute walk south of the park), the Thai *Supatra* restaurant (☎ 84 29 20) makes a refreshing change. It's next to the EDP (electricity company) headquarters at Rua General Amílcar Mota and is closed on Mondays.

Caldas is horrid for dieters: its sweet cavacas tarts are too good to miss and pastelarias seem to be everywhere. Try the popular *Pastelaria Machado* at Rua de Camões 14, or *Pastelaria Baia* and *Pastelaria Casa das Cavacas*, both near the spa hospital.

Entertainment

A new casa da musica (music theatre) has been built just inside the Porta da Vila to host various musical events.

Getting There & Away

Bus There are nine express buses a day to Lisbon (less at weekends), taking 1½ hours. There are four buses a day to Coimbra and five to Porto.

Train Three trains daily stop at Caldas to make the two-hour run south to Lisbon, and seven trains daily run north to the end of the line at Figueira da Foz (via Leiria and São Martinho do Porto).

FOZ DO ARELHO

The nearest beach to Caldas da Rainha (just eight km away), Foz lies on the northern shore of the Lagoa de Óbidos and is still surprisingly undeveloped. Its main drawback is the lack of shade. There's a fairly well-equipped camping ground (☎ 062-97 91 01) just before the town (sample rates: 300$00 per person, 250$00 to 500$00 per tent, 250$00 per car, 75$00 for a shower), and there are a few pensões and restaurants.

Getting There & Away

Around eight buses a day connect Foz with Caldas da Rainha (fewer on weekends).

SÃO MARTINHO DO PORTO

• postcode 2465 • area code ☎ 062

An almost perfectly enclosed bay, ringed by a sandy beach, has made this seaside resort 17 km north-west of Caldas da Rainha one of the most popular south of Nazaré: swimming here is calm and warm (a plus for families with kids). The resort itself has a Mediterranean appearance and atmosphere and seems fairly low key, but summer crowds quickly pack the place out.

Orientation & Information

The seaside Avenida 25 de Abril (also called Avenida Marginal) is the main drag, with the turismo (☎ 98 91 10) at the northern end. It's open in summer from 9 am to 7 pm on weekdays and from 9 am to 1 pm and 3 to 6 pm on weekends (from 10 am in winter). The train station is a short walk east of the beach.

Places to Stay

Camping Open year-round, the Colina do Sol camping ground (☎ 98 97 64) is a couple of km north of town.

Hostels The São Martinho pousada de juventude (☎ & fax 99 95 06) is actually

about four km inland at Alfeizerão, just off the main N8. Take any Caldas da Rainha-bound bus to get here.

Private Rooms There are plenty of private quartos available, usually for about 5000$00 a double. If the touts don't find you first, ask at the turismo.

Pensões & Residencials One of the most popular places is the Pensão Americana (☎ 98 91 70; fax 98 93 49). It's a friendly, well-run place just back from the beach at Rua Dom José Saldanha 2. Doubles with breakfast start at 6000$00. More mainstream is Pensão Carvalho (☎ 98 96 05), a block from the beach at Rua Miguel Bombarda 6, which has doubles with breakfast from 8000$00.

Places to Eat

Among the seafront restaurants on Avenida 25 de Abril, the most tempting choice is Casa Restaurante Wine Bar & Marisqueira (☎ 98 96 33) which has a huge selection of fish dishes, most from around 1300$00.

For humbler fare, retreat inland to the restaurant at the Pensão Americana.

Getting There & Away

From Caldas, the 15-minute train ride (almost a dozen times a day) is a better choice than the bus service, which runs seven times daily, taking 25 minutes. For Nazaré, however, choose the bus: on weekdays, it makes the 20-minute run at least six times daily.

Getting Around

Mountain bikes are available for rent at the Pensão Americana for 500$00 an hour.

NAZARÉ

• pop 10,000 • postcode 2450 • area code ☎ 062

Brash and bold, Nazaré has successfully shed its image of cute little fishing village to become one of the most hard-selling seaside resorts on the Atlantic coast. As soon as you arrive at the bus station you'll be pounced on by a band of aggressive local fisherwomen,

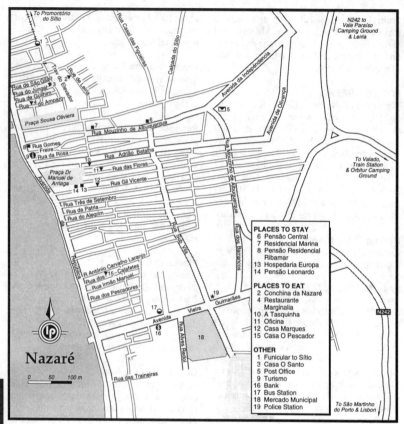

Nazaré

0   50   100 m

PLACES TO STAY
6   Pensão Central
7   Residencial Marina
8   Pensão Residencial
    Ribamar
13 Hospedaria Europa
14 Pensão Leonardo

PLACES TO EAT
2   Conchina da Nazaré
4   Restaurante
    Marginalia
10 A Tasquinha
11 Oficina
12 Casa Marques
15 Casa O Pescador

OTHER
1   Funicular to Sítio
3   Casa O Santo
5   Post Office
9   Turismo
16 Bank
17 Bus Station
18 Mercado Municipal
19 Police Station

many of them dressed in their traditional seven-petticoated skirts and coloured scarfs, touting for private rooms. Where once the old fishermen pushed their boats out to sea along the sweeping stretch of beach, they now sell trinkets and souvenirs to tourists, backed up by another band of no-nonsense women selling sweaters, pistachios and dried fruits.

Until the 18th century, when the sea covered the beach and present-day town of Nazaré, the locals lived inland at the hilltop Pederneira and the nearer Promontório do Sítio. Today, both play second fiddle to

Nazaré and its seafront Avenida da República, which is the main focus of activity. Stretching inland from here is a fishers' quarter of narrow lanes, but new town development is rapidly encroaching from the south and east.

Undeniably, Nazaré looks impressive, especially seen from the town's original site on the Promontório do Sítio (accessible by funicular). But, in summer the beach is packed with sunbathers and their tents (the sea is often too rough for swimming) and the streets are clogged with cars and tour buses. Come here for the sand and seafood if that's what you fancy, but don't expect charm, tradition or tranquillity.

Orientation

While the train station is six km inland, the bus station is fairly centrally located on Avenida Vieira Guimarães, about 150m uphill from Avenida da República.

Information

Coming from the bus station, turn right when you hit Avenida da República and you'll eventually reach the turismo (☎ 56 11 94), just after Praça Dr Manuel de Arriaga. The staff of this small office almost outdo their colleagues in Lagos for surliness: you'll get minimal help here (and no smiles).

Banks with ATMs are scattered around liberally, mostly along Avenida Vieira Guimarães. The main post office, at Avenida da Indepéndencia 2, is a 10-minute walk inland from the turismo. The police station (☎ 55 12 68) is on Rua Sub Vila. There are two options for medical emergencies: a *centro de saúde* (medical centre; ☎ 55 11 82) in Nazaré on the eastern outskirts of town, or the main hospital (☎ 56 11 16) in Sítio.

The *mercado municipal* is just across the road from the bus station.

Sítio

The Sítio clifftop area, perched 110m above the beach, is popular for its tremendous views, and among Portuguese devotees for its religious connections. According to legend it was here that a statue of the Virgin brought back from Nazareth – known as Nossa Senhora da Nazaré – was finally found after being hidden in the 18th century.

Even more famously, an apparition of the Virgin is said to have been seen here one foggy day in 1182 when a local nobleman, Dom Fuas Roupinho, was out hunting a deer. When the animal disappeared off the edge of the Sítio precipice, with the nobleman's horse in hot pursuit, Dom Fuas cried out to the Virgin for help and his horse miraculously managed to stop just in time.

The small **Hermida da Memória** chapel, on the edge of the belvedere, was built by Dom Fuas to commemorate the event. It was later visited by a number of VIP pilgrims, including Vasco de Gama. The nearby baroque 17th-century **Igreja de Nossa Senhora da Nazaré** replaced an earlier one and is decorated with attractive Dutch azulejos.

An *elevador* (funicular) climbs up the hill to Sítio throughout the day from 7 am to 1 am during summer and until midnight in winter; the fare is 80$00. The station is five minutes walk north of the turismo, in Rua do Elevador.

Special Events

The Nossa Senhora da Nazaré *romaria* is Nazaré's big religious event of the year. It takes place every 8-10 September in the square facing the church of the same name in Sítio. It features everything from sombre processions to folk dances and bullfights in the nearby bullring.

During July and August, bullfights take place here almost every weekend; check with the turismo on times and ticket availability.

Places to Stay

Camping The nearest camping grounds are just three km away:*Vale Paraíso* (☎ 56 15 46), off the N242 to the north; and Orbitur's *Valado* (☎ 56 11 11), off the Valado road to the east.

Private Rooms Officially, there are over 120 rooms for rent in Nazaré. The turismo keeps a complete list (though they won't make bookings or recommendations) so if the touts don't find you first, check the turismo list. Expect to pay at least 4500$00 for a double in high season.

Pensões & Residencials There's a bunch of rather scruffy, cheap pensões, including *Pensão Leonardo* (☎ 55 12 59), at Praça Dr Manuel de Arriaga 28, where doubles range from 2500$00 without bath to 4500$00 with. Next door, the *Hospedaria Europa* (☎ 55 15 36) offers a deal of 10,000$00, including meals, for rooms without private bath.

ESTREMADURA

Other options can be found along the busy Rua Mouzinho de Albuquerque, including *Residencial Marina* (☎ 55 15 41) at No 6, which has doubles from 5000$00; and the long-established *Pensão Central* (☎ 55 15 10) at No 85, which has rooms from 5000$00 to 7000$00.

Seaview hotels are inevitably pricey (and the ones in the centre of Avenida da República can often be noisy): expect to pay at least 12,000$00 in high season for bright, breezy double rooms in places like *Pensão Residencial Ribamar* (☎ 55 11 58; fax 56 22 24) at Rua Gomes Freire 9.

Places to Eat

As you'd expect, there are dozens of seafood restaurants in Nazaré, though the ones along the seafront tend to be touristy and over-priced. Snoop around the back lanes for less pretentious places which serve other dishes as well as seafood, such as the simple *Conchina da Nazaré* (☎ 56 15 97), at Rua da Leiria 17D, where budgies squawk in the corner and the price of dishes rarely rises higher than 1000$00. Around the corner, at Travessa do Elevador 11, start the evening with beer and amêijoas (clams) at *Casa O Santo*, a rustic nook with tables on the street outside. Even more down-to-earth, *Oficina* (☎ 55 21 61), at Rua das Flores 33, is a locals' bar and café where you can get an arroz de marisco for a bargain 1500$00. Nearby, at Rua Gil Vicente 37, *Casa Marques* (☎ 55 16 80) is run by a friendly troika of typically Nazarean women who dish up hearty meals for under 1200$00.

Slightly more up-market is the small and rustic *Restaurante Marginalia* (☎ 56 22 03) at Rua do Amparo 13, or the justifiably popular *A Tasquinha* (☎ 55 19 45) at Rua Adrião Batalha 54. *Casa O Pescador* (☎ 55 33 26), at Rua Carvalho Laranjo 18A, has become more touristy in recent years but can still deliver a great caldeirada (fish stew) for 900$00.

Getting There & Away

Since the nearest train station is six km inland at Valado (connected by frequent bus services), you'll generally be best off with direct buses. There are regular runs to/from Lisbon, Caldas da Rainha and Alcobaça; half a dozen trips daily to Coimbra and Leiria; and two or three buses daily to Aveiro, Fátima and Batalha.

ALCOBAÇA
• pop 5400 • postcode 2460 • area code ☎ 062

One of Portugal's greatest architectural masterpieces (and one of Europe's most significant medieval Cistercian monuments) dominates this low-key town 26 km northeast of Caldas da Rainha. The 12th-century Cistercian monastery, Mosteiro de Santa Maria de Alcobaça – a UNESCO World Heritage Site – is worth going miles out of your way to see. Although the town offers little else to detain you, it's pleasant enough for a one-night stopover.

Orientation

From the bus station in the new town, turn right along Avenida dos Combatentes to cross the Rio Alcôa and reach the monastery, a 10-minute walk away. The turismo, restaurants and hotels are all near the monastery.

Information

The turismo (☎ 423 77), on Praça 25 de Abril, opposite the monastery, is open from 9 am to 7 pm on weekdays and 10 am to 1 pm and 3 to 6 pm on weekends. The post office is almost next door, and there are several banks with ATMs in the praça as well.

The hospital (☎ 59 74 16) is on the eastern edge of the new town, off Rua Afonso de Albuquerque. The police station (☎ 433 88) is on Rua de Olivença.

Mosteiro de Santa Maria de Alcobaça

The monastery was founded in 1153 by Dom Afonso Henriques to honour a vow he'd made to St Bernard after the capture of Santarém from the Moors in 1147. The king entrusted the construction of the monastery to the monks of the Cistercian order, also giving them a huge area around Alcobaça to develop and cultivate.

Building started in 1178 and by the time the monks actually moved in, some 40 years later, the abbey estate had already reaped the rewards of its land-holdings to become one of the richest and most powerful in the country. In these early days the monastery is said to have housed no less than 999 monks who held Mass nonstop, in shifts.

Switching from farming to teaching in the 13th century, the monks later used the estate's abundant rents to carry out further enlargements and changes to the monastery: altars were remodelled to suit the fashion of the day, one of the largest libraries in the country was built, and the kitchen (which was already huge) underwent further alterations. Towards the 17th century, the monks turned their talents to pottery and the sculpting of figures in stone, wood and clay.

But although their revived agricultural efforts in the 18th century made the Alcobaça area one of the most fertile and productive in the land, it was the monks' growing decadence which became famous, thanks to the bitchy writings of 18th-century travellers such as William Beckford, who, despite his own decadence, was shocked at the 'perpetual gormandising…the fat waddling monks and sleek friars with wanton eyes, twanging away on the Jew's harp'.

It all came to an abrupt end in 1834 with the dissolution of the religious orders.

The monastery is open daily from 9 am to 7 pm (closing at 6 pm in winter). You can enter the church for free, but to see the rest there's an admission fee of 400$00.

The Church Modelled on the French Cistercian abbey of Cîteaux, the Alcobaça abbey church is far more impressive inside than out. Much of the original façade was altered (including the addition of wings on either side) in the 17th and 18th centuries, leaving only the main doorway and rose window unchanged. But step inside and the combination of Gothic simplicity and Cistercian austerity hits you immediately: the nave is a breathtaking 106m long but only 23m wide, with huge pillars and truncated columns. All later decorations and alterations have been removed, leaving only beams of light filtering through from the aisle and rose windows.

Tombs of Dom Pedro & Dona Inês Occupying the south and north transepts are these intricately carved 14th-century tombs, the church's greatest possession. Perhaps it's the contrast with the surrounding simplicity that makes the tombs so especially stunning. Or perhaps it's because of the tragic, romantic tale they represent.

Although the tombs themselves were badly mutilated by rampaging French troops in search of treasure in 1811, they still show extraordinary detail and are embellished with a host of figures and scenes from the life of Christ. The Wheel of Fortune at the foot of Dom Pedro's tomb and the gruesomely

Love & Revenge

Portugal's most famous love story revolves around Dom Pedro, son of Dom Afonso IV, who fell in love with his wife's Galician lady-in-waiting, Dona Inês de Castro. Even after his wife's death he was forbidden by his father to marry Inês because of her Spanish family's potential influence. Various suspicious nobles continued to pressure the king until he finally sanctioned her murder in 1355, unaware that the two had already married in secret.

Two years later, when Pedro succeeded to the throne, he exacted his revenge by ripping out and eating the hearts of Inês' murderers. He then exhumed and crowned her body, and (so the story goes) compelled the court to pay homage to his dead queen by kissing her decomposing hand.

On Pedro's orders, the lovers now lie foot to foot in the Mosteiro de Alcobaça so that on the Day of Judgement they will see each other as soon as they rise. ■

realistic Last Judgement scene at the foot of Inês' tomb are especially striking.

Kitchen & Refectory The grand kitchen, described by Beckford as 'the most distinguished temple of gluttony in all Europe', owes its immense size to 18th-century alterations (which were presumably necessary to keep up with the greedy monks' lifestyle). A water channel was also built through the middle of the room so that a tributary of the Rio Alcôa could provide a constant source of fresh fish.

Even now, it's not hard to imagine the scene when Beckford was led here by the grand priors ('hand in hand, all three together') and saw 'pastry in vast abundance which a numerous tribe of lay brothers and their attendants were rolling out and puffing up into a hundred different shapes, singing all the while as blithely as larks in a corn field'.

The adjacent refectory, huge and vaulted, is where the monks ate in silence, while the Bible was read to them from the pulpit. Opposite the entrance is a 14th-century *lavabo* (bathroom) embellished by a dainty hexagonal fountain.

Claustro do Silencio & Sala dos Reis The beautiful Cloisters of Silence date from two eras: the intricate lower storey, with their arches and traceried stone circles, were built by Dom Dinis in the 14th century. The upper storey, typically Manueline in style, was added in the 16th century.

Off the north-east corner of the cloisters is the 18th-century Kings' Room, so called because statues of practically all the kings of Portugal line the walls. Below them are azulejo friezes depicting relevant historic moments such as the siege of Santarém and the life of St Bernard. A huge army soup cauldron, captured from the Spanish at the battle of Aljubarrota in 1385, is also on display here; once used to feed an army it was no doubt a useful addition to the monks' own kitchen.

Museu do Vinho
A down-to-earth alternative to the monastery, this museum provides an absorbing portrait of the region's famous wine-making history, with everything from huge vats and old winepresses to samples of wine to buy. Housed in a spacious adega, it's about a km east of town, on the Leiria road, and is open daily from 8.30 am to 12.30 pm and 2 to 5.30 pm. Admission is free.

Places to Stay
Camping The municipal camping ground (☎ 422 65) is on Avenida Professor Vieira Natividade on the northern outskirts of town.

Pensões & Residencials The cheapest option is the dozy *Pensão Mosteiro* (☎ 421 83) on the busy Rua Frei Estevão Martins. Spacious doubles without bath are 3000$00. On the equally noisy Rua Frei António Brandão, at No 39, is *Pensão Restaurante Corações Unidos*, where you can get a double (with breakfast) from 4000$00; the quieter rooms at the back are 4500$00 to 5000$00 (with private bath).

If visiting the monastery has given you illusions of grandeur, there's palatial accommodation at the *Challet Fonte Nova* (☎ 59 83 00; fax 59 68 39), a 19th-century mansion on Estrada Fonte Nova, which has six bedrooms for around 20,000$00 each.

Places to Eat
Both the pensões have good restaurants with standard hearty Portuguese dishes. More casual is the basement bar of *António Padeira Cervejaria-Restaurante* (☎ 422 95), just off the Praça 25 de Abril at Travessa da Cadeia 27. It's closed on Wednesdays.

For more comfort and frills, there's the *Cervejaria O Cantinho* (☎ 434 71), at Rua Engenheiro Bernardo Villa Nova (off the main Rua 15 de Outubro), and the well-hidden *Celeíro dos Frades* (☎ 422 81) in Arco de Cister, under the arches near the north side of the monastery; there's a popular bar here too. The restaurant is closed on Thursdays.

ESTREMADURA

Getting There & Away

There are frequent buses to Nazaré and Batalha and up to six a day to Leiria and Porto de Mós. Connections to Lisbon are also good, with six express buses daily. The nearest train station is five km north-west of town at Valado dos Frades and is connected to Alcobaça by regular buses.

BATALHA

The Gothic-Manueline Mosteiro de Santa Maria da Vitória – usually known as Batalha ('Battle Abbey') – is another architectural giant, rivalling those other national masterpieces, the Mosteiro dos Jerónimos at Belém and the Mosteiro de Santa Maria de Alcobaça. Like them, Batalha boasts UNESCO World Heritage status (though that hasn't yet convinced authorities to move the shockingly close N1 motorway). You'd be hard pressed to choose which is the finest monument of the three, but for ornate decoration and mind-boggling flamboyance, our vote goes to Batalha.

Unlike Alcobaça, there's no decent town around the abbey so you'd be better off coming here en route to (or on a day trip from) Leiria, 11 km to the north, or Alcobaça, 20 km south-west.

Mosteiro de Santa Maria da Vitória

Like Alcobaça's monastery, the abbey was founded as the result of a battle vow, though the stakes at the 1385 Battle of Aljubarrota (fought four km south of Batalha) were considerably higher than Alcobaça's Santarém battle. On one side was the 30,000-strong force under Juan I of Castile, who was claiming the Portuguese throne; on the other was the 6500-weak Portuguese army of rival claimant Dom João of Avis, commanded by Dom Nun' Álvares Pereira and supported by a few hundred English. Defeat for João meant Portugal would slip into Spanish hands. He called on the Virgin Mary for help and vowed to build a superb abbey in return for victory. The battle was duly won and work on the Dominican abbey started three years later.

Most of the monument – the church, royal cloister, chapter house and founder's chapel – was completed by 1434 in Flamboyant Gothic style but the dominant theme is one of Manueline flamboyance, thanks to additions made in the 15th and 16th centuries. Work at Batalha only stopped in the mid-16th century when Dom João III turned his attention to expanding the Convento de Cristo in Tomar.

The abbey is open from 9 am to 6 pm daily and entry is 400$00. A turismo (☎ 044-968 06) in the nearby modern shopping complex is open in summer from 10 am to 1 pm and 3 to 7 pm daily (closing at 6 pm on weekends).

The Exterior Set in an empty concrete plaza below the motorway, the abbey at first seems like an apparition bizarrely out of place. But confronted with the detail of the building's architecture you quickly forget the surroundings: the ochre limestone monument is all pinnacles and parapets, flying buttresses and balustrades, intricately carved windows in Gothic and flamboyant styles and octagonal chapels and massive columns reflecting the English perpendicular style. There's no bell tower (the Dominicans didn't like them); catching the eye instead is the main western doorway, where layers of arches are packed with carvings of the Apostles, various angels, saints and prophets, and topped by Christ and the Evangelists.

The Interior The vast vaulted Gothic interior is deceptively plain, long and high like Alcobaça's church, and is warmed by light from modern stained glass windows. But step to the right as you enter and the scene changes dramatically: the Capela do Fundador (Founder's Chapel) is a beautiful star-vaulted square room, covered by an octagonal lantern. In the centre is the joint tomb of João I and his English wife, Philippa of Lancaster, whose marriage in 1387 established the special alliance that exists between Portugal and England to this day.

The tombs of their four younger sons line the south wall of the chapel: furthest to the left is that of Dom Fernando who died as a

ESTREMADURA

hostage in Ceuta (Morocco); second from the right is that of Henry the Navigator.

Claustro Real The Royal Cloisters were first built in a restrained Gothic style by Afonso Domingues, the master of works at Batalha during the late 1380s. But it's the later addition of Manueline embellishments by the father of Manueline art, Diogo de Boitac, which really takes the breath away. Every arch here is a tangle of detailed stone carvings of typically Manueline symbols such as armillary spheres and crosses of the Order of Christ, entwined with marine motifs such as ropes, pearls and shells and exotic flowers. The overall effect is probably the finest marriage of Gothic and Manueline art in Portugal.

Claustro de Dom Afonso V The sober Dom Afonso V Cloister seems dull by comparison. It's a plain Gothic affair and its appeal lies in its austerity.

Sala do Capítulo To the east of the Claustro Real is the early 15th-century Chapter House. Its huge unsupported vault, 19m square, was considered so outrageously dangerous to build that only prisoners on death row were employed in its construction. More traditional is the beautiful 16th-century stained glass east window, which is all purples, pinks and greens. The chapter house contains the tomb of the unknown soldiers – one killed in Flanders in WWI, the other in Africa – now watched over by a constant guard of honour.

Capelas Imperfeitas The roofless Unfinished Chapels at the east end of the abbey are perhaps the most astonishing and tantalising part of Batalha. Only accessible from outside the abbey, the octagonal mausoleum with its seven chapels was commissioned by Dom Duarte (João I's eldest son) in 1437. But as with the Royal Cloister, later Manueline additions (by architect Mateus Fernandes) have overshadowed everything else, including the Renaissance upper balcony.

Although Fernandes' plan (an upper octagon supported by buttresses) was never completed, the staggering ornamentation gives a hint of what might have followed: not only are the unfinished pillars covered with carvings, so too is the 15m-high doorway, a mass of stone-carved thistles, ivy, flowers, snails and all manner of 'scollops and twistifications', as William Beckford noted. Dom Duarte can enjoy this extraordinary panorama for eternity – his tomb (and that of his wife) lies opposite the door.

Getting There & Away
There are regular buses from Batalha to Alcobaça and Leiria and three a day to Fátima.

LEIRIA
• *pop 13,000* • *postcode 2400* • *area code* ☎ *044*
Despite its impressive medieval hilltop castle and location beside the Rio Lis, Leiria is a disappointingly dull town with little to get excited about except an attractive old cobbled quarter. The town was a good deal more important in medieval times: Dom Afonso III called a *cortes* (parliament) here in 1254; Dom Dinis established his main residence in the hilltop castle in the 14th century; and in 1411 the sizeable Jewish community built Portugal's first paper mill in the town.

Today, its main attraction to travellers is as a convenient base for visiting Alcobaça, Batalha and Fátima or the nearby beach of São Pedro de Muel – all easily accessible by bus.

Orientation
The life of the town focuses on the Praça Rodrigues Lobo and its elegant shops, and the livelier Largo Cândido dos Reis to the south-west near which are numerous little lanes of restaurants, shops and guesthouses. The castle perches above it all, on a wooded hilltop to the north.

Leiria train station is four km north-west of the centre; there's no shuttle bus into town but taxis are usually available.

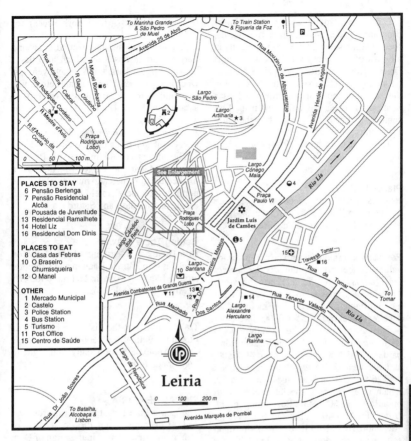

PLACES TO STAY
6 Pensão Berlenga
7 Pensão Residencial Alcôa
9 Pousada de Juventude
13 Residencial Ramalhete
14 Hotel Liz
16 Residencial Dom Dinis

PLACES TO EAT
8 Casa das Febras
10 O Braseiro Churrasqueira
12 O Manel

OTHER
1 Mercado Municipal
2 Castelo
3 Police Station
4 Bus Station
5 Turismo
11 Post Office
15 Centro de Saúde

Leiria

Information

Arriving at the bus station, you'll be just across the Praça Paulo VI from the riverside Jardim Luís de Camões. On the other side of this little park you'll find a useful regional turismo (☎ 82 37 73), the head office for the surrounding Rota do Sol region. It's open weekdays from 9 am to 7 pm and weekends from 10 am to 1 pm and 3 to 7 pm (to 6 pm in winter).

The post office is nearby on Avenida Combatentes da Grande Guerra. The centro de saúde (medical centre; ☎ 81 22 15) is across the river to the east, on Travessa Hospital,

while the police station (☎ 81 37 99) is at Largo Artilharia 4.

Castelo

This long-inhabited hilltop site got its first castle in the time of the Moors. After this was captured by Afonso Henriques in 1135 it stood at the front line of the Christian kingdom until Santarém and Lisbon finally fell in 1147. The town continued to live within the castle walls until Dom Dinis decided to establish a royal residence here in the 14th century, at which time the town began to spread down towards the river.

ESTREMADURA

Dom Dinis' Gothic royal palace, with its panoramic gallery, is still here, though it's been restored several times, most recently at the turn of this century by Swiss architect Ernesto Korrodi. Parts of the palace are now frequently used for exhibitions. Also within the walls is the ruined Igreja de Nossa Senhora da Penha, originally built in the 12th century, and rebuilt by João I in the early 15th century.

The castle is open daily from 9 am to 6.30 pm; admission is 130$00.

Places to Stay

Hostels There's an excellent pousada de juventude (☎ & fax 318 68) right at the heart of town at Largo Cândido dos Reis 7D.

Pensões & Residencials The best place for value, service and hospitality is *Residencial Dom Dinis* (☎ 81 53 42), up the steep Travessa de Tomar at No 2, where you'll get a comfortable modern double (including an excellent breakfast) for 5000$00. Two other pensões downtown are the friendly *Pensão Berlenga* (☎ 82 38 46) at Rua Miguel Bombarda 3, which has doubles from 4000$00, and the nearby *Pensão-Residencial Alcôa* (☎ 326 90) at Rua Rodrigues Cordeiro 20, which offers nothing-special doubles with breakfast for 5000$00. For fading glory, *Hotel Liz* (☎ 81 40 17; fax 243 10), at Largo Alexandre Herculano 10, overlooks the main square and has doubles with breakfast for 6000$00. A more modern choice favoured by business travellers is the similarly priced *Residencial Ramalhete* (☎ 81 28 02) at Rua Dr Correia Mateus 30.

Places to Eat

The pedestrianised Rua Dr Correia Mateus has several good restaurants to choose from, including *O Manel* (☎ 321 32) at No 50, which boasts a huge fish menu and other main dishes from 1000$00. At Rua Mestre d'Avis 33, *Casa das Febras* (☎ 323 21) is a locals' favourite, serving hearty dishes at cheap prices, including the house speciality,

febras grelhadas (grilled pork slices) for 750$00.

Another good hunting ground is around Largo Cândido dos Reis which also has a bunch of lively bars. On Sunday evenings, when many of Leiria's restaurants close, you can find some great take-away frangos assados (grilled chicken) and rice dishes (as well as beer, wine and soft drinks) at *O Braseiro Churrasqueira* (☎ 258 66) at Avenida Combatentes da Grande Guerra 41.

The attractive old market on Rua Dr Correia Mateus no longer functions as a market: the new mercado municipal is in the north of town near Hotel Dom João III and is best on Tuesdays and Saturdays.

Getting There & Away

Bus There are at least eight buses daily (on weekdays) to Fátima, Batalha and Coimbra; around five to Alcobaça; and three to Mira de Aire, via Porto de Mós.

Train Leiria is on the Lisbon to Figueira da Foz line, with three services to Lisbon's Santa Apolónia station daily and eight to Figueira da Foz.

PINHAL DE LEIRIA

The Leiria Pine Forest, stretching for over 11,000 hectares along the coast west of Leiria, was first planted in the reign of Dom Afonso III, some 700 years ago. But it was his successor, Dom Dinis, who expanded and organised the forest (subsequently called the Pinhal do Rei or Royal Pine Forest) so that it would serve not only as a barrier against the encroaching sands but so that it would also supply timber for the maritime industry – especially welcome during the Age of Discoveries.

Today the pine-scented forests, stretching from Pedrógão in the north to São Pedro de Muel in the south, are one of the most delightful areas in the province. They are popular for their picnic and camp sites and several excellent beaches.

Orientation & Information

The nicest and nearest beach to Leiria, 20 km west, is São Pedro de Muel. Two other popular beach resorts 16 km north of here – Praia de Vieira and Pedrógão – have both become rather developed. The town of Marinha Grande, halfway between Leiria and São Pedro de Muel, has a useful turismo (☎ 56 66 44), as do São Pedro de Muel (☎ 59 91 52), Praia de Vieira (☎ 69 52 30) and Pedrógão (☎ 69 54 11), the latter open July and August only.

The telephone code for this area is ☎ 044.

Places to Stay & Eat

Camping There are two decent sites at São Pedro de Muel: one belonging to *Inatel* (☎ 59 92 89) on Avenida do Farol; and the other, nearby, an *Orbitur* site (☎ 59 91 68). Praia de Vieira has a roadside municipal site (☎ 69 53 34), open June to mid-September only. The municipal site in the forest at nearby Pedrógão (☎ 69 54 03) is nicer.

Pensões & Residencials São Pedro de Muel is your best bet for accommodation and restaurants, though the other beach resorts also have several pensões and restaurants. The turismo at Marinha Grande or São Pedro de Muel can help you locate these or private rooms in high season when accommodation can get tight.

Getting There & Away

There are a couple of direct buses daily from Leiria to São Pedro de Muel (last one back around 7 pm) and several others which involve a change at Marinha Grande. The resorts further north are served by infrequent buses from Marinha Grande.

FÁTIMA

Before 13 May 1917, no-one paid any attention to this unremarkable little place 22 km south-east of Leiria. But on that day something happened to transform Fátima into one of the most important places of pilgrimage in the Catholic world. It now rivals Lourdes in popularity and is visited by over four million pilgrims a year. The town itself is more of a shrine to religious commercialisation than to the Virgin: it's packed with boarding houses for the pilgrims, and shops selling every kind of tasteless souvenir imaginable. Undeniably, there's an extraordinary atmosphere at the sanctuary itself, though you'd probably want to avoid coming anywhere near the place around 12-13 October or 12-13 May, when up to 100,000 pilgrims arrive to commemorate the first apparitions.

Orientation & Information

The focus of the pilgrimages, where the apparitions occurred, is Cova da Iria, just a km or so east of the A1 motorway. Where once sheep grazed there's now a vast, one-km-long esplanade dominated by a huge white basilica and surrounded by streets filled with shops, restaurants and hostels.

Apparitions & Miracles

On 13 May 1917, three shepherd children from Fátima – Lúcia, Francisco and Jacinta – claimed they saw an apparition of the Virgin. Only 10-year-old Lúcia could hear what the holy lady said, including her request that they return on the 13th of every subsequent month for the next six months. The word spread and by October 13th some 70,000 devotees had gathered. What happened then has been described as the Miracle of the Sun – intense lights shooting from the sun, followed by the miraculous cure of disabilities and illnesses suffered by some of the spectators.

What the Virgin apparently told Lúcia must have seemed equally potent in those WWI days: her messages described the hell that resulted from 'sins of the flesh' and implored the faithful to 'pray a great deal and make many sacrifices' to secure peace. The most controversial of the messages claimed that if her request were heeded, 'Russia [would] be converted and there [would] be peace'. One final message remains secret, known only to the pope. ■

ESTREMADURA

The sprawling town of Fátima itself lies to the south-east, though Cova da Iria is invariably referred to as Fátima too.

Fátima's train station lies 25 km away, to the east. Buses arrive at Avenida Dom José Alves Correia da Silva in Cova da Iria, a short walk from the sanctuary. Also on the Avenida is a turismo (☎ 53 11 39).

The telephone code for Fátima is ☎ 049.

The Sanctuary

The 1953 basilica may be gross to look at, but the efforts of many of the pilgrims to reach it tend to choke any criticism. On any day of the year you're likely to see suppliants, usually women, shuffling across the esplanade on their padded knees. Others count the rosary or murmur prayers. En route, they usually stop at the **Chapel of the Apparitions**, the site where the Virgin appeared, which is packed with devotees offering flowers and lighting candles.

Inside the basilica the focus of attention is the tombs of Francisco (died 1919) and Jacinta (died 1920) – both victims of a flu epidemic. Lúcia, who entered a convent in Coimbra in 1928, is still alive.

Places to Stay & Eat

There are dozens of reasonably priced pensões and boarding houses, many geared for groups of hundreds. Among the smaller, cheaper places are *Pensão Santa Isabel* (☎ 53 12 95) on Rua de São José, and *Pensão Santa Clara* (☎ 53 11 83) at Rua Santa Isabel 27, both offering doubles for around 5000$00. Restaurants abound, most offering good food at reasonable prices, as you'd expect of a place swarming with discriminating Portuguese – try those on Rua de São José.

Getting There & Away

Bus Buses make the 25-minute run from Leiria at least eight times daily. There are four to five buses daily from Batalha, Coimbra and Lisbon. Fátima is often referred to as Cova da Iria on bus timetables.

Train Fátima is on the Lisbon to Porto line; a dozen trains daily stop here (change at Entroncamento coming from Lisbon and at Coimbra coming from Porto).

PORTO DE MÓS

At the northern tip of the Parque Natural das Serras de Aire e Candeeiros, nine km south of Batalha, Porto de Mós is an insignificant but pleasant little town beside the Rio Lena, dominated by a 13th-century hilltop castle.

At the heart of a region once inhabited by dinosaurs (you can see dinosaur bones in the town's museum), Porto de Mós was an important Roman settlement. The Romans used the Rio Lena for ferrying mill stones hewn out of a nearby quarry and, later, iron from the mine some 10 km south at Alqueidão da Serra (where you can still see a Roman road). Today, the town serves as a convenient base for visiting the caves in the area or exploring the park.

Orientation & Information

The town spreads out from a cluster of streets just below the castle to a newer area further south around the bus station on Avenida Dr Francisco Sá Carneiro. Walk west from the bus station towards the Rio Lena and you'll hit Alameda Dom Afonso Henriques. The turismo (☎ 49 13 23) is at the top of this road in the *jardim público*. Its eager staff can provide maps of the park and the town. It's open daily from 10 am to 1 pm and 3 to 7 pm (to 6 pm in winter).

The telephone code is ☎ 044.

Castelo

The distinctive green-towered castle, originally a Moorish possession, was conquered in 1148 by Dom Afonso Henriques and rebuilt in 1450. It's open daily from 10 am to noon and 1 to 5 pm (free admission).

Museu Municipal

This little museum, just off Largo Machado dos Santos, is a treasure trove of the region's prehistoric remains, with everything from fossils of turtles and dinosaur bones to polished Neolithic stones and Palaeolithic flint stones. There are also some Moorish and

Parque Natural das Serras de Aire e Candeeiros

This park stretching south of Porto de Mós occupies the most extensive and diversified limestone range in Portugal. The landscape ranges from high plateaux and peaks to huge rocky hollows and depressions. Home to the rare red-billed jackdaw and to several working windmills, the park is also famous for its network of caves. One of the most spectacular parts of the park is the high plateau of Serra de Santo António (in the area of the caves) where the sweeping farmland is divided by dry stone walls.

The park operates several *casas de abrigo* (shelters) in the southern part of the park for groups of up to 12 people: to rent a six-person casa for the night costs 4200$00. Officially, this accommodation has to be booked a week in advance (and note that prices almost double at weekends). There's also a summer-only camping ground (☎ 044-45 05 55) in the park at Arrimal, about 17 km south of Porto de Mós.

For further information and to book shelters, contact the park headquarters (☎ 043-919 68; fax 043-926 05) at Jardim Municipal, Rio Maior (just south of the park). ∎

Roman objects and a small exhibition of local crafts.

It's open daily, except Mondays, from 10 am to 12.30 pm and from 2 to 5.30 pm.

Places to Stay & Eat

There's only one pensão in town, the friendly *Residencial O Filipe* (☎ 40 14 55) on the central Largo do Rossio at No 41. Its doubles (with bath) are 5000$00. A pleasant alternative is the *Quinta de Rio Alcaide* (☎ 40 21 24), a km south-east of town. This converted farmhouse has one room and five small self-catering apartments (including one in a former windmill) which cost 8500$00 per day. There's a swimming pool here too.

There are some reasonable restaurants along Avenida Dr Francisco Sá Carneiro and Alameda Dom Afonso Henriques and around the market on Avenida de Santo António.

Getting There & Away

There are about three buses daily to Porto de Mós from Leiria via Batalha. Coming from Alcobaça or Rio Maior, ask to be dropped at São Jorge, on the N1 about five km north-west of Porto de Mós, where you can pick up local bus connections.

MIRA DE AIRE

Portugal's largest cave, the Mira de Aire, lies 14 km south-east of Porto de Mós and is the most easily accessible of the caves in the area. It was discovered in 1947 but was only made open to the public in 1971. The 45-minute guided tour leads you down through a series of colourfully lit caverns dripping with stalactites and stalagmites. The last cavern, 110m down, has a huge lake with a dramatic fountain display.

Near the exit of the cave is the **parque aquático**, a summer-only water-slide park (admission fee included in the cave fee).

Mira de Aire is open daily from 9.30 am to 6 pm in winter and 9 am to 7 pm in summer (until 8 pm in July and August). Admission is 500$00.

Grutas de Alvados & Grutas de Santo António

These caves lie about 15 km south-east of Porto de Mós, and about three km and seven km, respectively, south of the N243, which runs from Porto de Mós to Mira de Aire. They're smaller, less touristy versions of Mira de Aire.

They're both open daily, from June to September, between 9.30 am and 8 pm (until 6 pm from October to March; until 7 pm during April and May; and until 9 pm during July and August). Admission is 300$00.

Getting There & Away

There are three buses daily on weekdays from Porto de Mós to Mira de Aire (two on weekends), and two returning. If you take the

ESTREMADURA

first bus out (around 9.30 am) you can easily make it a day trip. Check the timetable with the Porto de Mós turismo.

There are no direct buses to the Alvados and Santo António caves – if you don't have your own transport, you'll have to take the Mira de Aire bus and then walk. Alternatively, a taxi from Porto de Mós should cost about 2000$00 return (including an hour's wait at the caves).

SANTARÉM
• *pop 20,000* • *postcode 2000* • *area code ☎ 043*
One of the most agreeable towns in this otherwise dull region, Santarém, the provincial capital, is 'a book made of stone,' wrote Portugal's famous 19th-century novelist Almeida Garrett, 'in which the most interesting and most poetical part of our chronicles is written'.

As well as the churches and mansions to which Garrett refers, today's Santarém is also famous for its bullfights and its various fairs and festivals, notably the huge agricultural fair held every June. Outside of festival season its breezy panoramas and abundance of restaurants still make it a great one-day stopover.

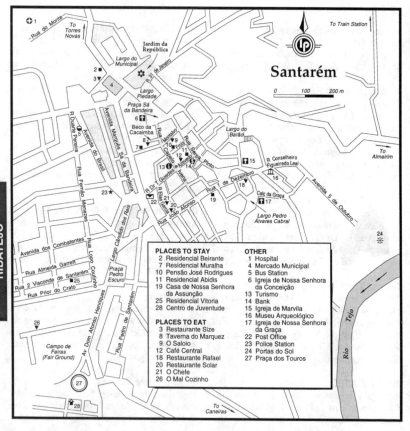

Santarém

0   100   200 m

PLACES TO STAY
2   Residencial Beirante
7   Residencial Muralha
10 Pensão José Rodrigues
11 Residencial Abidis
19 Casa de Nossa Senhora
    da Assunção
25 Residencial Vitoria
28 Centro de Juventude

PLACES TO EAT
3   Restaurante Size
8   Taverna do Marquez
9   O Saloio
12 Café Central
18 Restaurante Rafael
20 Restaurante Solar
21 O Chefe
26 O Mal Cozinho

OTHER
1   Hospital
4   Mercado Municipal
5   Bus Station
6   Igreja de Nossa Senhora
    da Conceição
13 Turismo
14 Bank
15 Igreja de Marvila
16 Museu Arqueológico
17 Igreja de Nossa Senhora
    da Graça
22 Post Office
23 Police Station
24 Portas do Sol
27 Praça dos Touros

History

The town's position in a fertile area high above the Rio Tejo made Santarém a prized possession even before the time of the Romans and Moors. It was captured by Dom Afonso Henriques in 1147 in one of the watershed successes of the Reconquista – the king built the Mosteiro de Alcobaça on the strength of the victory. Subsequently, Santarém became a favourite royal residence (partly because of its good hunting opportunities) and its palace served as the meeting place of the cortes (parliament) during the 13th, 14th and 15th centuries. Four hundred years later, in 1833, it was again favoured by royalty when Dom Miguel used Santarém as his base during his brief (and unsuccessful) war against brother Pedro.

Orientation

Overlooking the Rio Tejo, Santarém commands some grand views of the Ribatejan plains. At the heart of the old town are the pedestrianised Rua Capelo e Ivens and Rua Serpa Pinto, where the turismo and most of the restaurants, shops and cheap accommodation can be found. Signposts to the Portas do Sol lookout lead visitors on a pleasant walk past most of the churches of interest.

The train station lies two km below the town to the north-east and there's no shuttle bus to the centre. The bus station is much closer – just west of the town centre on Avenida do Brasil.

Information

Tourist Office The helpful turismo (☎ 39 15 12) is at Rua Capelo e Ivens 63 and can provide information about the region as well as about Santarém.

Money There are banks with ATMs along the central Rua Guilherme Azevedo and nearby Rua Serpa Pinto.

Post & Communications The main post office is at the end of Rua Dr Teixeira Guedes, near Largo Cândido dos Reis.

Medical Services The hospital (☎ 37 05 78) is on the northern edge of town, off the road to Torres Novas.

Emergency The police station (☎ 220 22) is on the west side of Largo Cândido dos Reis.

Igreja de Nossa Senhora da Conceição

This baroque 17th-century Jesuit seminary church, built on the site of the former royal palace, dominates the town's most impressive square, Praça Sá da Bandeira. Inside the church, which now serves as the town's cathedral, are the usual baroque frills, including a painted ceiling and gilded, carved altars.

Igreja de Marvila

Dating from the 12th century, but with 16th-century overlays, the most outstanding features of this endearing little church, redolent with wood polish, are its Manueline doorway and glowing 17th-century azulejos.

It's at the end of Rua Serpa Pinto and open daily, except Monday, from 9.30 am to 12.30 pm and 2 to 6 pm (6.30 pm on weekends).

Igreja de Nossa Senhora da Graça

Just south of the Igreja de Marvila, on Largo Pedro Álvares Cabral, is Santarém's most impressive church. It was built in the early 15th century and features a magnificent rose window. It houses the tombs of Pedro Álvares Cabral (the 'discoverer' of Brazil) and Dom Pedro de Menses (the first governor of Ceuta, who died in 1437). Probably because the de Menses family founded the church, Dom Pedro's tomb is considerably more ornate than that of the explorer.

The church, which sometimes has exhibitions, is open daily, except Monday, from 9.30 am to 12.30 pm and from 2 to 5.30 pm.

Museu Arqueológico

Back on the main route towards Portas do Sol, on Rua Conselheiro Figueiredo Leal, the recently tarted-up archaeological museum (complete with piped classical music) is housed in the 12th-century Igreja de São João de Alporão. Among the stone carvings, azulejos, old chains and keys and other dusty relics, the showpiece is undoubtedly the elaborately carved tomb of Dom Duarte de Menses, who died in 1464 in a battle against the Moors in North Africa. The only bit of him that was saved for burial – a single tooth – used to be on display too, but seems to have been removed during the latest prim cleanup.

The museum (admission 200$00) is open daily, except Monday, from 9.30 am to 12.30 pm and from 2 to 6 pm.

Portas do Sol
The 'gates of the sun', on the site of the Moorish citadel on the south-east edge of town, is the town's best panoramic and picnic site. There is a walled-in garden with aviaries and a pond, and a fantastic view over the Rio Tejo and plains beyond.

Special Events
Santarém's Feira Nacional da Agricultura (National Agriculture Fair) is famous nation-wide for its horse races, bullfights and night-time bull-running in the streets. It lasts for 10 days, from the first Friday in June, and takes place a couple of km west of the centre.

Gourmets should take note of the Festival Nacional de Gastronomia, a 10-day affair at the end of October, which encourages you to eat as much traditional Portuguese fare as you can. Various handicraft displays also take place at the same time.

Accommodation during both these events can be tight: you'd be wise to book ahead.

Places to Stay
Camping The nearest camping ground (☎ 543 99) is at Alpiarça, 10 km to the east.

Hostels The centro de juventude (☎ 33 32 92; fax 278 55) is at Avenida Dom Afonso Henriques 109, on the south-west edge of town.

Pensões & Residencials There's a good range right in the centre, including the popular little *Pensão José Rodrigues* (☎ 230 88), at Travessa do Froís 14 (a few steps from the turismo), which has doubles from

3500$00. In the 5000$00 to 6000$00 range are the old-fashioned, Art Deco *Residencial Abidis* (☎ 220 17) at Rua Guilherme de Azevedo 4, and the more up-market *Residencial Muralha* (☎ 223 99) at Rua Pedro Canavarro.

Away from the centre are the *Residencial Beirante* (☎ 225 47), near the market at Rua Alexandre Herculano 3, which is better than it looks from the outside, with doubles from 5000$00 (7000$00 with bath); and the similarly priced *Residencial Vitoria* (☎ 225 73; fax 282 02) at Rua 2 Visconde de Santarém 21, south-west of the centre.

Among several attractive Turihab properties that the turismo can arrange for you, the most central is the delightful *Casa de Nossa Senhora da Assunção* (☎ 250 48), right in the heart of the historic area at Rua 1 de Dezembro 55. It has just two rooms at 12,000$00 each, and a slightly more expensive suite.

Places to Eat
Even on a budget you'll do well in Santarém: the place is chock-a-block with cheap restaurants. The best of the rather scruffy options around the market area is *Restaurante Size* (☎ 230 30) at Rua do Mercado 24B. It's a jolly, busy lunch-time place where you'll be hard pushed to spend more than 900$00 a dish.

In the turismo area is the *Taverna do Marquez* (☎ 229 37), a cosy nook at Beco da Cacaimba 9, and the popular *O Saloio* (☎ 276 56), down the opposite lane, Travessa do Montalvo 11, which has generous half-portions from 800$00. The friendly and well-advertised *O Chefe*, in Largo Emilio Infante da Câmara (off Rua Elias Garcia), is a family-run place with daily specials starting from 750$00. It's open until 2 am. Nearby, at No 9 on the same Largo, is the posher *Restaurante Solar* (☎ 222 39), which is popular for business lunches, as is the long-established chrome and Art Deco *Café Central* (☎ 223 03) at Rua Guilherme de Azevedo 32. A smaller place which catches the passing tourist trade is the attractive *Restaurante Rafael* (☎ 265 17), at Rua 1 de

Fishy Stuff in Santarém
There's a curious culinary speciality in Santarém: *fataça na telha* – mullet fish grilled on a tile – which occasionally appears on menus. Apparently only a few people know how to cook it properly, including a village woman from Caneiras, five km south of town. The turismo can sometimes persuade her to cook it by special arrangement if you're really interested. ∎

Dezembro 3, where dishes cost around 1300$00. Similarly priced is the long-popular *O Mal Cozinho* (☎ 235 84) at Campo de Feiras, near the bullring south of town.

Getting There & Away
Bus There are hourly buses to Lisbon (taking an hour and 20 minutes) plus a couple of quicker express services a day. Around six buses a day run to Caldas da Rainha, Fátima, Abrantes and Tomar, and four run to Setúbal.

Train There are five Alfa *intercidade* services between Lisbon's Santa Apolónia station and Santarém (taking 45 minutes) as well as frequent local services to Lisbon (taking an hour and 10 minutes). Taxis charge around 500$00 for the trip between the town and the station.

TOMAR
• *pop 15,000* • *postcode 2300* • *area code* ☎ *049*
This attractive and historically outstanding town is an oasis of interest in the Ribatejo. Not only is its Convento de Cristo, former headquarters of the Knights Templar, one of the most significant architectural and religious monuments in the land, but Tomar is also home to one of the country's few remaining medieval synagogues, and hosts the unique Festa dos Tabuleiros (Festival of the Trays).

The town itself, straddling the Rio Nabão, is a fine place to wander around, with its delightful old quarter of cobbled lanes and the extensive Mata Nacional dos Sete Montes (Sete Montes National Forest) at the foot of the Convento de Cristo. If you have your own transport, the town also makes a perfect base for exploring the surrounding area, including the nearby Castelo de Bode reservoir which is set in some very pretty countryside.

Orientation
It's easy to get your bearings in Tomar: the Rio Nabão neatly divides the town, with new development largely on the east bank and the old town on the west side. The *convento* looks down on it all from its wooded hilltop above town to the west.

The bus and train station are together at the southern end of town. To get to the centre of town from here, walk north 300m past the tree-bordered Várzea Grande square and you'll reach Avenida Dr Cândido Madureira, the southern edge of the old town.

Information
Tourist Office The excellent turismo (☎ 32 26 03, ☎ 32 24 27), at the western end of Avenida Dr Cândido Madureira, can supply a comprehensive town map and help with accommodation. It's open weekdays from 9.30 am to 12.30 pm and 2 to 6 pm and on weekends from 10 am to 1 pm and 3 to 6 pm (from 1 October to 31 May it closes on Saturday afternoons and all day Sunday. For information about other places nearby, head for the regional turismo (☎ 32 31 13; fax 31 46 77) at Rua Serpa Pinto 1.

Money There are numerous banks around town with ATMs, including those on Rua Serpa Pinto and the new town's Rua Marquês de Pombal.

Post & Communications The main post office is by the river on Avenida Marquês de Tomar.

Medical Services In addition to a couple of medical centres, Tomar also has a district

RIBATEJO

hospital (☎ 32 11 00) halfway along Avenida Dr Cândido Madureira.

Emergency The police station (☎ 31 34 44) is on Rua Dr Sousa.

Convento de Cristo

Set on the wooded slopes above town, and enclosed within its 12th-century walls, the former headquarters of the Knights Templar reflects perfectly all the power and mystique that this religious military order wielded from the 12th to the 16th century. The monastery was founded in 1160 by Gualdim Pais,

the Templars' Grand Master. Its various chapels, cloisters and chapter houses, added over the centuries by successive kings and grand masters, reveal the changing architectural styles in spectacular fashion.

From 1 July to 30 September the convent is open daily from 9.15 am to 12.15 pm and 2 to 5.45 pm (to 5.15 pm in May and June, to 5 pm from October to April). Admission is 400$00.

Charola This extraordinary 16-sided Templar church dominates the convento. Built in the late 12th century, its round design is

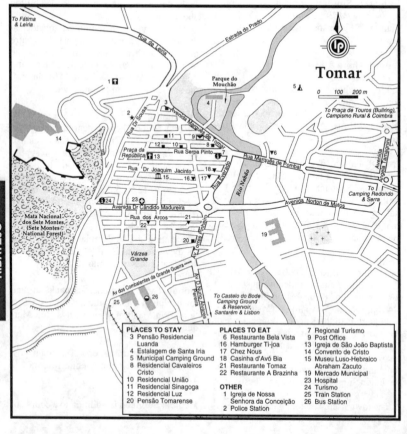

Tomar

0   100   200 m

PLACES TO STAY
3 Pensão Residencial Luanda
4 Estalagem de Santa Iria
5 Municipal Camping Ground
8 Residencial Cavaleiros Cristo
10 Residencial União
11 Residencial Sinagoga
12 Residencial Luz
20 Pensão Tomarense

PLACES TO EAT
6 Restaurante Bela Vista
16 Hamburger Ti-joa
17 Chez Nous
18 Casinha d'Avó Bia
21 Restaurante Tomaz
22 Restaurante A Brazinha

OTHER
1 Igreja de Nossa Senhora da Conceição
2 Police Station
7 Regional Turismo
9 Post Office
13 Igreja de São João Baptista
14 Convento de Cristo
15 Museu Luso-Hebraico Abraham Zacuto
19 Mercado Municipal
23 Hospital
24 Turismo
25 Train Station
26 Bus Station

The Order of the Knights Templar

This religious military order was founded around 1119 by a clutch of French knights who decided to devote themselves to the protection of pilgrims visiting the Holy Land from bands of marauding Muslims. King Baldwin of Jerusalem housed them in a part of his palace that was once a Jewish temple – hence the name of the order.

It soon became a strictly organised semireligious affair headed by a grand master. Each Templar took vows of poverty and chastity, and to emphasise their religious vows, the knights wore white coats emblazoned with a red cross. By 1139, they were placed directly under the pope's authority and soon became the leading defenders of the Christian crusader states in the Holy Land. In Portugal, their main role was in helping to expel the Moors from the country.

Rewarded with land, castles and titles, the order quickly grew very rich, owning properties all over Europe, the Mediterranean and the Holy Land. This network, and their military strength, gave them another influential role: that of bankers to kings and pilgrims alike.

By the mid-13th century, however, the primary *raison d'être* of the order was in question – the Christians had recaptured all of Portugal – and by 1300 the Moors had taken the last remaining crusader stronghold in the Holy Land. There was talk of merging the order with their age-old rivals, the Hospitalers (another military religious order), but the axe finally fell as a result of rumours and scandals involving the order's practices, probably stirred up by their enemies.

In 1307, King Philip IV of France – either eager for the order's wealth or afraid of its power – initiated an era of persecution (supported by the French pope Clement V), arresting all the knights, accusing many of heresy, and seizing their property. In 1314, the order's last grand master was burned at the stake.

In Portugal, however, things didn't go nearly so badly for the order. Dom Dinis did follow the trend by dissolving the order in 1314, but a few years later he cannily re-established it as the Order of Christ, under the control of the throne. It was largely thanks to the wealth of the order that Prince Henry the Navigator (grand master from 1417 to 1460) was able to fund the launch of the Age of Discoveries. Dom João III took the order into a humbler phase, shifting it towards monastic duties. From the 17th century its power diminished and in 1834, together with all the other religious orders, it finally broke up. ■

based on the Church of the Holy Sepulchre in Jerusalem. It's said that the Templars arrived here for Mass on horseback. Sadly, the restoration work that has been going on for years means you can't go inside to see the circular aisle, the high altar enclosed within a central octagon, or the early 16th-century paintings.

Dom Manuel was responsible for tacking on the nave to the west side of the Charola and commissioning Diogo de Arruda to build a chapter house, with a *coro alto* (choir) above. The main western doorway into the nave – a splendid example of Spanish Plateresque style – is the work of the Spanish architect João de Castilho, who later repeated his success at Belém's Mosteiro dos Jerónimos.

Claustro do Cemitério & Claustro da Lavagem

These two azulejo-decorated cloisters to the east of the Charola were built

during the time when Prince Henry the Navigator was Grand Master of the order. The Claustro do Cemitério (burial-ground cloister) contains two 16th-century tombs, while the water tanks of the two-storey Claustro da Lavagem (ablutions cloister) are now full of plants.

Chapter House Even if you've seen photos or postcards of it before, the famous west-side chapter-house window, best seen from the roof of the adjacent Claustro de Santa Bárbara, blows you away: here is the supreme expression of Manueline art, the confidence of that seafaring Age of Discoveries made tangible in stone. Created by an anonymous genius around 1510, it's an exuberant celebration of tangled ropes and seaweed, coral and cork floats, topped by the Cross of the Order of Christ and the royal arms and armillary spheres of Dom Manuel. An almost equally fantastic window on the

RIBATEJO

south side of the chapter house is frustratingly obscured by the Claustro Principal.

Claustro Principal The elegant Renaissance Great Cloisters are in striking contrast to the flamboyance of the convento's Manueline architecture. Commissioned during the reign of João III, they were probably designed by the Spanish Diogo de Torralva but completed in 1587 by an Italian, Filippo Terzi. These 'foreign' architects were among several responsible for introducing a delayed Renaissance style into Portugal. The Great Cloisters are arguably the country's finest expression of that style: a sober ensemble of Greek columns and Tuscan pillars, gentle arches and sinuous, spiralling staircases.

The outlines of a second Chapter House, commissioned by João III but never finished, can be seen from the cloister's south-west corner.

Museu Luso-Hebraico Abraham Zacuto

In a charming cobbled lane of the old town, at Rua Dr Joaquim Jacinto 73, you'll find the best preserved medieval synagogue in Portugal. Built between 1430 and 1460, it was used as a Jewish house of worship and meeting place for only a few years before Dom Manuel's edict of 1496 forced the Jews of Portugal to convert to Christianity or leave the country. The synagogue subsequently served as a prison, chapel, hay loft and warehouse until it was classified as a national monument in 1921.

Largely thanks to the efforts of Luís Vasco (who comes from one of two Jewish families left in Tomar), the small, plain building now serves as a Luso-Hebraic museum, displaying various tombstones engraved with 13th and 14th-century Hebraic inscriptions, as well as gifts from Jewish visitors from around the world. In the house next door, women's ritual baths, discovered during 1985 excavations, are now on display under glass.

The synagogue (free admission) is open daily, except Wednesdays, from 9.30 am to 12.30 pm and 2 to 6 pm (5 pm in winter).

Igreja de São João Baptista

The old town's most striking church faces Praça da República, itself an eye-catching ensemble of 17th-century buildings. The church, mostly dating from the late 15th century, has an octagonal spire and richly ornamented Manueline doorways on the north and west sides. The six panels hanging inside were painted specially for the church by Gregório Lopes, one of the finest of Portugal's 16th-century artists.

Igreja de Nossa Senhora da Conceição

Just downhill from the convento lies this little Renaissance basilica which is striking in its simplicity. It was probably built by Francisco de Hollanda, one of Dom João III's favourite architects, in the middle of the 16th century.

It's only open from 11 am to 12.15 pm daily. At other times, ask for the key at the entrance to the convento.

Special Events

Tomar's most famous event is its unique Festa dos Tabuleiros. Another important reli-

---

Festa dos Tabuleiros

Tomar's unique Festival of the Trays probably traces its roots to a pagan fertility rite, though officially it's related to the saintly practices of Dona Isabel (Dom Dinis' queen) and has been held in its present form since the 17th century. These days the colour and spectacle of the event – all the attendant music, dancing and fireworks – are the most memorable aspects.

The highlight of the festival is a procession of about 400 young white-clad women (traditionally they should be virgins!) bearing enormously tall tray-headdresses stacked with loaves, decorated with colourful paper flowers and topped by a white paper dove. Young male attendants, dressed in black and white (apparently *they* don't have to be virgins) help the girls balance the load, which can weigh up to 15 kg. The following day, bread and wine, blessed by the priest, are handed out to local families.

The festival is held every three or four years. The last time was in 1995 but the 1999 event may be brought forward to coincide with Expo '98. ■

gious festival is the Nossa Senhora da Piedade candle procession, which is held on the first Sunday in September in alternate years. During this festival, floats decorated with paper flowers are paraded through the streets.

Activities

Adventure Sports With advance planning, you could take advantage of an ambitious range of adventure sports and other activities organised by ADIRN (Associação para o Desenvolvimento Integrado do Ribatejo Norte or Association for the Integrated Development of Northern Ribatejo). Their programme includes everything from walking, biking and canoeing day trips to parachuting, caving, 'paint ball' (a game of 'strategy' in which you shoot paint at your opponents) and hot-air balloon trips. Even the walking trips have to be booked a week in advance, however. Contact ADIRN (☎ 32 19 60; fax 32 17 20) at Alameda 1 de Marco, Centro Commercial Templários.

Horse Riding If you'd like to go riding, contact Paulo Mota at the Turihab Quinta de Anunciada Velha (☎ 34 54 69), three km south-west of town.

Water Sports Although most water sports are no longer allowed on the nearby Castelo de Bode reservoir, 14 km east of Tomar, there are a couple of operators who arrange canoe and boat trips on the Rio Zêzere (which feeds into the reservoir). Try Centro Nautico Lago Azul (☎ 36 15 85; fax 36 16 60), which is based in Castenheira (17 km north-east), or A Barcaça (☎ 37 16 17), near Serra (10 km east). The biggest operator in the area is Centro Naútico do Zêzere (☎ 074-997 45; fax 074-997 60), offering jet skis, yachts, water-skis, canoes and kayaks from its centre in Palhais, 45 km north-east of Tomar.

Places to Stay

Camping Tomar's municipal camping ground (☎ 32 26 07) is across the river from the post office and next to the football stadium and municipal swimming pool.

There are other good camping grounds east of town: *Campismo Rural* (☎ 30 18 14), seven km north-east at Pelinos (poor bus connections); *Camping Redondo* (☎ & fax 37 64 21) at Poco Redondo, near Serra, 10 km east, which has a swimming pool, bar and restaurant (and reasonably good bus connections); and *Castelo de Bode* (☎ 99 22 62), 14 km south-east (with a few buses a day from Tomar).

Pensões & Residencials One of the longest established cheap pensões in town, *Pensão Tomarense* (☎ 31 29 48), on the noisy Avenida Torres Pinheiro at No 13, still offers bargain rooms for 3500$00, but they're pretty seedy. The nearby *Pensão Nun' Alvares* is currently under renovation. The next best options are in the heart of the old town. *Residencial Luz* (☎ 31 23 17), at Rua Serpa Pinto 144, has doubles for 5500$00. Get a room at the back and you'll be serenaded by cooing pigeons and a caged blackbird. Better value is the popular *Residencial União* (☎ 32 31 61; fax 32 12 99), down the road at No 94, where doubles with breakfast are 6000$00.

In the next price bracket is the modern *Pensão Residencial Luanda* (☎ 32 32 00; fax 32 21 45), overlooking the river at Avenida Marquês de Tomar 15. Doubles here are 7000$00. There's also a bunch of posher, modern residencials with doubles for around 8000$00, such as *Residencial Cavaleiros Cristo* (☎ 32 12 03; fax 32 11 92) at Rua Alexandre Herculano 7; and the central *Residencial Sinagoga* (☎ 31 67 83; fax 32 21 96), at No 31 in the quiet residential Rua Gil Avo, which has all the frills (including satellite TV).

Top of the range in town is the *Estalagem de Santa Iria* (☎ 31 33 26; fax 32 10 82) in the island's Parque do Mouchão, where you can splurge on a suite from 14,000$00 or a humbler double from 10,000$00. For around the same price there are also several lovely Turihab properties in the area. The nearest is *Quinta da Anunciada Velha* (☎ 34 52 18; fax 32 13 62), three km south-west. The turismo has details of this and others.

RIBATEJO

Places to Eat

Winning the prize for looks and location, at Rua Fonte do Choupo 6 (next to Ponte Velha) is *Restaurante Bela Vista* (☎ 31 28 70). Overlooking the river's weir, it has outdoor tables under the shade of wisteria flowers. The menu has reasonably priced dishes from around 1000$00. It's closed on Mondays.

Restaurante Tomaz (☎ 31 25 52), at Rua dos Arcos 31, has dour service but large helpings at cheap prices (half-portions from 650$00). Further up the road at No 55, *Restaurante A Brazinha* (☎ 31 30 20) is a posher option with fancy dishes starting from 1500$00. It's closed on Saturdays. Cosier and cheaper is the cutely decorated *Casinha d'Avó Bia* (☎ 32 38 28), at Rua Dr Joaquim Jacinto 16, with half-portions from 800$00. The nearby *Chez Nous*, at No 31, is an expensive place specialising in French delicacies such as filet mignon. It's closed on Sundays. *Hamburger Ti-joa*, at Rua dos Moinhos 49, serves burgers and English breakfasts.

To buy fresh fruit and vegetables, head for the mercado municipal, just across the river by Rua Santa Iria. It takes place daily except Sundays, but is at its biggest and best on Fridays.

Getting There & Away

Bus Three to five buses daily go to Lisbon, Batalha, Fátima and Santarém and two daily go to Nazaré and Leiria.

Train On weekdays there are hourly trains to/from Lisbon's Santa Apolónia station (about eight a day on weekends), taking two hours.

Getting Around

There are several car-rental agencies in town, including Listartour (☎ 32 23 58) and Nabantur (☎ 32 29 68).

The Beiras

At the heart of Portugal lies the Beira region, and at the heart of the Beira is the country's highest mountain range and most prominent geophysical landmark, the beautiful Serra da Estrela. This and the region's lesser ranges help to define the three Beira provinces – *litoral* (coastal), *alta* (upper) and *baixa* (lower) – that mirror Portugal's own multiple personalities.

Air masses from the Atlantic Ocean tumble against these granite ranges, spilling their moisture and giving birth to several major river systems which have laid down a rich subsoil in and west of the mountains. Unlike most of Portugal's better known rivers, which have their headwaters in Spain, the Rio Mondego, rising in the Serra da Estrela, is the longest exclusively Portuguese river.

Beira Litoral's splendid coastline has so far escaped serious development; the only major resort is at cheerful Figueira da Foz. Aveiro and Ovar preside over a vast and complex estuary at the mouth of the Rio Vouga, with an important wildlife refuge at São Jacinto. From the coast a fertile, sometimes boggy plain reaches 30 km inland to the Gralheira, Caramulo and Buçaco hills and, in the south, 50 to 90 km into the foothills of the Serra da Estrela.

Elegant Coimbra – the provincial head-

quarters and the biggest town in the Beiras – is, with Lisbon and Porto, one of Portugal's historic capitals and a major centre of culture and learning. Around it lie the spa town of Luso, the holy forest of Buçaco and, at Conimbriga, Portugal's finest Roman ruins.

Beira Alta, hemmed around by mountains, was the heartland of the Lusitani who, under the legendary Viriathus or Viriato – Portugal's original national hero – put up stubborn resistance to the Romans. Its dour people see few visitors other than those who stumble upon Viseu or the provincial capital, Guarda. Most visitors head, via Seia or Gouveia, straight into the Serra da Estrela. Robbed of rain, the eastern parts of the province are sparsely populated and thinly cultivated.

Beira Baixa, though hilly in the north, is much like the Alentejo, with modest, good-natured people, ferocious summer weather and hypnotically flat landscapes of cork oaks, olive groves and giant agricultural estates. Like most of the Beira Alta, it's of minimal interest except to lovers of vast, quiet, open spaces; even the capital, Castelo Branco, has little to offer. A conspicuous exception is the proud, handsome hilltop town of Monsanto.

Cuisine of the Beiras
Coimbra likes its roast suckling pig, and Aveiro its fried eels, but the cuisine of the region is perhaps most strongly defined by the hearty, warming food of the mountains – roast lamb, roast kid and grilled trout; smoked ham, sausages and bacon; roast chestnuts and several varieties of *feijoacas* (little beans); rye bread and stout yellow corn bread; and the strong, semisoft cheese of the Serra da Estrela. Finish your meal with an *aguardente* made from honey or juniper berries. ■

BEIRAS

The Beira Litoral

COIMBRA
• *pop 85,000* • *postcode 3000* • *area code* ☎ *039*

Perched high above the Rio Mondego, midway between Lisbon and Porto, Coimbra is renowned as the 'Oxford of Portugal'. Its ancient university, founded in 1290, is still the focus of life here, though the city has an abundance of other cultural attractions, some dating back to the time when Coimbra served as Portugal's capital some 850 years ago.

Although modern development and appalling traffic have eroded the city's charm, it's still a great place to hang out for a few days: transport is good, there are plenty of reasonably priced restaurants and places to stay, and there are some attractive day-trip destinations nearby, including the country's best Roman ruins at Conimbriga. If you're here in May, you can throw yourself into the spirit of Coimbra's biggest bash – the students' Queima das Fitas, which celebrates the end of the academic year with boisterous revelry.

BEIRAS

All in all, this is a thoroughly enjoyable destination. It's romantic and cultured (Coimbra even has its own version of fado), lively and fun.

History

The Romans founded a major settlement at nearby Conimbriga and the Moors settled in Coimbra itself, until the Christians booted them out in the 12th century. Afonso Henriques made the city his new capital in 1145 but, just over a century later, Afonso III decided to move to Lisbon. Coimbra wasn't forgotten – although Coimbra University, the first in the country (and among the first in Europe), was actually founded in Lisbon by Dom Dinis in 1290, it settled here for good in 1537, attracting a steady stream of teachers, artists and intellectuals from all over Europe.

The 16th century was a particularly cultured time for Coimbra thanks to Nicolas Chanterène, Jean de Rouen (João de Ruão) and several other French sculptors who helped create a school of sculpture which was to influence styles all over Portugal.

Today, though the university has fewer students than Lisbon's, it's still considered the most prestigious in the country. Coimbra itself, though respected as a traditional centre of art and culture, prospers these days thanks to its textile, tannery and tourism industries.

Orientation

Crowning Coimbra's hilltop site is the university, with the old town clustered below in a tangle of lanes. Most places of interest are in this area and within easy (if steep) walking distance from one another. The new town sprawls around the bottom of the hill and along the Rio Mondego. The main hubs of activity are Largo da Portagem and its nearby pedestrianised street, Rua Ferreira Borges; and the student haunt, Praça da República. There are only a few sights of interest across the river; you can walk there via Ponte de Santa Clara.

The main bus station is at the north-west end of town, on the riverside Avenida Fernão de Magalhães, about 15 minutes walk from

the centre. There are three train stations: the central Coimbra A; the main Coimbra B, a couple of km to the north-west; and Coimbra Parque, five minutes walk south of the centre. You'll probably arrive at Coimbra B; a shuttle service connects this with Coimbra A. If you're arriving by car, be prepared for worse than usual driving habits and appalling parking facilities.

You're best off parking across the river (Avenida de Conimbriga is a good bet).

Information

Tourist Office The rude regional turismo (☎ 330 19; fax 255 76) at Largo da Portagem is open on weekdays from 9 am to 6 pm and on weekends from 10 am to 1 pm and 3 to 5.30 pm.

Far more amenable and efficient are two municipal turismos. The one at Praça Dom Dinis (☎ 325 91) by the university is open on weekdays from 9 am to 6 pm and on weekends from 9 am to 12.30 pm and 2 to 5.30 pm. The other turismo (☎ 332 02), below the university in Praça da República, is open from 10 am to 6.30 pm on weekdays only. Pick up a copy of the informative town map from any of these offices.

Money There are banks (most with ATMs) along Avenida Fernão de Magalhães, the riverside Avenida Emídio Navarro and the main shopping street, Rua Ferreira Borges. Outside banking hours, the Hotel Astoria, at Avenida Emídio Navarro 21, can also change currency.

Post & Communications The main post office (☎ 281 81) is at Avenida Fernão de Magalhães 223, 10 minutes walk from Largo da Portagem. It's open weekdays from 8.30 am to 6.30 pm and on Saturdays from 9 am to 12.30 pm. Another conveniently central branch is near the mercado municipal, on Rua Nicolau Rui Fernandes.

Travel Agencies For student cards and youth travel discounts, head for Tagus Travel (☎ 349 99; fax 349 16) in the students' Associação Academica de Coimbra (AAC), on Rua Padre António Vieira, just off Praça da República. The agency is open weekdays only from 9.30 am to noon and 2 to 5 pm. Other reliable agencies include Abreu (☎ 270 11) and Intervisa (☎ 238 73).

Bookshops There's a cluster of good bookshops along Rua Ferreira Borges, including a branch of Livraria Bertrand.

Campuses The historic Velha Universidade (Old University) is the heart of the university campus and its most interesting area. The dull modern faculty additions have few

student rendezvous areas; the AAC (Associação Academica de Coimbra) on Rua Padre António Vieira serves that role better, with a canteen and student-oriented shops.

Cultural Centres The British Council (☎ 235 49) at Rua de Tomar 4 (and Rua Alexandre Herculano 34) is open Mondays, Thursdays and Fridays from 10 am to 12.30 pm and 2 to 8 pm. Its library stocks English newspapers.

Medical & Emergency Services The University of Coimbra's hospital (☎ 40 04 00) is on Praça Professor Mota Pinto. The police

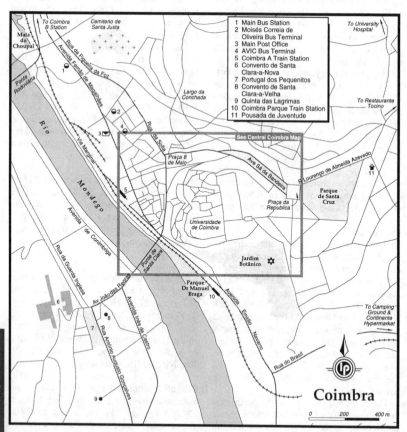

1 Main Bus Station
2 Moisés Correia de Oliveira Bus Terminal
3 Main Post Office
4 AVIC Bus Terminal
5 Coimbra A Train Station
6 Convento de Santa Clara-a-Nova
7 Portugal dos Pequenitos
8 Convento de Santa Clara-a-Velha
9 Quinta das Lagrimas
10 Coimbra Parque Train Station
11 Pousada de Juventude

To Coimbra B Station
Cemiterio de Santa Justa
Mata do Choupal
Rua da Figueira da Foz
Avenida Fernão de Magalhães
Largo da Conchada
Ponte Rodoviária
Rio Mondego
Via Marginal
Rua da Sofia
Praça 8 de Maio
See Central Coimbra Map
Ave Sá da Bandeira
R Lourenço de Almeida Azevedo
To University Hospital
To Restaurante Tocino
Parque de Santa Cruz
Avenida de Conimbriga
Praça da República
Universidade de Coimbra
Rua da Guarda Inglesa
Ponte de Santa Clara
Jardim Botânico
Av João das Regras
Avenida Inês de Castro
Rua António Augusto Gonçalves
Parque Dr Manuel Braga
Avenida Emídio Navarro
To Camping Ground & Continente Hypermarket
Rua do Brasil

Coimbra

0   200   400 m

station (☎ 220 22) is on Rua Nicolau Rui Fernandes, opposite the *câmara municipal*.

Quercus An enthusiastic branch of the environmental organisation Quercus (☎ & fax 257 15) is at Avenida Emídio Navarro 81 (4th floor, room G); Fernando Remão, a staff member, speaks good English.

Upper Town

The steep climb to the university from Largo da Portagem gets you into the heart and soul of Coimbra. Turn right off the smart pedestrian shopping street Rua Ferreira Borges to pass under the **Arco de Almedina**, once part of the old city wall and now a popular venue for quality buskers.

Around the corner to the left, at the end of Rua Sub Ripas, is the **Torre de Anto Memória da Escrita**, a converted tower now displaying the literary works of famous Coimbra writers and poets. It's open Tuesday to Friday from 10 am to 12.30 pm and 2 to 7 pm and Saturdays from 2.30 to 7 pm. En route, you'll see a magnificent Manueline doorway, part of the former **Palácio de Sub Ripas**. Backtrack and climb to the Sé Velha (Old Cathedral; see the following section). One last haul up narrow Rua Borges Carneiro and you reach the **Museu Nacional Machado de Castro** (see the following section) and the dull 'new' campus, much of it founded by the aggressively efficient Marquês de Pombal in the 18th century. Dominating Largo da Sé Nova in front of the museum is the **Sé Nova** (New Cathedral), a severe building started by the Jesuits in 1598 but only completed a century later. The **Velha Universidade** (Old University) is a short walk south of here, along Rua São João. For a taste of student life, take any of the alleys around the Sé Velha or below the Sé Nova (eg Rua de São Salvador). Flags and graffiti identify the cramped houses known as *repúblicas*, each housing a group of students – traditionally 12 or 13, usually from the same region or faculty.

Velha Universidade

The Old University, packed with cultural treasures from the 16th to 18th centuries, lies within a compact square, the Patio das Escolas (sadly used as a car park). The square's most eye-catching feature is the much-photographed 18th-century clock tower, nicknamed *a cabra* (the goat) by students. In the centre of the square a statue of João III turns his back to a superb view of the city and river. It was João III who re-established the university in Coimbra in 1537 and set it on course for serious academic pursuits by inviting renowned international scholars to teach here.

As you enter the courtyard take the stairway to the right (follow the *reitoria* sign) to the **Sala dos Capelos**. The walls of this former examination room (now used for degree ceremonies) are covered with dull portraits of Portugal's kings, but the catwalk around the outside offers brilliant views of the city below. Just below the clock tower is the entrance to the **Capela de São Miguel**, a small, ornate chapel with a gargantuan, gilded baroque organ. But everything pales before the **Biblioteca Joanina** (João V Library) which is behind an imposing baroque doorway next door (visits are staggered so you may have to wait to get in). A gift from the extravagant João V in the early 18th century, the three rooms of the library are totally unsuitable for study, thanks to their distracting riches: tables of ebony, rosewood and jacaranda; wood made to look like marble; Chinoiserie designs etched in gilt; and ceilings covered with frescoes. The 300,000 books on the shelves (most of them ancient leather-bound tomes) are dedicated to law, philosophy and theology. At the far end, firmly catching the eye, is a portrait of the patron himself. It costs 250$00 to visit each of these places, except for students and teachers (from anywhere, not just here – provided you can prove it); tickets are available outside the Sala dos Capelos. Opening hours are from 9.30 am to noon and 2 to 5 pm daily.

Sé Velha

At first glance you'd hardly call Coimbra's chunky Old Cathedral attractive. It looks

Central
Coimbra

PLACES TO STAY

3	Pensão Santa Cruz
12	Casa Pombal Guesthouse
28	Residencial Ideal
29	Residencial Lusa Atenas
30	Pensão Residencial Madeira
31	Hotel Oslo
33	Pensão Residencial Internacional
34	Pensão Lorvanense
36	Pensão Restaurante Vitória
37	Residencial Domus
38	Residencial Moderna
42	Pensão Residencial Rivoli
48	Hotel Astoria
50	Pensão Residencial Larbelo
51	Hospedaria Simões
58	Pensão Residencial Antunes
59	Santa Cruz Residencial

PLACES TO EAT

4	Café Santa Cruz
13	Restaurante Sá da Bandeira
15	Cartola Esplanade Café
24	Restaurante O Trovador
39	Restaurante Viela
40	Restaurante Funchal
41	Restaurante Zé Neto
43	Café Praça Velha
46	Café Arcadia
47	Restaurante Zé Manel
60	Restaurante-Bar AAC/OAF

OTHER

1	Igreja do Carmo
2	Bar Diligência
5	Igreja de Santa Cruz
6	Câmara Municipal
7	Mosteiro Santa Cruz
8	Police Station
9	Jardim da Manga
10	Post Office
11	Mercado Municipal
14	Cambridge School

16	Turismo
17	Tropical
18	AAC & Tagus Travel
19	Dom Dinis Bar
20	Sé Nova
21	Museu Nacional Machado de Castro
22	Aqui Há Rato
23	Sé Velha
25	Boémia Bar
26	Palácio de Sub Ribas
27	Torre de Anto Memória da Escrita
32	Coimbra A Train Station
35	Centro Velocipédico de Sangalhos
44	Arco de Almedina
45	Café-Galeria Almedina
49	Livraria Bertrand
52	Regional Turismo
53	Quercus
54	Biblioteca Joanina
55	Capela de São Miguel
56	Sala dos Capelos
57	Municipal Turismo
61	British Council

more like a fortress – and deliberately so, since it was built in the late 12th century when the Moors were still a threat. Little has been done to it since then – even the Renaissance doorway added to the north side in the 16th century has eroded so badly you hardly notice it. What you see is pure, austere Romanesque, and one of the finest Portuguese cathedrals of its time. The interior is equally simple: the most elaborate piece of decoration is an early 16th-century carved and gilded altarpiece.

The cathedral is open daily in summer from 9.30 am to 12.30 pm and 2 to 5.30 pm (hours are irregular in winter). There's a charge of 100$00 to visit the Gothic cloisters.

Museu Nacional Machado de Castro

In this attractive former bishop's palace, which has a 16th-century loggia overlooking the rooftops of the cathedral and old town, is one of the most important collections of 14th to 16th-century sculpture in the country. Coimbra itself was a magnet for sculptors during this period, thanks in part to a plentiful supply of soft, easily carved Ança limestone.

The museum has several magnificent limestone pieces, including the Gothic *Virgin & Child* by Master Pero. There is also an anonymous medieval knight on his horse, and the lovely Renaissance *A Virgem Anunciada* by Nicolas Chanterène. The museum's collection of paintings and ceramics is also very impressive, especially the 16th and 17th-century Flemish and Portuguese paintings, including two panels by Quentin Metzys. Much preferred by school groups is the extensive *cryptoporticus* in the museum's basement, a series of galleries which probably served as the foundation for a Roman forum. The museum has been undergoing major restoration and several sections are closed. The rest is open daily, except Mondays, from 9.30 am to 5.30 pm; entry is 250$00.

Mosteiro de Santa Cruz

After walking the length of Rua Ferreira Borges and Rua Visconde da Luz, with their trendy shops and pastelarias, the 16th-century Santa Cruz church (originally founded in the 12th century) plunges you back into the Manueline and Renaissance eras.

Step through the Renaissance porch and flamboyant 18th-century arch and you'll find some of the Coimbra School's most impressive sculpture, including a wonderfully ornate pulpit and the elaborately designed tombs of Portugal's first kings, Afonso Henriques and Sancho I, probably carved by Nicolas Chanterène. The most striking of the Manueline works here is the restrained Cloister of Silence, designed in 1524. In the *coro alto* (choir stalls) above is a frieze showing Portuguese ships at their fighting best. At the back of the church is the **Jardim da Manga** (once part of the monastery's cloisters) with a bizarre domed and buttressed fountain. The church is open daily from 9 am to noon and 2 to 5.45 pm. There's a 200$00 fee to see the cloisters.

Jardim Botânico

A pleasant place to catch your breath on the cultural sightseeing trail is the botanical garden that runs alongside Alameda Dr Júlio Henriques, a 10-minute walk downhill from the university. Established by the Marquês de Pombal in the shadow of the 16th-century Aqueduto de São Sebastião, it's a combination of formal flower beds, meandering paths and elegant fountains.

Across the River

Convento de Santa Clara-a-Velha Crossing the Ponte de Santa Clara (an ideal afternoon location for photographing Coimbra), you'll soon notice the *convento* on the left, currently being cleared of the river mud that has drowned it since the 17th century. The church has famous connections: it was founded in 1330 by Dona Isabel (Dom Dinis' wife), whose tomb later lay here beside that of Dona Inês de Castro, the murdered mistress of Dom Pedro (see the boxed aside in the Estremadura & Ribatejo chapter).

BEIRAS

Quinta das Lágrimas According to legend, Inês was killed in the gardens of this privately owned *quinta*, some 200m away down Rua António Augusto Gonçalves. The quinta is closed to the public, but you can visit the gardens and Fonte dos Amores (Lovers' Fountain) where the dastardly deed is said to have taken place.

Convento de Santa Clara-a-Nova Inês' tomb now lies in the Mosteiro de Santa Maria de Alcobaça (see the Estremadura & Ribatejo chapter for details), while Isabel's is up the hill from Santa Clara-a-Velha in the Santa Clara-a-Nova Convent, an unattractive 17th-century complex, most of which now serves as an army barracks. The church which contains Isabel's solid silver tomb is devoted almost entirely to the saintly queen's memory: a series of panels shows how her tomb was moved here, wooden panels in the aisles tell her life story, and some of her clothes hang in the sacristy. Her statue here is also the focus of the Festa de Rainha Santa (see Special Events).

The convent church is open daily from 9 am to 12.30 pm and 2 to 5.30 pm.

Portugal dos Pequenitos At this over-rated theme park nearby, coachloads of kids debouch to clamber over models of Portugal's most famous monuments. Several displays on the former colonies seem permanently closed and many models need a lick of paint. It's open daily in summer from 9 am to 7 pm (until 5.30 pm in winter); entry is 500$00 (200$00 for children under 10).

Hiking

If you fancy walking in the wild and beautiful Serra de Lousã area south of Coimbra but don't fancy going it alone, contact Dutch resident Maryke Kramer (☎ & fax 99 52 54) who organises guided walks for around 2200$00 per person. Quercus (see Information) also organises walks in this area.

Canoeing

During the summer, O Pioneiro do Mondego (☎ 47 83 85 from 1 to 3 pm and 8 to 10 pm)

rents out kayaks at 2500$00 a day for paddling down the Rio Mondego from Penacova (a free minibus whisks you up to the starting point at 10 am). The 25-km trip takes about three hours. Contact their information kiosk in the riverside Parque Dr Manuel Braga.

Boat Trips

Basófias (☎ 71 44 37, mobile ☎ 0676-35 81 31) operates 75-minute boat trips on the Rio Mondego throughout the year, daily except Mondays, for around 1000$00 per person. They leave from beside Parque Dr Manuel Braga.

Horse Riding

Trot around Mata do Choupal (Choupal Park) on the north-west edge of town by contacting the Coimbra Riding Centre (☎ 376 95).

Language Courses

The university (☎ 41 09 99) runs a month-long Portuguese-language course every July for 80,000$00. There are also several private schools with Portuguese-language courses, including the Cambridge School (☎ 349 69; fax 339 16) at Praça da República 15, which has a six-week course for 76,000$00.

Special Events

Queima das Fitas The 'burning of the ribbons' festival in May is when Coimbra's students celebrate the end of the academic year by burning their faculty ribbons (each faculty has a different colour). The students traipse through the streets in their black gowns and hats, and sing fado day and night (they've even taken to joining other student celebrations around the country, so don't be surprised to find gowned, beribboned fado singers far from Coimbra around this time). If you arrive soon after it's over, you'll find all of Coimbra in a state of utter exhaustion.

Festa de Rainha Santa This major religious festival, held in even-numbered years around 4 July, commemorates the queen-saint Isabel with a procession that takes her statue from Santa Clara-a-Nova to Igreja do

Carmo and back. Events during the festival (which coincides with the Festa da Cidade or Town Festival) include folk music and dancing, and fireworks by the river.

Places to Stay – bottom end

Camping The municipal camping ground (☎ 70 14 97) is currently next to the municipal swimming pool and stadium, off Rua General Humberto Delgado on the east side of town; take bus No 5 from Largo da Portagem. There are plans to move it to the riverside, four km east.

Hostels Coimbra's pleasant pousada de juventude (☎ 229 55) is at Rua Dr António Henriques Seco 12-14, on the north-east side of town. Take bus No 5 from Largo da Portagem or No 7 from Coimbra A train station.

Pensões & Residencials The spartan cubicles at the central *Hospedaria Simões* (☎ 356 38) at Rua Fernandes Tomáz 69 are a bargain at 2000$00/3000$00 for a single/double with bath. Similarly priced but a fair bit seedier is *Pensão Lorvanense* (☎ 234 81) at Rua da Sota 27, not far from the train station.

The nearby *Pensão Restaurante Vitória* (☎ 240 49), at Rua da Sota 9 and 19, is a friendlier, brighter option, with doubles (minus bath) from 3000$00. The old-style *Residencial Ideal* (☎ 222 37), at Largo das Olarias 2, has adequate rooms without bath for 2500$00/3500$00. *Pensão Residencial Internacional* (☎ 255 03), on noisy Avenida Emidio Navarro at No 4, has a similar run-down charm, with small doubles from 3000$00 (without bath). In the university area at Rua Castro Matoso 4, *Santa Cruz Residencial* (☎ 236 57) has characterless rooms from 2500$00/3000$00.

Places to Stay – middle

Among the old-fashioned residencials along busy Avenida Fernão de Magalhães, the *Madeira* (☎ 205 69), at No 26, offers doubles with bath for around 5000$00. Similarly priced but with more character is *Residencial*

Lusa Atenas (☎ 264 12; fax 201 33) at No 68; some rooms (eg No 101) have fantastic stucco ceilings, though all are prey to traffic noise. More modern and frilly are *Residencial Domus* (☎ 285 84), at Rua Adelino Veiga 62, where doubles start at 4500$00; and the equally businesslike *Residencial Moderna* (☎ 254 13; fax 295 08), at No 49, where all doubles (6700$00) have bath, air-con and satellite TV.

Other central choices include *Pensão Residencial Larbelo* (☎ 290 92; fax 290 94), surprisingly inexpensive for its location at Largo da Portagem 33: doubles with bath are 5000$00. A great people-watching place is the 3rd-floor *Pensão Santa Cruz* (☎ 261 97), on Praça 8 de Maio (opposite Mosteiro de Santa Cruz), where bright singles/doubles go for 3500$00/4500$00. At Praça do Comércio 27, the 1st to 3rd-floor rooms of *Pensão Residencial Rivoli* (☎ 255 50) are wonderfully quiet at the back, and good value at 4500$00 a double (with unreliable shower). The university area has few options. *Pensão Residencial Antunes* (☎ 230 48; fax 383 73), at Rua Castro Matoso 8, has doubles with bath and breakfast from 7500$00 (and some without bath from 4800$00), plus parking spaces. In the tangle of lanes at the top of the hill, at Rua das Flores 18, is the friendly, Dutch-run *Casa Pombal Guesthouse* (☎ & fax 351 75), a cosy household of single/double rooms at 3800$00/6000$00 including a huge Dutch-style breakfast.

Places to Stay – top end

The efficient *Hotel Oslo* (☎ 290 71; fax 206 14), at Avenida Fernão de Magalhaes 25, has air-con rooms for 7000$00/9000$00 (and private parking). More attractive but rather snobby is the Art Deco *Hotel Astoria* (☎ 220 55; fax 220 57), at Avenida Emidio Navarro 21, where doubles go for 15,000$00.

The nearest Turihab property is *Casa dos Quintas* (☎ 43 83 05), six km south in the hamlet of Carvalhais de Cima, near Assafarge. It's in a fantastic setting overlooking Coimbra and has three doubles in the main house and a detached apartment with kitchen

BEIRAS

and lousy plumbing. The rooms are over-priced (at least 7000$00 for the doubles and 9000$00 for the apartment) but negotiable.

Places to Eat

Restaurants The lanes off Praça do Comércio and Praça 8 de Maio are the places to head for cheap, filling fare. Take your pick of male-dominated dives in Rua Direita or more amenable budget restaurants in Rua das Azeiteiras, including *Restaurante Zé Neto* (☎ 267 86), at No 8, which has a homey atmosphere and standard favourites for under 1200$00; and *Restaurante Funchal* (☎ 241 37), at No 18, with a great chanfana carne de cabra à regional (goat stewed in wine) for 1300$00. The tiny *Restaurante Viela* (☎ 326 25), at No 33, does a brisk local trade, as does *Restaurante Vitória* (☎ 240 49) at Rua da Sota 9, where generous portions are under 1000$00.

The wacky *Zé Manel* (☎ 237 90), at No 12 in the dark Beco do Forno, is packed with knick-knacks, scribbled ditties and poems. This unique eccentricity doesn't come cheaply: dishes are about 1800$00 (though some half-portions are available). Try the excellent feijoada à leitão (beans and suckling pig). Come early or be prepared to wait. In the university area, behind walls at the south end of Rua Castro Matoso, is a popular student hang-out, *Restaurante-Bar AAC/OAF* (☎ 242 51), jointly named after the students' academy and a local football club. Bargain combinados (a main dish plus salad and chips) are 550$00. An up-market choice for traditional Portuguese fare is *Restaurante Sá da Bandeira* (☎ 354 50), at Avenida Sá da Bandeira 89, where dishes average around 1500$00. Near the youth hostel, at Rua Bernardo de Albuquerque 120, is the Italian *Restaurante Tocino* (☎ 359 89) where you can fill up on pasta for 1200$00 a dish. If you've got your own transport, there are two recommended restaurants serving the local speciality, leitão da bairrada (roast suckling pig), six km north at Sernadelo, on the IC2/N1 road: *Rui dos Leitões* (☎ 91 34 13) and *Meta dos Leitões* (☎ 221 70) dish out the

piggy by weight (600 grams is enough for two) and serve it with french fries and salad.

Cafés Coimbra has some seductive cafés, including *Café Arcadia*, at Rua Ferreira Borges 144, beloved of the chic shopping set, and *Café Praça Velha* at Praça do Comércio, which is great for watching pigeons, tourists and the setting sun. Our vote for one of the most alluring cafés in Portugal, though, goes to *Café Santa Cruz*, a vaulted annexe of the Mosteiro de Santa Cruz: sit on creased leather chairs inside or at watch-the-world-go-by tables outside.

Market For self-caterers, the mercado municipal is by Rua Nicolau Rui Fernandes, behind the Mosteiro de Santa Cruz.

Entertainment

Coimbra's version of fado is more serious and intellectual than the Lisbon variety. More traditional too: a fracas erupted in Coimbra in 1996 when a woman announced plans to record a CD of Coimbra-style fado, which is supposed to be sung by men only (see the boxed aside in the Facts about the Country chapter).

You're most likely to hear fado sung by students themselves during Queima das Fitas (see Special Events), but there are several fado restaurants and bars too. One of the most congenial is *Bar Diligência* (☎ 276 67), at Rua Nova 30, where singers tend to pop in around 11 pm on Fridays and Saturdays. You can eat here, too, but check your bill: there have been reports of tourists being overcharged. The *Restaurante O Trovador* (☎ 254 75), at Largo da Sé Velha, is more up-market (expect to pay around 1800$00 a dish), with fado on Fridays and Saturdays. You may also hear fado at *Boémia Bar* (☎ 345 47), around the corner at Rua do Cabido 6. For less traditional sounds and a disco-dance floor, *Aqui Há Rato* (☎ 248 04), at Largo da Sé Velha 20, is hot.

Students also flock to the *Tropical* bar on Praça da República and the huge *Dom Dinis Bar* in the university, off Praça Marquês de Pombal. Attracting a more varied clientele is

Café-Galeria Almedina (361 92), dug into the old town walls at Arco de Almedina.

Things to Buy

A bright workshop-cum-gallery called Galeria de Artes e Oficios Tradicionais, upstairs at Rua Ferreira Borges 83, displays excellent basketry, textiles, pottery (for which Coimbra is particularly famous) and more. On Wednesdays, you can watch some of the artisans working here. It's open Tuesday to Friday from 10 am to 7 pm and on weekends from 3 to 6.30 pm.

Getting There & Away

Bus Rodoviária Beira Litoral (☎ 270 81), at the main bus station on Avenida Fernão de Magalhães, caters for most domestic and international destinations. At least a dozen coaches a day go to Lisbon, with frequent expresses to Porto, Évora and Faro, and at least six a day to Braga. In winter there are frequent services to Beira Alta destinations such as Seia and Guarda.

The AVIC terminal (☎ 237 69) at Rua João de Ruão 18 runs buses to Cantanhede, Condeixa and Conimbriga, and Tocha and Mira beaches. A third terminal, Moisés Correia de Oliveira (☎ 282 63), is at Rua João Machado 23, and has services to Figueira da Foz and Montemor-o-Velho.

Train Coimbra has three train stations: the main one is Coimbra B, linked to the more central Coimbra A (called 'Coimbra' on timetables) by a shuttle service. Only direct Figueira da Foz trains leave from Coimbra A. Coimbra Parque is only for Lousã and the *Rápido Sud-Expresso*.

There are frequent trains to Lisbon (via Santarém) and Porto (via Aveiro), including three Alfas, six *intercidades* and four *interregionals*. The Lisbon-Irún-Paris *Rápido Sud-Expresso* calls at Coimbra daily.

Getting Around

Bus Although walking is the best way to see Coimbra's old town, you'll probably want a bus for places on the outskirts. The most useful services are No 1 from Coimbra A

train station to the university, via the town centre; No 7 from Coimbra A or No 5 from Largo da Portagem to the youth hostel (No 5 also goes to the camping ground); and Nos 11 and 24, which run past the university and aqueduct to the shopping hypermarket, Continente, on the southern outskirts.

You can buy tickets on board but if you plan to use buses a lot, pick up a *senha* (block of 10 tickets) from kiosks around town, most conveniently in Largo da Portagem.

Bicycle You can rent bikes for around 1500$00 a day from Centro Velocipédico de Sangalhos (☎ 246 46), Rua da Sota 23, or mountain bikes for 3000$00 a day from O Pioneiro do Mondego (☎ & fax 47 83 85), with an information kiosk in Parque Dr Manuel Braga (see Canoeing).

Car Car-rental agencies include Avis (☎ 347 86), Hertz (☎ 374 91) and Salitur (☎ 205 94).

CONIMBRIGA

The Roman ruins of Conimbriga, 16 km south-west of Coimbra, are the finest you'll see in Portugal and among the best preserved in the entire Iberian peninsula. The site actually dates back to Celtic times (*briga* is a Celtic term for a defended area) but when the Romans settled here in the 1st century AD, they developed it into a major city on the route from Lisbon (Olisipo) to Braga (Bracara Augusta).

In the 3rd century, threatened by invading tribes, the townsfolk hurriedly built a huge defensive wall right through the town centre, abandoning the residencial area. But it wasn't enough to stop the Suevi seizing the town in 468. The inhabitants fled to nearby Aeminius (Coimbra), thereby saving Conimbriga from destruction.

Museum

It's worth visiting the small museum first to get a grip on Conimbriga's history and layout. Unfortunately there are no English labels, but the displays are magnificent and present every aspect of Roman life, from

BEIRAS

rings and hairbands to needles and hoes. Murals and mosaics, carved fragments from temples, statues and tombstones are some of the site's artistic treasures.

The museum is open daily, except Mondays, from 10 am to 1 pm and 2 to 6 pm. The admission fee of 350$00 includes entry to the site itself. There's a very pleasant café-restaurant at the back of the museum.

Ruins

The defensive wall slices through the site like a scar. Outside it, to the right, is the so-called Casa dos Repuxos (House of the Fountains) which was partly destroyed during the wall's construction. But the layout of ponds and rooms is still obvious and there are some striking mosaic floors showing the four seasons and various hunting scenes. The site's most important villa, on the other side of the wall, is said to have belonged to Cantaber (whose wife and children were seized by the Suevi in an attack in 465). It's a palace of a place, with its own private baths, a series of pools (one encircled by columns) and a sophisticated underground heating system. Even humbler houses nearby have mosaic floors.

Excavations are continuing in the outer areas of the city. Among eye-catching features are the remains of a three-km-long aqueduct which led up to a hilltop bathing complex, and a forum, once surrounded by covered porticoes (the museum has a model). The site – which becomes something of a playground for raucous school groups in term-time – is open daily, except Mondays, from 9 am to 1 pm and 2 to 8 pm (6 pm in winter). The 350$00 admission fee includes entry to the museum.

Getting There & Away

Buses run frequently from Coimbra to Condeixa, one km from the site, or you can take a direct bus (245$00) at 9.05 am or 9.35 am (9.35 am only at weekends) from the AVIC terminal at Rua João de Ruão 18; the bus returns at 1 pm or 6 pm (on weekends at 6 pm only).

LUSO & THE BUÇACO FOREST

The small spa town of Luso, 24 km northeast of Coimbra, is quaint and rather old-fashioned. Portuguese tourists have been coming here for decades to soak in the hypotonic waters (a balm for everything from gout to asthma). It's an easy day trip from Coimbra, usually tagged onto a visit to the Mata Nacional do Bussaco (Bussaco, or Buçaco, National Forest) three km up the road. If you're tempted by the forest's walks to linger longer, Luso makes a suitably relaxing base. Try to avoid weekends and holidays, when you'll be swamped by hundreds of Portuguese visitors.

Orientation & Information

The town nestles around the spa, stretching out uphill north and south. Coming from the train station, on the northern outskirts, it's a 20-minute walk downhill, via Rua Dr António Granjo, to the town centre. Tree-shaded Avenida Emidio Navarro, stretching south of the centre, is where the bus stops.

The efficient turismo (☎ & fax 93 91 33), nearby on Rua Emídio Navarro, can provide accommodation information and good maps of the town and forest. Serious botanists and historians should ask for the specialist 'pedestrian circuit' leaflets which detail the forest's flora and points of historical interest. The office is open from 9.30 am to 8 pm from June to September and from 10 am to 12.30 pm and 3 to 6 pm in other months. The telephone code for the area is ☎ 031.

Termas de Luso

Unlike many of Portugal's spas, this one is open to casual visitors as well as those taking a cure. The simplest and cheapest therapies are a water-pressure treatment for 650$00 or a jacuzzi-like bath for 850$00 – great for relaxing limbs after a walk in the forest. A sauna and shower will cost you 1350$00 and a half-hour massage is 2000$00.

You can fill up your water bottle for free at the adjacent Fonte de São João.

Casino

The former casino, next to the Fonte de São

DAMIEN SIMONIS

JULIA WILKINSON

TONY WHEELER

Estremadura & Ribatejo
Left: Obidos
Right: Batalha monastery
Bottom: Nazaré

BETHUNE CARMICHAEL

JULIA WILKINSON

TONY WHEELER

DAMIEN SIMONIS

JULIA WILKINSON

BETHUNE CARMICHAEL

BETHUNE CARMICHAEL

Tiles

João, is now a venue for exhibitions, folk dancing and fado. It's open only at weekends, from 3 pm to 11 pm (from 4 pm in winter).

Mata Nacional do Bussaco (Buçaco)

The 105-hectare Buçaco Forest, on the slopes of the Serra do Buçaco, is no ordinary collection of trees. For centuries it's been a religious haven; a place of sanctity and peace. Even today, overrun by picnickers at weekends and tourists in the summer, it still has a mystical appeal. There's an astounding 700 different species of trees, including huge Mexican cedars, giant ferns and ginkgo trees.

History The area was probably used as a refuge for early Christians in the 2nd century although the earliest known hermitage was established in the 6th century by Benedictine monks.

In 1628 the hermitage was sold to the Barefoot Silent Carmelites, who embarked on an extensive programme of forestation, introducing all kinds of exotic species, marking out cobbled paths and enclosing the forest within walls. It became so famous that in 1643 Pope Urban VIII decreed that anyone who damaged the trees would be excommunicated.

Twenty years earlier, his predecessor had ensured that the monks tending the trees were protected from distracting influences: he forbade women to even enter the forest. In 1810, during the Peninsular War, the peace was briefly disrupted when Napoleon's forces under Masséna unsuccessfully clashed with the Duke of Wellington's Anglo-Portuguese army who were cunningly hidden behind the ridge above the forest. In 1834, when religious orders throughout Portugal were abolished, the forest became state property and even more new tree species were introduced.

Walks The forest is threaded with trails, dotted with crumbling little chapels and crosses, and enhanced by ponds and fountains. Some of the most popular and well-trodden trails lead to areas of great beauty, such as the Vale dos Fetos (Valley of Ferns), but you can get enjoyably lost on smaller, more overgrown trails which eventually join up to the main trails. There are several superb viewpoints, especially 545m Cruz Alta, and along the path leading to it (known as Via Sacra) are several chapels with figures depicting the stages of the Cross.

Mosteiro dos Carmelites A tiny 17th-century church, almost overshadowed by the adjacent Hotel Palace do Buçaco, is all that remains of the Carmelite monastery. There's not much to see: a few cork-lined cells (in one of which Wellington spent the night before the 1810 battle) and a frieze of azulejos depicting the battle. It's open daily, except Fridays, from 10 am to noon and 2 to 6 pm in summer and in winter from 9 am to noon and 1 to 5 pm. Admission is 100$00.

Hotel Palace do Buçaco This zany wedding cake of a building – all turrets and spires, arches and neo-Manueline ornamentation – was built in 1907 on the site of the monastery to serve as a royal summer residence. Three years later, the monarchy was abolished so the royals hardly got a look-in. Now a very posh hotel (see Places to Stay), it's surprisingly tolerant of the hordes of tourists who wander in to gawp at the décor.

Museu Militar Military historians interested in the details of the 1810 Battle of Buçaco will find maps, weapons and other paraphernalia in this small museum on the eastern outskirts of the forest, just beyond Portas da Rainha. It's open daily, except Mondays, from 10 am to 5 pm; entry is 200$00.

Places to Stay

The cheapest and grottiest place to stay is the *Buçaco Pensão* (☎ 93 92 74), at the top of Rua Dr António Granjo (300m up from the town centre), with a grumpy owner who rents out plain doubles with shower for 3000$00. You're better off looking around for 'alugam-se quartos' signs (or ask to see the list kept by the turismo); private rooms are about 4000$00 a double. Try the central *Café-Bar O Caracol* (☎ 93 94 05) on Rua Dr Francisco Diniz.

Alternatively, there are several reasonable pensões: across the main square on Avenida Emídio Navarro, the popular *Pensão Central* (☎ 93 92 54) has doubles without bath for 4500$00 (or 6000$00 with bath) including breakfast. The rather run-down *Pensão Astória* (☎ 93 9182), next to the turismo on Rua Emídio Navarro, has similar prices. For more genteel accommodation, try the delightful *Pensão Alegre* (☎ 93 02 56) beyond the Pensão Central on Avenida Emídio Navarro, a 19th-century manor house (with swimming pool) where doubles with breakfast start at 7000$00. For palatial indulgence there's the *Hotel Palace do Buçaco* (☎ 93 01 01; fax 93 05 09) where a double will set you back at least 30,000$00.

Places to Eat

Most of the pensões have reasonable restaurants: in summer the outdoor patio restaurant at *Pensão Central* is very pleasant. The lovely Art Deco salão de chá (tea room) next to the Fonte de São João captures the spa town atmosphere of Luso perfectly: this is the place to come for tea and cakes.

Heartier meals are available at *Restaurante O Cesteiro* (☎ 93 93 60) on the N234, a 500m hike uphill in the direction of the train station. The menu features several regional specialities, including the ubiquitous leitão a bairrada (roast suckling pig). If you get hooked on this, there are several restaurants at Sernadelo (near Mealhada), en route back to Coimbra, which specialise in almost nothing else – see the Coimbra Places to Eat section for details.

For a serious splurge, head for the restaurant at the Hotel Palace do Buçaco, where you can dine in splendour for about 5000$00 per person.

Getting There & Away

There are three trains daily from Coimbra to Luso and four back: you'd need to catch the 10.35 am from Coimbra B to make a day trip feasible (the last train back is at 6.18 pm).

Bus connections between Coimbra and Luso are more convenient: there are five daily during the week and two at weekends. These all continue to Buçaco (stopping outside the Hotel Palace). Car drivers are charged 500$00 entry to the forest.

Getting Around

During the summer, horse and carriage rides are available in Luso and Buçaco from 1 pm to 8 pm on Tuesdays, Thursdays, Saturdays and Sundays. It costs 750$00 for a one-hour circuit in Luso and 1500$00 for a return trip from the Hotel Palace do Buçaco to Portas de Coimbra. Discounts are available for residents of the operator, Pensão Alegre (see Places to Stay).

FIGUEIRA DA FOZ
• *pop 18,000* • *postcode 3080* • *area code* ☎ *033*

Once top of the list for Spanish beach-seekers, this old-fashioned seaside resort and fishing port 43 km west of Coimbra, at the mouth *(foz)* of the Rio Mondego, still has a faithful, mostly Portuguese, following. Some come for the casino, some for the surf (this was a venue in the 1996 World Surfing Championships) and some just to loll on the huge stretch of sand. There is plenty of accommodation, as well as restaurants and bars, but you'll be hard pushed to find a cheap room in high season.

Orientation

From Coimbra, you pass salt pans and rice fields and ugly industrial outskirts before you reach the best bit of Figueira da Foz – the beach fronting the Avenida 25 de Abril, near the mouth of the Rio Mondego. Guarding the estuary is the 16th-century Forte de Santa Catarina and inland from here is the tourist part of town: a cluster of streets (several of them pleasantly pedestrianised) where you'll find most of the accommodation and restaurants (and the casino). Seafront development continues all the way to Buarcos, a former fishing village three km

Figueira da Foz

0   250   500 m

1 Bus Station	10	Restaurante Aquario
2 Museu Municipal do		Marisqueira
Dr Santos Rocha	11	Pensão Central
3 AFGA Agência de Viagens	12	Pensão & Restaurante Astória
4 Turismo	13	Mercado Municipal
5 Pensão Residencial Universal	14	Post Office
6 Café Sylmar	15	Pensão Residencial Moderna
7 Pensão Residencial	16	Residencial Sãozinha
Bela Figueira	17	Pensão Figueirense
& Restaurante Bela Figueira	18	Train Station
8 Hotel Wellington	19	Castrotour Boat Tours
9 Casino		

north along the coast, now just an extension of Figueira.

North-east of the tourist part of town, on the other side of Parque Abadias, is a more down-to-earth district. The train station is at the far end, 1.5 km from the turismo (a good 20-minute walk along the seafront). The bus station, on Rua Gonçalvo Velho, is slightly closer.

Information
The enthusiastic municipal turismo (☎ 226 10; fax 285 49) is conveniently located in the Edifício Atlântico on Avenida 25 de Abril (next to the Hotel Atlântico). It's open daily in summer from 9 am to midnight and in winter from 9 am to 12.30 pm and 2 to 5.30 pm on weekdays and from 10 am to 12.30 pm and 2 to 6.30 pm at weekends.

There's a smaller turismo (☎ 330 19) in Buarcos, on Largo Tomás Aquino, which is open daily in summer from 9 am to 8 pm and in winter from 9 am to 12.30 pm and 2 to 5.30 pm on weekdays only.

There's a bunch of banks in Praça 8 de Maio (en route to the train station) and a couple more along the seafront Rua 5 de Outubro. Most have ATMs. The main post office is on Rua Infante Dom Henrique, across the other side of the *jardim municipal*.

Casino
At the heart of the tourist part of town, at the junction of Rua Bernardo Lopes and Rua Dr Calado, the casino is a focus of activity and is open daily from 3 pm to 4 am. For the roulette section you must pay an entrance fee of 513$00 and wear suitable shoes (ie no sandals or sports shoes). Daily in the night-club, and on Fridays and Saturdays in the festivities hall, there's a musical show at 11 pm and 1 am.

Museu Municipal do Dr Santos Rocha
This modern museum, just off Rua Calouste

BEIRAS

Gulbenkian beside the Parque Abadias (a 10-minute walk north of the turismo), houses a particularly rich archaeological collection as well as some less impressive paintings and sculptures. It's open daily, except Mondays, from 9 am to 12.30 pm and 2 to 5.30 pm (free admission).

Beaches

Once notorious for its polluted seas, Figueira has now cleaned up its act considerably. In recent years the beaches have boasted European Blue Flag approval, though you might check with the turismo on the current situation.

The main town beach is vast and shadeless, packed and scorching hot in August – unless you've got shoes on, you'll need to stick to the boardwalks that cross the very wide beach to the sea. For more fishing village character and surfing action, head for Buarcos. Just around the Cabo Mondego from Buarcos (eight km north of Figueira) you'll find considerably more seclusion at Praia de Quiaos (accessible by bus from Figueira). In the opposite direction, across the mouth of the Rio Mondego is the popular Praia de Cabedelo (a prime site for surfing) and a little further south (four km from Figueira) is Praia de Gala, with clean seas and an Orbitur camping ground (see Places to Stay). Both beaches are accessible by buses from town.

Serra de Boa Viagem

If you've got your own transport, this wooded range of pines, eucalypts and acacias four km north of Figueira is a great place for panoramic ocean views, cool walks and picnics in the woods; there's even a fantastic wooden playground at one of the main picnic sites in the forest.

Take the coast road to Buarcos and turn right at the cape's lighthouse, following the signs to Boa Viagem.

Special Events

The Festival Internacional de Cinema has been held in Figueira da Foz for over 25 years. It takes place in the casino during the first 10 days of September.

Places to Stay

Camping The municipal camping ground (☎ 330 33) is on the northern edge of town, a couple of km from the beach (but there's an adjacent swimming pool). Buses to Casal da Areia pass close by. To stay at the well-situated *Foz do Mondego* site (☎ 314 96) near Cabedelo beach, you must belong to the Federação Portuguesa de Campismo e Caravanismo. A little further south is an *Orbitur* site (☎ 314 92) at Praia de Gala, a km's walk from the nearest bus stop. There's another great seaside site (☎ 91 04 99) north of Figueira, at Praia de Quiaos (open 1 June to 30 September only) which is cheaper than Orbitur's.

Private Rooms The turismo has details of six officially recognised quartos (including an apartment) which usually go for around 4500$00 a double. Touts may approach you at the bus or train station with their own offers.

Pensões & Residencials The cheapest bets are near the train station. *Pensão Figueirense* (☎ 224 59), at Rua Direita do Monte 10, is better than it looks from the outside and has doubles (including breakfast but no private bath) for 4500$00. The nearby, quieter *Residencial Sãozinha* (☎ 252 43), at Ladeira do Monte 43, has comfortable doubles with bath for 5000$00. Overlooking shady Praça 8 de Maio at No 61 is the spacious old *Pensão Residencial Moderna* (☎ 227 01), which has a touch of Indian décor and doubles from 4500$00.

Similarly priced but right in the tourist centre is *Pensão Astória* (☎ 222 56) at Rua Bernardo Lopes 45. *Pensão Central*, opposite at No 36, is slightly pricier – big old doubles are 6000$00 (pity about the fibreglass bathroom units). At the smarter *Pensão Residencial Universal* (☎ 206 12; fax 204 97), Rua Miguel Bombarda 50, doubles with breakfast are 6500$00. At No 13 on the same road is the popular *Pensão*

Residencial Bela Figueira (☎ 227 28), which charges 7850$00 for doubles in August.

Hotel Wellington (☎ 267 67; fax 275 93), at Rua Dr Calado 23, is an old and comfortable favourite, just a few steps from the casino. Its doubles (all with air-con and satellite TV) cost 9000$00.

Places to Eat

Younger visitors hang out at *Café Sylmar* (☎ 229 71) on Esplanada Silva Guimarães (above the turismo) – its outdoor tables are a great afternoon suntrap. There are several good restaurants attached to pensões, including the *Astória* at Rua Bernardo Lopes 55 and *Restaurante Bela Figueira* (☎ 227 28) at Rua Miguel Bombarda 13, which has Indian-Portuguese fare that makes a delicious change. Opposite the casino, *Restaurante Aquario Marisqueira* (☎ 269 30), at Rua Bernardo Lopes 85, is very good value (combinados dishes start from 650$00) and is open until 4 am.

Seafood is inevitably expensive, but prices are probably better in Buarcos than the town centre – try *Dory Negro* (☎ 213 33), at Largo Caras Direitas 16, where you can eat well for under 2000$00. For self-caterers the mercado municipal, big and bountiful, is a short walk from the turismo at the far end of Rua Dr António Dinis.

Getting There & Away

Bus Most services use the main terminal, including about five buses daily to Aveiro and Mira and at least seven to Leiria.

AVIC express buses to/from Lisbon (twice-daily on weekdays) stop in the town centre opposite the turismo. The one express bus a day to Porto goes from AFGA Agência de Viagens at Rua Miguel Bombarda 79. AVIC buses to Buarcos, Cabo do Mondego and Casal da Areia leave from the train station. For Praia de Cabedelo and Praia de Gala (across the river), AVIC buses leave every half-hour from the mercado municipal and the train station.

Train There are two services daily to

Figueira from Lisbon via Caldas da Rainha and Leiria, with several more from Cacém. Services from Coimbra are far better than the bus, with frequent trains that take an hour or so.

Getting Around

Bicycle You can rent a bike from AFGA Agência de Viagens (☎ 289 89), at Avenida Miguel Bombarda 79, for about 1500$00 a day. In high season the municipal camping ground (☎ 330 33) usually rents out bikes as well.

Boat Trips Three different motorboat trips up the Rio Mondego or around the coast are offered by Castrotour (☎ 280 52). The boats leave from the Doca de Recreio (just off the seafront Rua 5 de Outubro). The turismo has current departure times and prices.

AVEIRO

• *pop 31,000* • *postcode 3800* • *area code* ☎ *034*

One of the most attractive towns in the Beira Litoral (once you get past the ugly outskirts), Aveiro lies on the south-eastern edge of a marshy lagoon known as the Ria. Canals lace through the town under humpbacked bridges, giving a genteel Dutch feel to the place. The area of narrow lanes around the fish market is especially picturesque, with pastel-coloured houses bordering the canals.

Apart from one superb convent-museum, there's little to see or do in town, but it makes a relaxing base for visiting several nearby beaches or the bird reserve at São Jacinto. The turismo's museum leaflet details other possibilities nearby, ranging from a museum of steam engines (in Águeda) to a collection of famous Vista Alegre porcelain (in Ílhavo).

History

Aveiro's prosperity as a seaport at the mouth of the Rio Vouga took off in the 16th century, thanks largely to its salt pans, fishing fleet and the growing trade in salt cod *(bacalhau)*. But in the 1570s a ferocious storm closed the mouth of the Vouga which had been gradually narrowed by encroaching coastal sandbanks. The river's winter flooding

BEIRAS

created fever-breeding marshes which helped decimate Aveiro's population from 14,000 to a low of 3500 by 1759.

In 1808, the old town walls were used to build the Barra Canal which re-established a passage through to the sea, draining the marshes to leave a network of salt lagoons. Aveiro quickly gained new importance as a fishing and industrial centre, its prosperity reflected in a spate of Art Nouveau houses and azulejo friezes around town. Today, salt is still a mainstay of its economy. At one time the harvesting of *molico* (seaweed) from the estuary for use as fertiliser was too, but it is on the decline. Many of the beautifully painted, high-prowed *moliceiros* boats tied up along the canals are now used for tourist jaunts through the Ria rather than for collecting seaweed.

Orientation

The azulejo-adorned train station is at the north-east end of the town's main street, Avenida Dr Lourenço Peixinho, just under a km from the central Praça Humberto Delgado (which straddles the Canal Central) and the nearby turismo.

Bus companies here seem to delight in

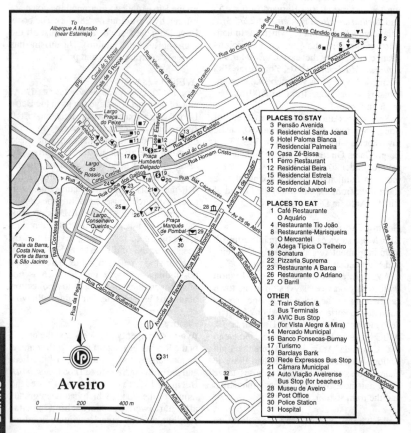

PLACES TO STAY
3 Pensão Avenida
5 Residencial Santa Joana
6 Hotel Paloma Blanca
7 Residencial Palmeira
10 Casa Zé-Bissa
11 Ferro Restaurant
12 Residencial Beira
15 Residencial Estrela
25 Residencial Alboi
32 Centro de Juventude

PLACES TO EAT
1 Café Restaurante O Aquário
4 Restaurante Tio João
8 Restaurante-Marisqueira O Mercantel
9 Adega Típica O Telheiro
18 Sonatura
22 Pizzaria Suprema
23 Restaurante A Barca
26 Restaurante O Adriano
27 O Barril

OTHER
2 Train Station & Bus Terminals
13 AVIC Bus Stop (for Vista Alegre & Mira)
14 Mercado Municipal
16 Banco Fonsecas-Burnay
17 Turismo
19 Barclays Bank
20 Rede Expressos Bus Stop
21 Câmara Municipal
24 Auto Viação Aveirense Bus Stop (for beaches)
28 Museu de Aveiro
29 Post Office
30 Police Station
31 Hospital

Aveiro

0   200   400 m

confusing visitors: at the last count, there were eight different companies with terminals scattered all over town. The major ones tend to congregate near the train station.

Information

Tourist Office The super-efficient regional turismo (☎ 207 60; fax 283 26), housed in one of the most ornate Art Nouveau houses in town, at Rua João Mendonça 8, has loads of information on Aveiro and the region. From mid-June through September it's open daily from 9 am to 9 pm. Other times, it's open weekdays from 9 am to 7 pm and on Saturdays from 9 am to 12.30 pm and 2 to 5.30 pm.

Money In addition to several banks (most with ATMs) on Avenida Dr Lourenço Peixinho, there's also the central Banco Fonsecas-Burnay bank on Praça Humberto Delgado, and a branch of Barclays just across the Canal Central from the turismo, on Rua Batalhau dos Caçadores.

Post & Communications The main post office is on Praça Marquês de Pombal, five minutes walk south of the turismo.

Medical Services The hospital is on the southern edge of town, off Avenida Artur Ravara.

Emergency The police station is on Praça Marquês de Pombal.

Museu de Aveiro

The former Convento de Jesus, opposite the cathedral, owes its best treasures to Princesa (later beatified and called Santa) Joana, a daughter of Afonso V. In 1472, seven years after the convent was founded, she 'retired' here and although she was forbidden to take full vows she stayed until her death in 1489.

Her 17th-century tomb is a masterpiece of marble mosaic and is placed in a chancel of equally lavish baroque ornamentation including azulejos on the life of the princess. Among the museum's paintings is another fine creation inspired by the saintly Joana, a

late 15th-century portrait attributed to Nuno Gonçalves. The museum is open daily, except Mondays, from 10 am to 12.30 pm and 2 to 5 pm. Admission is 250$00.

Beaches

They're not the most spectacular beaches you'll find along the Costa de Prata but Praia da Barra and nearby Costa Nova are fine for a summer day's outing from Aveiro (13 km east). Although packed at weekends they're still surprisingly undeveloped. Costa Nova is the prettier of the two resorts and its beachside street is lined with small restaurants and candy-striped cottages.

Buses leave regularly for both resorts from the station, stopping at the more convenient bus stop on Rua Clube dos Galitos, across the canal from the turismo. Pop into the turismo for the exact timetable. Wilder and less easily accessible is the São Jacinto beach, on the northern side of the lagoon from Barra. To get here, you first have to take a bus (from the Rua Clube dos Galitos stop) to Forte da Barra and then a small passenger ferry across the lagoon to the port of São Jacinto. The vast beach of sand dunes is a 1.5 km walk from here, through the ugly modern residential area at the back of town.

Reserva Natural das Dunas de São Jacinto

Between the sea and the N327 coastal road stretching north from São Jacinto to Torreira and Ovar is this small wooded nature reserve (☎ 33 12 82) equipped with trails and birdwatching hides. Badly scarred by a fire in 1995, it's still looking rather ragged, but there are guided three-hour walks twice a day on weekdays (10 am and 2 pm) for 200$00 if you're interested (it's best to phone ahead to confirm the time).

From the ferry pier in São Jacinto, it's a 1.3 km walk along the Torreira road (head for the beach and turn right). The entrance is poorly signposted: look for the Snack Bar Portela opposite.

Special Events

The Festa da Ria is Aveiro's big celebration

BEIRAS

of its canals and moliceiros boats. Lasting several weeks from mid-July to the end of August, its highlight is a moliceiros race, backed up by folk dancing in the streets and *praças*.

Places to Stay
Camping There are camping grounds at all the nearby beach resorts. At Barra, there's a municipal site (☎ 36 94 25) and at Costa Nova a smaller private site (☎ 36 98 22). You've got two choices at São Jacinto: a municipal site (☎ 33 12 20), 2.5 km from the pier along the Torreira road, or the better equipped and more expensive *Orbitur* site (☎ 482 84) 2.5 km further on. There's no bus service along this road.

Hostels The centro de juventude (☎ 38 19 35; fax 38 23 95) on Rua das Pombas has beds for about 1500$00.

Pensões & Residencials There's a generous sprinkling of budget places near the train station and (more conveniently central) around Largo Praça do Peixe. Two minutes walk from the train station, at Avenida Dr Lourenço Peixinho 259, try the elegantly stuccoed *Pensão Avenida* (☎ 233 66), which has bright singles/doubles for a bargain 2500$00/4000$00. At No 227 the friendly *Residencial Santa Joana* (☎ 286 04) offers doubles with bath from 6000$00.

Cheaper rooms, attached to restaurants, can be found near Largo Praça do Peixe – at *Casa Zé-Bissa* (☎ 222 77), at Rua dos Marnotos 26, which has doubles from 3000$00, and the trendier *Ferro Restaurant* (☎ 222 14) across the street at No 39, where doubles are 4000$00. For more comforts in this area, head for the neat, family-run *Residencial Palmeira* (☎ 225 21), at Rua da Palmeira 7, where doubles without/with bath go for 4000$00/6000$00. Near the turismo, on Rua José Estevão, are two businesslike residencials, *Residencial Beira* (☎ 242 97) at No 18 and *Residencial Estrela* (☎ 238 18) at No 4, both offering doubles with bath and breakfast from 6000$00. For more frills *Residencial Alboi* (☎ & fax 251 21), at No 6

in the quiet Rua da Arrochela, has doubles with breakfast from 8000$00. The most attractive place in town is undoubtedly *Hotel Paloma Blanca* (☎ 38 19 92; fax 38 18 44), at Rua Luís Gomes de Carvalho 23. It's an elegant mansion with doubles at 13,500$00.

An unusual rural alternative, 18 km north of Aveiro and five km from Estarreja station in the farming hamlet of Bunheiro, is the French-run *Albergue A Mansão* (☎ 460 00). Spacious doubles with dinner and breakfast are 9500$00. Huge, delicious dinners are served à la famille, so expect long, conversational evenings (French-speakers will feel right at home). There's plenty of space in the garden if you want to put up your tent (5000$00 with breakfast and dinner). You can be met at Estarreja station if you call ahead.

Places to Eat
Tucked away in the backstreet Rua 31 de Janeiro are two popular and good-value restaurants, the best of which is *O Barril* (☎ 284 55) at No 37 where you can eat a quick snack at the counter or more leisurely meal out the back. At the top of the lane (actually at Rua Capitão Sousa Pizarro 4) is *Restaurante O Adriano* (☎ 208 98), with a slightly pricier menu including an excellent cabrito assado a regional (roast kid) for 1100$00.

Near the train station are several cheapies, including *Restaurante Tio João* (☎ 72 17 85), at Avenida Dr Lourenço Peixinho 235, a casual, noisy restaurant with everything from tripe and hamburgers to carapau (horse mackerel) and rojões (pork pieces). Around the corner at Rua Almirante Cândido dos Reis 139, *Café Restaurante O Aquário* (☎ 250 14) is larger and brighter, with dishes from 650$00. Closer to the turismo, at Rua Clube dos Galitos 6, vegetarians can find arroz integral (brown rice) at the rather dour *Sonatura* (☎ 244 74). *Pizzeria Suprema* (☎ 217 77), at Rua José Rabumba 7, offers attractive alternatives to Portuguese fare, and has tables outside.

The best grilled fish in town can be found at *Restaurante A Barca* (☎ 260 24) next door at No 5, while seafood splurges are most reliably enjoyed at the popular *Restaurante-Marisqueira O Mercantel* (☎ 280 57) at Rua António Lé 16, a huge place often packed at weekends. Try the local speciality, enguias fritas (fried eels). Cheaper fare in more bohemian surroundings is available at the nearby *Adega Típica O Telheiro* (☎ 294 73) at Largo da Praça do Peixe 22.

Getting There & Away

Bus If you're forced to use the bus, check timetables and stops with the turismo beforehand as they can be confusing. The services you're most likely to use include Rede Expressos to Figueira da Foz (two per day), Nazaré and Caldas da Rainha (one daily); AVIC to nearby Vista Alegre (six times daily) and on to Mira (twice daily); and Auto Viação Aveirense to Praia de Mira (five times daily in summer), Barra and Costa Nova (hourly from 8 am to 8 pm), and Forte da Barra (almost hourly from 7 am to 7 pm). Note that services are reduced at weekends and on holidays.

All these companies also have convenient stops in the town centre; see the map.

Train Since Aveiro is on the main Lisbon-Porto line there are good connections north and south including four interregionals and seven Alfas (taking two hours 40 minutes to Lisbon via Coimbra and just under an hour to Porto).

Getting Around

From mid-June to mid-September the turismo organises daily motorboat trips on the Ria. They leave from Aveiro's Canal Central at 10 am and head up to the seaside resort of Torreira (13 km north), where you'll have a few hours to eat lunch or laze on the beach before returning by 5 pm. Tickets, at 2000$00 per person, are available at the turismo.

Privately organised trips on traditional moliceiros to São Jacinto (two hours) are also usually available in summer. They leave several times a day from the Canal Central and cost around 1500$00 per person. To buy tickets, look for the kiosk by the canal or ask at the turismo.

The Beira Alta

Some northern Beira Alta towns along the Rio Douro are covered in the East of Peso da Régua section of the Douro chapter.

VISEU

• *pop 21,000 • postcode 3500 • area code* ☎ *032*

Seldom-visited Viseu, capital of Beira Alta province, is a lively commercial hub, a town with the noise and swagger of a city. In the middle is a compact – one could almost say cosy – old centre gathered around a hulking granite cathedral, symbolic of Viseu's status as a bishopric ever since Visigothic times. Its very old, crowded and partly pedestrianised market zone, punctuated with stoic 17th and 18th-century townhouses, is a pleasure to squeeze through.

Viseu was the 16th-century home of an important school of Renaissance art that gathered around the painter Vasco Fernandes (known as O Grão Vasco), and the town's biggest drawcard is a rich museum holding his and his students' best works. You could do Viseu justice in less than a day, though with an overnight stop you can while away an evening in one of several good restaurants and, if you like, the wee hours as well in a *casa de fado*.

History

The Romans built a fortified camp just across the Rio Pavia, and several well-preserved stretches of their roads survive nearby. The town, conquered and reconquered in the struggles between Christians and Moors, was finally taken by Dom Fernando I in 1057.

Viseu's sturdy walls were completed by Afonso V around 1472. The town soon spread beyond them, having grown large and wealthy from agriculture and trade. An annual 'free fair' declared by João III in 1510 has since grown into one of the region's

BEIRAS

Wines of the Dão Region

The red wines of the Dão region (an area demarcated in 1907, roughly within the watershed of the Rio Mondego in the south-west corner of the Beira Alta) have had a solid reputation since the 16th century and are today considered among Portugal's best. Vines have been cultivated here since the time of the Phoenicians and Carthaginians, over 2000 years ago, and possibly even before then (palaeobotanists have found vine pollens over 5000 years old in the Lagoa Comprida lagoon, near Seia), though serious wine production only began with the Romans.

Although white Dão wines are available, the full-bodied reds are by far the best (and strongest in alcohol content). There are several *adegas* where you can try these velvety 'Burgundies of Portugal' including the Adega Cooperativa de Vila Nova de Tázem (☎ 038-461 82) and the Adega Cooperativa de São Paio (☎ 038-421 01), both near Gouveia. It's best to phone ahead to confirm visiting times. ■

biggest agricultural and handicrafts expositions. Much of the town's wealth these days comes from the excellent wines of the Dão region (south-west Beira Alta), near Viseu.

Orientation

Surrounded by pine-covered hills, Viseu sits on the south bank of the Rio Pavia, a tributary of the Mondego. In the very middle of town is the handsome Praça da República, known to all as the Rossio. From here the shopping district stretches east along Rua Formosa and Rua da Paz, and north into the 'historical zone' along Rua do Comércio and Rua Direita. At the town's highest point and historical heart is the cathedral, enclosed to the north, east and south by a warren of narrow lanes.

From the bus station the Rossio is uphill (south-east) along Avenida Dr António José de Almeida. Drivers should avoid the old town, with its harrowing one-way lanes.

Information

Tourist Office The well-organised turismo (☎ 42 20 14) on Avenida Calouste Gulbenk-

ian is open on weekdays from 9 am to 12.30 pm and 2 to 6 pm, and on weekends from 10 am to noon and 3 to 5.30 pm. A recommended purchase for town explorers is the small *Viseu Tourist Guide* (250$00), which is available from the turismo.

Money There are numerous banks with exchanges and Multibanco ATMs, especially along Rua Formosa.

Post & Communications The post office is at the east end of Rua da Paz.

Bookshops The best bookshop in the centre looks to be Livraria Domingos Agostinho on Rua Formosa, though its maps don't include Viseu and its books don't include much in English!

Medical Services The district hospital (☎ 241 24) is 1½ blocks east of the turismo on Rua do Hospital.

Emergency The police station (☎ 260 41) is on Rua Alves Martins.

Dangers & Annoyances South of the Rossio is the big Parque da Cidade, potentially a good place for kids to play, but with shrubs that barely conceal couples at play at any hour of the day or night. In any case, it looks like a pretty dodgy place at night.

If you're driving and get as far as the Adro da Sé (Cathedral Square) – now a parking lot – you'll have plenty of 'help' from enterprising down-and-outers who wave you into the space you have just found by yourself and then expect a tip.

Rossio & Around

Praça da República (Rossio), shady almost to the point of seeming indoors, is a stately place to begin your wandering after you've been fortified by coffee and sweets from the good snack bar in the middle.

At the south end of the square the late 18th-century **Igreja dos Terceiros** has azulejo panels portraying the life of St Francis. Beyond this stretches the **Parque** da **Cidade** (see Dangers & Annoyances), also called Parque Aquilino Ribeiro. On the west side is the rather grand 19th-century **câmara municipal** (town hall). Fine modern **azulejos** at the north end of the Rossio depict fairs and other scenes from regional life.

Beyond the azulejos wall is the odd, sloping **Jardim das Mães** (Mothers' Garden), centred on a bronze statue of a sleeping child. The most elegant route into the old town is this way, up past the marginally interesting **Casa Museu Almeida Moreira**, where the first director of the Museu de Grão Vasco (see The Old Town section) decided

to make his house, furniture and knick-knacks into a museum too.

Old Town

Just north of the Casa Museu Almeida Moreira you pass through the **Porta do Soar de Cima**, beneath a small bit of Afonso V's town walls, into the old town. Bear right into the huge Adro da Sé (or Largo da Sé), the cathedral's forecourt, its grandeur lost in a bleak sea of parked cars.

Sé Resplendent on a rock above the whole town is the granite Sé (cathedral), with a

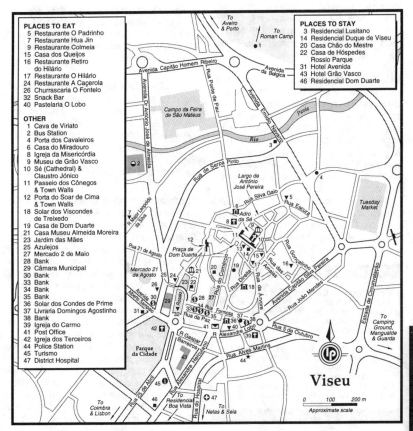

PLACES TO EAT
5 Restaurante O Padrinho
7 Restaurante Hua Jin
9 Restaurante Colmeia
15 Casa dos Queijos
16 Restaurante Retiro do Hilário
17 Restaurante O Hilário
24 Restaurante A Cacerola
26 Churrascaria O Fontelo
32 Snack Bar
40 Pastelaria O Lobo

OTHER
1 Cava de Viriato
2 Bus Station
4 Porta dos Cavaleiros
6 Casa do Miradouro
8 Igreja da Misericórdia
9 Museu de Grão Vasco
10 Sé (Cathedral) & Claustro Jónico
11 Passeio dos Cônegos & Town Walls
12 Porta do Soar de Cima & Town Walls
18 Solar dos Viscondes de Treixedo
19 Casa de Dom Duarte
21 Casa Museu Almeida Moreira
23 Jardim das Mães
25 Azulejos
27 Mercado 2 de Maio
28 Bank
29 Câmara Municipal
30 Bank
33 Bank
34 Bank
35 Bank
36 Solar dos Condes de Prime
37 Livraria Domingos Agostinho
38 Bank
39 Igreja do Carmo
41 Post Office
42 Igreja dos Terceiros
44 Police Station
45 Turismo
47 District Hospital

PLACES TO STAY
3 Residencial Lusitano
14 Residencial Duque de Viseu
20 Casa Chão do Mestre
22 Casa de Hóspedes Rossio Parque
31 Hotel Avenida
43 Hotel Grão Vasco
46 Residencial Dom Duarte

Viseu

BEIRAS

magnificently gloomy 17th-century Renaissance façade that conceals a splendid 16th-century interior, including a carved and painted Manueline ceiling. The building itself dates from the 13th century. The north chapel is graced with 18th-century azulejos.

Stairs in the north transept climb to the choir, from where you can enter the upper gallery of the stately **Claustro Jónico** (Ionian Cloister), with a chapter house with 17th-century azulejos outside, 18th-century azulejos inside, as well as a collection of ecclesiastical treasures, some quite lovely. The original, lower level, is one of Portugal's earliest Italian Renaissance structures. Return to the church through a Romanesque-Gothic portal only rediscovered in this century. The church is open most of the time (except lunch time, this being Portugal) and admission is free.

Museu de Grão Vasco Adjoining the Sé is a great square granite box, the Paço de Três Escalões (Palace of Three Steps), probably contemporary with the cathedral. It was originally the bishop's palace, then a seminary, then the bishop's palace again. In 1916 it proudly reopened as a museum for the works of Viseu's own Vasco Fernandes, one of Portugal's seminal Renaissance painters (see the boxed aside).

These and other works of the 'Viseu School' are on the 2nd floor. Most impressive are Grão Vasco's own *St Peter* as Renaissance man; and 14 panels (which once

Grão Vasco & the Viseu School
Viseu and Lisbon were the main centres of a uniquely Portuguese style of Renaissance art in the 16th century. The brightest lights in the so-called 'Viseu School' of painting were Vasco Fernandes – known as O Grão Vasco, 'the Great Vasco' (1480-1543) – and Gaspar Vaz. Grão Vasco's works, heavily influenced by the Flemish masters, feature a range of direct, luminous, extra-realistic paintings done for the Sé and other churches. Most of them are now at home in the Museu de Grão Vasco. ■

hung above the altar of the Sé next door) by Grão Vasco and his students, including the *Adoration of the Magi* which depicts the third wise man as an Indian from (then newly discovered) Brazil. Other displays in the museum include 13th to 18th-century sculpture, 16th to 19th-century furniture, 19th to 20th-century Portuguese paintings, Oriental and Portuguese ceramics, and more. The Grão Vasco Museum (☎ 42 20 49) is open daily except Mondays and holidays, from 9.30 am to 12.30 pm and 2 to 5.30 pm; entry is 250$00 (but free on Sundays until 12.30 pm) and guided tours are available.

Igreja da Misericórdia Facing the cathedral across the Adro da Sé is the 1775 Misericórdia Church. It's rococo, symmetric and blindingly white outside, and neoclassical, severe and dull inside.

North of the Cathedral On the north side of the Sé and the museum is Largo de António José Pereira (named after a 19th-century Viseu artist). Behind it, down along Rua Silva Gaio, is the longest stretch of the old town walls. At the bottom, across Rua Emídio Navarro, is another old town gate, the **Porta dos Cavaleiros**.

South of the Cathedral Snug beneath the Passeio dos Cônegos (Curates' Walk) on a segment of the old wall is **Praça de Dom Duarte**, named for the Portuguese monarch (brother of Prince Henry the Navigator) who was born in Viseu. Southward along Rua Dom Duarte is a house with a beautiful Manueline window, the **Casa de Dom Duarte**, which tradition regards as the king's birthplace. On and around the square, several old **mansions** show off their wrought-iron balconies and genteel contours.

Rua Augusto Hilário (formerly Rua Nova), after passing eastward through Viseu's 14th to 16th-century **judiária** (Jewish quarter), crosses Rua Direita, certainly Viseu's most appealing street and once the most direct route to the hilltop. It's now a lively gauntlet of cluttered shops, souvenir stands, cafés, restaurants and old townhouses.

Old Mansions

The handsomest of Viseu's many old townhouses is the 18th-century **Solar dos Condes de Prime** (the counts of Prime being its last owners), also called Casa de Cimo de Vila. Its interior is full of azulejos, and there is a little chapel and a ballroom. This will eventually be the home of a new municipal history museum. It's on Rua dos Andrades, an extension of Rua Direita.

Among other venerable stately homes are the 18th-century **Solar dos Viscondes de Treixedo** on Rua Direita (now a bank office), and the 16th-century **Casa do Miradouro** just off Largo de António José Pereira.

Roman Remains

On a shady embankment north of the centre are the remains of a Roman **military camp**, dating from about the time (139 BC) when Viriathus (Viriato), cunning chief of the Lusitani tribe (who put up the most ferocious resistance to the Romans; see History in the Facts about the Country chapter), was double-crossed and murdered. Legend says that at some point he took refuge in a cave here, though there appears to be no factual basis for this story. At any rate, there's a statue of him here, and the place is called Cava de Viriato.

A long hike or a car ride south-east of the town centre is **Via Romana de Coimbrões**, a well-preserved stretch of Roman road. Take the Mangualde road to Fraguzela village, turn right, and follow signs to Parque Industrial de Coimbrões; there is also an access from São João de Lourosa, on the Nelas road. Another segment, north-east of the town centre, is **Via Romana de Ranhados**, in the village of Ranhados. Ask at the turismo for detailed directions. There are no bus services to or near these sites.

Tuesday Market

Every Tuesday from 8 am to 2 pm a big Gypsy market sprawls across an open area a few blocks north-east of the centre.

Special Events

Viseu's biggest annual event is the Feira de São Mateus (St Matthew's Fair), a wine-growing, agricultural and handicrafts fair that carries on for a month from mid-August to mid-September. It includes folk music and dancing, traditional food, amusements and fireworks as well. This direct descendant of the town's old 'free fair' still takes place on the Campo da Feira de São Mateus which was set aside for the event by João III in 1510.

Places to Stay

Camping The well-equipped, shady *Fontelo* Orbitur camping ground (☎ 261 46) is open from mid-January to mid-November. It's near the municipal stadium, about one km east of the Rossio. Sample rates are 550$00 per person, 450$00 to 840$00 for a tent, and 470$00 per car. The camping ground is wheelchair-accessible.

Rooming Houses Bottom of the heap is *Casa Chão do Mestre* (☎ 279 91), a claustrophobic rooming house at Rua Chão do Mestre 109-C, where rooms with shared shower and loo are 2000$00/3000$00.

Pensões & Residencials You'll do much better for a bit more at *Residencial Lusitano* (☎ 42 30 42), at Avenida Emídio Navarro 167. Its spacious, carpeted and street-noisy rooms are 3000$00/4000$00 with shared facilities or 4000$00/5500$00 with your own, all with breakfast. Our mid-range choice is the dignified *Casa de Hóspedes Rossio Parque* (☎ 42 20 85) at Rua Soar de Cima 55, in a nice position above the Rossio. It has a small restaurant and doubles are 5500$00 (without bath) or 7000$00 (with).

Two sober, child-friendly but rather noisy residencials south on Rua Alexandre Herculano are the *Dom Duarte* (☎ 42 19 80; fax 42 48 25) at No 214 (around the corner from the turismo), and the *BelaVista* (☎ 42 20 26; fax 42 84 72), about 400m further out at No 510. A double with shower and TV at either is about 6500$00, including breakfast; the Bela Vista also has doubles with bath for

7000$00. Try for a quieter room at the back of either of these places.

Your best bet in the upper bracket is the small *Residencial Duque de Viseu* (☎ 42 12 86), upstairs at Rua das Ameias 22, right below the Sé. Rooms cost 5000$00/8000$00 with toilet and small bath, TV and air-con and are small, but those at the rear are sunny and quiet.

Hotels Within sight of the Rossio is the good *Hotel Avenida* (☎ 42 34 32; fax 256 43), at Avenida Alberto Sampaio 1, where a room with bath and TV is 7000$00/9500$00. Top of the line here is the big *Hotel Grão Vasco* (☎ 42 35 11; fax 42 64 44), on Rua Gaspar Barreiros, which has singles/doubles for 11,300$00/13,000$00.

Turihab There are numerous Turihab properties in the surrounding countryside; ask at the turismo.

Places to Eat

Viseu is awash in good food. For a hit of coffee and a huge choice of tempting pastries, go to *Pastelaria O Lobo* (☎ 279 59) at Rua Francisco Alexandre Lobo 37. Don't overlook the cheerful snack bar in the middle of the Rossio.

Our favourite restaurant, and not just because it's child-friendly, is *Casa dos Queijos* (☎ 42 26 43), just off Rua Direita at Travessa das Escadinhas da Sé 7-9. It has delicious trutas grelhados (grilled trout), decent cozidos (stews), lots of greens and great pudim. Another commendable place is *Churrascaria O Fontelo* (☎ 42 42 21), at Rua Conselheiro Afonso de Melo 45, which has a big selection of grilled chicken (half for 800$00), meat (to 1200$00) and fish (to 1400$00). We also like *Restaurante A Caçerola* (☎ 42 10 07) at Travessa Major Teles 3, just off the Rossio. It's bright, tiled, clean and simple, with a good selection of pratos do dia for under 1450$00, half-portions under 850$00, and mini-portions for 450$00. For a little fado with dinner, try *Restaurante Retiro do Hilário* (☎ 42 84 25), Rua Gonçalinho 42, off Rua Direita. It's

open daily, except Sundays, from 7 pm to 2 am and has a small, pricey menu with a minimum charge of 1000$00 (1500$00 on Fridays and Saturdays). It probably gets booked out for lunch. It may be no coincidence that there's a former casa de fado, *Restaurante O Hilário* (☎ 265 87), at Rua Augusto Hilário 35, where no course is over 1000$00. Other worthwhile places in the old town are *Restaurante O Padrinho* (☎ 42 26 65), at Rua Escura 46, with lunch, snacks, dinner and takeaways, and occasional fado in the basement; and *Restaurante Colmeia* (☎ 42 37 18) at Rua das Amaias 12-14. For a change, try the peaceful Chinese *Restaurante Hua Jin* (☎ 42 12 62), at Rua Major Leopoldo da Silva 36, which has an immense menu of dishes under 1000$00. Self-caterers will find fruit, vegetables and other goodies in Mercado 2 de Maio, the old town market on Rua do Comércio.

Things to Buy

Handicrafts here are noticeably cheaper than in more touristed towns. Among local specialities are black pottery, basketware and lace. Look for small handicrafts shops on or near Rua Direita, or venture into the huge, dumbbell-shaped Mercado 21 de Agosto in the street of the same name.

Getting There & Away

Viseu is no longer on a passenger railway line. CP still runs buses to Viseu from the Coimbra-Porto line at Sernada and from the Coimbra-Guarda line at Mangualde, and two private bus lines have links with Mangualde (25 minutes away), but the journey ends up being rather complicated.

Bus transport can be daunting too. As in other towns in the region, the bus station is just a collection of private ticket offices – chiefly Rede Expressos or RE (through Rodoviário de Beira Litoral, ☎ 42 28 22), Beira Alta (through Marques Turismo, ☎ 278 06), Joalto (☎ 42 60 93) and Barrelhas – each with its own routes. The most frequent connections (all with at least two buses a day) are Coimbra (800$00) and Lisbon (1300$00) with Beira Alta or RE; Aveiro

(800$00) and Porto with Beira Alta or Joalto; Braga with Joalto or RE; Guarda and Covilhã with Joalto; and Mangualde (about 300$00) with Barrelhas.

SERRA DA ESTRELA

The Serra da Estrela, a glacially scoured plateau forming a conspicuous natural boundary between south and north, is the highest mountain range in Portugal (topping out at 1993m Torre). At higher elevations it is decidedly alpine, with rounded peaks, boulder-strewn meadows, icy lakes and deep valleys. Lower down, the land furrows into stock trails, terraced fields lined with drystone walls, and pine plantations. The range gives birth to, and is then circumscribed by, two rivers: the Mondego (the longest river rising within Portugal) to the north and the Zêzere (a tributary of the Tejo) to the south.

Mountain people – some still living in traditional one-room stone *casais* thatched with rye straw, but now mostly concentrated in valley hamlets – raise sheep (for wool, meat and milk); grow rye, vegetables and potatoes; and increasingly depend upon touristic variants of their traditional activities, for instance the selling of woollen goods and tasty, pungent *queijo da serra*, and the renting out of rooms. Town-dwellers are concentrated at the north-east end, around Guarda.

The Parque Natural da Serra da Estrela (PNSE, or Serra da Estrela Natural Park) was founded in 1976 to preserve not merely habitats and landscapes but the plateau's rural character and its people's cultural identity. Straddling Beira Alta and Beira Baixa provinces, it's about 1000 sq km in size, with more than half of it above 700m.

Crisp, hyperclean air and immense vistas make this a very fine place for serious hiking, and there's greater scope for it here than anywhere else in the country, thanks to a system of well-marked trails, and maps to go with them. Remoteness, harsh winters, and the umbrella of 'natural park' status have fairly well preserved the range's natural beauty and its human character.

This is not to say the Serra is empty and untouched. Enough snow falls in winter to ski on and there are modest facilities at Torre and Penhas da Saúde. Every weekend (and all week in July and August), Portuguese families come up by car and bus in their thousands to play in the snow or picnic, ripping branches from the trees for bonfires and creating huge high-altitude traffic jams around Torre. Torre itself has been defaced with a radar station and a shopping complex. Sabugueiro and a few other formerly quiet villages now bristle with pensões and souvenir shops. But for the rest of the week, and off the road almost any time, the mountains do indeed seem empty.

The weather constantly goes to extremes – even scorching summer days give way to frigid nights, and chilling rainstorms can arise with little warning. Mist is a big hazard, because it obscures walking routes and landmarks (not to mention views) and because it can stealthily chill you, even to the point of hypothermia. You may set out on a warm, cloudless morning and in the middle of the day find yourself shivering and with zero visibility, so always pack for the cold and the wet too.

Wildflowers bloom in late April. The best walking is from May to October. Winter is harsh, with snow at upper elevations from November/December to April/May.

Information

Tourist Offices There are park information offices at Seia, Gouveia and Manteigas. Manteigas is the head office, though all are equally helpful – but don't count on English being spoken at any of them.

We found the most competent turismos to be the Beira Baixa regional office at Covilhã and the local office at Seia. There is also a Beira Alta regional office at Guarda, and local offices at Gouveia, Guarda, Manteigas and elsewhere.

Books & Maps If you're serious about exploring the park, pick up the excellent 1:50,000, three-colour topographic map called *Carta Turística: Parque Natural da Serra da Estrela*, which is marked with

BEIRAS

Parque Natural da Serra da Estrela

0   5   10 km

roads, walking routes, camp sites, shelters and more. It costs 1050$00 and is available from any park office or the Covilhã, Manteigas and Seia turismos. It's also available at the Instituto Português de Cartográfia e Cadastro in Lisbon and the Porto Editora bookshop in Porto (see the Information sections for those cities). Its sole drawback is the paper it's printed on, which tends to decompose when wet.

The essential companion to this is a good English-language booklet, *Discovering the Region of the Serra da Estrela*, which describes all the park's official walking routes, along with background information, flora and fauna basics, facilities, trail profiles, walking times and relevant sections of the *Carta Turística*. This is for sale at the same offices for 840$00. Those with a more detailed interest in the park's flora and fauna can also pick up the booklet *Estrela: A Natural Approach* for 630$00.

Walking

Serra da Estrela is the only *parque natural* with a system of well-marked walking trails and good maps to go with it. Surprisingly few people actually use these trails, even in summer, and walkers often have the wonderful impression that they have the whole park to themselves. The park's traditional villages and agricultural way of life make a trek additionally rewarding. Unless you're an experienced winter camper, stick to the summer months.

Within a zone of special protection that takes in almost everything above about 1200m, camping and fires are prohibited except at a few designated camp sites, all of them on main trails. Cutting trees and picking plants are also prohibited in this zone.

Routes There are three main official routes that you can easily enter and leave at numerous points. T1 runs the length of the park, about 90 km from Vide to Guarda, taking in every kind of terrain, including the summit of Torre. T2 and T3, both around 80 km, run respectively along the western and eastern slopes of the Serra. Each main route has branches and variants.

It's feasible to assemble anything from a day hike to a week-long circuit of the park, or to cut right across the middle of it. The trails and variants all run through towns and villages in the park; thus, reaching the trails is relatively easy and there are sometimes accommodation options other than camping.

Manteigas is probably the best base for walkers, as many of the most attractive hikes start there, including the one up the beautiful Vale do Zêzere towards Nave de Santo António (anything from a day hike to an overnight; 7½ to eight hours return); the one to Poço do Inferno waterfall (3½ to four hours return); to Penhas Douradas (3½ to four hours return); and that to Folgosinho (about 10 hours return) or on to Linhares (an additional seven hours return). A good alternative base, close to Torre, is Penhas da Saúde.

Guided Walks Passeios a Pé no PNSE (Walks in the PNSE) is a programme of customised walks guided by park staff, by advance arrangement with the Manteigas park office. Amazingly, there is no charge for

the guide service, only for food, accommodation and other expenses. They are, however, mainly in Portuguese.

Serious hikers might also want to contact the enthusiastic Clube Nacional de Montanhismo (☎ 075-32 33 64; fax 075-31 35 14; see Covilhã Information) which, despite its name, is a local club that organises weekend walking, camping, skiing and other expeditions. It has its own camp site at Penhas da Saúde and *casas de abrigo* (shelter-houses) at Penhas da Saúde and Torre.

Horse Riding
If you'd like to go riding contact Pedro Manuel Fazendeiro (☎ 075-92 18 94) in Terlamonte (about 10 km north-east of Covilhã).

Skiing
The ski season typically runs from January through March, with the best conditions in February. Gentle slopes and modest facilities are available at Torre (including three lifts) and at Penhas da Saúde. Equipment can be rented (2500$00 per day for skis, poles and boots), and lift-ticket prices are about 2000$00 per weekday or 3000$00 on Saturdays, Sundays and holidays. Another source of equipment rental is Ski Clube de Montanha (☎ & fax 038-31 11 02, mobile ☎ 0936-757237) in Sabugueiro. The Clube Nacional de Montanhismo (☎ 075-32 33 64; fax 075-31 35 14; see Covilhã Information) also organises ski trips.

Other Activities
Ski Clube de Montanha (see Sabugueiro Information) rents out mountain bikes and canoes in summer.

Places to Stay
The most convenient bases for exploration of the Serra are Gouveia and Seia on the west side (within driving distance of many camping grounds), Covilhã on the east side (with more accommodation options, including a youth hostel at nearby Penhas da Saúde), and Manteigas in the middle (less well equipped but close to Torre and the beautiful Vale do Zêzere).

BEIRAS

While camping grounds either close or drop their rates outside the summer season, many hotels, pensões and residencials actually *raise* theirs in winter to cover the extra cost of heating; at others there is no seasonal variation. Everything tends to be pricier than, for example, down in Coimbra.

Camping There are at least seven camping grounds near the centre of the park: Curral do Negro and Quinta das Cegonhas (see Gouveia); Covão da Ponte, Covão da Ametade and Valhelhas (see Manteigas); Pião (see Covilhã); and Penhas da Saúde. Several more are further out: Guarda; Ponte do Ladrão and Monte Alto (both east of Celorico da Beira); São Gião, Ponte das Três Entradas and Pomares (all near Oliveira do Hospital, west of the park); and Quinta do Convento (west of Fundão). Only Covão da Ponte is significantly far (six to seven km) from a sealed road.

Hostels The Serra's only HI/YHA pousada de juventude (youth hostel; ☎ 075-253 75) is at Penhas da Saúde. There is also a centro de juventude with some hostel accommodation at Guarda.

Casas de Abrigo Scattered around the park are several fairly isolated casas de abrigo (shelter-houses) for use by park staff. At least two of these, at Covão da Ponte (north of Manteigas) and Videmonte (west of Guarda), are also open to the public on a self-catering basis. Each has two rooms, with four to six beds, though you could book all the beds in one room (5000$00 per room, plus 500$00 per person for bed linen) for yourself. Each has a shared, fully equipped kitchen, plus a fireplace and central heating.

They can be booked through the park office at Manteigas, with a 50% payment in advance. Prices are the same year-round. Both are accessible by car (at least by prior arrangement), and on foot, on poor municipal tracks.

The Clube Nacional de Montanhismo operates its own casas de abrigo at Penhas da Saúde and near Torre, which can be booked

with the club in Covilhã (see Covilhã Information).

Turihab The Turismo Habitação scheme, which is relatively new to this area, is concentrated along the Seia-Gouveia axis but spreading rapidly. Rates vary from mid-range (eg a big castle-like place in Sortelha for 6000$00) to top-end places (eg one room plus a kitchenette in Fundão for 10,000$00). They can be booked through local turismos or through ADRUSE (Associação de Desenvolvimento Rural da Serra da Estrela, or Serra da Estrela Rural Development Association; ☎ 038-49 11 23; fax 038-402 50) at Largo do Mercado in Gouveia.

Pousadas de Portugal Two top-end places with world-class views are the *Pousada de São Lourenço* (see Manteigas), and the *Pousada de Santa Barbara* (☎ 038-595 51; fax 038-596 45) at Póvoa das Quartas, five km east of Oliveira do Hospital on the N17, where doubles are 19,000$00.

Things to Buy
Souvenir shops in Serra towns sell tasty Serra da Estrela cheese, heavy round loaves of rye bread *(pão de centeîo)* and corn bread *(pão de milho)*, honey, smoked hams and sausages.

Non-edible regional items include wool hats, slippers, rugs, coats and waistcoats (mostly made in Manteigas, Gouveia, São Romão and Folhadosa), baskets used for carrying cheese and bread (Vale de Azares and Vinhó), and miniature barrels and wooden tubs made by local wine-barrel makers (Gouveia and Seia).

Getting There & Away
There are several express coaches each day from Coimbra to Seia, Guarda and Covilhã, as well as from Aveiro, Porto and Lisbon to Guarda and Covilhã.

From Lisbon and Coimbra, twice-daily intercidade trains go to Guarda via Celorico da Beira. Two additional interregional trains each day also stop at Gouveia (2½ hours from Coimbra or five hours from Lisbon).

BEIRAS

Serra da Estrela Cheese

Creamy, semisoft queijo da serra is made, usually in one to two-kg rounds, during the cold, humid months from November to April. Curing takes a fairly brief 40 days or so. A healthy by-product is curd cheese, made from the liquid drained in cheese manufacture.

Most serra farming families make their own cheese, though gradually the process is becoming industrialised, with certified cheese factories (offering tours and sales) around the region. Towns with the most cheese factories include Celorico da Beira, Linhares, Carrapichana, Vale de Azares, Cadafaz, Algodres, Arcozelo, Folgosinho and São Romão.

Cheese fairs take place all over the region from November to mid-April. Best known are those at Fornos de Algodres (every other Monday), Celorico da Beira (every other Friday) and Carrapichana (every Monday); as well as those on Carnival Saturday in Seia, Carnival Sunday in Gouveia, and Carnival Tuesday in Manteigas. But you've got to rise early: they're typically in full swing by sunrise and all over by 9 am. ∎

Covilhã is on the Lisbon-Paris mainline, with two intercidades from Lisbon as far as Covilhã (4½ hours) and numerous regional services on to Guarda, plus connections from Porto.

Getting Around

There are regular regional bus services from Guarda down both sides of the park – two to four trips daily to Gouveia and Seia and a similar number to Covilhã, plus two a day to Manteigas. No buses go right across the park, though you can go around the south end between Covilhã and Seia, via Unhais da Serra, twice a day. On weekends, only in July and August, a few buses run from Covilhã as far as Penhas da Saúde and Nave de Santo António.

Hitching appears to be pretty good, especially up from Covilhã to Penhas da Saúde. Driving can be hairy, thanks to mist and wet or icy roads at high elevations, and often stiff winds. The Gouveia-Manteigas road is one of the wiggliest we saw in Portugal, although the immense views are – for better or worse – guaranteed to distract you. Another especially scenic drive is up the Vale do Zêzere from Manteigas.

Do not expect to find empty roads up there on weekends, especially around Torre. On a weekend drive from Seia to Covilhã in April we found ourselves in a traffic jam that stretched over the horizon and lasted for hours.

GUARDA
• *pop 16,500* • *postcode 6300* • *area code* ☎ *071*

The traditional description of Guarda – *fria, farta, forte e feia* (cold, rich, strong and ugly) – hardly makes it sound very enticing. And to be frank, it doesn't have much trouble living up to its reputation. Even in early summer this district capital of Beira Alta seems grey, dour and distant – and since it's at an altitude of over 1000m (making it the highest fully fledged city in Portugal), it's nearly always cold.

Hardly an ideal first impression for visitors arriving overland in Portugal at Vilar Formoso (40 km to the east) from Spain or France. And despite the fact that the city has an 800-year history (it was founded in 1199 to guard the frontier), there's little actually to see or do here. So why come? Guarda makes a good base for exploring the rugged frontier hinterland, which is scattered with remote medieval fortified towns. It's also a jumping-off point for the untouristy north-eastern parts of the Parque Natural da Serra da Estrela. There's plenty of decent accommodation and restaurants, as well as efficient transport connections. Just be sure to bring your jumper and woolly hat.

Orientation

Arriving at the bus terminal on Rua Dom Nuno Álvares Pereira, you're at the southeast edge of town, about 800m from the old town's Praça Luís de Camões (also called

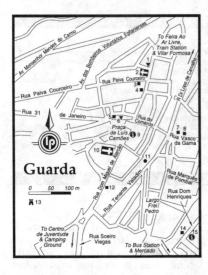

Guarda

0   50   100 m

1   Restaurante Belo Horizonte
2   Igreja de São Vicente
3   Pensão Belo Horizonte
4   Casa dos Frangos
5   Casa da Sé
6   A Brasileira Mini-Bar Restaurante e
     Cervejaria
7   Restaurante Residencial Felipe
8   Pensão Aliança
9   Municipal Turismo
10   Sé
11   Torre dos Ferreiros
12   Solar de Alarcão
13   Castelo
14   Residencil Beira Serra
15   Regional Turismo & Câmara Municipal

Praça Velha). Most accommodation, restaurants and places of interest are near here. The train station is four km north of town.

Information
Tourist Offices There are two turismos. The unhelpful municipal one (☎ 22 22 51), by Praça Luís de Camões on Rua Dom Miguel de Alarcão, is open weekdays from 9 am to 12.30 pm and 2 to 5.30 pm, and closed on weekends. The regional turismo (☎ 22 18 17), on Rua Infante Dom Henrique, is better,

though its opening hours are flakey; officially it's open Tuesday to Saturday from 9.30 am to noon and 2 to 6 pm. You can get information about the Parque Natural da Serra da Estrela here.

Money There are several banks with ATMs around the turismo and Rua Marquês de Pombal.

Quercus A branch of the environmental organisation Quercus (☎ & fax 23 08 30) operates from an office in the bus station on Thursdays only.

Sé
This grey granite fortress of a cathedral in Praça Luís de Camões is daunting to look at on a cold, rainy day. It's basically in a sober Gothic style, with the earliest parts dating from 1390, but as it took 150 years to finish there are several Manueline and Renaissance additions such as ornamented doorways and windows and interior vaulting. The flying buttresses and pinnacles are reminiscent of Batalha abbey in the Estremadura (the same architect, Mateus Fernandes, worked on both). Keep an eye out for the whimsical gargoyles which provide a nice touch of devilry.

Inside, the most striking feature is a 16th-century Renaissance altarpiece attributed to Jean de Rouen (one of the French team of sculptors who set up a very influential school of sculpture in Coimbra). There's a charge of 100$00 to climb the tower to the roof (open daily, except Mondays, from 10 am to noon and 2 to 5.30 pm).

Old Town
Praça Luís de Camões, the cathedral square, is the most attractive in Guarda, thanks to its 16th to 18th-century mansions (see Places to Stay for one you can sleep in).

There's not much left of the **castelo** (castle), which sits on a hilltop just above the cathedral, except a simple tower (which was closed to visitors when we were there). Of the old town walls and gates, the 17th-

BEIRAS

century **Torre dos Ferreiros** (Blacksmiths' Tower), along Rua Tenente Valadim, is still in stalwart condition. For the best old-town atmosphere, poke among the lanes north of the cathedral and Rua do Comércio. At the heart of this area, around Igreja de São Vicente, was the city's former **judiaria** (Jewish quarter).

Market

A big open-air market, the Feira Ao Ar Livre, is held on the first and third Wednesdays of the month on the northern outskirts of town.

Places to Stay

Camping If you're equipped for cold nights, you'll find the *Orbitur* camping ground (☎ 21 14 06) pleasant enough. It's in the municipal park on the western edge of town, next to a swimming pool and a stadium. It's closed from mid-November to mid-January.

Hostels There's a centro de juventude (☎ 21 25 33; fax 21 27 56) on Avenida Alexandre Herculano. Although geared to youth groups, you may be able to get a cheap bed (about 1500$00) here.

Private Rooms There are a few private quartos advertised around town, including basic doubles (without bath) for 2000$00 at *Restaurante Casa dos Frangos* (see Places to Eat).

Pensões & Residencials In the atmospheric old town area, some of the cheapest rooms are at *Pensão Belo Horizonte* (☎ 21 10 36), on Rua de São Vicente next to the church, where a double is 3000$00. Closer to the cathedral, at Rua Augusto Gil 17, *Casa da Sé* (☎ 21 25 01) has renovated doubles with TV and bath for 5500$00 (4500$00 without bath). Similarly priced is *Pensão Aliança* (☎ 22 22 35; fax 22 14 51) at Rua Vasco da Gama 8A (rates here include breakfast). At No 9 is the more up-market *Restaurante Residencial Filipe* (☎ 22 36 58) where doubles start at 5500$00 (including breakfast).

In the newer part of town, opposite the câmara municipal at Rua Infante Dom Henrique 35A, is the very pleasant *Residencial Beira Serra* (☎ 21 23 92) which has doubles from 6500$00 (7500$00 with bath), including breakfast. For historic surroundings, the Turihab *Solar de Alarcão* (☎ 21 43 92) is unbeatable: situated close to the cathedral, at Rua Dom Miguel de Alarcão 25, this handsome 17th-century granite mansion, with its own courtyard and loggia, has just three rooms for rent; they start from 10,000$00.

Places to Eat

The small, friendly *Casa dos Frangos* (☎ 21 27 04), at Rua Francisco de Passos 47, offers a refuge from the cold, with hearty servings from 800$00 (but, horror of horrors, instant coffee). *Restaurante Belo Horizonte* (☎ 21 14 54), at Largo de São Vicente 1, is packed at lunch time with locals enjoying excellent regional specialities (all under 1000$00). *Pensão Aliança* (☎ 22 22 35), at Rua Vasco da Gama 8A, is another local favourite, with an excellent cabrito assado na brasa (roast kid) for 1300$00 and pratos do dia (daily specials) for 900$00.

A Brasileira Mini-Bar Restaurante e Cervejaria (☎ 21 22 38), opposite the cathedral at Praça Luís de Camões 17, is a little too keen to attract tourists but has a cosy atmosphere and an appealing menu, with most dishes under 1000$00.

Getting There & Away

Bus At least four different bus companies operate from the bus terminal, and there's no central information booth to help you sort them out. Some services advertised by the smaller companies are actually run by Rede Expressos.

Beira Alto Expressos (☎ 22 18 81) has coaches twice a day on weekdays to Viseu, Aveiro and Lisbon and four times daily to Gouveia and Seia. Rede Expressos (☎ 21 27 20) has two coaches a day to Seia (four times per day in winter), continuing to Coimbra; at least five a day to Lisbon via Covilhã, Castelo Branco and Santarém); and at least three a day to Braga via Viseu and Porto.

The Estrela Mountain Dog
The great shaggy cão da Serra da Estrela is a breed perfectly suited to its mountain environment. It's strong, fierce (thanks to wolf ancestry) and able to endure the cold. Though they're not all long-haired, they're all pretty big – an adult can weigh up to 50 kg. Traditionally used by farmers to protect their flocks from wild animals, the breed was, until recently, in danger of dying out. Now they're popular enough to have their own breeding kennel (a few km south of Gouveia off the N232) where the pedigree is preserved. ∎

Joalto (☎ 21 19 76) runs three buses a day to Porto and Braga (plus one express service); two to Lisbon via Covilhã and Castelo Branco; four to Aveiro via Viseu; and two to Manteigas.

Train Guarda is served by two lines from Lisbon. On the Beira Alta line, via Coimbra, there are five trains daily, taking five hours; change at Pampilhosa for Porto. There are three services daily (taking an hour longer) on the Beira Baixa line, via Castelo Branco and Santarém, though you must change at Covilhã (and at Entroncamento for Porto).

There are regular shuttle buses between the train station and the bus terminal, with a stop at Rua Marquês de Pombal.

The daily Paris-Lisbon *Rápido Sud-Expresso* train (via Irún and Vilar Formoso) stops at Guarda at 7.24 am en route to Lisbon and 11.13 pm the other way. There are also four local trains daily to/from the border town of Vilar Formoso, taking an hour.

GOUVEIA

On the north-west edge of the Parque Natural da Serra da Estrela, five km off the N17 between Coimbra and Celorico da Beira, this small, dozy mountain town has little to offer beyond a beautifully manicured children's park. But, with rural surroundings and dreamy views of hills and meadows, at least you feel you're in the country, and it's got enough accommodation and restaurants (and

reasonable transport) to serve as a base for exploring this side of the Parque Natural da Serra da Estrela.

Orientation

The town centre, Praça de São Pedro, is at the junction of five streets. One, Avenida 25 de Abril, climbs north-east to the câmara municipal (town hall) and on to the turismo. South of the praça, Avenida Bombeiros Voluntários de Gouveia passes the park information office and the mercado municipal.

Long-distance buses stop in the praça. Local buses have a terminal a few minutes walk south-west; to reach the town centre, cross the bridge over the Ribeira de Gouveia and follow Rua Cardeal Mendes Belo to the right. The train station is 14 km north, near Ribamondego.

Information

The turismo (☎ 421 85) is temporarily, and inconveniently, located on the north-east edge of town, in a tiny lodge in the Jardim Lopes de Costa. It's open daily except Sundays, from 9.30 am to 12.30 pm and 2.30 to 6 pm. It's currently of little use except for accommodation information and a town map.

The Parque Natural da Serra da Estrela information office (☎ 424 11) is in the 16th-century Casa da Torre at Avenida Bombeiros Voluntários de Gouveia 8. It's open weekdays only from 9 am to 12.30 pm and 2 to 5 pm. The staff try their best, though their English is limited. The head office of ADRUSE (☎ 49 11 23; fax 402 50) which, among other things, organises rural accommodation and supports local handicrafts, is at Largo do Mercado.

The telephone code for the Gouveia area is ☎ 038.

Parque Infantil

This enchanting children's park above the town hall has clusters of swings and seesaws surrounded by wisteria and sculpted hedgerows – it's a showcase of topiary skills as well as a delight for kids and picnicking adults. It got a 10-out-of-10 vote from our toddler.

Abel Manta Museu de Arte Moderna

Gouveia's most famous son, Abel Manta (1888-1982), was an accomplished painter whose works now fill the elegant former manor house of the counts of Vinhós in Rua Direita (off Praça de São Pedro). Also on display are paintings by better known 20th-century painters including Vieira da Silva. The museum is open daily, except Mondays, from 10 am to 12.30 pm and 2 to 5 pm (free admission).

Don't confuse this museum with a gallery next to the town hall, which is called Espaço João Abel Manta. It's named after the painter's son and features temporary exhibitions.

Museu Arqueologia e Etnográfico

Behind the impressive câmara municipal (a former Jesuit college) is this museum with a charming, small miscellany of Roman remains and medieval sculpted stones. It's open Mondays and Thursdays only, from 9.30 am to 12.30 pm and 2 to 5.30 pm (free admission).

Places to Stay

Camping The municipal *Parque Curral do Negro* camping ground (☎ 49 10 08) is three km east of Gouveia on the road to Folgosinho (heading uphill, turn right after the câmara municipal and right again).

Quinta das Cegonhas (☎ & fax 458 86) is a fine rural camping ground with a swimming pool and washing facilities in the grounds of an old quinta which its Dutch owners are slowly restoring. It's six km north-east of Gouveia, between the villages of Nabais and Melo.

Private Rooms The turismo has details of a couple of private places in town which cost about 4000$00 a double.

Pensões & Residencials *Pensão Estrela do Parque* (☎ 421 71), at Rua da República 36 (the main road into Praça de São Pedro

from the west), has fine Gothic stone windows in its inner yard and less glamourous doubles (with bath and breakfast) for 5500$00.

Hotels The modern *Hotel de Gouveia* (☎ 49 10 10; fax 413 70) is at Avenida 1 de Maio (off Rua da República). Its dull doubles are 8500$00.

Turihab There's far more atmosphere in several Turihab options, including *Casa da Rainha* (☎ 421 32; Lisbon fax 01-387 7314) at Rua Direita 74. It's a grand old mansion with six apartments for two to six people; summer prices range from 8500$00 to 22,000$00. The turismo and ADRUSE have details of other places.

Places to Eat

Standard fare for standard prices is available at *Pensão Estrela do Parque*'s restaurant (☎ 421 71) at Rua da República 36. Or check out *Restaurante O Jardim* (☎ 404 27), just below Jardim Lopes de Costa at Rua do Alto Concelho 5, which has an 1800$00 tourist menu and a good cabrito assado (roast kid) for under 1000$00.

The town's best restaurant is probably *O Júlio* (☎ 421 42), at Travessa do Loureiro 1 (an alley just before the market). It's a comfortable place with Abel Manta prints on the walls and a large menu of regional specialities, including cabrito a serrana (mountain kid) and trutas do Mondego (Rio Mondego trout). Prices start at about 1000$00.

Self-caterers will find the mercado municipal, which is off Avenida Bombeiros Voluntários de Gouveia, at its best and biggest every Thursday. You can get good regional cheeses including queijo de ovelha (sheep's milk cheese) here. Or try the tiny, well-stocked grocery store called Cabaz Beirão; it's on Rua da Cadeia Velha.

Getting There & Away

Bus There are four buses daily to Seia and to Guarda, and two to Viseu and Coimbra

BEIRAS

(one of which, an express service to Coimbra, continues to Lisbon).

Train Gouveia is 'on' the northern Lisbon to Guarda line (the station is 14 km from town); five trains daily include an evening service originating in Coimbra. There's no bus connection to/from the station; taxis charge around 2000$00.

SEIA

Once a simple mountain village, Seia is now a popular stop for weekend tourists seeking an easy taste of the serra. It's just a couple of km from the Coimbra-to-Guarda N17 road and has some well-stocked shops and comfortable accommodation. Use it as a base for exploring the Parque Natural da Serra da Estrela (there's a park information office here) or simply as a convenient source of souvenirs.

Orientation & Information

The central Praça da República (where buses stop) is an attractive square bordered by handsome mansions and shops. Restaurants and pensões are all within walking distance of this square. The small, friendly park office (☎ 255 06; fax 256 06) at No 28 has literature and information on the park. It's open weekdays only, from 9 am to 12.30 pm and 2 to 5 pm.

The telephone code for Seia is ☎ 038.

Places to Stay

The cheapest place around is *Café Tamanquinhas* (☎ 226 17), 1.5 km down towards the N17, with basic doubles for around 3000$00. A nicer option right in the town centre is *Café Residencial Serra da Estrela* (☎ 255 73; fax 251 35), at Rua Dr Simões Pereira, which has doubles (including breakfast) for about 6000$00. A more up-market choice is *Hotel Camelo* (☎ 225 55), at Rua 1 de Maio, where you'll pay at least 7000$00 a double.

Places to Eat

Several restaurants around Praça da República offer tempting regional specialities, including *Snack Bar O Favo* (☎ 31 16 33), at Esplanada Combatentes de Grande Guerra 6, with a downstairs restaurant with dishes from 800$00.

For takeaway serra cheeses, the Casa do Pastor grocery store, at Rua da República 56, has one of the best selections, including the more unusual queijo Torre, a cheese made from a mixture of cow's and sheep's milk.

Getting There & Away

There are four buses daily from Gouveia and two to five daily from Covilhã via Guarda (continuing to Coimbra). Two to three buses daily also run to/from Lisbon (via Coimbra).

The Rede Expressos ticket office is at Rua da República 52.

SABUGUEIRO

Sabugueiro, 11 km above Seia on the N339 to Torre, is a typical Serra da Estrela mountain village, with chickens on the paths and sturdy mountain farmer-shepherd families living in slate-roofed houses. But it's the highest village in Portugal (1050m) and has therefore become a standard tourist magnet.

Pensões and souvenir shops are sprouting along the highway, and the village increasingly survives on tourist money. In fact, this is not a bad place to pick up Serra da Estrela cheese, local smoked ham, rye bread, juniper-berry firewater or fleecy slippers or vests of Serra sheep's wool. Aside from a brief wander into the older part of the village there's little else to do but snack and move on. Should you want to stay, accommodation is pricey in winter but good value in summer, and the village is quiet on weekdays.

Information

SCM or Ski Clube de Montanha (☎ & fax 038-31 11 02; mobile ☎ 0936-75 72 37; Seia ☎ 038-244 59) rents skis in winter and mountain bikes and canoes in summer. It's on the highway beside Estalagem O Abrigo da Montanha.

Places to Stay & Eat

Our choice, the small, friendly *Casa do Serrinho* (☎ 038-243 04), just off the highway on Largo Nossa Senhora da Fátima, has four rooms and a communal kitchen-dining area above a shop and café; a double is 4000$00 (6000$00 in winter). In a modern building on the highway, *Estalagem O Abrigo da Montanha* (☎ & fax 038-252 62) has well-equipped doubles for 5000$00 (10,000$00 in winter) with breakfast, and a good restaurant. Down the road, above a large shop, *Residencial Monte Estrela* (☎ 038-229 84) has doubles with breakfast for 5000$00.

Getting There & Away

A single bus goes to Sabugueiro from Seia each week. It departs from Seia on Wednesdays at 12.45 pm and returns from Sabugueiro the next day at 8 am.

MANTEIGAS
• pop 4000 • postcode 6260 • area code ☎ 075

Manteigas is the best possible base for exploring the Serra da Estrela – right in the middle of the parque natural, with a good park information office, adequate supplies, pretty decent food and comfortable accommodation for such a remote place.

Set in a deep valley at the 700m-high confluence of the Rio Zêzere and several of its tributaries (and just three km as the crow flies from the Rio Mondego as well), it's also one of the most picturesque towns in the range. Though devoid of interesting architecture, this typical whitewashed mountain town is collectively pretty. All around are dizzyingly steep, terraced hillsides clad in pine and dotted with rugged stone casais (huts), beehives and little meadows. The closest big attraction is the cathedral-like Vale do Zêzere – the glacial valley of the Zêzere, carpeted with small fields and ascending straight as an arrow for eight km south-west of town to the foot of Torre.

There has been a settlement here since at least Moorish times – perhaps because of the hot springs around which the nearby spa of Caldas de Manteigas has grown. Its name ('butter') presumably refers to good local dairy products. The main sources of work for local people are three textile mills, and forestry jobs.

Orientation

From Seia or Gouveia you approach Manteigas down a near-vertical switchback road that takes 17 km to cover just three km across the landscape. The town hardly seems to have a centre in any sense, though a good reference point is the turismo, which is also where the bus from Guarda sets you down.

Information

The turismo (☎ 98 11 29), on Rua Dr Esteves de Carvalho near the GALP petrol station, is open Tuesday to Friday from 9.30 am to noon and 2 pm to 6 pm, and Saturdays to 8 pm. It's closed on Sundays and – annoyingly – on Mondays. In any case it's not really very useful.

Go instead to the Parque Natural da Serra da Estrela office (☎ 98 23 82; fax 98 23 84) at Rua 1 de Maio 2, a three-minute walk from the turismo, just beyond the petrol station. Little English is spoken, but they try hard. Among much reading matter, mostly in Portuguese, are the excellent *Discovering the Region of the Serra da Estrela* booklet and *Carta Turística: Parque Natural da Serra da Estrela* map. There are several banks with exchange counters along the main street, Rua 1 de Maio (turn left as you approach the park office).

Caldas de Manteigas

Two km south of Manteigas itself is this tidy spa centre. It's open from May through October with a spa hotel, heated pool and two springs at 19° C and 42° C – helpful, it's said, for rheumatic, respiratory and skin ailments. Six km east of the spa, on a rough track, is **Poço do Inferno** (Hell's Well), a waterfall on the little Ribeira de Leandres.

Places to Stay

Camping Five km up the switchback road to Seia, and about five km further up a rough track, is the park-run camping site of *Covão da Ponte,* at 960m on the lush banks of the Rio Mondego. There are no facilities, and for the moment it's free. Also here is one of the park's two basic casas de abrigo or shelters (see the section on the Parque Natural da

BEIRAS

Serra da Estrela), which can be booked at the park office in Manteigas. There is no public transport.

Another free camp site, set in an amphitheatre of peaks – a day's walk or a short drive up the Vale do Zêzere – is *Covão da Ametade*, which is open in summer only. It has picnic tables, a small snack bar and lots of flat places among the birch trees, but nothing else. Unfortunately it's only a short walk from the road and very popular with picnickers and school groups, though you'd have it to yourself on a spring or autumn weekday. Shepherds say it's also plagued with mosquitoes and midges in summer.

The *Parque de Campismo de Valhelhas* (☎ 075-481 60) is about 18 km east of Manteigas on the road to Belmonte. From Manteigas, hitch or take any Guarda or Belmonte bus (see Getting Around).

Private Rooms Just below (east of) the turismo, the Restaurante Santa Luzia (☎ 982 83) advertises dormidas (rooms).

Pensões & Residencials On Rua 1 de Maio (go left at the park office), at No 15, is *Pensão Serradalto* (☎ 98 11 51), which has adequate doubles for 5500$00 (with bath) or 4500$00 (without). On the road above this (bear right at the park office), *Residencial Estrela* (☎ 98 12 88), at Rua Dr Sobral 5 by a church, has more comfortable doubles with bath for 6500$00 (7500$00 in the winter high season), and a good restaurant. Breakfast is included at both places.

Turihab At last, here's a cheap, central and recommendable Turihab place (Turismo Rural in this case): *Casa de São Roque* (☎ 98 11 25, ☎ 98 14 76) at Rua de Santo António 67 (first left beyond Pensão Serradalto). It has big, nicely furnished doubles with bath for 5000$00 (4500$00 for stays longer than one night). Breakfast is served in an elegant dining room, and there is an outdoor patio with mountain views.

Pousadas The deluxe but low-key *Pousada de São Lourenço* (☎ 98 24 50; fax 98 24 53) is 13 km above town at the highest of the hairpin bends, on a 1285m ridge with stupendous views up the Vale do Zêzere, down to Manteigas and, on a clear day, east into Spain. High-season doubles are 14,500$00.

Places to Eat
Boasting a member of the Academie de Gastronomie Brillat-Savarin, the restaurant at *Residencial Estrela* aspires to higher standards (and prices) than elsewhere in town. But *Pensão Serradalto's* restaurant also serves good meals, and for reasonable prices, as does *Café-Restaurante A Cascata* (☎ 98 21 39) at Rua 1 de Maio 10. Trutas de Mondego (trout from the Rio Mondego), the local speciality, is cheapest (900$00) at A Cascata.

Things to Buy
For camping gas and other supplies go to the Matos, Martins & Lopes shop (☎ 98 11 31), on Rua 1 de Maio opposite Pensão Serradalto.

Getting There & Away
From Guarda, Joalto buses leave for the 40-km trip to Manteigas at around 11 am and 5 pm, and return from Manteigas at about 7 am and 1 pm. In Covilhã, change from a Joalto Guarda-bound bus at Vale Formoso to a Guarda-Manteigas or Belmonte-Manteigas bus (connections three times a day). During school term there is also one direct Covilhã-Manteigas bus. A ticket for Guarda or Covilhã is 480$00.

Buses to Guarda and to Belmonte (two a day to each) pass near the Valhelhas camping ground.

SORTELHA
• pop 550 • postcode 6320 • area code ☎ 071
Sortelha is the oldest of a string of rock fortresses guarding the frontier east of Guarda and Covilhã. A 12th-century walled village, with Arab origins and built into a hillside's rocky boulders, it's also one of the most stunning. It's less immediately dramatic and less well known than Monsanto – its hilltop site is practically hidden from the

newer village on the road below – but it boasts similarly grand views over the surrounding wild and barren landscape and there is some fantastic accommodation.

Tourism is rapidly changing the scene: there are already a number of tourist-geared restaurants and when we were there power and telephone cables were being put underground, while at the top of the village several old houses were being remodelled into a hotel to cater to the mostly Portuguese and Spanish visitors. But it remains wonderfully quiet midweek, with villagers returning home on their donkeys at dusk, clattering up the steep cobbled alleys and disappearing into humble granite cottages.

Orientation & Information
The newer part of Sortelha, below the medieval hilltop fortress, borders the Santo Amaro to Sabugal road. Here you'll find a restaurant and several Turihab properties. The fortress itself is a 10-minute walk up a rough road.

Old Village
The main entrance to the old fortified village is through a grand Gothic gateway. From the square inside, a lane leads up to the heart of the village, where there is a pelourinho (pillory) in front of the remains of an old tower to the left and the parish church to the right.

Higher still is the bell tower. Climb right up to the bells to look over the entire village, or tackle the ramparts around the village (but beware of some precarious drops). You can reach the walls quickest by turning immediately right after entering the village and following the steep Rua da Fontinha to the top.

Special Events
The big bash of the year is a *festa* of folk dancing and merry-making on 15 August. In some years there are bullfights too, with bulls running through the streets.

Places to Stay
Sortelha has several extraordinary Turihab

properties as well as private accommodation, including some of the most atmospheric bargains in the Beiras.

On the road below the old village is *Casa da Cerca* (☎ 681 13; fax 685 00), a handsome 17th-century mansion with doubles (including bath, air-con and breakfast) for 10,000$00, and an apartment that sleeps four in the adjacent *Casa do Pateo* cottage for 14,000$00. The same owners have a cottage inside the walls, *Casa da Vila*, with room for eight, though two can rent it for the half-price deal of 10,000$00. Also inside the walls is *Casa Arabe* (☎ 682 76, ☎ 681 29), a cosy one-bedroom cottage which costs 6000$00. Similarly priced is *Casa do Palheiro* (☎ 681 82). All have lashings of medieval atmosphere (including immense stone walls and less than perfect heating), but the most remarkable place is *Casa do Vento Que Soa* (☎ 681 82), a castle-like, four-bedroom house built into the rocks on Rua da Fontainha – a dream bargain for 6000$00 (including logs for the massive fire). Sadly, renovations are on the cards, so prices (and heat) may increase and atmosphere diminish.

Places to Eat
On the main road, *Restaurante Bar O Celta* (☎ 682 91) doesn't hold a candle in ambience to the two restaurants inside the walls, but it does serve a hearty ensopada de javali (wild boar stew) for 2200$00.

Inside the village walls, the *Restaurante-Grill Dom Sancho* (☎ 682 67) is an up-market, oddly out-of-place establishment with bar and log fire downstairs and a pricey restaurant upstairs (closed on Tuesdays). More in keeping with the character of the village is *Restaurante Típico Alboroque* (☎ 681 29, ☎ 682 83), on Rua Dá-Mesquita beyond the church, with all the trappings of a medieval inn and a menu to match (lots of wild boar and kid). It's closed on Mondays. The *As Boas Vindas*, a bar just below the Restaurante Típico Alboroque, has satellite TV. It's open until midnight and draws a steady stream of visitors on weekends and holidays.

BEIRAS

Things to Buy

The simplest souvenirs are reed basket trinkets made and sold by several old dears who hang out around the village entrance. More enticing antiques – from old keys and crockery to rural furniture and carved wooden bedsteads – can be found at a shop near the pillory square, as well as at Casa da Cerca.

Getting There & Away

It's almost impossible to get here easily by public transport: there's a once-a-day bus service to/from Sabugal but it only runs regularly during school term.

Probably your best option is to take a Lisbon to Guarda train (three a day, with a change at Covilhã) to Belmonte-Manteigas station, 12 km to the north-west, and then call the local taxi service (☎ 681 82) owned by Dona Maria Conceição, who manages two of the Turihab properties (but speaks little English). The charge will be around 2000$00.

Getting Around

The Estrela-Raia Clube de Turismo (Lisbon ☎ 01-726 6907; fax 01-726 6175) has its eye on Sortelha: as well as operating the Restaurante-Grill Dom Sancho and funding the new hotel in the village, it also organises mountain-biking, jeep and horse-riding trips in the region. These might be available from the new hotel; it's worth asking.

The Beira Baixa

COVILHÃ

• *pop 22,000* • *postcode 6200* • *area code* ☎ *075*

This dour, polluted university town on the southern edge of the parque natural is of minor interest in itself, but it's the closest urban centre to the heart of the Serra da Estrela. With shops, some modestly priced pensões and restaurants, and a sometimes-helpful turismo, it makes a good base for exploring the mountains.

Covilhã's only historical claim to fame is as the birthplace of one Pêro de Covilhã, a young Arabic-speaking Portuguese who went east in search of spice markets, and perhaps to find the legendary Christian priest-king Prester John, on behalf of Dom João II. Disguised as a Muslim trader, he journeyed through Egypt, India and even to the holy cities of Mecca and Medina. He was finally detained by a Coptic Christian king in what is now Ethiopia, where he married and lived out his days.

His is the statue in the town's main square, beside a huge granite map showing his travels.

Orientation

Covilhã seems pinned to the side of the Serra da Estrela foothills. Long-distance buses arrive at one of several stations around Largo das Forças Armadas, just below the town's centre, Praça do Município.

The train station, however, is far below the centre, and a climb up will give you a feel for how steeply pitched things are. From the station, walk 150m up to the nearest roundabout, head right (north) on Rua Mateus Fernandes for 100m to Ramal da Estação, then turn left. This becomes a combination path and stairway up to the centre, an awful climb of something like a km. Alternatively, catch bus No 2 (Rodrigo) from the roundabout (it runs every 20-30 minutes and the fare is 120$00) to the police station, which is just up Rua António Augusto de Aguiar from Praça do Município. Going the other way, the bus stand at the roundabout near the station is called Tribunal. Don't get lost: the streets are poorly marked.

Information

Service at the regional tourist office, the Região de Turismo da Serra da Estrela (☎ 32 21 70; fax 31 33 64) on Praça do Município, ranges from excellent to absolutely hopeless. It's open daily, except Sundays, from 9 am to noon and 2 to 8 pm (to 6 pm in winter). There is no municipal turismo.

Several banks on and near Praça do Município have exchange desks and Multibanco ATMs. The post office is across the square from the turismo.

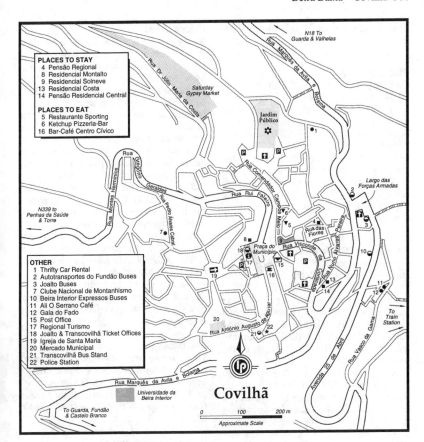

PLACES TO STAY
4 Pensão Regional
8 Residencial Montalto
9 Residencial Solneve
13 Residencial Costa
14 Pensão Residencial Central

PLACES TO EAT
5 Restaurante Sporting
6 Ketchup Pizzeria-Bar
16 Bar-Café Centro Cívico

OTHER
1 Thrifty Car Rental
2 Autotransportes do Fundão Buses
3 Joalto Buses
7 Clube Nacional de Montanhismo
10 Beira Interior Expressos Buses
11 Ali O Serrano Café
12 Gala do Fado
15 Post Office
17 Regional Turismo
18 Joalto & Transcovilhã Ticket Offices
19 Igreja de Santa Maria
20 Mercado Municipal
21 Transcovilhã Bus Stand
22 Police Station

Covilhã

0   100   200 m
Approximate Scale

The Clube Nacional de Montanhismo (☎ 32 33 64; fax 31 35 14), upstairs at Rua Pedro Álvares Cabral 5, is a totally noncommercial, Covilhã-based club that organises regular outings, mainly walking and mountaineering, occasionally horse riding (plus bridge and an annual auto rally; its cycling 'department' was dormant when we visited). It also runs a summer-only camping ground at Penhas da Saúde, and casas de abrigo at Penhas da Saúde and Torre. The lack of English spoken by staff is offset by great enthusiasm, and the club's events are open to all. Call by for a copy of its calendar, on weekdays from 10 am to 5 pm. The club also runs its own Candelas Café (and bar) there in the evenings.

The regional university, the Universidade da Beira Interior, is south of the centre on Rua Marquês da Avila e Bolama.

Things to See

There isn't much to look at, although the narrow, wiggly streets west of Praça do Município have a plain, quiet charm. In the midst of them is the azulejo-fronted **Igreja de Santa Maria**.

A big Gypsy market sprawls across the

BEIRAS

plaza beside Rua Dr Júlio Maria da Costa every Saturday morning.

Places to Stay

Camping The year-round *Pião Camping* (☎ 31 43 12), run by the Clube de Campismo e Caravanismo de Covilhã, is about five km up the twisting N339 towards Penhas da Saúde. Typical rates are 330$00 per person, 330$00 to 420$00 per tent, 250$00 per car, and 100$00 for a shower. There are other camping sites further into the park at Penhas da Saúde and Covão da Ametade and there is the summer-only *Valhelas* municipal site (☎ 075-481 60) about 20 km north of Covilhã.

Pensões & Residencials The *Pensão Residencial Central* (☎ 32 27 27), run by a quirky old dear at Rua Nuno Álvares Pereira 14, has good-value doubles for 3500$00 (with shower) and 4000$00 (with shower and loo). Next door at No 16, the *Residencial Costa* (☎ 32 20 50) has huge, mouldy doubles with shower for 4000$00. Both have splendid views to the east, but noise on the west (street) side.

A very central, well-run place is *Residencial Solneve* (☎ 32 30 01; fax 31 54 97), at Rua Visconde da Coriscada 126. It's really a hotel, with a good restaurant, a parking garage (worth its weight in gold in this congested town) and comfortable doubles with TV and bath for 5500$00 (6500$00 on weekends and 7500$00 in winter), including breakfast. Another good place is *Residencial Montalto* (☎ 32 76 09; fax 31 54 24), at Praça do Município 1, where similar doubles are 5000$00. The quiet *Pensão Regional*, at Rua das Flores 4, has rooms for 3500$00/ 5000$00 (without bath) and 4000$00/ 6000$00 (with). It also has a good restaurant downstairs.

Turihab The nearest Turihab properties are well south of Covilhã in Fundão and Sortelha. The regional turismo can help you book one.

Places to Eat

Meaty *Restaurante Solneve* (☎ 32 30 01) is in the basement of the residencial of the same name. Around the corner on Rua Comendador Mendes Veiga is a better deal, *Restaurante Sporting* (☎ 241 84). Open daily from noon to 3 pm and 7 to 10 pm, it has two or three specials for 700$00, plus other meat and fish plates for under 1200$00. *Restaurante Regional*, below the pensão of the same name, has a nice mixed menu of meaty standards at 900$00 to 1400$00 per course, plus burgers and omelettes.

The name of the *Ketchup Pizzeria-Bar*, Rua Comendador Campos Melo 42, speaks for itself: cheap, mediocre pizza, pasta, salads, burgers and sandwiches, with snail's-pace service. You'll find a cheerier setting at *Bar-Café Centro Cívico*, a student hang-out in front of the Caixa Geral de Depósitos bank on Praça do Município.

Self-caterers will find fruit and vegetables on most mornings at the mercado municipal (town market) on Rua António Augusto de Aguiar.

Entertainment

There are two tiny casas de fado in the lower reaches of town, where the music doesn't begin till 10 pm or so: *Ali O Serrano Café* (☎ 32 36 11), at Rua Vasco da Gama 61, and *Gala do Fado* (☎ 251 93), next door at No 59.

Getting There & Away

Covilhã has a small airport, but it has no scheduled flights.

Bus Three small bus ticket offices cluster around Largo das Forças Armadas: Beira Interior Expressos (☎ 249 14) at Rua Vasco da Gama 27, Joalto (☎ 32 35 13) at Rua Vasco da Gama 3, and Autotransportes do Fundão in the station on Rua Marquês da Avila e Bolama. Joalto also has a ticket office (express coaches only) beside the turismo on Praça do Município; it's open weekdays from 8.45 am to 12.30 pm and 2 to 6.45 pm, and Saturdays from 8.30 am to 1 pm.

Beira Interior runs four or five express

coaches a day to/from Coimbra (1300$00), Porto (1350$00) and Lisbon (1400$00); Joalto also has connections, though fewer and slower. Joalto is the one for Guarda (650$00) and Aveiro, with two to five buses a day to each. Autotransportes do Fundão operates mainly in the Covilhã area, but also has twice-daily connections to Seia via Unhais da Serra at the south end of the parque natural.

Twice a day on weekends in July-August, local Transcovilhã buses climb to Penhas da Saúde and Nave Santo António. For schedules of this and local services, go to the office Transcovilhã shares with Joalto, beside the turismo.

Train Two intercidade trains run to/from Lisbon (4½ hours) with connections to Porto. There is no easy train link from Coimbra. The regional turismo has train timetables posted in the window.

Car Thrifty Car Rental (☎ 31 34 44) is north of the town centre, at Rua Conde de Covilhã 43.

PENHAS DA SAÚDE

Penhas da Saúde isn't a town at all, but the site of an old high-altitude tuberculosis sanatorium which burned down some years ago. It's now a weather-beaten collection of prefab ski chalets and other facilities for mountain-heads at the foot of the Barragem do Viriato dam, 10 km up the N339 from Covilhã.

Turistrela (☎ 249 33 in Covilhã; also with an office in the Hotel Serra da Estrela) operates a winter-sports centre here which rents out skis, sleds, snowboards and other gear. It also has skiing lessons and a health club with sauna, Turkish bath and jacuzzi (2000$00 an hour). It also has facilities at Torre.

Supplies are limited; if you're going walking in the mountains, buy what you need down in Covilhã.

Places to Stay & Eat

Facilities include the Quality Inn *Hotel Serra da Estrela* (☎ 075-31 38 09; fax 075-32 37

89), which is built on the site of the old sanatorium; the *Pensão O Pastor* (☎ 075-32 38 10; fax 075-31 40 35); and two cafés.

Also here is the good *Pousada de Juventude das Penhas da Saúde* (☎ 075-253 75), an HI/YHA youth hostel with facilities for meals (theirs or do-it-yourself) and dormitory accommodation. The Clube Nacional de Montanhismo (see the Covilhã Information section) runs a casa de abrigo here – four rooms with six beds each, plus kitchen and common room – plus a spartan camping ground (☎ 075-32 23 82), open from June through September (it also operates the *Casa Abrigo dos Covões de Louriga* near Torre).

Getting There & Away

In July and August, local buses come up twice a day (on weekends only) to Penhas da Saúde, and on to Nave de Santo António, from the stand beside the police station in Covilhã. The timetable is posted at an office to the right of the Covilhã turismo. Otherwise you'll have to take a taxi (expensive), hitch (fairly safe and easy), cycle or walk. Except for the ever-expanding views across the flatlands to the east, this looks like a miserable climb on foot from Covilhã, much of it along the road.

MONSANTO

• *pop 2100* • *postcode 6090* • *area code* ☎ *077*

Once the most remote and least visited of Portugal's medieval fortress villages, Monsanto is now well on the tourist map, and making the most of its reputation as (allegedly) the oldest settlement in the country. Things have changed rapidly in recent years: Portuguese 'outsiders' from as far afield as Lisbon have bought up many of the abandoned houses and flocks of tourists now arrive here daily. But despite the inevitable gentrification (fancy street lighting, souvenir shops and even a pousada), this fortified rock settlement is still stunning.

Orientation & Information

Monsanto is so small all you have to do is follow the path uphill to reach the castle. Signs en route point to the *gruta* (a cavern

BEIRAS

where local men used to drink). The castle is a short climb above this.

Village

Near the entrance to the village, the houses are surprisingly grand, some even sporting Manueline doorways and stone crests. Since Monsanto won an award in 1939 for 'the most traditional village in Portugal', building restrictions have largely put a stop to creeping cement modernisation.

As the path winds upwards, cottages, chicken coops and animal sheds are built right in among the boulders of the rugged granite hill. Stone crosses appear at every turn as the narrow lane wriggles up to the ruins of the once-massive castle.

Castelo

There was probably some kind of fortress here even before the time of the Romans, but after Dom Sancho I booted out the Moors in the 12th century it became more substantial. Dom Dinis refortified it but after centuries of attacks from across the border it finally fell into ruin. Now it's a strikingly beautiful site full of lizards and wildflowers.

Just below the entrance is a cement square which is used for folk dances at festival time. To the right is a ruined Renaissance church. and bell tower and five stone tombs carved into the rock.

Views from the castle's 800m eyrie are tremendous, including Spain to the east and the Barragem da Idanha lake to the southwest. But the sight of the village below, fading into the rock, is even more striking, an insight into medieval Portugal at its toughest and truest.

Special Events

Monsanto celebrates a unique festival on 3 May, the Festa das Cruzes. This commemorates a medieval siege that failed thanks to a clever trick by the starving villagers: they threw their last calf over the walls, so disheartening their attackers (who thought the villagers were being starved into submission) that the siege was called off. These days, young girls throw baskets of flowers instead, after which there's dancing and singing under the castle walls.

Places to Stay

At the time of writing, there was only one place to stay in the village, the *Pousada de Monsanto* (☎ 344 71; fax 344 81), a simple but comfortable 10-room inn near the entrance where doubles cost 14,500$00.

Surprisingly, there don't seem to be any private rooms for rent but you could ask at the Café Snack Bar, 1.5 km down the hill in Relva about possibilities there.

Places to Eat

The *Café Monsantinho* (☎ 321 51), near the entrance, on Rua de Nossa Senhora do Castelo, serves drinks and snacks, while just outside the village walls is *Café O Granito*, which serves adequate food. Some souvenir shops sell delicious home-made honey cakes, an energy boost as you make your way up to the castle.

Getting There & Away

There are only one or two buses daily between Castelo Branco and Monsanto, making a day trip tricky. During school time, there's also a bus between Penamacor (24 km to the north) and Relva (the village 1.5 km below Monsanto).

CASTELO BRANCO
• *pop 25,000* • *postcode 6000* • *area code ☎ 072*

The provincial capital of Beira Baixa is pretty and prosperous but amazingly dull. Its excuse is that proximity to the frontier (just 20 km south) made it the target of so many attacks over the centuries – including an especially vicious one by the French in 1807 – that few historic monuments remain.

The city's real value for travellers is as a base for visiting the spectacular fortress village of Monsanto (48 km to the northeast). While you're here, have a peek at the whimsical gardens of the bishop's palace.

Orientation & Information

It's easy enough to get your bearings: turn right out of the bus station and follow Rua

BETHUNE CARMICHAEL

JULIA WILKINSON

BETHUNE CARMICHAEL

JULIA WILKINSON

BETHUNE CARMICHAEL

JULIA WILKINSON

BETHUNE CARMICHAEL

Windows

JULIA WILKINSON

JULIA WILKINSON

The Beiras
Top: Aveiro
Bottom: Praia de Mira

do Saibreiro to the central Alameda da Liberdade. The train station is half a km south of the Alameda, at the far end of Avenida Nuno Álvares. In a park adjacent to the Alameda is the turismo (☎ 210 02), which is open weekdays only from 9 am to 12.30 pm and 2 to 5.30 pm.

The remains of the town's castle are roughly half a km west of here, and the bishop's palace is the same distance to the north.

Jardim do Antigo Palácio Episcopal

The Palácio (or Paço) Episcopal (Bishop's Palace), in the north of town on Rua Frei Bartolomeu da Costa, is a sober 18th-century affair housing the Tavares Proença Museu Regional, which is currently closed for long-term renovations. But outside are formal gardens that are a delightfully lively baroque creation of little granite statues among clipped box hedges and ornamental pools. The statues represent all manner of themes and personalities, ranging from naked cherubic zodiac figures to a line-up of the kings of Portugal. Note the two who are deliberately smaller than the others – the Spanish imposters, Felipe I and II.

The gardens are open daily from 9 am to 7 pm.

Castelo

There's little left of the castle, which was originally built by the Knights Templar in the 13th century and extended by Dom Dinis. But the Miradouro de São Gens garden, which has taken the place of the walls, providing extensive views over the town and surrounding countryside, is a marvellous spot for a picnic. The old lanes leading back down to the centre are very picturesque.

Places to Stay

Camping The municipal camping ground (☎ 216 15) is three km to the north of Castelo Branco, just off the N18 to Covilhã. It's spartan and cheap.

Private Rooms The turismo has details of a few private quartos costing about 3500$00 a double.

Pensões & Residenciais The best deal in town is probably *Pensão Martinho* (☎ 217 06), right in the centre at Alameda da Liberdade 41, with doubles for around 4000$00. Alternatively, there's the more comfortable *Residencial Arraiana* (☎ 216 34), at Avenida 1 de Maio, where doubles are around 6000$00.

Places to Eat

There's not a lot to get excited about food-wise. You'll find a reasonable selection of restaurants around Alameda da Liberdade. Or pick up your own supplies from the market on Avenida 1 de Maio.

Getting There & Away

Bus At least three Rede Expressos buses daily travel to Braga (via Covilhã, Guarda, Viseu and Porto) and two to Coimbra. There are around two buses daily between Guarda and Lisbon (via Covilhã) with a stop in Castelo Branco.

Train Castelo Branco is on the Lisbon to Guarda line, with six trains daily going to Lisbon and seven to Covilhã (where you must change for Guarda).

BEIRAS

The Douro

The Douro province is dominated by Portugal's second-largest city, Porto, and by its best known river, the Douro. Rising in Spain, the Rio Douro ('River of Gold') defines the Spain-Portugal border from just north of Miranda do Douro (in Trás-os-Montes) down to Barca de Alva, and then runs for about 200 km across Portugal to Porto. It's in the area from the Spanish border to Peso da Régua, known as the Alto Douro, that the famous port-wine grapes are grown on steep terraced hillsides of schist that trap the region's intense summer heat.

In the early days of the port-wine trade the Douro region, especially the mountain-ringed valley itself, was rough and wild. Travellers were at the mercy of bandits, and accommodation was so primitive that British port-wine traders searching for new sources had to sleep 'on ye tables for reason of ye insects'.

Even the journey to Porto from the coastal town of Viana do Castelo (where the earliest wine traders got their start) had its perils. 'We bestrode mules with awkward straw stuf'd saddles,' wrote a young Yorkshireman, Thomas Woodmass, in 1700. 'It was our intention to stay over ye night at Villadecon [Vila do Conde] but it was not so to be, for 6 arm'd men did stop us in ye King's name, and examined our pockets, taking all we had; our guides running away at first sight of them.'

Today the Douro valley is one of Portugal's most popular tourist destinations. The river, tamed by five dams in the 1980s, is now navigable all the way to Barca de Alva, allowing passenger cruises to slip through dramatic gorges into the heart of the port-wine country. The Douro railway, which opened in 1887 and runs from Porto to Pocinho, is another fine way to travel. Although its picturesque narrow-gauge branch lines have been truncated or amputated altogether in recent years, bits remain that are well worth travelling (see Getting

HIGHLIGHTS

- the atmospheric city of Porto and its spectacular bridges
- sampling port in Vila Nova de Gaia's port-wine lodges
- Lamego and its terraced vineyards
- a ride on the narrow-gauge railway Linha de Tâmega to the handsome town of Amarante

Around under East of Peso da Régua, in this chapter).

Porto, of course, makes an excellent base for exploring this region. The beaches north and south of the city are some of the most polluted in Portugal, but Vila do Conde's fine beaches are less than an hour's train ride away. And, as far as we could discover, 'ye insects' are no more.

PORTO
• pop 325,000 • postcode 4000 • area code ☎ 02
Portugal's second-largest city, Porto is a vibrant contrast to Lisbon: whereas the capital likes to revel in its elegance, Porto is grimy, down-to-earth and hard working. This is the heart of Portugal's most important economic area, where most manufacturing and some of the largest private enterprises are based. Porto folk are proud of their work ethic, quoting an old saying, 'Coimbra sings, Braga prays, Lisbon shows off and Porto works'. The refreshingly unpretentious people of Porto, traditionally mocked by *lisboêtas* as *tripeiros* (tripe-eaters), refer to the southerners in turn as *alfacinhas* (lettuce-eaters).

Despite its go-getting populace, Porto

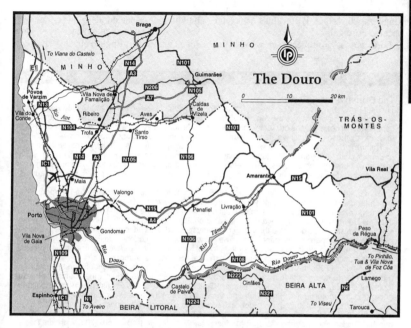

itself (only foreigners call it Oporto, which literally means 'the port') is surprisingly old-fashioned. Built on steep granite hills above the Rio Douro, its heart is a 19th-century tangle of gritty alleys and lanes tumbling down to the riverside. Spanning the river are five dramatic bridges to Porto's 'other half', Vila Nova de Gaia, which is the historic home of the port-wine lodges and Porto's biggest tourist attraction.

The city's cultural attractions are pretty thin (many of its museums seem permanently under renovation), but what it lacks in churches and monuments it makes up for in eclectic atmosphere. The riverside Ribeira district is a beguiling mix of run-down fishing quarter and tourist haunt, with chic restaurants alongside bohemian bars. The central Mercado do Bolhão (Bolhão market), a bustling, no-nonsense affair, is surrounded by smart shops. And everywhere are the leg-aching steep streets with their blend of grand old mansions and back-alley dives.

You'll need several days to soak up this atmosphere (not to mention the port wine). Porto also makes a good base for exploring the beautiful Douro valley and a host of attractive places further north in the Minho, which is easily accessible by train or bus.

History

Linguistically, Porto is the cradle of the country. In Roman times a Lusitanian settlement called Cale, on the left bank of the Douro near the river's mouth, became an important crossing point on the Lisbon to Braga road. As traffic increased, a settlement called Portus (harbour) grew on the opposite bank. Portus-Cale later became the capital of the county of Portucalia, which lay between the Minho and Douro rivers. This was the county given to Henri of Burgundy on his marriage to the daughter of the King of León in 1095. From here his son Afonso Henriques launched the Reconquista against the Moors, finally establishing an independent kingdom which took Portucalia's name and became Portugal.

Porto's own prominence grew with the building of a cathedral in 1111, and was sealed with later royal favours: here Dom João I married his English queen, Philippa of

The British, Port & Porto

The first British traders to set up shop in Porto in the 13th century weren't even aware they were sitting on a gold mine of port. It was the region's olive oil, fruit and cork they were interested in (though their compatriots at nearby Viana do Castelo dabbled a bit in the local crisp red wine known as 'red portugal'), exchanging these goods for woollen cloth and wheat from England and dried cod from Newfoundland.

The turning point came in 1667 when Louis XIV's protectionist minister, Colbert, forbade the import of English cloth into France. Charles II retaliated by stopping the import of French wines into England – a heavy blow for English gents who were very fond of their claret. The English 'rag merchants' in Viana and Porto saw a chance to make big bucks and shipped as much red portugal to England as they could find.

Demand grew for a stronger wine and in 1678 – so the story goes – two sons of a Liverpool wine merchant decided to investigate the upper Douro valley. They found what they wanted in a Lamego monastery (Portugal's monks had long been expert wine-makers) and shipped gallons of this new Douro red to England, via Porto. It was probably a rich, sweet wine known as 'priest's port', although the story also goes that the young man may have added a bit of brandy to the wine to enable it to travel better (thereby 'inventing' port as we know it today). In fact, the addition of brandy to arrest fermentation, retain sweetness and raise the alcohol level was not standard practice until 1850, and happened only gradually in order to meet demand from English consumers.

By the early 1700s the Viana wine merchants were on the Douro trail: among the first to establish a base in Porto and regularly make the hazardous journey up to the Douro wine country were the founders of today's Taylor Fladgate & Yeatman, Croft's and Warre's. The English had already clinched enormous commercial privileges in Portugal, thanks to a 1654 treaty between Cromwell and João IV, and the new 'factory' of English and Scottish traders soon constituted the most powerful group of wine merchants in Porto. There was a trickle of competition from American, Dutch and German wine traders, but the English had a stranglehold on the increasingly profitable trade. The 1703 Methuen Treaty between England and Portugal secured even greater profits by reducing the duty on Portuguese wines imported to Britain to a third less than that imposed on French wines.

By the 18th century, port had become so popular in England that it was considered quite indispensable among all proper Englishmen ('claret is the liquor for boys; port for men,' proclaimed Dr Johnson). But as supply failed to meet demand, the wine-growers soon resorted to various malpractices (mixing port with sweet Spanish wine or heavy doses of brandy, for instance) and by 1755 there was a crisis: the English factory refused to buy the wine unless the adulteration stopped.

The fracas reached the ears of the powerful Marquês de Pombal who seized the opportunity to loosen the English merchants' hold on the trade. He declared that henceforward a state monopoly company (Companhia Geral da Agricultura dos Vinhos do Alto Douro, also known as the Companhia Velha or 'Old Company') would control the entire port-wine trade and that only port from a specific region in the Alto Douro (the world's first demarcated wine region) could be exported.

Naturally, the English wine merchants yelped in protest. But though the company's rules were strict, there was room for corruption (even Pombal managed to pass off wine from his own vineyards on the Tejo as port). The improved port wines regained favour in England and by the late 18th century the English merchants had settled down again to a business that remained steadily profitable right up until WWII, thanks largely to port's increasing popularity in Britain as a working person's drink (mixed with lemonade and drunk in bars by the mug).

When port came back onto the market after the war, it found stiff competition from sherry and cheap 'British wines' (a mixture of imported wine and grape juice). This meant unprecedented tough new times in Porto and many companies sold out or amalgamated into larger groups. Others, notably Sandeman, whose symbol – a black-hatted Spanish don – was a startling innovation, decided the future lay in advertising (hitherto considered ungentlemanly) under the firm's own name.

Today's port market is very different from that of the 1700s. Ironically, the French – indirectly responsible for the English infatuation with port – are now the world's biggest consumers, drinking three times as much port as the English. They love it as an apéritif, but the English still corner the market for vintage port, followed closely these days by the Americans. Vintage port may gain an even more up-market niche following a 1996 Portuguese ruling banning bulk shipments of port, which will prevent the bottling of cheap blends abroad. ■

Lancaster, in 1337; and here their most famous son, Henry the Navigator, was born in 1394. While Henry's explorers were groping their way round Africa to discover the sea route to India, British traders were finding a foothold in Porto with their trade in port wine.

Over the following centuries, Porto developed a reputation for rebelliousness. In 1628 a group of Porto women attacked the minister responsible for a tax on linen. In 1757 a 'tippler's riot' against the Marquês de Pombal's strict new control of the port-wine trade was savagely put down. In 1808 Porto citizens arrested their French governor and set up a provisional junta. The French army which re-established a foothold in the following year was booted out by the British under the future Duke of Wellington, but Porto radicals soon turned against British 'control' of Portugal, demanding a new liberal constitution – subsequently adopted in 1822.

When the absolutist Miguel I usurped the throne in 1828, Porto stood by its principles, supporting Miguel's constitutionalist brother, Dom Pedro. Miguel's forces laid siege to the city in 1832 after Pedro arrived from Brazil, but the liberal cause won through when Miguel's fleet was captured off Cabo São Vicente in 1833. Porto continued to break out in rebellions in support of liberals throughout the 19th century. In 1878 the country's first republican deputy was elected here.

Orientation

Old Porto clambers up the rocky gorge of the Rio Douro about nine km from the river's mouth. 'New' Porto has expanded to embrace the polluted seashore of Foz do Douro (at the mouth of the river) and now bumps up against the industrialised suburb of Matosinhos (about five km north of Foz). Vila Nova de Gaia, the port-wine centre across the river, has been so much a part of Porto's history that it's also considered part of the city, although strictly speaking it's a separate municipality.

Porto's most distinctive landmarks are its bridges *(pontes)* across the Douro: from west to east, the modern Ponte da Arrábida linking Porto to the Lisbon highway; the striking two-level Ponte de Dom Luís I to Vila Nova de Gaia; two railway bridges, the Eiffel-designed Ponte de Maria Pia and adjacent Ponte de São João to/from Campanhã station; and the newest highway bridge, Ponte Freixo.

The axis of the city is Avenida dos Aliados, a broad avenue enclosing a patch of pigeon-pecked greenery, with the *câmara municipal* (town hall) dominating Praça do General Humberto Delgado at its northern end. Here are the municipal *turismo*, post office, banks and much reasonably priced accommodation. To the east and north-east is a busy shopping district (including the Mercado do Bolhão).

At the southern end of the avenue is Praça da Liberdade, a crowded café and bus-stop venue. A steep climb west up Rua dos Clérigos brings you to central Porto's best *miradouro* (lookout): the tower of the Igreja dos Clérigos. The university area is just west of the tower. South-east from Praça da Liberdade, up Avenida de Vimara Peres, is the Sé (cathedral). Atmospheric old alleys and lanes tumble south and west from the cathedral to the riverside Cais da Ribeira.

All these areas are within steep but reasonable walking distance of one another. Municipal buses run to most other places of interest, including the Centro Comercial Brasília shopping complex at Praça Mouzinho de Albuquerque (commonly known as Boavista), the nearby Cidade do Porto shopping complex and the camping ground to the north-west.

Porto's international airport, Aeroporto Francisco Sá Carneiro, is about 20 km north-west of the centre. There are three train terminals: Campanhã, two km east of the city centre; São Bento, near the south-east corner of Praça da Liberdade; and Trindade station, a few blocks north of the câmara municipal. See the Getting There & Away section for destinations served by each.

Bus terminals are also scattered all over: the Rede Expressos terminal is at Rua

DOURO

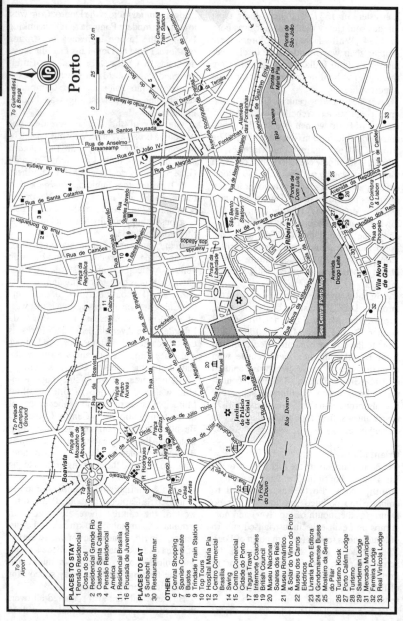

Porto

To Guimarães & Braga

To Airport

0   25   50 m

To Prelada Camping Ground

Boavista

To Coqueiro

Praça de Mouzinho de Albuquerque

Rua da Boavista

Rua da Alegria

Rua de Santa Catarina

Rua de Santos Pousada

Rua de Anselmo Braaneanp

Rua de D João IV

Av. Fernão de Magalhães

R Duque de Saldanha

Rua do Bonfim

To Campanhã Train Station

Rua do Heroísmo

Rua da Terceira

Alameda das Fontainhas

Avenida de Gustavo Eiffel

Ponte da Maria Pia

Ponte de São João

Rio Douro

Ponte de Dom Luís I

Avenida de Alvares Cabral

Avenida da República

To Coimbra & Lisbon

Rua Cândido dos Reis

Rua do Choupelo

Vila Nova de Gaia

To Foz do Douro

Rio Douro

Jardim do Palácio de Cristal

Avenida Diogo Leite

Ribeira

São Bento Station

Av. de Vimara Peres

Praça da Liberdade

Cedofeita

See Central Porto Map

Praça da República

Rua de Camões

Rua Gonçalo Cristóvão

Rua Álvares Cabral

Rua dos Bragas

Rua da Torrinha

Rua de Júlio Dinis

Praça de Pedro Nunes

Praça da Galiza

Praça Campo Alegre

R Rodrigues Lobo

Rua de Vilar

Rua Dom Pedro V

Rua de Dom Manuel II

Rua da Restauração

Rua da Alegria

Alexandre Herculano 370. Several companies operate from Praça Dona Filipa de Lencastre, while long-distance Renex buses congregate on Rua Carmelitas. The regional operator Rodonorte is at Rua Ateneu Comércial do Porto 19. See the Getting There & Away section for destinations served by these.

Maps The turismo's free 1:20,000 *Porto* map isn't totally up-to-date but is fine for most purposes. A very out-of-date bus route map is sometimes available at the turismo too, but it's hardly worth having. Bookshops (especially Livraria Porto Editora at Rua da Fábrica 90) and street kiosks have other Porto maps, but few are reliable: the best is the 1:16,500 *Porto: Mapa Turístico* published by Dinternal. Porto Editora's 1:14,000 *Planta da Cidade* has a street index.

If you're planning a trip along the Rio Douro, an excellent schematic map with bilingual notes, *Rio Douro*, is available for 1000$00 from bigger bookshops.

Information

Tourist Offices The very helpful municipal turismo (☎ 31 27 40; fax 208 4548), temporarily located in the câmara municipal, is due to return across the street to its renovated home at Rua Clube dos Fenianos 25. In summer (July to September) it's open weekdays from 9 am to 7 pm, Saturdays from 9 am to 4 pm and Sundays from 10 am to 1 pm. In winter it's open weekdays from 9 am to 5.30 pm and Saturdays from 9 am to 4 pm.

There's also a small national (ICEP) turismo (☎ 31 75 14; fax 31 32 12) at Praça Dom João I 43 which can deal with both Porto and national enquiries. It's open weekdays from 9 am to 7.30 pm (to 7 pm in winter) and weekends from 9 am to 3.30 pm.

There are also turismos at the airport (☎ 941 25 34), open from 8 am to 11.30 pm daily, and at Vila Nova de Gaia (see that section for details).

Listings The municipal turismo usually stocks the free monthly *Metro* magazine (in Portuguese only), with music, theatre,

cinema and bar listings. Similar listings – plus information on everything from babysitters and football to takeaway restaurants and late-night pharmacies – can be found in local editions of *Público* and *Jornal de Notícias*, which are on sale at newsagents.

Foreign Consulates Consular offices in Porto include the following. (See Embassies in the Facts for the Visitor chapter for offices in Lisbon.)

Austria
   Praça General Humberto Delgado 267 (☎ & fax 208 47 57)
Belgium
   Alameda de Basílio Teles 26 (☎ 600 12 45)
Denmark
   Rua Eugénio de Castro 280 (☎ 609 45 84; fax 609 97 46)
France
   Rua Eugénio de Castro 352 (☎ 609 48 05; fax 606 42 05)
Greece
   Rua Eugénio de Castro 280 (☎ 609 89 68)
Israel
   Rua da Fábrica Social (☎ & fax 32 09 48)
Italy
   Rua da Restauração 409 (☎ 606 22 92; fax 600 65 62)
Japan
   Rua de Júlio Dinis 803 (☎ 609 46 98; fax 609 09 61)
Netherlands
   Avenida Diogo Leite 26, Vila Nova de Gaia (☎ 371 15 75)
Spain
   Rua de Dom João IV 341 (☎ 56 39 15; fax 510 19 14)
Sweden
   Largo do Terreiro 4 (☎ 32 25 87; fax 31 49 55)
Switzerland
   Rua de Gondarém 1427 (☎ 618 97 06; fax 610 50 79)
UK
   Avenida da Boavista 3072 (☎ 618 47 89; fax 610 04 38)

Money There are Multibanco automatic-teller machines (ATMs) all over Porto, most conveniently at the Praça da Liberdade end of Avenida dos Aliados. Exchange machines can be found at Avenida dos Aliados 21 and 138. The best rates with travellers cheques are at private exchange bureaus such as

DOURO

Portocambios, Rua Rodrigues Sampaio 193 (open from 10 am to 6 pm weekdays and 10 am to 1 pm weekends) and Intercontinental at Rua de Ramalho Ortigão 8. American Express travellers cheques can be cashed with no commission at Top Tours (see Travel Agencies in this section), Porto's Amex representative.

Other useful exchanges are at the airport's Totta e Açores bank (open daily from 9 am to 8 pm), and Banco Espírito Santo in the Cidade do Porto shopping centre (open weekdays from 9 am to 10 pm) on Rua Gonçalo Sampaio, near Boavista.

Post The main post office (which is the place to collect poste restante) is by the câmara municipal on Praça General Humberto Delgado. It's open weekdays from 8 am to 9 pm, and weekends and holidays from 9 am to 6 pm. American Express credit card and travellers cheque holders can have mail sent to the less central Top Tours (see Travel Agencies in this section).

Telephone & Fax The most convenient place to make long-distance or international calls is the Portugal Telecom office at Praça da Liberdade 62. It's open weekdays from 8

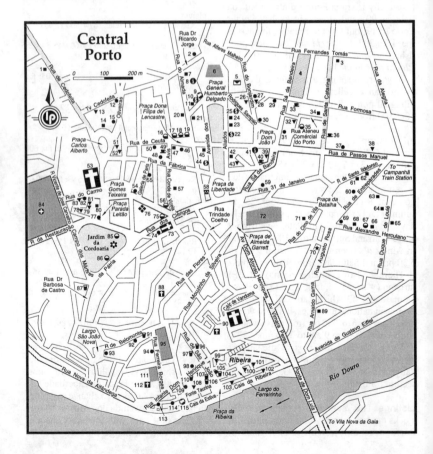

am to midnight, Saturdays from 8.30 am to midnight (to 9 pm for operator assistance) and Sundays from 10 am to 1 pm and 2 pm to midnight (2 to 6 pm for operator assistance). There's also a telephone office (open 9 am to 6 pm weekdays only) in the main

DOURO

PLACES TO STAY
1	Pensão-Residencial Estoril
3	Pensão do Norte
7	Pensão e Restaurante Europa
11	Residencial Vera Cruz
14	Pensão São Marino
20	Pensão Porto Rico
21	Pão de Açucar
23	Pensão Chique
24	Residencial Paulista
34	Grande Hotel do Porto
42	Residencial Universal
45	Residencial dos Aliados
47	Hotel Infante de Sagres
57	Residencial União
61	Residencial Belo Horizonte
62	Residencial Santo André
63	Pensão Aviz
64	Residencial Afonso
65	Pensão Residencial Henrique VIII
66	Residencial Antígua
68	Residencial Dom Filipe I
71	Pensão Mondariz
80	Pensão-Residencial Douro
89	Pensão Astória

PLACES TO EAT
13	Bakery
26	Pedro dos Frangos
28	Conga Casa das Bifanas
32	Restaurante Abadia do Porto
33	Confeitaria do Bolhão
36	Café Majestic
38	Restaurante Tripeiro
39	Restaurante Snack-Bar Girassol
40	Café & Restaurante A Brasileira
43	Restaurante e Adega Flor dos Congregados
49	Aviz Salão de Cha
51	Restaurante Carlos Alberto
52	Solar Moinho de Vento

78	Retiro do Jardim
79	Casa Zé Bota
81	Restaurante O Padeiro
83	Restaurante A Tasquinha
99	Restaurante da Alzira
100	Restaurante do Terreirinho
101	Casa de Pasto Snack Bar Dura Sempre
102	Taverna dos Bêbodos
103	Casa Filha da Mãe Preta
108	Casa Cardoso

OTHER
4	Mercado do Bolhão
5	Main Post Office
6	Câmara Municipal
8	Municipal Turismo
9	Austrian Consulate
10	Intercontinental Currency Exchange
12	Casa dos Plásticos
16	IASA Coaches
17	REDM Coaches
18	AV Minho Coaches
19	João Terreira das Neves Coaches
22	Currency Exchange Machine
25	Portocambios Currency Exchange
27	Casa Januário
29	Apérola do Bolhão
30	Luciano Matos
31	Casa Coelho
35	Rodonorte Coaches
41	ICEP Turismo
44	Currency Exchange Machine
46	Livraria Porto Editora
48	Livraria Porto Editora
50	Jumbo Expresso
53	Igreja do Carmo
54	Livraria Lello e Irmão
55	Livraria ASA Material Didáctico
56	Renex Coaches
58	Telephone Office
59	Livraria Bertrand
67	Rede Expressos Coaches at Paragem Atlântico
69	Cinema Batalha
70	Police Station

72	São Bento Train Station
73	Igreja dos Clérigos & Torre dos Clérigos
74	Casa Oriental
75	Renex Coaches
76	Clérigos Shopping
77	Ervanário
82	Garrafeira do Carmo
84	Hospital Santo António
85	Airport Bus Stop (Night)
86	Airport Bus Stop (Day)
88	Igreja da Misericórdia & Santa Casa da Misericórdia
90	Sé (Cathedral)
94	Instituto do Vinho do Porto
95	Mercado Ferreira Borges Exhibition Hall
105	Quercus Loja do Ambiente (Environmental Shop)
109	Casa do Infante
111	Palácio da Bolsa (Stock Exchange)
112	Igreja de São Francisco
113	Lavandaria São Nicolau
114	Centro Regional de Artes Tradicionais
115	Swedish Consulate

ENTERTAINMENT
2	Cinema Trindade
15	Auditório Nacional Carlos Alberto
37	Coliseu do Porto
60	Sinatra's
87	Glam Gay Club
91	Pinguim Café
92	Teatro de Belomonte
93	O Fado Restaurante Típico
96	Cosa Nostra
97	Oporto Rock Bar
98	Real Feytoria
	Café-Teatro
104	Taverna Filha da Mãe Preta
106	Meia Cave
107	Aniki Bóbó
110	Capítulo Final Bar Grill

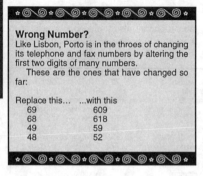

post office. Both places, as well as many kiosks and newsagents, sell Portugal-wide Credifone cards and the TLP telephone cards used in Lisbon and Porto only (for more on these see Post & Communications in the Facts for the Visitor chapter). In Porto, TLP telephones are more common than Credifones.

Faxes can be sent from the post office.

You can rent a mobile telephone from Novarent (☎ 610 76 99; fax 610 76 87) for about 1200$00 a day (plus 115$00 per minute for national calls and 500$00 per minute for international calls).

Travel Agencies Youth-oriented Tagus Travel (☎ 609 41 46; fax 609 41 41), at Rua Campo Alegre 261, sells discounted plane and train tickets, as well as ISIC and Cartão Jovem cards. They're open weekdays from 9 am to 6 pm and Saturdays from 10 am to 1 pm. They also have a small camping shop on the premises.

Another youth specialist is Jumbo Expresso (☎ 208 15 61; fax 208 14 35), at Rua de Ceuta 47, which can also arrange discounts on car rental. They're open weekdays from 9 am to 6.30 pm and Saturdays from 9.30 am to 12.30 pm.

Top Tours (☎ 208 27 85), Rua Alferes Malheiro 96, is Porto's American Express representative. If you have American Express credit cards or travellers cheques you can get commission-free currency exchange here and have mail and faxes held

or forwarded. It's open weekdays only from 9 am to 12.30 pm and 2.30 to 6 pm.

Bookshops Porto's most useful chain of bookshops is Livraria Porto Editora, with a branch at Praça Dona Filipa de Lencastre 42 (☎ 200 76 81), another – best for maps and some foreign-language books – round the corner at Rua da Fábrica 90 (☎ 200 76 69), and a third in the university area at Rua da Restauração 343 (☎ 606 25 02). The best bookshop for English and French-language books is Livraria Bertrand (☎ & fax 200 43 39) at Rua 31 de Janeiro 65.

An excellent source of educational children's books, toys and Portugal wall maps is Livraria ASA Material Didáctico (☎ 200 71 35), which is combined with Livraria Infantile Juvenil at Rua Galeria de Paris 118.

Even if you're not looking for books, don't miss the gorgeous Livraria Lello e Irmão (☎ 200 20 37) at Rua Carmelitas 144, a turn-of-the-century Art Deco gem stacked floor to ceiling with new, second-hand and antique books, in lavish quarters more suited to a gentlemen's club.

Campuses The Universidade de Porto is just north of Jardim da Cordoaria (also known as Jardim de João Chagas). Various faculty buildings also line Rua da Restauração to the west.

Cultural Centres The British Council (☎ 207 30 60; fax 207 30 68) is at Rua do Breiner 155. Its library, with a good selection of English-language books and newspapers, is open Mondays from 10 am to noon and 2.30 to 5.30 pm; Tuesdays from 2.30 to 5.30 pm; Wednesdays from noon to 5.30 pm; Fridays from 5 to 7.30 pm; and Saturdays from 10 am to noon. It's closed on Thursdays.

Laundry Pinguim Lavandaria (☎ 609 50 32), in the basement of the Centro Comercial Brasília on Praça Mouzinho de Albuquerque (in Boavista), has laundry and dry-cleaning facilities. It's open daily, except Sundays, from 10 am to 10.30 pm. To wash and dry a normal load it costs 1500$00.

The much cheaper (900$00) municipal Lavandaria São Nicolau (☎ 200 78 15) is an underground complex which also includes public showers; it's at the junction of Rua da Reboleira and Rua Infante Dom Henrique. It's open daily, except Sundays, from 8 am to 7 pm.

Medical Services There are dozens of *farmácias* all over Porto; see *Público*, or call ☎ 118, for a list of 24-hour places. Hospital Santo António (☎ 200 52 41 day; ☎ 200 73 54 night) on Rua Vicente de José Carvalho has some English-speaking staff. There's also a special children's hospital, Hospital Maria Pia (☎ 609 98 61), at Rua de Boavista 82.

Emergency The police station (☎ 200 21 85, ☎ 200 68 21) is on Rua Augusto Rosa.

Dangers & Annoyances Porto has more than its fair share of seedy, dimly lit alleys that are best avoided after dark, in particular the run-down riverside areas off Rua Nova da Alfândega and Avenida de Gustavo Eiffel.

Even Porto's most central parks and squares (eg Praça Gomes Teixeira and Praça da Batalha) have plenty of weirdos, drunks and oddballs. We never had any hassles during the day, though solo women travellers might feel uncomfortable taking a lunchtime picnic. São Bento train station and the popular night-time Ribeira district are other areas where you might not want to hang around by yourself late at night.

Don't go anywhere near the beach at Foz do Douro: it's appallingly, dangerously filthy. No beach is really clean until Vila do Conde (26 km north) or Ovar (40 km south).

Quercus The Porto branch (☎ 32 03 24; fax 200 33 90) of the national environmental organisation Quercus is one of the most active in the country. There is a *centro de educação ambiente* or environmental education centre (☎ 208 78 98); the Centro de Acolhimento do Palácio de Cristal, a bird

sanctuary in the Jardim do Palácio de Cristal, mostly for birds of prey; and a *loja do ambiente* (environmental shop) at Praça da Ribeira 23, with various environmental publications, mostly in Portuguese. The shop is open daily, except Mondays and Wednesdays, from 2 to 7 pm.

Torre dos Clérigos
One of the best places to get your bearings and photographs of the city is this 75m-high baroque tower, south-west up Rua dos Clérigos from Praça da Liberdade. The Italian architect Nicolau Nasoni designed both the 240-step tower and the adjoining oval-shaped Igreja dos Clérigos in the mid-18th century (he died in Porto 10 years after the tower was completed, having put his hand to several other monuments in the city). The tower is open daily, except Wednesdays, from 10.30 am to noon and 2.30 to 5 pm; entry is 100$00.

Sé
This formidable fortress of a cathedral dominates central Porto from high ground above São Bento station. It was founded in the 12th century but rebuilt the following century and extensively changed during the 18th century. Only a Romanesque rose window and the 14th-century cloisters remain from its earlier incarnation. The rest is mostly baroque, including a loggia on the north face (probably the work of Nicolau Nasoni) and most of the interior.

There's nothing much memorable here, though the 17th-century silver altarpiece is worth a look. Best of all, perhaps, is the upper storey of the cloisters (reached by a Nasoni-designed stairway), which is decorated with 18th-century azulejos and affords some fine views.

The cathedral is open daily, except Sundays, from 9 am to 12.30 pm and 2.30 to 5.30 pm. Admission to the cloisters is 200$00.

Ribeira
The riverside Ribeira district is the most fascinating part of Porto. It's still largely

undeveloped and ungentrified – and despite its growing popularity as a venue for bars, restaurants and flocks of tourists – it's the guts of Porto's past, with a cluster of boats at the quayside and all grit and grime in its narrow lanes and alleys.

Henry the Navigator is said to have been born here, in the so-called **Casa do Infante** on Rua da Alfândega, which now serves as an historical archive and exhibition hall.

Palácio da Bolsa

The 19th-century neoclassical Bolsa (Stock Exchange), facing Praça do Infante Dom Henrique, is a pompous monument to Porto's money merchants, and the official headquarters of Porto's Commercial Association. The Great Hall near the entrance is where the stock exchange once took place; it's an impressive glass-domed space with international coats of arms covering the upper walls.

You can see this hall without joining the guided tours, but the highlight of a tour is the ballroom known as the Arabian Hall (copying, in style, the Alhambra at Granada) which took 18 years to build. This goes completely over the top with its gilded stucco (18 kg of gold was used) and detailed wall decorations, including Arabic inscriptions glorifying Maria II, who commissioned the building.

The Bolsa is open weekdays from 9 am to 1 pm and 2 to 6 pm and weekends from 10 am to 1 pm and 2 to 7 pm. In winter it's closed at weekends. The guided tours cost 550$00 (250$00 for children and students).

Igreja de São Francisco

You wouldn't guess by looking at it, but this plain-faced Gothic church next to the Bolsa houses one of the most incredible displays of baroque and rococo gilt decoration in the country. Nearly 100 kg of gold leaf was used to plaster the dozens of carved figures and coiling foliage which cover the altars, pillars and ceiling. The extravagance was obviously too much for devotees: the church no longer holds services and is packed instead with tour groups.

There's a boring little museum in the catacombs below, with a few ecclesiastical furnishings from the Franciscan monastery which once stood on the site, and a pit full of human bones dating back to the 19th century (creepier ossuary chapels are at Évora and Faro).

The church and museum are open daily from 9 am to 6 pm; entry is 500$00.

Santa Casa da Misericórdia

Hidden away in this museum at Rua das Flores 15 is the superb *Fons Vitae* (Fountain of Life) Renaissance painting by an unknown painter, showing Dom Manuel I and his wife and children around a fountain of blood from the crucified Christ. The museum is open weekdays from 9 am to noon and 2.30 to 12.30 pm and 2 to 5 pm. Admission is 200$00.

Museu Nacional Soares dos Reis

Porto's most important museum – recently reopened after years of 'renovation' – is in the former Palácio das Carrancas on Rua de Dom Manuel II. This grand 18th-century neoclassical mansion, once the home of a wealthy Jewish family, was later sold to Dom Pedro V. During the Peninsular War the French general Marshal Soult briefly set up his headquarters here, but he was evicted so suddenly by troops of the future Duke of Wellington that he left an unfinished banquet behind, which the Duke and his officers duly polished off.

Transformed into a museum in 1940 its most notable items are works of the 19th-century sculptor Soares dos Reis (see especially his famous *O Desterrado*, The Exile) and his pupil Teixeira Lopes; and the naturalistic paintings by the 19th-century artists of the so-called Porto school, Henrique Pousão and Silva Porto. There's also a fine collection of Bohemian glass and Vista Alegre porcelain.

The museum is open daily, except Mondays, from 10 am to 12.30 pm and 2 to 5.30 pm. Admission is 350$00 (140$00 for students) and is free on Sunday mornings.

Jardim do Palácio de Cristal

This large, leafy park – named after a 19th-century crystal palace which no longer exists – has a huge domed pavilion in the centre used for sports and occasional exhibitions. On the grounds are a children's playground, a small pond and roving peacocks. The pavilion has a reasonable self-service restaurant. The park is about 800m west of Jardim da Cordoaria (the main entrance is on Rua de Dom Manuel II).

Museu Romántico

On the west side of the Jardim do Palácio de Cristal at Rua Entre Quintas 220 is the Quinta da Macieirinha, where the abdicated King of Sardinia, Carlos Alberto, lived in 1849. It's now a 'Romantic Museum' of marginal interest, with the king's belongings on display among dainty furnishings. Opening hours are Tuesday to Saturday from 10 am to noon and 2 to 5 pm and Sundays from 2 to 5.30 pm (100$00 admission). The Solar do Vinho do Porto, housed in the same building, is described under Bars in this section.

Museu de Arte Moderna

Housed in the Casa de Serralves, a 1930s palace off Rua de Serralves (seven km west of the city centre), this collection administered by Lisbon's Fundação Calouste Gulbenkian is an impressive display of some of the country's best modern art and architectural design. The palace gardens are worth seeing too.

The museum's collection is organised into temporary exhibitions so check with the turismo first to see whether the museum is closed for its two-week rehanging period. From April through October the museum and gardens are open Tuesday to Friday from 2 to 8 pm; the gardens are also open on weekends from 10 am to 8 pm. The rest of the year, the museum and gardens are open Tuesday to Sunday from 2 to 6 pm. Admission is 300$00 (free on Sundays from 10 am to 2 pm). Take bus No 78 from the Jardim da Cordoaria or Palácio de Cristal.

Museu dos Carros Eléctricos

The Tram Museum, a cavernous former switching-house with dozens of restored old trams, is beside the STCP building on Alameda de Basílio Teles, on the No 18 tram line. It's open Tuesday to Saturday from 9 am to noon and 2 to 5 pm; admission is 100$00.

Vila Nova de Gaia

Vila Nova de Gaia's main function is to serve as an entrepôt for port wine. Since the mid-18th century, bottlers and exporters of this highly prized, highly regulated tipple have been obliged to have their 'lodges', for storage and maturing of the wine prior to shipment, in this enclave across the Rio Douro from Porto.

The lodges, presently numbering around 60, are crammed cheek-by-jowl from the waterfront to the top of the steep slope, the oldest and biggest of them sporting huge signs. Most are open to visitors, and many offer tours and tastings. This is the only reason to go over to Vila Nova de Gaia. Despite its crumbling Georgian façades, the part of Vila Nova down around the lodges is unattractive and full of speeding cars, loitering men and venal kids.

Port-wine types and vintages are discussed in the Drinks section of the Facts for the Visitor chapter.

Orientation & Information Some buses cross the lower deck of the Ponte de Dom Luís I to the riverfront Avenida Diogo Leite, stopping in front of Vila Nova's turismo beside the Sandeman lodge. This polite office (☎ & fax 30 19 02), open from 9 am to 12.30 pm and 2 to 5.30 pm on weekdays and from 2 to 6 pm on Saturdays, has a map showing lodges open for tours, and a list of their hours. The map is of dubious accuracy, but you need only say the name of a lodge and local people will point you to it.

Buses across the bridge's top deck go into Vila Nova's small town centre, inconveniently far above and beyond the lodges. However, a little turismo kiosk (☎ 371 25 87) is open in July and August in Jardim do

Morro, right at the end of the bridge. From there you can work your way down through narrow lanes to the riverfront.

Wine Tasting & Tours About two dozen lodges are open for tours and tastings on weekdays and Saturdays. In high season (roughly June through mid-September) the larger ones run visitors through like clockwork and you rarely have to wait more than 10 or 15 minutes to join a tour. Outside the summer months, most will accommodate you more or less on the spot.

Of the old English-run lodges, the venerable Taylor's (Taylor Fladgate & Yeatman, a 10-minute walk up Rua do Choupelo) offers abundant information and a taste of the top-of-the-line LBV (Late Bottled Vintage) wine. Among older Portuguese-run lodges, Ferreira (600m west of the turismo along the riverfront) has a good tour. Recommended small, independent lodges include Porto Calém (on the river near the bridge) and Rozès (a stiff 600m climb up Rua Cândido

dos Reis past the railway, then right at Rua da Cabaça). Sandeman, Osborne and Real Vinícola also have tours on Sundays.

(If you can't be bothered crossing the river, the Solar do Vinho do Porto, run by the Instituto do Vinho do Porto, is a posh and pricey 'pub' in Porto where you can taste port from all the lodges; see Bars in the Entertainment section.)

Mosteiro da Serra do Pilar Vila Nova de Gaia's one architectural monument is this severe 16th-century monastery on a crowning hill beside the Ponte de Dom Luís I. The future Duke of Wellington made his headquarters here – probably because of the view of Porto – before crossing the river and chasing the French out of the city in 1809. Much of the monastery, including a striking circular cloister, now belongs to the army and is off limits, though you could see the church – also round – when Mass is sung on Sunday morning. Take a bus via the upper deck of the bridge.

Getting Port to Market

In 1756 the Marquês de Pombal got to grips with English domination of the port trade, and with the deteriorating quality of Douro valley wines, by founding a Portuguese company with monopoly control over port-wine standards and prices, and by demarcating the region where port wine could legally be produced. This probably included the designation of Vila Nova de Gaia as the place where it was to be stored, aged and bottled prior to shipment overseas.

For centuries young port wine was brought to Vila Nova from the wine estates by river (in February and March, following the autumn harvest). It came in barrels stacked on the decks of *barcos rabelos* – handsome, flat-bottomed boats with billowing square sails. But progress, initially in the form of a railway line down the valley, caught up with them. The last commercial journey by a barco rabelo was in 1956, and tanker trucks now speed the wine down modern highways. Every summer the most river-worthy of the old boats, navigated by company officials, compete in a race. Aside from that they just serve as floating advertisements for the lodges and add colour to the quays.

Port wine is stored, fortified, lovingly checked and fine-tuned in huge vats or 25,000-litre oak casks in the lodges' cool, dark *armazéns* (warehouses). It is then matured in the cask or in black glass bottles, depending on the quality of the harvest. Though the bottling and shipping firms still like to project a 'family-owned' image, many have gobbled one another up or are in the hands of multinational companies.

Since 1986 it has been legal to store and age port in the Douro valley as well. A small entrepôt has grown up at Peso da Régua (see the Douro Valley section), and some *quinta* owners now market their own 'estate-bottled' products.

To learn more about port wine and the port-wine region, visit the Instituto do Vinho do Porto – a private organisation dedicated to maintaining the quality of port wine and the reputation of the port appellation – which has several good booklets and brochures at the front desk of their headquarters (☎ 200 65 22; fax 208 04 65), opposite the Mercado Ferreira Borges exhibition hall on Rua Ferreira Borges, in Porto. ∎

'The Old Company'
The monopoly company formed by the Marquês de Pombal to clamp down on the port-wine trade was called Companhia Geral da Agricultura dos Vinhos do Alto Douro, nicknamed Companhia Velha, the 'Old Company'. Its direct modern descendant is Real Vinícola (properly, Real Companhia Vitivinícola do Norte de Portugal), the old quarters of which are the grubby pink buildings with 'est 1756' on the outside, west along the riverfront, just before Ferreira. Their tours, however, are of their new quarters up on Rua Luís de Camões. ∎

Ponte de Dom Luís I The bridge is almost reason enough to go to Vila Nova de Gaia if you have the energy and the nerve to walk across the upper deck. It offers some of the most spectacular views of Porto.

Places to Eat There is a depressing group of grotty eateries on Avenida Diogo Leite in the block west of the mercado municipal, itself about 300m west of the turismo. But one good-value exception is *Restaurante Imar* (☎ 379 27 05), before the market at No 56. It's popular and clean, serving delicious regional specialities. A meia dose (half-portion) at 450$00 to 1200$00 is plenty for one person. They also have good caldo verde.

Several lodges, including Sandeman and Taylor's, serve lunch in their own posh and pricey restaurants.

Getting There & Away Bus Nos 57 and 91 from Praça de Almeida Garrett (by São Bento station) go via the lower deck of the bridge, right to the riverfront turismo (and back); other buses are convenient only for going back. Bus Nos 82 and 84 from Boavista, Praça da República and Praça da Liberdade cross the upper deck to the centre of Vila Nova de Gaia.

City Tours Gray Line (☎ 31 65 97) runs 4500$00, half-day city tours four times a week from April through October and twice

a week during the rest of the year. These can be booked, and you can be picked up, at most upper-end hotels.

River Cruises Several outfits offer 45 to 60-minute 'Five Bridges' cruises around six times a day in summer, in what pass for traditional barcos rabelos, the colourful boats once used for carrying port wine down from the vineyards.

Get aboard on the Porto side at Praça da Ribeira; tickets are 1500$00. Over at Vila Nova de Gaia, cruises leave from near the Ponte de Dom Luís I and cost 1200$00. Children up to 12 years old go free. Turis-douro (☎ & fax 30 63 89), with the Sandeman port-wine lodge, also organises trips. The Ferreira lodge (☎ 370 00 10, ext 300 or 354) runs them too.
Via d'Ouro (☎ & fax 938 81 39), who run the 'Five Bridges' trips from the Porto side, also go to Entre-os-Rios for 10,000$00 and to Peso da Régua for 13,000$00. See East of Peso da Régua in this chapter for information on longer cruises along the Douro.

Special Events
Porto's biggest bash is the Festa de São João (St John's Festival, also called the Festa da Cidade or City Festival) on 23-24 June, when the whole city erupts in merry-making – dancing, drinking and hitting one another over the head with huge plastic hammers.

Throughout the year, there's a stream of cultural festivals; check with the turismo for exact dates. Among those worth catching are:

February
    Fantasporto or Festival Internacional de Cinema Fantástico (International Festival of Fantastic Cinema)
March
    Festival Intercéltico do Porto (International Celtic Festival)
May
    Queimas das Fitas (student week)
    Festival de Marionetas (Puppet Festival)
June
    Festival Internacional de Folclore do Porto (International Folklore Festival)
    Festival Ritmos (Rhythm Festival)

August
    Noites Ritual Rock (Rock Festival)
September
    Grande Noite de Fado (Grand Night of Fado)
    festival
October
    Festival de Jazz do Porto (Jazz Festival)
December
    Semana do Cinema Europeu (Week of European
    Cinema)

Places to Stay – bottom end

Camping Porto's nearest camping ground, *Parque de Campismo da Prelada* (☎ 81 26 16), is about five km north-west of the city centre on Rua Monte dos Burgos. Take bus No 6 from Praça de Liberdade or bus No 50 from Jardim do Cordoaria.

Three other local sites are near one another across the river: *Campismo Salgueiros* (☎ 781 05 00), near Praia de Salgueiros, is open May to September only. Slightly more expensive, *Campismo Marisol* (☎ 713 59 42) is at the next beach south, Praia de Canide, and open year-round. Vila Nova de Gaia's new municipal *Campismo Madalena* (☎ 711 59 42) is close by at Praia da Madalena and is open from June to December. Take bus No 57 to any of them from Praça de Almeida Garrett. Note that the sea at these places is far too polluted for swimming.

If everything is full, the year-round *Parque de Medas* (☎ 02-986 01 61) is 25 km up the Douro on the N108. If you don't have wheels you can catch a bus for 370$00 from the small Gondomarense bus company office at Rua do Duque da Terceira 112. The camping ground is 50 minutes away at the end of the Formiga/Campidouro route; get off at Formiga, not Medas. There are a dozen buses daily on weekdays but only three or four on weekends and holidays.

Youth Hostel Porto's 50-bed pousada de juventude (☎ 606 55 35) is a couple of km from the centre at Rua Rodrigues Lobo 98. Reservations are essential. Take bus No 3, 20 or 52 from Praça da Liberdade.

Pensões & Residencials Some of Porto's cheapest hostelries are around Praça da Batalha, a short walk east of São Bento station. *Pensão Mondariz* (☎ 200 56 00), at Rua do Cimo de Vila 139, is the best of the bunch in this seedy lane, with singles/ doubles without bath from 1500$00/ 3000$00. Near the Rede Expressos bus station on noisy Rua de Alexandre Herculano is a string of residencials including the adequate *Residencial Dom Filipe I* (☎ 31 78 79), at No 384, with doubles for 3500$00, and the more pleasant *Residencial Antígua* (☎ 31 55 19), at No 314, where doubles with bath are 4000$00.

On nearby Rua Duque de Loulé at No 233, *Residencial Afonso* (☎ 31 54 69) has grotty rooms without bath for 2500$00/3500$00. A better bet is *Pensão Residencial Henrique VIII* (☎ 200 65 11), at No 168, where bright doubles with bath and breakfast are just 5000$00 (book ahead in summer). You'll find smaller, more modern rooms in two functional residencials in Rua de Santo Ildefonso: *Belo Horizonte* (☎ 208 34 52) at No 100 and *Santo André* (☎ 31 58 69) at No 112. The cheapest doubles at either are around 2500$00 (without bath).

A hidden gem 10 minutes walk downhill from here is the quiet *Pensão Astória* (☎ 200 81 75) at Rua Arnaldo Gama 56. Its 10 elegant rooms (some with great views of the river) are a bargain 3000$00/5000$00, minus bath but including breakfast (book well ahead in summer).

In the shopping district north of Praça da Batalha, the rambling old-fashioned *Pensão do Norte* (☎ 200 35 03), at Rua de Fernandes Tomás 579 (opposite the azulejo-covered Capela da Santa Catarina), has rooms from 1800$00/3000$00 without bath (plus pricier ones with bath).

Residencial União (☎ 200 30 78), at Rua Conde de Vizela 62, is better inside than it looks from outside; no-frills doubles start at 2000$00 without bath, 3500$00 with. Along the more congenial Rua do Almada, *Pensão Porto Rico* (☎ 31 87 85), at No 237, has rooms without bath for 3000$00/3500$00. Similarly priced is the simple but welcoming *Pensão e Restaurante Europa* (☎ 200 69 71) at No 396.

Places to Stay – middle
Around Avenida dos Aliados *Residencial Vera Cruz* (☎ 32 33 96; fax 32 34 21), Rua Ramalho Ortigão 14, has smart singles/doubles with bath for 5500$00/7000$00, including breakfast. *Pão de Açucar* (☎ 200 24 25; fax 31 02 39), at Rua do Almada 262, is a popular Art Deco residence with a terrace on the top floor. Rooms start from 5500$00/7500$00 and go quickly in summer; reservations are essential.

There is a row of impressive old hostelries on the east side of the Avenida, including *Residencial Paulista* (☎ 31 46 92; fax 600 72 76), on the 2nd floor at Avenida dos Aliados 214, where rooms are 5000$00/6000$00 with breakfast. *Pensão Chique* (☎ 32 29 63), at No 206, has small rooms but a friendly atmosphere: singles/doubles are 4500$00/6500$00 with breakfast. The renovated *Residencial Universal* (☎ 200 67 58; fax 200 10 55), at No 38, is one of the poshest in the row, with a startling modern interior and doubles with breakfast for 7500$00.

North of Avenida dos Aliados At the quieter end of Rua do Bonjardim at No 977 is *Residencial Grande Rio* (☎ 59 40 32; fax 550 32 26), with well-equipped singles/doubles for 4000$00/5000$00. At the north end of Rua Santa Catarina are a string of residencials, including the businesslike *Pensão Residencial América* (☎ 200 83 57; fax 208 38 62) at No 1018 and *Pensão Residencial Costa do Sol* (☎ 59 33 44; fax 550 19 51) at No 1432. Rooms with bath and breakfast are 6500$00/7000$00 at both places (garage parking is free at the América).

Porto's most extraordinary hostelry, *Castelo Santa Catarina* (☎ 59 55 99; fax 550 66 13), is in this area, at Rua Santa Catarina 1347. A turn-of-the-century pseudo-Gothic castle in a palm-shaded garden, it is rich with azulejos and has its own private chapel to boot. The rooms, at least in the castle (there are others in a modern annexe), are small and gloomy for the 6000$00/7000$00 price tag (with breakfast). Car parking is available.

Bus No 9 runs to this area regularly from Praça Marquês de Pombal.

Around Praça da Batalha One of the best value places in this area is the efficient and welcoming *Pensão Aviz* (☎ 32 07 22; fax 32 07 47), at Avenida de Rodrigues de Freitas 451, where rooms with bath and breakfast are 5000$00/6000$00. Garage parking is available at 600$00 for 24 hours.

University Area *Pensão-Residencial Estoril* (☎ 200 27 51; fax 208 24 68), at No 193 on a pedestrianised stretch of Rua de Cedofeita, is a 15-minute walk from the centre but its rooms with bath at 4000$00/5000$00 are good value. *Pensão-Residencial Douro* (☎ 208 12 01), above a lively student café of the same name at Praça Parada Leitão 41, has rooms with bath for 4500$00/5500$00.

Popular with business people, the prim *Pensão São Marino* (☎ 32 54 99), at Praça de Carlos Alberto 59, has comfortable doubles with bath (some overlooking the praça's small park) for 6000$00.

Near Praça da República The child-friendly *Residencial Brasília* (☎ 200 60 95; fax 200 65 10) is the best of several rambling residencials on traffic-clogged Rua Álvares Cabral, at No 221. Spacious doubles with breakfast start from 6500$00. Garage parking is 800$00 for 24 hours.

Places to Stay – top end
The grand-looking *Residencial dos Aliados* (☎ 200 48 53; fax 200 27 10), at Rua Elísio de Melo 27, has old-fashioned charm but noisy rooms; doubles with bath are 8500$00. The *Grande Hotel do Porto* (☎ 200 81 76; fax 31 10 61), on pedestrianised Rua de Santa Catarina at No 197, has deluxe doubles for 14,000$00.

Poshest of all is the *Hotel Infante de Sagres* (☎ 200 81 01; fax 31 49 37) at Praça Dona Filipa de Lencastre 62, which is stuffed with antiques and an air of opulence; doubles are a steep 27,500$00.

DOURO

Places to Eat

Around Avenida dos Aliados Near São Bento station at Travessa dos Congregados 11, the rustic *Restaurante e Adega Flor dos Congregados* (☎ 200 28 22) offers regional specialities like tripas a moda do Porto (tripe Porto style) and bacalhau a moda de Braga for around 1400$00 (some half-portions are available for 950$00).

At Rua do Bonjardim 219 is *Pedro dos Frangos* (☎ 200 85 22), which is very popular at lunch time for its frango no espeto (spit-roasted chicken) and house wine on tap. Opposite at No 320 is the equally casual *Conga Casa das Bifanas* (☎ 200 01 13) where bifanas (small steaks) with potatoes and rice is 700$00. Another hot lunch spot is *Restaurante Snack-Bar Girassol* (☎ 200 73 93) at Rua Sá da Bandeira 131, which has 560$00 specials and 1200$00 main dishes.

Restaurante Abadia do Porto (☎ 200 87 57), a cavernous, azulejo-lined place at Rua do Ateneu Comércial do Porto 22, is a long-established favourite of business folks where you can be sure of getting your tripe right; prices are surprisingly reasonable. The spacious *Restaurante Tripeiro* (☎ 200 58 86), at Rua de Passos Manuel 195, has hearty helpings of lunch-time specials from 450$00; main dishes in the evening cost around 1500$00.

University Area Travessa do Carmo has a few bargain restaurants. Our favourite is the homely *Restaurante O Padeiro* (☎ 200 74 52), at No 28A, which serves up the usual fare with a smile; filling daily specials are 1200$00. Next door, at No 20, is the larger, brisker *Casa Zé Bota* (☎ 31 46 97), which has excellent fish dishes (try the grilled salmon).

At Rua do Carmo 23, the folksy *Restaurante A Tasquinha* (☎ 32 21 45), with a dessert menu almost as long as the wine list, is popular with students and families; it's closed on Sundays. A bargain place for lunch is the nearby *Retiro do Jardim* (☎ 31 12 44), at Campo dos Mártires da Pátria 44, where pratos do dia are a mere 550$00. In Praça de Carlos Alberto are several more cheap options. The most popular is *Restaurante Carlos Alberto* (☎ 200 17 47), with a menu scribbled on the blackboards outside (prices from 650$00). The venerable *Solar Moinho de Vento* (☎ 31 11 58), on Largo do Moinho de Vento, offers a range of tasty dishes, though most are fairly pricey.

Ribeira Some of the cheapest eats in this neighbourhood are at the *Casa de Pasto Snack Bar Dura Sempre* (☎ 200 84 88), at Rua da Lada 106, with tables in the lane and a family ambience inside. There's no menu, just two pratos do dia for around 800$00 a half-portion. It's closed on Mondays. Another unpretentious place (but with prices at around 1300$00 per dish) is *Restaurante da Alzira* (☎ 200 50 04) at Viela do Buraco 3; follow the signs into a grubby alley. At Rua de Fonte Taurina 58, *Casa Cardoso* (☎ 31 86 44) is in an old high-ceilinged house and has a menu of half-portions from 650$00 and main dishes from around 1200$00.

Most riverfront restaurants in this popular district are overpriced and touristy, but the most congenial of the lot is *Casa Filha da Mãe Preta* (☎ 31 55 15) at Cais da Ribeira 39, with upstairs river views. It's closed on Sundays. The long-popular *Taverna dos Bébodos* (☎ 31 35 65), at Cais da Ribeira 24, still has a great old-inn atmosphere though prices are steep. It's closed on Mondays and for the first two weeks of September. One of the poshest places around is the salubrious *Restaurante do Terreirinho* (☎ 208 81 58), at

---

A Load of Tripe

For most of us it's something to be avoided, but Porto folk can think of nothing nicer than a rich stew of tripe. This affection dates back to 1415 (so the story goes), when Henry the Navigator was preparing to sail for Ceuta in Morocco. The loyal citizens of Porto sent their best meat, keeping the offal for themselves – since then they have been nicknamed tripeiros (tripe-eaters). ■

Largo do Terreirinho 7, where you can expect to pay around 1800$00 a dish.

Vegetarian Restaurants As you'd expect of a city famous for tripe, vegetarians are badly catered for. One possibility is a small macrobiotic place called *Suribachi* (☎ 56 28 37) at Rua do Bonfim 136, though it's only open from noon to 2 pm.

There are several health-food shops, including *Augusto Coutinho* (☎ 31 11 56) at stall 12-14 in the Mercado do Bolhão, and *Ervanário* (☎ 200 86 82) at Praça Parada Leitão 21-33.

Confeitarias & Cafés One of the yummiest selections of local sweets, including pão de ló (a sponge cake) and bolo rei (a rich fruit cake), is at *Confeitaria do Bolhão* at Rua Formosa 339, opposite the Mercado do Bolhão. For the best pão de ló go to the bakery at Travessa de Cedofeita 20B, where the baking methods have hardly changed in centuries.

An unpretentious turn-of-the-century tea salon is *Aviz Salão de Cha* at Rua de Avis 17. *A Brasileira*, at Rua do Bonjardim 116, is an Art Deco gem with a pavement café and a stuffier indoor restaurant. It's packed with business people at lunch time.

Porto's most famous café is the renovated *Café Majestic*, at Rua de Santa Catarina 112, where gold-braided waiters serve you a set breakfast for 1500$00 or afternoon tea for 1100$00. The interior is all prancing cherubs and gilded woodwork; splurge on a coffee (200$00) and have a look around.

Entertainment
Porto is a lively place day and night, with a huge calendar of cultural festivals (see the Special Events section, earlier). Pick up the turismo's free monthly programme or the Portuguese-language *Metro* magazine to find out what's going on.

Cinemas Porto has a generous supply of cinemas, often featuring dubbed or subtitled English-language films. Among newer multiscreen theatres are those at Central

Shopping (☎ 510 27 85) at Campo 24 de Agosto 145A, and Cidade do Porto (☎ 600 91 64) on Rua Gonçalo Sampaio in Boavista. Other central theatres are *Cinema Batalha* (☎ 202 24 07), on Praça da Batalha, and *Cinema Trindade* (☎ 200 44 12), on Rua Dr Ricardo Jorge.

Discos Most of Porto's discos are on the outskirts, some as far away as Foz do Douro or Matosinhos. The largest is *Terminal X* (☎ 610 72 32), at Avenida de Fontes Pereira de Melo 449, in the north-west industrial area; take bus No 44 from Jardim da Cordoaria. Slightly more central, on Avenida Sidónio Pais, is *Via Rapida*, while *Swing* (☎ 609 00 19), at Praceta Engenheiro Amaro da Costa 766 (off Rua de Júlio Dinis), is popular for easy bopping. In Foz do Douro, *Indústria* (☎ 617 68 06), at Avenida do Brasil 843, pulls in the biggest crowds; take bus No 78 from Avenida dos Aliados to Casa das Artes.

Theatres & Concert Halls The main venues for classical music, plays and occasional exhibitions are the Auditório Nacional Carlos Alberto (☎ 200 45 40), at Rua das Oliveiras 43, and the Casa das Artes (☎ 600 61 53), at Rua de António Cardoso 175.

Larger scale dance, rock and other musical performances are usually held at the Coliseu do Porto (☎ 200 51 96) on Rua de Passos Manuel. Teatro de Belomonte (☎ 208 33 41) at Rua de Belomonte 57, also called Teatro de Marionetas do Porto, specialises in puppet shows.

Fado Porto isn't as famous as Lisbon or Coimbra for fado, but there are several places where you can enjoy this melancholic bluesy music. *Sinatra's* (☎ 31 20 42), at Rua de Entreparades 37, is a plain café-restaurant with live fado and guitar music on Saturdays from 9.30 pm (there's a minimum charge of 1500$00). Much more up-market is *O Fado Restaurante Típico* (☎ 202 69 37), at Largo de São João Novo 16, which charges a 5000$00 minimum.

For funkier surroundings, check out *Real*

Feytoria Café-Teatro (☎ 200 07 18), at Rua Infante Dom Henrique 20, which has occasional fado as well as films and other entertainment.

There's a Grande Noite de Fado (Grand Night of Fado) festival in September; check with the turismo for exact dates.

Brazilian Music Porto's favourite venue for Brazilian music is *Coqueiro* (☎ 609 90 09) at Avenida da Boavista 1588, 6th floor.

Bars The most lively bar area is around Ribeira, especially along Rua de Fonte Taurina and Rua de São João. The bars usually open at 10 pm and close at around 3 am (later on weekends). Some have a minimum charge (anything from 500$00 to 1000$00).

Among the more enticing of the trendy bars in Rua de Fonte Taurina is *Aniki Bóbó* (☎ 32 46 19), at No 36, which often features live rock and Portuguese pop; it's open nightly except Sundays. Around the corner at Praça da Ribeira 6, *Meia Cave* (☎ 32 32 14) is a posher, pricier bar with rock, salsa, acid jazz (Wednesday nights) and techno (Thursdays). *Capítulo Final Bar Grill* (☎ 208 36 40), at Rua Infante Dom Henrique 35, is a popular student haunt and is open nightly from 11 pm to 4 am. If it's down-to-earth locals you want to hang out with, *Taverna Filha da Mãe Preta*, at Rua Canastreiros 26 (a back alley off the Cais da Ribeira), is a grubby stand-up bar with cheap snacks and cheap booze.

Along Rua de São João, bars come thick and fast: check out *Cosa Nostra* at No 76 and *Oporto Rock Bar* at No 89. At Rua de Belomonte 67, *Pinguim Café* (☎ 32 31 00), apart from being a popular bar, is a great cultural rendezvous point, with everything from poetry readings and art exhibitions to live jazz and rock. It starts warming up at around 11 pm.

The most salubrious place to drink port wine is *Solar do Vinho do Porto* (☎ 609 47 49) at Rua Entre Quintas 220, beside the Jardim do Palácio de Cristal. This comfortable bar with a riverview terrace is

surprisingly welcoming to novice port drinkers: the waiters help you choose from hundreds of varieties (prices start from around 150$00 a glass). It's open weekdays from 10 am to 11.45 pm and Saturdays from 11 am to 10.45 pm.

Gay & Lesbian Bars Porto's highest profile gay bar ('for gay boys 'n girls 'n cool straights') is the *Glam Gay Club* (☎ 208 71 07) at Rua Dr Barbosa de Castro 63. The music varies nightly, with special guests on Wednesday nights. More discreet is *Bustos* (☎ 31 48 76), at Rua Guedes de Azevedo 203; it's open weekends only from 10 pm to 4 am.

Spectator Sports
Porto's football (soccer) team, FC Porto, is a major rival to Lisbon's Benfica, and is frequently league champion. You can watch them at Porto's Estádio das Antas (take bus No 6 from Praça da Liberdade).

Things to Buy
Porto is a great place to shop, even if you don't end up buying anything: establishments range from funky to chic and there are entire streets specialising in particular items (eg, Rua Galeria de Paris for fine art, Rua da Fábrica for bookshops).

Modern malls are multiplying, though they're thankfully still few and far between. Among popular ones are Centro Comercial Brasília on Praça Mouzinho de Albuquerque in Boavista; the underground Clérigos Shopping off Rua Carmelitas; and the newest megacomplex, Centro Comercial Cidade do Porto, on Rua Gonçalo Sampaio in Boavista.

Port & Wine Port is the obvious purchase in Porto. If you can't get to the port-wine lodges of Vila Nova de Gaia, you'll find plenty of alternative sources in Porto – often with cheaper prices for run-of-the-mill stuff. A photogenic port speciality shop is Casa Oriental, at Rua dos Clérigos 111, which has bacalhau dangling outside. Other good sources are Casa Januário, at Rua do Bonjardim 352, and Garrafeira do Carmo at

Rua do Carmo 17 (the latter specialises in vintage port and high-quality wines).

Camping Supplies Porto's best camping shop is Casa Coelho (☎ 200 57 22; fax 32 03 40) at Rua Sá da Bandeira 200. Nearby Luciano Matos (☎ 200 48 80), at Rua do Bonjardim 278, has more general kitchen and camping equipment. Tagus Travel (see Travel Agencies under Information) has a small camping shop.

Handicrafts The Centro Regional de Artes Tradicionais (Regional Centre for Traditional Arts & Crafts, or CRAT) has a select display of handmade textiles, puppets, toys, glass and pottery. It's in the Ribeira district at Rua da Reboleira 37 and is open Tuesday to Friday from 10 am to noon and 1 to 6 pm, and at weekends from 1 to 7 pm. The Mercado do Bolhão also has basketry and ceramics, and in Praça da Batalha there are jewellery and craft stalls.

Shoes Porto has some great shoe bargains. You'll find *sapatarias* (shoe shops) everywhere, especially along Rua Mouzinho da Silveira, Rua 31 de Janeiro and Rua de Cedofeita.

Speciality Items For delightful speciality shops selling cork items, brushes and fishing tackle, check out Rua Mouzinho da Silveira. At Rua Formosa 279, the beautiful Art Deco Apérola do Bolhão is the place to pick up nuts, dried fruits and other quality groceries. If you want to throw yourself into the spirit of Porto's Queimas das Fitas student week in May, you'll find all the necessary silly plastic gadgets and party gear at Casa dos Plásticos, Rua das Oliveiras 87.

Markets For cheese, olives, fresh bread, strawberries and other luscious fruit, you can't beat the bustling municipal Mercado do Bolhão, which is off Rua Sá da Bandeira. It's open weekdays from 7 am to 5 pm and Saturdays from 7 am to 1 pm.

Among the city's flea markets (best on Saturday mornings) the most rewarding one is at Alameda das Fontaínhas, south-east of Praça Batalha. There's also a scrawny one full of junk and cheap clothes and shoes in Calçada de Vandoma, below the cathedral, and a touristy market along the Cais da Ribeira (good for t-shirts, woollen jumpers, tacky souvenirs and some traditional toys).

Getting There & Away

Air Both international and domestic flights use Francisco Sá Carneiro airport (☎ 948 21 41 for flight information), which is about 20 km north-west of the city centre.

Domestic links include daily Portugália and TAP flights to/from Lisbon and a weekly direct Portugália flight to Faro (but none back), plus TAP flights to/from Funchal daily, Porto Santo weekly and Ponta Delgada every other day. Direct international connections include one or more on most days from London, Paris, Frankfurt, Amsterdam, Brussels and Madrid. Refer to the Getting There & Away and Getting Around chapters for more details

Useful booking numbers in Porto include TAP (☎ 608 02 10) and Portugália (600 82 80). Country-wide numbers are also available for TAP (☎ 0808-21 31 41, at local rates from anywhere in Portugal) and British Airways (☎ 0500-1251, toll-free from anywhere in Portugal).

Bus – Domestic Connections There are at least four places to catch long-distance coaches to points within Portugal.

With the fewest intermediate stops, Renex (☎ 200 33 95; fax 31 04 01), at Rua Carmelitas 7 and 32, is the best option for Lisbon (1800$00), with about a dozen express departures per day. They also go to the Algarve (eg Faro for 3000$00) several times a day, with a change at Lisbon, as well as north to Braga. The ticket office at No 32 is open 24 hours a day. Coaches depart from near this office.

The best bet for express *(rápidas)* connections to the Minho is one of three lines operating from the north side of Praça Dona Filipa de Lencastre. Rodoviária de Entre Douro e Minho, or REDM (☎ 200 31 52), goes mainly to Braga (610$00), with over 20 departures a day. Autoviação do Minho or AV Minho (☎ 200 61 21) runs mainly to Viana do Castelo (750$00), with five departures. João Terreira das Neves (☎ 200 08 81) concentrates on Guimarães (610$00), with eight departures. Weekend services are pretty limited.

From the Paragem Atlântico terminal at Rua Alexandre Herculano 370, Rede Expressos (☎ 200 69 54; fax 208 76 12) goes all over Portugal – eg Braga (about 10 a day, 700$00), Viana do Castelo (three services, 900$00), Vila Real (three, 800$00), Bragança (three, 1250$00), Lisbon (10, 1800$00) and the Algarve. Under the name RBL (Rodoviária da Beira Litoral) it goes to Aveiro, Coimbra and other points in the Beiras. Across the road at No 339 is an office for a line called Valpi (☎ 200 75 55), which goes several times a day to Amarante (690$00) with a change at Penafiel.

Rodonorte (☎ & fax 200 56 37), at Rua Ateneu Comércial do Porto 19, has around eight express coaches a day to Amarante and Vila Real (880$00), and several to Bragança (1350$00). Its office is open weekdays from 7.30 am to 8 pm, Saturdays from 10 am to 2 pm and 3.30 to 7 pm, and Sundays from 10 am to noon and 1.30 to 8 pm. It's also open on Friday and Sunday evenings from 8.30 pm to midnight.

Bus – International Connections Northern Portugal's main international carrier is Inter-

norte, a Eurolines affiliate with connections throughout Europe (see the Getting There & Away chapter). Although they have an office (☎ 69 32 20; fax 609 60 16) at Praça da Galiza 96, most travel agencies in town can book their long-distance coaches. An affiliated regional line, Rodonorte (see Domestic Connections), links Porto to Valladolid (in Spain) on weekdays for 3900$00.

IASA (☎ 208 43 38; fax 31 01 91), at Praça Dona Filipa de Lencastre 141, runs coaches five times a week between Paris and Porto (via Braga) for about 13,500$00.

Train Porto, a rail hub for northern Portugal, has three major train stations. Most international connections, and all *intercidade* links throughout Portugal, start at Campanhã, the largest station, two km east of the centre.

Interregional and regional connections start from either Campanhã or the very central São Bento station, just off the bottom of Praça da Liberdade. All lines from São Bento also pass through Campanhã, though some trains only start at Campanhã. Bus No 35 runs frequently between these two stations.

Trindade station, a few blocks north of the câmara municipal, has trains to Póvoa de Varzim and Guimarães only.

At São Bento you can book tickets for any destination and any station. São Bento and Campanhã have competent information offices which are open from 8.30 am to at least 7.30 pm every day. For information by telephone (all trains and all stations) call ☎ 56 41 41 from 8 am to 11 pm daily.

Trains & Azulejos
The last place you'd expect to find some of Portugal's finest azulejos is in a railway station. But check out the splendid entry hall of São Bento station, which has tiles, painted in 1930 by Jorge Colaço, depicting everything from everyday scenes to historic Portuguese battles.

Other train stations serving as azulejo art galleries are at Aveiro (see the Beiras chapter) and Pinhão (see East of Peso da Régua in this chapter). ■

Car The best per-day, unlimited-mileage rate we found – about 5000$00 a day for under a week, 4200$00 a day for longer – was from City Tour, whose only pick-up point (☎ 941 74 64; fax 941 74 65) is at the airport. Other agencies with low rates are Nova Rent (☎ 610 76 97), AA Castanheira (☎ 606 52 56), Kenning (☎ 81 43 40) and Rupauto (☎ 32 52 58). Mainstream agencies include Avis (toll-free in Portugal ☎ 0500 10 02), Hertz (☎ 31 23 87), Europcar (☎ 31 83 98) and Budget (☎ 609 81 13).

Motorcycle At Gesrent (☎ 550 77 39) a Yamaha 50 is 3300$00 per day (for up to three days), 3000$00 a day (for up to a week) or 2800$00 a day (for more than a week).

Getting Around
The Airport Bus No 56 (160$00) runs between the airport and the south side of Jardim da Cordoaria (also called Jardim de João Chagas) from 6 am to midnight, about every half-hour during the day and hourly in the early and late hours. This is the only central-area stop until 9 pm, when buses move to the other side of the park and also stop at the bottom of Praça da Liberdade. A taxi from Praça da Liberdade to the airport is 2500$00 to 3000$00, plus possible baggage charges of 300$00. The trip normally takes about 45 minutes; during peak traffic time, allow an hour or more.

Bus Porto's municipal transport agency, Serviços de Transportes Colectivos de Porto or STCP, operates an extensive bus system from hubs at Jardim da Cordoaria (also called Jardim de João Chagas), Praça de Liberdade and Praça Dom João I. Individual 160$00 tickets are sold on the bus. From STCP kiosks near bus stops you can get a *caderneta* of 20 tickets for 1400$00 or a *bilhete diário* (day pass) for 350$00. The STCP kiosk (☎ 606 82 26) opposite São Bento station, open daily from 8 am to 7.30 pm, sells a four-day (1700$00) or one-week (2200$00) Passe Turístico. Discounts are offered to student-card holders.

Tram Porto's trams used to be one of the delights of the city, but only one is left: the No 18, trundling from Carmo out to Foz do Douro and back to Boavista (about 45 minutes in all) every quarter-hour from 6 am to 9 pm – except Sundays and holidays when a No 18 bus does the route. The fare is 85$00, or you can use a bus pass (the conductor sells day passes). Sentimental fans can stop en route at the Tram Museum (see Museu dos Carros Eléctricos).

Dial-a-Ride STCP, the Portuguese Red Cross (CVP) and the regional social-security agency (CRSS) jointly operate a dial-a-ride minibus service for disabled people. It's available daily from 7 am to 9 pm. Call CVP at ☎ 606 68 72 or CRSS at ☎ 606 66 46.

Taxi Taxis are good value and fairly easy to flag in the central area (except at meal times). Figure on about 500$00 for Boavista to Praça da Liberdade. An additional charge is made if you cross the Ponte de Dom Luís I to Vila Nova de Gaia or leave the city limits.

Car & Motorcycle Driving in the city centre is a pain, thanks to gridlocked traffic, one-way streets and scarce parking.

Bicycle Porto is best discovered on foot, although bikeless but determined visitors can rent mountain bikes from Nova Rent (☎ 610 76 97) or Gesrent (☎ 510 36 36). It costs 3900$00 for a weekend and 1700$00 per day for up to a week or 8400$00 per week.

VILA DO CONDE
• *pop 20,100* • *postcode 4480* • *area code* ☎ *052*
Once a quiet ship-building port, and famous for its lace, Vila do Conde has become a popular seaside resort and handicrafts centre. Its beaches (a couple of km to the south) are some of the best north of Porto (26 km away) and connections are easy enough to make a day trip feasible.

The town itself, at the mouth of the Rio Ave, remains charmingly unaffected by the fuss at the beach, offering a far less touristy atmosphere than the over-developed beach resort of Póvoa do Varzim four km to the north.

Orientation & Information
The town is dominated by the Mosteiro de Santa Clara and adjacent aqueduct. The train station is a five to 10-minute walk across the river from the town centre. The bus terminal is in the town centre, on Rua 5 de Outubro. There's a small turismo (with handicrafts for

sale) opposite the bus station, but the main turismo (☎ 64 27 00; fax 64 18 76) is around the corner in an ivy-clad cottage at Rua 25 de Abril 103. From June to September it's open daily from 9 am to 12.30 pm and 2 to 5.30 pm; at other times it's open on weekdays only.

There's an excellent market every Friday opposite the main turismo.

Mosteiro de Santa Clara

This fortress-like convent was founded in 1318 by Dom Afonso Sanches but considerably altered and enlarged in the 18th century. At one time over 100 nuns lived here but after the 1834 decree abolishing religious orders only a few were allowed to stay; the last one died here in 1893. The convent served as a prison from 1902 to 1944, and since then has been a reformatory for teenage boys. The imposing aqueduct which brought water to the convent from Póvoa de Varzim apparently once had 999 arches.

The fortified church outside the main complex is the only part to have retained its severe Gothic style. Nuns' tombstones line the route to the church door. Inside are the carved tombs of Dom Afonso, Dona Teresa Martins (his wife) and their children. A painting in the sacristy tells of the 'election' of an unpopular nun as Mother Superior on the strength of votes from the dead. Remains of a fine 18th-century cloister are also worth seeing; its fountain is the terminal for the aqueduct.

The church (with one of the boys from the reformatory school as a guide) is open daily from 9 am to noon and 2 to 5.30 pm.

Igreja Matriz

This impressive Manueline parish church dates from the early 16th century. Its ornately carved doorway shows a distinctly Spanish Plateresque style (reflecting the work of Spanish *plateros* or silversmiths) thanks to its Basque artist, João de Castilho. The bell tower dates from the 17th century. Outside the church is a striking *pelourinho* (pillory), remodelled in the 18th century, with the arm

of justice sticking out the top and brandishing a sword.

School of Lace-making

Long famous for its lace, Vila do Conde is one of the few places in the country with an active school of the art, founded in 1918. Children as young as four or five come to learn from local experts such as Maria Beatrix Estrela, who started learning from her mother when she was three. Among a display of finished products is one sample which, using 1400 bobbins, took over two years to make. To visit the school, on Rua de São Bento, ask the turismo.

Beaches

The two best beaches, Praia da Forno and Praia de Nossa Senhora da Guia, a couple of km south of town, have lots of sand and calm seas suitable for families with young kids. Plenty of cafés and kiosks offer refreshments and meals.

Special Events

Suitably for a town known for handicrafts, a major regional *feira de artesanato* (handicrafts fair) is held here in the last week of July and first week of August.

The biggest religious festival is the Festa de São João on 23 June, when a candle-lit procession winds through the streets to the beach.

Places to Stay

Camping The closest camping ground (☎ 63 32 37) is about three km south of town, near the village of Árvore. It's open year-round and is close to the beach.

Private Rooms The turismo has a list of rooms, which get snapped up quickly in summer. Expect to pay 4500$00 for a double.

Pensões & Residencials One of the best budget places is *Le Villageois* (☎ 63 11 19), at Praça da República 94, where clean, quiet rooms (with shower) cost around 3500$00 a double. *Pensão Patarata* (☎ 63 18 94) is a cute riverside house at Cais das Lavandeiras

18. It has doubles for around 5000$00 (with bath) and a restaurant.

The best up-market choice is the central *Estalagem do Brasão* (☎ 64 20 16), on Avenida Dr João Canavarro, where an elegantly furnished double is around 9000$00, with breakfast.

Places to Eat
In addition to the locally popular restaurants at *Le Villageois* and *Pensão Patarata*, there are several chic options along the riverside and on Rua 5 de Outubro.

Things to Buy
The Centro de Artesanato (handicrafts centre) on Rua 5 de Outubro is the best place to pick up pottery, wooden toys, basketry, embroidered linen and, of course, lace. Local lacemakers sometimes work here too.

The Friday market sells everything from woollen socks and lace collars to freshly made brown bread.

Getting There & Away
Bus Two express coaches run each weekday from Lisbon to the northern border town of Moncão, with stops at Coimbra, Porto, Vila do Conde and Viana do Castelo. About five buses also run each day from Porto.

Train Vila do Conde is on the Porto to Famalição line. Trains leave at least hourly from Porto's Trindade station for the 50-minute run.

AMARANTE
• *pop 4900 • postcode 4600 • area code ☎ 055*
This is a place to visit purely for its setting. It's a gracious town straddling the Rio Tâmega by way of a handsome, historical stone bridge. The river is dotted with swans and rowing boats and the banks are lined with willows. Sturdy, balconied houses rise in tiers up the steep banks. Anchoring it all at one end of the bridge is a church and monastery dedicated to the town's patron saint, Gonçalo. Amarante is also known for its eggy pastries – and not only the phallic

cakes that appear during the cheerful festivals of São Gonçalo.

The most fitting and delightful way to get here is on the narrow-gauge Linha da Tâmega railway (see Getting There & Away).

History
The town may date back to the 4th century BC, but archaeological records are scanty. Gonçalo, a 13th-century hermit, is credited with everything from the founding of the town to the construction of its first bridge. His hermitage grew into the trademark church by the bridge.

Amarante's strategic position on the Tâmega and on the roads to Porto, Braga and Trás-os-Montes was nearly its undoing in 1809, when the French lost their brief grip on Portugal. Marshall Soult's troops retreated north-eastward after abandoning Porto, plundering as they went. On 18 April a detachment under Generale Loison arrived at Amarante in search of a river crossing, but plucky citizens and troops led by General Francisco da Silveira (the future Count of Amarante) held them off, allowing residents to escape to the far bank and bringing the French to a standstill. The French retaliated by trashing the upper town and burning much of it to the ground, and it was two weeks before they managed to trick their way across. Loison withdrew from the area about a week later and the French were soon in full retreat across the Minho and Trás-os-Montes.

Amarante has also suffered frequent natural invasions by the Tâmega. Little *cheia* (high-water level) plaques in Rua 31 de Janeiro and Largo Conselheiro António Cândido tell the harrowing story. The last big flood was in 1962.

Orientation
The Tâmega, which flows south-west through the middle of town, is spanned by the old Ponte de São Gonçalo and a huge modern highway bridge upstream. Planted on Praça da República at the west end of the old bridge is the Igreja de São Gonçalo. In the former cloisters behind it are the câmara

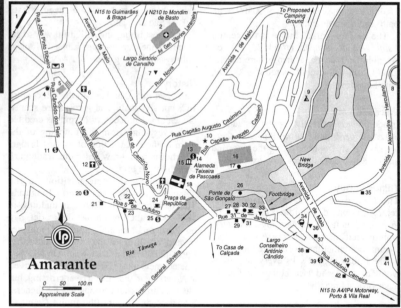

Amarante

0   50   100 m
Approximate Scale

municipal (town hall) and the turismo, facing east onto the market square, Alameda Teixeira de Pascoaes.

Buses stop in Largo Conselheiro António Cândido, 300m east of the bridge. The small train station is an 800m walk north-west of the bridge.

Information

The very helpful turismo (☎ 43 22 59), facing Alameda Teixeira de Pascoaes, is open daily from 9.30 am to 7 pm (without a lunch break in summer).

Several banks with ATMs are along Rua 5 de Outubro, and at least one is on the other side in Rua António Carneiro. The telephone office (open weekdays from 9 am to 12.30 pm and 1.30 to 5 pm) is a short walk up Rua 5 de Outubro. The tiny post office (open weekdays from 8.30 am to 12.30 pm and 1.30 to 6 pm) is near the train station on Rua João Pinto Ribeiro.

The hospital (☎ 43 76 31) is on Largo

Sertório de Carvalho. The police station (☎ 43 20 15) is at the top of Alameda Teixeira de Pascoaes, near the turismo.

The biggest days at the mercado municipal (town market), just east down the hill from the turismo, are Wednesdays and Saturdays.

Ponte de São Gonçalo

The granite São Gonçalo Bridge is Ama-

Souza Cardoso

Amarante's Amadeo de Souza Cardoso (1887-1918) is probably the best known Portuguese artist of this century. A friend of Modigliani and a student of Cézanne during his eight years spent in Paris, he bucked the trend among his contemporaries, abandoning naturalism for cubism and a home-grown variety of impressionism. ■

PLACES TO STAY		28	Restaurante Zé de	10	Police Station
9	Municipal Camping		Calçada	11	Bank
	Ground	31	Kilowat	12	Igreja de São Pedro
21	Albergaria Dona	32	Tinoca	13	Câmara Municipal
	Margaritta (Hotel	33	O Chico Café	14	Turismo
	Silva)	36	Restaurante A Quelha	15	Museu Amadeo de
27	Residencial Estoril	37	Residencial Raposeira		Souza Cardoso
29	Casa Zé de Calçada	40	Adega Regional de	16	Mercado Municipal
35	Casa da Cerca d'Além		Amarante	17	Boat Rental
37	Residencial Raposeira			18	Igreja de São Gonçalo
38	Residencial Príncipe			19	Igreja de São Domin-
41	Hotel Residencial	**OTHER**			gos
	Amaranto	1	Train Station	20	Bank
42	Hotel Navarras	2	Hospital	22	Telephone Office
		3	Post Office	23	Pharmacy
		4	Pharmacy	25	Bank
PLACES TO EAT		5	Solar dos Magalhães	26	Boat Rental
7	Restaurante A Taberna	6	Igreja da Misericórdia	30	Valpi Bus Ticket Office
24	Café	8	Bullring	34	Rodonorte Bus Station
27	Residencial Estoril			39	Bank

rante's visual centrepiece, and a historical symbol (the defence against the French is marked by a plaque at the south-east end). It also offers one of the best views of town. The original bridge, allegedly built at Gonçalo's urging in the 13th century, collapsed in a flood in 1763; this one was completed in 1790.

Igreja de São Gonçalo

The Mosteiro de São Gonçalo and its prominent, rather dour church, which is topped with a brick-red cupola, were founded in 1540 by João III, though the buildings weren't finished until 1620.

Beside the church's multitiered, Italian Renaissance side portal (with a carved figure of Gonçalo in a niche) is an arcaded gallery with 17th-century statues of Dom João and the other kings who ruled while the monastery was under construction – Sebastião, Henrique and Felipe I. The bell tower was added in the 18th century.

Inside are finely carved and gilded baroque altar and pulpits, an organ casing held up by three giants, and Gonçalo's tomb in a tiny chapel to the left of the altar. Gonçalo is also patron saint of marriages, and tradition has it that the not-so-young-anymore in search of a mate will get their wish within a year if they touch the statue on

the tomb. Its limestone toes, fingers and face have been all but kissed and rubbed away.

Through the north portal is the peaceful Renaissance cloister – two cloisters actually, one still attached to the church and the other occupied by the town hall.

The church is open during daylight hours, daily.

Other Churches

Up a switchback path and steps beside São Gonçalo is the round, 18th-century Igreja de São Domingos, with a little museum of church furnishings that never seems to be open. Up on Rua Miguel Bombarda, the baroque-fronted Igreja de São Pedro has a nave decorated with 17th-century blue and yellow azulejos.

Museu Amadeo de Souza Cardoso

In part of the cloisters facing the market square is a delightful, eclectic collection of contemporary art, a surprise in such a small town and a bargain at 200$00 for entry. It's named for and dominated by favourite son Souza Cardoso, with sketches, cartoons, portraits and abstracts. But there's more: don't overlook the very still portraits and landscapes of António Carneiro, and Jaime Azinheira's touching *Escultura*. Upstairs around the cloister are Roman pottery, millstones and tools.

The museum is open daily, except Mondays and holidays, from 10 am to 12.30 pm and 2 to 5.30 pm (last entry at noon and 5 pm). At the rear of the ground floor is the small, well-thumbed Gulbenkian Library.

Solar dos Magalhães
A stark, uncaptioned memento of the 'French fortnight' is the burned-out skeleton of an old manor house above Rua Cândido dos Reis, near the train station.

Casa de Calçada
Behind high walls at the south-east end of Ponte de São Gonçalo is Casa de Calçada, the manor house and estate of a prominent local family (who apparently own most of Rua 31 de Janeiro, once part of the estate). There were plans (and some site work) to build a five-star hotel here, but that was suspended and the grounds are presently closed to the public.

Activities
You can potter around the phlegmatic Rio Tâmega in paddle boats or rowboats, which are available for rent along the riverbank between the old and new bridges, accessible from below the market or via a narrow walkway from the other side. Follow the *barcos e gaivotas* signs. There are several beaches upstream, but the river is pretty polluted.

Special Events
Amarante lets go during the Festas de Junho, which is held on the weekend of the first Saturday in June, with an all-night drum competition (the winners are the ones who last the longest), livestock fair, children's parade, handicrafts market, bullfights and fireworks, all rounded off with a procession from the Igreja de São Gonçalo. This is also a *romaria* in honour of São Gonçalo. The town gets into the spirit during the previous week too, with concerts, exhibitions and elaborate street lighting. Accommodation, not surprisingly, is hard to find at this time.

During the Festas de Junho (and on São Gonçalo's day, 13 January), unmarried men and women swap little phallic-shaped pastry cakes called *falus de Gonçalo* or *bolos de Gonçalo* – a delightfully frank tradition probably descended from a pre-Christian fertility cult. Gonçalo is the patron saint of marriages, and this is the time to pray for a partner.

Places to Stay
Except during the Festas de Junho, there's plenty of accommodation, most of it overpriced. Try to avoid street-side rooms, which are noisy everywhere.

Camping The small, fairly cheap municipal *Quinta dos Frades* camping ground (☎ 43 21 33) is on the riverbank just beyond the market. This site is due to be replaced by a big new one about 1.5 km upstream, though it has been under construction for years and nobody is holding their breath.

Pensões & Residencials Two threadbare residencials face one another across Largo Conselheiro António Cândido near the bus station. The *Raposeira* (☎ 43 22 21), at No 41, has doubles for 3500$00 without bath or 5000$00 with, and the *Príncipe* (☎ 43 29 56), across at No 78, has doubles for 4000$00 with shower or 5000$00 with bath and toilet. Both have their own restaurants and snack bars.

More comfortable, romantic and pricey is *Residencial Estoril* (☎ 43 12 91, ☎ 43 18 92), on Rua 31 de Janeiro, where a street-facing double with bath is 7000$00, while one with a balcony over the river is 8000$00, all with breakfast.

Hotels The best hotel bargain is the small, polite *Albergaria Dona Margaritta* (☎ 43 21 10; fax 43 79 77), formerly the *Hotel Silva*, at Rua Cândido dos Reis 53, west of the bridge. Air-conditioned doubles with bath and TV are 6000$00 on the street side, and

8000$00 to 9000$00 depending on facilities on the river side, with breakfast.

Uphill from the bus station, on Rua António Carneiro, is *Hotel Navarras* (☎ 43 10 36; fax 43 29 91). It has a swimming pool and spotless, boring doubles with everything (including breakfast) for 12,000$00. Across Avenida 1 de Maio is the more or less equivalent *Hotel Residencial Amaranto* (☎ 44 92 06; fax 42 59 49).

Turihab *Casa Zé de Calçada* (☎ 42 20 23), on Rua 31 de Janeiro, a former townhouse oddly categorised 'Turismo Rural', has a few elegant doubles for at least 8000$00, but street noise destroys the atmosphere. Check in at the restaurant of the same name across the street.

Better value and more peaceful are several converted manor houses around Amarante, including *Casa da Cerca d'Além* (☎ 43 14 49), on Avenida Alexandre Herculano, where doubles with bath, bedroom and sitting room are 8000$00 to 10,000$00, with breakfast. Ask at the turismo.

Places to Eat

Amarante has at least three cheap, plain and very good restaurantes regionais that would make the town worth a stop even if it weren't pretty. Our favourite is *A Quelha*, a mini-adega with smoked hams dangling above half a dozen wooden tables and benches. It's tucked behind the bus station on Rua da Olivença. A plate of local queijo (cheese) and presunto (ham), plus soup, is about 750$00. Big half-portions are about the same and petiscos (snacks) are 350$00 to 600$00. Wash it down with beer or a mug of red wine, and add your card or poem to hundreds stuck on the wall.

Plainer but equally packed out at lunch is *Adega Regional de Amarante*, opposite the Hotel Navarras on Rua António Carneiro. A good 10-minute climb above the river through the old town, but worth the effort, is *Restaurante A Taberna* (☎ 43 16 70) on Rua Nova (or up the back steps from Largo Sertório de Carvalho, opposite the hospital). It's open daily from 10 am to midnight and

has friendly vibes and first-rate regional cooking.

Rua 31 de Janeiro is lined with cafés and restaurants, notable and otherwise. *O Chico Café* at No 197 is at least cheap: 500$00 for the prata do dia plus soup, bread and a glass of wine. *Tinoca*, a teahouse with a river view at No 137, is full of local-style pastries. Amarante's most idiosyncratic eatery is a grumpy tasca called *Kilowat* at Rua 31 de Janeiro 104. It has hams hanging by the door and sells only sandwiches of local ham, and wine by the mug. It's open daily until about 9 pm.

More style than substance is *Restaurante Zé de Calçada* (☎ 42 20 23), at the west end of Rua 31 de Janeiro, with courses for 2500$00 to 3000$00 at lunch, and more in the evening.

Most residencials have restaurants of average quality. Those at both the *Raposeira* and the *Príncipe* have half-serves of Portuguese standards for under 1000$00, plus ground-floor cafés with sandwiches and snacks. *Residencial Estoril* also has a restaurant.

Entertainment

Numerous pubs and disco-bars are on Avenida General Silveira, the downstream extension of Rua 31 de Janeiro. The bullring is out on Avenida Alexandre Herculano.

Getting There & Away

Bus Rodonorte coaches on the Porto-Vila Real route stop at the station on Largo Conselheiro António Cândido about 15 times a day; Porto (700$00) is 1¼ hours away and Vila Real (650$00) is 40 minutes away. Rodonorte goes to Mirandela and Bragança about seven times a day, and to Coimbra and Lisbon twice on most days.

Rede Expressos also comes through en route to Porto, Vila Real and Bragança at least twice a day; ask at the snack bar of Residencial Príncipe. Valpi (☎ 43 24 01) is a regional line with connections all day to Porto, but with a change at Penafiel; it's at Rua 31 de Janeiro 107.

Train The pokey narrow-gauge connection from the Douro valley mainline at Livração up to Amarante takes 25 minutes and costs 100$00. There are seven to nine trains a day, of which most have good mainline connections. The two-hour journey between Porto and Amarante (five or six a day) is 590$00.

LAMEGO
• *pop 10,000* • *postcode 5100* • *area code* ☎ *054*
Calling itself the 'cultural capital of the Douro', Lamego, 12 km south of the Rio Douro, is a rich, handsome town surrounded by terraced hills of vineyards and fruit orchards. Though officially in the Beira Alta, it belongs in spirit and tradition to the Douro: the road linking it to Peso da Régua was built by the Marquês de Pombal in the 18th century specifically so that Lamego's famously fragrant wine ('smelling wine' as turismo brochures call it) could be shipped to Porto.

Today Lamego's Raposeira sparkling wine (the best of Portugal's few such wines) gives it unique status among wine connoisseurs. The stunning baroque stairway of the Igreja de Nossa Senhora dos Remédios puts it on the cultural map. Well worth a digression from the Rio Douro trail, Lamego also makes a pleasant base for exploring the surrounding countryside and its half-ruined monasteries and medieval chapels.

History
Lamego was considered an important centre even in the time of the Suevi, who made it a bishopric, a status re-established in 1071. In 1143, the country's first *cortes,* or parliament, was held here, confirming Afonso Henriques as king of Portugal.

The town's wealth grew from its position on east-west trading routes and from its wines, which were already famous in the 16th century. Some of its most elegant mansions date from this time, while others date from the 18th century, when Lamego's wine production took off commercially.

Orientation
The town is overlooked by two hills: on the

northern hill stands the ruins of a 12th-century castle, and on the south-western one is the Igreja de Nossa Senhora dos Remédios. The church's monumental baroque stairway descends to Avenida Dr Alfredo de Sousa, a boulevard with a shady park in the middle. This is just a few minutes walk from the heart of town, which is dominated by the Sé (cathedral). Nearby, behind the Museu de Lamego, is the bus station.

Information
The conscientious turismo (☎ 620 05; fax 640 14) on Avenida Visconde Guedes Teixeira is headquarters for the Região de Turismo do Douro Sul and has plenty of information on both Lamego and the region as a whole. It's open weekdays from 10 am to 12.30 pm and 2 to 6 pm, and Saturday from 10 am to 12.30 pm. From July through September its hours are extended to 7 pm on weekdays and from 10 am to 12.30 pm and 2 to 5.30 pm on Saturday and Sunday.

Igreja de Nossa Senhora dos Remédios
This 18th-century church is a major pilgrimage site, especially during the Festas de Nossa Senhora dos Remédios (see Special Events), when devotees arrive in their thousands. The church itself is of little interest and is completely overshadowed by a fantastic stairway (similar to the one at Bom Jesus near Braga) that zigzags up the hill and is decorated with azulejos and urns, fountains and statues.

Sé
The cathedral has little left of its 12th-century origins except for the base of its square belfry. The rest, including a brilliantly carved Renaissance triple portal and a lovely cloister, dates mostly from the 16th and 18th centuries.

Museu de Lamego
Housed in the grand 18th-century former episcopal palace is one of Portugal's best regional museums. The collection features some remarkable pieces: a series of five works by the renowned 16th-century Portu-

Lamego

0   50   100 m

PLACES TO STAY
1 Albergaria do Cerrado
3 Ana Paula Dormidas
13 Pensão Solar da Sé
14 Residencial Império
16 Pensão Silva
19 Maria Assunção Lapa
    Monteiro Dormidas
22 Pensão Residencial Solar
    do Espírito Santo
25 Hotel Parque

PLACES TO EAT
8 Casa de Pasto Vítor Pinto
9 Casa de Pasto Albino
   Alves Teixeira
15 Casa Filipe
18 Restaurant Tás da Sé
20 Restaurant Avenida

OTHER
2 Castle
4 RBL Bus Stop
5 Bus Station
6 Museu de Lamego
7 Market
10 Totobolo Shop
    (for RBL Bus Tickets)
11 Turismo
12 Sé
17 Turismo Santa Cruz
    (for Rodonorte Bus Tickets)
21 Post Office
23 Capela do Desterro
24 Igreja de Nossa
    Senhora dos Remédios

guese painter known as Grão Vasco, richly worked Brussels tapestries from the same period, and heavily gilded 17th-century chapels rescued in their entirety from the long-gone Convento das Chagas.

The museum is open daily, except Sunday afternoon and Mondays, from 10 am to 12.30 pm and 2 to 6 pm (to 5 pm from October through May). Admission is 250$00 (free on Sunday mornings).

Castelo
Climb Rua da Olaria behind the turismo and head along Rua de Almacave to narrow Rua

do Castelinho on the right, which leads to the castle. What little remains of the 12th-century castle – some walls and a tower – now belongs to the boy scouts, who made it their local headquarters after a heroic 1970s effort to clear the site of rubbish.

In summer it's usually open daily (on weekends only during the rest of the year). If you're lucky, a scout may give you a guided tour. Nip up to the roof for spectacular views.

Caves da Raposeira
Portugal's best known sparkling wines are

DOURO

produced by the Seagram company in Lamego (the only other champagne-like wine comes from the Bairrada region of Coimbra). The winery (☎ 65 50 03) is a couple of km west of town on the Viseu road. Free guided tours and tastings are held on weekdays at 10 and 11 am and 2, 3 and 4 pm.

Special Events
Lamego's Igreja de Nossa Senhora dos Remédios is the focus of the biggest festival of the year, the Festa de Nossa Senhora dos Remédios, which manages to last several weeks from the end of August to the middle of September. The highlight is a procession on 7 and 8 September when ox-drawn carts carrying religious scenes parade through the streets, and devotees climb the stairway to the church on bended knee. Less religious aspects of the festival include rock concerts, folk dancing and car racing. The turismo has full details.

Places to Stay
Camping The nearby *Dr João de Almeida* camping ground (☎ 620 90) at Turissera has closed with no hint of when it might reopen. Your next option is a site (☎ 68 92 46) run by an international development organisation called Instituto dos Assuntos Culturais (ICA), which is 20 km south of Lamego in Mezio. Take any Viseu-bound bus.

Private Rooms The turismo has details of several attractive dormidas, including the small, clean rooms of *Maria Assunção Lapa Monteiro* (☎ 625 56), at Rua Santa Cruz 15, which cost around 4000$00 a double. For an apartment, contact the multilingual *Ana Paula* (☎ 630 22, ☎ 632 01), who also has doubles, at Avenida 5 de Outubro 143, for around 5000$00.

Pensões & Residencials *Pensão Silva* (☎ 620 60) on Largo da Sé, within bell-ringing earshot of the cathedral, has cosy doubles (without bath) from 4000$00. The rather dull *Residencial Império* (☎ 627 42), at Travessa dos Loureiros 6, has singles/doubles for 4000$00/6000$00. *Pensão Residencial Solar do Espírito Santo* (☎ 643 86), with entrances on Avenida Dr Alfredo de Sousa and Rua Alexandre Herculano, has air-conditioned rooms with private bath for 4000$00/7000$00, including breakfast. At *Pensão Solar da Sé* (☎ 620 60), opposite the cathedral on Largo da Sé, several of the functionally furnished rooms (all with bath) have splendid, if noisy, views of the cathedral; they're 4800$00/7800$00, with breakfast.

Hotels The *Hotel Parque* (☎ 621 05; fax 277 23) has an unrivalled location in a wooded park by the Igreja de Nossa Senhora dos Remédios; singles/doubles are 6500$00/ 8000$00. The modern, canary-coloured *Albergaria do Cerrado* (☎ 631 64; fax 654 64), out on the Peso da Régua road, is the top choice if you want your comforts; doubles are 12,000$00.

Turihab The turismo has details of several properties in the region. Among the closest to Lamego is the modern *Quinta da Timpeira* (☎ 628 11; fax 651 76), three km west of town, with swimming pool and tennis courts. Expect to pay around 10,000$00 for a double.

Places to Eat
Behind the cathedral are several budget options including *Restaurant Tás da Sé* (☎ 624 68) at Rua Tás da Sé, where jovial locals come for feijoada (bean stew), cabrito estufado (stewed kid) and other favourites. Prices are around 900$00 per dish. Equally jolly is *Casa Filipe* (☎ 624 28), on the same street, with half-portions for 700$00.

Another clutch of reasonably priced places is on Rua da Olaria. The tiny 1st-floor *Casa de Pasto Albino Alves Teixeira* (☎ 633 18), at No 1, is packed at lunchtime. *Casa de Pasto Vitor Pinto* (☎ 629 74), at No 61, is slightly cheaper. Also in this street are several grocery shops that sell Lamego's famous hams and wines – perfect for a picnic.

For up-market dining, try *Restaurant Avenida* (☎ 623 44) on Avenida Dr Alfredo de Sousa, with prices per dish from 900$00 to 1400$00.

Getting There & Away

The most convenient way to travel between Lamego and Porto (or other destinations in the Douro valley) is by bus to Peso da Régua, where you can pick up trains running on the Douro railway line.

Three companies operate from separate offices in Lamego's bus station. Empresa Automobilista de Viação e Turismo or EAVT (☎ 621 16) has regular links with Peso da Régua, and goes twice daily to Celorico da Beira on the edge of the Serra da Estrela. Empresa Soares (☎ 637 27) has buses three times a day to Porto. Empresa Guedes (☎ 626 04) has express coaches to/from Lisbon (via Viseu and Coimbra) twice daily, and local services to Peso da Régua and Viseu.

Rodonorte and Rodoviária Beira Litoral (RBL) express coaches pass through twice daily en route between Lisbon and Peso da Régua, stopping at Rua do Regimento de Infantaria 9. You can buy Rodonorte tickets from travel agents such as Turismo Santa Cruz (☎ 621 03) at Rua Pádua Correira 2, and RBL tickets from the Totobolo shop near the turismo.

AROUND LAMEGO

Capela de São Pedro

This lovely chapel is hidden away in the hamlet of Balsemão, three km east of Lamego by the Rio Balsemão. Originally built by the Suevi in the seventh century, it features ornate 14th-century additions, many commissioned by the Bishop of Porto, Dom Afonso Pires. The bishop's tomb, surrounded by capitals and supported by angels, dominates the otherwise simple interior.

The chapel is open the same hours as the Museu de Lamego although the custodian, Dona Prazeres (☎ 65 56 56), closes it one weekend a month (usually the last). It's a pleasant walk from Lamego: from the 17th-century Capela do Desterro at the end of Rua da Santa Cruz, cross the river and follow the road to the left.

Mosteiro de São João de Tarouca

Fourteen km south-east of Lamego in the quiet, wooded Barosa valley below the Serra de Leomil are the remains of Portugal's first Cistercian monastery. It was founded in 1124 and left to fall into ruin when religious orders were abolished in 1834.

Only the church, considerably altered in the 17th century, stands intact among the eerie ruins of the monks' quarters. Inside are treasures including the imposing 14th-century tomb of the Count of Barcelos (Dom Dinis' illegitimate son), carved with scenes from a boar hunt; a larger-than-life 14th-century granite Virgin and Child; gilded choir stalls; and some fine 18th-century azulejos. The church's most famous possession, a painting by Grão Vasco, was taken away in 1978 for restoration.

Ponte de Ucanha

Just north of Tarouca, off the N226, is the unremarkable village of Ucanha. But follow the lane down to the Rio Barosa to a huge 12th-century fortified bridge. The chunky tower was added by the Abbot of Salzedas in the 15th century, probably as a tollgate. Stonemasons' initials are clearly visible on almost every block.

Under the bridge are medieval washing enclosures made of stone – one for suds, one for rinsing. They're long since defunct, though village women still use the arch of the bridge to dry their laundry.

Mosteiro de Salzedas

Three km further up the Rio Barosa valley are the ruins of a Cistercian monastery. It was one of the grandest in the land when it was built in 1168 with funds from Teresa Afonso, governess to Dom Afonso Henriques' five children. The church, extensively remodelled in the 18th century, dominates the humble village around it. Black with mould and rancid with decay, it seems past hope of restoration, though students conscientiously

DOURO

work here in the summer to bring the complex back to life.

Getting There & Away
From Lamego, Empresa Automobilista de Viação e Turismo (EAVT) runs buses to São João de Tarouca a dozen times a day and to Ucanha three times a day.

PESO DA RÉGUA
• pop 5500 • postcode 5050 • area code ☎ 054
This small, busy town at the confluence of the Douro and Corgo rivers is at the western edge of the demarcated port-wine region. As the largest town in that region with river access to Porto, it quickly grew into a major port-wine entrepôt. Its traditional status as capital of the trade has shifted to Pinhão, 25 km to the east.

There's little to actually see or do here, other than honing up on (and tasting) port wine at a local lodge. But Régua (its common name) is a good place from which to visit the vineyard country, cruise the Rio Douro or ride the Corgo railway line to Vila Real.

Orientation & Information
From the train and bus station it's a 10-minute walk west along Rua dos Camilos to the turismo (☎ 238 46; fax 32 22 71) at Rua da Ferreirinha 505. It's open from June through September on weekdays from 9 am to 12.30 pm and 2 to 6 pm and weekends from 10 am to 12.30 pm and 2 to 6.30 pm.

The older part of Régua is a steep climb from the two main streets: Rua da Ferreirinha, with a market and shops, and Rua dos Camilos, which has most of the accommodation and restaurants.

Instituto do Vinho do Porto
If you haven't visited the lodges of Vila Nova de Gaia, this slick branch of the Port Wine Institute (☎ 32 11 75), at Rua dos Camilos 90, is a good place for an introduction to port-wine production in the Douro region. Watch a 20-minute slide show or pick up books about wine and the valley. Nearby are the headquarters of Casa do Douro, the watchdog organisation that supervises all port-wine viticulture. The institute is open weekdays only, from 9 am to 12.30 pm and 2 to 4.30 pm.

Quinta de São Domingos
This port-wine lodge belonging to Ramos Pinto (one of the biggest port-wine companies) is the nearest and easiest to visit, and offers free tours and tasting. It's on the Vila Real road, and is open from 9 am to 12.30 pm and 2 to 5 pm, on weekdays only.

Places to Stay
Pensões & Residencials There are several cheapies along Rua dos Camilos between the train/bus station and the turismo. Pensão Douro (☎ 32 12 31), at No 105, is crumbling, leaky and heavily perfumed, but has the cheapest rooms in town at 2500$00 a double (without bath). Better value but further away, at Avenida Sacadura Cabral 1 (a 10-minute walk beyond the turismo), is Residencial Don Quixote (☎ 32 11 51), the only guesthouse overlooking the river. Its singles/doubles with bath are 3000$00/4500$00. Another modern place, a step away from the train/bus station at Rua José Vasques Osorio 8, is Residencial Império (☎ 32 01 20; fax 32 14 57), where rooms with bath are 3500$00/6000$00, including a big breakfast.

Turihab The turismo has details of some properties in the area. For a complete list of Turihab properties in the Douro valley, contact Quintas do Douro (☎ & fax 32 27 88).

Places to Eat
Restaurante O Maleiro (☎ 236 84), opposite the post office on Rua dos Camilos, is a friendly place with prices from 800$00 and a big wine list. Restaurante Muxima, at Rua dos Camilos 28, has tasty grilled offerings and regional fare. For a more up-market menu, head for the welcoming Restaurante Cacho d'Oiro (☎ 32 14 55), just west of the turismo on Rua Branca Martinho, where you can splurge on fillet mignon à Princesa Diana for 1650$00 or cabrito no churrasco (grilled kid) for 1400$00.

Getting There & Away

There are 15 trains daily to/from Porto (a 2½-hour trip) and five to seven onward to Tua. Five trains daily leave for Vila Real on the Corgo railway line. From the train station, buses run hourly to Lamego and Vila Real.

River Cruises

Cruises along the Douro are operated by Companhia Turística do Douro (☎ 628 11). Their shortest trip (1½ hours) is from Cais da Barragem de Bagaúste, just upstream from Régua, to Pinhão; it costs around 2000$00. Call ahead to reserve a place. See Getting There & Away in the next section for information on cruises from Porto to Peso da Régua.

EAST OF PESO DA RÉGUA

The Rio Douro east of Peso da Régua, defining the border between Trás-os-Montes and the Beira Alta, is not actually part of Douro province. We include it here because it's an integral part of the region and because you'll most likely travel through the valley from Porto (the entire train journey to the end of the line at Pocinho takes just four hours).

The area is entirely dominated by terraced vineyards wrapped around every precipitous, crew-cut hillside, and dotted with the port-wine lodges' bright-white quintas. Villages are small and cultural sights are few and far between. Come here for the dramatic landscape, the port, or the recently discovered Palaeolithic rock carvings near Vila Nova de Foz Côa – or simply for the train ride, which offers fantastic views once it enters the valley, some 60 km east of Porto.

Maps Refer to the Beiras map or the Trás-os-Montes map in this book for the eastern end of the Douro valley. *Rio Douro*, a handsome and useful schematic colour map of the entire Douro valley within Portugal, is available for 1000$00 from bigger bookshops, at least in Porto.

Pinhão

This small town 25 km east of Peso da Régua is now considered the centre of quality port-wine production. It's completely surrounded by terraced vineyards and dominated by large signs of several lodges; even the train station has azulejos depicting the wine harvest.

If you have your own wheels, a 12-km hop north-east up the N322-3 to Favaios will reward you with the discovery of a little-known moscatel, one of only two produced in Portugal (the other comes from Setúbal).

Death in the Douro Rapids

Squeezed into the Douro gorge nine km above Tua, the dramatic Barragem (dam) de Valeira marks the site of the dreaded Cachão da Valeira rapids. Here, in May 1862, Baron Joseph James Forrester, one of the most remarkable men in the history of the port trade, died when his boat capsized.

Forrester first entered the Porto scene in 1831 to work in his uncle's firm, Offley Forrester & Co. He soon became thoroughly involved in the port industry and devoted his considerable artistic and cartographic talents to producing outstanding maps of the Douro region (in recognition of which he was made Barão de Forrester by the king).

In 1844, 33-year-old Forrester turned his attention to the widespread but controversial practice of adulteration of port wine with brandy, sugar, elderberry juice and other 'pollutants' – in Forrester's opinion, a practice that had got out of hand. His *A Word or Two on Port Wine*, accusing the trade of encouraging the practice and of corruption among the official tasters of the Companhia Velha, caused a storm of protest.

There certainly seemed to be grounds for his accusations, but his purist approach would have meant the end of port as we know it: without the addition of brandy to stop fermentation, 'port' would simply be a thin, inferior wine. The furore eventually died down, adulteration decreased and the Companhia Velha was itself reformed in 1848. When Forrester met his death (his money belt full of gold sovereigns probably carried him right to the bottom), nearly all of Porto mourned the loss. ∎

Victory for Rock Art

In the rugged valley of the Rio Côa (a tributary of the Douro), 15 km from the Spanish frontier, is an extraordinary Stone Age art gallery which is reckoned to be the world's largest open-air Palaeolithic site. Thousands of rock engravings of deer, fish, horses and other animals 10,000 to 25,000 years old were found along a 19-km stretch of the valley in 1994, after construction had started on a US$366 million hydroelectric dam.

The discovery immediately challenged existing theories about humankind's earliest art – smaller open-air sites have been found elsewhere in France, Spain and Portugal, but nothing on this scale or covering such a time span. It was probably the valley's resistant schist bedrock and Mediterranean microclimate which saved this site from Ice Age destruction.

The discovery of the site also triggered a battle between the electricity company building the dam (which would have flooded the valley) and archaeologists who insisted the engravings were of worldwide importance and had to be preserved. Only after an international campaign was launched and the socialist government came to power in 1995 was the half-built dam abandoned and plans announced to turn the site into a 200-sq-km natural park.

The Parque Arqueologia de Foz Côa (Côa Valley Archaeological Park) was officially launched in August 1996 with the opening of two visitor centres (one on each side of the valley) in Vila Nova de Foz Côa and in Castelo Melhor. A company (ProCoa) was also established to set up the infrastructure (including 12 new roads and a study institute) to cope with the expected influx of tourists. Local entrepreneurs have got into the spirit of things by naming their local white wine 'Vinho Paleolítico'.

Guides at the centres take visitors to some of the engravings. To make a booking or check on opening times, call ☎ 079-76 43 17. ∎

Tua

The only reason for stopping here is to pick up the narrow-gauge Linha da Tua railway line, which runs north to Mirandela. It once went all the way to Bragança but a bus service now copes with the rest of the journey from Mirandela.

Vila Nova de Foz Côa

This remote-feeling town, nine km south of Pocinho, has been put on the map by the discovery of thousands of Palaeolithic rock carvings nearby. The town itself has a few Manueline highlights, including a granite pelourinho topped by an armillary sphere, and the Igreja Matriz, which has an elaborately carved portal and painted ceiling.

Places to Stay

In addition to the few pensões in Pinhão and Vila Nova de Foz Côa, there are dozens of Turihab properties in the area, many marketed by a Peso da Régua company called Quintas do Douro (central booking office ☎ & fax 054-32 27 88). The turismo in Peso da Régua should have details.

The *Pousada Barão de Forrester* (☎ 059-95 92 15, or the central reservation service in Lisbon at ☎ 01-848 12 21) is at Alijó, 15 km north-east of Pinhão. Renovated doubles are 14,500$00.

Getting There & Away

Train The finest way to see the upper Douro valley is by train. The track runs beside the river and clings dramatically to the valley wall. Around 15 trains a day run from Porto up to Peso da Régua, with at least seven carrying on to Tua (three hours from Porto) and four to Pocinho (four hours from Porto).

Two narrow-gauge trains still climb out of the valley from the main line, offering slow, charming diversions. From Livração the Linha da Tâmega runs to Amarante (see Amarante). From Tua the Linha da Tua ascends for two hours to Mirandela; the 5½-hour Porto-Mirandela trip (three or four trains a day) is 1170$00 (2nd class). This line once continued from Mirandela to Bragança; CP now runs buses on this stretch, though you can still use rail passes and train tickets.

Car, Motorcycle & Bicycle Wheeled travellers have a choice of snaky, river-hugging roads (N108 and N222) along both banks to Peso da Régua and along the south bank (N222) to Pinhão, though on weekends they're crowded with Porto escapees, driving infuriatingly slowly or suicidally fast.

Beyond Pinhão only the train keeps to the valley floor, while the roads climb in and out. One of the most dramatic crossings in the valley is on a local road between Linhares and São João de Pesqueira – it plunges to the Barragem de Valeira dam fast enough to make your ears pop.

Organised Tours

Gray Line (☎ 31 65 97) runs day-long tours of the Douro valley from Porto every Sunday for 13,000$00. They can be booked (and you can be picked up) at most upper-end hotels in Porto.

River Cruises Numerous outfits in Porto offer cruises up and down the Rio Douro mostly in summer. Douro Azul (☎ 02-208 32 94; fax 02-208 34 07) has day-long return trips every Saturday from March through November. Boats go from Porto to Peso da Régua (12,500$00) and from Porto to Pinhão (16,500$00). Douro Azul also organises one-way day cruises from Barca de Alva down to Porto – the entire length of the Douro in Portugal – for 20,000$00, as well as Pinhão-Porto, Peso da Régua-Porto and Pinhão-Peso da Régua trips.

Vistadouro (☎ 02-938 79 49; fax 02-938 79 50) has a day-long return trip from Porto to Peso da Régua (15,000$00), and a weekend overnight trip (27,000$00). Via d'Ouro (☎ & fax 02-938 81 39), who run the 'Five Bridges' trips from Porto, also go from Porto to Entre-os-Rios (10,000$00) and to Peso da Régua (13,000$00).

The Minho

The north-west corner of Portugal is traditional, conservative and very beautiful. Tucked under the hem of Spanish Galicia, its inland mountains provide it with plentiful rain while its rich soil encourages intensive farming, with smallholdings of maize and vegetables divided by low stone walls covered with trailing vines. Despite recent injections of funding from the EU, this remains a largely poor agricultural area where many farmers still rely on their lyre-horned oxen to pull their creaking carts and plough their fields. Generations of sons have left their homes to seek fortunes elsewhere, mostly in France and Germany, returning to flaunt their wealth by building fancy new houses for their retirement.

The Minho clings to its rural traditions: you'll see some of Portugal's most vibrant country markets here (most famously in Barcelos) and throughout the year there are dozens of festivals and religious processions commemorating local saints. Religion also continues to play an important part in life here: the Easter celebrations at Braga, Portugal's 'ecclesiastical capital', are an extraordinary combination of merry-making and devotional fervour. Minhotos are proud of their history too. This is where the kingdom of Portugal began – Guimarães was birthplace of Portugal's first king, Afonso Henriques, and the place from which he launched the Reconquista against the Moors. In almost the same place over a millennium earlier, the Celto-Iberians maintained their last stronghold against the Romans: the Citânia de Briteiros. Today this is one of the country's most fascinating archaeological sites.

These three major destinations – Barcelos, Guimarães and Citânia de Briteiros – all lie within easy reach of each other in the southern part of the province. The Costa Verde (Green Coast), which is lashed by cold Atlantic seas, has fewer attractions, though Viana do Castelo is a jovial resort with good

beaches, and the stretch of coastline north of it has plenty of deserted spots.

But the Minho's real pull is inland – along the Rio Minho (which forms the northern frontier with Spain) and the dreamy Rio Lima (so alluring the Romans reckoned it was the mythical Lethe, the river of oblivion) – where you'll find Portugal's highest concentration of Turismo Habitação (Turihab) accommodation. These provide the chance to stay in palatial manor houses as guests of local grandees or in converted farmhouses well off the beaten track. Further inland still is the Parque Nacional da Peneda-Gerês, Portugal's only true 'national' park – which is really several parks in one – with the closest thing the country has to true wilderness, some of its most appealing treks and other sports, and several competent outfits ready to show you around. Don't plan on rushing through the Minho: in addition to the density of its attractions, the pace of life is slow and the distractions are numerous – not least the local *vinho verde*, the young, sparkling wine that is among Portugal's most addictive.

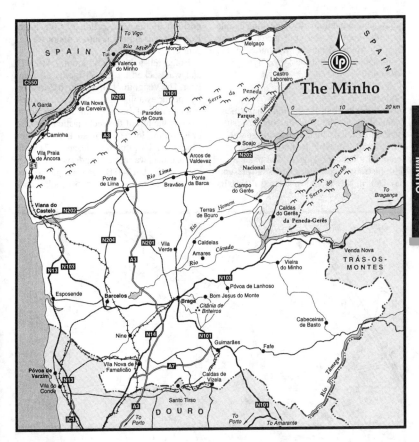

The Minho

Southern Minho

BRAGA

• *pop 65,000* • *postcode 4700* • *area code* ☎ *053*

The Minho's capital is one of the oldest settlements in Portugal and has genuine Celtic roots. More importantly to the Portuguese, Braga is their religious capital, with a Christian pedigree dating from the 6th century. From the 11th to the 18th century this was the seat of archbishops who each considered themselves 'Primate of All Spain' or at any rate 'Primate of Portugal'

(these days they minister as far south as Coimbra).

Brochures go on about 'the Portuguese Rome', though the comparison is silly. Braga overflows with churches – at least 35 of them – but only its ancient cathedral merits much attention, having survived wholesale baroque renovations that smothered most of the others in the 18th century. The city's best known attraction, Bom Jesus do Monte, isn't actually in the city at all (see Around Braga), but Braga does have a relaxing and attractive centre. The Universidade do Minho adds youthful leavening to an otherwise proud, pious, somewhat dour city. One thing people do smile about is the gold medal won by Braga's own Manuela Machado in the women's marathon at the 1996 Olympics in Atlanta.

History

It is thought that Braga may have been founded by a tribe of Celto-Iberians called Bracari (hence its ancient name, Bracara). In about 250 BC the Romans moved in, renamed it Bracara Augusta and made it the administrative centre of Gallaecia (present-day Douro, Minho and Spanish Galicia). Its

position at the intersection of five major Roman roads turned it into a major trading centre.

Braga fell to the Suevi around 410 AD, and was sacked by the Visigoths 60 years later. The Visigoths' conversion to Christianity and the establishment of an archbishopric in the middle of the following century put the town at the top of the ecclesiastical pecking order on the Iberian Peninsula. Though the Moors gained a foothold in about 715, the Reconquista was already underway in northern Spain and in 740 Braga was again seized by Christian forces. The Moors took it back

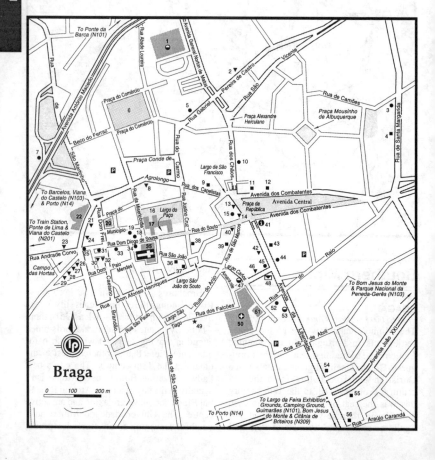

Braga

0   100   200 m

in 985, only to be finally dislodged in 1040 by Fernando I, King of Castile and León. Fernando's son Alfonso VI called for help from European crusaders to drive the Moors south, and to one of these, Henri of Burgundy (Dom Henrique to the Portuguese), he later gave his daughter Teresa in marriage, throwing in Braga as dowry. The archbishopric was restored in 1070, though prelates bickered with their Spanish counterparts for the next five centuries over who was 'Primate of All Spain', until the pope ruled in Braga's favour. The sturdy elegance of its churches and palaces reflects its subsequent prosperity and power, only curtailed when a separate Lisbon archdiocese was created in the 18th century. It was from straight-backed Braga that the 1926 coup was launched which eventually put António de Oliveira Salazar in power and introduced Portugal to half a century of dictatorship.

Orientation

From the bus station it's 600m south along Avenida General Norton de Matos and Rua

dos Chãos to Praça da República. From the train station, walk east for just over a km, via Rua Andrade Corvo, the old town gate and the shopping district of Rua Dom Diogo de Sousa and pedestrianised Rua do Souto, to Praça da República.

This square and the long park to the east beside Avenida dos Combatentes (both park and street are sometimes called 'Avenida Central'), are the heart of Braga. Most things of use or interest are within walking distance of the centre – except for the big municipal park 1.5 km to the south, which includes the camping ground, Estádio 1 de Maio (stadium), and the Largo da Feira exhibition grounds.

Information

Tourist Office In the decaying Art Deco headquarters at Avenida da Liberdade 1 (on the corner of Praça da República), the polite and fairly dependable *turismo* (☎ 225 50) endures the city's tourists daily from 9 am to 7 pm. It has a decent city map and can help with accommodation too.

PLACES TO STAY		
4	Pousada de Juventude	
9	Residencial dos Terceiros	
11	Hotel Francfort	
12	Hotel Residencial Centro Comercial Avenida	
36	Casa Santa Zita	
37	Hotel-Residencial Dona Sofia	
38	Residencial Inácio Filho	
39	Residencial São Marcos	
43	Grande Residência Avenida	
54	Hotel de Turismo	
55	Hotel Carandá	
56	Hotel João XXI	

PLACES TO EAT		
2	Retiro da Primavera	
8	Lareira do Conde	
13	Café Viana	
14	Café Astória	
21	Restaurante Biscaínhos	
23	Restaurante A Moçambicana	
24	Casa Grulha	
26	Restaurante Inácio	
27	Restaurante Bem-Me-Quer	
28	Restaurante Cruz Sobral	
29	Restaurante O Alexandre	
30	Casa de Pasto Pregão	
32	Taberna Rexío da Praça	
40	Café Brasileira	
42	Café Jolima	
46	Café Pachá	

OTHER		
1	Bus Station	
3	Livraria Diário do Minho	
5	Avic Travel Agency	
6	Mercado Municipal	
7	Parque Nacional da Peneda-Gerês Headquarters	
10	Shell Franchise Shop	
15	Torre de Menagem	
16	Jardim de Santa Bárbara	
17	Antigo Paço Episcopal (Former Archbishop's Palace)	
18	Livraria Bertrand-Cruz	
19	Tagus Travel & Oficina d'Aventura	
20	Câmara Municipal	
22	Museu dos Biscaínhos	
25	Arco da Porta Nova	
31	Arsenal do Minho	
33	Lavandaria Confiança	
34	Anglers' Shop	
35	Sé (Cathedral)	
41	Tourist Office	
44	Gold Center	
45	Teatro Circo	
47	Bus Stand for Bom Jesus do Monte	
48	Post Office	
49	Police Office	
50	Hospital de São Marcos	
51	Casa do Raio	
52	Fonte do Idolo	
53	Bus Stands for Municipal Park & Camping Ground	

MINHO

Park Office The headquarters of the Parque Nacional da Peneda-Gerês (☎ 61 31 66; fax 61 31 69) is in the former Quinta das Parretas on Avenida António Macedo, north-west of the centre. The public information office, in the modern building at the back, is open weekdays only from 9 am to noon and 2 to 5.30 pm. It has a good park map and a booklet (in English) on the park's human and natural features; most other information is in Portuguese.

Money The city has numerous banks with foreign-exchange desks and Multibanco ATMs, including several around Largo de São Francisco, at the northern end of Praça da República.

Post & Communications The post and tele-communications office is a block south of Praça da República on Avenida da Liberdade.

Travel Agencies Tagus Travel (☎ 21 51 44), at Praça do Município 7, makes budget-minded hotel and transport bookings, sells ISIC and Cartão Jovem cards, and organises some trips in Portugal and Spain through local specialist agencies. It's open weekdays only from 9 am to 1 pm and 2.30 to 6 pm. Also at this address is a camping shop called Oficina d'Aventura (see Things to Buy later in this section).

Bookshops The best bookshop is Livraria Bertrand-Cruz at Rua Dom Diogo de Sousa 129-133.

Another good one is Livraria Diário do Minho on Rua de Santa Margarida.

Campuses The Universidade do Minho, founded here in 1973, has administrative headquarters (☎ 61 22 34) in part of the former Archbishop's Palace on Largo do Paço. Science, economics, education, man-agement and arts faculties are along Rua do Castelo (behind Praça da República) and Rua Abade Loureira (behind the bus station). There is a separate engineering campus at Guimarães.

Laundry Lavandaria Confiança (☎ 269 07) is at Rua Dom Diogo de Sousa 46.

Medical Services The Hospital de São Marcos is a block west of Avenida da Liber-dade, and is accessed via Rua do Raio or Rua 25 de Abril.

Emergency The police station (☎ 61 32 50) is on Rua dos Falcões, two blocks south of the cathedral.

Praça da República
This broad square with computer-controlled fountains is a good place to start or finish your day. In an arcaded building on the western side are two of Portugal's best watch-the-world-go-by spots, Café Astória and Café Viana, with a tiny chapel in between and several well-stocked news-stands in front. The Astória is smaller, wood-panelled, a bit more elegant and less touristy.

The square crenellated tower visible at the back of the building is the Torre de Menagem (castle keep), the only survivor of a fortified palace built in 1738.

Sé
Braga's cathedral – the oldest in Portugal, begun after the restoration of the archdiocese in 1070 and completed in the following century – is a rambling complex of chapels and little rooms in a jumble of architectural styles. You could spend half a day probing its corners and sorting the Romanesque bits from the Gothic attachments and the baroque icing.

The original Romanesque survives in the overall shape, in the Porta do Sol entrance on the south side, and in the marvellous west or main entrance, carved with scenes from the medieval legend of Reynard the Fox (this is now sheltered inside a Gothic porch, so you have to look for it). The cathedral's most appealing and visible feature is its filigree Manueline towers and roof. Also outside, in a niche on the west side, is a lovely statue of Nossa Senhora do Leite (the Virgin suckling the Christ child), thought to be by the 16th-century expat French sculptor Nicolas Chanterène. You enter, not straight into the church but via a courtyard on the north side which gives access to the church, several Gothic chapels and, via a cloister, more chapels and the two-storey *tesouro* or treasury. The most interesting of the chapels is the Capela dos Reis (Kings' Chapel), with the tombs of Dom Henrique (Henri of Burgundy) and Dona Teresa, parents of the first king of the Portuguese, Afonso Henriques. Not surprisingly for a cathedral of such stature, the treasury is a rich collection of ecclesiastical booty – sorry, sacred art – including a 10th-century ivory casket in Arabic-Hispanic style and a plain iron cross used to celebrate the first Mass in newly discovered Brazil. In the church itself, note the fine Manueline carved altarpiece, a little chapel to the left with *azulejos* bearing scenes from the life of Braga's first bishop, and the extraordinary twin baroque organs.

A ticket from the official at the entrance, admitting you to the treasury, Coro Alto (choir), Capela dos Reis and several other chapels with archbishops' tombs in them, is 300$00.

The complex is open daily from 8.30 am to 1 pm and 2 to 6.30 pm. This is the only church in town of any real interest, and everybody else will be heading for it too, so get there early.

Antigo Paço Episcopal & Around

Across Rio do Souto from the cathedral is the sprawling former Archbishop's Palace. Begun in the 14th century and enlarged in the 17th and 18th centuries, it's now occupied by the municipal library, the Braga district archives and the university rectory and administration. The gilt-ceilinged library, one of the country's wealthiest, is full of ancient documents from a score of monastic libraries.

Outside the spiky-topped north wing is the **Jardim de Santa Bárbara** which dates, like this wing of the palace, from the 17th century. Beside it, several pedestrianised blocks of Rua Justino Cruz and Rua Fran-

cisco Sanches are filled on sunny days with buskers, balloon sellers and café tables.

At the western end of neighbouring Praça do Município is Braga's *câmara municipal* (town hall), with one of Portugal's best baroque façades, by architect André Soares da Silva. A more extrovert piece of Soares work is **Casa do Raio**, with a rococo front covered in azulejos; it is up Rua do Raio by the hospital.

Arco da Porta Nova

This 18th-century arch on the west side of the old centre was for some time the city's main gate. It bears the coat of arms of its builder, Archbishop Dom José de Bragança. East from here to Praça da República, Rua Dom Diogo de Sousa and Rua do Souto form a narrow little shopping district, heavy on religious paraphernalia.

Museu dos Biscaínhos

In a 17th-century aristocrat's palace on Rua dos Biscaínhos is the municipal museum (☎ 276 45). Surrounded by 18th-century gardens full of statuary and a fountain, this museum has an attractive collection of Roman relics, 17th to 19th-century pottery, furniture and furnishings. It is open daily, except Mondays, from 10 am to 12.15 pm and 2 to 5.30 pm; entry is 250$00.

The most interesting exhibit is the building itself, a solid, handsome mansion with painted or wood-panelled ceilings and 18th-century azulejos featuring hunting scenes (these reveal much about the life of the nobility of the time). The ground floor is an extension of the street and was paved with ribbed stones so carriages could drive right in, deliver their passengers and continue to the stables.

Fonte do Idolo

This startling little 1st-century AD Roman sanctuary, carved into solid rock, is down some stairs near the corner of Avenida da Liberdade and Rua do Raio.

Special Events

Braga may no longer be the religious capital,

but it's still the capital of Portuguese religious festivals. Easter Week here is a particularly serious and splendid affair. The city blazes with lights and roadside altars representing the Stations of the Cross, and the churches deck themselves out with banners. Most amazing is the torch-lit Senhor Ecce Homo procession of barefoot, black-hooded penitents on Maundy Thursday evening.

The Festas de São João on 23 and 24 June (and continuing into the wee hours of the 25th) is a pre-Christian solstice bash dressed up to look like holy days, but is still full of pagan energy. It features medieval folk plays, processions, dancing, bonfires and illuminations, a funfair in the city park, and mysterious little pots of basil everywhere.

Places to Stay

Accommodation tends to be pricey here, except for the camping ground and two hostels. Bom Jesus do Monte (see Around Braga) has several additional upper-end hotels.

Camping The year-round *Parque da Ponte* municipal camping ground (☎ 733 55) is almost two km south of the centre in the big municipal park. Typical high-season rates are 320$00 per person, 240$00 to 780$00 for a tent, 260$00 per car and 160$00 for a shower. From Avenida da Liberdade, city buses labelled Arcos pass the park every half-hour (or take anything that stops at Pinheiro da Gregório); ask for 'campismo'.

Hostels The *Pousada de Juventude de Braga* (☎ 61 61 63) is a 10-minute walk from the turismo, at the northern end of the building at Rua de Santa Margarida 6. Doors open from 9 am to 1 pm and 6 pm to midnight. The closest restaurants are along Avenida Central.

Casa Santa Zita (☎ 61 83 31) is a somewhat gloomy hostel for pilgrims (and for others at non-pilgrimage times) behind the cathedral at Rua São João 20. Spartan rooms without bath are 2750$00 per bed. It's unmarked but for a small tile plaque that says

'Sta Zita'; the owners are not very good about answering the door.

Pensões, Residencials & Hotels Categories are muddled, with some places calling themselves 'hotel/residencials', so we've put them all in one category.

Perhaps the best bargain in town is the faded but charming old *Hotel Francfort*, (☎ 226 48), at Avenida dos Combatentes (Avenida Central) 7, where huge rooms, sparsely equipped with creaky old furniture, are looked after by ladies of similar vintage. A single/double is 2500$00/3500$00 without bath or 4000$00/5000$00 with. They claim to take no reservations so you'd have to arrive early in the day, at least in summer.

Stuffy and precious, but clean and homey, is *Residencial Inácio Filho* (☎ 238 49), at Rua Francisco Sanches 42, where a double with shower is 5000$00.

The *Grande Residência Avenida* (☎ 229 55, 230 99), on the 3rd floor at Avenida da Liberdade 738, is good value too: comfortable doubles with TV are 4500$00 without bath and 6000$00 with.

The *Hotel Residencial Centro Comercial Avenida* (☎ 757 22; fax 61 63 63) is big, sterile and weirdly located above a centro comercial (shopping mall) at Avenida dos Combatentes (Avenida Central) 27-37. But it's good value: singles/doubles with bath, TV and air-con start at 5000$00/6500$00 (with breakfast), plus there are some doubles with kitchenette for 7500$00. It has its own lift at the back end of the mall.

Residencial São Marcos (☎ 771 87; fax 771 77), at Rua de São Marcos 80, has carpeted rooms with bath and TV for at least 5500$00/7000$00.

Residencial dos Terceiros (☎ 704 66; fax 757 67), at Rua dos Capelistas 85, has charmless rooms with bath, which are overpriced at 7500$00/8400$00 (with breakfast), it's mainly for tour groups.

The *Hotel-Residencial Dona Sofia* (☎ 231 60; fax 61 12 45), at Largo São João do Souto 131, is distinguished by the fact that its clean, boring rooms (7500$00/9000$00 with bath,

TV and minibar) come with an English breakfast, which should set you up for the day.

A further clutch of upper-end hotels is about 800m south of the centre at the intersection of Avenida da Liberdade and Avenida João XXI. Cheapest of these is *Hotel João XXI* (☎ 61 66 30; fax 61 66 31), where a double with bath is about 7000$00. The others are the *Hotel Carandá* (☎ 61 45 00; fax 61 45 03) and the *Hotel de Turismo* (☎ 61 22 00; fax 61 22 11).

Places to Eat

Around the corner from the bus station, at Rua Gabriel Pereira de Castro 100, is *Retiro da Primavera* (☎ 724 82). It is plain, unpretentious and clean, and offers lots of meat dishes under 1000$00 and fish under 1500$00; a half-portion does very nicely. This is one of the best bargains in town. It's open daily, except Saturdays, from noon to 10 pm.

Rustic, congenial and very good value is the family-run *Casa Grulha* (☎ 228 83), at Rua dos Biscaínhos 95, with excellent cabrito assado (roast kid). Just around the corner on Rua Andrade Corvo is *Restaurante A Moçambicana* (☎ 222 60), another good place with a big, meaty menu of dishes costing 1200$00 to 1700$00 and generous half-portions. Other, less notable places in the area include *Restaurante Biscaínhos* (☎ 61 14 91) at No 45, with regional specialities for around 1200$00 per dish. On the south side of Campo das Hortas is a row of stuffy restaurants with overpriced Portuguese standards (1700$00 to 2800$00 per dish): *Inácio* (☎ 61 32 35) at No 4, *Bem-Me-Quer* (☎ 220 95) at No 6, *Cruz Sobral* (☎ 61 66 48) at No 7-8 and *O Alexandre* (☎ 61 40 03) at No 10.

Inside the Arco da Porta Nova on Praça Velha are two plain, cheerful, good-value eateries with dishes under 1000$00: *Taberna Rexío da Praça* at No 17, with just two tasty daily pratos (open daily, except Sundays, from 10 am to midnight), and casa de pasto *Pregão* (☎ 772 49) at No 18, with a larger menu. A better-than-average churrasqueira

(grill) is the friendly, clean and cheap *Lareira do Conde* (☎ 61 13 40) at Praça Conde de Agrolongo 56.

On Avenida da Liberdade, *Café Jolima* is a giant, chrome-plated, self-serve restaurant, pizzeria, teahouse and confeitaria with a huge selection of munchies, but zero atmosphere. Around the corner at Rua Gonçalo Sampaio 12-14 is *Café Pachá*, a little sandwich bar that assembles big sandwiches, plus omelettes and drinks, from 10 am to 8 pm daily except Sundays.

For light meals, coffee or beer at Braga's best people-watching venue, settle down at *Café Astória* or *Café Viana* on Praça da República (see the Praça da República section). Around the corner on Rua do Souto is the locally favoured alternative, *Café Brasileira*, where grumpy waiters serve drinks and surprisingly awful coffee from 7 am to midnight, daily except Sundays. Self-caterers can go to the mercado municipal in Praça do Comércio, which bustles daily, except Sundays, from 8 am to 6 pm (Fridays 7 am to 5 pm, Saturdays 7 am to 1 pm).

Entertainment

The city's main drama theatre is *Teatro Circo* on Avenida da Liberdade. The *Gold Center* across the road has several cinemas.

By night, *Café Pachá* (see Places to Eat), at Rua Gonçalo Sampaio 12-14, reveals a modest basement disco (☎ 736 85) from 1 to 7 am on Tuesday, Wednesday, Friday and Saturday nights (plus live blues, jazz or acid jazz from 1 to 3 am Saturday), and from 4 to 8 pm on Saturdays and Sundays.

Things to Buy

A big weekly market is held on Tuesdays at the Largo da Feira exhibition grounds in the big park south of the centre. Take an 'Arcos' city bus from Avenida da Liberdade, running every half-hour.

Those planning to trek in the Parque Nacional da Peneda-Gerês can stop in at Oficina d'Aventura (☎ 21 53 01; fax 21 51 94), a small shop within Tagus Travel (see the earlier Information section) that stocks western name-brand packs, sleeping bags, clothes, shoes and tents, as well as topographic maps. ISIC or Cartão Jovem cards get a 10% discount. Numerous sports shops also peddle cheap rucksacks (backpacks); one, Arsenal do Minho at Rua Dom Diogo de Sousa 22, is next door to an appliance shop that sells camping stoves. An anglers' shop at Rua Dom Diogo de Sousa 104 has sturdy macs. Gaz (camping gas) is sold at a Shell franchise at Rua dos Chãos 48.

Getting There & Away

Bus The bus station on Avenida General Norton de Matos is a confusing gauntlet of private operators, including Avic/Joalto (☎ 226 23), REDM/Rede Expressos (☎ 61 60 80), Renex (☎ 770 03), AMI/Rodonorte, João Carlos Soares, and Empresa Hoteleira do Gerês (☎ 61 58 96). Several are agents for the international operator Internorte.

For Peneda-Gerês go to gate 18, where Empresa Hoteleira do Gerês runs every 1½ to 2½ hours daily to Rio Caldo and Caldas do Gerês (530$00). The best bet for Guimarães (350$00) is João Carlos Soares which has at least seven buses a day, or Rodonorte which has about 10. To Porto (about 700$00), REDM (Rodoviária de Entre Douro e Minho) has over 20 express coaches a day, Renex 10 (continuing to Lisbon) and Joalto two or three. AMI/Rodonorte goes directly to Vila Real and Bragança (1450$00) on Friday and Sunday evenings. It also has services five times a day with a change at Guimarães. For the Serra da Estrela, Avic/Joalto runs at least twice a day to Viseu, Guarda and Covilhã.

Train Though Braga station (☎ 221 66) is at the end of a branch line from Nine, services are not bad from major centres. Intercidades trains arrive twice a day from Lisbon (under five hours), Coimbra (2½ hours) and Porto (one hour). From Porto's São Bento station there are also suburban trains: eight a day direct (one to two hours) and as many more with a change at Nine.

Car & Motorcycle Completion of the A3/IP1 motorway has made Braga an easy day trip from Porto. The Automóvel Club de Portugal has a branch office (☎ 21 70 51; fax 61 67 00) in Braga.

The Avic travel agency (☎ 21 64 60; fax 21 41 66) on Rua Gabriel Pereira de Castro is an agent for Hertz Rent-a-Car.

AROUND BRAGA
Bom Jesus do Monte

Bom Jesus, about five km east of the centre of Braga on the N103, is the goal of legions of pilgrims every year. This sober, twin-towered church at the site of a (long-gone) 15th-century sanctuary is on a forested hill with fine views across the countryside. It was designed in neoclassical style by Carlos Amarante and built between 1784 and 1811.

It stands atop an astonishing, and considerably more famous, granite and plaster baroque staircase, the Escadaria do Bom Jesus, presumably built to concentrate the minds of the devout as they climb to the church. It's actually several staircases, from several centuries, built one after another: the lowest one is lined with chapels representing the Stations of the Cross, and also has fountains and startlingly lifelike terracotta figures; then there is the double zigzag Stairway of the Five Senses, with allegorical fountains and over-the-top Old Testament figures; and at the top is the Stairway of the Three Virtues, whose further chapels and fountains represent Faith, Hope and Charity. You can ascend by the staircase itself, as all pilgrims do (though you needn't go on your knees, as they usually do), and enjoy the finest views of the whole scene; or cheat and ride up in a few minutes on an adjacent *elevador* (funicular); or drive up a twisting road to the top. The whole area has become something of a resort, with upper-end hotels, tennis courts, a little lake with boats for hire, and the woods for walking. Go on a weekday if you can; it's quieter.

Places to Stay Accommodation is pricey, and usually pretty full, but it's hard to see why a non-pilgrim would want to stay more than a few hours anyway.

Hotel Sul-Americano (☎ 053-67 66 15)

has singles/doubles with bath and great views from 5500$00/7500$00, breakfast included. More expensive alternatives are *Hotel do Parque* (☎ 053-67 66 07), *Hotel do Elevador* (☎ 053-67 66 11) and *Aparthotel Mãe d'Água* (☎ 053-67 65 81). All are within a short walk of the stairway. Two Turihab properties are *Casa dos Lagos* (☎ 053-67 67 38) and *Casa dos Castelos* (☎ 053-67 65 66; fax 053-61 71 81).

Getting There & Away Buses run to Bom Jesus via the N103 every half-hour all day (175$00) from Largo Carlos Amarante in Braga. If you have wheels, a longer but far more scenic route leaves the city south-eastwards on the N309.

Citânia de Briteiros
Scattered all over the Minho are the remains of Celtic hill settlements called *citânias*, dating back at least 2500 years. One of the best preserved and most spectacular of these is the one at Briteiros, 15 km north of Guimarães and 12 km south-east of Braga.

The 3.75 hectare site, inhabited from around 300 BC to 300 AD, was probably the last stronghold of the Celto-Iberians against the invading Romans. When archaeologist Dr Martins Sarmento excavated the rocky hillside in 1875, he discovered the foundations and ruins of more than 150 mostly round stone huts, linked by paved paths and surrounded by the remains of multiple protective walls. Sarmento spent years clearing away the debris, and reconstructed two huts, creating one of the country's most evocative archaeological sites. Some striking remains, such as carved stone lintels and ornamental portals, are now on display in the Museu Martins Sarmento in Guimarães. The detailed site plan (available at the entrance) points out the most significant features, including a fountain, a circular community house, and the so-called 'funerary monument' (follow the path down the hill towards the road). This deep trench was initially thought to be a burial chamber when it was discovered in 1930. The more mundane recent explanation is that it was probably the bathhouse. The site is open daily from 9 am to 6 pm (5 pm in winter); entry is 200$00.

Getting There & Away Buses run to the site from Braga (Praça Alexandre Herculano, regularly all day) and from Guimarães (seven daily but only four returning, the last at 5 pm).

BARCELOS
• *pop 10,400 • postcode 4750 • area code ☎ 053*
The Minho is famous for its traditional markets, geared to the agricultural community, and none is more famous in the province than the one in this ancient town on the banks of the Rio Cávado, 22 km west of Braga. Indeed the Feira de Barcelos, held every Thursday, has become so well known that tourists now arrive by the coach load and cheap rooms can be hard to find on Wednesday and Thursday nights.

There are a few other cultural attractions, a thriving pottery tradition and several major festivals, but the town itself soon disintegrates into seedy and industrial outskirts. The market is its saving grace: if you don't make it here on a Thursday, it's scarcely worth coming.

Orientation
From the train station, it's a 10 to 15-minute walk south-west on Avenida Alcaides de Faria to the heart of town, Campo da República (also called Campo da Feira), a huge shady square where the market is held. Various bus companies have terminals north-east or south of the Campo.

The medieval part of town, with its museums and parish church, is clustered on the slopes above the river, 10 minutes walk south-west of the Campo. Restaurants and accommodation are in this district and around the Campo.

Information
The turismo (☎ 81 18 82; fax 82 21 88) shares the Torre de Menagem (the former castle keep) on Largo da Porta Nova with a large *centro de artesanato* (handicrafts and souvenir shop). Both are open daily from 9

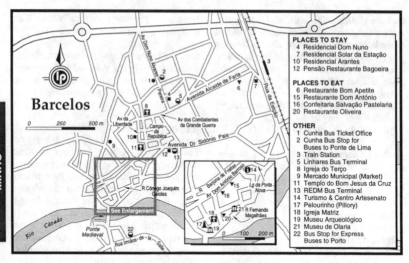

PLACES TO STAY
4 Residencial Dom Nuno
7 Residencial Solar da Estação
10 Residencial Arantes
12 Pensão Restaurante Bagoeira

PLACES TO EAT
6 Restaurante Bom Apetite
15 Restaurante Dom António
16 Confeitaria Salvação Pastelaria
20 Restaurante Oliveira

OTHER
1 Cunha Bus Ticket Office
2 Cunha Bus Stop for
  Buses to Ponte de Lima
3 Train Station
5 Linhares Bus Terminal
8 Igreja do Terço
9 Mercado Municipal (Market)
11 Templo do Bom Jesus da Cruz
13 REDM Bus Terminal
14 Turismo & Centro Artesenato
17 Pelourinho (Pillory)
18 Igreja Matriz
19 Museu Arqueológico
21 Museu de Olaria
22 Bus Stop for Express
  Buses to Porto

am to 12.30 pm and 2.30 to 6 pm (except on Thursday when they are open from 9 am to 6 pm) and from 9 am to 4 pm on weekends and holidays.

Feira de Barcelos

Despite increasing attention from tourists, the market is still basically a local, rural affair. Villagers come from miles around to sell everything from a few scrawny chickens to mounds of fruit and vegetables, fresh bread or hand-embroidered linen. Notice the huge cow bells, hand-woven baskets, beautifully carved ox yokes, and the pottery – especially the distinctive yellow-dotted *louça de Barcelos* ware and the gaudily coloured figurines in the style of Rosa Ramalho, a local potter who put Barcelos firmly on the pottery map in this century. And of course there's the trademark Barcelos cockerel everywhere – on pots and tea towels, key rings and bottle-openers and in pottery form in every size.

The tour groups arrive by mid-morning and the market starts to wind down after midday, so it's best to get here in the early morning.

Museu Arqueológico

On a high ledge overlooking an attractive stretch of the Rio Cávado and a restored 15th-century bridge are the roofless ruins of the former palace of the counts of Barcelos and Dukes of Bragança (the eighth count became the first duke). The palace was practically obliterated by the 1755 earthquake and now serves as an alfresco archaeological museum.

Among mysterious phallic stones, Roman columns, medieval caskets and bits of 18th-century azulejos from around the region, the most famous item is a 14th-century stone cross, the Crucifix O Senhor do Galo, depicting the 'Gentleman of the Cockerel' story and said to have been commissioned by the lucky pilgrim himself. Near the entrance is a late Gothic *pelourinho* (pillory) topped by a granite lantern. The site is open daily from 9 am to noon and 2 to 5.30 pm (free admission).

Museu de Olaria

Near the Museu Arqueológico, on Rua Cónego Joaquim Gaiolas, is a pottery museum featuring many of Portugal's regional styles, from Azores pots to proudly displayed figurines from Barcelos, Estremoz and Miranda do Corvo, and some striking pewter-grey pottery from Bisalhães. There's also an exhibit on techniques (though the labels are unfortunately all in Portuguese). The museum is open daily, except Mondays, from 10 am to 12.30 pm and 2 to 6 pm (with no lunch break on Thursdays). The 250$00 charge also covers changing temporary exhibitions.

Igreja Matriz
It's worth peeping inside the stocky Gothic parish church, next to the Museu Arqueológico, to see the splendid 18th-century azulejos and gilded baroque chapels inside.

Templo do Bom Jesus da Cruz
On the south-west corner of the Campo is this striking circular church, also called Igreja do Senhor da Cruz. It was built in 1705, probably by João Antunes (the same architect who designed Lisbon's Igreja da Santa Engrácia) and overlooks a garden of obelisks.

Igreja do Terço
This deceptively plain church, once part of an 18th-century Benedictine monastery, contains some striking azulejos on the life of St Benedict, designed by the 18th-century master, António de Oliveira Bernardes.

Competing for attention are the richly carved and gilded pulpit and the ceiling of painted panels with more scenes from the saint's life.

Special Events
The Festas das Cruzes (Festival of the Crosses) on 3 May turns Barcelos into a fairground of coloured lights, flags, flowers and street decorations. The Festival de Folclore, a celebration of traditional folk song and dance, is held on the last Saturday of July.

Places to Stay
The first choice for market days is *Pensão Restaurante Bagoeira* (☎ 81 12 36; fax 82 45 88) at Avenida Dr Sidónio Pais 495; frilly double rooms start at 4000$00 without bath. Next best is the homey, plant-adorned *Residencial Arantes* (☎ 81 13 26), at Avenida da Liberdade 35, where singles/doubles are 2900$00/3900$00 without bath or 3900$00/6000$00 with bath, including breakfast.

The *Residencial Solar da Estação* (☎ 81 17 41), right by the train station (the peach-coloured building to the left as you exit), has rooms with bath for 2500$00/5000$00.

The poshest but dullest choice in town is *Residencial Dom Nuno* (☎ 81 50 84; fax 81 63 36), at Avenida Dom Nuno Álvares Pereira 76, where modern rooms with bath are 5000$00/7000$00, including breakfast.

MINHO

The Barcelos Cockerel
The cockerel motif that you see all over Portugal – especially in pottery form in every turismo office – has its origins in a 16th (some say 14th) century 'miracle'. According to the story (which also crops up in Spain), a Galician pilgrim on his way to Santiago de Compostela was wrongfully accused of theft while passing through Barcelos. Though pleading his innocence, he was condemned to hang at the gallows. In his last appearance at the judge's house the pilgrim declared that the roast cockerel that the judge was about to eat would stand up and crow to affirm his innocence. The miracle occurred, the pilgrim was saved, and the cockerel gradually became the most popular folk art motif in the country, akin to a national symbol. ■

Places to Eat

Pensão Restaurante Bagoeira (see Places to Stay), the traditional market-day rendezvous for both shoppers and stall-holders, manages to cope with an incredible amount of jovial chaos. Even on non-market days it's worth coming for regional favourites such as rojões ã moda do Minho (a casserole of marinated pork pieces). Prices are under 1500$00 a dish.

At Largo do Município 17, *Restaurante Oliveira* (☎ 81 47 75) is a cheerful, child-friendly place with generous portions and prices under 1300$00 a dish. Simpler and cheaper is *Restaurante Bom Apetite* (☎ 81 54 14), near the train station at Avenida Alcaide de Faria 35: pratos do dia lunch-time specials here are under 700$00.

Restaurante Dom António (☎ 81 22 85), at Avenida Dom António Barroso 85, is a long-time favourite, with pratos do dia under 1000$00 and main dishes around 1400$00. *Confeitaria Salvação Pastelaria*, at No 137 on the same road, is worth a peek for its old engraved till and the famous almond sweets and cakes that have been sold here for decades.

Getting There & Away

Bus Three companies operate from Barcelos: REDM (☎ 81 43 10), at Avenida Dr Sidónio Pais 445, has services to/from Braga almost hourly from 7 am to 7 pm on weekdays (fewer at weekends) and to/from Ponte de Lima five times daily. REDM is also the agent for Internorte and Renex; Renex express coaches pass through Barcelos en route to Porto and Lisbon three times daily, stopping across the river on Rua Irmãos de la Salle.

Linhares (☎ 81 15 71), at Avenida dos Combatentes 50, runs coaches to Vila do Conde, Porto and Viana do Castelo around four times daily. Domingos da Cunha (☎ 81 58 43), on Avenida Dom Nuno Álvares Pereira (but with its major stop at the train station), has services to Ponte de Lima, Ponte da Barca and Arcos de Valdevez five to six times daily.

Train Barcelos is on the Porto-Valença line, with 11 services daily from Porto (half continuing to Valença and half to Viana do Castelo). There are also three local services from Nine (the junction to/from Braga), continuing via Barcelos to Viana do Castelo.

GUIMARÃES
• *pop 22,000* • *postcode 4800* • *area code* ☎ *053*

Known as 'the cradle of the Portuguese nation', Guimarães is chock-a-block with history. It was here, in 1110, that Afonso Henriques was born and from here, some 20 years later, that he launched the Reconquista against the Moors. Officially acknowledged as king of his new kingdom of 'Portucale' in 1143, Afonso made Coimbra the official capital, but Guimarães considers itself the first de facto capital.

Although its outskirts are now an ugly mass of industries, the historic core of Guimarães is a finely preserved enclave of medieval monuments, including two convents housing two excellent museums. As a university town (with a very successful football team) Guimarães also has a friendly, lively atmosphere which explodes into full scale merry-making during its annual Festas Gualterianas (see Special Events). There's enough here to warrant a full day's sightseeing – possibly as a day trip from Braga since cheap accommodation is thin on the ground. For those with escudos to spare, its two pousadas are among the finest in the land.

History

Guimarães caught the royal eye as early as 840 AD, when Alfonso II of León convened a council of bishops here, but it only started to grow in the 10th century after a powerful local noblewoman, Countess Mumadona, gave it her attention. A monastery was founded and a castle built. Henri of Burgundy, Count of Portucale (the region between the Minho and Douro) chose Guimarães for his court, as did his son Afonso Henriques until making Coimbra the capital of his new kingdom in 1143.

Even in medieval times, the town was

famous for its linen production, as it still is today. Other industries which contribute to its continuing prosperity are cutlery, kitchenware production and crafts such as gold and silversmithing, embroidery and pottery.

Orientation

The recently demarcated *zona de turismo* (tourist area), the heart of the old town, lies in the north-east part of modern-day Guimarães and includes nearly all the points of interest. At the northern end of the zone is the castle, and at the southern end is a strip of public gardens in three sections variously called Alameda da Resistência do Fascismo, Alameda da Liberdade, and Alameda de São Dâmaso. Between the castle and these gardens lies a tangle of medieval streets, fine monuments and shady squares. At the southwestern corner of the zone is handsome Largo do Toural, with restaurants, banks and hotels nearby.

From the train station on Avenida Dom João IV, it's a 10-minute walk north up Avenida Dom Afonso Henriques to the zona de turismo; the turismo (tourist office) is on the right, just before the gardens. From the bus station at the end of the uninspiringly

MINHO

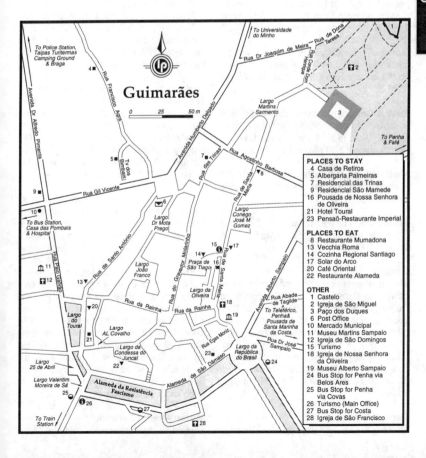

Guimarães

PLACES TO STAY
4 Casa de Retiros
5 Albergaria Palmeiras
7 Residencial das Trinas
9 Residencial São Mamede
16 Pousada de Nossa Senhora de Oliveira
21 Hotel Toural
23 Pensaõ-Restaurante Imperial

PLACES TO EAT
8 Restaurante Mumadona
13 Vecchia Roma
14 Cozinha Regional Santiago
17 Solar do Arco
20 Café Oriental
22 Restaurante Alameda

OTHER
1 Castelo
2 Igreja de São Miguel
3 Paço dos Duques
6 Post Office
10 Mercado Municipal
11 Museu Martins Sampaio
12 Igreja de São Domingos
15 Turismo
18 Igreja de Nossa Senhora da Oliveira
19 Museu Alberto Sampaio
24 Bus Stop for Penha via Belos Ares
25 Bus Stop for Penha via Covas
26 Turismo (Main Office)
27 Bus Stop for Costa
28 Igreja de São Francisco

modern Avenida Conde de Margaride, it's a 20-minute walk east to the centre.

Information

Tourist Office The main turismo (☎ 41 24 50) is at Alameda de São Dâmaso 86, at the junction with Avenida Dom Afonso Henriques. It's open weekdays only from 9 am to 12.30 pm and 2 to 5.30 pm. There's a smaller but more enthusiastic turismo (☎ 51 51 23, ext 184) right at the heart of the old town, above an art gallery in Praça de São Tiago. From June to August this is open from 9 am to 7 pm on weekdays and from 10 am to 1 pm and 3 to 5 pm on weekends; the rest of the year it's open from 9 am to 12.30 pm and 2 to 5.30 pm on weekdays only.

Money There are plenty of banks on the outskirts of the old town, especially in Largo do Toural and Rua Gil Vicente. Most have ATMs.

Post & Communications The post office, at the top of Rua de Santo António, is open from 8.30 am to 6.30 pm on weekdays and from 9 am to 12.30 pm on Saturdays.

Medical Services The hospital (☎ 51 26 12) is north of the main bus station, off Avenida Conde de Margaride.

Emergency The police station (☎ 51 33 34) is on the northern edge of town, on Rua Texieira de Pascoais.

Castelo

The striking seven-towered castle looks down over the northern part of the old town from a grassy hilltop. Built by Henri of Burgundy in about 1100, it's reputed to be the birthplace of his son Afonso Henriques. The little Igreja de São Miguel nearby is where Afonso was probably baptised. Castle and chapel are open daily, except Mondays, from 10 am to 12.30 pm and 2 to 5.30 pm (free admission).

Paço dos Duques

Downhill from the Igreja de São Miguel is the gross Ducal Palace, easily distinguished by its host of brick chimneys. Built in 1401 by Dom Afonso, the future first Duke of Bragança, it served as the ducal residence but fell into ruin after the family moved to Vila Viçosa in the Alentejo.

In 1933, during the Salazar era, it was tastelessly restored and has since become a museum. The only points of interest in a rather tedious tour are some fine 16th to 18th-century Flemish tapestries, and a couple of paintings attributed to Josefa de Óbidos (see the boxed aside under Óbidos in the Estremadura & Ribatejo chapter for more details on his work).

From June to August the palace is open daily from 9 am to 7 pm (entry 300$00); the rest of the year it's open from 10 am to 5.30 pm (200$00). Entry is free for students, and for all on Sunday mornings.

Igreja de Nossa Senhora da Oliveira

The main attraction in the lovely medieval Largo da Oliveira, at the heart of the old town, is this 14th-century convent-church founded by Countess Mumadona in the 10th century. It was rebuilt by João I four centuries later to honour a vow he made before his decisive 1385 battle against the Spanish at Aljubarrota.

In front is a Gothic canopy and cross which allegedly marks the spot where Wamba the victorious Visigoth (but reluctant ruler) drove his spear into the ground beside an olive tree, refusing to reign as king unless the tree immediately sprouted – which of course it did. Another legend, however, recounts that an olive tree growing here suddenly sprouted leaves as the porch of the church was being completed – hence the name of the church, Our Lady of the Olive Tree. Although the exterior still has some fine details, including a Manueline tower and a Gothic pediment over the main doorway, the interior, renovated this century, has little of interest. It's open daily from 7.15 am to noon and 3.30 to 7.30 pm.

Museu Alberto Sampaio

Housed in the conventual buildings of the

Igreja de Nossa Senhora da Oliveira, around the beautiful 13th-century Romanesque cloister, is this superb collection named after a prominent sociologist. Highlights include a 14th-century silver gilt triptych, allegedly part of booty taken from the Castilians after the Battle of Aljubarrota; a 16th-century silver Manueline cross; and the tunic said to have been worn by João I at Aljubarrota.

In July and August the museum is open daily, except Mondays, from 10 am to 12.30 pm and 2 to 7 pm. At other times it closes at 5.30 pm. Admission costs 200$00 but is free to students, and to all on Sunday mornings.

Museu Martins Sarmento

This excellent collection of Celto-Iberian items from the nearby citânias of Briteiros and Sabroso is named after the archaeologist who excavated the Briteiros site in 1875. The larger pieces are scattered around the adjacent cloister of the 14th-century Igreja de São Domingos.

There are some extraordinary and mysterious items here, in particular the so-called Pedra Formosa – a slab of carved stone which was probably the front of a funerary monument – and the arresting, three-metre-high Colossus of Pedralva, an anonymous figure with one arm stretched up to the sky. The museum is open daily, except Mondays, from 9.30 am to noon and 2 to 5 pm. Admission costs 200$00 (free to students).

Igreja de São Francisco

The Church of St Francis of Assisi, south of the public gardens, is worth visiting for its 18th-century azulejos on the life of St Francis. First founded in the 13th century, the church underwent considerable alterations over the following centuries, the most successful addition being a lovely Renaissance cloister.

Penha & Mosteiro de Santa Marinha da Costa

Seven km to the south-east is the wooded hill of Penha, overlooking Guimarães at 617m, the highest point in the Serra de Santa Catarina. On the lower slopes is the former Mosteiro de Santa Marinha da Costa, now one of Portugal's most luxurious pousadas, parts of which are open to the public. The trip makes a delightful break from the city, especially if you take the Teleférico da Penha (cable car) to the top.

The monastery dates from 1154 when the wife of Afonso Henriques commissioned it for the Augustinian Order to honour a vow to Santa Marinha, the patron saint of pregnant women. In 1528 the order was replaced by the Order of São Jerónimo. The monastery was almost entirely rebuilt in the 18th century, suffered a serious fire in 1834 and was finally sold to the government in 1951. It was opened as a flagship pousada in 1985.

Non-guests can visit the chapel and extensive gardens, while guests get to wander around a lovely cloister, encounter 18th-century azulejos by the tile-master Policarpo de Oliveira Bernardes (son of the equally renowned tile-master António de Oliveira Bernardes), and sleep in elegantly converted monks' cells.

The cable car goes from the end of Rua de Dr José Sampaio between 10 am and 7 pm, for 300$00 each way. There are also bus routes: the most convenient for the pousada is the service to São Roque, which leaves every half-hour between 7 am and 11 pm from the south side of the public gardens. Get off at Costa, a short walk from the pousada.

Special Events

The Festas Gualterianas (Festival of Saint Walter) takes place on the first weekend of August, celebrating a free fair (market) which has been held in Guimarães since 1452.

Places to Stay

Camping The municipal camping ground (☎ 51 74 51) is six km south-east of town, on the Penha hill. It's open from May to October and has a small swimming pool. Take the Mondinese bus that goes via Covas (from the stop opposite the turismo) or the one via Belos Ares (from the stop in Largo da República do Brasil).

Alternatively, eight km to the north-west

by the Rio Ave at Caldas das Taipas is the slightly more expensive *Taipas Turitermas* site (☎ 57 62 74), open from June to September. Take any Braga-bound bus.

Hostels One of the cheapest and starkest options in town is *Casa de Retiros* (☎ 51 15 15; fax 51 15 17) at Rua Francisco Agra 163. Run by the Redentoristas missionaries, its rules include payment on arrival, entry to rooms after 6 pm only and a curfew at 11.30 pm. But at 3000$00/5000$00/7000$00 a single/double/triple (including breakfast), the hardship is bearable. Dormitory beds, at 2000$00, are often booked by youth groups but it's worth asking.

Pensões & Residencials The *Pensão-Restaurante Imperial* (☎ 41 51 63), Alameda São Dãmaso 111 (and Rua Egas Moniz 57), has plain singles/doubles from 2000$00/ 3000$00 without shower or 3000$00/ 5000$00 with shower. Some rooms overlook the gardens.

Near the bus station, at the junction of Avenida Conde de Margaride and Rua de São Goncalo, is the soulless, modern *Residencial São Mamede* (☎ 51 30 92; fax 51 38 63) where dull doubles range from 3500$00 without bath to 6500$00 with bath (including breakfast). Far better value are the doubles for 6000$00 (with bath and breakfast) of *Residencial das Trinas* (☎ 51 73 58; fax 51 73 62) at Rua das Trinas 29, in an atmospheric old lane near the post office.

Hotels Hidden away on the 4th floor of the modern Centro Comercial das Palmeiras, off Rua Gil Vicente, is *Albergaria Palmeiras* (☎ 41 03 24; fax 41 72 61), where well-equipped, comfortable rooms are 9000$00/ 12,000$00 (including breakfast and free car parking). The entrance is difficult to find: take the side entrance to the Centro (down Travessa dos Bimbais) and the first lift on the left inside.

Far more congenial is the modernised *Hotel Toural* (☎ 51 71 84; fax 51 71 49) at Largo do Toural (the entrance is behind, in Largo AL Carvalho). Singles/doubles here are 11,000$00/13,000$00.

Pousadas Guimarães has two pousadas: the *Pousada de Nossa Senhora de Oliveira* (☎ 51 41 57; fax 51 42 04) is a 16th-century house on Rua de Santa Maria, in the heart of the old town, with beautifully furnished doubles for 18,000$00. The *Pousada de Santa Marinha da Costa* (☎ 51 44 53; fax 51 44 59), three km from town on the slopes of Penha, is the jewel in the pousada crown. Doubles here cost 23,000$00.

Turihab The only property in town is *Casa das Pombais* (☎ 42 19 17), a 17th-century manor house with peacocks strutting in its little garden, incongruously surrounded by shops and housing estates. There are only three rooms (at 11,000$00 a double including breakfast), so book well ahead.

Places to Eat
Old Town Several workers' taverns serving cheap snacks are along Rua Egas Moniz. A more mixed crowd patronises *Cozinha Regional Santiago* (☎ 51 66 69) at Praça de São Tiago 16, a surprisingly medium-priced restaurant given its location, with a bar favoured by local footballers. The menu features regional specialities such as rojões à Minhoto, for under 1200$00 a dish.

In the attractive Largo da Condessa do Juncal are several more restaurants: among the cheapest and friendliest is *Restaurante Alameda* (☎ 41 23 72), with Portuguese standards from around 1000$00. A notch smarter but equally welcoming is *Restaurante Mumadona* (☎ 41 90 41), at Rua de Santa Maria 48, with half-portions from 650$00. At the other end of this street is the up-market *Solar do Arco* (☎ 51 30 72; closed Sunday) where you'll pay around 2000$00 a dish from a select menu, mostly seafood. For a real treat, head for the elegant dining room of the *Pousada de Nossa Senhora de Oliveira* (☎ 51 41 57) where you can kiss goodbye to at least 3000$00 per person for a fixed-price menu.

Elsewhere A popular choice is *Café Oriental* (☎ 41 40 48) overlooking Largo do Toural. It's neither a café nor very Oriental, but serves reasonably priced Portuguese fare until 2 am. The nearby *Vecchia Roma* (☎ 51 52 48), at Rua Santo António 21, is a trendy place for pizzas and delicious gelados (ice creams); it's open until 11.30 pm.

For takeaway supplies, the mercado municipal is at the top of Rua Paio Galvão.

Getting There & Away

Bus Several bus companies operate from the main terminal: REDM (☎ 51 62 29) has four daily coaches to Viana do Castelo and six (including two express) to Chaves. Rodonorte's services include about 10 daily coaches to Braga, six to Amarante and 10 to Ponte de Lima. João Ferreira das Neves (☎ 51 31 31) has about seven express services daily to Porto. João Carlos Soares (☎ 51 24 93) has at least seven daily coaches to Braga, 10 to Porto and three expresses to Lisbon.

Train Guimarães is at the end of a line via Santo Tirso from Porto's Trindade station (520$00). Trains run about hourly and take just under two hours.

Coastal & Northern Minho

VIANA DO CASTELO
• *pop 15,200* • *postcode 4900* • *area code ☎ 058*
This is the Minho's largest and liveliest resort, an elegant town of Manueline and Renaissance houses and rococo palaces which stretches along the north bank of the Rio Lima estuary. Famous for its traditional festivals (especially the Romaria de Nossa Senhora da Agonia, held in August), and with a wide range of accommodation and restaurants, it's a perfect base for exploring the Lima valley or simply for hanging out at the excellent beach across the river.

History
Viana's Celtic roots lie on the wooded slopes and hilltop of Monte de Santa Luzia at the northern edge of town. The remains of a Celto-Iberian citânia or fortified hilltop settlement can still be seen here, though there's little evidence of the Romans, Suevi, Visigoths and Moors who followed. The Romans called the place Diana, which over the years changed to Viana.

The town by the river was 'created' by special charter in 1258 by Dom Afonso III, who wanted an urban and fishing centre at the mouth of the Rio Lima. In the 16th century the well-fortified town found fame and fortune in the seafaring activities of its sailors, who fished for cod off Newfoundland. The resulting prosperity led to a flurry of Manueline mansions and monasteries and the building of a fort at the mouth of the river. By the mid-17th century Viana was northern Portugal's biggest port, its merchants trading as far afield as Russia. It was during this time that British cloth merchants who had settled here began to export large quantities of the local 'red portugal' wine to England (see the boxed aside 'Getting Port to Market' in the Porto section of the Douro chapter).

More money flooded into Viana in the 18th century, thanks to the Brazilian sugar and gold trade. With Brazil's independence and Porto's increasing prominence as a wine-exporting port, Viana fell into decline. It has since revived to become a prosperous deep-sea fishing and industrial centre and an increasingly popular tourist destination.

Orientation
Viana is dominated by wooded Monte de Santa Luzia to the north, crowned by an ugly modern basilica. From the train station at the foot of the hill, it's a 10-minute walk straight down the broad Avenida dos Combatentes da Grande Guerra (usually shortened to Avenida dos Combatentes) to the river. To the left (east) of the Avenida is the old town, with its major sights of interest around Praça da República. To the right (west) lies the old fishing quarter, with the Castelo de São Tiago da Barra at the western edge of town.

From the bus station, at the eastern end of Rua da Bandeira, it's a 20-minute walk to the

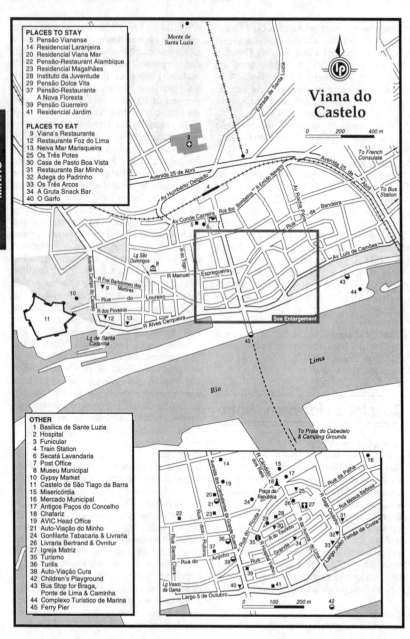

PLACES TO STAY
5   Pensão Vianense
14 Residencial Laranjeira
20 Residencial Viana Mar
22 Pensão-Restaurant Alambique
23 Residencial Magalhães
28 Instituto da Juventude
29 Pensão Dolce Vita
37 Pensão-Restaurante
    A Nova Floresta
39 Pensão Guerreiro
41 Residencial Jardim

PLACES TO EAT
9   Viana's Restaurante
12 Restaurante Foz do Lima
13 Neiva Mar Marisqueira
25 Os Três Potes
30 Casa de Pasto Boa Vista
31 Restaurante Bar Minho
33 Adega do Padrinho
34 A Gruta Snack Bar
40 O Garfo

OTHER
1   Basilica de Sante Luzia
2   Hospital
3   Funicular
4   Train Station
6   Secatá Lavandaria
7   Post Office
8   Museu Municipal
10 Gypsy Market
11 Castelo de São Tiago da Barra
15 Misericórdia
16 Mercado Municipal
17 Antigos Paços do Concelho
18 Chafariz
19 AVIC Head Office
21 Auto-Viação do Minho
24 Gonfilarte Tabacaria & Livraria
26 Livraria Bertrand & Ovnitur
27 Igreja Matriz
35 Turismo
36 Turilis
38 Auto-Viação Cura
42 Children's Playground
43 Bus Stop for Braga,
    Ponte de Lima & Caminha
44 Complexo Turístico de Marina
45 Ferry Pier

Viana do Castelo

MINHO

centre, but many buses stop beside the gardens which border the river directly south of Praça da República.

Information

Tourist Offices Viana is headquarters for the Região de Turismo do Alto Minho, with an administrative office (☎ 82 02 71; fax 82 97 98) in the Castelo de São Tiago da Barra. The turismo (☎ 82 26 20; fax 82 78 73) for general enquiries, however, is in the centre of the old town on Praça da Erva, in a building which was founded in 1468 to shelter pilgrims and travellers and later became a hospital. The office is open Monday to Saturday from 9.30 am to 12.30 pm and 2.30 to 6 pm; on Sundays it's open in the mornings only except in August when it's also open from 3 to 8 pm. As well as a comprehensive town brochure and map it should also have copies of the free monthly *Agenda Cultural* with details of cultural events.

Foreign Consulates There's a French consulate (☎ 82 22 56) on Rua Dr da Rocha Páris, east of the centre.

Money Banks with ATMs are along Avenida dos Combatentes and in the Praça da República.

Post & Communications The post office, with telephone and fax facilities, is at the top of Avenida dos Combatentes.

Travel Agencies Ovnitur Viagens e Turismo (☎ 82 03 33), at Largo do Instituto Histórico do Minho 36, can organise most things. For regional bus tours, see Getting There & Away.

Bookshops There is a branch of the good Livraria Bertrand at Rua de Sacadura Cabral 32. Foreign-language newspapers are available at newsagents, including Gonfilarte Tabacaria & Livraria on Praça da República.

Laundry Secatá Lavandaria, at Rua dos Rubins 111, can do a load of wash-and-dry within a day, if pushed. It's open weekdays from 9 am to 12.30 pm and 4.30 to 7 pm, and Saturdays from 9 am to 1 pm.

Medical Services The hospital (☎ 82 90 81) is off Avenida 25 de Abril, on the northern edge of town beyond the railway station.

Praça da República

This, the heart of the old town, is Viana's most picturesque spot, a finely preserved area of handsome mansions and monuments.

Chafariz The centrepiece of the old town square is this elegant Renaissance fountain built in 1554 by João Lopes the Elder. At the top of its sculptured basins are the famous Manueline motifs, an armillary sphere and the cross of the Order of Christ.

Antigos Paços do Concelho The fortress-like old town hall facing the square is another 16th-century creation, though it has since been restored, its arcade often serving as a craft hawkers' venue.

Misericórdia This former almshouse at right angles to the old town hall is the biggest eye-opener. Designed in 1589 by João Lopes the Younger, it features an arched colonnade with two tiers of loggias above supported by monster caryatids. The adjoining Igreja de Misericórdia, rebuilt in 1714 and featuring 18th-century azulejos, is open on Sundays from 11 am to 12.30 pm, and every day in August.

Igreja Matriz

The parish church (also referred to as the Sé or cathedral), south of Praça da República, dates from the 15th century but has undergone several modifications. Its most interesting features are the sculpted Romanesque towers and a Gothic doorway carved with figures of Christ and the Evangelists.

Museu Municipal

Housed in the imposing 18th-century Palacete Barbosa Maciel on Rua Manuel Espregueira is an outstanding collection of azulejos, ceramics (especially blue Portuguese china) and furniture (especially Indo-Portuguese tables and chests of ivory, teak and ebony) from the 17th and 18th centuries. The museum is open daily, except Mondays, from 9.30 am to noon and 2 to 5 pm; entry is 200$00.

Castelo de São Tiago da Barra

The grandiose castle overlooking the mouth of the river at the western edge of town started its life in the 15th century as a smallish fort, later integrated into a larger one which Philip II of Spain (at that time also Felipe I of Portugal) commissioned in 1592 to guard the prosperous port from pirates. Several offices are now based in the converted buildings inside, including the regional turismo.

Monte de Santa Luzia

There are two good reasons to climb Viana's hill. The dull modern basilica isn't one, but the view from the top of it is; look for the side entrance marked 'Zimbório'. The second draw is the ruins of a Celto-Iberian citânia, dating from around the 4th-century BC, in a fenced-off area behind the basilica. The site is poorly maintained but you should be able to make out the remains of walls and circular stone huts.

To get to the top you can either climb through pine woods (cross the railway track to find the trail beside a large white building called Misericórdia de Viana) or take the funicular from Avenida 25 de Abril, on the other side of the railway track. It runs on the hour from 9 am to noon and then every half-hour until 7 pm (except at 1 pm). The seven-minute trip costs 100$00 each way.

Children's Playground

There's an excellent children's adventure playground along the riverfront near Largo 5 de Outubro.

Markets The main mercado municipal is east of the centre, on Rua Martim Velho. A huge Gypsy market takes place every Friday in the wasteland beside the Castelo de São Tiago da Barra – a good opportunity to pick up cheap clothes and shoes or local handicrafts.

Beaches

Viana's beach, Praia do Cabedelo, on the other side of the river, is one of the best in the Minho: lots of sand and surf and little else but a windsurfing school and a couple of cafés by the dock. The easiest way to get there is by ferry from the pier south of Largo 5 de Outubro, which makes the five-minute hop across the river every half-hour (every hour in winter) from 8.30 am to 6.30 pm, for 100$00. Buses also go there half a dozen times daily. The last bus and ferry back leave at around 7 pm.

North of Viana, all the way to Caminha, is a string of beautiful undeveloped beaches and villages, such as Afife and Moledo do Minho, with a low-key resort at Vila Praia de Âncora. You can reach them on a day trip by either train or bus: there are four daily train services stopping at all the villages en route and regular bus services from Viana to Caminha via Afife and Vila Praia de Âncora.

Organised Tours

AVIC (☎ 82 97 05) runs several regional bus tours including one on Thursdays to Barcelos, with time to visit the market.

Boat Trips Trips up the Rio Lima run fairly regularly during the summer from the pier south of Largo 5 de Outubro. They can last anywhere from 30 minutes to three hours (the latter includes lunch). Call ☎ 84 22 90 for more details or check at the pier for information.

Special Events

Viana's Romaria de Nossa Senhora da Agónia (Our Lady of Sorrows) is one of the most spectacular of the Minho's many festivals. It starts on the Friday nearest 20 August and lasts for three days, featuring everything from sombre religious processions (especially on the first day) to merry parades of bands, floats and huge carnival figures, and nightly fireworks. The streets are decorated with coloured sawdust, the women come out in their gold jewellery and traditional dress, the men drink like there's no tomorrow and when it's all over the whole town seems to collapse with a massive hangover.

Accommodation is inevitably tight during this time – you'll need to book well ahead.

Places to Stay

Camping There are two camping grounds on Praia do Cabedelo. Closest to the beach is one run by *Inatel* (☎ 32 20 42), open to Inatel members and holders of the Camping Card International only. The more expensive *Orbitur* site (☎ 32 21 67), open mid-January to 15 November, is shady and has bungalows for rent. Both are packed out in summer. They're within walking distance of the ferry pier.

Hostels There's an instituto da juventude (elsewhere called a centro da juventude; ☎ 82 88 82) on Rua do Poço. It's heavily used by groups of kids though you may strike it lucky and find a cheap bed available.

Private Rooms The turismo keeps a list of private rooms around town – probably your only chance of accommodation during August (and during the Romaria). Expect to pay at least 5000$00 a double at these times.

Pensões & Residencials *Pensão Guerreiro* (☎ 82 20 99), at Rua Grande 14, has basic singles/doubles without bath for 2000$00/4000$00. The similarly priced *Pensão Vianense* (☎ 82 31 18), at Avenida Conde da Carreira 79, is a notch higher in comfort. For its wide range of rooms (from 3500$00 to 6000$00 a double, with bath) the welcoming *Residencial Laranjeira* (☎ 82 22 61; fax 82 19 02), at Rua General Luís do Rego 45, is an excellent choice. In a similar price range (doubles for 5000$00) are two places on pedestrianised Rua Manuel Espregueira: *Pensão-Restaurant Alambique* (☎ 82 38 94) at No 86, and the popular *Residencial Magalhães* (☎ 82 32 93) at No 62, where prices include breakfast. *Pensão Dolce Vita* (☎ 248 60), opposite the turismo

at Rua do Poço 44, has clean modern doubles with bath (above its Italian restaurant) for 5000$00.

Pricier and more comfortable options include the *Pensão-Restaurante A Nova Floresta* (☎ 82 23 86), at Rua do Anjinho 34, where doubles with bath cost 7000$00; the friendly *Residencial Viana Mar* (☎ & fax 82 89 62), at Avenida dos Combatentes 215, where they're 6500$00 (5000$00 without bath); and the elegant *Residencial Jardim* (☎ 82 89 15; fax 82 89 17) where river-view doubles with bath are 8500$00 (including breakfast).

Turihab The turismo has details of several rural cottages and manor houses nearby (most of them difficult to get to unless you have your own transport). Expect to pay at least 8000$00 for a double.

Places to Eat

All the Pensões-Restaurantes under Places to Stay are open to non-guests and offer reasonable food at good prices. Recommended is the 1st floor *Restaurante Guerreiro* at Rua Grande 14; it's better than its tacky menu suggests, and is popular with locals. Also on this road is the trendy *A Gruta Snack Bar* (☎ 82 02 14) at No 87, which is popular with students and has a small menu of dishes mostly under 1000$00. The cheap and cheerful *Casa de Pasto Boa Vista* (☎ 239 83), at Rua do Poço 13, is an easy-going place with a small menu but attractive prices. On the same street at No 44, the pasta and pizza at *Dolce Vita* (☎ 248 60) makes a refreshing change.

Restaurante Bar Minho (☎ 82 32 61), at Rua Gago Coutinho 103, is a family-style restaurant with generous portions. A more up-market family option is the *Adega do Padrinho* (☎ 269 54), at No 162, where you can fill up on traditional specialities such as ensopada de coelho (rabbit stew) for around 1300$00 a dish.

The unpretentious *O Garfo* (☎ 82 94 15), at Largo 5 de Outubro 28, has a similar range of dishes (offal-lovers will like the blood-and-meat concoction called sarrabulho).

MINHO

Top-of-the-range restaurants include *Os Três Potes* (☎ 82 99 28), at Beco dos Fornos 7, which draws in the tourists with folksy décor and Saturday night folk dancing; and *Os Três Arcos* (☎ 240 14), at Largo João Tomás da Costa 25, renowned for seafood. It's expensive, but at the adjoining cervejaria you can get half-portions from 500$00. Both restaurants are closed on Mondays.

The fisherfolk quarter between the castelo and Largo Vasco da Gama has several worthwhile restaurants, including *Foz do Lima* (☎ 82 92 32), at Rua dos Poveiros, with an excellent caldeirada de peixe (fish stew) for 1200$00. At *Viana's Restaurante* (☎ 247 97), Rua Frei Bartolomeu dos Martires 179, you can eat your fill of bacalhau, for which the restaurant is justifiably famous.

Opposite the fish market at Largo Infante Dom Henrique 1 (actually at the corner of Largo de Santa Catarina) is another fish restaurant, *Neiva Mar Marisqueira* (☎ 82 06 69). It looks oddly out of place with its fake lawn, but the large seafood menu is strong on grilled dishes, with prices at around 1400$00.

Getting There & Away
Bus Several companies operate from the main terminal (☎ 82 13 92) but they also have stops along Avenida dos Combatentes where you can buy tickets and board the long-distance coaches. Coaches to nearer destinations (eg Braga, Ponte de Lima and Cabedelo) stop by the riverside gardens, near the defunct Complexo Turístico de Marina (marine complex).

Auto-Viação do Minho or AV Minho (☎ 82 88 34) at Avenida dos Combatentes 181 has daily services to Ponte de Lima and express coaches to Porto (five daily), Coimbra and Lisbon. Auto-Viação Cura (☎ 82 93 48) at No 81 goes to Ponte de Lima and Arcos de Valdevez, and has express services to Porto, Monção and Lisbon. Turilis (☎ 82 93 48) at No 107 concentrates on northern destinations such as Melgaço, Monção and Vila Praia da Áncora. AVIC (☎ 82 97 05) is the largest local operator, with several offices along the Avenida and

its head office at No 206. It runs four express services daily to Lisbon via Vila do Conde, Porto and Coimbra.

Train Viana is on the Porto-Valença line, with 10 services daily from Porto's São Bento station, of which six continue to Valença (three are local services, and three international services with connections to Vigo in Spain). Coming from Braga, there are frequent services to Nine where you can pick up connecting trains to Viana.

Getting Around
Taxis hang out along Avenida dos Combatentes. Cars can be rented from Ovnitur (see Travel Agencies), Avis (☎ 82 39 94) and Hertz (☎ 82 22 50).

VALENÇA DO MINHO
• *pop 2500* • *postcode 4930* • *area code* ☎ *051*
From its grassy hilltop position, the 17th-century fortified citadel of Valença do Minho (commonly called Valença) overlooks the Rio Minho frontier with Spain. A dull new town has spread out below, but it's the old *fortaleza* which is the focus of attention for Spanish day-trippers. They troop across the river from Tuy in their hundreds to buy cheap linen and towels from the souvenir shops lining the cobbled streets. Once they've gone, the silence seeps up over the walls from the riverbank and the citadel regains its tranquillity and sense of isolation.

Orientation
Arriving by train or bus (they share the same terminal), you'd hardly guess there was anything worthwhile to see: the station is in the new part of town, half a km south of the citadel, and there are no signs to direct you. Head straight out onto Avenida Espanha, the main street running through the new town, and turn right. At the crossroads, turn left to enter the citadel at its southernmost gateway, Portas da Coroada. Or continue straight ahead to find the turismo, bearing left along Avenida dos Combatentes da Grande Guerra to enter the citadel at its most commonly

used pedestrian entrance, Portas do Meio: a 'Centro Histórico' sign points the way.

If you're arriving from Spain, you'll cross the Eiffel-inspired Ponte Internacional (also called Ponte Velha), built in 1886, to arrive at the northern end of Avenida Espanha. Drivers can also approach by the A3/IP1 motorway, which crosses the Rio Minho on a new bridge, slightly downstream from Ponte Velha.

Information

The turismo (☎ & fax 233 74) is in a poorly signed wooden building in a small wooded park just off Avenida Espanha (behind the Centro Histórico sign). It's open daily from 9 am to noon and 2 to 6 pm (morning only on Sundays).

There's a Spanish consulate (☎ 221 22) a little north of the turismo on Avenida Espanha.

Fortaleza

A fortress existed on this site from at least the 13th century, guarding Portugal's northern frontier. At that time, Valença was called Contrasta (the fortress across the river at Tuy provided its counterpart). The perfectly preserved fortress that you see today dates from the 16th century, its design inspired by the French military architect Vauban, as were several others in northern Portugal (eg in Chaves). In fact there are two fortresses, each with six bastions, several watchtowers and powder magazines and massive gateways, all enclosed by defensive bulwarks. The two are separated by a deep ditch and joined by a single bridge.

The ancient churches and elegant Manueline mansions which line the cobbled streets reveal how successful the fortifications were: the fortaleza escaped unscathed from several sieges, even during the 19th century. The larger, northern fortress contains most historic items of note, including the 14th-century Igreja de São Estevão with its Renaissance façade, the nearby Roman milestone (taken from the Roman Braga-Astorga road at its Rio Minho crossing) and, outside the Capela de Bom Jesus, a statue of Santo Teotónio, a 12th-century local holy man venerated by Dom Afonso Henriques.

Places to Stay

Fortaleza Although there may occasionally be private rooms available, and summer campers often set up tents below the western ramparts, there are only two official places to stay inside the citadel and both are expensive. The 15-room *Pousada de São Teotónio* (☎ 82 40 20; fax 82 43 97) was built in 1962 at the northern end of the fortress, with superlative views of the river and Spanish Galicia on the other side. High-season doubles cost 16,500$00.

The nearby *Casa do Poço de Valença* (☎ 82 52 35; fax 82 54 69), at Travessa da Gaviarra 4, is an 18th-century house which once lodged the sick from the nearby Misericórdia hospital. Recently restored by a Dutchman, its five deluxe double rooms cost 15,000$00. Artwork by leading contemporary Portuguese and Spanish artists gives a fresh, modern feel to the place, which features a downstairs library and billiard room and an upstairs living room with a fantastic river view.

New Town One of the cheapest options is *Pensão Rio Minho* (☎ 223 31), opposite the train station at Largo da Estação. Run-down singles/doubles with bath are 3500$00/ 5000$00. En route to the fortaleza is *Residencial São Gião* (☎ 232 66), on the 1st floor of Centro Comercial Alvarinho, where doubles with bath start from 5500$00 (including breakfast). *Residencial Val Flores* (☎ 82 41 06; fax 82 41 29), in the adjacent Centro Val Flores, has singles/doubles with bath for 3800$00/5800$00 (including breakfast), although this rockets to 4500$00/ 7000$00 in August.

Places to Eat

Eating inside the fortaleza with Spanish tour groups isn't as bad as it sounds if you like a jolly atmosphere. *Restaurante Monumental* (☎ 235 57) is tucked inside the walls of the southern Portas da Coroada and serves a variety of local specialities (eg roast kid and

MINHO

salmon, or trout from the Minho) in a spacious, easy-going setting. Two other popular places are *Restaurante Bom Jesus* (☎ 220 88), in Largo do Bom Jesus, which has everything from ameijoa à espanhola (Spanish-style clams) to rojões à moda do Minho for under 1400$00. Its sister establishment, *Restaurante Beluarte* (☎ 82 40 42), in Rua Apolinário da Fonseca, is more casual and has especially enticing desserts.

At the northern end, *A Gruta* (☎ 222 70) is a small, simple restaurant-bar built into the walls just before Largo da República. Try its filling feijoada (beans and meat stew) for 900$00.

Getting There & Away

Bus Two companies operate from the train station terminal: Empresa de Transportes Courense (☎ 82 41 75) and António Serra (☎ 231 20). Between them, they run seven daily services to Viana do Castelo (two on weekends) and around 10 a day to Monção (five on weekends). Auto-Viação do Minho express coaches pass through en route to Viana do Castelo three times daily, and AVIC has three express runs to Viana, Porto, Coimbra and Lisbon.

There are three buses daily, except Sundays, to Tuy and on to Vigo.

Train Valença is at the end of the line from Porto, with two regional services a day (taking just under four hours) and three international services (taking 2¼ hours and continuing to Spain). A couple of other regional services involve changes at Nine or Caminha.

The three daily international train services from Porto continue across the border to Tuy, Vigo, Santiago and La Coruña.

MONÇÃO
• *postcode 4950* • *area code* ☎ *051*
This pleasant riverside town, 16 km east of Valença do Minho, is a popular spot among local tourists thanks to its nearby spa, a couple of km to the east. There's little left of its 14th and 17th-century walled fortifications but the heart of the old town is an

atmospheric place to wander, with narrow lanes and shady squares, and there's plenty of good food and wine to sample.

Monção's most famous daughter is one Deu-la-Deu Martins, who tricked a force of Castilians into calling off a siege in 1368 by scrabbling together enough flour from the starving town to make some cakes. She threw these to the Castilians in a brazen show of plenty and the disheartened force retreated.

Orientation
From the defunct train station, now serving as the main bus terminal, it's a five-minute walk straight ahead along Rua General Pimenta de Castro to the first of the town's two major squares, Praça da República. Praça Deu-la-Deu and the heart of the old town lie a few minutes walk further on.

Auto-Viação do Minho has a separate terminal beside the GALP petrol station, just a minute's walk down Avenida 25 de Abril from the former train station, outside the town's southern gateway, Portas do Sol. If you're driving from Spain, you'll cross from Salvaterra via a new bridge.

Information
The turismo (☎ 65 27 57) is on the 1st floor of the restored Casa do Curro, which also houses the town library. There are entrances on Praça Deu-la-Deu next to the Café Escondidinho, and on Praça da República. It's open daily from 9.30 am to 12.30 pm and 2 to 7 pm (to 6 pm in winter).

Deu-la-Deu
Following the Deu-la-Deu history trail leads you through the most attractive parts of town. Start in chestnut-shaded Praça Deu-la-Deu, where her statue tops a fountain, and head east down an arched side street to her birthplace, next to a butcher's shop. Her tomb is in the Romanesque Igreja Matriz at the end of this street.

Igreja da Misericórdia
Dominating the southern end of Praça Deu-la-Deu, this church has a fine coffered

ceiling painted with cherubs and walls of azulejos.

Special Events

The town's biggest bash is the Festa de Corpo de Deus on 18 June, celebrated with a religious procession that includes a horseman and his 'dragon' who subsequently do battle in a re-enactment of the St George and the Dragon story.

Places to Stay

There are a number of unofficial private rooms available (look for *dormidas* signs): some of the cheapest are at *Taberna A Ponte de Lima* (☎ 65 22 23), at Praça da República 72, where singles/doubles above the crusty old tavern cost 2000$00/3000$00 (without bath). *Dormidas O Abrigo* (☎ 65 23 29), at Rua Bispo de Lemos 2 (just off Praça Deu-la-Deu), offers more comfort and less friendliness; doubles are 2500$00 without bath or 3000$00 with. Rooms above *Croissanteria Raiano* (☎ 65 35 34), at Praça Deu-la-Deu 34, have showers or bath and an abundance of plastic flowers (No 7 overlooks the square); they're 3500$00/5000$00 without breakfast (though there are plenty of croissants and cakes downstairs).

Two up-market establishments are on Rua General Pimenta de Castro: *Pensão Residencial Esteves* (☎ 65 23 86) has a cheery patron and modern rooms from 4500$00 for a double with bath. *Pensão Residencial Mané* (☎ 65 24 90), at No 5, has singles/doubles for 7000$00/9000$00. For upper-bracket comfort, ask the turismo about Turihab properties around town: the closest is *Casa de Rodas* (☎ 65 21 05), an elegant family house one km to the south on the grounds of a large estate producing Alvarinho grapes.

Places to Eat

Monção serves up great local specialities including salmon, shad and trout from the Rio Minho, and lamprey eels (in season from January to March). Wash them down with local Alvarinho wine, arguably the best of the Minho's vinhos verdes (though fairly pricey).

Some of the cheapest and most ordinary fare can be found opposite the Auto-Viação do Minho bus stop, just downhill from the old train station: *Restaurante-Bar Pepe* (☎ 65 25 60) is the cheeriest of several places here, with dishes from 800$00. There's more atmosphere at *Taberna A Ponte de Lima* (see Places to Stay), a benches-and-tables dive where the 700$00 prato do dia can be washed down with strong local wine on tap.

For classier menus and surroundings, head for *Restaurante Central* (☎ 65 28 05) on the eastern corner of Praça Deu-la-Deu (enter from the lane behind); it has good-value dishes from around 1000$00.

One of the best places for fish is nearby *Restaurante Cabral* on Rua do 1 Dezembro. A salubrious and pristine place en route to the spa is *Flor do Minho* (☎ 65 14 20) in Largo São João de Deus, which has many regional specialities for around 1200$00 a dish.

Getting There & Away

Two bus companies, Empresa de Transportes Courense and Salvador Alves Pereira, operate from the former train station (and post their timetables on the door). On weekdays they run about 10 buses a day to Valença do Minho (five on weekends); five to Braga and Arcos de Valdevez (three on weekends to Arcos only) and five to Viana do Castelo (two on weekends).

Auto-Viação do Minho and AVIC stop at the GALP station on express runs to Valença do Minho and Viana do Castelo three times daily on weekdays (four on Sundays); to Braga once a day via Arcos de Valdevez and Ponte da Barca; to Guimarães once on Sundays; and to Lisbon, via Valença do Minho, Viana do Castelo, Porto and Coimbra three times daily (twice on Sundays).

PONTE DE LIMA

• pop 2700 • postcode 4990 • area code ☎ 058

This dreamy market town reclining on the south bank of the Rio Lima, 23 km east of Viana do Castelo, is a relaxing and attractive place to hole up for a few days. When the Romans reached this point on their march

MINHO

through Iberia they had a great deal of trouble leaving because the soldiers were convinced the Rio Lima was the River Lethe – the mythical river of oblivion – and that if they crossed it they would forget everything. It was only after their leader, Decimus Junius Brutus, plunged ahead and shouted back their legionaries' names that they braved the waters.

The Roman bridge after which Ponte de Lima is named supposedly marks the very spot, and is part of the Roman road from Braga to Astorga in Spain. It's just one of several well-preserved historical features which give the town its character, though there's no pressure for major sightseeing here: the charm of the place lies in its sandy riverbank (the site of fantastic bimonthly markets and annual fairs) and shady riverside walks, its rural surroundings and laid-back atmosphere. As the headquarters of Turismo de Habitação, it also offers more Turihab properties than any other town. Unfortunately for traditionalists, a golf course and racecourse have recently opened too, marking Ponte de Lima's coming-of-age in up-market tourism.

Orientation
The bus station and market are a few steps from the Alameda, a riverside pedestrian-only avenue of huge plane trees. Turn right along it for the main square, Largo de Camões, with cafés, restaurants and an 18th-century fountain. The Roman bridge crosses the Rio Lima here, connecting Ponte de Lima with Arcozelo on the other side. Further downstream is the modern Ponte de Nossa Senhora da Guia, carrying the Braga to Valença N201 highway.

A newer part of town stretches uphill, south and east of Praça da República, but all sights of interest are in the old town along the riverside.

Information
Tourist Office The cheery, helpful turismo (☎ & fax 94 23 35) is on Praça da República, a few minutes walk south-east of the river via Rua Cardeal Baraiva. It's open daily from 9.30 am to 12.30 pm and from 2 to 6 pm (mornings only on Sundays). There's a small display of local handicrafts here too.

Turismo de Habitação The head office of Turihab (☎ 74 16 72; fax 74 14 44) is upstairs from the turismo, open daily, except Sundays, from 9 am to 12.30 pm and 2 to 6.30 pm. It has comprehensive information on Turihab properties around the country, though turismos here and elsewhere also have all the information you need.

Money There are several banks with ATMs, including one on Largo de Camões.

Post & Communications The post office is just across from the turismo on Rua Cardeal Baraiva.

Laundry Lavandaria Ibérica (☎ 74 14 74) in Centro Ibérico, a small shopping mall by the bus station, charges 350$00 per kg for wash-and-dry.

Medical Services The Centro de Saúde is off Avenida António Feijo, the broad street running uphill from Praça da República.

Emergency The police station is on Rua Dr Luís da Cunha Nogueira, east of the old town.

Roman Bridge
The 31-arched bridge across the Lima actually dates from the 14th century, when the original Roman bridge was rebuilt and extended. It was restored again the following century. The section on the north bank is the oldest. The bridge is off limits to motor traffic, but watch out for horse riders who often gallop across the bridge at dusk, instantly plunging the scene back into medieval days.

Museu dos Terceiros
Downstream from the bridge, just off the Alameda, is the Renaissance Igreja de São António dos Frades (formerly part of a convent). Adjacent to this is the 18th-century

The Douro
Left: Porto
Right: Ponte de Dom Luís I, Porto
Bottom: The Douro valley in spring

JULIA WILKINSON

TONY WHEELER

JULIA WILKINSON

Markets

Left: Ceramic roosters, Barcelos
Right: Hand-painted plates, Évora
Bottom: Shopping for bread, Barcelos

Igreja de São Francisco dos Terceiros, now a rambling museum of ecclesiastical and folk treasures. The highlight is the church itself, with gilded baroque altars and pulpits. The museum offers guided tours daily, except Tuesdays, from 9 am to noon and 2.30 to 5 pm. Ring the bell and wait for the curator to emerge. Admission is 200$00.

Igreja Matriz

The parish church, off Rua Cardeal Baraiva, is one of several eye-catching medieval monuments in this part of town. It dates from the 14th century but was remodelled in the 18th century. A fine Romanesque doorway remains from earlier days.

Torre

The 14th-century crenellated tower that faces the river just below the Roman bridge was once part of the town's walled fortifications. Later used as a prison, it now serves as a handicraft and souvenir shop, where you can see embroidered linen and cotton being made.

Markets

The huge Monday market, held twice a month, spreads from the market area along the riverbank downstream from the Roman bridge. It offers everything from agricultural implements, baskets and wine barrels to fresh fruit, cheese and bread, shoes, hats and t-shirts.

Activities

Walking Ponte de Lima's turismo has produced *Trilhos*, a folio of half a dozen easy, illustrated walks ranging from seven to 14 km (though the maps and details are not totally reliable). Almost everywhere around Ponte de Lima offers enticing walks through villages and cobbled lanes trellised with vines. Take a picnic, though: cafés and restaurants are few and far between.

Golf Campo de Golfe de Ponte de Lima (☎ 82 89 43; fax 82 88 81) is a couple of km south of town, off the Braga road. The 18-hole, par 71 course covers the wooded slopes

above town, commanding grand views. The clubhouse includes a restaurant and golf supplies shop.

Horse Riding At Clube Equestre (☎ 94 24 66), across the river in Arcozelo, you may be able to hire a horse for an hour or so.

Wine-Tasting The Adega Cooperativa de Ponte de Lima (☎ 74 14 49), east of the centre on Rua Conde de Bertiandos, is open weekdays for wine-tasting tours. The adega produces both red and white varieties of vinho verde, as well as two brands of *aguardente* firewater.

Special Events

Feiras Novas Like the Monday market, the so-called New Fairs have been held in Ponte de Lima since 1125, when Dona Teresa (wife of Henri of Burgundy, Count of Portucale) granted Ponte de Lima a royal charter. Held over three days in mid-September, Feiras Novas is a combined market and fair featuring folk dances, fireworks, brass bands and much merry-making. You'll need to book accommodation well ahead if you want to be around at this time.

Vaca das Cordas Held in early June, this centuries-old tradition is a form of bull-running, where crowds of young men goad the bull (restrained by a long rope or *cordas*) as it runs through the town and down to the river. The following day's Festa do Corpo de Deus has more religious overtones and features patterns of flowers carpeting the streets.

Places to Stay

Pensões & Residencials The run-down *Pensão Morais* (☎ 94 24 70), at Rua da Matriz 8, has peeling paintwork and damp rooms but it's the cheapest in town at 2000$00/3500$00 for a single/double (or 10,000$00 for a six-bed room).

Pensão Beira Rio (☎ 94 34 71), at Passeio 25 de Abril 10, on the riverfront, has riverview doubles for 6000$00, or doubles at the back for 4000$00. Similar in style but further from the river is *Pensão São João* (☎ 94 12 88), at Largo de São João, with rooms from 2500$00/4500$00 including breakfast.

Just under a km east of town, on the Ponte da Barca road, is the modern *Restaurante Residencial O Garfo* (☎ & fax 74 31 47) where comfortable doubles cost 6000$00 including breakfast.

Poshest of all in town is the dull modern *Albergaria Império do Minho* (☎ 74 15 10; fax 94 25 67) in a shopping complex on the riverfront Avenida dos Plátanos. Singles/doubles with bath, satellite TV, and air-con are 7500$00/9000$00 with breakfast.

Turihab There are some 30 Turihab properties in the area, ranging from modest farmhouses to fabulous mansions. You can book through the Turihab association, the turismo or (often more cheaply) directly with the owners. An official price list orders properties according to quality and elegance: figure on at least 8500$00 for a double or a small self-catering cottage. For more about the Turihab scheme, see the Accommodation section in the Facts for the Visitor chapter.

Among the more affordable choices near Ponte de Lima are *Casa de Crasto* (☎ 94 11 56), a 17th-century house a km east, off the Ponte da Barca road, and *Casa do Arrabalde* (☎ 74 24 42), across the bridge in Arcozelo, a restored 18th-century manor house with additional apartments in the grounds.

Our favourite is *Quinta da Aldeia* (☎ 94 22 68), a secluded manor house a couple of km east, off the Ponte da Barca road, with four cottage-apartments, plenty of outdoor space for kids and even a miniature playhouse. It's a microcosm of the region: buffalo carts creak down the cobbled lane while modern concrete houses are being built around the corner.

Places to Eat
Both *Pensão São João* and *Pensão Beira Rio* (see Places to Stay) have popular and reasonably priced restaurants, run by a bevy of mums and grannies. Also worth checking out are *Restaurante Manuel Padeiro* (☎ 94 16 49) on Rua do Bonfim, near the market, and *Restaurante Casa Gaio* (☎ 94 12 51) on nearby Rua Agostinho José Taveira. Both serve the local speciality, rojões de sarrabulho (a minced pork and pork blood dish) and local sável (shad fish) in season. Prices are in the 1000$00 to 1500$00 per dish range at both.

A popular market-watching spot is *Restaurante Encanada* (☎ 94 11 89) on Passeio 25 de Abril (above the market). Tucked away up Rua Formosa (head inland from Largo de Camões and turn left up a narrow lane) is *Restaurante Tulha* (☎ 94 28 79), a smart place favoured by late-night diners, with prices around 1300$00 per dish. The best cafés for watching the world go by are in the Largo de Camões, especially the old *Confeitaria Havaneza*.

Getting There & Away
There are frequent buses to Viana do Castelo and Ponte da Barca. There are around six daily to Barcelos, three to Braga and four to Porto.

PONTE DA BARCA
• *postcode 4980 • area code* ☎ *058*
This pretty riverside town is a smaller and drowsier version of Ponte de Lima, 18 km to the west. Named after the *barca* which used to ferry passengers (frequently pilgrims on their way to Santiago de Compostela) across the river, its old town area has a picturesque 15th-century bridge and a pleasant riverside promenade. The place comes marvellously to life on alternate Wednesdays when a huge market spreads along the riverside.

This makes a fine overnight stop or a base for longer stays if you fancy rambling around the countryside.

Orientation
Immediately east of the bridge, the old town is packed into narrow lanes on both sides of the main road, Rua Conselheiro Rocha Peixoto. East of here, along the road's continuation, Rua António José Pereira, is an ugly new town extension. Buses stop near the bridge.

Information

The turismo (☎ & fax 428 99), a few minutes walk east of the bridge at Largo do Misericórdia 10 (below Rua Conselheiro Rocha Peixoto), is open daily, except Sundays, from 9 am to 12.30 pm and 2.30 to 6 pm from June to September (mornings only on Saturdays the rest of the year). You can pick up a town map and accommodation information here.

Upstairs from the turismo is ADERE, the Associação de Desinvolvimento das Regiões (☎ 422 50; fax 424 50), a consultancy involved in culturally sensitive development in and around the Parque Nacional da Peneda-Gerês. It's open weekdays from 9 am to 1 pm and 2 to 7 pm. For more on its work, including traditional-style accommodation in the park area, see Information in the Parque Nacional da Peneda-Gerês section later in this chapter.

Banks with ATMs can be found in the new part of town, along Rua António José Pereira.

The post office is here too, on Rua das Fontainhas.

Ponte & Jardim dos Poetas

The lovely 10-arched bridge across the Rio Lima was first built in 1543 but restored several times later, most recently in the 19th century. Next to it is the former arcaded marketplace and a little garden, Jardim dos Poetas, dedicated to two 16th-century poets, Diogo Bernardes and his brother Agostinho da Cruz, born in Ponte da Barca.

Walks

The turismo can suggest walking routes in the area, including a strenuous 18-km hike just within the national park, starting from Entre Ambos-os-Rios, 12 km east of Ponte da Barca. The details are actually photocopied from *Landscapes of Portugal: Costa Verde* (see Books in Facts for the Visitor chapter), which isn't entirely up to date, though the old villages described en route have changed very little.

A shorter, simpler walk is westwards four km to Bravães, a roadside hamlet famous for

its Romanesque Igreja de São Salvador, whose doorways are covered with intricate carvings of animals, birds and human figures.

Places to Stay

Camping The nearest camping ground (☎ 683 61) is a simple riverside site at Entre Ambos-os-Rios. It is open from May to September. To get there take any Lindoso-bound bus.

Pensões & Residencials *Pensão Gomes* (☎ 422 88, 421 29), at Rua Conselheiro Rocha Peixoto (near the bridge), is the cheapest and cosiest place in the old town, with simple singles/doubles without bath for 2000$00/3500$00 and a rooftop terrace for river views. Other cheap options with less atmosphere are in the new town, including *Pensão Carvalho* (☎ 422 68), on Praça Dr António Lacerda, where spartan doubles without bath go for 3000$00; and the modern *Residencial Fontainhas* (☎ 424 42), on busy Rua António José Pereira, which has rooms with bath for 3500$00/5000$00 including breakfast.

Up-market options range from the swanky *Residencial Os Poetas* (☎ 435 78), at Jardim dos Poetas (you can't miss its eyesore roof sign), where doubles under renovation will probably cost at least 7000$00, to *Casa Nobre* (☎ 421 29), a private manor house opposite the turismo (behind the arched town hall) whose two doubles cost 9000$00 each.

Turihab There are five Turihab properties within five km of town, including *Quinta da Prova* (☎ 431 86) on the river's north bank, with three two-room apartments. The turismo has full details of this and others.

Places to Eat

The restaurant attached to *Pensão Gomes* serves tasty regional fare, including truta à Rio Lima (river trout) for 990$00. There are several cheaper places in the new town along Rua António José Pereira. Our favourite is the friendly *Café Snack Bar O Nicola* (☎ 432 86), at No 32, which has good-value pratos

452 Coastal & Northern Minho – Arcos de Valdevez

do dia for 600$00 until 2 pm, and other dishes under 1000$00.

For a splurge, head down to the smart riverside *Restaurant Bar do Rio* (☎ 425 82) where you can dine on escargot, arroz de marisco (seafood rice) and other luxuries for around 1800$00 a dish.

Getting There & Away
Frequent buses go to Arcos de Valdevez and Braga, eight daily to Ponte de Lima and two or three to Lindoso. The relevant bus stops are scattered around the bridge area: the start of the Ponte de Lima road (Rua Diogo Bernardes) for Ponte de Lima; opposite Pensão Gomes for Lindoso and Braga; and outside Pensão Gomes for Arcos de Valdevez.

ARCOS DE VALDEVEZ
Though Arcos does have two comely old churches in a small, seemingly tourist-free old centre, and a pleasant location above the Rio Vez (a tributary of the Lima), it doesn't merit a special trip. But you have to change buses here for the trip from Braga to Soajo or Lindoso, and there is a competent Parque Nacional da Peneda-Gerês information office a stone's throw from the bus stand. This is one gateway by road into the northern part of the park.

Orientation & Information
The park office (☎ 653 38) is right beside the 'Avenida' bus stop at the edge of the old town (if you end up at Arcos' bus station it's back along the main road). Like the other park offices, this one (open weekdays from 9 am to 12.30 pm and 2 to 5.30 pm) has a park map and a booklet on the park's human and natural features, but little else of interest unless you read Portuguese.

The polite turismo (☎ 660 01), about 200m south (downstream) of the park office, is open from 9 am to 12.30 and 2.30 to 6 pm on weekdays, plus Sunday mornings. It can give you a glossy map-brochure about Arcos and help you find a place to stay.

The town centre is Praça Municipal, a block uphill from the park office. Arco's

telephone code is ☎ 058. Every other Wednesday is market day here, alternating with Ponte da Barca.

Churches
If you've got time on your hands, from the turismo walk a block north and then left up Rua Placido Abreu into Largo da Lapa, which embraces the oval and oddly pretty baroque Igreja da Nossa Senhora da Lapa (1767). Bear right and watch to the left for its neighbour, the little Romanesque Capela da Nossa Senhora da Conceição (also called Capela da Praça), which dates from 1372.

Places to Stay
At the lower end (doubles for 3000$00 and 4000$00) are the very plain *Pensão Flôr do Minho* (☎ 652 16), at Rua da Valeta 106-108, down behind the Praça Municipal (take the lane along the left side of the Igreja da Nossa Senhora da Lapa), and gloomy *Pensão Ribeira* (☎ 651 74), on Largo dos Milagres, just across the river from the turismo, on the right. Only Flôr do Minho's pricier double has an attached bath.

Residencial Tavares (☎ 662 53) opposite Nossa Senhora da Lapa has doubles with bath for 6000$00. Two more distant residencials suggested by the turismo, with doubles for 6000$00, are the *Costa do Vez* (☎ 52 12 26), on the Monção road about half a km north of the park office, and the *Dom António* (☎ 52 10 10), on Rua Dr Germano Amorim, 250m south of the turismo, around to the right just before the river bridge to Braga.

Places to Eat
Restaurante A Cozinha da Aldeia, at Rua da Valeta 75 (between Capela da Nossa Senhora da Conceição and Pensão Flôr do Minho), dishes up Portuguese standards for 750$00 to 1200$00 per plate.

Getting There & Away
From Viana do Castelo, Auto-Viação Cura has regular services to Arcos via Ponte de Lima. Empresa de Transportes Courense and Salvador Alves Pereira run five times a day

on weekdays (three on weekends) from Braga and from Monção, and AV Minho runs once a day. From Barcelos, Domingos da Cunha runs to Arcos five to six times a day via Ponte de Lima and Ponte da Barca. Renex comes here from Lisbon three times a day.

Buses run from Arcos to Lindoso (20 minutes) at least three times a day, with numerous extra services on Wednesdays (market day in Arcos or Ponte da Barca).

Parque Nacional da Peneda-Gerês

Peneda-Gerês National Park, Portugal's first protected area, was established in 1971 to protect both the country's natural riches and the rural way of life of its people. At 72,000 hectares, it's the second-largest protected area in the country, after the Parque Natural da Serra da Estrela.

The crescent-shaped park takes in four major granite massifs – the Serra da Peneda, Serra do Soajo, Serra da Amarela and Serra do Gerês – largely in north-eastern Minho but with one end in Trás-os-Montes. It's crossed by one river, the Rio Lima, which rises in Spain; almost dissected by the Rio Homem, which rises high in the park; and deeply etched by many more streams. Two rivers help define its boundaries: the Rio Laboreiro between the Serra da Peneda and Spain, and the Rio Cávado which runs along the entire south-eastern end of the park. Five hydroelectric dams back up big reservoirs within the park, three of them on the Cávado.

The heights close to the Spanish frontier, especially in the Serra do Gerês where several peaks rise over 1500m, are almost free of human activity other than summertime transhumance (temporary migration of entire villages, with their sheep, goats and cattle, to high pastures). The outer part of the crescent includes some 115 villages totalling around 15,000 people.

The park, sharing 80 km of frontier with

Spain's Orense province, embraces a corresponding Spanish reserve, the Parque Natural Serra do Xures. Peneda-Gerês, especially the accessible southern Serra do Gerês, offers fine hiking and other sports, some attractive rural accommodation, and a window on a vanishing rural way of life.

Needless to say, this area is very popular. The main base is the little spa town of Caldas do Gerês. If your time is short and you plan to base yourself there, do it midweek if you can: Portuguese day-trippers swarm up on summer weekends (though they tend to stick to the main camping areas). There's no fee to enter the park.

Flora & Fauna

In a transition zone between Mediterranean and Euro-Siberian zones, the park has a striking diversity of climate, habitat and landscape, nourished by heavy rainfall (the Serra da Peneda gets more rain than anywhere else in Portugal). In sheltered valleys are stands of arbutus, laurel and cork oak. Forests of black oak, English oak and holly give way at higher elevations to birch, yew and Scots pine, and in alpine areas to juniper and sandwort. In a small patch of the Serra do Gerês grows the Gerês iris, found nowhere else in the world.

In remoter areas there are wolves, wild boars, foxes, badgers, polecats and otters, as well as roe deer and a few wild ponies. Closer to the ground are grass snakes and the occasional venomous black viper. Birds include red kites, buzzards, goshawks, golden eagles and several species of owls. The park's best known domestic animal is the sturdy Castro Laboreiro sheepdog.

Traditional Culture

Many of the park's oldest villages are truly in a time warp, with oxen being trundled down cobbled streets by black-clad old women, and horses being shoed in smoky blacksmith shops. The practice of moving sheep, goats and cattle (and even entire villages) up to high pasture for up to five months in the warm season still goes on in the Serra da Peneda and Serra do Gerês,

MINHO

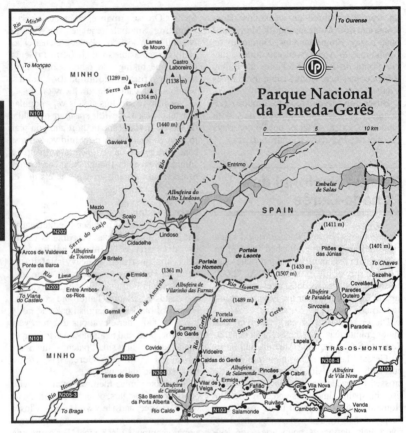

though it's giving way to the use of silage and purchased feed.

But despite the founding of the park, the building of roads and other efforts by the government and private development agencies, this rustic scene is fading away as young people desert the region for the cities. Statistics say that an astonishing 75% of the local people now are over 65. The road between Cabril and Paradela, for example, reveals a deeply ironic picture – a string of sparsely populated, decaying villages, surrounded by grand scenery, fertile soil, pristine air and clean water.

Information

Park Offices The park's headquarters (☎ 053-600 34 80) in Braga has a public information office. Somewhat better stocked are offices in Arcos de Valdevez (☎ 058-653 38), Caldas do Gerês (☎ 053-39 11 81) and Montalegre (☎ 076-522 81). Caldas is the most helpful, Montalegre the least. English is spoken except at Montalegre, though you may have better luck with French. There are also small interpretative centres, with basic information and occasionally exhibits, at Lamas de Mouro and Mezio.

All the offices sell a park map (530$00)

showing some roads and tracks (but not trails), and a booklet (105$00) on the park's human and natural features. Most other information – including much on habitats, flora and fauna, and school and children's materials – is in Portuguese. The Caldas office also has a beautiful satellite photo-montage of the park for 530$00.

ADERE The Associação de Desenvolvimento das Regiões do Parque Nacional da Peneda-Gerês is an organisation involved in preservation of the region's traditional way of life through the encouragement of culturally sensitive but profitable development. Among other things it has started (in Soajo) a Turihab-like project called Turismo de Aldeia or Village Tourism, offering funding and advice if at least six owners in a village

will restore their houses in traditional style and rent rooms to visitors. It also acts as a central booking office for 10 *casas de abrigo* (shelters) in the park that lie near villages (and thus contribute to the local economy), and for Turihab properties in the five *concelhos* (counties) that cover the park.

Its reservations office (☎ 058-422 50; fax 058-424 50) is in Ponte da Barca, upstairs from the turismo at Largo da Misericórdia 10, and is open weekdays from 9 am to 1 pm and 2 to 7 pm.

Other Resources Some switched-on private outfits offer reliable tips on sights, accommodation and recreation, especially if you make use of their services. These include Água Montanha Lazer at Rio Caldo, Montes d'Aventura at the youth hostel in Campo do

MINHO

Protected Areas

Peneda-Gerês is a parque *nacional* (while all Portugal's other parks are called *natural*) because it meets certain conditions of the International Union for the Conservation of Nature (IUCN), a body set up to establish standards for protected areas. Among other things, this means that Peneda-Gerês includes ecosystems of scientific, educational or recreational value which remain fairly untouched by human activities, and which the government has taken steps to protect.

The result is an inner *área de ambiente natural* (natural environmental area) at higher elevations close to the border, parts of which are set aside for research and off limits to the general public. This is surrounded by a buffer *área de ambiente rural* (rural environment area) peppered with small villages, where controlled development is permitted. The park's roads, tracks and trails are largely in the latter area.

The most assiduously protected part of the park – upon which its 'national' status heavily depends – is an area of virgin oak, chestnut and mistletoe forest called the Mata de Albergaria, north of Caldas do Gerês. Ironically, it's traversed by the N308 highway which, as it serves an EU-anointed international border crossing, cannot simply be closed. Satisfying both the IUCN and the EU presents park officials with a ticklish job. On a six-km stretch of the twisting road above Caldas, from the Portela de Leonte pass to the border at Portela do Homem, motorised traffic is tolerated but not allowed to linger. At checkpoints at either end, each driver gets a time-stamped ticket and has 15 minutes to turn it in at the other end. This stretch is patrolled, and the checkpoints staffed, seven days a week from July to September, and on weekends the rest of the year. Two sideroads are also no-go for vehicles: south-west down the Rio Homem valley (except for residents), and east from Portela do Homem into the high Serra do Gerês.

The rules on camping – essentially that you can only camp at designated sites unless you're on a mountaineering expedition – are most strictly enforced in heavily trafficked areas. Signs warn against *campismo clandestino*, and park rangers are more like police than the cheerful helpers foreign visitors might expect.

The only restrictions on walking are those on camping, ie if you can't get as far as a designated camping ground then you're expected to come back out. Nevertheless it seems private guides do take people on multi-day treks through remote areas that apparently have no official camping grounds. There are also restrictions on boats in the park's five *albufeiras* (reservoirs): motorised boats of all kinds are allowed on the Caniçada, only electric motors on the Lindoso, only non-motorised boats on the Salamonde, and no boats at all on the Vilarinho das Furnas and Paradela. ■

Gerês, and Trote-Gerês near Cabril; see the Getting Around section.

Maps Military topographic maps covering the park at 1:25,000 are on sale for about 900$00 per quadrangle from Oficina d'Aventura, a shop on the premises of Tagus Travel in Braga. Montes d'Aventura, based at the youth hostel in Campo do Gerês, also has these, as well as 1:50,000 civilian topos (for more on topographic maps of Portugal, see Planning in the Facts for the Visitor chapter). The civilian maps show some trails and are more current, but lack the detail and precision of the military ones, which also show more old roads. None are up to date enough to show the reservoirs.

A small, detailed orienteering map of the region around Campo do Gerês is available for 300$00 from the Cerdeira camping ground there, and occasionally from park offices.

The park's own map is suitable for orientation, but not reliable enough for hiking.

Megaliths

There are Stone Age dolmens (temple-tombs) on the high plateaus of the Serra da Peneda and Serra do Gerês; near Castro Laboreiro, Mezio, Paradela, Pitões das Júnias and Tourém. If you read Portuguese you can learn more about them from a booklet sold at least at the Arcos de Valdevez park office.

Roman Road

A 350-km Roman military road between Bracara Augusta (Braga) and Asturica Augusta (Astorga in Spain) ran up the valley of the Rio Homem, and a two-km stretch – a candidate for UNESCO World Heritage status – is still visible along the south side of the Albufeira de Vilarinho das Furnas. Milestones remain at least at Miles XXIX, XXX and XXXI, and others have been haphazardly collected at Portelo do Homem. A brochure about the park's Roman remains (in Portuguese) is on sale at the Arcos de Valdevez park office.

Hiking & Mountain Biking

The scenery, the crisp air, the rural panorama and local hospitality make walking a treat in Peneda-Gerês. There's still a certain amount of dead reckoning involved, though tracks of some kind (animal or vehicle) are everywhere in the área de ambiente rural, most of which lead within a half-day's walk to a settlement or a main road. Local people claim streams at higher elevations are safe to drink from, though anything below farmed areas is suspect.

An official long-distance footpath *(trilho pedestre de longo curso)* is gradually being developed, with eight linked itineraries to span the park, mostly following traditional roads or tracks between villages where you can stop for the night. Park offices sell detailed 300$00 map-brochures in Portuguese for two of these itineraries (Lamas de Mouro to Soajo, and Cabril to Paradela), plus one for a short interpretive trail at Pitões das Júnias that's also suitable for children. At the time of research, these and two others (Campo do Gerês to Vidoeiro, and Paradela to Pitões das Júnias) had been scouted and apparently marked. Day hikes around Caldas do Gerês are popular but crowded; see that section for details. Further afield, Ermida and Cabril make excellent goals, and both have simple accommodation and food. The high-elevation trek directly between Portela do Homem and Pitões das Júnias is said to be the finest in the park, though park maps don't show a trail there.

Água Montanha Lazer (see Rio Caldo) sells western-brand shoes, jackets, tents and other camping gear; Braga is also a good place for equipment. Essential food and other supplies can be bought in smaller towns closer to the park. See Getting Around for information on organised walks and bike trips, and bike rental. Two useful books setting out routes in the park are *Walking in Portugal* and *Landscapes of Portugal*; see Books in the Facts for the Visitor chapter.

Horse Riding

The national park operates horse-riding facilities (☎ 053-39 11 81) beside its

Vidoeiro camping ground near Caldas do Gerês. A minimum of three horses must be hired, at 1300$00 each per hour (half of it paid up front), for fixed time slots (10 to 11 am, 2 to 3 pm and 3.30 to 4.30 pm).

Rather more flexible are two private outfits. Equi Campo (☎ 053-35 70 22) at Campo do Gerês rents horses for 1200$00 per hour. Low/high season rates at Trote-Gerês (☎ & fax 053-65 98 60) near Cabril are 1500$00/1850$00 per hour or 6000$00/8000$00 per day.

Canoeing & Other Water Sports

There's no easily accessible whitewater in the park. Water sports are all on its reservoirs. Rio Caldo, eight km south of Caldas do Gerês, is the base for the Albufeira da Caniçada. English-run Água Montanha Lazer (☎ 053-39 17 40) rents single/double kayaks at 600$00/1000$00 for the first hour, four-person canoes for 1500$00, pedal-boats and small outboard boats. It also organises water-skiing jaunts, and sells water sport gear.

For paddling the Albufeira de Salamonde, Trote-Gerês (☎ & fax 053-65 98 60) rents canoes from its camping ground at Cabril. Prices for a two-person canoe in the low/high season are 800$00/1000$00 per hour or 5000$00/6000$00 per day. There's a swimming pool in Caldas do Gerês' Parque das Termas.

Organised Tours

Montes d'Aventura, with a weekend base at the Campo do Gerês youth hostel and a home office in Porto (☎ 02-208 81 75, ☎ 02-937 13 10, mobile ☎ 0936-67 37 39 or ☎ 0936-97 36 65 for French-speakers) organises customised mountaineering, trekking, horse riding, canoeing and bike trips in the park. At the time of research a trek was about 1000$00 per person per day (including equipment), plus food. This outfit knows the Serra do Gerês and Serra da Amarela best.

From its camping ground near Cabril, Trote-Gerês (☎ & fax 053-65 98 60) also arranges walking trips, for around 1750$00 per person per day plus food.

Parque de Campismo de Cerdeira (☎ 053-35 70 65; fax 053-35 10 05), at Campo do Gerês, has its own good programme of walks and other events.

Rafael Lima (☎ 053-67 64 76), at Rua José Antunes Guimarães in Braga, offers a schedule of guided, small-group weekend trips including walking, climbing, canoeing, cycling and orienteering.

The Associação de Cicloturismo do Minho (☎ 053-69 11 57 in José; ☎ 053-60 42 02 in Jorge) in Braga organises cycling trips around the Minho.

For a spin through the major sights in the park, Agência no Gerês (☎ 053-39 11 12), at the Hotel Universal in Caldas do Gerês, does two to five-hour minibus trips for 1000$00 to 1250$00 per person, from June to August. It also has an office in Braga (☎ 053-61 58 96).

The AVIC bus company is reputed to have Saturday tours for a stiff 5000$00 plus lunch, but staff at its offices in Viana do Castelo (☎ 058-82 97 05) and Barcelos (☎ 053-82 45 98) were unhelpful.

Places to Stay

Unless you're camping, cheap accommodation is hard to find in the park. Campo do Gerês has a youth hostel. The national park runs fairly basic camping grounds at Lamas do Mouro, Mezio, Entre Ambos-os-Rios and Vidoeiro (just north of Caldas do Gerês); all are open from May or June to September or October, depending on the weather and the whims of the park service. Pricier, private camping grounds open year-round are at Campo do Gerês and Cabril. Both are a cut above the rest: the former runs its own activities in the park, while the latter rents horses, bikes and canoes.

A righteous alternative is to track down private rooms (ask turismos, park offices or the Ponte da Barca office of ADERE), which gives a minor but appropriate boost to the local economy. Ten plain casas de abrigo (shelters) around the park, formerly for park staff, can now be booked through ADERE in Ponte da Barca (see Information); each has baths, hot water and heating and four doubles. The entire house must be rented, at rates that depend on season and duration

MINHO

(from about 10,000$00 per night for a week in the low season, or 15,000$00 for shorter periods in the high season). Visits of less than a week can only be booked a week in advance. Meals cannot be cooked in the houses, but all the houses are in or near villages where food is available.

The park also operates two shelters for groups of 25 to 30 at Dorna and Vidoeiro, which can only be booked at the park headquarters in Braga.

Caldas do Gerês has many pensões, but they tend to get booked out in summer by spa patients and tourists. Booking ahead is a good idea. These and other options are noted under individual towns in this section.

ADERE in Ponte da Barca is the place to book one of at least 10 houses in Soajo. These have been restored under ADERE's Turismo de Aldeia programme (see the earlier Information section) and all cost under 7000$00 for two people. ADERE also operates at least a dozen Turismo em Espaço Rural (Turihab) properties in the concelhos of Ponte da Barca and Arcos de Valdevez.

Things to Buy
Local honey (mel) is on sale everywhere. The best – unpasteurised and unadulterated with syrup – is from small dealers (look for signs on private homes). Much of it bears a faint piney taste, from certain evergreen flowers.

Getting There & Away
Bus From Braga, Empresa Hoteleira do Gerês runs coaches every 1½ to 2½ hours daily to Caldas do Gerês (530$00), and REDM has at least three a day to Campo do Gerês (510$00). For access to the northern end of the national park, Salvador Alves Pereira has connections from Braga to Arcos de Valdevez and Monção. Coming from the east, a few buses run from Montalegre to Paradela on weekdays only, with other Paradela connections at Cambedo from Montalegre-Braga coaches.

Car & Motorcycle There are entry roads at Lamas de Mouro (from Monção and Mel-

gaço), Mezio (from Arcos de Valdevez), Entre Ambos-os-Rios (from Ponte de Lima and Ponte da Barca), Covide, Rio Caldo and Salamonde (from Braga) and Sezelhe, Paradela and Vila Nova (from Montalegre). Four roads cross the (unstaffed) border from Spain as well.

Getting Around
Annoyingly, there appear to be no buses operating within the park, only external connections to a few points in or near it. To get around inside the park without your own wheels you must bag a taxi (scarce), hitch or walk. Back roads in the park can be axle-breakers, even when the map suggests a reliable dirt road. Note the restrictions on travel through the Mata de Albergaria (see the 'Protected Areas' boxed aside earlier in this section).

Even with a car there's no practical way to travel between the Peneda and Gerês sections except outside the park – most conveniently via Spain, where the main roads are about as good as they are on the Portuguese side.

Bicycle Mountain bikes can be hired from Água Montanha Lazer (☎ 053-39 17 40) in Rio Caldo for 2100$00 per day; from Pensão Carvalho Araújo (☎ 053-39 11 85) in Caldas do Gerês for 2400$00 per day; or from Trote-Gerês (☎ & fax 053-65 98 60) at its camping ground near Cabril for 3700$00 per day.

RIO CALDO
Just inside the national park on the Albufeira de Caniçada, Rio Caldo is little more than a base for water sports on the reservoir. It makes a nice fall-back if everything is booked out in Caldas. An English-run shop called Água Montanha Lazer (☎ 053-39 17 40; ☎ 053-39 17 01, 24 hours; fax 053-39 15 98), about 100m from the roundabout on the road to Campo do Gerês, is a good source for park information, accommodation, and boat and mountain bike rental.

About 2.5 km further along the N304 is São Bento da Porta Alberta, a startling knot of overpriced accommodation and trinket stands, surrounding a church to which bus loads of pilgrims come all day long. The village is filled with oddly clean-cut and usually older visitors, and police. That's it; even the former convent to which the church was attached is now an inn. The views of the reservoir are brilliant, but who would want to stay here?

Places to Stay
A few hundred metres from the roundabout on the Amares road is the ho-hum *Pensão do Cávado* (☎ 053-39 11 57), where a double is 3500$00/4000$00 without/with bath. It also has a house near Rio Caldo with doubles for 6000$00.

The owners of Água Montanha Lazer have four fully equipped houses in the Rio Caldo area. The two-bedroom ones are roughly 9000$00/12,000$00 per night in the low/high season and the four-bedroom ones start from 15,000$00/22,000$00.

Scattered along the road from Rio Caldo to São Bento da Porta Alberta are lots of pensões with doubles from 4000$00 to 6000$00. In the former convent at São Bento is the terribly deluxe *Estalagen São Bento da Porta Alberta* (☎ 053-39 11 06; fax 053-39 11 17) where a double with the works is 8000$00.

CALDAS DO GERÊS
If the Gerês end of the national park has a 'centre', it is the somnolent spa town of Caldas do Gerês (or just 'Gerês'). Wedged into the valley of the Rio Gerês, it is a centre only because of its position, bus connections and an earnest park office. The spa, the spa-owned park and many, but not all, pensões are closed from October to April.

Orientation
The town is built on an elongated loop of road with the spa centre *(balneário)* in the plain pink buildings in the middle. The original hot spring, some baths, the turismo, a bar and an ice-cream parlour are in the very staid *colunat* (colonnade) 150m away at the upper end. Buses stop about 50m below the spa, on

Avenida Manuel F Costa, opposite the twin hotels Universal and Termas.

Information
The turismo (☎ 053-39 11 33), open in the colunat from 9 am to noon and 2 to 6 pm daily (mornings only on Sundays), has a bit of information about the town but little of use on the park. For that, go a block uphill to the park information office (☎ 053-39 11 81; fax 053-39 14 96); it's open daily from 8 am to 8 pm, year-round.

The post office, and Banco Espírito Santo, with an exchange desk and a Multibanco ATM, are on Avenida Manuel F Costa below the bus stand. Mountain bikes can be hired for about 2400$00 per day from Pensão Carvalho Araújo (see Places to Stay).

Caldas do Gerês' telephone code is ☎ 053.

Walks
The turismo or the park office can suggest local strolls. One pleasant (but not free) option is the spa-owned Parque das Termas, through the gate opposite the turismo. Admission is 130$00 (half-price for kids under 12 years old). The swimming pool costs 700$00 on weekdays or 1100$00 on weekends and holidays (less for kids under seven years old), and there's a little lake with boats for hire at 600$00 for half an hour.

About one km up the N308 is Parque do Merendas, the start of a short and popular 'Miradouro' walk, with good views to the south. Or you can walk, hitch or take a taxi up the N308 to the 862m pass at Portela de Leonte (about six km).

From Albergaria, where the Rio Homem crosses the road (10 km above Caldas do Gerês), a walk up the river takes you to a picturesque waterfall. At the 757m Portela do Homem border post (13 km from Caldas do Gerês) is a cluster of Roman milestones.

A good choice (with swimming possibilities) is to head south-west from Albergaria down the Rio Homem and the Albufeira de Vilarinho das Furnas for eight km to Campo do Gerês. Several clusters of Roman milestones dot this route, a section of a Roman road. Walking all the way from Caldas do

Gerês takes one very long and rugged day, so you're better off bagging a ride as far as Albergaria.

Spa

You can drink the local mineral water, or soak in it at several different temperatures – hottest at the colunat, cooler at the balneário – daily, except Sundays, from 8 am to noon and 3 to 6 pm. Tourists are welcome for one-off visits; buy a ticket at the main entrance opposite the petrol station on Avenida Manuel F Costa. A hot bath is 700$00, a sauna or steam bath 1000$00, a full massage 2000$00; serious devotees can also try various arcane and uncomfortable 'intubations'.

Places to Stay

Camping One km north of Caldas do Gerês at Vidoeiro is the good park-run *Parque Campismo Vidoeiro* (☎ 053-39 12 89), open at least in summer.

Private Rooms There are lots of private rooms available in summer, for around 4000$00 to 5000$00 per double, with owners approaching travellers at the bus stand and around town.

Pensões & Residencials Caldas has plenty of pensões, though in summer you may find some block-booked for spa patients, and the others may fill up a month or more ahead. But with all the competition, bargaining is definitely in order outside the high season; we paid 3000$00 for a 5000$00 room in May.

A line of at least 10 pensões – most with TV, heating, bath, breakfast, some sort of restaurant, and their own parking – climbs the west side of the valley. Beside the roaring river on Rua da Boa Vista, *Pensão da Ponte* (☎ 39 11 21) looks like good value with plain, clean doubles for 6000$00 without bath or 7000$00 with. Run by the same people, the *Príncipe*, just up the hill, has the same rates.

Further up, the rather posh *Carvalho Araújo* (☎ 39 11 85; fax 39 12 25) has doubles for 8000$00. Doubles at the glum *Horizonte do Gerês* (☎ 39 12 60) and *Flôr de Moçambique* (☎ 39 11 19) are about 7000$00 with bath. At the top of the hill, the least stuffy and with the best views is *Pensão Maria Adelaide Ribeiro*, or just Pensão Adelaide (☎ 39 11 88, 39 12 56), where doubles in summer start at 4000$00/5000$00 without/with bath. At *Pensão Restaurante Baltazar* (☎ 39 11 31), above the restaurant of the same name by the park office, mouldy doubles are 3000$00/5000$00 without/with bath. More pensões are downstream from the bank, and a gauntlet of others lines the road up from Rio Caldo.

Hotels At the twin hotels *Universal* and *das Termas* (☎ 39 11 41, 39 11 70; fax 39 11 02), owned by the Empresa Hoteleira do Gerês bus company, doubles are 14,500$00 in August, 11,600$00 from May to October, and 9250$00 in winter.

Places to Eat

Most pensões provide hearty meals, and these are usually available to non-guests too; *Pensão Adelaide* is popular. Though its geriatric residencial contingent lends it a funereal air, *Pensão Restaurante Baltazar* (☎ 39 11 31), next to the park office, does a decent lunch or dinner with very big portions of fish or meat starting at about 900$00, plus omelettes for under 700$00. Enjoy its entertaining English menu too, featuring 'boiled Portuguese' (cozido à Portuguesa), 'head-chop' (costeletas à chef) and 'plate-stick' (prago no prato).

Several restaurants, cheap cafés, food shops and pastelarias are at the lower end of town. One is *Restaurante Capela*, about half a km from the turismo, with a sizeable menu and modest prices. At the bottom of the town is a cheerful fast-food place called the *Green House*, with burgers and other grill items, sandwiches and ice cream, and outdoor tables.

AROUND CALDAS DO GERÊS

About 11 km from Parque do Merendas above Caldas do Gerês is **Ermida**, a sturdy village of small farms and stone houses clinging to steep hillsides. Spartan rooms (dormidas) are available for around 2500$00 for a double with shared loo. Six km on eastward is **Fafião**, which also has some rooms; ask at the *Retiro do Gerês* café beside the small post office.

CAMPO DO GERÊS

Campo do Gerês – called São João do Campo on some maps, and just 'Campo' by nearly everybody – is barely more than a hamlet, near the Albufeira de Vilarinho das Furnas dam, with a compact old centre that seems entirely made of the same rugged square blocks of sandstone. The youth hostel and camping ground here make very good bases for hikes.

Orientation & Information

Recent development is spread thinly around Campo. The bus from Braga stops beside the Museu Etnográfico and then continues 1.5 km to the old village centre. The youth hostel is a km up a sideroad from the museum. About 200m before the centre, the road to the dam branches to the right, and the camping ground is about 700m in this direction.

The telephone code for Campo do Gerês is ☎ 053.

Roman Road

The old Roman road runs past the reservoir. The nearest of several milestones is about a km beyond the camping ground, with others further along towards Albergaria on the N308 (see Caldas do Gerês).

Vilarinho das Furnas & Museum Etnográfico

The village of Vilarinho das Furnas was, by all accounts, an extraordinary place – a democratic community with a well-organised communal life, shared property and decisions taken by consensus. Even during the Salazar years, Vilarinho maintained its principled, independent way of life. The village was submerged by the reservoir in 1972, and its people moved elsewhere, but in summer when the reservoir

level usually falls, its empty walls rise like spectres from the water and the near shore.

In anticipation of the end of their old way of life, villagers donated many articles for a proposed museum, and they are now on view at an excellent and rather moving ethnographic museum (☎ 35 11 35), where the road forks to the youth hostel and to Campo. Admission is 100$00, and it's open daily from 8 am to noon and 2 to 5 pm (from 10 am on weekends). This is an especially worthwhile stop if you plan to visit the spooky remains of the village itself, about 2.5 km beyond the dam, a comfortable three-hour return trip walk from Campo or the camping ground.

Guided Walks & Other Programmes

The Parque Campismo de Cerdeira (see Places to Stay) organises interpretive walks in the area, typically three or four hours long, two or three times a week in summer – eg to Vilarinho das Furnas, the museum and the Roman road. It also runs some longer trips in the park, as well as hosting orienteering competitions. Most interestingly, it has made an effort to arrange its own events in connection with local festivals – eg Matança do Porco (a communal pork meal and other events) in January; tree-planting in March; and the Desfolhada Minhota (harvest festival) in October.

Places to Stay

The sprawling pousada de juventude or youth hostel (☎ 35 13 39) was originally a camp for dam-construction workers. In addition to dormitory-style beds at 1600$00, it has four-person rooms with bath for 1800$00 per person, doubles with/without bath for 4500$00/3600$00, and a few bungalows sleeping four or five people, each with kitchenette and bath. Booking ahead is wise, though one or two drop-in visitors can always be accommodated.

North of the centre is the good *Parque Campismo de Cerdeira* (☎ 35 70 65; fax 35 10 05). Typical rates are 500$00 per person, 400$00 to 800$00 per tent and 450$00 per car.

It also has bungalows for two with kitchenettes for 8000$00 in July-August or 6000$00 the rest of the year. Walk-in prospects are poor in July-August but good the rest of the year.

Pensão Stop (☎ 35 12 91), near the turnoff for the dam, has doubles with bath for 4000$00, including breakfast. A café and shop called *Casa Batista*, a few paces from the bus stand in the centre, might be able to help find a cheap room in a pinch. The horserental outfit Equi Campo, about 700m north of the museum and youth hostel turn-off, has a café and a few rooms for 2000$00 per person.

Places to Eat

The *Parque Campismo de Cerdeira* has its own cheerful, no-frills restaurant with Minho specialities like bersame (a pork and vegetable stew), rojões à moda do Minho and cabrito (kid) at 1200$00 to 2000$00 for four people (the minimum available serving), as well as omelettes, hamburgers and other snacks.

Getting There & Away

REDM coaches stop by the museum, the camping ground and in the centre. When many hostel-bound passengers are aboard or the weather is foul, drivers have been known to drive out to the hostel as well.

CABRIL

Though it hardly looks the part, this tiny village happens to be the administrative centre of Portugal's biggest *freguesia* (parish) stretching from Fafião to Lapela and up to the Spanish border. It also makes a fine place to stay for a few days. Set with outlying hamlets in a wide, fertile bowl, it is peaceful and pretty, with access on foot to hardy villages like Pincães, which are struggling to maintain a traditional lifestyle but are short on young people.

An old bridge, submerged by the Salamonde reservoir half a century ago, rises partly out of the water in summer; the 'new' bridge beside it looks quite old too. Four km away at Vila Nova is another handsome old bridge.

Orientation & Information

The village's reference point is a tiny square with a pillory and the Tasquinha do Guarda café-bar. Off to one side is a grimy but pretty little church (said to have been moved around five centuries ago, brick by brick, by

---

Pillory Power

Portugal's *pelourinhos*, or pillories, are a distinctive feature of nearly every town and village, especially in the northern Minho and Trás-os-Montes provinces. Believed to have originated in Roman times, these stone columns became prominent in Portugal around the 12th century and were in use for some 500 years. Originally, they were devoid of decoration and served as a form of punishment: criminals were chained from hooks at the top (earlier versions had cages) or locked into attached handcuffs. But increasingly, pillories became a symbol of municipal power – which is why you'll see most of them beside town halls, cathedrals or monasteries, the most common seats of jurisdiction at the time. During the 16th-century Manueline era, pillories became elaborate works of art and were often topped by Dom Manuel's motifs of an armillary sphere and cross of the Order of Christ, while the stone column itself was carved into rope-like coils.

Some of the more unusual pillories in Portugal include the 16th-century one in Elvas, covered with stone dots; a hexagonal pillory in Barcelos, topped by a graceful granite lantern; and the curiously pagan pillory of Soajo, carved with a crude smiling face. ■

villagers of nearby São Lourenço in search of a more propitious locale). On a rise beyond the church is a small national park work station and information office (no telephone); it's open weekdays roughly from 9 am to 5 pm.

Places to Stay

The small, year-round *Outeiro Alto* camping ground is 1.2 km up from the village square, across the bridge and in the direction of Pincães and Ermida (follow the signs showing a rearing horse). Typical rates are 400$00 per person and 450$00 per tent, with no charge for cars. This is part of a 'leisure-time collective' called Trote-Gerês (☎ & fax 053-65 98 60), which also rents horses, bikes and canoes (and runs a good-value pousadinha in Paradela).

Private rooms are available in the village for 2000$00 to 2500$00 for a double; ask at the Restaurante de Ponte Nova de Cabril by the bridge, at Tasquinha do Guarda in the square, or Café Aguia Real, about 250m from the square towards Paradela.

Getting There & Away

There are no buses to Cabril at all. The best option is to get off any Braga-Montalegre bus (five or six a day, fewer at weekends) at Salamonde and ask about a taxi at the Retiro da Cabreira café. The only crossing into the park for miles is across the Salamonde reservoir dam, way down below the highway. Once a week, on Mondays, there is a bus between Salamonde and Fafião, but you'd have to walk or hitch between there and Cabril. Trote-Gerês might also be willing to collect you from Salamonde.

PARADELA

There is nothing to do here but walk. Trote-Gerês (see Cabril) operates the plain and friendly *Pousadinha de Paradela* beside the little parish church, where comfortable doubles without/with bath are 4200$00/5500$00 including breakfast (book ahead in summer). It is good value, except for the hourly church bell all night. Other meals are available on request for 1300$00.

Less snug but equally friendly (run by an English-speaking Portuguese woman) and with better views (at the back) is *Restaurante Sol Rio* (☎ 076-561 67), 300m out along the road to Montalegre. Doubles are 3000$00 without bath or 4000$00 to 5000$00 with.

Getting There & Away

There are buses to Paradela at 1.15 and 6.50 pm on weekdays from Cambedo on the Braga-Montalegre road (REDM has five or six daily buses on this route). There is only one direct Montalegre-Paradela bus on weekdays, departing Montalegre at 12.30 pm. There are no buses to Paradela from anywhere on weekends.

SOAJO & LINDOSO

These two sturdy and remote villages are close together on either side of the Rio Lima valley. They are best known for their *espigueiros* or **stone granaries** – huge slatted granite caskets on stilts – for storing maize or winnowed grain and protecting it from rats. Dating from the 18th and 19th centuries, many are still used for this purpose. Clustered on rises above their villages, grizzled with moss and topped with little crosses (perhaps an indication of the traditional sacredness of their contents), they look like miniature cathedrals, or giants' tombs. The brass-belled cows grazing around them and the washing lines tied to them do little to dispel their eerie appearance.

Lindoso also has its own small, restored **castle**, founded in the early 13th century by Afonso III, beefed up in the 14th by Dom Dinis, occupied by the Spanish in 1662-64, and used as a military garrison until 1895. Now it's 'garrisoned' by the national park and has an information office and tantalising but poorly captioned exhibits on the castle, its excavations and the traditional way of life of the village. It's open daily, except Mondays, from 9.30 am to noon and 1.30 to 6 pm; entry is 200$00. Walk through the stony old villages, too, to see the remnants of traditional life here.

MINHO

Places to Stay

Soajo is the home of an ADERE pilot programme called Turismo de Aldeia (see the introduction to the national park section), under which at least 10 village houses have already been renovated and adapted for tourist accommodation. There is one for two people at 7000$00, and others for four at 13,000$00, six at 18,000$00 or eight at 24,000$00. Book these through ADERE (☎ & fax 058-674 27 in Soajo or 058-422 50; fax 058-424 50 in Ponte da Barca). Failing that, you could ask about quartos at Café Videira near the bus stand.

About half a km beyond the Lindoso turn-off on the N203 (heading towards Spain) is the *Restaurante Alto Lindoso* (☎ 058-674 22). It has a few doubles with shared bath for 3000$00. You may also have some luck at the nearby *Café Carril*.

Getting There & Away

On weekdays only, buses depart from Arcos de Valdevez for Soajo and separately for Lindoso at least twice a day – at approximately midday and 6 pm to each destination – returning about 7 am and 1 pm; the Lindoso connections start at Ponte da Barca. Check with the Arcos or Ponte da Barca turismo for exact times. Extra services are laid on each Wednesday, which is market day alternately in Arcos and Ponte da Barca. The fare to Arcos-Soajo is 300$00 and to Ponte da Barca-Lindoso it's 370$00.

Trás-os-Montes

Portugal's north-east province is well off the main tourist trail, and largely ignored even by most Portuguese who consider it the most backward and pagan part of the country. Its name, 'beyond the mountains', reflects more than its geographical isolation, cut off from the neighbouring Minho province by the Serras do Gerês, Alvão and Marão. Here, too, you'll encounter the country's most extreme range of temperatures: in the north, a *terra fria* where winter temperatures drop to freezing and last for several months; in the south (officially, the Alto Douro), a *terra quente* of searing summers which help to ripen its olives, almonds, fruit and rye, and the Douro and Tua valleys' port-wine grapes.

The isolation and harsh living conditions have bred mysterious practices and beliefs, as well as an incredible self-sufficiency. In this vast province – almost twice the size of the Minho, with less than half the population – you can still find villages where EU funds have failed to filter through and where farmers struggle to make ends meet, ploughing the fields with oxen, living in the humblest of granite houses with their pigs and hens and donkeys.

For an adventurous traveller, this austere lifestyle and often harsh landscape are the province's major attractions. Few places in Europe have such a sense of space and remoteness. But getting around can be a problem: the long-haul bus network is largely limited to the major cities of Vila Real, Chaves, Bragança, and Miranda do Douro (with local services often disappearing entirely on weekends and outside the school term from July to mid-September). The Linha da Corgo train only gets you as far as Vila Real, and the narrow-gauge Linha da Tua as far as Mirandela. While these cities are useful as bases for exploring further afield and have their own points of interest – especially Chaves for its spa and Roman bridge, and Bragança for its old walled citadel – it's the smaller villages that are the

more memorable. To discover these you'll need either your own transport or plenty of time to wait for bus connections.

Hikers will find the province's two natural parks – Parque Natural do Alvão near Vila Real and Parque Natural de Montesinho near Bragança – some of the most rewarding areas to explore. Neither are as well equipped with trails or facilities as the Parque Nacional da Peneda-Gerês, but you won't find nearly as many tourists visiting them either. If you're planning some serious hiking, be sure to check into the parks' relevant offices in Vila Real and Bragança for all the information you can get; this is no place to get lost.

Destinations in the valley of the Rio Douro, where it forms the province's southern border with Beira Alta – Peso da Régua, Pinhão and Tua – are covered in the Douro chapter.

Western Trás-os-Montes

VILA REAL
• pop 13,000 • postcode 5000 • area code ☎ 059
High above the confluence of the Rios Corgo

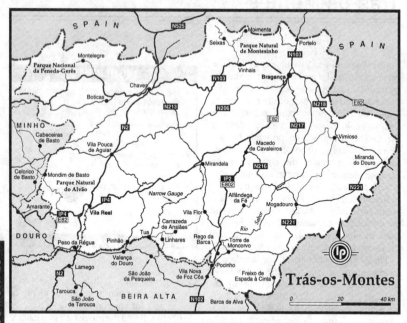

and Cabril is the district capital of Vila Real, a busy little university and industrial town. It's surrounded by the splendid mountainous scenery of the Serra do Marão to the west and Serra de Alvão to the north, with parts of the latter incorporating the Parque Natural do Alvão.

The town itself has few cultural attractions, though the Palácio (or Solar) de Mateus is a couple of km away and worth a visit. For hikers interested in exploring the surrounding countryside, the town can serve as a useful base for a few days. Otherwise it's best considered as a stop-over en route to the wilder and more intriguing parts of Trás-os-Montes.

Orientation

From the train station on the eastern edge of town, it's a 20-minute walk across the Rio Corgo to the central Avenida Carvalho Araújo, running north-south. The main Rodonorte bus station (beside the Hotel Cabanelas) is five minutes walk north of the Avenida. Local Auto-Viação do Tâmega buses stop south of the Avenida. Most accommodation, restaurants and places of interest are in the Avenida area.

Information

Tourist Office Vila Real is the administrative headquarters for the Região de Turismo da Serra do Marão. The turismo for general enquiries (☎ 32 28 19; fax 32 17 12) is at Avenida Carvalho Araújo 94, in a striking Manueline building. From June to October it's open daily from 9.30 am to 7 pm, and the rest of the year daily, except Sundays, from 9.30 am to 12.30 pm and 2 to 5 pm (to 7 pm in April and May).

Park Office The head office of the Parque Natural do Alvão (☎ 241 38; fax 738 69) is on the 3rd floor at Rua Alves Torgo 22, and is open weekdays only from 9 am to 12.30 pm and 2.30 to 5 pm. It can provide leaflets in English on the park's flora and fauna, handicrafts and local products, as well as some information on walks.

Money There are banks with ATMs along Avenida Carvalho Araújo (including one next to the turismo).

Post & Communications The post office, with fax and telephone facilities, is at the top of Avenida Carvalho Araújo.

Campuses The Universidade de Trás-os-Montes e Alto Douro (☎ 32 16 31; fax 744 80) is on the southern edge of town, half a km or so beyond the train station.

Medical Services The hospital (☎ 34 10 41) is on the north-western edge of town, across the IP4/E82 motorway.

Emergency The police station (☎ 32 20 22) is just west of Avenida Carvalho Araújo.

Sé
Once part of a 15th-century Dominican monastery, the cathedral is an unremarkable remnant, although if you're staying in one of the pensões opposite you'll remember its clanging bells well enough.

Miradouro de Trás-do-Cemitério
There's a fantastic view from the promenade at the southern tip of town, just beyond a small cemetery and chapel, which looks down over the plunging gorge of the Rio Corgo and its confluence with the Rio Cabril.

Palácio de Mateus
More commonly known as Solar de Mateus, and famously depicted on bottles of Mateus rosé, this frilly baroque creation four km east of Vila Real was probably designed and built by the Italian Nicolau Nasoni in the mid-18th century. The house's granite and white-washed wings ('advancing lobster-like towards you,' wrote English poet and critic Sacheverell Sitwell) shelter a cobbled fore-court dominated by an ornate balustraded

stairway, and overlooked by rooftop spires and statues.

Instead of the swan shown on the wine labels, the pond in front now holds a half-submerged statue of a naked lady by the contemporary sculptor João Cutileiro. Behind the palace is perhaps the best bit of all – an Alice-in-Wonderland garden of tiny box hedges, prim statues and a well-trimmed cypress tunnel, dark and fragrant. Inside the house, you get to see just a few rooms, heavy with velvet drapes and fussy 18th-century furnishings. As for the Mateus rosé, it's actually made by the Sogrape company down the road, though the palace does produce its own range of jams and wines, sold at a shop on the premises.

The palace is open daily from 9 am to 1 pm and 2 to 7 pm (to 6 pm in winter). Admission fees are exorbitant: 900$00 for the interior and 600$00 for the garden. Take the bus marked 'Timpeira e Mateus', which leaves five times daily from near the police station, and ask for palácio; it's a five-minute walk from the crossroads where you'll be dropped.

Special Events
The Festa de São Pedro on 28 and 29 June is one of the town's liveliest events, with a huge market held in the streets east of the turismo. This is a good time to pick up the region's unusual black pottery as well as other local handicrafts.

Places to Stay
Camping The Clube de Campismo camping ground (☎ 32 47 24) has a prime spot right by the river, north-east of the centre. There are good facilities, including a swimming pool, but you need a carnet or Camping Card International (see Documents or Accommodation in the Facts for the Visitor chapter) to stay.

Hostels There's an Instituto Português de Juventude (☎ 722 01) hostel– elsewhere these are sometimes called centros de juventude – in a large youth complex on Rua Dr Manuel Cardona near the camping

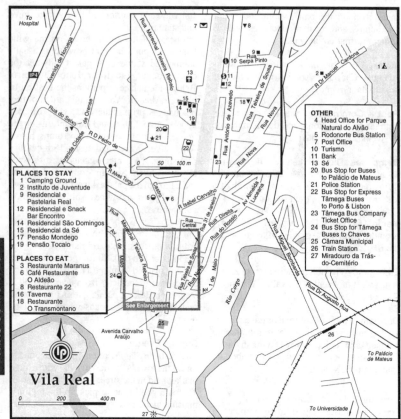

PLACES TO STAY
1 Camping Ground
2 Instituto de Juventude
9 Residencial e Pastelaria Real
12 Residencial e Snack Bar Encontro
14 Residencial São Domingos
15 Residencial da Sé
17 Pensão Mondego
19 Pensão Tocaio

PLACES TO EAT
3 Restaurante Maranus
6 Café Restaurante O Aldeão
8 Restaurante 22
16 Taverna
18 Restaurante O Transmontano

OTHER
4 Head Office for Parque Natural do Alvão
5 Rodonorte Bus Station
7 Post Office
10 Turismo
11 Bank
13 Sé
20 Bus Stop for Buses to Palácio de Mateus
21 Police Station
22 Bus Stop for Express Tâmega Buses to Porto & Lisbon
23 Tâmega Bus Company Ticket Office
24 Bus Stop for Tâmega Buses to Chaves
25 Câmara Municipal
26 Train Station
27 Miradouro da Trás-do-Cemitério

Vila Real

ground. You may be able to get a cheap dormitory bed if youth groups haven't pre-booked them all.

Pensões & Residencials A trio of budget places is right beside the cathedral in Travessa de São Domingos, well within earshot of the cathedral bells: cheapest is *Pensão Mondego* (☎ 32 30 97; fax 32 20 39) at No 11, where fraying singles/doubles are 2000$00/2500$00 without bath or 2700$00/3500$00 with. Under the same management, at No 33, is *Residencial São Domingos* (☎ & fax 32 20 39), where cosy singles/doubles

are 3000$00/4000$00 with bath. Smartest is *Residencial da Sé* (☎ 32 45 75) at No 19, with rooms for 2000$00/3000$00 without bath or 3000$00/5000$00 with bath, the latter with breakfast.

Another popular cheapie is *Residencial e Snack Bar Encontro* (☎ 32 25 32) at Avenida Carvalho Araújo 76, with good-value rooms with air-con but no bath for 3000$00/3500$00. A double with bath or a small suite minus bath is 5500$00. Overlooking pedestrianised Rua Central at No 5 is *Residencial e Pastelaria Real* (☎ 32 58 79; fax 32 46 13), with neat singles/doubles/triples for 4500$00/6500$00/9000$00, including bath and breakfast. A notch down is the deceptively grand-looking *Pensão Tocaio* (☎ 32 31 06; fax 716 75) at Avenida Carvalho Araújo 45, where 1960s rooms (with bathrooms often bigger than the bedrooms) are 4000$00/6000$00/8000$00 with breakfast.

Turihab There are several Turihab properties near town, including a 1922 mansion, *Casa Agrícola da Levada* (☎ 32 21 90; fax 34 69 55), 1.5 km north-east near the Rio Corgo. It's part of an estate breeding wild boar and producing its own bread, jam and honey. Expect to pay around 10,000$00 a double. The turismo has details of other possibilities.

Places to Eat

An unnamed tavern at Travessa de São Domingos 17 is worth a look for its fantastic bottle collection. But for drinks and dinner in jovial local company, head for *Restaurante 22* (☎ 32 47 94) at Rua António de Azevedo 22, with a bar in the front and a restaurant at the back serving hearty fare for 900$00 to 1400$00 a dish. *Café Restaurante O Aldeão* at Rua Dom Pedro de Castro 70 is another popular place where you can eat well for under 1200$00 a dish. More touristy, but serving good regional fare, is *Restaurante O Transmontana* (☎ 32 35 40) at Rua da Misericórdia 35; bacalhau, veal and kid dishes are recommended.

Restaurante Snack Bar Maranus (☎ 32 15 21), at Lote 2 in the shopping complex, Quinta do Seixo, on the western edge of town, looks an unlikely venue but serves great grilled dishes and even fondues for around 1200$00.

Getting There & Away

Bus Two companies operate from Vila Real. Auto-Viação do Tâmega (☎ 32 29 28), with a ticket office at Avenida Carvalho Araújo 26 and bus stands nearby, runs local and long-distance services including two expresses daily to Porto and Lisbon via Amarante and Coimbra, and one to Lisbon via Lamego and Viseu. Local services include nine daily to

Chaves and four to Peso da Régua. Express services of Rodonorte (☎ 32 32 34), at Rua Dom Pedro de Castro 19, include three daily runs to Chaves, Lisbon and Porto, two to Bragança and Mirandela, and three to Mondim de Basto.

Train Vila Real is at the end of the Linha da Corgo from Peso da Régua: five services daily connect with trains to/from Porto.

PARQUE NATURAL DO ALVÃO

This 7220-hectare park (Portugal's smallest) occupies the western slope of the Serra do Marão between Vila Real and Mondim de Basto. In a transitional zone between the humid coastal region and dry interior, the park has diverse fauna and flora. But it's the harsh, higher-elevation landscape that is most striking, especially around Lamas de Olo, a village of traditional slate and schist architecture at 1000m. An extensive granite basin here is the source of the Rio Olo (a tributary of the Tâmega), and a 550m drop to Ermelo gives rise to the spectacular Fisgas de Ermelo waterfalls, the park's major tourist attraction.

Exploring on your own is tricky as there is minimal public transport and few maps. Before setting out on foot, visit the park office at Vila Real or Mondim de Basto for descriptive leaflets in English, and information on park-run accommodation at Arnal in the south-eastern corner of the park. There's an *escola ecológica* between Arnal and Galegos da Serra, mainly geared for school groups.

Information

The park's head office (☎ 059-241 38; fax 738 69) is at Rua Alves Torgo 22 in Vila Real. Two other offices are in Mondim de Basto: an administrative office (☎ 055-38 12 09) at Avenida da Igreja, Block 1, and an information centre at Zona do Barrio, Sitío de Retiro. All are open weekdays from 9 am to 12.30 pm and 2 to 5.30 pm. Mondim de Basto's turismo is also a useful source of park information.

TRÁS-OS-MONTES

Walks

A three-hour hike from Agarez to Arnal is described in the park leaflet *Guia do Percurso Pedestre*, which details traditional farming activities in the area, as well as geology, flora and fauna. Another possibility is a nine-km uphill route to Fisgas de Ermelo waterfall via the attractive village of Ermelo, just off the Vila Real to Mondim de Basto road; there's little shade en route so take sun protection and water. Lamas de Olo village is another popular goal: from Anta, on the park's northern boundary, it's a four-km walk.

Places to Stay & Eat

The park's accommodation at Arnal is a 12-bed cottage, which costs 1300$00 per person with your own sleeping bag or 2000$00 with linen. The minimum charge is 5200$00, and bookings must be made in advance through the park office.

In Lamas de Olo, *Restaurante A Cabana* (☎ 059-34 17 45) has one double for around 4000$00. The restaurant is renowned for its trout dishes. Ermelo has three cafés where you could ask about private rooms.

If you've got your own transport, two Turihab properties called *Casa da Cruz* and *Casa do Mineiro* (☎ 059-729 95 or 97 92 45; fax 729 95) at Campeã, 12 km west of Vila Real, make a fine base for exploring the park. The remodelled granite cottages with three rooms each are owned by an enthusiastic local teacher who has files of information on the area, including walking maps. The cottages cost around 8000$00 a night (less for longer stays).

Getting There & Away

Auto-Viação do Tâmega buses run from Vila Real to Vila Marim, via Agarez, around six times a day. Rodonorte/Auto-Viação Mondinense goes from Vila Real to Mondim de Basto three times daily on weekdays (twice on Saturdays, none on Sundays), via the turning to Ermelo; the village itself is just up from the main road. Two km beyond this turning is a picnic site and the turning to Fisgas de Ermelo waterfall.

There are no buses to Lamas de Olo: taxis from Vila Real cost around 1500$00 one way. Taxis are also available in Lamas de Olo.

School term sees additional services to the villages of Fervença and Varzigueto, at the heart of the park. Check with the park or turismo offices in Vila Real or Mondim de Basto for timetables.

MONDIM DE BASTO
• *postcode 4880* • *area code* ☎ *055*

This little mountain town near the intersection of Douro, Minho and Trás-os-Montes provinces, 22 km north-east of Amarante, is an unattractively modernised place. However, it's saved by mountain surroundings, friendly folk, and a strong local wine for which this so-called Terras de Basto region is famous. Although the town isn't worth a special detour, it makes a suitable base for exploring this little-known area, including the Parque Natural do Alvão.

Orientation & Information

The town sprawls in all directions with little sense of a central point. Arriving by bus you'll find yourself near the market, from where it's a short walk west to the turismo (☎ 38 14 79) at Praça 9 de Abril, and what remains of the old town. From July to September the efficient little turismo is open daily from 9.30 am to 12.30 pm and 2 to 5.30 pm; in other months it closes on weekends. As well as the usual help with accommodation and transport information it can supply photocopied maps showing regional walks and points of interest.

See the Parque Natural do Alvão section for information on park offices in Mondim.

Walks & Swimming

One of the most popular walks is to the Capela de Senhora da Graça, on top of Monte Farinha, 13 km east of town. It takes two to three hours to reach the pine-clad summit, and you can reward yourself with lunch (see Places to Eat) once you get there. The turismo can provide a rough map.

Two km south of town, just off the N304,

is a delightful swimming spot at Senhora da Ponte, beside the Rio Cabril (follow signs to the camping ground and then take the track to the right). River water still powers an old flour mill by the rocky site. Follow the river upstream for shady picnic spots and walks.

By taking the 7 am bus from Mondim you could also tackle the nine-km walk to Fisgas de Ermelo waterfall in the Parque Natural do Alvão (see previous section). The last bus back from the N304 turn-off to the waterfall is at 7 pm (2.20 pm on weekends), but check this with the turismo first.

Wine Tasting
The nearest 'Basto' *vinho verde* wine is produced by Quinta do Fundo (☎ 38 12 91) in Vilar de Viando, just over two km south of town across the Rio Cabril (see Places to Stay). Two other labels come from a few km west of town, at Quinta da Veiga (☎ 36 12 12) in Gagos and Quinta da Capela (☎ 02-49 10 76) in Veade. Check with the turismo on opening hours for wine tasting.

Places to Stay
Camping There's an excellent camping ground (☎ 38 16 50) beside the Rio Cabril, two km south of town, open only to holders of a carnet or Camping Card International (see Documents or Accommodation in the Facts for the Visitor chapter).

Pensões & Residencials Two decent places on Avenida Dr Augusto Brito (just west of the turismo) offer singles/doubles for around 3000$00/4000$00: *Residencial Carvalho* (☎ 38 10 57) near the petrol station, and *Residencial Arcadia* (☎ 38 14 10) further south.

Turihab *Casa das Mourôas* (☎ 38 13 94) is a converted 19th-century hayloft near the turismo on Rua José Carvalho Camões, with singles/doubles for 5500$00/6500$00. *Quinta do Fundo* (☎ 38 12 91; fax 38 20 17) is a considerably grander affair, two km south of town at Vilar de Viando (just off the N304 to Vila Real). As well as bottling its own wine, the quinta has a tennis court,

swimming pool, and horses and bikes for rent. Singles/doubles cost around 7500$00/8500$00, including breakfast.

Places to Eat
Restaurante Transmontana (☎ 38 16 82), on Avenida da Igreja, offers a good selection of regional fare at reasonable prices. Atop Monte Farinha is *Restaurante Senhora da Graça* (☎ 38 14 04), where the prices are steeper but the views are fantastic.

Best value of all is *Adega São Tiago* (☎ 38 22 69), just above the turismo on Rua Velha – a rustic little place with daily specials for a bargain 700$00, served in a jovial and welcoming atmosphere. It's closed on Sundays.

Getting There & Away
Auto Mondinense (☎ 38 20 41) runs buses to/from Vila Real, skirting the Parque Natural do Alvão near Ermelo: three a day on weekdays, two on Saturdays and none on Sundays. Two buses a day go to Amarante, five to Porto via Guimarães, and one to Lisbon (two on Sundays).

MONTALEGRE
• *postcode 5470* • *area code* ☎ *076*
You're only likely to call in on this small town if you're on the way between Chaves and the Parque Nacional da Peneda-Gerês (see the Minho chapter). There's a marginally useful park information office here. Presiding over the town and the surrounding plains is a restored castle, one of Dom Dinis' necklace of frontier outposts. Wellington rested here after chasing the French from Porto.

Orientation & Information
The town hall sits foursquare on a new-looking square at the top of a rise. The turismo is across the road to the south, by the traffic roundabout, but we found it unstaffed and with no posted hours. A bank with exchange facilities and a Multibanco ATM is on the square in front of the town hall, and another is on the square behind it.

The park office (☎ 522 81) is at Rua do Regioso 17 – turn left at Banco Crédito

Predial Português (behind the town hall) and go to the end of the street, then jog right a few metres to a low stone building set back from the street. You may have to hammer on the door at the back, and the staff will probably be annoyed to be disturbed. It's open on weekdays only from 9 am to 12.30 pm and 2 to 5.30 pm.

Castelo
The castle, consisting mainly of a restored, 28m-high keep, three smaller turrets and some walls in a misshapen oval, is on the heights about 400m north-east of the town hall, with high views of the countryside (and of the fairly ugly new town). Built in the 12th century by Dom Dinis, the castle was enlarged (including the addition of the biggest of the towers) by his son Afonso IV.

Places to Stay & Eat
There's little obvious accommodation beyond the *Residencial Fidalgo* (☎ 524 62), about 300m up Rua da Corujeira (the Braga road) from the centre, at No 34. Clean doubles with bath and TV are 5000$00.

A further 200m up is *Restaurante Florestal* (☎ 524 20), a bit pricey for the locale (fish and meat dishes from 900$00 to 1300$00) but clean and earnest. On Rua dos Ferradores, near the park office, is the basic *Café-Restaurante Terra-Fria*, and across the road is *Pizzeria-Restaurante O Cantinho*.

Getting There & Away
A furniture store in a building called – mysteriously – 'Casa Australiana', across the roundabout from the town hall, is also the information and ticket office for regional and long-distance buses, mainly REDM. Braga-Chaves coaches stop here about five times a day on weekdays and three times a day on weekends and holidays. Change at Chaves for Vila Real and Bragança.

CHAVES
• *pop 11,500* • *postcode 5400* • *area code* ☎ *076*
This attractive regional capital and spa town, 10 km south of the Spanish frontier, spans the Rio Tâmega in a particularly fertile valley and is renowned among local visitors not only for its waters but also for its smoked ham *(presunto)* and sausages. It's a friendly place with an appealing end-of-the-road atmosphere, well worth an overnight stay as you delve into Trás-os-Montes or head to Spain.

The town's name ('keys') reveals its strategic importance as gateway both to Portugal and to the northern frontier: Romans, Suevi, Visigoths, Moors and, later, the French and Spanish have all squabbled over Chaves. The Romans, who founded it in 78 AD, called it Aquae Flaviae after the spa and their emperor, Flavio Vespasianus. They built a 16-arched bridge across the river, which is still a major feature of the town, together with an old medieval quarter, a 14th-century castle keep and two fortresses.

Orientation
From the bus station (beside the defunct train station) it's a five to 10-minute walk to the town centre. Leaving the station, walk straight ahead to reach the turismo and turn left to reach the Roman bridge and southern part of town, where you'll find most of the accommodation.

Information
The turismo (☎ 33 30 29; fax 214 19) is at Terreiro de Cavalaria, a garden at the northern end of Rua de Santo António. It's open on weekdays from 9 am to 7 pm and on weekends from 9 am to 12.30 pm and 2 to at least 6.30 pm.

Banks with Multibanco ATMs are along Rua de Santo António and Rua Direita. The district hospital (☎ 33 20 12 or 33 22 11) is on Avenida Sá Carneiro, north-west of the centre. The police station (☎ 231 25) is on Avenida dos Bombeiros de Voluntariós, near the turismo.

Ponte Romana
The Roman bridge was built between 98 and 104 AD by Emperor Trajan (hence its other common name, Ponte Trajano) and probably served as a link in the important Braga to Astorga road. Walk out to the middle of it to

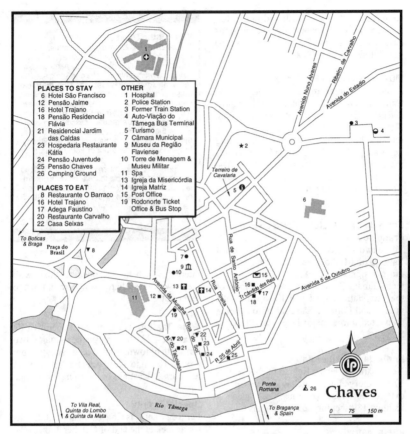

PLACES TO STAY
6 Hotel São Francisco
12 Pensão Jaime
16 Hotel Trajano
18 Pensão Residencial
   Flávia
21 Residencial Jardim
   das Caldas
23 Hospedaria Restaurante
   Kátia
24 Pensão Juventude
25 Pensão Chaves
26 Camping Ground

PLACES TO EAT
8 Restaurante O Barraco
16 Hotel Trajano
17 Adega Faustino
20 Restaurante Carvalho
22 Casa Seixas

OTHER
1 Hospital
2 Police Station
3 Former Train Station
4 Auto-Viação do
   Tâmega Bus Terminal
5 Turismo
7 Câmara Municipal
9 Museu da Região
   Flaviense
10 Torre de Menagem &
   Museu Militar
11 Spa
13 Igreja da Misericórdia
14 Igreja Matriz
15 Post Office
19 Rodonorte Ticket
   Office & Bus Stop

To Boticas & Braga — Praça do Brasil

Terreiro de Cavalaria

Ponte Romana

To Vila Real, Quinta do Lombo & Quinta da Mata

Rio Tâmega

To Bragança & Spain

Chaves

0   75   150 m

TRÁS-OS-MONTES

see engraved Roman milestones on both sides of the road.

Spa

The warm (73°C) sodium-bicarbonated waters of the Chaves spa are famous for treating rheumatism, nutritional disorders, liver complaints and high blood pressure, but the stuff actually tastes pretty awful. Have a free cupful at the spa gardens. Most residencials in town are full of elderly patients on long courses of treatment: four cups of spa water a day for two weeks is the recommended dose for rheumatism.

Torre de Menagem & Museu Militar

The Torre de Menagem (keep) is the only bit left of a castle built by Dom Dinis in the 14th century and originally enclosed within defensive walls (parts of which can still be seen). After Dom João triumphed at Aljubarrota in 1385, he gave the castle to his valiant constable, Dom Nun' Álvares Pereira. It was inherited by the House of Bragança when Nun' Álvares' daughter Beatriz married the Count of Barcelos, the future Duke of Bragança.

Today the keep, which is set in manicured gardens with fine views of the surrounding countryside, houses a small and rather dull military museum, open daily, except Mondays, from 9 am to 12.30 pm and 2 to 5.30 pm. Admission is 100$00.

Museu da Região Flaviense

Around the corner from the keep, in Praça de Camões, is this collection of archaeological and ethnographical material from the region. Not surprisingly, there are a lot of Roman remains but perhaps the most interesting items are prehistoric stone menhirs and carvings, some dating back over 2500 years. The museum is open daily, except Mondays, from 9 am to 12.30 pm and 2 to 5.30 pm, for 100$00.

Forte de São Neutel & Forte de São Francisco

These two 17th-century forts, like the one at Valença do Minho, were built in the style of those designed by the French military architect Vauban. Forte de São Neutel, north of the bus station, isn't usually open to the public, and Forte de São Francisco is being converted into a major hotel (see Places to Stay).

Igreja da Misericórdia

Next to the Museu da Região Flaviense, this 17th-century church catches the eye with its exterior porch and columns. Peek inside at its huge 18th-century azulejo panels.

Igreja Matriz

The Romanesque parish church was completely remodelled in the 16th century, though the doorway and belfry still show Romanesque features. There's little of interest in the renovated interior.

Activities

Horse Riding At an Escola de Esquitação (mobile ☎ 0936-80 52 39) in Curalha, four km south-west of town, you can take riding lessons or hire horses.

Mountain Biking The BTT Clube de Chaves (☎ 32 25 55, ☎ 274 91; fax 33 21 67) organises regular group outings to places of

Wine of the Dead

Some 23 km south-west of Chaves, in the unremarkable little town of Boticas, you can sample Portugal's most bizarrely named brew: *vinho dos mortos* (wine of the dead). This rough red wine (generously described by the local turismo as 'famous, tasty clarets') takes its name from an incident in 1809 when villagers hid their hoard of wine from the invading French by burying it underground. Discovering afterwards that it tasted rather better than before, they have continued the practice to this day, burying wine in deep underground cellars for up to a year.

There are a number of cafés in Boticas where you can sample this earthy wine, including Café de Armindo on Rua de Sangunhedo, or ask at the turismo (☎ 076-423 53) on Rua 5 de Outubro. ∎

interest, which might appeal to those with their own bikes (there's nowhere in town to rent one).

Wine Tasting The Adega Cooperativa de Chaves (☎ 221 83) on Avenida Duarte, two km south of town, is open on weekdays from around 10 am to 12.30 pm and 2.30 to 5 pm for tours and tastings of its strong local wine.

Special Events

Feira de Santos is Chaves' major fair. It lasts for a week at the end of October, though the biggest days are 31 October and 1 November when there's music and dancing, and market stalls fill the streets.

Dia de Cidade on 8 July is another big bash, with brass bands, parades, fireworks, and laser lights. One of the most important religious events is a 15-km pilgrimage to the Sanctuario de São Caetano on the 2nd Sunday of August.

Places to Stay

Camping The municipal *São Roque* camping ground (☎ 227 33) is on the south bank of the river near the Roman bridge. It's open from April to October.

Pensões & Residencials There are plenty of cheap (and often old-fashioned) residencials geared to the spa clientele, though they're heavily booked in summer. One of the cheapest is *Pensão Residencial Flávia* (☎ 225 13) at Travessa Cândido dos Reis 12, where basic singles/doubles without bath are 2500$00/2900$00. The restaurant is gloomy but there's a delightful courtyard garden.

Along Rua do Sol is a string of restaurants-cum-pensões built into the old town walls. *Pensão Juventude* (☎ 267 13), at No 8, is a pretty blue-and-white house with eight clapboard-walled singles/doubles for around 2500$00/4000$00 (try bargaining). It's clean and quiet and the owners are a jolly bunch. The *Hospedaria Restaurante Kátia* (☎ 244 46), at No 28, is newer and slicker, with rooms for 4500$00/5000$00 including bath and breakfast.

More traditional spa lodgings, where you'll rub shoulders with ageing patients, include the rambling *Pensão Chaves* (☎ 211 18), on Rua 25 de Abril, with rooms for 2500$00/4000$00 without bath or 3800$00/5500$00 with; and the duller but more up-to-date *Pensão Jaime* (☎ 212 73), on Avenida da Muralha (and Rua da Família de Camões), with rooms for 2500$00/ 3500$00 without bath, 3500$00/4500$00 with.

A notch up is the friendly and efficient *Residencial Jardim das Caldas* (☎ 33 11 89), among modern hotels on Alameda do Tabolado, where rooms are 3000$00/4500$00 without bath, 4000$00/6500$00 with.

Hotels *Hotel Trajano* (☎ 33 24 15; fax 262 14) on Travessa Cândido dos Reis is a comfortable old favourite with doubles for around 9000$00.

The *Hotel do Forte de São Francisco* (☎ 33 37 00; fax 33 37 01), converted from the old Forte de São Francisco, is due to open mid-1997. Room rates weren't available at the time of research but they'll probably be pricey.

Turihab If you've got your own transport it's worth enquiring about nearby Turihab places. The nearest are *Quinta do Lombo*

(☎ 214 04), a stone house with six rooms and a swimming pool, two km south-east off the Valpaços road; and *Quinta da Mata* (☎ & fax 962 53), a 17th-century manor house two km further out on the same road, with tennis courts and a sauna. Expect to pay around 10,000$00 a double.

Places to Eat
A regular clientele of spa patients ensures that most residencials and many other restaurants serve generous portions of standard Portuguese fare at reasonable prices. *Hotel Trajano*'s restaurant is very popular among better-heeled patrons. At the lower end of the scale is the modest and unsignposted *Casa Seixas* (☎ 235 70) at Rua do Sol 38, with a simple menu and a homely atmosphere.

More unusual is *Adega Faustino* (☎ 221 42) on Travessa Cândido dos Reis. It's a cavernous former adega (winery) with huge wine barrels behind the bar, and a menu of snacks for around 500$00, ranging from salads and spicy sausage to pig's ear in vinaigrette sauce. Another taberna típica worth the 10-minute walk away from the centre is *O Barraco* (☎ 250 66), a restored stone cottage incongruously alone on a busy main road off Praça do Brasil. Daily specials (mostly regional meat dishes cooked in a traditional oven) are served in a wood-beamed tavern where customers have stuck poems and ditties on the walls. It's closed on Mondays.

One of the most renowned places in town is *Restaurante Carvalho* (☎ 217 27), which has moved several pegs up-market since its days as a one-room café opposite the camping ground. Now it's a posh place with bow-tied waiters, in the modern complex on Alameda do Tabolado, but it still serves great food, at around 1200$00 a dish. It's closed on Thursdays.

Getting There & Away
From the main bus station Auto-Viação do Tâmega (☎ 33 23 51) operates local and long-distance services (often in conjunction with REDM), including 11 buses daily to Vila Real, five to Caldas do Gerês in the

TRÁS-OS-MONTES

Parque Nacional da Peneda-Gerês, two to Bragança, five to Braga via Montalegre (three on weekends) and four express services to Porto.

Rodonorte (☎ 33 34 91) on Alameda do Tabolado has four weekday express services to Lisbon (two via Porto and two via Viseu), one on Saturdays and three on Sundays, a daily service to Bragança, and four to Vila Real and Amarante. The ticket office is open on weekdays from 7.30 am to 7 pm and 9 to 9.30 pm, Saturdays from 8 am to noon and 2 to 6 pm, and Sundays from 8 to 11 am, 3 to 7 pm and 9 to 10 pm. Buses leave from outside the ticket office.

Auto-Viação do Tâmega has an express from Porto to Orense (Spain) on Thursdays and Sundays, calling at Chaves around 1 pm; buy your ticket the day before. Nine local services daily go to the frontier, where you can pick up Spanish buses to Orense.

Eastern Trás-os-Montes

BRAGANÇA
• pop 15,000 • postcode 5300 • area code ☎ 073

From the 15th century onward, the name Bragança rings down through Portuguese history. In 1442 Dom João I created a duchy here as a reminder to the Spanish that this remote corner was indeed part of the Portuguese kingdom. Though the dukes of Bragança came to prefer their vast holdings in the south (see Vila Viçosa and the boxed aside in the Alentejo chapter), their hometown's splendid isolation remained a kind of symbol of national determination, especially after they ascended the throne in 1640, to rule until the fall of the monarchy in 1910.

Thanks to mountains, bad roads and poor communications, the isolation continued right into the late 20th century, until an EU-designated motorway, the E82, arrived from Porto and Vila Real in the early 1990s, completing a major link with Spain. Bragança is now – rather suddenly – a few hours from Porto as well as Madrid, and in summer its

sober streets fill with Portuguese tourists and jolly Spaniards.

But despite an air of self-importance – and a walled citadel that presents, from afar, one of the most stirring views in northern Portugal – the town itself is surprisingly modest in scale, at heart a backwater where donkey-carts still trundle within a few blocks of its little cathedral.

Why come all this way? Bragança still has a dollop of medieval atmosphere and one of the country's best museums, and it makes a natural base for a spin through the underrated Parque Natural de Montesinho. If you're driving or cycling, a roundabout route to Bragança through eastern Trás-os-Montes reveals some of Portugal's loveliest and least-seen landscapes.

History
The town has Celtic roots, as Brigantia or Brigantio. The Romans fortified it and called it Juliobriga. Trashed during repeated Christian and Moorish campaigns, it was solidly rebuilt in the early 12th century by one Fernão Mendes, an in-law of Afonso Henriques, as the capital of a semi-independent fiefdom. It wasn't long (1199) before its brand-new fortress was attacked and unsuccessfully besieged by Alfonso IX of León.

In 1442 Dom João I, determined to keep a grip on the region, assumed direct control of it, creating the duchy of Bragança – a thumb in the eye of Castile and León – and declaring his bastard son Afonso the first Duke of Bragança. The House of Bragança soon rose to become one of the wealthiest and most powerful families in the country.

Jews fled from the Spanish Inquisition to Bragança in large numbers in the 16th century, to a rather milder Portuguese version which was hardly felt in Trás-os-Montes. Unfortunately, few traces remain of the town's old Jewish community.

In 1640 the Portuguese decided 60 years of Spanish rule was enough. They booted out Philip II's garrisons, and the eighth Duke of Bragança reluctantly took the Portuguese throne as João IV. In his quest for alliances against the Spanish he gave his daughter

Catherine in marriage to Charles II of England.

Spain and France invaded Trás-os-Montes in 1762 on the pretext of freeing Portugal from English domination. Bragança and other towns were besieged for a time before being bailed out by Portuguese and English troops. Shortly afterward, Bragança scored an ecclesiastical coup when the bishopric at Miranda do Douro was moved here.

Orientation

Bragança sits in undulating countryside, at around 670m, on the edge of the Parque Natural de Montesinho. Beside it runs the Rio Fervença, a tributary of the Rio Sabor, which runs right across eastern Trás-os-Montes to the Douro. The approach to the town from Braga and Chaves is through ugly outskirts, but with the citadel always floating above the scene like a mirage.

If Bragança has a centre at all, it is Praça da Sé, in front of the modest cathedral. From here one road runs to the citadel, one to Spain and one to the rest of Portugal. The axis of town is Avenida João da Cruz (where most long-distance coaches start and stop), Rua Almirante Reis and Rua Combatentes da Grande Guerra (usually called just Rua Combatentes).

Where streets are signposted, house numbers seem scarce, and vice-versa.

Information

Tourist Offices Bragança's very helpful and well-organised turismo (☎ 38 12 73) on Avenida Cidade de Zamora is open daily from 9 am to 12.30 pm and 2 to 7 pm (mornings only on Sundays). An unwelcoming regional tourism office (☎ 33 10 78) on Largo do Principal has nothing the city turismo doesn't.

Park Office A Parque Natural de Montesinho information office (☎ 38 14 44, ☎ 38 12 34; fax 38 11 79) is among other park offices at No 5 in Bairro Salvador Nunes Teixeira, a residential district east beyond the turismo. It's open weekdays only, from 9 am to 12.30 pm and 2 to 5.30 pm. Some ICN

Pig Mysteries

Scattered around Trás-os-Montes and the Zamora region of Spain are hundreds of crudely carved granite pigs or boars known as berrões (singular berrão). Some date back over 2000 years, others to the 2nd or 3rd century AD. No one knows what they were for, though there are plenty of theories: they may be fertility or prosperity symbols, or grave guardians or offerings to, or representations of, Iron Age gods. Or they may have marked the boundary of someone's land.

You can take a close look at these mysterious pigs in museums in Chaves, Bragança and Miranda do Douro, or in situ in Bragança castle where there's a pig – pierced through its middle by a pillory. ■

(park service) publications in Portuguese are for sale; there's nothing in English except a free schematic park map showing villages, roads and tracks, points of interest, camp sites and accommodation, but no trails. However, staff are very helpful, and willing to share their expertise with interested amateurs.

Money Several banks with foreign exchange desks and Multibanco ATMs are along Rua Almirante Reis. The private Neves currency exchange at Rua Combatentes 222 has what look like lousy rates.

Post & Communications The post and telecommunications office is at the top of Rua Almirante Reis.

Travel Agencies Sanvitur (☎ 33 18 26; fax 275 36), at Avenida João da Cruz 38, is the local agent for Rede Expressos and other remnants of the old national coach lines, and is competent at other services too. Santos, at Rua 5 de Outubro 5, beside the Banco Nacional Ultramarino, is a travel agent, a regional coach line for Trás-os-Montes, and an agent for Internorte coaches.

Bookshops There is a small bookshop, Livraria Popular, at Rua Almirante Reis 16.

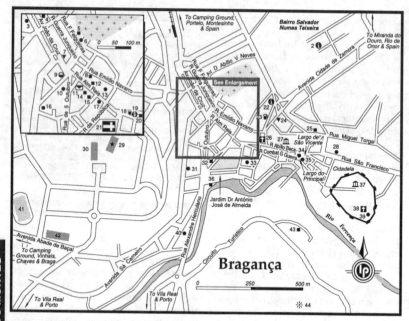

Medical & Emergency Services The district hospital is over a km west of the centre, on Avenida Abade de Baçal. In the same complex, behind the câmara municipal, is the police office.

Sé

Don't get your hopes up. This old but forgettable church, which started life in 1545 as the Igreja de São João Baptista, was declared a cathedral in 1770 when the bishopric was moved here from Miranda.

Museu do Abade de Baçal

This museum of regional archaeology, ethnography and art is one of Portugal's best museums, with a wide-ranging, high-minded and well-presented collection based on that of its namesake, the Abbot of Baçal, Francisco Manuel Alves (1865-1947), a dedicated scholar of regional history and architecture. It's in the 16th-century Paço

Episcopal (former Bishop's Palace) on Rua Abílio Beça, just off Largo de São Vicente.

Drift through three wood-ceilinged halls downstairs, past ancient pottery, stone and bronze tools, the mysterious stone pigs called berrões (see boxed aside) and other animal totems, a handsome assembly of Roman funeral stones (plus Roman milestones, tools and coins), papal bulls proclaiming the diocese of Miranda in the 16th century and moving it to Bragança in the 18th, plus paintings of *pelourinhos* (pillories) and the daily life of the region.

In six halls upstairs are the remnants of the palace's own chapels, luminous wooden church statues and other ecclesiastical furnishings. An elegant garden at the back is dotted with more tombstones and stone animals.

In a small audio-visual area you can watch a video about the Trás-os-Montes region. The only real disappointment is that there is no information at all in English. The museum

PLACES TO STAY		36	O Bolha Restaurante	23	Petrol Station
4	Residencial Classis			26	Igreja da Misericórdia
5	Residencial Tulipa	**OTHER**		27	Museu do Abade de
8	Residencial Tic-Tac	1	Train Station		Baçal
12	Hospedaria	2	Rodonorte/Internorte	28	Igreja de São Bento
	Internacional		Kiosk	29	Police Office
14	Hospedaria Brigantina	3	Parque Natural de	30	Câmara Municipal
15	Pensão Rucha		Montesinho Office	31	Embaixada Disco
16	Hotel Bragança	6	IP4 Disco	33	Mercado Municipal
20	Residencial Poças	9	Bus Stop to Meixedo	34	Igreja de São Vicente
25	Residencial São Roque		(& Municipal	35	Regional Turismo
32	Residencial Santa		Camping Ground)	37	Museu Militar
	Isabel	10	Santos Travel Agency	38	Igreja de Santa Maria
43	Pousada de São	11	Post & Telecommunica-	39	Domus Municipalis
	Bartolomeu		tions Office	40	Bruxa Disco
		13	Moderna Disco	41	Market Area, at Sports
PLACES TO EAT		17	Livraria Popular		Ground
7	Restaurante Xavier	19	Neves Currency	42	District Hospital
18	Café		Exchange	44	Lookout
24	Restaurante Arca de	21	Sé		
	Noé	22	Turismo		

is open daily, except Mondays, from 10 am to 5 pm (weekends to 6 pm) for 250$00, and there's a café downstairs.

Largo de São Vicente & Around

Facing this small, pretty square is the Igreja de São Vicente, Romanesque in origin but rebuilt in the 17th century. Tradition has it that the future Dom Pedro I secretly married Inês de Castro here around 1354 (see the boxed aside Love & Revenge about this star-crossed and ultimately grisly affair, under Alcobaça in the Estremadura & Ribatejo chapter).

Bragança's most attractive church is about a block east on Rua São Francisco: the Igreja de São Bento, with a Renaissance stone portal, a Renaissance trompe l'oeil ceiling over the nave and an Islamic-style inlaid ceiling over the chancel.

Cidadela

From Largo de São Vicente follow cobbled Rua Trindade Coelho or Rua Serpa Pinto up to the walled and amazingly well-preserved *cidadela* (citadel). People still live along the few narrow lanes inside, now sharing the area with *artesanatos* and posh restaurants. There used to be more houses in pre-Salazar days.

At the rear of the inner town is an irregular five-sided building called the **Domus Municipalis**. This odd, severe structure, which dates from the 12th or 13th century, is one of the few examples of non-church Romanesque architecture in Portugal, and the country's oldest town hall. Upstairs in a single arcaded room, Bragança's medieval town council met to settle land or water disputes; below it is the citadel's precious cistern. It's been tidied up a bit too much, and unfortunately roofed with incongruous red tiles.

It's usually locked, but the woman who has the key lives more or less opposite; just ask around: *Por favor, gostaria de visitar a domus por dentro* (please, I'd like to go inside the domus). She may also be able to open the door – covered with carved vines – of the early 16th-century **Igreja da Santa Maria** next door, said to have an 18th-century trompe l'oeil ceiling showing the Assumption.

Within the walls of the citadel are what remains of the castle, built in 1187 by Dom Sancho I and beefed up by João I for the dukes of Bragança. The massive, square **Torre de Menagem** or keep (built as a residence too; note the Gothic window upstairs) was garrisoned in the 19th and early 20th

TRÁS-OS-MONTES

century, and now houses the marginally interesting **Museu Militar**, which is open daily, except Thursdays, from 9 to 11.45 am and 2 to 4.45 pm, for 200$00 (free on Sunday mornings). Out in front is an extraordinary and primitive pelourinho, atop a granite boar like the berrões found all over the province.

The best view of the citadel is from the Pousada de São Bartolomeu across the valley (see Places to Stay), the road beyond it or, best of all, a lookout near the old Mosteiro de São Bartolomeu. Cross the river on Rua Alexandre Herculano and take the first left.

Market
A big thrice-monthly market, with animals as well as the usual clothes and homewares, takes over the municipal sports ground west of the centre on Avenida Abade de Baçal, on the 3rd, 12th and 21st of each month (or on the following Monday when any of these falls on a Saturday or Sunday).

Places to Stay
Camping The municipal *Parque de Campismo do Sabor* (☎ 33 15 35; fax 272 52), open from May to October, is six km north of the centre on the Portelo road. Typical rates are 200$00 per person, 200$00 to 300$00 for a tent and 200$00 per car. On weekdays only, municipal (STUB) bus No 7 goes to/from Meixedo via the camping ground, departing from the bottom of Avenida João da Cruz at 12.44 and 5.44 pm (and during school term at 2.10 pm), and stopping at the camping ground en route back to Bragança at 7.38 am and 1.34 pm (and during school term at 6.16 pm). From the old train station the Rodonorte bus to Portelo departs weekdays only at 1.30 pm, passing the camping ground. Check first for current times.

The next nearest camping ground is at Gondesende, 12 km west on the Vinhais road; see the Parque Natural de Montesinho section.

Private Rooms The municipal turismo can

make suggestions, and the Livraria Popular bookshop at Rua Almirante Reis 16 has a few accommodation notices in the window.

Pensões & Residencials Bragança is plagued with street noise, thanks to unmuffled motorbikes in its canyon-like streets late at night, so try for back rooms.

Most residencials are around the axis between the old train station and the cathedral. Best value at the bottom of the range is peaceful *Pensão Rucha* (☎ 33 16 72), above the Banco Totta & Açores building at Rua Almirante Reis 42, where small doubles with shared bath and toilet are 3500$00.

Two threadbare hospedarias also face one another across this street. The *Brigantina* (☎ 243 21) at No 48 has dreary doubles with shared facilities for 3000$00, and all the charm of a hospital ward; better value is the *Internacional* (☎ 226 11) at No 47, where the same price (or 3500$00 with shower) gets you a modicum of atmosphere and a small restaurant.

Residencial Poças, over the restaurant of the same name at Rua Combatentes 200, was under renovation when we were there. Once a good cheapo, it will doubtless emerge with attached baths and higher rates. It's under the same management and has the same booking number as *Residencial São Roque* (☎ 33 14 27), rather far from the centre on Rua Miguel Torga, on the 7th and 8th floors of an ugly block, where comfortable doubles with bath, TV and excellent views (and no motorcycle noise) are 6500$00. A third place under this management is *Residencial Santa Isabel* on Rua da República, which was closed when we called by.

Not far from where long-distance coaches unload are three smartly run residencials where characterless but clean and comfortable doubles with bath and TV are 7000$00 and up, including breakfast: *Classis* (☎ 33 16 31; fax 234 58) at Avenida João da Cruz 102; *Tic-Tac* (☎ 33 13 73; fax 33 16 73) at Rua Emídio Navarro 85; and *Tulipa* (☎ 33 16 75; fax 278 14) at Rua Dr Francisco Felgueiras 8-10, the last one a warren of over

The Minho
Top: Bridge over the Rio Cávado, Barcelos
Bottom: Storm clouds over Monção

JOHN KING

JOHN KING

JOHN KING

JOHN KING

JULIA WILKINSON

Trás-os-Montes

A: Stone granary
B: Northern longhorn cow
C: Farm couple, Campeã
D: Almond plantations, Sabor valley
E: House in Friexo de Espada à Cinta

80 rooms, like a hotel but with marginally more personality.

Hotels The *Hotel Bragança* (☎ 33 15 78; fax 33 12 42), at Avenida Sá Carneiro 11-15, has singles/doubles with the works (including breakfast) for 7750$00/10,000$00. Some old signs say Estalagem Bragança.

Pousadas If you have a bit of cash to burn, splash out at the *Pousada de São Bartolomeu* (☎ 33 14 93; fax 234 53), with splendid views across the valley to the citadel. It has posh high-season doubles for 14,500$00 and is 1.5 km from the centre (cross the river on Rua Alexandre Herculano and take the first left).

Turihab Among places the turismo can tell you about are *Moinho do Caniço* (☎ 235 77), a converted water mill that sleeps four to six and has two baths, a kitchen and a fireplace. It's by the Rio Baceiro at Castrelos, 12 km west of Bragança on the N103.

Places to Eat

You won't starve in Bragança; there are plenty of very ordinary cafés, pastelarias and pizzerias – including a string of them with sunny outdoor seating on the eastern side of Avenida João da Cruz. One of the few places along here for a decent meal is the restaurant at the back of *Restaurante Xavier* (☎ 239 68) at No 12, with dishes for around 1200$00 and a good-value, weekday-only special plate for 700$00. Residencials *Tic-Tac* and *Tulipa* have their own restaurants, serving adequate versions of Trás-os-Montes specialities. At the sharp end of Praça da Sé is a cheerful café with no sign to be seen, popular with local people and cool in summer.

Several places do rise above the rest. You may find the service rather too attentive at *O Bolha Restaurante* (☎ 232 40), on the corner of Jardim Dr António José de Almeida, but, for the price, the food was some of the best we had in Portugal: a small menu of carefully prepared northern and Portuguese specialities, typically 1200$00 per dish, some with 750$00 half-portions. The staff like to remind you that they're famous in various guidebooks for their feijoada (broad bean and pork stew), but we liked their rojões do Transmontana (a casserole of marinated pork pieces).

Restaurante Poças, at Rua Combatentes 200, has a big menu of fish and meat dishes for 800$00 to 1300$00; nothing is typically northern but the food is deservedly well known and the service polite and unpretentious. A restaurant, marisqueira and adega called *Arca de Noé* or Noah's Ark (☎ 38 11 59), on Avenida Cidade de Zamora, has a big, pricey seafood menu, but some dishes are under 1500$00 and the lunch-time special (800$00 for soup, salad, fish, rice and a glass of wine) is good value. It's open daily from 11 am to 3 pm and 5.30 pm to whenever.

Entertainment

There are at least four discos in town: *IP4* on Rua Dr Francisco Felgueiras, *Moderna* in a shopping arcade on Rua Almirante Reis, *Embaixada* on Avenida Sá Carneiro, and *Bruxa* on Rua Alexandre Herculano.

Getting There & Away

Air Bragança has an aerodrome, nine km out on the Rio de Onor road, but there are no scheduled flights to it.

Bus Tickets for Rodonorte (and affiliates Alfandegense and the Spanish operator Empresa Francisco Ledesma) are sold at a kiosk on upper Avenida João da Cruz. Rede Expressos tickets are sold at the Sanvitur agency (☎ 33 18 26; fax 275 36), down the road at No 38. For Trás-os-Montes services, go to Santos at Rua 5 de Outubro 5.

Rodonorte has a nine-hour express to/from Lisbon via Viseu and Coimbra once each weekday, an overnight run each weekend and a slower daily service via Mirandela, Vila Real, Peso da Régua, Viseu and Coimbra. Rede Expressos does Bragança-Lisbon two or three times a day; Coimbra is 1800$00, Lisbon 2200$00. Rede Expressos runs between Bragança, Braga and Porto once or twice a day, with additional weekend services from October to June. Rodonorte does Bragança-Porto daily via Amarante.

Once each weekday, Ledesma (Rodonorte) runs from Porto to Zamora (2050$00) and Valladolid (3895$00) in Spain, passing through Bragança about 3.15 pm (Mondays at 10.45 am). The return journey, also once each weekday, via Bragança, Vila Real, Amarante and other points to Porto, passes through Bragança at about 5.15 pm (Mondays at 6.15).

Rodonorte and Santos are also agents for Internorte/Eurolines, which goes to further European destinations (see the Getting There & Away chapter).

For destinations inside the Parque Natural de Montesinho, STUB (the municipal bus company) departs from a stand at the bottom of Avenida João da Cruz, opposite Caixa Geral de Depósitos bank. Rodonorte also has some services. See the Parque Natural de Montesinho section.

Train Passenger trains don't run to Bragança anymore, but don't rule it out: CP buses run two to four times a day from Bragança's old train station to Mirandela (2½ hours), with connections on the narrow-gauge Linha da Tua to Tua (two hours), from where you can pick up ordinary trains to Porto (3¼ hours).

Car At the time of writing, the IP4's Bragança bypass was still under construction, so drivers had to go through the town en route to/from Spain. Elsewhere in both directions, the IP4 is one of the best and emptiest highways in the country.

PARQUE NATURAL DE MONTESINHO

Projecting into Spain, in what looks like an annex of north-eastern Trás-os-Montes, is Montesinho Natural Park, a modest and very lived-in park with dozens of small, lean villages sprinkled across 75,000 hilly hectares of grassland and deciduous forest. Its appeal is this very mixture of gentle human and natural landscapes – both of which the park seeks to protect – and minimal tourist development.

Though it was founded in 1979, regional tourist literature seems oddly silent on the park, in what could almost be a conspiracy of silence – or perhaps people simply take it for granted. Certainly on summer weekends, every family in north-eastern Portugal seems to go there for a picnic.

The park includes two slatey massifs: the lusher, wetter Serra da Corôa in the central west and the Serra de Montesinho in the central east. The finest landscapes are in these highland areas and the complex watershed between them. Elevations range from 438m on the Rio Mente at the western end of the park, to 1481m near the Rio Sabor at its northernmost point.

The most convenient base from which to see the park is Bragança. There is also some accommodation at villages within the park, though transport is limited.

Flora & Fauna In the park's immense forests of Iberian oak and chestnut, or among riverside alders, willows, poplars and hazel, you may spot roe deer, otter or wild boar. In its grasslands are partridge, kite and hunting kestrel. Above about 900m the otherwise barren ground is carpeted in heather and broom. Stands of birch grow at the highest elevations of the Serra de Montesinho.

Huge state plantations of pine mar the eastern limb of the park. Nevertheless, this and the Serra de Montesinho have the richest diversity of animals. The north-eastern corner of the park, along with the Reserva Nacional de Sierra Culebra on the Spanish side, is the last major refuge for the endangered Iberian wolf (for more on the Iberian wolf, see Flora & Fauna in the Facts about the Country chapter). Other threatened species here are the royal eagle and black stork.

There are no specially restricted zones in the park except for golden eagle nesting areas (there are three near the Spanish border), which are off-limits to rock climbers. Motorised boats are not permitted anywhere in the park.

Traditional Culture There has been settlement in this area for thousands of years. Iron

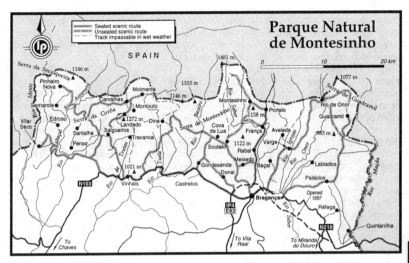

Parque Natural de Montesinho

Age foundations, adapted by the Romans, have been found in a number of places. Many of the park's 92 villages bear distinctly Germanic names, given to them by Visigothic settlers. In an attempt to create a sustainable fabric of life in this remote terra fria, with its extremes of climate, early Portuguese rulers established a system of collective land tenure, and communal practices persist today.

The park's overall population is only about 9000, which works out at an average of less than 100 souls per village. The park was founded in part to protect and revitalise this fragile social structure and its unique cultural heritage, but many of the more remote villages are on the decline, deserted by their young people. The main exception is Moimenta, the park's biggest village. It's the first stop for many of these young people and therefore it is growing healthily.

Villages are more concentrated towards the park's lusher western end. Many shelter in deep valleys, peaceful gems easily overlooked by the casual visitor. To counter the spread of ugly stucco and red-tile *emigrante* construction, help is on offer to those who will restore traditional slate-roofed stone structures, including not only houses but also churches, forges, water mills and the conspicuous, charming *pombals* (dovecotes).

Villages which have successfully retained at least some of their traditional appearance include Pinheiro Novo, Sernande, Edroso, Santalha and Moimenta in the west, and Donai, Varge, Rio de Onor and Guadramil in the east. Edroso, Santalha and Moimenta also have handsome medieval bridges. One place to see the failure of this effort, where traditional houses continue to be displaced by ugly *emigrante* versions, is Rabal, nine km from Bragança.

Information

There is a good park information office in Bragança (see Bragança Information), and at the time of research another one (☎ 073-724 16) was about to open in the old-town centre of Vinhais, the region's other *concelho* or county seat. Publications on flora and fauna and the park's cultural and architectural heritage are in Portuguese, but English-speaking staff are very willing to answer questions.

Maps The free schematic park map shows villages, roads and tracks, points of interest, camp sites and rural accommodation, but no trails. Some two dozen military topographic maps cover the park at 1:25,000, but nobody seems to be selling these or the 1:50,000 civilian versions. The park office in Bragança has these maps and will photocopy them at your expense. The sensible thing for serious hikers would be to bring maps from Porto or Lisbon.

Rio de Onor

Little Rio de Onor, 22 km up the N308 from Bragança, is one of the most interesting villages in the park, not only because of its well-preserved stone buildings but because it has held on staunchly to the independent-minded communal lifestyle once typical of the region.

On top of that, the Portuguese-Spanish border runs right through the middle of the village (marked only by a stone marker with 'P' on one side and 'E' on the other), and nobody pays it a blind bit of notice. People on both sides speak a dialect that's neither quite Portuguese nor quite Spanish, and have more in common with one another than with Lisbon or Madrid.

The Rio Onor itself – just a trickle here – flows at right angles to the border. The road from Bragança ends at the village, and a footpath branches left to cross the border or right to cross the river. East over the bridge is the prettiest part of the village.

Visiting without your own wheels is tricky: bus No 5 departs Bragança's Praça da Sé on weekdays only at 5.44 pm, but at 6.40 pm, 15 minutes after arriving at Rio de Onor, it heads back. It probably comes again in the evening, as there's another trip to Bragança at 7.10 am. So you either look the place over in 15 minutes or stay the night.

With the permission of the village *presidente* (ask at the *casa de povo* or common house above the village on the east side of the river), you could pitch your tent on common land or possibly stay in the casa de povo itself. The only place to eat is *Cervejaria Prato*, across the bridge.

During the school term only, an additional bus leaves Bragança at 2.11 pm, which would allow you about 3½ hours at the village. A taxi from Bragança and back would probably be about 3000$00 with a wait.

Walks

Spring and summer are best for walking here, though visually the park is at its best in the chilly autumn. Few if any trails have been established with hikers in mind, but a network of roads and dirt tracks pushes out to villages in many remote corners. The prettiest areas with the least paved roads are the Rio Sabor watershed north of Soutelo and França, and the Rio Tuela between Dine and Moimenta. The park operates its own fairly comfortable *abrigos de montanha* or mountain shelters in these areas (see Places to Stay).

Horse Riding

A park-run *centro hípico* or pony trekking and riding centre (☎ 073-911 41) is at França, from where numerous routes go into the park. Horses can be hired for 900$00 per hour. The centre is open daily, except Mondays, from 8 am to noon and 2 to 6 pm. França is 15 km up the Portelo road from Bragança, and the centre is 800m down a track from the upper end of the village, past a restored mill. The Rodonorte bus to Portelo stops in França, departing from Bragança's old train station at 1.30 pm on weekdays only.

Organised Tours

Lanius (☎ & fax 01-225 77 76) in Lisbon is an environmental travel agency that does specialised small-group walks in the park – including deer and birdwatching, and hunting for golden eagle nests and signs of wild boar and wolves. Its English-speaking Bragança contact is Luís Moreira (☎ 38 10 01), who says walks can be arranged on fairly short notice.

Places to Stay & Eat

Camping The small, year-round *Cepo Verde* camping ground (☎ 073-993 71) is 12 km west of Bragança on the N103 and 0.6 km north off the highway, just before Gondesende village. Typical rates are 500$00 per person, 300$00 to 500$00 for a tent and 300$00 per car (20% less from November to May). On weekdays only, Rodonorte's Bragança-Vinhais bus passes the camping ground twice a day.

There is also a camping ground just north of Bragança; see the Bragança section. Villagers, if asked, will sometimes allow free camping on common land.

Abrigos de Montanha For hikers especially, the park operates at least eight year-round 'mountain shelters' of various sizes – one at Montesinho, one between Montesinho and Soutelo, one between Dine and Landedo, two at Moimenta and three at Montouto, ranging from 5000$00 for two people to 20,000$00 for nine. All have sheets, blankets and towels, hot water, equipped kitchens, fireplaces and firewood. Book them well ahead, at the park office in Bragança or Vinhais, with a 50% deposit.

Private Rooms Private rooms are not plentiful in the park, but it's possible to find them in a few park villages; ask at cafés and shops, or check (in person or by phone) with the park officers in Bragança or Vinhais for their recommendations. Montesinho, a friendly village of 35 people, has around 10 beds. In July and August they're all booked out, while from October to May you don't have to book at all. Montesinho is 23 km from Bragança (bus almost to Portelo, plus a fine five-km walk).

Other places we saw or heard of with a few rooms include *Café Turismo* in França, *Snack Bar O Careto* (☎ 073-912 69) in Varge and *Restaurante Fraga dos Três Reinos* (☎ 073-641 74) in Moimenta.

Hotels *Hospedaria da Senhora da Hera* (☎ 073-994 14 or ☎ 073-249 54), near Cova de Lua, has nine doubles for 7000$00 and four triples for 8000$00, with bath; there's also a restaurant, bar and swimming pool. It's about one km off the N308 to Dine. Rodonorte's weekday-only bus to Dine departs from opposite Bragança's old train station at 1.30 pm.

Turihab The Turismo Rural bandwagon is on the way, with villagers restoring old houses: in Montesinho there's a place for two for 6000$00, and a house for about 8000$00; contact Maria Rita on ☎ 073-912 29, or the Café Montesinho on ☎ 073-912 19.

Getting There & Away
Main roads enter the park at around a dozen places, mainly via Bragança and Vinhais. There are also three roads to/from Spain (plus a footpath through Rio de Onor), all of them open 24 hours a day.

Getting Around
The tracks on the map are mainly fire roads, and sometimes dicey in bad weather. The unsealed scenic routes are in marginally better condition. All make suitable hiking routes, but if you plan to drive on any of them, check on current conditions with the park office.

Bus Public buses within the park are scarce, and normally run on weekdays only. Schedules also depend on the school term, with many services disappearing in July, August and early September.

STUB, Bragança's municipal bus company, has routes near Bragança, departing from the bottom of Avenida João da Cruz. Useful routes are No 7, a loop to Meixedo via the municipal camping ground, and No 5 to Rio de Onor. The turismo can provide current timetables.

Rodonorte goes elsewhere in the park, from various points in Bragança, for about 300$00 to 600$00. Routes include:

Vinhais, 11.55 am and 5.25 pm, from the Rodonorte kiosk; change at Vinhais for Penso and Moimenta
Portelo, 1.30 pm, from opposite the old train station
Dine, 1.30 pm, from opposite the old train station
Guadramil, Mondays only, at 1.45 and 5.25 pm, from opposite the petrol station on Avenida Cidade de Zamora

Check Rodonorte's kiosk on Avenida João da Cruz for current schedules and fares.

Bicycle Given a bit of notice and a 1000$00 deposit, the park service rents mountain bikes through its abrigos de montanha (see Places to Stay) at Montesinho, Moimenta and Montouto, and through its horse-riding centre at França. The cost is 300$00 for the first hour plus 100$00 per hour after that.

Minibus For trips within the park only, groups of about 10 or more can hire minibuses from the park office, complete with a guide-driver, for about 5000$00 per day.

MIRANDA DO DOURO
• *pop 1600* • *postcode 5210* • *area code* ☎ *073*
This sleepy town facing Spain across the Rio Douro gorge, in the furthest corner of Trás-os-Montes, is one of Portugal's (and Europe's) smallest cities – for despite its small population, a 'city' is what history made it. That history is one of Miranda's few present claims to fame.

This is also the easternmost town of any size in Portugal, more accessible from Spain than from Portugal, and in a sense more Spanish than Portuguese. Local people speak *mirandês*, a dialect descended almost straight from Latin but sounding rather like that of rural Castile and León.

What is there to see? The uninteresting ruins of its medieval castle; views of the Douro, dammed here into a silent lake; a cathedral without a diocese; and an amateurish but charmingly eclectic ethnographic museum. Its famous Pauliteiros stick-dancers (see boxed aside) are hard to find anymore.

The cobbled streets of the old town, lined with identical, blindingly whitewashed 15th and 16th-century houses, echo with the chatter of Spanish tour groups in summer and on weekends. New-town Miranda is for these day-trippers what the Algarve is for many English: a sanitised gauntlet of handicraft shops and pricey restaurants.

Miranda would make a pleasant day trip if it were closer to anywhere else in Portugal. You can see everything worth seeing in a couple of hours, but public transport makes it almost essential to spend longer. Don't come on Monday, when the museum and cathedral are closed.

History
Strategic Miranda was an important bulwark during the first two centuries of Portuguese independence, and the Castilians had to be chucked out at least twice: in the early days by Dom João I, and in 1710 during the Wars of the Spanish Succession. In 1545, perhaps as a snub to the increasingly powerful House of Bragança, a diocese was created here, an oversized cathedral built, and the town declared a *cidade*.

During a siege by French and Spanish troops in 1762, the castle's powder magazine blew up, pulverising most of the castle, killing 400 people and leaving almost nothing to besiege. Twenty years later, shattered Miranda was kicked while it was down, with the transfer of its diocese to Bragança. No one ever saw fit to rebuild the castle, and nobody paid much attention to Miranda again until the Barragem de Miranda dam was built in the 1950s.

Orientation
From Largo da Moagem, a roundabout on the N218 from Bragança (where the buses stop), the new town is down to the left (north-east) – consisting mainly of Rua 1 de Maio, parallel to the highway, and Rua 25 de Abril and Rua do Mercado, perpendicular. Here there are handicraft shops, pensões, restaurants, cafés (those on Rua do Mercado have views across the gorge) and, a few hundred metres down Rua do Mercado, the mercado municipal.

About 200m uphill from the roundabout are the old walls and castle ruins, and beyond them the old town and what was once the citadel. The axis is Rua da Mousinho da Albuquerque; crossing it just inside the walls and then curving parallel to it is Rua de Dom Turíbio Lopes. Between them, halfway along, is the centre of the old town, Praça de Dom João III. On a triangular *largo* at the end of Rua de Dom Turíbio Lopes is the cathedral.

Information

A small turismo beside the roundabout on the highway is open on weekdays only, from 9 am to 12.30 pm and 2 to 5.30 pm. Several banks with ATMs are near Largo da Moagem, and there's one beside the post office, facing the cathedral at the back end of Rua da Mousinho da Albuquerque.

Museu de Terra de Miranda

The municipal ethnographic museum on Praça de Dom João III offers a charmingly miscellaneous look at the region's past, laid out with the innocence of a school project. Upstairs, past a Roman tombstone and an old wooden loom, the museum is divided into several halls.

Highlights of the Sala de Arqueologia are a barely recognisable berrão (stone pig) and 14th and 15th-century stones with Hebrew inscriptions. The Sala do Traje e do Artesanato features rough woollen Mirandês wear, and the Sala das Armas has old pistols, muskets and traps. A highlight of the museum is the marvellous, musty collection of musical instruments, masks and ceremonial costumes (including those of the Pauliteiros) in the Sala das Figuras Rituais do Solsticío de Inverno. Other rooms have farm tools, kitchen furnishings and a scrawny assembly of Portuguese and Spanish regional pottery.

The museum is open daily, except Mondays, from 10 am to 12.45 pm and 2.30 to 5.45 pm, for 150$00.

Old Town

The backstreets of the old town are all alike, save for a few old but dignified (and unwhitewashed) 15th-century façades, which punctuate Rua da Costanilha, running west off Praça Dom João III, and a Gothic gate at the end of it.

The severe, twin-towered, granite Sé (cathedral), dating from the founding of the bishopric in the 16th century, is unremarkable except for its size. Inside is a very grand gilded main altarpiece. In a case in one transept stands the arresting Menino Jesus da Cartolinha, a Christ child in a top hat, whose wardrobe has more outfits than Imelda Marcos, thanks to local devotees. The cathedral is closed to tourists on Mondays and when Mass is in progress.

From beside the cathedral are some of the best views down over the gorge and the dead river. Behind the cathedral are the roofless remains of the former bishop's palace, which burned down in the 18th century.

Barragem de Miranda

A road crawls across the 80m-high dam and on to Zamora, 55 km away. This dam is one of five on the Douro along the Spanish border, the upper three for use by Portugal. About 20 km south-west on the N221 is the Barragem de Picote, and 35 km away is the Barragem da Bemposta, the latter also a border crossing.

Places to Stay

Camping The modest municipal camping ground (☎ 411 96), open from June to September, is among the few camping grounds we found that are free of charge. It's west of the old town across the ravine of the little Rio Fresno, 1.3 km from the Rua da Costanilha gate or 1.8 km from the roundabout, at the end of a residential street. Some houses nearby also advertise private rooms.

Pensões & Residencials Many pensões appear to close outside high summer, including two on Rua do Mercado – *Hospedaria Flor do Douro* at No 7-9 and *Pensão Vista Bela* further on. *Residencial Planalto* (☎ 413 62; fax 427 80) at Rua 1 de Maio 25 has 40 rooms with bath, TV and telephone; singles/doubles are 2950$00/3950$00, with breakfast. Further on at No 49, restaurante *Casa Pimentel* (☎ 426 78) advertises dormidas, though we found it closed.

In the old town, at Rua Abade de Baçal 61, just off the largo by the castle ruins, is the prettified *Pensão Santa Cruz* (☎ 413 74), where singles/doubles with small baths are 3200$00/4000$00 and a double with full bath and TV is 4500$00, all with breakfast.

For a deluxe treat and yawning views, take a room at the *Pousada de Santa Catarina* (☎ 410 05; fax 410 65), just east off the roundabout and perched at the edge of the gorge. High-season doubles are 14,500$00.

Places to Eat

Most pensões have a restaurant of some description, open at fixed meal times.

The casual *Restaurante & Pizzeria O Moinho* (☎ 411 16) at Rua do Mercado 47-D, less pricey than others on the street and with views across the gorge, has a big menu with paella for 1250$00, salads under 500$00, pizzas under 750$00, and Portuguese standards for 1000$00 to 1400$00 per dish; it's open daily from about 10 am.

Restaurants in the old town include *São Pedro* at Rua da Mousinho da Albuquerque 20, with a vast menu of meat and fish dishes for 700$00 to 1500$00, and *Buteho*, upstairs at Rua da Mousinho da Albuquerque 55. The Buteho also has a cheerful café and ice-cream parlour on the corner of Praça de Dom João III.

Getting There & Away

On summer weekdays Rodonorte departs Bragança for Miranda at 6 and 11 am and 1 and 5 pm, for 790$00. By car, the quickest road from Bragança to Miranda is the N218, a tortuous 85 km trip. The 100-km route to Miranda from the IP4/E82 motorway via Macedo de Cavaleiros and Mogadouro (N216 and N221) is one of the loveliest – and wiggliest – in Portugal. It crosses a *planalto* (high plain) dotted with almond and olive groves, with a dramatic descent into the Rio Sabor valley.

FREIXO DE ESPADA À CINTA
• *postcode 5180* • *area code* ☎ *079*

Just three km from the Rio Douro where it marks the Spanish border, and a world away from anywhere, Freixo de Espada à Cinta encapsulates Trás-os-Montes 'beyond the mountains' feeling. Surrounded by wild hills where black kites soar, it was once a sanctuary for fugitives and released prisoners who were allowed to settle here to promote the development of the strategically placed town. That was in Dom Afonso Henriques' day, over 800 years ago. A century later, Dom

Dinis gave the town its bizarre name (which means 'ash tree of the girth-sword') when he stopped here for a rest and hung his sword in an ash tree (or so the story goes).

Today, it's famous in spring for its blossoming almond trees, which draw hundreds of Spanish tourists. Otherwise the little town is so remote it hardly sees anyone – which in itself is a big attraction. There are unpublicised surprises, too: an elaborate parish church, a heptagonal 13th-century tower, an attractive old town of Manueline houses, and a small silk industry, with the finished products for sale in the town.

Orientation & Information

The old town centres around the Igreja Matriz (parish church) and landmark Torre de Galo, with narrow streets winding their way to the N221 and the town's modern outskirts. From the bus station near the main road, head for the Torre de Galo and you'll find all the places of interest nearby.

Igreja Matriz

The local villagers like to compare the interior of their 16th-century parish church to the monumental Mosteiro de Jerónimos in Belém, and there's certainly some resemblance, with three naves of elaborate vaulting. The highlight, though, is the altarpiece of 16 paintings attributed to the renowned Grão Vasco (see boxed aside in the Beiras chapter).

Torre de Galo

Above the parish church is the landmark keep known as the Cockerel's Tower. It was built by Dom Dinis and is all that remains of the town's medieval defences. There are some superb views from the top if you can gain access.

Casa da Bicha da Seda

The House of Silk Worms at Largo do Outeiro 6 is just that: a house where thousands of silkworms munch on mulberry leaves grown in the yard at the back. The silk thread is hand-woven into cotton or linen-backed items, some of which are for sale here. Or check out the weaving room, in the arched building by the church, where more items are for sale.

To find Largo do Outeiro, follow Rua Sacadura Cabral from beside the Igreja Matriz.

Places to Stay & Eat

There's not much choice in the old town itself, though you could try knocking on the doors of *Pensão Paris* (☎ 627 86), in Largo do Outeiro, where rooms (when it's open) are 25000$00 for a double without bath. A more reliable option is the *Residencial Restaurante Cinta de Ouro* (☎ 625 50), on the N221 just south of town, where doubles with shower are around 45000$00. This is the best place to eat, too.

Getting There & Away

A handful of buses connect Freixo with Miranda do Douro daily.

TRÁS-OS-MONTES

Glossary

See the Food Glossary in the Facts for the Visitor chapter for a listing of culinary terms.

abrigo de montanha – mountain shelter
adega – a cellar, especially a wine cellar; also means a winery, or a traditional wine bar likely to serve wine from the barrel
Age of Discoveries – the period during the 15th and 16th centuries when Portuguese explorers ventured across the seas, 'discovering' and colonising various territories, exploring the coast of Africa, and finally charting the sea route to India
aguardente – strongly alcoholic firewater
albergaria – an up-market inn
albufeira – reservoir or lagoon
aldeia – village
almoço – lunch, lasting at least two hours (usually from 1 to 3 pm)
arco – arch
armillary sphere – a model of the celestial sphere used by early astronomers and navigators to determine the position of stars; appears in the Portuguese coat of arms
artesanatos – handicraft shops
azulejos – hand-painted tiles, often blue and white, used to decorate buildings

bacalhau – salted cod
bagagem – baggage office
bairro – town district
balcão – counter in a bar or café
balneário – health resort or spa
barragem – dam
beco – cul de sac
berrões – stone pigs found in Trás-os-Montes
bica – short black espresso coffee
bicyclete tudo terrano (BTT) – mountain bike

câmara municipal – town hall
cartões telefónicos – plastic phonecards

casa de abrigo – 'shelter-house', mainly for national park staff but sometimes open to the public
casa de banho – same as *sanitários*
casa de chá – teahouse
casa de hóspedes – similar to a *hospedaria* or boarding house; prices are lower than at a *pensão* or *residencial*, and showers and toilets are usually shared
casa de pasto – a casual eatery with cheap, simple meals
casa de povo – 'common house', a place in small villages where you can stay, with the permission of the mayor
castelo – castle
castro – fortified hill town
Celto-Iberians – the race of people living on the Iberian peninsula, particularly the northern part of Portugal, who emerged after the arrival of the Celts in the area around 600 BC
centro de saúde – state-administered medical centre
centro infantil – kindergarten
centros de juventude – state-funded youth-activity centres which sometimes have lodgings
cerveja – beer
cervejaria – literally a beer house; also serves snacks
chouriço – spicy smoked sausage
churrasqueira or **churrascaria** – literally a barbecue or grill, usually a restaurant serving grilled foods, especially chicken
cidade – city
citânia – Neolithic or Celtic fortified village
claustro – cloisters
conta – bill (check)
coro alto – choir stalls overlooking the nave in a church
Correios – post office
cortes – parliament
couvert – cover charge added to the bill to pay for bread and butter
cromlech – a circle of Neolithic standing stones
cruzeiro – cross

direita – right; abbreviated as D, dir or Dta
dolmen – megalithic tomb dating from the Neolithic Age
Dom, Dona – honorific titles (Sir, Madam) given to kings, queens and other nobles
dormida – rooming house
duplo – room with twin beds
elevador – lift (elevator) or funicular

ementa turística – tourist menu
entrada – entrée or starter
ementa – menu
esplanada – terrace or seafront promenade
esquerda – left; abbreviated as E, esq or Esqa
estação – station (usually train station)
estalagem – like an *albergaria*, but even pricier

fado – the haunting, melancholy Portuguese equivalent of the blues
farmácia – pharmacy
feira – fair
festa – festival
fiambre – ham
FICC – Fédération Internationale de Camping et de Caravanning
fortaleza – fort
FPCC – Federação Portuguesa de Campismo e Caravanismo
freguesia – parish

gelado – ice cream
GNR – Guarda Nacional Republicana, the national guard; acting police force in major towns
gruta – cave
Gypsy markets – huge outdoor markets specialising in cheap clothes and shoes, and largely operated by Portugal's Gypsies

hipermercado – hypermarket
horário – timetable
hospedaria – boarding houses; prices are lower than at *pensões* or *residencials*, and showers and toilets are usually shared

ICEP – Investimentos, Comércio e Turismo de Portugal; the government umbrella organisation for Portugal's national tourism body; there are ICEP *turismos* in most major cities (in addition to the municipal *turismos*)
igreja matriz – parish church
igreja – church
ilha – island
infantário – children's daycare centre
intercidade – express intercity train
interregional – fairly fast train without too many stops

jantar – evening dinner
jardim – garden
judiaria – a Jewish quarter where Jews were segregated
junta de turismo – see *turismo*

largo – small square
latifúndios – Roman system of large farming estates
lavandaria – laundry
lista – same as *ementa*
livraria – bookshop
loggia – a covered area on the side of a building

Manueline – a unique and elaborate style of art and architecture that emerged during the reign of Manuel I in the 16th century
marisqueira – seafood restaurant
meia dose – half-portion of a dish
menir – menhir; individual standing stone dating from the late Neolithic Age
mercado municipal – municipal market
mesa – table
minimercado – grocery or small supermarket
miradouro – lookout
Misericórdia – from Santa Casa da Misericórdia (Holy House of Mercy), a charitable institution founded in the 15th century to care for the poor and the sick
mosteiro – monastery
mouraria – Moorish quarter where Moors were segregated after the Christian *Reconquista*
mudéjar – Moorish-influenced art or decoration
museu – museum

paço – palace

paços de concelho – town hall (an older name for a *câmara municipal*)

parque de campismo – camping ground

parque infantil – children's playground

pastelaria – pastry and cake shop

pelourinho – stone pillory, often ornately carved; from the 13th to 18th centuries, pillories were used, particularly in northern Portugal, not only as a symbol of justice but also to chain up criminals for whipping and abuse

pensão (s), **pensões** (pl) – guesthouse; the Portuguese equivalent of a bed and breakfast (B&B), but breakfast is not always included

pequeno almoço – breakfast, which is traditionally just coffee and a bread roll (often taken in a café)

planalto – high plain

pombal – dovecote; a structure for housing pigeons

portagem – toll road

posto de turismo – see *turismo*

pousada de juventude – youth hostel

pousada – government-run hotel (in a programme called Pousadas de Portugal) offering up-market accommodation, often in a converted castle, convent or palace

praça – square

praça de touros – bullring

praia – beach

prato do dia – dish of the day

PSP – Polícia de Segurança Pública; the local police force

quarto de casal – room with a double bed

quarto individual – single room

quarto particular (or simply **quarto**) – room in a private house

queijo – cheese

quinta – country estate or villa; in the Douro wine-growing region it often refers to a wine lodge's property

Reconquista – Christian reconquest of Portugal begun in 718 and completed in 1249

rés do chão – ground floor; abbrieviated as R/C

residencial – guesthouse; often slightly more expensive than a *pensão* and usually serving breakfast

ribeiro – stream

rio – river

romaria – religious pilgrimage

rua – street

salão de cha – teahouse

sandes – sandwiches

sanitários or **casas de banho** – public toilets

sé – cathedral, from the Latin for 'seat' (sedes), implying an episcopal seat

selos – stamps

sem chumbo – unleaded petrol

serra – mountain or mountain range

solar – manor house

sopa – soup

talha dourada – gilded woodwork

tasca – a simple tavern, often with rustic décor

termas – spa

torre de menagem – castle tower or keep

tourada – bullfight

Turihab – short for Turismo Habitação, an association marketing private accommodation (particularly in northern Portugal) in country cottages, historic buildings and manor houses

turismo – tourist office

vila – town

vinho da casa – house wine

vinhos verde – semisparkling young wine

Index

MAPS

TEXT

LONELY PLANET JOURNEYS

JOURNEYS is a unique collection of travel writing – published by the company that understands travel better than anyone else. It is a series for anyone who has ever experienced – or dreamed of – the magical moment when they encountered a strange culture or saw a place for the first time. They are tales to read while you're planning a trip, while you're on the road or while you're in an armchair, in front of a fire.

JOURNEYS books catch the spirit of a place, illuminate a culture, recount a crazy adventure, or introduce a fascinating way of life. They always entertain, and always enrich the experience of travel.

THE GATES OF DAMASCUS
Lieve Joris

Translated by Sam Garrett

This best-selling book is a beautifully drawn portrait of day-to-day life in modern Syria. Through her intimate contact with local people, Lieve Joris draws us into the fascinating world that lies behind the gates of Damascus. Hala's husband is a political prisoner, jailed for his opposition to the Assad regime; through the author's friendship with Hala we see how Syrian politics impacts on the lives of ordinary people.

Lieve Joris, who was born in Belgium, is one of Europe's leading travel writers. In addition to an award-winning book on Hungary, she has published widely acclaimed accounts of her journeys to the Middle East and Africa. *The Gates of Damascus* is her fifth book.

'Expands the boundaries of travel writing' – **Times Literary Supplement**

KINGDOM OF THE FILM STARS
Journey into Jordan
Annie Caulfield

Kingdom of the Film Stars is a travel book and a love story. With honesty and humour, Annie Caulfield writes of travelling in Jordan and falling in love with a Bedouin. Her book offers fascinating insights into the country – from the traditional tent life of nomadic tribes to the first woman MP's battle with fundamentalist colleagues. *Kingdom of the Film Stars* unpicks some of the tight-woven Western myths about the Arab world, presenting cultural and political issues within the intimate framework of a compelling love story.

Annie Caulfield, who was born in Ireland and currently lives in London, is an award-winning playwright and journalist. She has travelled widely in the Middle East.

'Annie Caulfield is a remarkable traveller. Her story is fresh, courageous, moving, witty and sexy!' – **Dawn French**

LONELY PLANET TRAVEL ATLASES

Lonely Planet has long been famous for the number and quality of its guidebook maps. Now we've gone one step further and in conjunction with Steinhart Katzir Publishers produced a handy companion series: Lonely Planet travel atlases – maps of a country produced in book form.

Unlike other maps, which look good but lead travellers astray, our travel atlases have been researched on the road by Lonely Planet's experienced team of writers. All details are carefully checked to ensure the atlas corresponds with the equivalent Lonely Planet guidebook.

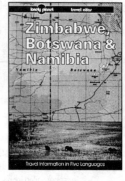

The handy atlas format means no holes, wrinkles, torn sections or constant folding and unfolding. These atlases can survive long periods on the road, unlike cumbersome fold-out maps. The comprehensive index ensures easy reference.

- full-colour throughout
- maps researched and checked by Lonely Planet authors
- place names correspond with Lonely Planet guidebooks
  – no confusing spelling differences
- legend and travelling information in English, French, German, Japanese and Spanish
- size: 230 x 160 mm

Available now:
Chile & Easter Island • Egypt • India & Bangladesh • Israel & the Palestinian Territories • Jordan, Syria & Lebanon • Kenya • Laos • Thailand • Vietnam • Zimbabwe, Botswana & Namibia

---

LONELY PLANET TV SERIES & VIDEOS

Lonely Planet travel guides have been brought to life on television screens around the world. Like our guides, the programmes are based on the joy of independent travel, and look honestly at some of the most exciting, picturesque and frustrating places in the world. Each show is presented by one of three travellers from Australia, England or the USA and combines an innovative mixture of video, Super-8 film, atmospheric soundscapes and original music.

Videos of each episode – containing additional footage not shown on television – are available from good book and video shops, but the availability of individual videos varies with regional screening schedules.

Video destinations include: Alaska • American Rockies • Australia – The South-East • Baja California & the Copper Canyon • Brazil • Central Asia • Chile & Easter Island • Corsica, Sicily & Sardinia – The Mediterranean Islands • East Africa (Tanzania & Zanzibar) • Ecuador & the Galapagos Islands • Greenland & Iceland • Indonesia • Israel & the Sinai Desert • Jamaica • Japan • La Ruta Maya • Morocco • New York • North India • Pacific Islands (Fiji, Solomon Islands & Vanuatu) • South India • South West China • Turkey • Vietnam • West Africa • Zimbabwe, Botswana & Namibia

The Lonely Planet TV series is produced by: **Pilot Productions** Duke of Sussex Studios 44 Uxbridge St London W8 7TG UK	*Lonely Planet videos are distributed by:* **IVN Communications Inc** 2246 Camino Ramon California 94583, USA 107 Power Road, Chiswick London W4 5PL UK

Music from the TV series is available on CD & cassette.
For video availability and ordering information contact your nearest Lonely Planet office.

PLANET TALK

Lonely Planet's FREE quarterly newsletter

We love hearing from you and think you'd like to hear from us.

When...is the right time to see reindeer in Finland?
Where...can you hear the best palm-wine music in Ghana?
How...do you get from Asunción to Areguá by steam train?
What...is the best way to see India?

For the answer to these and many other questions read PLANET TALK.

Every issue is packed with up-to-date travel news and advice including:

* a letter from Lonely Planet co-founders Tony and Maureen Wheeler
* go behind the scenes on the road with a Lonely Planet author
* feature article on an important and topical travel issue
* a selection of recent letters from travellers
* details on forthcoming Lonely Planet promotions
* complete list of Lonely Planet products

To join our mailing list contact any Lonely Planet office.

Also available: Lonely Planet T-shirts. 100% heavyweight cotton.

LONELY PLANET ONLINE

Get the latest travel information before you leave or while you're on the road

Whether you've just begun planning your next trip, or you're chasing down specific info on currency regulations or visa requirements, check out the Lonely Planet World Wide Web site for up-to-the-minute travel information.

As well as travel profiles of your favourite destinations (including interactive maps and full-colour photos), you'll find current reports from our army of researchers and other travellers, updates on health and visas, travel advisories, and the ecological and political issues you need to be aware of as you travel.

There's an online travellers' forum (the Thorn Tree) where you can share your experiences of life on the road, meet travel companions and ask other travellers for their recommendations and advice. We also have plenty of links to other Web sites useful to independent travellers.

With tens of thousands of visitors a month, the Lonely Planet Web site is one of the most popular on the Internet and has won a number of awards including GNN's Best of the Net travel award.

http://www.lonelyplanet.com

LONELY PLANET PRODUCTS

Lonely Planet is known worldwide for publishing practical, reliable and no-nonsense travel information in our guides and on our web site. The Lonely Planet list covers just about every accessible part of the world. Currently there are eight series: *travel guides*, *shoestring guides*, *walking guides*, *city guides*, *phrasebooks*, *audio packs*, *travel atlases* and *Journeys* – a unique collection of travel writing.

EUROPE

Austria • Baltic States & Kaliningrad • Baltic States phrasebook • Britain • Central Europe on a shoestring • Central Europe phrasebook • Czech & Slovak Republics • Denmark • Dublin city guide • Eastern Europe on a shoestring • Eastern Europe phrasebook • Finland • France • Greece • Greek phrasebook • Hungary • Iceland, Greenland & the Faroe Islands • Ireland • Italy • Mediterranean Europe on a shoestring • Mediterranean Europe phrasebook • Paris city guide • Poland • Prague city guide • Portugal • Russia, Ukraine & Belarus • Russian phrasebook • Scandinavian & Baltic Europe on a shoestring • Scandinavian Europe phrasebook • Slovenia • Spain • St Petersburg city guide • Switzerland • Trekking in Greece • Trekking in Spain • Ukrainian phrasebook • Vienna city guide • Walking in Britain • Walking in Switzerland • Western Europe on a shoestring • Western Europe phrasebook

NORTH AMERICA

Alaska • Backpacking in Alaska • Baja California • California & Nevada • Canada • Florida • Hawaii • Honolulu city guide • Los Angeles city guide • Mexico • Miami city guide • New England • New Orleans city guide • Pacific Northwest USA • Rocky Mountain States • San Francisco city guide • Southwest USA • USA phrasebook • Washington, DC & the Capital Region

CENTRAL AMERICA & THE CARIBBEAN

Bermuda • Central America on a shoestring • Costa Rica • Cuba • Eastern Caribbean • Guatemala, Belize & Yucatán: La Ruta Maya • Jamaica

SOUTH AMERICA

Argentina, Uruguay & Paraguay • Bolivia • Brazil • Brazilian phrasebook • Buenos Aires city guide • Chile & Easter Island • Chile & Easter Island travel atlas • Colombia • Ecuador & the Galápagos Islands • Latin American Spanish phrasebook • Peru • Quechua phrasebook • Rio de Janeiro city guide • South America on a shoestring • Trekking in the Patagonian Andes • Venezuela

Travel Literature: Full Circle: A South American Journey

ANTARCTICA

Antarctica

ISLANDS OF THE INDIAN OCEAN

Madagascar & Comoros • Maldives & Islands of the East Indian Ocean • Mauritius, Réunion & Seychelles

AFRICA

Arabic (Moroccan) phrasebook • Africa on a shoestring • Cape Town city guide • Central Africa • East Africa • Egypt • Egypt travel atlas • Ethiopian (Amharic) phrasebook • Kenya • Kenya travel atlas • Morocco • North Africa • South Africa, Lesotho & Swaziland • Swahili phrasebook • Trekking in East Africa • West Africa • Zimbabwe, Botswana & Namibia • Zimbabwe, Botswana & Namibia travel atlas

Travel Literature: The Rainbird: A Central African Journey • Songs to an African Sunset: A Zimbabwean Story